ADOLESCENT BEHAVIOR AND SOCIETY: *A book of readings*

ADOLESCENT BEHAVIOR AND SOCIETY:

A book of readings

ROLF E. MUUSS   EDITOR

Goucher College

RANDOM HOUSE   NEW YORK

PREFACE

This book is designed for courses in psychology, education, and sociology concentrating on the growth and development of the adolescent and his relationship to society. Evolving out of reading assignments made by the editor in his own course in adolescent development, the book attempts to provide the reader with an in-depth survey of contemporary perspectives on the psycho-social correlates of adolescence, that is, the interrelationship between the psychological forces within the adolescent and the dynamics of the social environment influencing his behavior. The exposure to a variety of interpretations and issues related to adolescence that is provided by this anthology will, hopefully, serve four purposes: to contribute to a better understanding of contemporary social and educational issues related to youth; to stimulate increased sensitivity in the reader to the needs and problems of individual adolescents as well as to stimulate some reflective thought on the reader's part and thereby to contribute to a better understanding of his own adolescence; to expose the reader to the processes of scientific inquiry, comparison, and evaluation; and finally, on a more practical level, to make easily available a diversity of articles and research studies which can be integrated effectively with lecture, class discussion, and textbook materials. Such diversity is seldom available in the library of a small college and may be scattered in departmental libraries in larger universities.

To achieve these purposes, forty-four articles were selected and organized into ten parts according to headings which frequently appear in general textbooks or course outlines. Each of the parts has a brief introduction in which the editor attempts to place the respective group of articles in a broader context: to integrate it with similar, related, and opposing knowledge, and to give in summary fashion the highlights of the articles so as to motivate the student and guide his reading.

The title *Adolescent Behavior and Society* implies that the selections are not limited to psychological, or even developmental, sources. The selections include a variety of disciplines and approaches: psychological, sociological, educational, physiological, anthropological, and medical. The problems and issues related to adolescent behavior have become truly interdisciplinary. The contributions of such diverse disciplines as biology and sociology to knowledge of youth has perhaps also added to such controversies as the relative importance of physical and social forces in adolescent development. Many controversial issues still plague present day thinking about adolescent development.

v

In several selections the issue is raised as to whether pubescence and adolescence are causally related or are independent phenomena. It is even questioned whether adolescence is a period of crisis, conflict, frustration, and storm and stress, or a continuous, relatively undisturbed extension of childhood and preparation for adulthood. In the sixties and early seventies, the question has been asked whether an independent "youth culture" is developing which is basically different from the larger society, not only in language, dress, manners, and entertainment preferences, but also in more fundamental values, attitudes, and morals. Are youth more susceptible to conformist behavior than their parents? Much controversy exists concerning the depth, intensity, and even the existence of a "generation gap." Finally, there is disagreement as to whether the problems of today's youth are different and more serious than the problems of adolescents of past generations. The reader who approaches the book with the hope of finding definitive answers to such and similar questions is likely to be disappointed. However, the reader who is mainly concerned with issues, problems, and hypotheses will find these readings rewarding.

The editor at one point considered making the organizing principle of the book a juxtaposition of such opposing and controversial articles, but decided against such an approach since certain topics—such as those listed above—would be overrepresented, while less controversial issues would be neglected. The student should be aware of opposing positions, such as the article by Albert Bandura (2)* in contrast to the article by Leon Eisenberg (3) and several others; also, the article by Robert Bealer, *et al.* (39) stands in sharp opposition to several others, especially James Coleman's study (40) of the adolescent subculture. It is the editor's assumption that such controversies result from the diverse approaches used by various disciplines, and that differences within a given discipline are rooted in dissimilar theoretical orientations. A theoretical commitment predisposes assumptions which can influence not only methodology but also interpretations of findings and observations. For a more thorough analysis of the relationship between different authors' theoretical assumptions and their conceptualizations of adolescence, the reader should consult the editor's earlier volume, *Theories of Adolescence* (2nd ed.), of which one chapter is included here.

Each article was selected to appeal to the social, educational, psychological, and personal interests of college students, to the contemporary student's demand for academic and social relevancy, and to the beginning student's need for experience in scientific approaches to data. The level of difficulty is such that a student who has had no more than an introductory course in psychology or sociology and only a limited exposure to statistical methods and interpretations can comprehend and benefit from the articles. Some selections are in-

---

* The numbers (1–44) in parentheses in the editor's introductions to each of the ten parts of the book refer to the chapter numbers in this book.

cluded because of the relevancy of the material to the late adolescent, the college student himself. For example, he may find that the articles by Allport (25), Halleck (29), Rubinstein (43), Seiden (34), Davis and Munoz (44), contribute to an understanding of his own behavior and development as well as that of his peers. College students by definition are on the threshold between late adolescence and youthful dependency, and adulthood, independence, and maturity. The college student involved in a search for identity may benefit from the knowledge about identity formation presented in the articles by Erikson (21, 22) and by Marcia (23).

The editor has attempted to include those topics most commonly found in courses in adolescent psychology and development, those articles most intimately concerned with the adolescent's relationship to a changing culture, and those excerpts which crystallize the thought and data of renowned researchers and theoreticians in the field of adolescent development. While there are obvious differences in the quality and value of the various selections, all authors are competent researchers or writers, and many of them are internationally known for their contribution to developmental psychology in general and adolescent development in particular. Further selection among the wide range of articles which satisfy these criteria for content was dictated by two subsidiary points: first, that the information in the article be either recently published and, consequently, in the forefront of work in its field, or as applicable to adolescents today as it was at the time of its publication; and second, that the book as a whole present a balance between empirical research studies focusing on specific issues, theoretical papers opening broad perspectives, and integrative articles synthesizing the information on a topic.

Finally, the editor selected articles that have satisfied his need as a teacher of adolescent psychology and development and that, consequently, reflect his personal and professional values, preferences, and biases.

Underlying all these criteria is the theme of the influence on the adolescent of his society, and particularly the effect on the developing youth of the home, peer group, and school, the three major agents through which socialization of the young is achieved. Special emphasis is placed on the significance of the school as an agent of society. There is good reason for this emphasis. The adolescent spends a great deal of his time in school under the influence of his teachers, the curriculum, extracurricular activities, school values, and his peer group. Furthermore, many college students enrolling in adolescent development courses are considering working with adolescents in school or in school-related activities and organizations; consequently a consideration of the impact of education during adolescence is not confined to Part Eight of the book, but appears also in a number of other sections.

The selection of articles and studies for inclusion in a book of readings is a difficult task and, in the final analysis, a subjective one. Many hundreds of articles were considered for inclusion, and the table of content has been changing until the last moment. A significant contribution in the selection of articles was provided by the editor's students in his course "Adolescent Development," who read and evaluated a list of articles and their alternatives and rated each according to its level of difficulty, its interest appeal, and its relevancy. In many instances, final selection has been guided by their judgment, although sole responsibility rests with the editor. Sincere appreciation is expressed to these young women and to the staff of the Goucher College Computer Center, who analyzed and summarized the students' data.

An expression of gratitude is also due to the authors of the articles, who generously granted permission to reprint their work. To these sensitive and devoted investigators of adolescence I humbly dedicate this work. I am also grateful to the publishers, who have permitted reproduction of their material; specific acknowledgment is included with each of these articles. Finally, I say thanks to my wife, Gertrude, without whose moral support and efforts in editing and proofreading, this book would never have seen the light of day.

CONTENTS

ONE THE NATURE, THEORY, AND HISTORY OF ADOLESCENCE *1* [1] *Rolf E. Muuss* THE PHILOSOPHICAL AND HISTORICAL ROOTS OF THEORIES OF ADOLESCENCE, 3 [2] *Albert Bandura* THE STORMY DECADE: FACT OR FICTION?, 22 [3] *Leon Eisenberg* A DEVELOPMENTAL APPROACH TO ADOLESCENCE, 31 [4] *David Elkind* EGOCENTRISM IN ADOLESCENCE, 39

TWO PHYSIOLOGICAL DEVELOPMENT AND ITS PSYCHOLOGICAL CORRELATES *49* [5] *Rolf E. Muuss* ADOLESCENT DEVELOPMENT AND THE SECULAR TREND, 51 [6] *Johanna Dwyer and Jean Mayer* PSYCHOLOGICAL EFFECTS OF VARIATIONS IN PHYSICAL APPEARANCE DURING ADOLESCENCE, 64 [7] *Franklyn N. Arnhoff and Ernest N. Damianopoulos* SELF-BODY RECOGNITION: AN EMPIRICAL APPROACH TO THE BODY IMAGE, 82 [8] *Alexander Frazier and Lorenzo K. Lisonbee* ADOLESCENT CONCERNS WITH PHYSIQUE, 88

THREE COGNITION, THOUGHTS, CONCEPTS, AND CREATIVITY IN ADOLESCENTS *99* [9] *Neal W. Dye and Philip S. Very* DEVELOPMENTAL CHANGES IN ADOLESCENT MENTAL STRUCTURE, 101 [10] *Jacob W. Getzels and Philip W. Jackson* THE HIGHLY INTELLIGENT AND THE HIGHLY CREATIVE ADOLESCENT: A SUMMARY OF SOME RESEARCH FINDINGS, 121 [11] *E. Paul Torrance and Dean C. Dauw* ATTITUDE PATTERNS OF CREATIVELY GIFTED HIGH SCHOOL SENIORS, *133*   [12] *Robert J. Havighurst* CONDITIONS PRODUCTIVE OF SUPERIOR CHILDREN, *139*

FOUR ATTITUDES, INTERESTS, AND VALUES *149*

[13] *Mary Cover Jones* A COMPARISON OF THE ATTITUDES AND INTERESTS OF NINTH-GRADE STUDENTS OVER TWO DECADES, *152*   [14] *John Paul McKinney* THE DEVELOPMENT OF CHOICE STABILITY IN CHILDREN AND ADOLESCENTS, *171*   [15] *Joseph Adelson and Robert P. O'Neil* GROWTH OF POLITICAL IDEAS IN ADOLESCENCE: THE SENSE OF COMMUNITY, *175*   [16] *Lawrence Kohlberg* MORAL EDUCATION IN THE SCHOOLS: A DEVELOPMENTAL VIEW, *193*

FIVE PARENT AND PEER GROUP INFLUENCES ON ADOLESCENTS *215*   [17] *Robert E. Grinder & Judith C. Spector* SEX DIFFERENCES IN ADOLESCENTS' PERCEPTIONS OF PARENTAL RESOURCE CONTROL, *217*   [18] *Clay V. Brittain* ADOLESCENT CHOICES AND PARENT-PEER CROSS-PRESSURES, *224*   [19] *Norman E. Gronlund* PERSONALITY CHARACTERISTICS OF SOCIALLY ACCEPTED, SOCIALLY NEGLECTED, AND SOCIALLY REJECTED JUNIOR HIGH SCHOOL PUPILS, *234*   [20] *Philip R. Costanzo & Marvin E. Shaw* CONFORMITY AS A FUNCTION OF AGE, *242*

SIX THE DEVELOPMENT OF EGO IDENTITY *251*

[21] *Erik H. Erikson* YOUTH AND THE LIFE CYCLE, *253*   [22] *Erik H. Erikson* A MEMORANDUM ON IDENTITY AND NEGRO YOUTH, *265*   [23] *James E. Marcia* DEVELOPMENT AND VALIDATION OF EGO-IDENTITY

STATUS, 277   [24] *Herbert A. Otto and Sandra L. Healy* ADOLESCENTS'

SELF-PERCEPTION OF PERSONALITY STRENGTHS, 291   [25] *Gordon W.*

Allport CRISES IN NORMAL PERSONALITY DEVELOPMENT, 298

SEVEN SEX DIFFERENCES, SEX ROLES, AND

SEXUAL DEVELOPMENT 307   [26] *Elizabeth Douvan*

SEX DIFFERENCES IN ADOLESCENT CHARACTER PROCESSES, 310   [27]

David B. Lynn THE PROCESS OF LEARNING PARENTAL AND SEX-ROLE

IDENTIFICATION, 318   [28] *Gordon Shipman* THE PSYCHODYNAMICS OF

SEX EDUCATION, 326   [29] *Seymour L. Halleck* SEX AND MENTAL

HEALTH ON THE CAMPUS, 339   [30] *Carlfred B. Broderick* SOCIAL

HETEROSEXUAL DEVELOPMENT AMONG URBAN NEGROES AND WHITES, 352

EIGHT THE ADOLESCENT'S ADJUSTMENT TO

SCHOOL 361   [31] *Thomas A. Ringness* IDENTIFICATION

PATTERNS, MOTIVATION, AND SCHOOL ACHIEVEMENT OF BRIGHT JUNIOR HIGH

SCHOOL BOYS, 363   [32] *Philip W. Jackson and Jacob W. Getzels*

PSYCHOLOGICAL HEALTH AND CLASSROOM FUNCTIONING: A STUDY OF THE

DISSATISFACTION WITH SCHOOL AMONG ADOLESCENTS, 376   [33] *David*

Gottlieb and Warren D. TenHouten RACIAL COMPOSITION AND THE SOCIAL

SYSTEMS OF THREE HIGH SCHOOLS, 384   [34] *Richard H. Seiden*

CAMPUS TRAGEDY: A STUDY OF STUDENT SUICIDE, 400

NINE SOCIO-CULTURAL BASIS OF ADOLESCENT

BEHAVIOR 419   [35] *Rolf E. Muuss*   PUBERTY RITES IN

PRIMITIVE AND MODERN SOCIETIES, 421   [36] *Urie Bronfenbrenner* RE-

SPONSE TO PRESSURE FROM PEERS VERSUS ADULTS AMONG SOVIET AND AMERI-CAN SCHOOL CHILDREN, 433   [37] *Georgene H. Seward and William R. Larson* ADOLESCENT CONCEPTS OF SOCIAL SEX ROLES IN THE UNITED STATES AND THE TWO GERMANIES, 442   [38] *Solomon Kobrin* THE IMPACT OF CULTURAL FACTORS ON SELECTED PROBLEMS OF ADOLESCENT DEVELOPMENT IN THE MIDDLE AND LOWER CLASS, 446

TEN THE ADOLESCENT SUBCULTURE *451*

[39] *Robert C. Bealer, Fern K. Willits and Peter R. Maida* THE REBEL-LIOUS YOUTH SUBCULTURE—A MYTH, 454   [40] *James S. Coleman* THE ADOLESCENT SUBCULTURE AND ACADEMIC ACHIEVEMENT, 463   [41] *Joseph S. Himes* NEGRO TEEN-AGE CULTURE, 476   [42] *William A. Schonfeld* ADOLESCENT TURMOIL: SOCIOECONOMIC AFFLUENCE AS A FACTOR, 486   [43] *Eli A. Rubinstein* PARADOXES OF STUDENT PROTESTS, 498 [44] *Fred Davis and Laura Munoz* HEADS AND FREAKS: PATTERNS AND MEANINGS OF DRUG USE AMONG HIPPIES, 511

INDEX, 523

ONE THE NATURE, THEORY, AND HISTORY OF ADOLESCENCE

Reacting to recent philosophical, psychological, social, and technological developments throughout the world, and stimulated by theoretical and empirical progress in their own discipline, developmental psychologists are reevaluating their conceptualizations of the nature of human development in general and adolescent personality development in particular. Not only college students but also experts in the field of psychology are challenged by the multiplicity of interpretations of basic psychological issues, as witness the intense responses to A. R. Jensen's article on the nature-nurture controversy, "Environment, Heredity and Intelligence" (1969). In order to help clarify the nature of the controversy related to adolescent development, the first group of articles exposes the reader to different interpretations of adolescent behavior.

The first selection [Rolf E. Muuss, (1)] gives a historical synopsis of basic philosophical interpretations of human development with emphasis on adolescent development. In the past, Muuss points out, adolescence was rarely isolated for particular consideration; youth was viewed as merely one stage of normal human growth. The current stress on the "youth culture," due to the prolonged period of transition between childhood and adulthood, is, therefore, a relatively recent phenomenon. Although the word "adolescence" itself appeared for the first time circa 1430, the term was rarely used until the late eighteenth century. Muuss notes that many of the "innovative" developmental theories presently in vogue may have their origin in ancient philosophical thought.

Albert Bandura (2), known for his contributions to social learning theory, challenges the widely accepted hypothesis of G. Stanley Hall, which describes adolescence as a time of storm and stress, or rebellion against authority, and of self-conflict. The social learning theory of development deemphasizes the biological nature of development and attacks the widely held "stage" concept. Bandura analyzes the origin and the fallacy of the mythology of adolescence. He summarizes his position by stating that "the sequence of developmental changes is considered in social learning theory to be primarily a function of changes in reinforced contingencies and other learning variables rather than an unfolding of genetically programmed response dispositions" (Bandura and F. J. McDonald, 1963). Furthermore, he feels that the childrearing patterns of the American middle class are consistent, and severe sexual tensions are not inevitable. On the contrary, adolescent rebellion may be a result of adult apprehension or the anti-social image of the adolescent as presented in the mass media. Bandura's view is not a popular one, as is obvious from other selections in this book, but it does provide a provocative alternative to the traditional theoretical position.

The third selection [Leon Eisenberg, (3)], takes still another point of view, serving as a contrast both to Bandura's (2) and Hall's interpretations of development. As a psychiatrist, Eisenberg sees adolescence as a "critical period," a span of life which can be "particularly stormy." Eisenberg's concern with the "acceleration of physiological growth" and the "acceleration of cognitive growth and personality development" implies the "stage" concept that Bandura rejects. Eisenberg declares that adolescence differs from adulthood not merely because of differences in social learning and social reinforcement, but also because of the interaction between social, psychological, and, especially, biological forces. Because he concentrates on a broad spectrum of topics rather than one particular issue, the article serves as a general introduction both to many of the topics covered in this book and to the main issues under study by developmental psychologists: the secular trend (5, 13), puberty rites (39), sexual roles (27), dating and courtship, peer group, identity (21, 22, 23), and idealism, and economic disadvantage (12, 38, 41).

David Elkind (4) offers a fourth viewpoint, writing specifically within the framework of Jean Piaget's theory of adolescent development. The concept of "egocentrism," previously associated only with the study of childhood behavior, is expanded to include adolescent development. Elkind defines "egocentrism in adolescence" as an adolescent's "belief that others are preoccupied with his appearance and behavior," and he hypothesizes that adolescent egocentrism finds expression in the contradictory behavior patterns of conformity and the struggle for identity. (See readings 20 through 23 for further discussion of conformity and the struggle for identity.) On a practical level, the adolescent's egocentric preoccupation "with what they appear to be in the eyes of others as compared with what they feel they are" (E. H. Erikson, 1950), becomes a genuine concern in many families and personal conflicts arise during the developmental years.

REFERENCES

Bandura, A., & F. J. McDonald, "Influence of Social Reinforcement and the Behavior of Models in Shaping Children's Moral Judgments." *Journal of Abnormal and Social Psychology*, 1963, 67, 274–281.

Erikson, E. H. *Childhood and Society*. New York: Norton, 1950.

Jensen, A. R. "How Much Can We Boost IQ and Scholastic Achievement?" *Harvard Educational Review*, 1969, 39, 1–123.

[1]   *Rolf E. Muuss*   THE PHILOSOPHICAL AND HISTORICAL ROOTS OF THEORIES OF ADOLESCENCE

Long before psychology became a science, there were philosophical, theological, educational, and psychological theories that contributed to an understanding of human nature and human development. G. Stanley Hall, with his famous two-volume *Adolescence* (10), is considered the father of a scientific "psychology of adolescence." Prior to Hall it was frequently the philosopher-educator who was especially concerned with a theory of human development with its implications for teaching. This was the case with Plato, Aristotle, Comenius, Rousseau, Herbart, Froebel, and Pestalozzi.

One difficulty in identifying prescientific theories of adolescent development is that prior to Hall adolescence was not considered a separate part or stage of human development and received no special emphasis. The word "adolescence" first appeared in the fifteenth century, indicating that historically adolescence was subordinated to theoretical considerations about the general nature of human development. Contemporary theories of adolescence frequently have their historical roots in general theories of development. Some important ideas about human development come from philosophers who are primarily concerned with the question: What is the nature of man? For example, what Locke and Darwin have to say about the nature of man is so profound that it is utilized and reflected in the writings of Rousseau and Hall respectively and thus constitutes a philosophical basis for a theory of development.

In classifying theories of development, Ausubel (6) distinguishes between preformationistic and predeterministic approaches to human development on the one side, and *tabula rasa* approaches on the other side. The preformationistic theory is reflected in the theological proposition of man's instantaneous creation, in the homunculus theory, and in the doctrine of man's basic sinfulness as well as in the more recent theories emphasizing instincts and innate drives. Predeterministic theories postulate universally fixed stages of development, but allow for environmental influences, as is obvious in Rousseau, Hall's theory of recapitulation, Freud's stages of psychosexual development, and Gesell's emphasis on maturation. In contrast to this are the *tabula rasa* ap-

FROM *Theories of Adolescence*, SECOND EDITION, BY ROLF E. MUUSS. COPYRIGHT © 1962, 1968 BY RANDOM HOUSE, INC. REPRINTED BY PERMISSION.

proaches that minimize the biological and genetic factors and place the emphasis on environmental determinants of human development. As the name implies, this includes Locke's *tabula rasa* theory, the humanistic approaches, and the related modern theories of behaviorism and cultural determinism.

Early Greek concern with human nature

An historical approach to a theory of adolescence must begin with the early Greek ideas about human development. Their influence remained prevalent through the Middle Ages and is still noticeable today. The philosophical idea of dualism, for instance, is essentially Greek. Plato (427–347 B.C.) made a clear distinction between two aspects of human nature: soul and body. He expounded that body and soul were different substances and that although there was some interaction between them the soul was an entity in itself, capable of leaving the body without losing its identity. It could perceive more clearly and reach higher realities when freed from the body; *soma sema* (the body is the grave of the soul) he declared. The body and sensuality are the fetters that hinder the soul in reaching those higher realities. Body is matter and has all the defects of matter. The idea of dualism between mind and body reappeared later in Christian theology and became of primary importance in the philosophical thinking of the seventeenth century, especially under Descartes, Leibnitz, and Spinoza.

Of greater interest from a developmental point of view is the idea of the layer structure of the soul which Plato developed in the dialogue *Phaedo* (15). According to Plato, the soul has three distinguishable parts, layers, or levels. Thus, probably for the first time in the history of psychology, a three-fold division of soul, mind, or psyche is advanced. The lowest layer of the soul is described as man's desires and appetites. Today we might describe this level in terms of drives, instincts, and needs, and its resmblance to Freud's concept "id" can hardly be denied. According to Plato, this part of the soul is located in the lower part of the body and is primarily concerned with the satisfaction of the physical needs ". . . it fills us full of love, and lusts, and fears, and fancies of all kinds, and endless foolery, and . . . takes away the power of thinking at all" (16). The second layer of the soul, the spirit, includes courage, conviction, temperance, endurance, and hardihood; aggressiveness and fierceness also originate here. Man has both the first and the second layer in common with the animal world. These two layers belong to the body and die with it. The third layer is divine, supernatural, and immortal; it constitutes the essence of the universe. This is the real soul, which Plato describes as reason and which has its temporary seat in the body. Plato's theory concerning the layer structure of the soul closely resembles several contemporary central European personality theories, which are developed on the assumption of a layer-like stratification of personality, especially those of Rothacker, Lersch, and Remplein. They perceive development as a process by which the lower layers mature earlier and are superseded by higher layers as the child grows older. Plato already postulated such a developmental theory. Reason is latent during the first stage when perception is most important. The second stage of development is characterized by conviction and understanding and brings the second layer of the soul, spirit, into the foreground of psychological development. The third stage, which we might identify with adolescence and maturity, but which, according to Plato, is not reached by all people, relates to the development of the third part of the soul, reason and intelligence.

Interspersed in most of Plato's dialogues—but particularly in *Laws* and in *The Republic*—are descriptive accounts of children and youth as well as advice concerning the control of their behavior. While this material does not constitute a theory of development as we understand it today, it does give insight into Plato's conception of the nature of development.

During the first three years of his life the infant should be free from fear and pain and sorrow. This point of view would be endorsed by many psychologists today. Interestingly enough, in the dialogue in *Laws* Cleinias suggests that in addition to freeing the infant from pain we ought to provide him with pleasure. This is in agreement with Plato's basic goal, which is the possession of happiness. However, the Athenian Stranger objects that this would spoil the child, since during the early years "more than at any other time the character is engrained by habit" (14). Character is formed at such an early age because the experiences and impressions leave a lasting influence. However, Plato does admit that "the characters of young men are subject to many changes in the course of their lives." The argument about the consistency of personality versus its modifiability has continued and proponents for both of Plato's statements can be found today.

From three to six the child needs sports and social contact with age-mates in order to get rid of his self-will. Plato would punish but not disgrace the child. Social development is taken into consideration at this age and children ought to come together in a kind of kindergarten arrangement under the supervision of a nurse. However, children should find for themselves the "natural modes of amusement" appropriate to their age.

Plato suggested a division of the sexes at six. "Let boys live with boys and girls . . . with girls." The boy now has to learn horsemanship, the use of bow and arrows, the spear, and the sling. Boys will not be allowed to drink wine until they are eighteen because of their easy excitability, "fire must not be poured upon fire." A related adolescent desire is argument for amusement's sake. In their enthusiasm they will leave no stone unturned and in their delight over the first taste of wisdom they will annoy everyone with their arguments. Plato believes that the character is formed through habit at a very early age.

Plato developed his educational philosophy in *The Republic* (16). He perceives education as the development of the soul under the influence of the environment "and this has two divisions, gymnastic for the body, and music for the soul." Reasoning in the young child is undeveloped, but since the young child is impressionable Plato suggested establishing "a censorship of the writers of fiction" since "anything that he receives into his mind is likely to become indelible and unalterable: and therefore . . . the talks which the young first hear should be models of virtuous thoughts" (16). Rational and critical thought develop mainly during adolescence. The training that began with music and gymnastics during childhood is continued through adolescence with mathematical and scientific studies. The latter bring out critical thought and dissatisfaction with direct sense-knowledge; during this training students would develop methods of finding the truth and of distinguishing truth from opinion. Plato speaks of education as "that training which is given by suitable habits to the first instincts of virtue in children; when pleasure, and friendship, and pain, and hatred are rightly implanted in souls not yet capable of understanding the nature of them, and who find them, after they have attained reason, to be in harmony with her" (14). The meaning of education is to provide experiences for children prior to the development of reason that are nevertheless in agreement with reason when it does develop during adolescence. Plato already recognized the importance of individual differences; children are born with different abilities and should be guided into those kinds of activities that are in line with their aptitudes.

Plato postulated that the attainment of knowledge might be explained by his doctrine of innate ideas. Though undeveloped, vague, and nebulous, innate ideas are nevertheless present at birth. Learning is a process of remembering these ideas, which once, probably before the soul entered the body, were clear. Sensations help in reawakening these partially lost ideas. The mind-body dualism is of relevance here since the body contributes sensation while the mind contains the ideas. In this way, Plato's theory of innate ideas opens the discussion about the influence of heredity and environment.

Aristotle (384–322 B.C.), in contrast to Plato, denied the separation of body and soul and returned to the older Greek idea of the unity of the physical and mental worlds. Body and soul for him were related in structure and function. The relationship between body and soul was the same as that between matter and form; body was matter and soul was form. Soul-life, for which Aristotle used the word *entelechy*, was the principle by which the body lives. Aristotle accepted Plato's idea concerning the levels of the soul-life; however, he viewed soul structure from a biological, almost evolutionary, point of view. The lowest soul-life form is that of the plant, the life-functions of which are supply of nourishment and reproduction. The next higher form of soul-life is also found in animals, its additional functions being sensation, perception, and locomotion. The third soul-life function is distinctly human and sets men apart from the animal world. It includes the ability to think and to reason. Consequently, there are three layers of soul-life, the food supplying or plant soul, the perceiving or animal soul, and the thinking or human soul. Aristotle further divided the thinking or human part of the soul into two different parts, the practical soul by which we "deliberate about those things which depend upon us and our purpose to do or not to do" (3) and the theoretical soul which deals with higher and abstract knowledge such as distinguishing between what is true and what is false.

Aristotle advanced a theory of development concerning the layer structure of the soul that appears to have some resemblance to Darwin's more scientific biological theory of evolution, even though it does not include the idea of evolution of one species to another. Furthermore, Aristotle made an impassable division between the different levels of soul-life. Plato, in describing the stages of development, held that the first (plant) soul level developed before the second (animal) soul level and this again was a prerequisite for the rational soul level. Aristotle followed this idea of the level structure of the soul and applied it to the development of the child, as becomes obvious from the following quotation:

As the body is prior in order of generation to the soul, so the irrational is prior to the rational. The proof is that anger and wishing and desire are implanted in children from their very birth, but reason and understanding are developed as they grow older. Wherefore, the care of the body ought to precede that of the soul, and the training of the appetitive part should follow; none the less our care of it must be for the sake of the reason, and our care of the body for the sake of the soul (4).

Aristotle divided the developmental period of the human being into three distinguishable stages of seven years each. The first seven years he named infancy; the period from seven to the beginning of puberty, boyhood; and from puberty to twenty-one, young manhood. This division of the period of development into three stages was generally accepted during the Middle Ages and recurs in some modern psychological theories of development, as advanced by Kroh, Remplein, and Zeller in Germany. Even in contemporary law twenty-one is the age at which the last limitations and protections of the "minor status" are removed.

Infants and animals are alike in that both are under the control of their appetites and emotions. "Children and brutes pursue pleasures" (1). Aristotle emphasized that moral character is the result of choice, "for by choosing what is good or bad we are men of a certain character. . . ." Even though young children are able to act voluntarily they do not have choice; "for both children and the lower animals share in voluntary action, but not in choice, and acts done on the spur of the moment we describe as voluntary, but not as chosen" (1). This seems to imply that children first go through an animal-like stage of development; what distinguishes them from animals is that children have the potential for higher development than animals, "though psychologically speaking a child hardly differs for the time being from an animal" (2). It is the characteristic of adolescence to develop the ability to choose. Only if the youth voluntarily and deliberately chooses will he develop the right kind of habits and this in the long run will build the right kind of character. Thus, by choosing the adolescent actively participates in his own character formation. Voluntarily and deliberate choice thus becomes an important aspect in Aristotle's theory of development, since it is necessary for the attainment of maturity. This idea is expressed today by modern writers. For example, both Margaret Mead and Edgar Friedenberg have stated that today with prolonged education and prolonged dependency we have reduced choices for adolescents to the extent that we interfere with their attainment of maturity.

Although Aristotle does not offer us a systematically stated theory of adolescence, he provides us with a rather detailed description of the "youthful type of character," part of which resembles descriptive statements that could have been written by G. Stanley Hall or Arnold Gesell. "Young men have strong passions, and tend to gratify them indiscriminately. Of the bodily desires, it is the sexual by which they are most swayed and in which they show absence of self-control" (5). Sexuality in adolescence is of concern in any contemporary text whether theoretically, empirically, or clinically oriented. Among the more recent theoretical positions, Otto Rank in particular describes promiscuity as an adolescent defense mechanism against sexual urges. Aristotle in his description of the adolescent comments on their instability: "They are changeable and fickle in their desires, which are violent while they last, but quickly over: their impulses are keen but not deep-rooted" (5). Lewin and Barker among the contemporary writers deal with the instability of the psychological field of the adolescent since he stands in a psychological no-man's-land. This makes many sociopsychological situations unclear, indefinite, and ambiguous and the resulting behavior is "changeable and fickle." "For owing to their love and honour they cannot bear being slighted, and are indignant if they imagine themselves unfairly treated" (5). Adolescent complaints about being "unfairly treated" in home, school, and society in general are so common today that they need no further elaboration. The list of quotes from *Rhetoric* in which Aristotle describes to his reader the characteristics of adolescence could be continued at length and further analogies to contemporary theory, observation, and empirical data would not be too difficult to find. Aristotle discusses, among other issues, adolescent desire for success, their optimism, trust, concern with the future rather than the past, their courage, conformity, idealism, friendship, aggressiveness, and gullibility.

In education, the adolescent was to study mainly mathematics including astronomy and theory of music and geometry, since these subjects teach abstraction but do not require the life experiences and wisdom necessary to be a philosopher or a physicist.

Under the early impact of Christian theology, Aristotelian thought seemed to get lost; however, it was later combined with Christian ideas by St. Thomas Aquinas. The Aristotelian Thomistic philosophy became dominant in the twelfth and thirteenth centuries and its influence was felt during the Middle

Ages—particularly in the form of scholasticism. Aristotle is also considered as influential in laying the foundation for a more scientific approach to science and psychology.

Medieval Christian view of human development

The theological view of human nature and development cannot as readily be identified in terms of one man, a specific period of time in history, or even a particular church. We find the idea of original sin expressed by Tertullian in the second century when he speaks of the depravity of human nature. It is emphasized by John Calvin in the sixteenth century and is prevalent in Catholic scholasticism, Protestant Calvinism, and American Puritanism.

The theological view of human nature and development as we find it in the medieval-early reformation period encompassed several ideas relevant to our topic:

1. Man's unique position in the universe, being created in the image of God.
2. Man's evil due to Adam's original sin.
3. Man's dualistic nature, a spiritual, immortal soul and a material, mortal body. Salvation and the life after death places the immortal soul on a higher level of importance.
4. Knowledge as revealed to man from without. It comes from God and is revealed to us through the Bible.
5. The homunculus idea of instantaneous creation. The last point is not so much biblical as medieval.

Most of these ideas can be found in biblical sources, but they are also influenced by Greek philosophy, especially Plato's dualism. We will see later that theories that follow in the seventeenth, eighteenth, and nineteenth centuries, especially those advanced by Locke, Rousseau, and Darwin, can partly be understood as antitheses to these earlier theological ideas.

The idea that God created man in his own image and thus gave him a unique position in the universe is expressed in Genesis 1:27-28, "And God created man to his own image: to the image of God he created him: male and female he created them." Furthermore, he gives them the power to rule over all living creatures. Prior to Darwin man was seen as being divinely created and basically different from the animal world.

The second important idea concerning the nature of man is the theological doctrine of human depravity. The human being was seen as having innate tendencies toward ungodliness and sinfulness. Man is fundamentally bad and his badness will become stronger during the developmental years if it is not counteracted by stern discipline. The idea of original sin as based on Genesis 3:6-7 relates the sinfulness of each individual to Adam's first sin. And "as sin came into the world through one man and death through sin, and so death spread to all men because all men sinned. . . . Yet death reigned from Adam to Moses, even over those whose sins were not like the transgression of Adam . . ."

(Romans 5:12–14). This pessimistic view of human nature, prevalent in Catholic theology before the Reformation, receives a new impetus with Calvin's theology and thus sets the intellectual climate for Puritanism. The educational objective in this theory is to bring forth the innate ideas which are God given— knowledge of his laws and commands. This was accomplished by stern mental and moral discipline. There is little room for individual differences, since the quality of the mind is the same for all individuals and the child who fails to learn is seen as willfully resisting the efforts of the teacher. The role of the teacher is defined by his authority and a belief that learning can be facilitated by physical punishment. The role of the child is defined by obedience. Calvin in particular expressed a strong faith in the value of education.

The theological point of view that man was the result of instantaneous creation results in preformationist thinking (6). It was believed that the child came into the world as a miniature adult. The difference between a child and an adult was only a quantitative one, not a qualitative one. Therefore girls wore long dresses and corsets of adult style, only smaller in size, as is obvious from many medieval paintings, just as mature women did. The qualitative difference in body build, body function, and mental abilities was disregarded. Growth was understood to be only a quantitative increase of all physical and mental aspects of human nature, not a qualitative one. This is a regression of thought during the Dark Ages when contrasted with the logical theories of Plato and Aristotle. The theory of preformationism held that children had the same interests as adults and therefore should be treated correspondingly, which meant that adult requirements were put upon them and were enforced by stern discipline. According to this view the child did not "develop," since he was preformed. This idea of "homunculism" was even utilized in prescientific theory of embryology.

It was seriously believed that a miniature but fully-formed little man (i.e., an homunculus) was embodied in the sperm, and when implanted in the uterus simply grew in bulk, without any differentiation of tissues or organs, until full-term fetal size was attained at the end of nine months (6).

This idea of homunculism was soon to be challenged by the beginning of modern science and advancements in the field of medicine. It was learned that the young child has qualitative and quantitative characteristics of his own and is not a miniature adult. One might speculate that the reason for the limited concern of pre-Hallian writers with the basic physiological changes that take place during pubescence—many of these changes are obvious to the keen observer and their detection does not require medical knowledge or technology —are due to the theoretical position that the child is a miniature adult. If one were to accept this point of view then it follows that there should be no difference in the physiological functions of the child and the adult. In the philosophical realm it was Rousseau who stated that "nature would have children be children before being man. If we wish to prevent this order, we shall produce precocious fruits which will have neither maturity nor flavor, and will speedily deteriorate; we shall have young doctors and old children" (17). Thus a new conception of human nature contributed to a more scientific concept of growth and development.

John Amos Comenius' development-centered theory of education

The Renaissance may be seen as a revolt against authoritarianism in church, school, and society. The Aristotelian logic, the presupposition of universal ideas, and scholasticism in general is challenged by Erasmus and Vives. Vives felt that one had "to begin with the individual facts of experience and out of them to come to ideas by the natural logic of the mind" (7). Learning is no longer seen as a deductive process, but as an inductive process beginning with experiences, and he suggests that an understanding of the learning process comes from psychology. Learning is determined by the mind of the learner and, therefore, education becomes concerned with individuality in pupils.

Comenius (1592–1670) accepted these new ideas of the Renaissance, combined them with Aristotle's classification of development, and advanced a theory of education that is based on psychological assumptions. In his *Great Didactic* (8) Comenius suggests a school organization based on a theory of development. Rather than dividing the developmental period into three stages of seven years, as Aristotle did, Comenius proposes four developmental stages of six years each and a different kind of school for each of these four stages.

The suggested school organization is based on assumptions concerning the nature of human development and a specific theory of learning, that of faculty psychology. Interestingly enough, present-day school organization in parts of the United States closely resembles this pattern. Comenius argued that the temporal sequence of the curriculum content should be borrowed from nature, in other words it should be suitable to the psychological development of the child. "Let our maxim be to follow the lead of nature in all things, to observe how the faculties develop one after the other, and to base our methods on this principle of succession" (8).

The child in the first six years of his life learns at home in the Mother-School at his mother's knee. He should exercise the external senses and learn to discriminate between the various objects around him. The nature of the development of the faculty of sense perception is such that it precedes all other faculties and, consequently, sensory experiences and sensory knowledge should be provided first. The significance of early sensory-motor experiences is emphasized in Piaget's contemporary theory of development.

The child from six to twelve attends the vernacular-school and receives a general well-rounded elementary education, which is provided for all children, rich or poor, boy or girl. Included in the curriculum are the correct use of the vernacular language, social habits, and religious training. The program at this level would emphasize training of the "internal senses, the imagination and memory in combination with their cognate organs." Comenius accepts the faculty psychology point of view in respect to memory. "The memory should be exercised in early youth since practice developes it, and we should therefore take care to practice it as much as possible. Now, in youth, labour is not felt, and thus the memory developes without any trouble and becomes very retentive" (8).

For the next six years, from twelve to eighteen, which includes the adolescent period as we understand it today, education is provided in the Latin school. The psychological purpose of the school at this age is to train the faculty of reasoning. The student learns to "understand and pass judgment on the information collected by the senses." Included are judgments about relationships of the things perceived, imagined, and remembered. Understanding here implies utilization of the principle of causality. The curriculum of the school is divided into six years, which results in the following six classes: Grammar, Natural Philosophy, Mathematics, Ethics, Dialectics, and Rhetoric.

The following six years from eighteen to twenty-four consist of university education and travel and it is at this point that the faculty of the will is to be trained. Considering our present conception of will this appears to be a strange notion and becomes more meaningful only if we consider that the concept of will, as used by Comenius, includes the self-direction of one's own life. Corresponding ideas can be found in the contemporary theories of Erikson and Nixon.

Comenius strongly advocates that the instructional procedure fits the level of comprehension of the child in contrast to the scholastic education, which he attacks. For Comenius, development is not uniform, continuous, and gradual— as the homunculus theory of development implies—but each stage of development has its own characteristics, "teachable moments" as Havighurst would say today. Development is a process in which the intellectual functions gain progressively more control over the other aspects of the soul.

To attempt to cultivate the will before the intellect (or the intellect before the imagination, or the imagination before the faculty of sense perception) is mere waste of time. But this is what those do who teach boys logic, poetry, rhetoric, and ethics before they are thoroughly acquainted with the objects that surround them. It would be equally sensible to teach boys of two years old to dance, though they can scarcely walk (8).

The right time for the education of each of the faculties must be chosen correctly and the sequence must be "borrowed from nature." In his continuous focus on what children can do, know, and are interested in at each stage of development, we seem to find the historical roots of a child-centered theory of education.

John Locke's empiricism

The idea of homunculism with its emphasis on preformationism and Plato's theory of innate ideas—a basic scholastic principle—was most seriously challenged and opposed by John Locke (1632–1704). Locke was influenced by Thomas Hobbes' idea that the human being, both body and mind, is part of the natural order; and further expanded Hobbes' theoretical position, known today as empiricism, that all of our knowledge is derived from sensation. Hobbes had stated that "there is no conception in man's mind, which has not at first, totally, or by parts, been begotten upon the organs of sense" (11). Locke further developed the theory that there are no innate ideas; ideas that we hold in our consciousness are either obtained through our senses directly or are derived from those ideas that have been obtained through sensations previously. The child's mind at the time of birth is, according to an analogy used by Locke, a *tabula rasa*, a blank tablet. He made the following famous statement concerning the nature of the human mind:

Let us then suppose the mind to be, as we say, white paper, void of all characters, without any ideas:—How comes it to be furnished? . . . To this I answer, in one word, from EXPERIENCE. In that all our knowledge is founded; and from that it ultimately derives itself. Our observation employed either, about external sensible objects, or about the internal operations of our minds perceived and reflected on by ourselves, is that which supplies our understandings with all the materials of thinking. These two are the fountains of knowledge, from whence all the ideas we have, or can naturally have, do spring (12).

This assumption has had far-reaching influence in social theory and has with amplification become the cornerstone of democracy. Since the minds of all men at birth are a *tabula rasa*, all ideas and all knowledge that men have come from experience; since present differences and inequalities that can be found in people are due to environment and experiences, men are completely equal at birth. Thus the principle of democracy is in part derived from a philosophical-psychological theory concerning the child's mind at birth. Locke discussed his views concerning democracy in *Treatise of Civil Government* (13). He blamed environmental conditions, such as poor education and poor social environment, for the human misery in the world and gave hope to those who lived under unfavorable conditions. Thus a theory emerged which is an expression of faith in the perfectibility of the human race.

Locke found rather enthusiastic followers in Helvetius and Condillac in France. They carried his empiricism to its extreme since for them even the powers of faculties of the mind are the result of sensation. Furthermore, since poor living conditions existed for the French lower and middle classes prior to the revolution, many people in France were especially susceptible to such ideas. Thus the words *liberté égalité, fraternité* became the powerful symbols of a new concept of human nature. A new hope emerged: that by changing the environment, human nature could be changed. Mankind could determine its own destiny.

Locke's proposition that there are no innate ideas and that the human mind is a *tabula rasa* contrasted sharply with several of the theories of human development already discussed. The more outstanding examples are:

1. The doctrine of human depravity and original sin appeared to be in open contradiction to Locke's new concept of the human mind. If our mind is formed by experience only, then it follows that whether a child becomes "good" or "bad" is due to environmental experiences. Locke's psychology stresses nurture rather than nature.

2. The medieval class system of Europe was based on what we would consider today as hereditary assumptions. The nobility was noble by birth, regardless of personal merits and qualities. This notion was challenged by the empiricist assumption that "all men are born equal." If all men are alike and begin life at the same point, everyone should have the same rights and opportunity to obtain better social position. King and subject, rich and poor, begin life at the same zero point. Therefore support for social mobility is found in this theory. Locke's early form of environmentalism, even though it is not directly related to behaviorism and cultural relativism, may be viewed as a historical forerunner to these schools of thought.

3. The doctrine of innate ideas was interpreted by the medieval period to imply that the child is a miniature adult and only grows quantitatively. Locke's *tabula rasa* concept implied that the child at birth is fundamentally different from the adult both qualitatively and quantitatively. If ideas are not innate then the newborn child is radically different from the adult in respect to intellectual properties. Locke pointed out that the child's personality is basically different from that of the adult and thus laid the foundation for a new theory of child development; he also urged the scientific study of human nature. Development, he believed, occurred in a gradual process from mental passivity in the early years of childhood to increased mental activity in adolescence. The rational faculty emerges toward the end of this developmental process and therefore is characteristic of the period of adolescence.

Locke himself, even though he advances many important ideas about human nature, foreshadows rather than develops a specific theory of human development. It is Rousseau who, influenced by Locke, proposes a new theory of child development.

Jean Jacques Rousseau's romantic naturalism

Rousseau (1712–1778) was greatly influenced by Locke's ideas, but he developed his own theoretical positions concerning human nature. While for Locke reason was the most important aspect of human nature, Rousseau considered human nature as primarily feeling. While Locke was concerned with constitutional government, Rousseau made a great plea for individualism and individual freedom and directed his criticism and attack against society and social institutions. Although he, too, was concerned with the social well-being of all, he distinguished between the "will of all" (majority will, determined by vote) and the "general will" (that which is really best for every member of the society). Rousseau was not truly democratic for he was afraid that a majority vote could be as bad as any monarchy. Ideally the majority will and the general will would coincide. This, however, was only possible if men were educated and wise.

Rousseau brought about a revolutionary change in thought concerning the nature of human development with its corresponding educational implications, the main ideas of which he expressed in *Emile* (17). The traditional approach toward childhood education had been to see the child from the adult point of view, adult interests, and adult social life. Rousseau claimed that such an approach is not only false, it may even be harmful. He started with the needs and interests of the child and saw development as a natural preplanned process. If one were to free the child from the restrictions, unnatural limitations, and rigid discipline of the adult world, nature would assure a harmonious and healthy development. The child was innately good, but the restrictions of adult society and poor education had corrupted the child. To correct this, he advocated a natural development in a sound and healthy environment, which for him was one that posed little restriction on the child, especially in the first twelve years. Rousseau was one of the strongest proponents of individualism in education, basing his proposition on a deep faith in the natural good of man.

Rousseau advocated a revision of the treatment children received at home and in school as well as changes in the methods of instruction; if development were left to the laws of nature the outcome would be most desirable. Each of the four stages of development has specific psychological characteristics. Consideration of these characteristics results in definite educational objectives, the attainment of which helps children grow toward maturity. The educational methods, the content to be taught, and the educational objectives at each age level are to be determined by the characteristics of the child at that developmental level. Learning is most effective if the child has freedom and can learn and grow according to his own impulses.

Rousseau most strongly opposed the homunculus idea and asserted that it was the plan of nature that children play, live, and behave like children before they become adults. "Childhood has its own way of seeing, thinking, and feeling, and nothing is more foolish than to try to substitute ours for them" (17). Rousseau advised teachers and parents, "You ought to be wholly absorbed in the child—observing him, watching him without respite, and without seeming to do so, having a presentiment of his feelings in advance" (17). Even though Rousseau himself had only limited and not always successful educational experiences—his five children lived in a foundling asylum—his theory had a tremendous impact on educational practice in the latter part of the eighteenth and most of the nineteenth centuries. Rousseau's ideas are obvious in the works of Pestalozzi, Froebel, Basedow, Spencer, Horace Mann, and John Dewey, and are reflected in a child-centered approach to education.

Rousseau, like Aristotle, saw the development of the child occurring in certain stages—however, he identified four stages rather than three—and believed that teaching and training should be in harmony with the developmental nature of each of these stages. According to Rousseau, these various stages are breaks in the developmental process and each can be distinguished because each has special characteristics and functions. He spoke of a metamorphosis that takes place when the child changes from one stage to another. Thus, Rousseau introduced a saltatory theory of human development according to which the nature of development is seen as change that is more sudden at certain age levels than at others. He, like G. Stanley Hall, speaks of puberty as a new birth. New functions may emerge rather suddenly and become dominant in the psychological organization. We might better understand this saltatory aspect of development in Rousseau's theory if we recall his own temperamental saltatory experiences.

The first stage, that of infancy, includes the first four to five years of life. The child is dominated by the feeling of pleasure and pain. This period is called the animal stage, because the child is like an animal in regard to its physical needs and undifferentiated feelings. This notion we encountered earlier in the writings of Aristotle. Education, such as training motor coordination, sense perception, and feeling, is primarily physical. He advocates to mothers that the method of nature be followed in everything and proposed the following rule: "Observe nature, and follow the route which she traces for you. She is ever exciting children to activity; she hardens the constitution by trials of every sort; she teaches them at an early hour what suffering and pain are."

The second stage, which Rousseau characterized as the savage stage, includes the years from five to twelve. Dominant during this stage is the faculty of sense. Sensory experiences are provided by play, sport, and games, and the curriculum is centered around the training of the senses. During this stage self-consciousness and memory develop and human life in the proper sense begins here. The child still lacks reasoning ability and is not yet sufficiently aware of moral considerations. Education during this stage should be free from external, social, and moral control. Formal training in reading and writing are seen as harmful and therefore postponed until the beginning of the third developmental stage. In the first twelve years education

. . . ought to be purely negative. It consists not at all in teaching virtues or truth, but in shielding the heart from vice, and the mind from error. If you could do nothing and allow nothing to be done, if you could bring your pupil sound and robust to the age of twelve years without his being able to distinguish his right hand from his left, from your very first lesson the eyes of his understanding would be open to reason (17).

Rousseau's method of "negative education," based on the assumption that there was an innate developmental plan in the organization which cannot be improved upon by environmental factors, finds its corresponding modern psychological concept in "maturation." The defenders of the maturational concept of development frequently advocate, as did Rousseau, a permissive and unrestricted atmosphere for childrearing.

The third stage, from the age of twelve to fifteen, is characterized by an awakening of the rational functions, including reason and self-consciousness. Youth at his age possess an enormous amount of physical energy and strength. The excess of energy leads to curiosity, which the school curriculum should utilize by encouraging exploratory behavior and the desire to discover what is true about the world. The only book that should be read during this stage was *Robinson Crusoe*. Rousseau saw in Crusoe the great model and ideal for the preadolescent, since his style of life was characterized by exploration of the world and a primitive curiosity and corresponds to the needs and interests of this developmental stage. The curriculum should be geared to the study of nature, astronomy, science, art, and crafts. Rousseau in agreement with contemporary educational theory emphasizes the learning process rather than the product. "He is not to learn science, he is to find out for himself." This is the age of reason; curiosity and personal utility are the main motives for behavior; social conscience and emotionality are still undeveloped. It is interesting to observe that, in opposition to other developmental theories, the rational aspect of personality develops prior to the emotional. Rousseau's theory was a reaction to the historically earlier philosophy of rationalism. Modern theory of personality stratification sees in emotionality the deeper and therefore the historically and developmentally earlier layer of personality.

The fourth period, adolescence proper, from the age of fifteen to twenty, finally culminates in the maturation of the emotional functions and brings about a change from selfishness to self-esteem and social consideration. The adolescent is no longer self-sufficient but develops a strong interest in other people and a need for genuine affection. This stage is characterized—late by comparison to knowledge about youth today—by the emergence of the sex drive, which Rousseau considered a second birth. "We have two births, so to speak—one for existing and the other for living; one for the species and the other for the sex" (17). Now conscience is acquired and morals and virtues become possible. This is the period of preparation for marriage, which ideally coincides with the attainment of maturity.

Maturity could be considered as a fifth stage in the process, but it appears to be less clearly defined. The faculty that becomes dominant during this period is will. The will is the faculty of the soul by which we choose between two alternatives.

These stages of development, according to Rousseau, correspond to certain stages in the development of the human race. Thus it was assumed by this recapitulation theory that the human race had gone through the stages of animal-like living, the stage of savagery, the stage of reason, and finally, through a stage of social and emotional maturity. He used the historical development of the race in order to explain the development of the individual child. This hypothesis was taken up again and further developed by educators, such as Froebel and Ziller, as well as by G. Stanley Hall and the Child Study Movement of America.

Critics have pointed out that Rousseau overemphasized the individual nature of human growth and development and underemphasized the importance that education, society, and culture have in the developmental process and especially in the formation of the human personality. He saw the influence of education and culture as negative forces in personality development which he wanted to remove to make possible the free natural development of what is good in the child.

Charles Darwin's theory of biological evolution

A new trend of thought concerning the nature of development results from the publication of Darwin's *Origin of Species* (9). Darwin's (1809–1882) idea of evolution—growth and development from the simpler to the more complex forms of organic life—has been one of the most revolutionary and influential ideas in man's thinking about himself and the nature of his development. Every living organism from the simplest organic structure to the most complex, man himself, is brought together under the lawfulness of natural explanation. The psychological implications resulting from this biological concept of development were accepted, elaborated, and applied to adolescent development by G. Stanley Hall, thus leading to a science of adolescent development.

Since Darwin's theory is well known, only its basic principles will be stated. Darwin collected substantial, though not complete, evidence for a theory which claimed that the evolution of biological life was continuous, from a single cell organism, through numerous higher developmental stages, to the complexity of human mind and body. This evolutionary theory assumed variability and adjustability in all organisms as well as the overproduction in the number of offspring of each species. Darwin showed that the overproduction of offspring outnumbered their capacity to survive. The result is a "struggle for existence." In this struggle of the selection of some and elimination of others, a "natural selection process" takes place by which the increase in population is checked. The stronger, healthier, faster, more immune, more intelligent, and physically better developed and adjusted organisms survive and reproduce, while the weak, sick, and less adaptable species perish. In time this leads to the "survival of the fittest." The qualities that account for the survival of the fittest are inherited by the offspring. Since the conditions for survival frequently differ in various kinds of environments basic changes in the organism occur. Thus in the selection process, variations, new kinds, new races, and eventually new organisms come into existence. This process began with the simple one cell organism, and from the lower forms of organic life more and more complex forms have developed. The last link in this biological evolution is the human being. Since the climate, geological and general life conditions change, the evolutionary process is a perpetual one.

This theory of evolution is in complete contrast to the theological doctrine of the Divine Creation of each individual. Through Darwin's theory man was placed in the order of nature. Most theological and many philosophical positions previous to Darwin,—e.g., Aristotle—had postulated an essential dichotomy between man and nature. This absolute distinction between human nature and the nature of the organic world was seriously challenged by Darwin. Man was now seen as part of the organic world, albeit a more advanced and more intelligent species.

G. Stanley Hall's biogenetic psychology of adolescence

G. Stanley Hall (1844–1924) was the first psychologist to advance a psychology of adolescence in its own right and to use scientific methods in his study of adolescence. It can be said that he bridged the philosophical, speculative approach of the past and the scientific, empirical approach of the present.

Hall expanded Darwin's concept of biological "evolution" into a psychological theory of recapitulation. In this theory he stated that the experiential history of the human species had become part of the genetic structure of each individual. The law of recapitulation asserted that the individual organism, during its development, passes through stages that correspond to those that occurred during the history of mankind. That is, the individual relives the development of the human race from early animal-like primitivism, through a period of savagery, to the more recent civilized ways of life which characterize maturity.

Hall assumed that development was brought about by physiological factors. He further assumed that these physiological factors were genetically determined, that internal maturational forces predominantly controlled and directed development, growth, and behavior; there was little room in this theory for the influence of environmental forces. It follows that development and its behavioral concomitants occur in an inevitable and unchangeable pattern which is universal, regardless of the sociocultural environment. Cultural anthropologists and sociologists were able to challenge this point and to show that Hall's position was extreme and untenable in the light of accumulated evidence. They further refuted the claim that the behavioral predispositions of physiological drives, as expressed in the recapitulation theory, are highly specific. Hall held that socially unacceptable types of behavior—those characteristic of earlier historical phases—must be tolerated by parents and educators, since they are necessary stages in social development. He advocated childrearing practices of leniency and permissiveness. However, he reassured parents and educators that unacceptable behavior would disappear in the following developmental stage without any corrective educational or disciplinary efforts. Remnants of this assumption can be found in Gesell's conception of maturation.

A corollary of Hall's theory of recapitulation is his concept of stages of human development; the characteristics of a certain age in the development of the individual correspond to some primitive historical stage in the development of the human race. Hall did not divide human development into three stages as advocated by Aristotle and many present-day "stage" psychologists. He followed a four-division pattern similar to that proposed by Comenius and Rousseau. Hall's developmental stages were infancy, childhood, youth, and adolescence.

The period of infancy includes the first four years of life. While the child is still crawling, he is reenacting the animal stage of the human race when the species was still using four legs. During this period, sensory development is dominant; the child acquires those sensory motor skills which are necessary for self-preservation.

The period of childhood—the years from four to eight—corresponds to the cultural epoch when hunting and fishing were the main activities of man. This is the time when the child plays hide-and-seek, cowboys and Indians, uses toy weapons, etc. The building of caves, shacks, and other hiding places parallels the cave-dwelling culture of early history.

Youth—from eight to twelve—includes the period which today is commonly referred to as "preadolescence." During this stage the child recapitulates the "humdrum life of savagery" of several thousand years ago. This is the period of life when the child has a favorable predisposition to practice and discipline, when routine training and drill are most appropriate.

Never again will there be such susceptibility to drill and discipline, such plasticity to habituation, or such ready adjustment to new conditions. It is the age of external and mechanical training. Reading, writing, drawing, manual training, musical technic, foreign tongues and their pronunciation, the manipulation of numbers and of geometrical elements, and many kinds of skill have now their golden hour, and if it passes unimproved, all these can never be acquired later without a heavy handicap or disadvantage or loss (10).

Adolescence is the period from puberty (about twelve or thirteen) until full adult status has been attained. According to Hall, it ends comparatively late, between the twenty-second and twenty-fifth years. Hall described adolescence as a period of *Sturm und Drang,* "storm and stress." In German literature, the period of *Sturm und Drang* includes, among others, the works of Schiller and the early writings of Goethe. It is a literary movement full of idealism, commitment to a goal, revolution against the old, expression of personal feelings, passion, and suffering. Hall saw an analogy between the objectives of this group of young writers at the turn of the eighteenth century and the psychological characteristics of adolescence. In terms of the recapitulation theory adolescence corresponds to a time when the human race was in a turbulent, transitional stage. Hall described adolescence as a new birth, "for the higher and more completely human traits are now born" (10).

The characteristics of adolescent *Sturm und Drang* are pictured in detail in the chapter "Feelings and Psychic Evolution." Hall perceived the emotional life of the adolescent as an oscillating between contradictory tendencies. Energy, exaltation, and supernatural activity are followed by indifference, lethargy, and loathing. Exuberant gaiety, laughter, and euphoria make place for dysphoria, depressive gloom, and melancholy. Egoism, vanity, and conceit are just as characteristic of this period of life as are abasement, humiliation, and bashfulness. One can observe both the remnants of an uninhibited childish selfishness and an increasing idealistic altruism. Goodness and virtue are never so pure, but never again does temptation so forcefully preoccupy thought. The adolescent wants solitude and seclusion, while he finds himself entangled in crushes and friendships. Never again does the peer group have such a strong influence over him. At one time he may exhibit exquisite sensitivity and tenderness; at another time, callousness and cruelty. Apathy and inertia vacillate with an enthusiastic curiosity, an urge to discover and explore. There is a yearning for idols and authority that does not exclude a revolutionary radicalism directed against any kind of authority. Hall implies these antithetical impulses of Promethean enthusiasm and deep sentimental *Weltschmerz* in his use of the concept of *Sturm und Drang*, which for him is so characteristic of the adolescent (10).

In late adolescence the individual recapitulates the stage of the beginning of modern civilization. This stage corresponds to the end of the developmental process: he reaches maturity. Hall's genetic psychology did not see the human being as the final and finished product of the developmental process; it allowed for indefinite further development.

REFERENCES

1. Aristotle. "Ethica Nicomachea." (W. D. Ross, trans.) in *The Basic Works of Aristotle* (R. McKeon, ed.). New York: Random House, 1941.
2. ———. "Historia Animalium." (D. W. Thompson, trans.) in *The Basic Works of Aristotle* (R. McKeon, ed.). New York: Random House, 1941.
3. ———. "Magna Moralia." (G. Stock, trans.) in *The Works of Aristotle* (W. D. Ross, ed.). Vol. IX. Oxford: Clarendon Press, 1925.
4. ———. "Politicia." (B. Jowett, trans.) in *The Basic Works of Aristotle* (R. McKeon, ed.). New York: Random House, 1941.
5. ———. "Rhetorica." (W. R. Roberts, trans.) in *The Basic Works of Aristotle* (R. McKeon, ed.). New York: Random House, 1941.

6. Ausubel, D. P. *Theory and Problems of Child Development.* New York: Grune & Stratton, 1958.
7. Boyd, W. *The History of Western Education.* New York: Barnes & Noble, 1965.
8. Comenius, J. A. *The Great Didactic* (M. W. Keating, ed. and trans.). London: A. & C. Black, 1923.
9. Darwin, C. R. *The Origin of Species by Means of Natural Selection.* London: J. Murray, 1859.
10. Hall, G. S. *Adolescence.* 2 vol. New York: Appleton, 1916.
11. Hobbes, T. *Leviathan.* Reprint of the Edition of 1651. Oxford: Clarendon Press, 1929.
12. Locke, J. *An Essay Concerning Human Understanding* (A. C. Fraser, ed.). Oxford: Clarendon Press, 1894.
13. ———. *Treatise of Civil Government.* New York: Appleton-Century-Crofts, 1937.
14. Plato. "Laws." (B. Jowett, trans.) *The Dialogues of Plato.* Vol. IV, 4th ed. Oxford: Clarendon Press, 1953.
15. ———. "Phaedo." (B. Jowett, trans.) *The Dialogues of Plato.* Vol. I, 3rd ed. New York: Random House, 1937.
16. ———. *The Republic.* (B. Jowett, trans.) Oxford: Clarendon Press, 1921.
17. Rousseau, J. J. *Emile.* (W. H. Payne, trans.) New York: Appleton-Century-Crofts, 1911.

[2] *Albert Bandura* THE STORMY DECADE: FACT OR FICTION?

If you were to walk up to the average man on the street, grab him by the arm and utter the word "adolescence," it is highly probable—assuming he refrains from punching you in the nose—that his associations to this term will include references to storm and stress, tension, rebellion, dependency conflicts, peer-group conformity, black leather jackets, and the like. If you then abandoned your informal street corner experiment, and consulted the professional and popular literature on adolescence, you would become quickly impressed with the prevalence of the belief that adolescence is, indeed, a unique and stormy developmental period (Gallagher & Harris, 1958; Hurlock, 1955; Josselyn, 1948; Mohr & Despres, 1958; Parsons, 1950; Pearson, 1958).

FROM *Psychology in the School,* 1964 *1,* 224–231. REPRINTED BY PERMISSION OF THE AUTHOR AND THE CLINICAL PSYCHOLOGY PUBLISHING COMPANY, INC.

The adolescent presumably is engaged in a struggle to emancipate himself from his parents. He, therefore, resists any dependence upon them for their guidance, approval or company, and rebels against any restrictions and controls that they impose upon his behavior. To facilitate the process of emancipation, he transfers his dependency to the peer group whose values are typically in conflict with those of his parents. Since his behavior is now largely under the control of peer-group members, he begins to adopt idiosyncratic clothing, mannerisms, lingo, and other forms of peer-group fad behavior. Because of the conflicting values and pressures to which the adolescent is exposed, he is ambivalent, frightened, unpredictable, and often irresponsible in his behavior. Moreover, since the adolescent finds himself in a transition stage in which he is neither child, nor adult, he is highly confused even about his own identity.

The foregoing storm and stress picture of adolescence receives little support from detailed information that Dr. Walters and I obtained in a study of middle class families of adolescent boys (Bandura & Walters, 1959). Let us compare the popular version of adolescence with our research findings.

PARENTAL RESTRICTIVENESS

At adolescence, parents supposedly become more controlling and prohibitive. We found the very opposite to be true. By the time the boys had reached adolescence, they had internalized the parents' values and standards of behavior to a large degree; consequently, restrictions and external controls had been lightened as the boys became increasingly capable of assuming responsibility for their own behavior, and in directing their own activities. The parents were highly trustful of their boys' judgment and felt that externally imposed limits were, therefore, largely unnecessary. The following interview excerpts provide some typical parental replies to inquiries concerning the restrictions they placed on their boys:

M. (MOTHER): I don't have to do anything like that any more.
   I think he's getting so mature now, he's sort of happy medium.
   I don't have to do much with him.
I. (INTERVIEWER): What are some of the restrictions you have for him? How about going out at night?
F. (FATHER): We trust the boy. We never question him.
I: Are there any things you forbid him from doing when he is with his friends?
F: At his age I would hate to keep telling him that he mustn't do this, or mustn't do that. I have very little trouble with him in that regard. Forbidding I don't think creeps into it because he ought to know at 17, right from wrong.
I: Are there any friends with whom you have discouraged him from associating?
F: No, not up to now. They are very lovely boys.
I: How about using bad language?
F: Only once, only once have I; of course I'm a little bit hard of hearing in one ear, and sometimes he gets around the wrong side and takes advantage of that.

The boys' accounts were essentially in agreement with those given by the parents. In response to our questions concerning parental demands and controls, the boys pointed out that at this stage in their development parental restraints were no longer necessary. An illustrative quotation, taken from one of the boys' interviews, is given below:

I: What sort of things does your mother forbid you to do around the house?
B: Forbid me to do? Gee, I don't think there's ever anything.
The house is mine as much as theirs. . . Oh, can't whistle, can't throw paper up in the air, and can't play the radio and phonograph too loud. Rules of the house; anybody, I mean, it's not just me. . .
I: Are you expected to stay away from certain places or people?
B: She knows I do. I'm not expected; I mean, she figures I'm old enough to take care of myself now. They never tell me who to stay away from or where. Well, I mean, they don't expect me to sleep down on Skid Row or something like that. . .

Since the boys adopted their parents' standards of conduct as their own, they did not regard their parents and other authority figures as adversaries, but more as supportive and guiding influences.

DEPENDENCE-INDEPENDENCE CONFLICTS

The view that adolescents are engaged in a struggle to emancipate themselves from their parents also receives little support from our study.

Although the boys' dependency behavior had been fostered and encouraged during their childhood, independence training had begun early and was, therefore, largely accomplished by the time of adolescence. A similar early and gradual decrease in dependency upon adults is reported by Heathers (1955), who compared the dependency behavior of two-year-old and of five-year-old children. He found that, even over this small age range, dependency on adults had declined, whereas dependency on other children had increased.

For most of the boys that we studied, the emancipation from parents had been more or less completed rather than initiated at adolescence. In fact, the development of independence presented more of a conflict for the parents, than it did for the boys. Some of the parents, particularly the fathers, regretted the inevitable loss of the rewards that their sons' company had brought them.

I: Do you feel that you spend as much time with Raymond as other fathers do with their sons, or more?
F: I would say about average, but perhaps I should spend more time with him, because as the years go by, I see that he's growing into manhood and I'm losing a lot of him every year. When he was younger, I think I was with him more than I am now. I think, as he gets older, he's had a tendency to get his pleasures from people his own age, this is fine as long as he makes home his headquarters. That's all I want.

Although the boys devoted an increasing amount of time to peer-group activities, they, nevertheless, retained close ties to their parents and readily sought out their help, advice, and support when needed.

PARENT PEER-GROUP CONFLICTS

The boys' primary reference groups were not selected indiscriminately. Since the adolescents tended to choose friends who shared similar value systems and behavioral norms, membership in the peer-group did not generate familial conflicts. In fact, the peer-group often served to reinforce and to uphold the parental norms and standards of behavior that the boys had adopted. Consequently, the parents were generally pleased with their sons' associates because they served as an important source of control in situations where the parents could not be present.

An essentially similar picture of adolescence, based on an intensive study of middle-class families, has been presented by Elkin and Westley (1955; 1956). They summarize their findings as follows:

Family ties are close and the degree of basic family consensus is high. The parents are interested in all the activities of their children, and the adolescents, except for the area of sex, frankly discuss their own behavior and problems with them. In many areas of life, there is joint participation between parents and children. . . . In independent discussion by parents and adolescents of the latters' marriage and occupational goals, there was a remarkable level of agreement. The adolescents also acknowledged the right of the parents to guide them, for example, accepting, at least manifestly, the prerogatives of the parents to set rules for the number of dates, hours of return from dates, and types of parties. The parents express relatively little concern about the socialization problems or peer group activities of their children (1955, p. 682).

Sources of the adolescent mythology

What are the origins of the mythology about adolescence, and why does it persist?

OVERINTERPRETATION OF SUPERFICIAL SIGNS OF NONCONFORMITY

The view that adolescence is a period of rebellion is often supported by references to superficial signs of nonconformity, particularly adolescent fad behavior.

It is certainly true that adolescents frequently display idiosyncratic fashions and interest patterns. Such fads, however, are not confined to adolescent age groups. Several years ago, for example, coon skin caps and Davy Crockett apparel were highly fashionable among pre-adolescent boys. When Davy Crockett began to wane a new fad quickly emerged—every youngster and a sizeable proportion of the adult population were gyrating with hoola-hoops. The hoola-hoop also suffered a quick death by replacement.

If pre-adolescent children display less fad behavior than do adolescents, this difference may be primarily due to the fact that young children do not possess the economic resources with which to purchase distinctive apparel, the latest phonograph records, and discriminative ornaments, rather than a reflection of a sudden heightening of peer-group conformity pressures during adolescence. The pre-adolescent does not purchase his own clothing, he has little voice in how his hair shall be cut and, on a 15-cent a week allowance, he is hardly in a position to create new fads, or to deviate too widely from parental tastes and standards.

How about adult fad behavior? A continental gentleman conducts a fashion show in Paris and almost instantly millions of hemlines move upward or downward; the human figure is sacked, trapezed, chemised, or appareled in some other fantastic creation.

At a recent cocktail party the present writer was cornered by an inquiring lady who expressed considerable puzzlement over adolescents' fascination for unusual and bizarre styles. The lady herself was draped with a sack, wearing a preposterous object on her head, and spiked high heel shoes that are more likely to land one in an orthopedic clinic, than to transport one across the room to the olives.

Fashion-feeders determine the styles, the colors, and the amount of clothing that shall be worn. It would be rare, indeed, to find an adult who would ask a sales clerk for articles of clothing in vogue two or three years ago. As long as social groups contain a status hierarchy, and tolerance for upward mobility within the social hierarchy, one can expect imitation of fads and fashions from below which, in turn, forces inventiveness from the elite in order to preserve the status differentiations.

MASS MEDIA SENSATIONALISM

The storm and stress view of adolescence is also continuously reinforced by mass media sensationalism. Since the deviant adolescent excites far more interest than the typical high school student, the adolescent is usually portrayed in literature, television, and in the movies as passing through a neurotic or a semi-delinquent phase of development (Kiell, 1959). These productions, many of which are designed primarily to generate visceral reactions or to sell copy, are generally viewed as profound and sensitive portrayals of the *typical* adolescent turmoil. Holden Caulfield, the central character in *The Catcher in the Rye* (Salinger, 1945), has thus become the prototypic adolescent.

GENERALIZATION FROM SAMPLES OF DEVIANT ADOLESCENTS

Professional people in the mental health field are apt to have most contact with delinquent adolescents, and are thus prone to base their accounts of adolescence on observations of atypical samples. By and large, the description of the modal pattern of adolescent behavior fits most closely the behavior of the deviant ten per cent of the adolescent population that appears repeatedly in psychiatric clinics, juvenile probation departments, and in the newspaper headlines.

Our study of the family relationships of adolescents also included a sample of antisocially aggressive boys. In the families of these hyper-aggressive adolescents there was indeed a great deal of storm and stress for many years. The boys' belligerance and rebellion, however, was not a unique product of adolescence. The defiant oppositional pattern of behavior was present all along, but because of their greater size and power the parents were able to suppress and to control, through coercive methods, their sons' belligerence during the early childhood years. By the time of adolescence, however, some of the boys had reached the stage where they were almost completely independent of the parents for the satisfaction of their social and physical needs. Moreover, they had developed physically to the point where they were larger and more powerful than their parents. With the achievement of the power reversal and the decrease of the parents' importance as sources of desired rewards, a number of the boys exhibited a blatant indifference to their parents' wishes about which they could now do little or nothing.

I: What sort of things does your mother object to your doing when you are out with your friends?
B: She don't know what I do.
I: What about staying out late at night?
B: She says, "Be home at 11 o'clock." I'll come home at one.
I: How about using the family car?
B: No. I wrecked mine, and my father wrecked his a month before I wrecked mine, and I can't even get near his. And I got a license and everything. I'm going to hot wire it some night and cut out.
I: How honest do you feel you can be to your mother about where you've been and what things you have done?
B: I tell her where I've been, period.
I: How about what you've done?
B: No. I won't tell her what I've done. If we're going out in the hills for a beer bust, I'm not going to tell her. I'll tell her I've been to a show or something.
I: How about your father?
B: I'll tell him where I've been, period.

The heightened aggression exhibited by these boys during adolescence primarily reflected response predispositions that became more evident following the power reversal in the parent-child relationship, rather than an adolescence-induced stress.

INAPPROPRIATE GENERALIZATION FROM
CROSS-CULTURAL DATA

It is interesting to note that many writers cite cross-cultural data as supporting evidence for the discontinuity view of child development in the American society. The reader suddenly finds himself in the Trobriand Islands, or among the Arapesh, rather than in the suburbs of Minneapolis or in the town square of Oskaloosa.

In many cultures the transition from child to adult status is very abrupt. Childhood behavior patterns are strongly reinforced, but as soon as the child reaches pubescence he is subjected to an elaborate initiation ceremony which signifies his abrupt transformation into adult status. Following the ceremonial initiation the young initiate acquires new rights and privileges, new responsibilities and, in some cultures, he is even assigned a new name and a new set of parents who undertake his subsequent social training in the skills and habits required to perform the adult role.

In our culture, on the other hand, except for the discontinuities in the socialization of sexual behavior, there is considerable continuity in social training. As was mentioned earlier, independence and responsibility training, for example, are begun in early childhood and adult-role patterns are achieved through a gradual process of successive approximations. This is equally true in the development of many other forms of social behavior.

It should be mentioned in passing, however, that cross-cultural studies have been valuable in demonstrating that stresses and conflicts are not inevitable concomitants of pubescence, but rather products of cultural conditioning. Indeed, in some societies, adolescence is one of the pleasant periods of social development (Mead, 1930).

OVEREMPHASIS OF THE BIOLOGICAL DETERMINATION OF
HETEROSEXUAL BEHAVIOR

With the advent of pubescence the adolescent is presumably encumbered by a powerful biologically determined sexual drive that produces a relatively sudden and marked increase in heterosexual behavior. The net result of the clash between strong physiological urges demanding release and even more substantial social prohibitions, is a high degree of conflict, frustration, anxiety and diffuse tension. In contrast to this widely-accepted biological drive theory, evidence from studies of cross-species and cross-cultural sexual behavior reveals that human sexuality is governed primarily by social conditioning, rather than endocrinal stimulation (Ford & Beach, 1951).

The cross-species data demonstrate that hormonal control of sexual behavior decreases with advancing evolutionary status. In lower mammalian species, for example, sexual activities are completely regulated by gonadal hormones; among primates sexual behavior is partially independent of physiological stim-

ulation; while human eroticism is exceedingly variable and essentially independent of hormonal regulation. Humans can be sexually aroused before
puberty and long after natural or surgical loss of reproductive glands. Thus,
one would induce sexual behavior in a rodent Don Juan by administering
androgen, whereas presenting him lascivious pictures of a well-endowed mouse
would have no stimulating effects whatsoever. By contrast, one would rely
on sexually-valenced social stimuli, rather than on hormonal injections for
producing erotic arousal in human males.

The prominent role of social learning factors in determining the timing,
incidence and form of sexual activities of humans is also clearly revealed in
the wide cross-cultural variability in patterns of sexual behavior. Sex-arousing
properties have been conditioned to an extremely broad range of stimuli, but
the cues that are sexually stimulating in one culture would, in many instances,
prove sexually repulsive to members of another society. A similar diversity
exists in the timing of the emergence of sexual interest and in the choice of
sexual objects. In cultures that permit and encourage heterosexual behavior
at earlier, or at later, periods of a child's development than is true for American
youth, no marked changes in sexual behavior occur during adolescence.

It is evident from the foregoing discussion that "sexual tensions" are not
an inevitable concomitant of pubescence. Furthermore, any significant increase in heterosexual activities during adolescence is due more to cultural
conditioning and expectations than to endocrinal changes.

STAGE THEORIES OF PERSONALITY DEVELOPMENT

Until recently, most of the theoretical conceptualizations of the developmental process have subscribed to some form of stage theory. According to the
Freudian viewpoint (1949), for example, behavioral changes are programmed
in an oral-anal-phallic sequence; Erikson (1950) characterizes personality development in terms of an eight-stage sequence; Gesell (1943) describes marked
predictable cyclical changes in behavior over yearly or even shorter temporal
intervals; and Piaget (1948, 1954), delineates numerous different stages for
different classes of responses.

Although there appears to be relatively little consensus among these theories concerning the number and the content of stages considered to be crucial,
they all share in common the assumption that social behavior can be categorized in terms of a relatively prefixed sequence of stages with varying degrees
of continuity or discontinuity between successive developmental periods.
Typically, the spontaneous emergence of these elaborate age-specific modes of
behavior is attributed to ontogenetic factors. The seven-year-old, for example,
is supposed to be withdrawn; the eight-year-old turns into an exuberant, expansive and buoyant child; the fifteen-year-old becomes remote and argumentative; parents are finally rewarded at sweet sixteen (Ilg & Ames, 1955).
In truth, all seven-year-olds are not withdrawn, all eight-year-olds are not
exuberant, expansive and buoyant, nor are all fifteen-year-olds aloof and argu-

mentative. I am also acquainted with sixteen-year-olds who are anything but sweet. The withdrawn five-year-old is likely to remain a relatively withdrawn eight- nine,- and sixteen-year-old unless he undergoes social-learning experiences that are effective in fostering more expressive behavior.

Although the traditional stage theories of child development are of questionable validity (Bandura & McDonald, 1963; Bandura & Mischel, 1963; Bandura & Walters, 1963), they have nevertheless been influential in promoting the view that adolescence represents a form of stage behavior that suddenly appears at pubescence, and as suddenly disappears when adulthood is achieved.

SELF-FULFILLING PROPHECY

If a society labels its adolescents as "teen-agers," and expects them to be rebellious, unpredictable, sloppy, and wild in their behavior, and if this picture is repeatedly reinforced by the mass media, such cultural expectations may very well force adolescents into the role of rebel. In this way, a false expectation may serve to instigate and maintain certain role behaviors, in turn, then reinforce the originally false belief.

In discussing our research findings with parents' groups I have often been struck by the fact that most parents who are experiencing positive and rewarding relationships with their pre-adolescent children are, nevertheless, waiting apprehensively and bracing themselves for the stormy adolescent period. Such vigilance can very easily create a small turbulence at least. When the prophesied storm fails to materialize, many parents begin to entertain doubts about the normality of their youngster's social development.

In closing, I do not wish to leave you with the impression that adolescence is a stress- or problem-free period of development. No age group is free from stress or adjustment problems. Our findings suggest, however, that the behavioral characteristics exhibited by children during the so-called adolescent stage are lawfully related to, and consistent with, pre-adolescent social behavior.

REFERENCES

Bandura, A., & McDonald, F. J. The influence of social reinforcement and the behavior of models in shaping children's moral judgements. *J. abnorm soc. Psychol.*, 1963, 67, 274–281.
Bandura, A., & Mischel, W. The influence of models in modifying delay-of-gratification patterns. Unpublished manuscript, Stanford Univer., 1963.
Bandura, A., & Walters, R. H. *Adolescent aggression*. New York: Ronald, 1959.
Bandura, A., & Walters, R. H. *Social learning and personality development*. New York. Holt, Rinehart & Winston, 1963.
Elkin, F., & Westley, W. A. The myth of adolescent culture. *Amer. sociol. Rev.*, 1955, 20, 680–684.

Erikson, E. H. *Childhood and society.* New York: Norton, 1950.

Ford, C. S., & Beach, F. A. *Patterns of sexual behavior.* New York: Harper, 1951.

Freud, S. *An outline of psychoanalysis.* New York: Norton, 1949.

Gallagher, J. R., & Harris, H. I. *Emotional problems of adolescents.* New York: Oxford Univer. Press, 1958.

Gesell, A., & Ilg, Frances. *Infant and child in the culture of today.* New York: Harper, 1943.

Heathers, G. Emotional dependence and independence in nursery school play. *J. genet. Psychol,* 1955, 87, 37–57.

Hurlock, Elizabeth B. *Adolescent development.* New York: McGraw-Hill, 1955.

Ilg, Frances L., & Ames, Louise B. *Child behavior.* New York: Harper, 1955.

Josselyn, Irene M. *Psychosocial development of children.* New York. Family Service Assoc. of America, 1948.

Kiell, N. *The adolescent through fiction.* New York: International Univer. Press, 1959.

Mead, Margaret. Adolescence in primitive and modern society. In V. F. Calverton, & S. D. Schmalhausen (Eds.), *The new generation.* New York: Macauley, 1930.

Mohr, G. S., & Despres, Marian A. *The stormy decade: adolescence.* New York: Random House, 1958.

Parsons, T. Psycho-analysis and social structure. *Psychoanal. Quart.,* 1950, 19, 371–384.

Pearson, G. H. J. *Adolescence and the conflict of generations.* New York: Norton, 1958.

Piaget, J. *The moral judgement of the child.* Glencoe, Ill.: Free Press, 1948.

Piaget, J. *The construction of reality in the child.* New York: Basic Books, 1954.

Salinger, J. D. *The catcher in the rye.* Boston: Little, Brown & Co., 1945.

Westley, W. A., & Elkin, F. The protective environment and adolescent socialization. *Social Forces,* 1956, 35, 243–249.

[3] *Leon Eisenberg* A DEVELOPMENTAL APPROACH TO ADOLESCENCE

Adolescence may be defined as a critical period of human development manifested at the biological, psychological, and social levels of integration, of variable onset and duration but marking the end of childhood and setting the foundation for maturity. Biologically, its onset is signaled by the acceleration

FROM *Children,* 1965, 12, 131–135. REPRINTED BY PERMISSION OF THE AUTHOR AND THE CHILDREN'S BUREAU, U.S. DEPARTMENT OF HEALTH, EDUCATION, AND WELFARE.

of physiological growth and the beginnings of secondary sexual development, its termination by the fusion of the epiphyses of the bones and the completion of sexual maturation. Psychologically, it is marked by an acceleration of cognitive growth and of personality formation, both of which continue to be subject to further evolution, though at a less marked rate, in subsequent stages of adulthood. Socially, it is a period of intensified preparation for the assumption of an adult role, and its termination is signaled when the individual is accorded full adult prerogatives, the timing and nature of which vary widely from society to society.

Adolescence is a "critical period" in development in being both a time of rapid and profound change in the organism and a time providing the necessary —but not sufficient—conditions for full maturation in adulthood. Optimal development in adolescence depends on successful accomplishment of the developmental tasks in infancy and childhood. Thus, clinical experience has indicated that adolescence is likely to be particularly stormy, prolonged, and sometimes poorly resolved if it follows a childhood marked by severe deficits.

Whether or not appropriate "experiential supplements" during adolescence can lead to successful negotiation of this period despite pathology in earlier life is not known. The heuristic hypothesis is to assume that repair can occur and that the task of the physician is to search for ways of encouraging optimal growth during the adolescence of a previously damaged child.

Although a rich, fulfilling adolescence provides the best groundwork for a successful adulthood, such an outcome is not automatic; it depends, in turn, on the provision of opportunities during adulthood for the creative exercise of the abilities achieved in adolescence.

The structural groundwork for adolescent development is laid by physical maturation. This developmental sequence is not preformed or automatic but depends upon an interaction between biological capacity and environmental stimulation. Just as growth requires adequate nutrition—being subject to delay or even cessation in the presence of starvation and to acceleration in the presence of optimal intake—so psychological maturation is dependent upon "psychological nutrition," that is, sequential opportunities for cognitive and social stimulation so timed that they promote further mental development.

Interdependent developments

Thus, adolescence is simultaneously a biological, a social, and a psychological phenomenon. Development at each of these levels of integration proceeds not independently but with significant interaction, with events at any one level to impede or to accelerate developments at each of the others.

For example, although the time at which the hypothalamic-pituitary axis initiates the biological sequence of adolescent growth is a function of individual heredity, it may, in a given individual, be delayed or advanced by environmental factors. Thus, the ultimate height attained by adolescents in economically developing countries has shown striking gains as nutrition has improved. Similarly, the time of menarche has shown a trend toward acceleration in countries in which increasingly better health of the children has been achieved. These physiological trends are the result of industrial and social organization.

Or again, biological maturation provides the increasing muscular strength and dexterity which permit the adolescent to participate successfully in the activities of his social group, thus acquiring a psychological sense of adequacy. At the same time, positive psychological motivation is a prerequisite for task perseverance and the search for variety of experience, which provide the conditions necessary for full muscular development through exercise.

Developments at the biological and psychological levels occur in a social framework, which may promote or retard them. Thus, unscientific notions about diet prevalent in a specific culture may lead to inadequate nutritional intake, and social prejudices against minority group members may deprive them of experiences necessary for full development.

The importance of such reciprocal influences is underscored by the fact that each society is dependent upon its adolescents as its future adults. Failure to provide them with the conditions necessary for optimal development will severely handicap the growth potential of that society.

Biological adolescence has fairly precise signs of its onset and termination, such as growth acceleration, sexual development, and epiphyseal fusion, but there is remarkable variation in the timing of their appearance in different individuals. Onset in normal children may occur as early as age 7 or 8 or as late as 17 or 18; termination as early as 15 or 16 or as late as 24 or 25. The timing seems to be a function both of internal factors, such as sex and inheritance, and external factors, such as nutrition or illness. In other words, the biological factors set wide limits for the onset, termination, and achievements of adolescence, the potential limits being subject to modification by environmental influences, among which both psychological and social factors play a role.

Social preparation

Adolescence as a social phenomenon, though restricted in range by biological considerations, is a function of cultural norms. In general, the more sophisticated the society is in its technology, the more prolonged is adolescence, since the complexity of the preparation required for the assumption of adult roles depends upon the demands the society sets. In the United States, for example, the long period of study required for specialized occupational roles delays the age of self-support, the opportunity for marriage, and the age of creative contribution to society—all attributes of the adult role.

In many cultures, the onset of adolescence is clearly signaled by puberty rites, usually in the form of tests of strength and courage, the completion of which entitles the individual to recognition as a young adult. In technologically advanced societies, such clear signification of the end of childhood is absent and the requirements for adulthood less clearly defined: the individual must, therefore, undergo a more prolonged and, at times, confused struggle to attain adult status.

Each culture provides experience specifically designated as part of the training of the adolescent, such as schooling and apprenticeship; other experiences, such as dating and courtship, which are for the most part limited to adolescence but are not formally organized; and other non-age-related opportunities for personal development which may be particularly meaningful for the adolescent, such as opportunities to participate in cultural and political life.

Deliberate social planning based on a scientific analysis of adolescents' needs has been relatively neglected, the forms and structures society provides having evolved empirically. Only within school systems has such planning been explicit, but even there with little careful research. Yet careful assessment of the needs of adolescents at all levels of developmental integration could lead to the design and provision of external conditions that would greatly accelerate the rate, and markedly increase the ultimate level, of the development of the human adolescent's full potentialities.

The idealism of adolescence

At a psychological level, the most striking attainment during adolescence is the ability to conceptualize at an abstract level. The future evolution of what Piaget calls the "concrete operations" of childhood[1] through interaction with increasingly more demanding intellectual tasks, provided both by formal schooling and informal social experience, leads to the ability to "think about thinking" and to analyze problems at a high level of generalization. It is here that the *Anlage* of scientific thought and creativity is to be found. This evolution of intellectual function requires appropriate environmental stimulation.

The adolescent's capacity for abstract thought accounts for his increasing concern with, on the one hand, national and international problems and, on the other, with the basic meanings and values of human existence. This "idealism" of adolescence is, of course, shaped by the cultural envelope which surrounds the individual, but its very existence leads to questioning, to examination of basic premises, and to dissatisfaction with the imperfections in the world adults have created. Its cultivation may be regarded as one of the most important tasks of society.

Fostering and strengthening this "suprapersonal" psychological trait in adolescents will lead to the creation of adults who will in turn enhance the society that bred them. The lack of adequate opportunity for its positive expression will warp the adolescent's normal development and lead to a generation of self-preoccupied adults who will fail to meet the challenge of history.

Personal identity

A second and related psychological theme of adolescence is the search for a sense of personal identity, to employ the terminology of Erikson.[2] No longer a child and not yet an adult, the adolescent is busily engaged in determining who he is and what he is to become.

In this effort, he examines his parents from a more critical perspective and leans more to peer groups for his sense of belonging. If his relations with his parents have been soundly constructed during earlier years, and if they meet his doubts and criticisms with sympathetic understanding, this temporary unsettling of his prior role as a child leads to a resynthesis of his relations with them on a firm and lasting basis, one marked by a reciprocal respect and by personal independence without abandonment of filial loyalty. Where the parent-child relationship has been one of excessive dependence or excessive hostility, the turmoil of adolescence may be prolonged and lead either to failure of emancipation or to rejection of family ties and a lasting sense of isolation.

Sexual role

A third key developmental task consists of the further evolution of sexual identity and role-appropriate behavior. Learning the social role of one's sex is firmly rooted in childhood—in culturally differentiated role assignments, in emulation of the like-sexed parent, and in peer interactions. These experiences provide a constant feedback, both by comparison of the self with others and by praise or blame from them, which informs the child as to what sex he is and what kind of behavior expectations this entails. These preliminary psychological structures are challenged by the adolescent's consciousness of his development of adult sexual characteristics and his experience of a bewildering array of new physical sensations, both of which lead to an upsurge of interest in physical sex and a psychological sensitization to a new aspect of interpersonal relationships. The forces in the social field then determine the further steps in his sexual development.

Comparative studies indicate that, as the evolutionary scale is ascended, sexual behavior is less dependent upon hormones and more upon learning. In man, the role of hormones is limited to priming the organism for biological sexual maturation and to influencing—but not solely determining—the level of libido; the direction, nature, and adequacy of sexual performance are controlled by psychosocial factors. Thus, the many investigations of the biology of sex deviants have failed to identify chromosomal, hormonal, or gonadal aberrations; and conversely, individuals with such biological incongruencies usually exhibit a sex-role identity conforming to sex-role assignment.

The remarkable variation in sexual behavior between societies as well as between social classes within a single society emphasizes the cultural determination of sexual behavior, given adequate biological maturation.

The ambivalence of Western society toward sexuality—manifested by the conflicts between official attitudes and private behavior, and the pervasive emphasis on sex side by side with sanctions against its expression—accounts for the difficulty, so common in adolescence, of attaining the basis for a sense of competence, freedom, and pleasure as a sexually functioning adult. Persons concerned with the development of adolescents have an important obligation to give them a clear and full explanation of biological function with emphasis on its *ethical significance* based upon a mutually meaningful relationship between human beings. Adolescents need a comprehensive knowledge of the physical and physiological differences between the sexes, of the development of sexuality, and of the appropriate stages of sexual experience en route to full maturity.

Commonly expressed fears that giving adolescents such information will lead to premature experimentation run contrary to clinical experience which indicates that ignorance and impoverishment of human relationships account for most sexual misadventures. A sense of inadequacy in sexuality not only impairs sexual function but also leads to disabilities in other adult roles and is an important source of psychological malfunction.

Origins of delinquency

The search for identity is markedly influenced by peer groups. If these are constructive social groups which provide creative outlets for adolescent energy, the result is a sense of meaningful membership in the community and identification with its larger goals. If the peer group is a delinquent gang, with values antagonistic to those of the larger society, the result is likely to be antisocial personality organization—especially if the adolescent is a victim of discrimination for religious, ethnic, political, or economic reasons.

The experience of growing up as a member of a disadvantaged minority group, with attendant humiliation and denial of opportunity, makes it difficult for the adolescent to identify with the values of the society at large and favors, instead, hostility toward its norms and a disposition to anarchistic individualism. However, even under these circumstances, leadership and social forms which permit the disadvantaged adolescent to employ his energy in efforts to change unjust social patterns can foster his emergence into creative adulthood. If such opportunities for constructive social action are denied, the distortion of development leads to a frustrating and progressively more embittering "individual war against society" characterized by criminal activities.

Some theorists focus upon family pathology in explaining the evolution of delinquent behavior. Their thesis is based upon the finding that family psychopathology is frequent in the history of delinquents. The family is indeed an important agent in transmitting the behavior pattern and values expected of the adolescent by society. Consequently, distortions in family structure, whether idiosyncratic or socially induced, will inevitably have profound effects upon individual development. However, the family-centered viewpoint fails to recognize that family psychopathology is closely related to social structure and that the adolescent is also molded by social experiences outside the family.

The social consequences of economic disadvantage—poor health and reduced longevity, poor education, extralegal marital arrangements, inability to plan for future contingencies, necessity for exploiting children economically —themselves erode family structure and are likely to cause the victims of these social circumstances, the genesis of which they do not understand, to turn on each other in destructive ways. The unemployed, drifting father and the unmarried, deserted mother not only fail to provide their children with adequate nurture but also serve as poor identification models.

However, even though family structure be distorted, the adolescent may attain a degree of normal development *if* provided adequate education and constructive peer group experience. Unfortunately, the aggregation of disadvantaged families in decaying neighborhoods is all too likely to reinforce family psychopathology and, by exposing the adolescent to delinquent gangs and ineffective schooling, heighten his growing sense of bitterness.

Hazards and symptoms

The sensitivity of the adolescent to the good opinion of his peers and the dependence of his sense of identity upon the attainment of competence in an adult role render him psychologically vulnerable to variation in physiological development, such as precocious or delayed growth, facial acne, obesity, enlarged mammary glands in the male, or inadequate or overabundant breast development in the female. These deviations from the expected pattern of maturation, though of no great medical significance, may, nonetheless, lead to major psychological trauma if not offset by sensitive guidance.

The adolescent with limited intellectual or physical capacity can develop a persisting and even irremedial feeling of inferiority if he is forced to compete in situations in which he experiences continual failure. The individualization of educational and vocational training for adolescents is essential, both to permit the talented individual to exploit his abilities, as well as to direct the youngster with specific limitations to activities which will develop what abilities he has.

Characteristic of adolescence is fluidity of psychological structure in the struggle to attain a new and more meaningful sense of identity. In consequence, the formation of transient symptoms, resembling many of the psychopathological syndromes of adulthood, is not uncommon during this period.

The clinician must exercise great caution lest he attribute too great a significance to the turbulent but temporary maladaptive patterns manifested by the adolescent. Incorrect diagnostic formulations may lead to social consequences —for example, withdrawal from school or institutionalization—that will freeze into permanence an otherwise readily correctable deviation in the growth pattern.

It is, of course, important to recognize that schizophrenia often first appears in adolescence, as does manic-depressive psychosis. However, these are uncommon disorders and may be simulated by panic reactions in the youngster who is confronted by overwhelming internal and external stimulation. If the recent trend toward a specialty of adolescent psychiatry has any justification, it lies in the opportunity for psychiatrists to acquire particular competence in the differential diagnosis and special management of adolescents' adjustment reactions. Experience with the psychiatric problems of adolescents leads to respect for their extraordinary range of individual variability and their remarkable restorative capacity under corrective and supportive experience.

The psychological basis for a sense of individual worth as an adult rests upon the acquisition of competence in a work role during adolescence. A sense of competence is not acquired on the basis of "reassurance," but rather upon the actual experience of succeeding in a socially important task. The challenge to the educator, therefore, is to stimulate abilities to the utmost without setting standards so high that they lead to an enduring sense of defeat.

The educational accomplishment must be matched by an opportunity for the individual to exercise his competence as a worker in the economic world. The sustained motivation necessary for mastering a difficult work role is only possible when there is a real likelihood of fulfilling that role in adult life and having it respected by others. The task of providing full employment in a world in which automation is revolutionizing traditional work roles provides a challenge to the abilities of leading thinkers in all societies.

The world's hope

No society can hope to survive that does not succeed in harnessing the constructive, searching suprapersonal and supranational drives of the adolescent. In recent world history, adolescents in underdeveloped countries have participated heroically in overthrowing the dead hand of the past and attaining the beginnings of a meaningful nationhood. The picture in the relatively developed countries is less clear and less heartening. As affluence is attained, societies tend to become frozen into traditional molds, with resultant trends toward self-preoccupation and egocentric goals that afford less challenge to adolescents. There are, fortunately, notable and inspiring exceptions to this self-preoccupation, as youngsters dedicate their energies to improving the lot of disadvantaged fellow citizens and to social betterment in underdeveloped countries far from their shores.

The capacity for engagement in meaningful social activity is clearly present in young people in every country of the world. The challenge to the behavioral scientist is to help his own country develop the forms and means to enable the adolescent to take a leading role in the struggle for the attainment of a world in which peace, freedom, and economic opportunity are omnipresent. No task is more suited to the adolescent. No task has greater potentiality for permitting the full flowering of his capacities.

Thus, the provision of an optimal framework for adolescent development is inseparable from the struggle to create a better world by helping to mold the citizens who will build it.

NOTES

1. Flavell, J. H.: The developmental psychology of Jean Piaget. Van Nostrand, New York. 1963.
2. Erikson, E. H.: Identity and the life cycle. *In* Psychological issues, monograph 1. International Universities Press, New York. 1959.

[4] *David Elkind* EGOCENTRISM IN ADOLESCENCE

Within the Piagetian theory of intellectual growth, the concept of egocentrism generally refers to a lack of differentiation in some area of subject-object interaction (Piaget, 1962). At each stage of mental development, this lack of differentiation takes a unique form and is manifested in a unique set of behaviors. The transition from one form of egocentrism to another takes place in a dialectic fashion such that the mental structures which free the child from a lower form of egocentrism are the same structures which ensnare him in a higher form of egocentrism. From the developmental point of view, therefore, egocentrism can be regarded as a negative by-product of any emergent mental system in the sense that it corresponds to the fresh cognitive problems engendered by that system.

Although in recent years Piaget has focused his attention more on the positive than on the negative products of mental structures, egocentrism continues to be of interest because of its relation to the affective aspects of child

FROM *Child Development*, 1967, 38, 1025–1034. © 1967 BY THE SOCIETY FOR RESEARCH IN CHILD DEVELOPMENT, INC. REPRINTED BY PERMISSION OF THE AUTHOR AND THE SOCIETY FOR RESEARCH IN CHILD DEVELOPMENT.

thought and behavior. Indeed, it is possible that the study of egocentrism may provide a bridge between the study of cognitive structure, on the one hand, and the exploration of personality dynamics, on the other (Cowan, 1966; Gourevitch & Feffer, 1962). The purpose of the present paper is to describe, in greater detail than Inhelder and Piaget (1958), what seems to me to be the nature of egocentrism in adolescence and some of its behavioral and experiential correlates. Before doing that, however, it might be well to set the stage for the discussion with a brief review of the forms of egocentrism which precede this mode of thought in adolescence.

Forms of egocentrism in infancy and childhood

In presenting the childhood forms of egocentrism, it is useful to treat each of Piaget's major stages as if it were primarily concerned with resolving one major cognitive task. The egocentrism of a particular stage can then be described with reference to this special problem of cognition. It must be stressed, however, that while the cognitive task characteristic of a particular stage seems to attract the major share of the child's mental energies, it is not the only cognitive problem with which the child is attempting to cope. In mental development there are major battles and minor skirmishes, and if I here ignore the lesser engagements it is for purposes of economy of presentation rather than because I assume that such engagements are insignificant.

SENSORI-MOTOR EGOCENTRISM (0–2 YEARS)

The major cognitive task of infancy might be regarded as *the conquest of the object*. In the early months of life, the infant deals with objects as if their existence were dependent upon their being present in immediate perception (Charlesworth, 1966; Piaget, 1954). The egocentrism of this stage corresponds, therefore, to a lack of differentiation between the object and the sense impressions occasioned by it. Toward the end of the first year, however, the infant begins to seek the object even when it is hidden, and thus shows that he can now differentiate between the object and the "experience of the object." This breakdown of egocentrism with respect to objects is brought about by mental representation of the absent object.* An internal representation of the absent object is the earliest manifestation of the symbolic function which develops gradually during the second year of life and whose activities dominate the next stage of mental growth.

PRE-OPERATIONAL EGOCENTRISM (2–6 YEARS)

During the preschool period, the child's major cognitive task can be regarded as *the conquest of the symbol*. It is during the preschool period that the

* It is characteristic of the dialectic of mental growth that the capacity to represent internally the absent object also enables the infant to cognize the object as externally existent.

symbolic function becomes fully active, as evidenced by the rapid growth in the acquisition and utilization of language, by the appearance of symbolic play, and by the first reports of dreams. Yet this new capacity for representation, which loosed the infant from his egocentrism with respect to objects, now ensnares the preschool children in a new egocentrism with regard to symbols. At the beginning of this period, the child fails to differentiate between words and their referents (Piaget, 1952b) and between his self-created play and dream symbols and reality (Kohlberg, 1966; Piaget, 1951). Children at this stage believe that the name inheres in the thing and that an object cannot have more than one name (Elkind, 1961a, 1962, 1963).

The egocentrism of this period is particularly evident in children's linguistic behavior. When explaining a piece of apparatus to another child, for example, the youngster at this stage uses many indefinite terms and leaves out important information (Piaget, 1952b). Although this observation is sometimes explained by saying that the child fails to take the other person's point of view, it can also be explained by saying that the child assumes words carry much more information than they actually do. This results from his belief that even the indefinite "thing" somehow conveys the properties of the object which it is used to represent. In short, the egocentrism of this period consists in a lack of clear differentiation between symbols and their referents.

Toward the end of the pre-operational period, the differentiation between symbols and their referents is gradually brought about by the emergence of concrete operations (internalized actions which are roughly comparable in their activity to the elementary operations of arithmetic). One consequence of concrete operational thought is that it enables the child to deal with two elements, properties, or relations at the same time. A child with concrete operations can, for example, take account of both the height and width of a glass of colored liquid and recognize that, when the liquid is poured into a differently shaped container, the changes in height and width of the liquid compensate one another so that the total quantity of liquid is conserved (Elkind, 1961b; Piaget, 1952a). This ability, to hold two dimensions in mind at the same time, also enables the child to hold both symbol and referent in mind simultaneously, and thus distinguish between them. Concrete operations are, therefore, instrumental in overcoming the egocentrism of the preoperational stage.

CONCRETE OPERATIONAL EGOCENTRISM (7–11 YEARS)

With the emergence of concrete operations, the major cognitive task of the school-age child becomes that of *mastering classes, relations, and quantities*. While the preschool child forms global notions of classes, relations, and quantities, such notions are imprecise and cannot be combined one with the other. The child with concrete operations, on the other hand, can nest classes, seriate relations, and conserve quantities. In addition, concrete operations enable the school-age child to perform elementary syllogistic reasoning and to formulate hypotheses and explanations about concrete matters. This system of concrete operations, however, which lifts the school-age child to new heights of thought, nonetheless lowers him to new depths of egocentrism.

Operations are essentially mental tools whose products, series, class hierarchies, conservations, etc., are not directly derived from experience. At this stage, however, the child nonetheless regards these mental products as being on a par with perceptual phenomena. It is the inability to differentiate clearly between mental constructions and perceptual givens which constitutes the egocentrism of the school-age child. An example may help to clarify the form which egocentrism takes during the concrete operational stage.

In a study reported by Peel (1960), children and adolescents were read a passage about Stonehenge and then asked questions about it. One of the questions had to do with whether Stonehenge was a place for religious worship or a fort. The children (ages 7–10) answered the question with flat statements, as if they were stating a fact. When they were given evidence that contradicted their statements, they rationalized the evidence to make it conform with their initial position. Adolescents, on the other hand, phrased their replies in probabilistic terms and supported their judgments with material gleaned from the passage. Similar differences between children and adolescents have been found by Elkind (1966) and Weir (1964).

What these studies show is that, when a child constructs a hypothesis or formulates a strategy, he assumes that this product is imposed by the data rather than derived from his own mental activity. When his position is challenged, he does not change his stance but, on the contrary, reinterprets the data to fit with his assumption. This observation, however, raises a puzzling question. Why, if the child regards both his thought products and the givens of perception as coming from the environment, does he nonetheless give preference to his own mental constructions? The answer probably lies in the fact that the child's mental constructions are the product of reasoning, and hence are experienced as imbued with a (logical) necessity. This "felt" necessity is absent when the child experiences the products of perception. It is not surprising, then, that the child should give priority to what seems permanent and necessary in perception (the products of his own thought, such as conservation) rather than to what seems transitory and arbitrary in perception (products of environmental stimulation). Only in adolescence do young people differentiate between their own mental constructions and the givens of perception. For the child, there are no problems of epistemology.

Toward the end of childhood, the emergence of formal operational thought (which is analogous to propositional logic) gradually frees the child from his egocentrism with respect to his own mental constructions. As Inhelder and Piaget (1958) have shown, formal operational thought enables the young person to deal with all of the possible combinations and permutations of elements within a given set. Provided with four differently colored pieces of plastic, for example, the adolescent can work out all the possible combinations of colors by taking the pieces one, two, three and four, and none, at a time.

Children, on the other hand, cannot formulate these combinations in any systematic way. The ability to conceptualize all of the possible combinations in a system allows the adolescent to construct contrary-to-fact hypotheses and to reason about such propositions "as if" they were true. The adolescent, for example, can accept the statement, "Let's suppose coal is white," whereas the child would reply, "But coal is black." This ability to formulate contrary-to-fact hypotheses is crucial to the overcoming of the egocentrism of the concrete operational period. Through the formulation of such contrary-to-fact hypotheses, the young person discovers the arbitrariness of his own mental constructions and learns to differentiate them from perceptual reality.

Adolescent egocentrism

From the strictly cognitive point of view (as opposed to the psychoanalytic point of view as represented by Blos [1962] and A. Freud [1946] or the ego psychological point of view as represented by Erikson [1959]), the major task of early adolescence can be regarded as having to do with *the conquest of thought*. Formal operations not only permit the young person to construct all the possibilities in a system and construct contrary-to-fact propositions (Inhelder & Piaget, 1958); they also enable him to conceptualize his own thought, to take his mental constructions as objects and reason about them. Only at about the ages of 11–12, for example, do children spontaneously introduce concepts of belief, intelligence, and faith into their definitions of their religious denomination (Elkind, 1961a; 1962; 1963). Once more, however, this new mental system which frees the young person from the egocentrism of childhood entangles him in a new form of egocentrism characteristic of adolescence.

Formal operational thought not only enables the adolescent to conceptualize his thought, it also permits him to conceptualize the thought of other people. It is this capacity to take account of other people's thought, however, which is the crux of adolescent egocentrism. This egocentrism emerges because, while the adolescent can now cognize the thoughts of others, he fails to differentiate between the objects toward which the thoughts of others are directed and those which are the focus of his own concern. Now, it is well known that the young adolescent, because of the physiological metamorphosis he is undergoing, is primarily concerned with himself. Accordingly, since he fails to differentiate between what others are thinking about and his own mental preoccupations, he assumes that other people are as obsessed with his behavior and appearance as he is himself. *It is this belief that others are preoccupied with his appearance and behavior that constitutes the egocentrism of the adolescent.*

One consequence of adolescent egocentrism is that, in actual or impending social situations, the young person anticipates the reactions of other people to himself. These anticipations, however, are based on the premise that others are as admiring or as critical of him as he is of himself. In a sense, then, the adolescent is continually constructing, or reacting to, *an imaginary audience*. It is an audience because the adolescent believes that he will be the focus of attention; and it is imaginary because, in actual social situations, this is not usually the case (unless he contrives to make it so). The construction of imaginary audiences would seem to account, in part at least, for a wide variety of typical adolescent behaviors and experiences.

The imaginary audience, for example, probably plays a role in the self-consciousness which is so characteristic of early adolescence. When the young person is feeling critical of himself, he anticipates that the audience—of which he is necessarily a part—will be critical too. And, since the audience is his own construction and privy to his own knowledge of himself, it knows just what to look for in the way of cosmetic and behavioral sensitivities. The adolescent's wish for privacy and his reluctance to reveal himself may, to some extent, be a reaction to the feeling of being under the constant critical scrutiny of other people. The notion of an imaginary audience also helps to explain the observation that the affect which most concerns adolescents is not guilt but, rather, shame, that is, the reaction to an audience (Lynd, 1961).

While the adolescent is often self-critical, he is frequently self-admiring too. At such times, the audience takes on the same affective coloration. A good deal of adolescent boorishness, loudness, and faddish dress is probably provoked, partially in any case, by a failure to differentiate between what the young person believes to be attractive and what others admire. It is for this reason that the young person frequently fails to understand why adults disapprove of the way he dresses and behaves. The same sort of egocentrism is often seen in behavior directed toward the opposite sex. The boy who stands in front of the mirror for 2 hours combing his hair is probably imagining the swooning reactions he will produce in the girls. Likewise, the girl applying her makeup is more likely than not imagining the admiring glances that will come her way. When these young people actually meet, each is more concerned with being the observed than with being the observer. Gatherings of young adolescents are unique in the sense that each young person is simultaneously an actor to himself and an audience to others.

One of the most common admiring audience constructions, in the adolescent, is the anticipation of how others will react to his own demise. A certain bittersweet pleasure is derived from anticipating the belated recognition by others of his positive qualities. As often happens with such universal fantasies, the imaginary anticipation of one's own demise has been realized in fiction. Below, for example, is the passage in *Tom Sawyer* where Tom sneaks back to his home, after having run away with Joe and Huck, to discover that he and his friends are thought to have been drowned:

But this memory was too much for the old lady, and she broke entirely down. Tom was snuffling, now, himself—and more in pity of himself than anybody else. He could hear Mary crying and putting in a kindly word for him from time to time. He began to have a nobler opinion of himself than ever before.

Still, he was sufficiently touched by his aunt's grief to long to rush out from under the bed and overwhelm her with joy—and the theatrical gorgeousness of the thing appealed strongly to his nature too—but he resisted and lay still.

Corresponding to the imaginary audience is another mental construction which is its complement. While the adolescent fails to differentiate the concerns of his own thought from those of others, he at the same time over-differentiates his feelings. Perhaps because he believes he is of importance to so many people, the imaginary audience, he comes to regard himself, and particularly his feelings, as something special and unique. Only he can suffer with such agonized intensity, or experience such exquisite rapture. How many parents have been confronted with the typically adolescent phrase, "But you don't know how it feels. . . ." The emotional torments undergone by Goethe's young Werther and by Salinger's Holden Caulfield exemplify the adolescent's belief in the uniqueness of his own emotional experience. At a somewhat different level, this belief in personal uniqueness becomes a conviction that he will not die, that death will happen to others but not to him. This complex of beliefs in the uniqueness of his feelings and of his immortality might be called *a personal fable*, a story which he tells himself and which is not true.

Evidence of the personal fable are particularly prominent in adolescent diaries. Such diaries are often written for posterity in the conviction that the young person's experiences, crushes, and frustrations are of universal significance and importance. Another kind of evidence for the personal fable during this period is the tendency to confide in a personal God. The search for privacy and the belief in personal uniqueness leads to the establishment of an I-Thou relationship with God as a personal confident to whom one no longer looks for gifts but rather for guidance and support (Long, Elkind, & Spilka, 1967).

*The concepts of an imaginary audience and a personal fable have proved useful, at least to the writer, in the understanding and treatment of troubled adolescents. The imaginary audience, for example, seems often to play a role in middle-class delinquency (Elkind, 1967). As a case in point, one young man took $1,000 from a golf tournament purse, hid the money, and then promptly revealed himself. It turned out that much of the motivation for this act was derived from the anticipated response of "the audience" to the guttiness of his action. In a similar vein, many young girls become pregnant because, in part at least, their personal fable convinces them that pregnancy will happen to others but never to them and so they need not take precautions. Such examples could be multiplied but will perhaps suffice to illustrate how adolescent egocentrism, as manifested in the imaginary audience and in the personal fable, can help provide a rationale for some adolescent behavior. These concepts can, moreover, be utilized in the treatment of adolescent offenders. It is often helpful to these young people if they can learn to differentiate between the real and the imaginary audience, which often boils down to a discrimination between the real and the imaginary parents.

The passing of adolescent egocentrism

After the appearance of formal operational thought, no new mental systems develop and the mental structures of adolescence must serve for the rest of the life span. The egocentrism of early adolescence nonetheless tends to diminish by the age of 15 or 16, the age at which formal operations become firmly established. What appears to happen is that the imaginary audience, which is primarily an anticipatory audience, is progressively modified in the direction of the reactions of the real audience. In a way, the imaginary audience can be regarded as hypothesis—or better, as a series of hypotheses—which the young person tests against reality. As a consequence of this testing, he gradually comes to recognize the difference between his own preoccupations and the interests and concerns of others.

The personal fable, on the other hand, is probably overcome (although probably never in its entirety) by the gradual establishment of what Erikson (1959) has called "intimacy." Once the young person sees himself in a more realistic light as a function of having adjusted his imaginary audience to the real one, he can establish true rather than self-interested interpersonal relations. Once relations of mutuality are established and confidences are shared, the young person discovers that others have feelings similar to his own and have suffered and been enraptured in the same way.

Adolescent egocentrism is thus overcome by a twofold transformation. On the cognitive plane, it is overcome by the gradual differentiation between his own preoccupations and the thoughts of others; while on the plane of affectivity, it is overcome by a gradual integration of the feelings of others with his own emotions.

Summary and conclusions

In this paper I have tried to describe the forms which egocentrism takes and the mechanisms by which it is overcome, in the course of mental development. In infancy, egocentrism corresponds to the impression that objects are identical with the perception of them, and this form of egocentrism is overcome with the appearance of representation. During the preschool period, egocentrism appears in the guise of a belief that symbols contain the same information as is provided by the objects which they represent. With the emergence of concrete operations, the child is able to discriminate between symbol and referent, and so overcome this type of egocentrism. The egocentrism of the school-age period can be characterized as the belief that one's own mental constructions correspond to a superior form of perceptual reality. With the advent of formal operations and the ability to construct contrary-to-fact hypotheses, this kind of egocentrism is dissolved because the young person can now recognize the arbitrariness of his own mental constructions. Finally, during early adolescence, egocentrism appears as the belief that the thoughts of others are directed toward the self. This variety of egocentrism is overcome as a consequence of the conflict between the reactions which the young person anticipates and those which actually occur.

Although egocentrism corresponds to a negative product of mental growth, its usefulness would seem to lie in the light which it throws upon the affective reactions characteristic of any particular stage of mental development. In this paper I have dealt primarily with the affective reactions associated with the egocentrism of adolescence. Much of the material, particularly the discussion of the *imaginary audience* and the *personal fable* is speculative in the sense that it is based as much upon my clinical experience with young people as it is upon research data. These constructs are offered, not as the final word on adolescent egocentrism, but rather to illustrate how the cognitive structures peculiar to a particular level of development can be related to the affective experience and behavior characteristic of that stage. Although I have here only considered the correspondence between mental structure and affect in adolescence, it is possible that similar correspondences can be found at the earlier levels of development as well. A consideration of egocentrism, then, would seem to be a useful starting point for any attempt to reconcile cognitive structure and the dynamics of personality.

REFERENCES

Bloss, P. *On adolescence.* New York: Free Press, 1962.

Charlesworth, W. R. Development of the object concept in infancy: methodological study. *American Psychologist,* 1966, **21,** 623. (Abstract)

Cowan, P. A. Cognitive egocentrism and social interaction in children. *American Psychologist,* 1966, **21,** 623. (Abstract)

Elkind, D. The child's conception of his religious denomination, I: The Jewish child. *Journal of genetic Psychology,* 1961, **99,** 209–225. (a)

Elkind, D. The development of quantitative thinking. *Journal of genetic Psychology,* 1961, **98,** 37–46. (b)

Elkind, D. The child's conception of his religious denomination, II: The Catholic child. *Journal of genetic Psychology,* 1962, **101,** 185–193.

Elkind, D. The child's conception of his religious denomination, III: The Protestant child. *Journal of genetic Psychology,* 1963, **103,** 291–304.

Elkind, D. Conceptual orientation shifts in children and adolescents. *Child Development,* 1966, **37,** 493–498.

Elkind, D. Middle-class delinquency. *Mental Hygiene,* 1967, **51,** 80–84.

Erikson, E. H. Identity and the life cycle. *Psychological issues.* Vol. 1, No. 1, New York: International Universities Press, 1959.

Freud, Anna. *The ego and the mechanisms of defense.* New York: International Universities Press, 1946.

Gourevitch, Vivian, & Feffer, M. H. A study of motivational development. *Journal of genetic Psychology*, 1962, **100**, 361–375.

Inhelder, Bärbel, & Piaget, J. *The growth of logical thinking from childhood to adolescence*. New York: Basic Books, 1958.

Kohlberg, L. Cognitive stages and preschool education. *Human Development*, 1966, **9**, 5–17.

Long, Diane, Elkind, D., & Spilka, B. The child's conception of prayer. *Journal for the scientific Study of Religion*, 1967, **6**, 101–109.

Lynd, Helen M. *On shame and the search for identity*. New York: Science Editions, 1961.

Peel, E. A. *The pupil's thinking*. London: Oldhourne, 1960.

Piaget, J. *The child's conception of the world*. London: Routledge & Kegan Paul, 1951.

Piaget, J. *The child's conception of number*. New York: Humanities Press, 1952. (a)

Piaget, J. *The Language and thought of the child*. London: Routledge & Kegan Paul, 1952. (b)

Piaget, J. *The construction of reality in the child*. New York: Basic Books, 1954.

Piaget, J. *Comments on Vygotsky's critical remarks concerning "The language and thought of the child" and "Judgment and reasoning in the child."* Cambridge, Mass.: M. I. T. Press, 1962.

Weir, M. W. Development changes in problem solving strategies. *Psychological Review*, 1964, **71**, 473–490.

TWO PHYSIOLOGICAL DEVELOPMENT AND ITS PSYCHOLOGICAL CORRELATES

Part II is devoted to a consideration of physical changes during adolescence, the influence of these changes on the adolescent, his self-evaluation and evaluation by his peers, the effect of differences in the endocrinological timing of physiological events, and the lasting effect of pubescent changes on adult personality. Changes which occur during pubescent growth are of profound importance to the adolescent, because the timing of sexual maturation and the sex appropriateness or inappropriateness of bodily development influence the adolescent's self-evaluation and evaluation by his peers. These pubescent changes are particularly significant in understanding the adolescent in Western society, where great emphasis is placed on physical beauty and sexual attractiveness. Helpful in understanding youth's preoccupation with his body is the previous article by Elkind (4), "egocentrism in adolescence," a theoretical construct which illuminates the adolescent male's search for the first hair to be shaved and the adolescent female's concern with breast development. The hours spent by the adolescent in front of the mirror reveal his awareness of the important role played by secondary sex characteristics in evaluations made by opposite sex peers concerning the individual's sexual attractiveness, sexual maturity, sex appropriateness, and general acceptability as a dating partner. Since the personality of the individual develops partially in response to his body, not only the physical changes themselves, but also the endocrinological timing of physiological events have profound influence on basic personality variables and on an individual's social-emotional adjustment. As shown by several studies, some of the psychological correlates of early and late maturation, especially in the male, carry over into adult life, when the physiological differences have disappeared.

The first selection, by Rolf E. Muuss (5), focuses on the historical changes in the patterns of man's physical development, particularly on a phenomenon which has been largely neglected in developmental literature: the earlier occurrence of adolescence today than a century ago. Today man grows faster, reaches his adult height and sexual maturity earlier, and becomes taller when an adult than in 1880. The disparity, for example, between the average physical growth curves for 1960 and 1880 is most noticeable during early adolescence (ages 10–15), as illustrated by Figure 1 of the article. Having established the fact of accelerated physiological change over the last century, Muuss, without attempting to establish a simple causal relationship, points to some of the broad social, educational, and medical implications of this accelerated development.

The Johanna Dwyer and Jean Mayer (6) article is concerned with the wide range of individual variations in the physical growth patterns of adolescence and the influence of these differences on the individual. Most of the individual variations that have been observed fall well within the range of normality from a strictly medical viewpoint. These differences, however, are frequently interpreted as abnormal by the adolescent who is guided by neither medical nor statistical knowledge. Consequently, under the influence of subtle and often overt reactions from his peers, the adolescent may develop considerable anxiety about his own deviation from the norm, an anxiety which is increased by an exaggeratedly idealistic vision of the human body. This idealization of the human body is not only reinforced by peer group evaluations, but even more through highly glamorized images in advertising, movies, fashion magazines, and beauty contests. An adolescent who is preoccupied with the impression he makes on others is likely to develop feelings of dissatisfaction with himself. This conclusion is supported by the finding that although only 16 percent of an adolescent group of girls studied were actually obese, 50 percent felt that they had weight problems, and 60 percent resorted to dieting. Dwyer and Mayer also discuss variations in physical development which have social-emotional implications relating to one's self-concept and personality, such as the asynchronism in development, the effects of early and late maturation, the sex appropriateness of one's physique, stature, and obesity. Alexander Frazier and Lorenzo K. Lisonbee (8) give further evidence that adolescents are overly concerned about and often unhappy with their bodies.

Although developmental literature abounds with references to the importance of an adolescent's evaluation of his own body, empirical evidence is less common. Research studies have focused largely on psychopathological conditions rather than on developmental changes that take place during adolescence. Franklyn N. Arnhoff and Ernest N. Damianopoulos (7) open the door to further study by providing an operational definition of the "body image"; the "visual memory-image one has of one's own body." The article suggests that, at least within the methodological structure of the study, males in late adolescence can effectively recognize the physical appearance of their own bodies. It might be of some value to apply the method and structure of this study to prepubescents, early adolescents, and adults, both male and female, in order to determine changes in the body image during adolescence. Such a study would help answer the question of whether the "body image" improves as a function of age, or whether the pubescent growth changes produce confusion and deterioration of the body image. In other words, is the "body image" less accurate during adolescence than during either latency or early adulthood? Such studies might result in evidence to support Kurt Lewin's theory of the "body image" which postulates that "during the normal developmental process body changes are so slow that the individual knows his own body. During adolescence, changes in body structure, body experiences, and new body sensations and urges are so drastic, that even the well-known life space of body image becomes unknown, unreliable, and unpredictable" (Muuss, 1968, p. 93.) The Arnhoff and Damianopoulos study gives some tentative indication that body awareness and recognition do not continue to improve as a function of age beyond adolescence, as illustrated by the fact that adults in their forties seem to engage in wishful thinking by maintaining an image of their physical appearance which has not changed since their early twenties.

Frazier and Lisonbee (8) investigated the preoccupation and dissatisfaction of tenth grade adolescents with their physical appearance. This study, too, may be interpreted to support David Elkind's (4) concept of "egocentrism in adolescence." The dissatisfaction with the appearance of one's body and the desire for positive change seems highly prevalent among tenth graders, and evidence from other sources indicates that this concern persists into early adulthood. Paradoxically, at a time in life when the body approaches aesthetic perfection, the individual, particularly the female, seems most displeased with physical appearance. Males, on the other hand, show exceptional concern with slow maturation, which penalizes them in their social, heterosexual, and emotional development. Dermatological imperfections seem to be the source of greatest dissatisfaction for both sexes. By suggesting that all adolescents suffer common unfounded fears and anxieties about their physical appearance, this article provides an effective tool for teachers, parents, and psychologists.

REFERENCES

Muuss, R. E. *Theories of Adolescence.* (2nd ed.) New York, Random House, 1968.

[5] *Rolf E. Muuss* ADOLESCENT DEVELOPMENT AND THE SECULAR TREND

Today's children grow faster, experience the adolescent growth spurt earlier, reach puberty earlier, and attain their adult height earlier. These patterns of accelerated physical growth are described as the "secular trend." Evidence indicates that the total process of growth is speeding up so that children and adolescents are taller and heavier than their coevals were sixty or seventy years ago. In addition, and less pronounced, the final adult height is increasing slowly, even though adult stature is reached at an earlier age. While there is

FROM *Adolescence*, 1970, 5, 267–284. REPRINTED BY PERMISSION OF LIBRA PUBLISHERS, INC.

some disagreement in respect to the specific amount of change which has taken place over any given historical period of time, there is no disagreement about the basic trend. Allowing for considerable individual variation and assuming the continuation of the present trend, it has been estimated that in the United States the normal healthy son will be as much as 1 inch taller and 10 pounds heavier than his father. The normal healthy girl will be ½ to 1 inch taller, 2 pounds heavier and will experience menarche about 10 months earlier than her mother. Boys are more strongly affected by the secular trend than girls, as boys in general react more strongly to various influences, "ranging from malnutrition in Central Europe to the effects of radiation in Hiroshima" (Tanner, 1968). The acceleration of physical growth appears to have its correlates in other areas of development as well. Attitudes, interests, dating patterns and heterosexual activities, educational changes, certain health problems, and even the legal recognition of the end of adolescence (e.g. voting age) are changing in the same direction, pointing to the close interrelatedness of physical, social, attitudinal, and educational development.

Data that support the secular trend in respect to change in body size, body weight and age of sexual maturation are not confined to the United States but come from different geographic regions of the globe and a large variety of national and ethnic groups: Chinese, Japanese, New Zealander, Italian, and Polish, as well as American Negroes and whites.

In a comprehensive review and analysis of all available data for American boys over an eighty year period, Meredith (1963) generalized that the stature of North American boys had increased. He found that fifteen year old white boys were 13.1 cm or 5¼ inches taller in 1955 than in 1870 which means an increase of 8.5% in relative stature. Negro youths, age fifteen, gained 9.5 cm or 5.8% in the period from 1890 to 1930. During the same period, Negro youths, age fifteen, increased their body weight by approximately 6.9 kg or 15.2 lbs. The average weight increase in white boys age fifteen, between 1870 and 1955, was 15 kg or 33 lbs., a change of 30% in body weight. (Figure 1)

In a Swedish study, school children above the age of seven were a year and a half more advanced in their overall physical development, and 8–17 cm taller in 1938 than school children in 1883. The adolescent growth spurt occurred a year earlier and the velocity of the height growth was greater for the 1938–39 group (Broman, Dahlberg & Lichtenstein, 1942). In Puerto Rico, eight to ten year old children attending private schools were found to be 4 cm taller than their coevals thirty years earlier (Knott & Meredith, 1963). Boys from socioeconomically favored families attending Marlborough College in England were measured at an average age of sixteen and a half in 1873 and averaged 65.5 inches tall. Eighty years later, boys of the same age in the same school, probably from families of similar socio-economic status were 69.1 inches tall, a gain of 4.1 inches or about ½ inch per decade. The relatively small gain for the last two groups might be explained on the basis that these children came from relatively wealthy families who seem to benefit less from the secular trend than

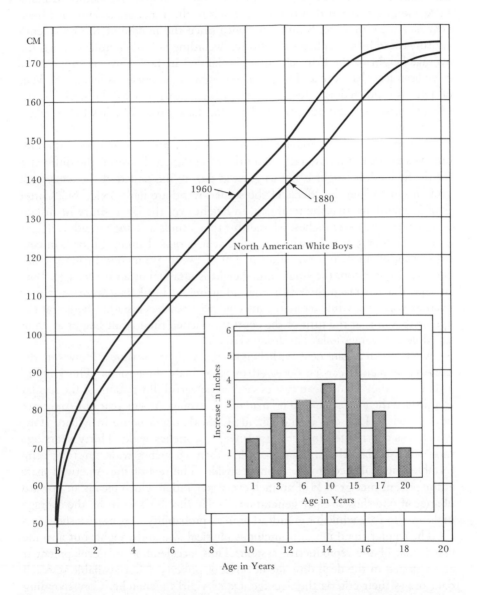

FIGURE 1 Schematic curves of mean stature for 1880 and 1960. Inset shows differences between the curves at selected ages.

From Meredith, H. V. "Change in the Stature and Body Weight of North American Boys During the Last 80 Years." In *Advances in Child Development and Behavior*. L. P. Lipsitt & C. C. Spiker (eds.), Vol. 1, p. 90. Copyright © 1963 by Academic Press, Inc. Reproduced by permission of the author and Academic Press.

children from the lower socio-economic classes (Tanner, 1962). Toronto school children of the age thirteen to fourteen were found to be 3 inches taller in 1939 than thirteen to fourteen year olds were in 1892. Comparative studies in Hamburg, Germany, report that twelve year olds in the 1960s are as large as fifteen year olds were in 1875. Similar evidence since the middle of the nineteenth century could be multiplied extensively. According to less scientific sources, the average height of the first colonists who landed in Jamestown is supposed to have been less than 5 feet. The average height of American sailors in the War of 1812 is estimated as 5 feet 2 inches, which explains why the decks of the USS Constitution did not need to be more than 5 feet 6 inches high (McV. Hunt, 1969).

The secular trend means that children not only grow faster at an earlier age but even as adults they are taller than their forefathers; however, the difference for the final adult height is not as great as during the period of the adolescent growth spurt when the effects of the secular trend are most noticeable. Carter (1966) maintains that the total gain in height over the last century in Britain is no more than 1–1½ inches; Meredith (1963) finds a change in adult height of 1.3 inches or 3.4 cm for an eighty-five year period; Tanner, (1968), in contrast, reported an increase in adult height of 2½ to 3½ inches during the last century. In addition, the final adult height is attained at an earlier age. Boys in 1880 did not reach their full final adult height until they were 23, 24, or even 25 years old, while today the average male reaches his adult height at the age of 18. Girls, at the turn of the century, reached their adult height at 18 or 19 while the average today has dropped to 16.

Most research data deal with height and weight measures. However, the same phenomenon can be observed in other body dimensions. The knights' armor in medieval European castles serve as powerful illustrations of the secular trend since the armor seem to be made to fit average 10–12 year old American boys of today. The seats in the famous La Scala opera house in Milan, Italy, which was constructed in 1776–1778 were 13 inches wide. Thirty years ago most states outlawed seats that were less than 18 inches wide. In 1975 comfortable seats will need to be 24 inches wide. The feet of the American male at the present time grow ⅓ of an inch every generation which means an upward change of one shoe size per generation. Today the shoes worn by the average male are 9 to 10B, while his grandfather in all probability wore a size 7 shoe.

The secular trend not only includes physical size and weight, but also the maturation of the reproductive system. Thus, acceleration in development is also reflected in the declining age of onset of puberty. Most available research data use as their criteria the average age of a girl's menarche. Corresponding acceleration of sexual maturation for boys has also been reported in the literature. A summary of the available evidence which has been collected from various sources, different national samples and different historical periods, has been presented by Tanner (1962) and is reproduced here (Figure 2). Even though

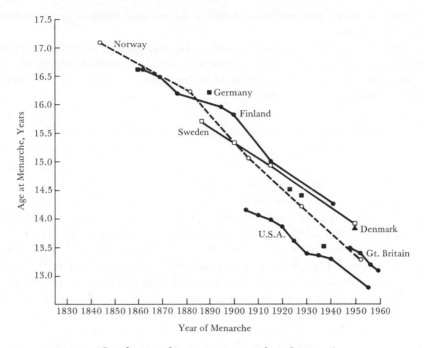

FIGURE 2 Secular trend in age at menarche 1830–1960.

From Tanner, J. M. *Growth at Adolescence*. Oxford: © Blackwell Scientific Publications Ltd., 1962, p. 153. Used by permission of the publisher.

there is some variation from one national sample to another, the overall pattern that emerges is an impressive illustration of the secular trend in sexual maturation. Menarche in the Norwegian data, which goes back to 1840, occurs on an average at the age of 17. Since then it has tended to occur approximately four months earlier per decade. By 1960 the reported average age of menarche was 13 and the trend continues so that today it already occurs in the twelfth year of life and may approach the age of 12 by the turn of the century.

The effects of the secular trend are most pronounced during pubescence as the comparison of Meredith's growth curves (Figure 1) clearly shows, and consequently height and weight comparisons during this developmental period yield more impressive differences than at an earlier or a later age. It is also during the pubescent period that the emotional impact and social awareness of generational differences in growth patterns are most pronounced. Parents may well remember the age when they attended their first dance, had their first date, received or gave their first kiss, and the mother, the age when she experienced menarche. And the frequently heard parental comparison "When I was your age . . ." may actually be accurate if one considered the chronological age alone, but is less appropriate if one considers the changes which are produced by the secular trend. Furthermore, the effects of the secular trend may be compounded by social pressure toward earlier dating and romantic involvement with the opposite sex.

Several interesting questions need to be raised concerning the secular trend, although answers to these questions need to be considered as hypotheses at best and some may be no more than interesting conjectures until more solid evidence becomes available.

1. WHEN DID THE SECULAR TREND BEGIN?

Apparently the change in man's growth pattern is a relatively recent phenomenon. Specific evidence to answer this question is hard to find since most available research studies compare data collected in the mid-twentieth century with data that were collected in the mid-nineteenth century. One study, to be cited in more detail later, indicates that there was relatively little height gain between 1740–1830, but that following 1830 the secular trend began and gained momentum after 1875 (Kiil, 1939). In agreement with this, Lenz (1959) quotes a Danish study which reported no change in height before 1845, but an acceleration of growth following that date. It has been proposed by Backman (1948), based on an extensive review of the literature, that the age of menarche was 14 to 15 years in ancient times and in the Middle Ages. The average age of menarche began to rise about 1500 and continued to increase until the end of the 18th century. At around 1800 the average age of menarche in Northern Europe was 17½ to 18 years. In the beginning of the nineteenth century with the impact of the industrial revolution the trend reversed itself and the age of menarche began to decline, an observation that is well supported by Tanner's (1962) data (Figure 2). In general, presently available evidence seems to place the acceleration of the adolescent growth spurt and the secular trend toward the end of the 18th or the beginning of the 19th century.

2. HOW LONG IS THE SECULAR TREND TO CONTINUE?

If one were to assume that the present rate of change of 1 inch gain per generation continues and then projects this trend to the year 4000, man would have doubled his standing height and have reached an average of 11 to 12 feet. And if the age of menarche would continue to decline by 4 months per decade, already by 2240 the average 4 year old would experience menarche. Krogman, a well known physical anthropologist, believes that there is a boundary to the ultimate size of man, just as other species seem to have size boundaries. He predicts that the secular trend will slow down when man reaches an average height of six feet. Jensen (1969) who approaches the issue from a genetic point of view, argues that the increase in heterozygosity—that is, the state of possessing genetically dissimilar genes in regard to a given characteristic—will wear off. Reduction in heterozygosity will slowly result in a leveling off effect of the secular trend. While some sources maintain that the secular trend continues unabated (Tanner, 1962), others maintain that the trend is already beginning to slow down, at least in the United States (Jensen, 1969).

3. WHAT IS RESPONSIBLE FOR THE CHANGE IN THE TIMING OF MAN'S GROWTH PATTERNS?

Two very different theories have been advanced to explain man's accelerated growth in physical development: 1. diet and environmental conditions, and 2. hybrid vigor. At the present time it appears to be impossible to say that one of these factors is entirely or even predominantly responsible while the other is not.

The most obvious factors that may contribute to the secular trend are nutritional considerations: better balanced diets, more emphasis on vitamins, proteins, and minerals rather than an increase in calories. However, the effects of the secular trend are more pronounced in the lower socio-economic classes than in the middle and upper classes, which are more likely to practice dietary knowledge. It is known that middle and upper class children are taller, heavier, and menstruate earlier than children from the lower socio-economic strata of society. Evidence to this effect can be found in the Broman, Dahlberg and Lichtenstein (1942) study; their data distinguish between elementary and secondary school pupils at least for the ages 10–14. Since Sweden at the time of the study had a dual track educational system, it can be assumed that many more children from the higher socio-economic strata of society attended secondary schools. On all measurements reported the secondary school pupils scored higher, an observation that is more pronounced in 1883 than in 1938. However, "the secular trend has over-ridden the social class differences, and though these still exist, the average boy of today is taller at all ages than the upper class boy of 1878" (Tanner, 1962, p. 147). In support of the nutritional hypothesis, it has been found that the secular trend is interrupted and even reversed during periods of famine and economic crises (Tanner, 1968). There are also other factors which are related to better health care, especially prenatal care, immunization against disease and reduction in serious childhood disease. Furthermore, it appears "that the mechanism which causes the secular shift must be operating within the first few years of life" (Donovan, 1965, p. 35) if not in the prenatal period of development. The change in family size from six children in the mid-nineteenth century to two or three children in the mid-twentieth century has also contributed to the secular trend. Children from small families have been found to be consistently larger and menstruate earlier than children from large families. However, this fact by itself does not constitute a sufficient explanation. It could account for some change but not for the phenomenon per se (Tanner, 1962). Since electricity has become widely available, children tend to spend more hours awake and under illumination— and if one can draw analogies from animal studies—this influences the rate of growth and accelerates sexual maturity. Other factors that may contribute to the secular trend include more leisure time, better child care, laws against child labor, improvement in housing and climate control, changes in temperature and humidity, as well as improvement in the standard of living in general.

As part of the hybrid vigor hypothesis it has been suggested that the invention of the bicycle in 1817, and the invention of the steam engine may have contributed to the secular trend. These technological inventions provided increasing freedom to travel and to select one's mate outside the narrow confines of the village. This change in the pattern of mate selection caused a progressive "breaking down of genetic isolates, that is, of the tendency for marriages to be contracted between members of the same village community" (Tanner, 1961, p. 150). Thus the change in the timing of the growth pattern and the change in the adult height receive a genetic explanation. "It has been estimated that 10 to 20 per cent of the variance in height is due to genetic dominance, so that the mean of the offspring of two parents will not be halfway between the parents but slightly closer to the taller parent. Outbreeding increases heterozygotes in the population with a consequent increase in height. This heterosis due to outbreeding also enhances growth rate and early maturation as amply demonstrated in numerous experiments in animal breeding" (Jensen, 1969, p. 229). One set of Norwegian data (Kiil, 1939), collected over a 200 year span, fit into the chronology of this hypothesis. Between 1740–1830 there was little evidence for gain in height. Between 1830–1875, with the availability of the bicycle, the height gain was found to be .3 cm per decade. After 1875 with the availability of better means of transportation the height gain increased further to .6 cm per decade. Additional support for this hypothesis can be found in the data presented by Hulse (1957). He observed in Swiss mountain villages that if both parents came from the same village their children, as adults, were 2 cm shorter than if the parents came from different villages.

The available evidence does not identify one specific factor which is responsible for the secular trend. The phenomenon is complex and in all probability the interaction of several of the factors discussed may contribute to it. A more definitive answer of the question of causation awaits further research.

4. WHAT ARE THE SOCIAL, ATTITUDINAL, AND EDUCATIONAL CORRELATES OF THE SECULAR TREND?

While the following discussion does not imply a simple cause-effect relationship, the secular trend in physical growth has its correlates in many other areas of development in that certain interest patterns and attitudinal changes as well as social sexual interests and social sophistication seem to occur at an earlier age today than even a generation ago. The effect of this change is most pronounced during the adolescent period and most noticeable in respect to the time when adult privileges are granted by parents or demanded by youths. Some of the contemporary adolescent problems and conflicts, especially the present concern with the "generation gap" may be better understood if one were to consider the earlier biological maturation of youth as contrasted with their chronological age which usually serves as the frame of reference for parents and teachers. On a more general level, even the structure of the curriculum, the amount and kind of knowledge acquired, and the changes in mental ability follow the direction of the secular trend in physical development.

Mary Cover Jones (1960)* gives evidence for this trend, even though, in contrast to the studies on physical growth patterns, her article covers a much shorter period of time historically speaking. Ninth graders in 1953 had attitudes and interests which were much like those held by eleventh graders 25 years earlier. The data from the more recent sample indicate that adolescents have become more serious, are more tolerant, show greater social sophistication and sexual interests than their coevals in 1935. Harris (1959) compared the interest patterns and concerns of junior and senior high school students in 1935 with those of subjects in 1957. For both sexes the more recent data reveal an increased interest in love, marriage, home and family, as well as a greater social concern as shown by a preference for the item "getting along with other people."

Broderick and Fowler (1961) reported that the frequently observed sex cleavage found in fourth grade sociometric tests and interpreted as a lack of interest in—if not outright hostility and antagonism toward—the opposite sex is disappearing. They found that the sex cleavage is being replaced by greater and earlier cross sex friendships, interest in the opposite sex, dating, romantic attachment, and kissing. 90% of this sample of fifth graders already had sweethearts, 65% had been kissed by the opposite sex, and 40% had already dated.

Kuhlen and Houlihan (1965), contrasting data on adolescent heterosexual interest obtained in 1942 with data obtained by the same procedure in 1963, provide further evidence for the fact that heterosexual interests have become significantly more pronounced in the more recent sample.

On a more practical level, considerable concern is expressed by many parents regarding their daughters' desire to use lipstick, nail polish, training bras, nylon stockings, perfume, and other paraphernalia of sex appeal, and their indications of sex interest at an earlier age. The changing patterns for boys is expressed in earlier smoking, drinking, use of drugs, having dates, and desiring physical intimacies on their dates. This concern with earlier sex appeal, heterosexual interest and sexual intimacy of today's adolescents has found expression in a number of articles which recently have appeared in the slick cover journals. Havighurst writes in 1963 "within the past generation, the ages at which boys and girls begin dating, going to boy-girl parties, learning to dance, and the other precursors of courtship and marriage have all decreased, so that junior high school is now a theater of rather active social life of a sort which formerly was thought more appropriate for the senior high school" (p. 160). Since then the pattern for junior high school as already been more widely accepted and the concern today is with the heterosexual interest in elementary school.

Curriculum changes in the public schools have also followed the patterns

* The study is reprinted as Chapter 13 of this book.

of the secular trend in physical development in that certain subject matters are being taught at an earlier age. Some of these changes are related to other factors, such as improved technology, new methods of teaching, and changing educational and psychological theory, as well as political and business reasons, nevertheless, the direction of change is the same as that of the secular trend. Content areas such as calculus, consumer education, or "personality and dating" are no longer the prerogatives of the college curriculum but are taught increasingly more in high schools, just as elementary school children learn different number systems, such as the binary system, and receive instruction about drugs as well as sex education.

The head width and the face width (Knott & Meredith, 1963), the size of the face (Hunter & Garn, 1969) and the circumference of the head have increased, which may well have resulted in an increase in the size of the brain. One might speculate whether this physical change could have contributed to the acceleration of children's ability to learn, to think and to reason. There is evidence that average mental test scores have increased from generation to generation in different cultures; e.g., World War II draftees scored approximately one standard deviation higher than World War I draftees (Tuddenham, 1948), and draftees in the 1960s scored ½ standard deviation higher than World War II draftees (Humphreys, 1969). To what extent changes in the patterns of physical development and changes in mental test scores are interrelated is hard to assess since increasing school attendance, better education and the mass media of communication and even increased exposure to and experience with testing would most likely contribute to increased intelligence test scores.

It is known that the period of adolescence is also expanding upward in that modern industrialized and computerized society requires increasingly more education thus prolonging the period of dependency and immaturity which the status of being a minor and being a student implies. "Without the challenge of independent responsibility . . . the duration of training tends to limit emotional maturity which is a vital component in the equipment of anyone who hopes to achieve wisdom" (Kubie, 1958). In addition, the increase of affluence in society permits the postponement of the assumption of responsibility in its young and makes possible the longer amount of schooling.

On the other hand, the overall effects of the secular trend and its social emotional correlates constitute a prolongation of the adolescent period downward since pubescence and adolescence begin considerably earlier today than at the turn of the century.

5. WHAT ARE THE BROADER IMPLICATIONS OF THE SECULAR TREND?

The social, medical, educational and psychiatric consequences of the secular trend and particularly of a continuation of the speeding up of man's physical and sexual development are hard to assess at this time. Although the phenomenon has already evoked some concern and a great deal of speculation it has stimulated only a limited amount of research. The interrelatedness of developmental acceleration with other social trends does not allow the singling out of the secular trend as the sole cause of any one contemporary social, medical, or psychiatric issue, and no claim is made here to that effect. Nevertheless, the direction of such changes are consistent with the secular trend in that there is an acceleration of the time schedule of social and educational phenomena and at least of some medical problems. Furthermore, knowledge of the secular trend may contribute to a better understanding of such social issues as the demand for the lowering of the voting age, the demand for student participation in the decision making processes of universities, colleges, and even high schools. The trend is also reflected in the dropping of the average age for marriages, which is preceded by a decline in the age of dating and courtship (Broderick, 1961), and a slow increase of physical intimacies and sexual intercourse at an earlier age. The resulting social-medical problems of increased venereal disease and illegitimate birth at an earlier age have been widely publicized. There is evidence that a new face shape and face size have emerged, which means "that present-day orthodontists may well be working towards cosmetic ideals thirty to fifty years old" (Hunter & Garn, 1969). Furthermore, the proportion of youngsters under 16 arrested for narcotic offenses, as well as the general phenomena of drug use and drug addiction, have increased drastically since 1950 in the adolescent age range and even in pre-adolescence.

Some biologists and geneticists have suggested that in order to solve the problems which man is facing due to the problems of over-population, lack of nutrition, and pollution of air and water we should not only continue to be concerned with changing the environment, but in addition, should consider changing man himself. Future man would be considerably reduced in size in order to change the ratio between the excessive size of man in relationship to the existing environment and the environmental resources. This then would constitute a drastic reversal of the secular trend.

Curriculum changes of the school reflect educational acceleration; in addition, the present reorganization of the public school system itself reflects the trend toward earlier maturation. In some school systems the sixth grade has been taken out of the elementary school structure and in combination with the seventh and eighth grade has resulted in a new educational concept: the middle school. Other school systems are contemplating similar moves. Schools recognize that the pubescent growth changes have been accelerated to the extent that the junior high school needs to be relocated age-wise and re-named.

Some authors with psychiatric or clinical orientations write about the discrepancy between an acceleration in physical, social, and educational development in today's youth with a simultaneous deceleration in emotional and ethical maturity. This developmental discrepancy is interpreted as one of the reasons for increased conflict and crises in adolescence. The available research evidence for such a discrepancy is sparse, and where the assessment of deceleration in emotional and ethical maturity has been attempted (Engelmann, 1962), the interpretations and generalizations seem to go beyond the data presented. Heath (1968) concludes on the basis of extensive personality test data which were obtained from entering Haverford freshmen since World War II: "Compared to the students of even just a decade ago, the contemporary student has become an increasingly intellectualized and inhibited person whose energies are directed more toward himself and his own interest than toward others with whom he has become progressively less emotionally involved" (p. 63). The similarity between Heath's (1968) and Engelmann's (1962) findings, even though obtained from different national groups, different age levels and by way of different methodology is noteworthy. Heath continues further in his analysis of historical changes. "In comparison to the student of the forties and fifties, the students of the sixties have become increasingly more over-controlled, inhibited, and tend to be more defensive and intellectually efficient" (p. 63). Quotes from the professional literature concerning the "psychological retardation of today's youth" (Seidmann, 1963) and "accelerated physical development and retarded emotional development" (Otterstädt, 1960) could be multiplied. If such a discrepancy between physical, intellectual, social-sexual development on the one hand and emotional, ethical and moral development on the other hand does exist during adolescence, it would be a significant conceptual contribution to the understanding of adolescent conflict, crises, and difficulties. However, while acceleration of physical, social, and educational development is well supported by available evidence, the simultaneous deceleration in emotional, ethical, moral or psychological development must be considered at this time as an interesting hypothesis which, even though it has some support, is in need of further empirical verification.

REFERENCES

1. Backman, G. "Die beschleunigte Entwicklung der Jugend. Verfrühte Menarche, verspätete Menopause, verlängerte Lebensdauer." *Acta Anatomica,* 1948, 4, 421–480.
2. Broderick, C. B. and S. E. Fowler. "New Patterns of Relationships Between the Sexes among Preadolescents." *Marriage and Family Living,* 1961, 23, 27–30.
3. Broman, B., G. Dahlberg, and A. Lichtenstein. "Height and Weight during Growth." *Acta Paediatrica,* 1942, 30, 1–66.
4. Carter, C. O. *Human Heredity.* Baltimore: Penguin, 1962.
5. Donovan, B. T. and J. J. Van Der Werff Ten Bosch. *Physiology of Puberty.* Baltimore: The Williams and Wilkins Company, 1965.
6. Engelmann, W. "Reifungsentwicklung und Reifungsveränderungen im

gefühlsbetonten Wertungsbereich unserer Jugend." *Psychologische Rundschau,* 1962, *13,* 131–140.

7. Harris, D. B. "Sex Differences in the Life Problems and Interests of Adolescents, 1935 and 1957." *Child Development,* 1959, 30, 453–459.

8. Havighurst, R. J. "Do Junior High-School Youth Grow Up too Fast?" *The Bulletin of the National Association of Secondary School Principles,* 1963, 47, 151–162.

9. Heath, D. H. *Growing Up in College.* San Francisco: Jossey-Bass Inc., Publishers, 1968.

10. Hulse, F. S. "Exogamie et Héterosis." *Archives Suisse D'Anthropologie Générale,* 1957, 22, 103–125.

11. Humphreys, L. "New Perspectives on Intelligence." Lecture delivered at the Maryland Psychological Association Annual Meeting, April 25, 1969.

12. Hunt, J. McV. "Has Compensatory Education Failed? Has it Been Attempted?" In *Environment, Heredity, and Intelligence.* Reprint Series No. 2 compiled from *Harvard Educational Review,* 1969, 130–152.

13. Hunter, W. S. and S. M. Garn. "Evidence for a Secular Trend in Face Size." *The Angle Orthodontist,* 1969, 39, 320–323.

14. Jensen, A. R. "Reducing the Heredity-Environment Uncertainty." In *Environment, Heredity, and Intelligence.* Reprint Series No. 2 compiled from *Harvard Educational Review,* 1969, 209–243.

15. Jones, M. C. "A Comparison of the Attitudes and Interests of Ninth-Grade Students over Two Decades." *Journal of Educational Research,* 1960, 51, 175–186.

16. Kiil, V. "Stature and Growth of Norwegian Men during the Past 200 Years." *Skr. Norske Vidensk. Akad.,* 1939, No. 6.

17. Knott, V. B. "Stature, Leg Girth, and Body Weight of Puerto Rican Private School Children Measured in 1962." *Growth,* 1963, 27, 157–174.

18. Knott, V. B. and H. V. Meredith. "Body Size of United States Schoolboys at Ages from 11 Years to 15 Years." *Human Biology,* 1963, 35, 507–513.

19. Kubie, L. S. *Neurotic Distortions of the Creative Process.* Lawrence: University of Kansas Press, 1958.

20. Kuhlen, R. G. and N. B. Houlihan. "Adolescent Heterosexual Interest in 1942 and 1963." *Child Development,* 1965, 36, 1049–1052.

21. Lenz, W. "Ursachen des gesteigerten Wachstums der heutigen Jugend." *Wissen. Veröff. deut. Gesellsch. Ernäh.,* 1959, 4, 1–33.

22. Meredith, H. V. "Change in the Stature and Body Weight of North American Boys during the last 80 Years." In *Advances in Child Development and Behavior.* L. P. Lipsitt and C. C. Spiker (Eds.), N.Y.: Academic Press, Vol. 1, 1963, 69–114.

23. Otterstädt, H. "Akzeleration und Stoffplan." *Psychologische Rundschau,* 1960, 11, 45–51.

24. Seidmann, P. *Moderne Jugend.* Zürich & Stuttgart: Rascher Verlag, 1963.

25. Tanner, J. M. "Earlier Maturation in Man." *Scientific American,* 1968, 218, 21–27.

26. Tanner, J. M. *Growth at Adolescence.* Oxford: Blackwell Scientific Publications, 1962.

27. Tuddenham, R. D. "Soldier Intelligence in World Wars I and II." *American Psychologist*, 1948, 3, 54–56.

[6] *Johanna Dwyer & Jean Mayer* PSYCHOLOGICAL

EFFECTS OF VARIATIONS IN PHYSICAL

APPEARANCE DURING ADOLESCENCE

Introduction

Recently Harms' (8) article in this journal called attention to the importance of the physical and organic side of the puberty period as a key to the understanding of the psychology of adolescence.

It is well known that adolescent growth patterns are extremely heterogeneous, whereas social and cultural pressures within the adolescent peer group stress homogeneity and conformity in matters of appearance. This situation leads to stress for many adolescents.

Physical variations in adolescent growth are commonly assessed by a variety of objective measurements which are then compared with standards. It can be arbitrarily decided that an unusual pattern of development is one occurring in 16% or less of adolescents of the same sex and chronological age. Since these variations are within the normal range from a medical point of view, physicians generally tend to disregard them. However, such patterns are often perceived as abnormal by the adolescents concerned and so may generate a great deal of anxiety and unhappiness. An awareness of the resultant social and psychological strains is thus essential for those who deal with and try to help adolescents through this difficult period.

We become aware of the importance of developmental variations during adolescence because of the extreme levels of anxiety and despair which were observed by us in our attempts to treat and understand obese adolescents.

The purpose of this paper will be to outline briefly some of the variations in physical appearance which commonly cause adolescents difficulty and then to take a more leisurely look within this framework at the problem of obesity during adolescence, which has been our major area of research over the past several years.

FROM *Adolescence*, 1968–69, 3, 353–380. REPRINTED BY PERMISSION OF THE SENIOR AUTHOR AND LIBRA PUBLISHERS, INC.

Characteristics of adolescent growth

PHYSICAL GROWTH

The physiological characteristics of adolescent growth explain much of the anxiety and upset of the teen years. During adolescence the velocity of growth (the overall rate of growth) suddenly rises from the slow and steady progress characterizing the previous years. The timing of this increase varies from person to person and depends on physiologic rather than chronological age. Normal variation for the start of accelerated growth covers a six-years span (from 8 to 14 years of age in girls and 9 to 15 years in boys). Variations in timing of maturation are natural and normal. Yet peers and parents may judge these variations less benignly than does the professional.

The total time necessary to complete growth also varies from one individual to another. Some adolescents are physically adults four to five years after the first signs of puberty, while others require seven years or more to reach the same end point.

Asynchronism or lack of coordination in development is sometimes present. Relative rates of development of different parts of the body are dissimilar in childhood, but these differences become more obvious at puberty. Asynchronisms usually disappear after a year, but while they last they may be excruciatingly embarrassing for the adolescent. Some adolescents whose growth is temporarily out of phase may be terrified that growth will cease, leaving them deformed for the rest of their lives. Others may fear that they will never stop growing. Probably the most common type of uncoordinated growth is short-waistedness due to growth of the legs disproportionate to that of the trunk. Other common asynchronisms include increase in hip width before shoulder width, or vice versa, growth of one part of the face before growth of another, and increase in muscle mass before increase in muscle strength.

During adolescence the velocity of genital and sex-linked anatomic changes far outstrips the rate of growth and change in other organ systems. Obviously the maturation of the procreative function has great social and psychological significance.

The adolescent phase of growth is also unique because of its finality. Children tend to assume that once they grow up their disabilities and problems will disappear. Teenagers are confronted with the reality of permanent differences, and some of them must come to terms with permanent defects or deficiencies in physical appearance. Previous differences such as those in size become more noticeable. A tall fourth grader and a short fourth grader differ by only a few inches; a tall man and a short may differ by as much as a foot.

A characteristic of physical growth which has potent social implications is that girls mature earlier than boys. Since our schools are run on the basis of chronologic rather than developmental age, boys are about two years behind girls of the same age in development throughout the adolescent period.

During adolescence psychological changes interact with the effects of physical variations in appearance. Certain social learning occurs simultaneously for all adolescents because of the similarity of school experiences. Other social learning may come earlier or later depending on the child's experiences outside of school. Thus the levels of physical, social and emotional maturation vary in adolescents of the same age.

Adolescents are acutely aware of the entire growth process and are almost always interested in it. Many are disturbed about their own growth as well. Longitudinal studies such as that of Stolz and Stolz (21) have shown that about one-third of all boys and one-half of all girls become sufficiently concerned about at least one aspect of their growth at some point that they spontaneously express their concern to the physician investigator. Actually, so many changes take place so fast during puberty that it is remarkable that more adolescents do not become unduly upset and worried about their development.

The adolescent has a greater sense of psychological and physical self-existence than does the small child. The exaggeration of individual differences in physique during the process of individual growth appears at the same time that self-awareness increases at a psychological level. The adolescent's more sophisticated thinking allows him to invest growth with symbolic meaning so that physical maturation may come to signify growth in other areas as well.

The desire to conform grows in the early teens. Peer acceptance becomes the motive for a great deal of behavior. Being different in appearance from one's peers often seems tantamount to being inferior.

A "sex-appropriate" appearance becomes particularly important in adolescence. Every country has ideals for male and female appearance. Most Americans think that men should be tall, large-shouldered, barrel-chested and narrow-hipped, while women should be petite, slender, and amply endowed in the bust. Sex-typed differences extend beyond the obvious primary and secondary sex characteristics to more subtle differences in manner of movement, hairiness, skin texture, and symmetry of features. Marked variations in any of these characteristics may adversely influence how a person is treated by others and how he thinks of himself.

Difficulties that arise from lack of sex-appropriateness in appearance can be divided into two categories. First is the transient problem of a sex-inappropriate phase of growth. Characteristics thought to be girlish may be present temporarily in the adolescent boy because of a slow change of voice, late maturation, or a feminine pattern of fat deposition. The fact that these conditions are transient makes them no less painful to the sufferer. More lasting and serious are the permanent problems arising from supposed lack of sex-appropriateness in the mature body. Such characteristics as lack of muscular strength, sparse beard, and frailness may become manifest as growth moves into the decelerating phase of later adolescence.

Adolescents are particularly sensitive to these types of nonconformity in appearance for several reasons. Doctor-patient communication is likely to be poor. Adolescents are unlikely to initiate a conversation about worries concerning maturation in the sexual area because of embarassment. Barring the presence of a gross abnormality, the physician may fail to mention a normal but unusual pattern of primary or secondary sexual development to his worried patient. He may also fail to reassure the adolescent about some condition that varies greatly from that of his peer group because he recognizes that it is simply due to a difference in the timing of maturation.

It is also important to realize that adolescent ideals of sex-appropriate appearance tend to be quite unrealistic. Adolescent girls long to look like fashion models; boys want to look like football pros. Sexual growth is particularly vulnerable to the tyranny of the often ignorant notions of normality that other adolescents possess, since the subject is so rarely discussed with parents, let alone with the doctor.

Teen-aged girls are even more interested in and concerned about their physical development than are boys. One reason is that outward appearance and the inward self are more closely bound together in females than in males. Women tend to interpret objective remarks about appearance, such as "You look awful," to mean "You are awful." Body awareness in men is more stable and less sensitive to chance remarks. Men seem to be more sensitive to remarks about physical performance and competence in using their bodies. Status in girls' groups and popularity with boys are two other reasons for the great amount of attention that adolescent girls devote to their appearance. Popularity with boys has for girls many of the competitive aspects that success in athletics has for boys. A common route to upward social mobility for a woman is to marry a man of higher social rank. Any positive attribute such as a pleasing appearance, a good voice or intelligence increase the chances of this happening.

The vulnerability of adolescent girls to worries about appearance makes wide variations in development potentially anxiety-provoking. Angelino and Mech (2) found that retrospective essays by 32 women 20 years of age on aspects of development causing the most anxiety mentioned tallness and overweight most frequently. The Stolzes (21), in their longitudinal study of 83 girls examined every six months for eight years, found that almost half of the subjects were disturbed about their development. Tallness and fatness accounted for the largest share of worries. Facial features and general physical appearance accounted for the next highest number of complaints. The combination of tallness or shortness with heaviness bothered several subjects. Glasses, thinness with flat chest, late development, acne, and tallness with thinness accounted for the rest of the difficulties.

The early maturer

Early maturers begin adolescence with attitudes toward their bodies which they have acquired during childhood and which differ from those of most children their age. Usually they have been larger and slightly more endomorphic or mesomorphic than their peers throughout childhood. During adolescence early and late maturers tend to have quite different social experiences. They are treated differently in terms of both privileges which are granted to them and behavior which is expected of them.

Most of the difficulties of the early maturer arise from the discrepancy between physiological changes and society's expectations of these changes. He faces a rapid physical change while his friends' growth is still relatively stable. He may feel bewildered and hesitant about growing up at this point, but once he has adapted to or accepted his early spurt, he may be pleased with his maturity.

The disadvantages of early maturation stem from the fact that the adolescent has acquired an adult body but may still think and act like a child. Some early maturers find that their mature appearance often pushes them into social situations for which they are not ready emotionally; they are expected to live up to adult standards appropriate to their size rather than to their age. Other early maturers encounter an entirely different problem. Their parents continue to treat them as small children, ignoring the fact that they look older and are treated by everyone else as though they really were older.

BOYS

The early maturing boy is at an advantage in three areas: athletics, heterosexual activity, and leadership. Early maturing boys are temporarily bigger and stronger than others of their own age and thus have a competitive advantage in sports. Latham's (14) study of junior high school boys called attention to the dominance of athletes in the leading crowds at school. Junior high boys who were more mature were taller, heavier and more muscular. These factors may have been the reason that they were more likely to be chosen as team captains. Patterns of association for junior high school boys often revolve around sports. Those who are successful in athletics have a chance to become popular and are more likely to become leaders. Athletic events of many American high schools are a focus of community interests, so that high school athletic prowess is a path to glory not only among peers but also among adults.

Timing of maturation also influences behavior and success in heterosexual areas. Early maturing boys tend to be more interested in girls (and girls in them) than are late maturing boys. During early adolescence, when separate groups of boys and girls begin to form heterosexual groups, the early maturer has a social advantage.

GIRLS

Early maturing girls are faced with the problem that few of the other girls and almost none of the boys are growing at a comparable rate. Therefore their physical changes stand out. Embarrassment among early maturing girls in the Stolz (21) longitudinal study centered about conspicuousness, bigness, tallness, complexion, and menstruation.

Peers of both sexes are often wary of early maturing girls because they are bigger and different from them physically. Older boys may befriend them since boys usually date girls who are younger. The lack of social and intellectual maturity in early-maturing girls and their potential competition in dating may preclude friendship with older girls who are closer to their physiological age.

The late maturer

BOYS

The late maturing boy is a laggard in development. Almost all of the girls and most of the boys mature physically before he does. The late maturing boys are not necessarily those who were small all through childhood; they are of average height in grammar school, but by junior high school they are smaller than their early maturing classmates. At the age of about 13 or 14 years the early maturing boys with their superiority in athletics and popularity with girls begin to crowd them out. The early maturing boys gain the prestige and adolescent laurels which the later maturers perhaps had in the past. For the next few years the late maturing boys are at a disadvantage.

The late maturing boy may lack interest in dating. If he is interested, he may find that the prettiest girls are dating older or more mature boys and that they ignore him except when they are in dire straits. When maturation finally comes, the late maturer's level of social and emotional development in the heterosexual area may be retarded in contrast to that of others of his age who have had more experience. For a while he may appear to be out of step and unsure in unfamiliar social situations. Thus it seems that a certain amount of strain in the social area is inevitable for very late maturing adolescents. If they try to be like their physically more advanced classmates and date, they may meet with rebuffs; if they ignore girls until they have grown up, they tend to be awkward from lack of experience.

This is not to say that adolescents who are less mature than others of their age are doomed to loneliness and misery. After school hours they may gravitate toward others who are younger or closer to their own level of physical development. At school, although they may find that they are not in the leading crowd of their grade with respect to athletics, leadership, or dating, they can still find a variety of extracurricular activities such as band or activity-oriented clubs (such as a math club) in which lack of physical maturity is not a major drawback if they have other talents. Late maturers can also achieve high status in recreational or institutional groups outside of school, such as the Boy Scouts or church youth groups. The effects of maturation level on leadership and status, therefore, depend largely on what groups the adolescent is trying to join. If he so chooses, he can move into a comfortable social setting in which he can obtain his share of social rewards, although we suspect that many late-maturing Eagle Scouts would give up all of their badges for the higher status accorded to the junior high school football star or the class Romeo.

GIRLS

In contrast to the large amount of attention that has been directed to late maturation in boys, little has been written about this in girls. Perhaps the girls have less pronounced problems because of their two-year advantage in physiological development, so that even the late-maturing girls grow up long before the last of the late-maturing boys. Since success in the heterosexual area is based partially on the appearance of sexual maturity, later-maturing girls may be at a slight disadvantage either because they are less interested in boys or less likely to be attractive to boys than are their early-maturing peers.

Measurable psychological consequences of maturation time

BOYS

Psychological differences between early and late-maturing boys are large during adolescence. Jones and Bayley (13), in their study of 13- to 15-year-old boys, assessed maturation by skeletal age of the hand and knee. They assessed social behavior by observing a large number of activities and studying peer ratings. The early maturers were the largest and strongest boys in their classes and the most advanced in skeletal age. Adults and other children treated them as being more mature. They tended to be more mesomorphic in build than later maturers, and this extra muscularity conferred an advantage in sports. They showed more mature interests, greater cleanliness, greater attractiveness in appearance, and less need to strive for status than did the later-maturing boys. Many of these early-maturers were student leaders. Their peers rated them as more grown-up, more assured, and more likely, to have older friends than their later-maturing classmates.

Mussen and Jones (17) examined differences in social behavior and thematic apperception test protocols of the same boys studied by Jones and Bayley, but at age 17. Although the test tended to present a somewhat more favorable psychological picture for the early-maturing boys, the only statistically significant difference was that the late-maturing boys gave responses which might indicate more feelings of inadequacy, rejection, dominance or rebelliousness toward their families. More of the early-maturers appeared to be self-confident and independent and to play an adultlike role in interpersonal relations. Although differences in these respects were not statistically significant, later maturers showed at age 17 a trend toward possessing the following characteristics: less attractive physique, less relaxation, less assurance in class, more animation, more eagerness, more uninhibitedness, more affectation, more restlessness, more behavior of an attention-getting nature, and fewer older friends. The early and later maturers did not differ significantly in observed popularity, leadership, prestige, poise, assurance, cheer or social effects in male groups. The late maturers were at a distinct disadvantage in mixed sex groups. The authors concluded that retarded maturation conferred a slight competitive disadvantage in the boys' world and a somewhat greater disadvantage in the very early heterosexual world.

Jones (12) used interviews and a variety of psychological tests (California Psychological Inventory and Edwards Personal Preference Schedule) to study the later careers and personalities of early-maturing and late-maturing boys. At age 33 the physical differences noted in adolescence had disappeared; the young adults who had matured early did not look more attractive or well groomed than the later-maturing group. There were no significant differences between the two groups in marital status, family size, or educational level. The early maturers tended to exhibit earlier success patterns. They scored higher on the "good impression" scale, which was an index of interest in and capacity for creating a good impression on others. Men who had been classified as physically retarded during adolescence by use of skeletal age criteria were found in interviews to be more expressive, and eager, and less settled at age 33 than their earlier-maturing colleagues. Objective psychologic tests showed few significant differences other than the fact that later-maturers did appear to be more "flexible," that is, more rebellious, touchy, impulsive, assertive, insightful, and self-indulgent. Jones concluded that although the overall effect of maturation time on personal life was small, the early maturers still tended to exhibit earlier success patterns.

GIRLS

Stone and Barker (22, 23) were among the first to study the differences in certain aspects of behavior and personality between early-maturing and later-maturing adolescent girls. They studied 1,000 junior high school girls 13 and 14 years of age, all white Anglo-Saxon, second generation Californians. The criterion of maturity was taken as the menarche. Admittedly the menarche is a rather ambiguous measure, since feminizing changes in body build begin long before and continue long after the first menses. However, the postmenarcheal sample undoubtedly was older in physiological age than the premenarcheal sample. The same questionnaire had been tested on older and younger subjects, so that the maturity level of the responses could be scored. The postmenarcheal group was made up of girls who matured early or at a normal rate. These girls favored responses indicating heterosexual interests, adornment or display of the person, disinterest in participating in games or activities requiring vigorous or strenuous physical effort, and greater interest in imaginary, or daydreaming activities. The two groups did not differ in attitudes toward the presence of family friction or revolt against family discipline.

More (16) studied the social behavior of early-maturing and later-maturing adolescent girls. Unfortunately, half of the sample was purposefully selected to include maladjusted adolescents, and it is difficult to know how many of the differences he reported were due to time of maturation and how many to unequal distribution of maladjusted subjects between early-maturing and late-maturing groups. Early-maturing girls were judged by peers to have a lower degree of motor activity and to be less quarrelsome, less demanding of attention, and less argumentative than late-maturing girls. Early-maturing girls were also regarded by their peers as participating more in peer life than late-maturing girls, and apparently their greater participation had contributed to their reputation for being bossy, assertive, and more forceful. They tended to be better groomed, more calm, and more physically integrated.

Stature

Stature is related to maturation, since early maturers tend to exceed others in height at one period of early adolescence. Final differences in stature persist throughout life and might be expected to have more lasting effects on personality than transient differences due to age at maturation.

BOYS

Boys want to be tall for many reasons. It is considered to be sex-appropriate in our culture for men to be big and tall; hence, tallness may symbolize masculinity to many boys and girls. There are also social advantages in being tall. All other things being equal, a tall boy or man has less difficulty in commanding the attention of strangers or of casual acquaintance than does a short one.

If a group of adolescents who do not know one another is asked to select a leader, the group tends to choose a large boy, and shorter adolescents are well aware of this. Shortness can be a real handicap in achieving prestige through athletic prowess in many of the more popular team sports. This does not mean that the short, wiry basketball player has no place, but it is true that in the sports height and weight are advantageous and shortness is disadvantageous. Short or late-maturing boys may be superb athletes, but they often excel in minor sports in the adolescent prestige hierarchy, such as golf, tennis, gymnastics, etc. This helps to enhance their reputation as "regular guys" but does not bring them the adulation accorded basketball or football heroes. Stolz (21) found that short boys did not achieve representation proportionate to their percentage in their grades in any of the sports which are most popular among adolescents.

Height is also often an excruciatingly embarrassing problem for adolescent boys in social relations with girls. The short, mature boy is often better off socially than the short, immature boy, but both often feel handicapped. In social dancing both sexes want the boy to be at least as tall as, and preferably taller than, the girl. Personality and all other attributes being equal, most girls probably prefer tall and handsome boys to those who are short and handsome.

Adolescent boys rarely worry about being too tall. The only boys who were upset about their tallness in the Stolz and Stolz study were the extremely thin boys over 6'3" and transiently tall early-maturers, who were disturbed because they were growing while nobody else was growing.

GIRLS

Girls seldom complain about shortness unless it is combined with heaviness so that they appear squat. They are more satisfied if they are short and petite. However, being tall bothers them a great deal. We have all seen early-maturing girls who have become stooped because of a self-conscious effort to compensate for their height. Many girls feel that their tallness hinders them in making friends with boys, especially in the early teens when the boys tend to be short. Even if they do manage to get short boys interested, tall girls may worry about how they look together, since it is the cultural ideal for women to be shorter than men.

Sex appropriateness of physique

The Stolzes (21) coined the term "sex-inappropriate physique" to describe a particular syndrome which gives rise to malaise in many teen-age boys. This syndrome is most likely to occur in puberty, especially in boys whose development is slow, and it usually passes quite rapidly. These boys tend to deposit a girdle of fat around the hips and thighs. This characteristic, together with small and slowly developing primary sex characteristics and the slight development of subcutaneous tissue about the nipples, makes these adolescents feel not only that they are deficient in acceptable male development but also that they are following a feminine pattern of growth. Certainly it is important for the physician to reassure these patients, since such growth is likely to be a topic of attention and ridicule from peers whose growth is more rapid and sex-appropriate.

Differences in genital changes in boys are visible and are obvious both to the boy himself and to other boys when they see each other in mens' rooms and showers. Female genital development is far less visible to the girl herself or to others because of the social strictures concerning modesty for girls.

BOYS

Both boys and girls worry about sex-inappropriateness of facial character-istics, but girls are able to do more about defects by using cosmetics. Among the characteristics which boys complained about as being unmasculine in the Stolz study were the following: eyeglasses, turned-up nose, dimples, receding chin, small rosebud mouth, lack of beard, protruding ears, tooth defects, hair problems such as cowlicks or early baldness, and acne. It goes without saying that physical competence in using the body for physical work is as important for the boy in defining his maleness as are some of the physical characteristics.

GIRLS

The adolescent girls in the Stolz study felt that the following characteristics were sex-inappropriate: extreme tallness, squatness, large hands or feet, thick ankles, underdeveloped or very large breasts, pigmented facial hair (especially when it formed a "moustache"), extreme thinness, fatness, heavy lower jaw, hairy arms and legs, and generally massive body build. Gracefulness and co-ordination were considered to be assets for girls, whereas strength and physical competence were not as highly prized in girls as they were in boys.

Facial features that many of the girls regarded as unfeminine included glasses, braces, large nose or mouth, receding chin, acne, moles, birthmarks, scars, oily skin, large pores, and freckles. However, for each individual who was upset about having such a characteristic, there were several other girls with the same characteristic who were not bothered at all.

A great deal of individual variation exists among adolescent girls as to which aspects of their figures they regard as being particularly invested with feminin-ity. Early in childhood girls become aware of their prettiness as compared with that of other girls and also of their particular physical features that are espe-cially attractive.

Development or lack of it in the breasts is particularly worrisome to many girls, because it is one of the first signs of maturity and because the breasts are objects of masculine interest. Our society tends to emphasize the breasts as being the repositories of sexuality. Menstruation is also of importance in the girl's definition of her femininity.

Obesity and overweight

Obesity is usually defined as the excessive accumulation of body fat. How much fat is excessive depends upon a variety of medical, social, and cultural factors. For our purposes obesity will be defined as the condition in which the triceps skinfold measurement is greater than the age and sex-appropriate mean for the population by one standard deviation or more. This means that

16% of a representative group of adolescents would be declared obese if these standards were used.

Obesity has several unique characteristics which distinguish it from other unusual physical variations during adolescence:

PREDATES AND POSTDATES ADOLESCENCE

Unlike some of the variations which have already been discussed, such as timing of maturation, obesity is often a lifelong affliction. Children who have gained somewhat more weight than appropriate for them during the school years are most likely to remain obese as adults. Obesity in adolescence is likely to become permanent if not treated. Obese children and adolescents are more likely to remain obese as adults and so constitute a major reservoir for obese people in adult life.

PATHOLOGICAL FROM MEDICAL STANDPOINT

Obesity holds a unique position among the variations which have already been discussed, because it is regarded by physicians as a health hazard which should be eliminated, rather than a normal variant of adolescent growth for which the only treatment necessary is reassurance and sympathy. Most physicians are concerned about the presence of obesity and overweight because of the well-known relationships between these conditions and chronic disease later in life. It is not yet clear whether the real health culprit is obesity or overweight, but since action can only be taken against the fat component of body weight, physicians commonly advise adolescents whose obesity has persisted beyond the prepubertal period to diet, or they at least regard the variation as one which deserves watching so that it can be nipped in the bud before it gets out of hand.

THE DANGER OF MISLABELING

Obesity is unique in that, unlike other developmental variations, there is a high probability of confusing the condition with overweight, instead of its being labeled correctly as overfatness. Overweight refers to body weight in excess of a standard, as opposed to obesity, which refers to fatness in excess of a standard. The relative contributions to overweight of bone, muscle, and fat vary from person to person, but the term "overweight" does not distinguish between them. Thus, the real cause of weight in excess of normal may not be clear to the individual. A football player can be overweight because of a heavy frame and well developed muscles, and still be far from obesity. Other persons may be overweight yet not obese.

The distinction between overweight and obesity is a crucial one, since it is possible to reduce excess weight due to extra fat by dieting and exercise, while it is not possible to reduce the bone and muscle components of weight.

Huenemann (11) showed that while adolescent girls attributed their overweight to overfatness, adolescent boys often attributed their overweight to build components other than fat (bone and muscle) and regarded this excess weight as desirable. These findings offer an explanation as to why most adolescent girls want to lose weight, while most adolescent boys want to gain weight.

One reason why overweight and obesity are so often thought to be synonymous is that there is an association of obesity with certain body types. Stuart (24) reported in his studies of children that there was a strong disposition to becoming obese which was associated with stoutness. The obese child often possessed such morphological characteristics as being tall for age, of broad and heavy skeletal build, and advanced in physical development. Seltzer and Mayer (19) found that the obese adolescent girls whom they studied differed from their nonobese age-mates, not only in fatness, but in other respects as well. They were characterized by a relative lack of ectomorphy and a predominance of endomorphy and mesomorphy. In other words, not only were the obese overfat, they were overweight in addition because of their frames and builds. The obese girls were the largest, stoutest, and fattest girls in the population.

Obese adolescent girls studied by Dwyer, Feldman, Seltzer, and Mayer (7) were asked to judge their standing in comparison to others in their class vis-à-vis weight, fatness, frame, and muscularity. They were also asked to compare real and ideal for body parts. The obese girls realized that they were larger as well as fatter than their peers. These girls wished to change not only the fatness components of weight, but also contributions from the muscle and bone components, so that they would be smaller in all of these respects. In contrast to this, boys wished to be larger in the bone and muscle components of weight.

Largeness with respect to build components other than fat was found by Dwyer, Feldman, and Mayer (6) to be a possible cause of dieting among certain adolescent girls. Girls who were actually below average in body fatness, but with large frames and builds, apparently mistakenly attributed their relative largeness and heaviness to fatness rather than to other components. They used this as a cue for dieting when it was really not called for. Such girls should devote themselves to more fruitful and rewarding enterprises than reducing diets which attempt to change characteristics of body build which cannot be changed by dieting. Since dietary modifications are used to treat a number of different conditions, such as skin problems, diabetes, etc., it is not surprising to find that some adolescent girls fancy that they can change their body builds through dieting.

Another labeling problem which is associated with body fat is that of making the distinction between amount and distribution of fat. The triceps skinfold measurement has been developed by Seltzer (20) as a quick and accurate measurement of body fatness. Adolescents who are far from being obese or even overweight may be displeased by the fat patterning on their bodies. When weight is lost, the size of all of the subcutaneous fat depots goes down. While dieting can reduce the total amount of fat on the body, it cannot change the pattern of fat distribution. Dieting may reduce the size of particularly disturbing fat depots on the body and, hence, enable dress size to be changed; but if the fat depots are unusually large to begin with, especially in certain areas such as thighs or hips, the reduction in size may not be enough to please the dieter.

SOCIOCULTURAL AND PSYCHOLOGICAL DIFFERENCES

Current cultural ideals for women, and to a lesser extent for men, link obesity with unattractiveness. It is unfortunate that adolescents in particular tend to favor ideals which are very much opposed to obesity. Many perfectly normal or even lean adolescents from a medical viewpoint consider themselves to be obese and wish to do something about it.

Dwyer, Feldman, Seltzer, and Mayer (7) showed silhouette pictures of different body types to several hundred senior high school students of an upper middle class suburb of Boston. The more ectomorphic silhouettes were overwhelmingly considered to be the ideal body type for the girls. For boys, the most mesomorphic body silhouette shown was regarded as ideal by the great majority of both girls and boys.

Sociocultural as well as medical attitudes are much more negative and crystallized toward obesity than they are toward other unusual variations in appearance. Others' expectations and behavior toward the obese adolescent may be strongly influenced by these attitudes. Folk knowledge holds that obesity is immoral, caused by gluttony and sloth. Supposedly the obese person is obese because of lack of determination, ambition, and willpower. Bullen et al. (3) distributed questionnaires to similar groups of obese and nonobese girls. The answers of the obese adolescents reflected these popular ideas about obesity. They said they ate more than the average-weight girls and they considered this to be the cause of their obesity. In actual fact these girls were characterized, not by an abnormally high food intake, but rather by an extremely low level of physical activity.

Obese adolescent girls seem to accept more blame and feel more guilty about their condition than do adolescents with other unusual variations in appearance such as extreme tallness. This is probably partially due to the fact that so often they fail to persist in their dieting efforts and blame themselves for it.

Obese adolescents are affected by negative social and cultural attitudes toward their condition. Monello and Mayer (15) studied obese and normal-weight girls. They found that obese adolescent girls showed personality characteristics strikingly similar to the traits of ethnic and racial minority groups, due to their status as victims of prejudice. They showed obsessive concern, heightened sensitivity toward obesity, and preoccupation with their obese status, in projective test responses to words such as diet, reducing, overweight, calories, and fat. They gave more passive responses in picture description tests. These responses illustrated the obese girls' isolation and feelings of rejection by their peers. Obese girls also showed acceptance of dominant values toward obesity in a sentence-completion test.

One case of possible discrimination against the obese adolescent has been described by Canning and Mayer (4). They showed that, although application rates to high-ranking colleges and academic qualifications did not vary between obese and nonobese seniors in an excellent suburban school system, the obese students, and particularly the obese girls, were not accepted in as great a number as nonobese seniors.

The bad effects of early exposure to negative sociocultural attitudes toward obesity is evident from the study of Stunkard and Mendelson (26). They found that obesity with onset in childhood or adolescence left more sensitivity and ill effects about it than did obesity of adult onset. Subjects who had been obese since childhood or adolescence had a more exaggerated preoccupation with weight. They judged people in terms of weight, felt contempt for fat persons, and admired slender persons. They considered their obesity a handicap and believed it to be responsible for all the disappointments they suffered. Subjects who had become obese in adulthood did not display such negative attitude.

In another study of obesity and body image, Stunkard and Mendelson (27) found that of the many behavioral disturbances to which the obese are subject, only two were unique to obesity: overeating and a disturbance of body image characterized by the feeling that the body was grotesque and loathsome and that others viewed it with hostility and contempt. This syndrome was found among emotionally disturbed persons whose obesity began prior to adult life, and it was found to persist even after weight reduction.

Stunkard and Burt (25) recently studied the age at onset of disturbances in body image reported by some obese persons. These workers hypothesized that being obese in adolescence was a necessary cause for body image disorder. If this hypothesis was correct, persons obese in childhood and adult life, but not during adolescence, would show a lower frequency of body image disturbance than persons obese in both childhood and adolescence, persons obese in adolescence but not in childhood, and persons obese only during adulthood. Unfortunately, not enough subjects could be found who were obese as children and adults, but of normal weight during adolescence. Again, they found that body image disturbances were more intense in those whose obesity was of early onset.

SEX DIFFERENCES—GIRLS

Disturbance over body fatness and overweight is much more widespread during adolescence for girls than it is for boys. Deisher and Mills' (5) study of high school students found that 28% of the boys and 48% of the girls they interviewed felt they had a weight problem. Another study, published recently in this journal by Adams (1), showed that while health was not an area of major concern for either sex, girls were twice as concerned as boys (2% of the boys and 4% of the girls regarding it as their own problem). The sex differences were chiefly accounted for by the female's fixation on problems of weight, particularly between the ages of 11 and 14. This study drew a sample from a larger sample of different ages, while Deisher and Mills' sample had very heavy representation from the 15- to 17-year-old age group. This probably partially accounts for the differences in frequency of disturbance for weight, since dieting and weight problems are extremely prevalent during the last few years in high school.

Hinton, Eppright, Chadderdon, and Wolins (10) studied eating behavior and dietary intakes of 140 12- to 14-year-old girls. They found that while 52% of the overweight girls were concerned about weight, 17% of the average-weight girls and 10% of the underweight girls were similarly concerned.

We (6) recently concluded a study on the physical characteristics and attitudes toward weight among 446 girls in the senior class of a high school in an upper middle class suburb of Boston. Both questioning of teachers and comparing measurements obtained for the rest of the class indicated that the sample of girls was representative of the total female population in the class. A precoded questionnaire was used to assess girls' attitudes. Using triceps skinfold measurements, the group was separated into four categories: obese, above-average fatness, below-average fatness, and lean. Among the obese, 97% had been on diets by this time of their lives and there was a 22-pound difference between means for reported and desired weights. In the above-average fatness category, 87% had dieted and there was a 10-pound difference between reported and desired weights. In the below-average fatness category, 53% had been on diets and there was a 4-pound difference between reported and desired weights. In the lean category, 27% of the girls had dieted to lose weight. Desired weights were 1 pound higher than reported weight means for the category.

Obesity in adolescent girls provides perhaps the best example of differences between medically defined and socially defined standards for normality. We discovered that while only 16% of the girls who were studied were found to be obese and presumably should be dieting, about 60% of the adolescent girls had been on reducing diets by the time they were seniors in high school. About 30% of them were on diets at the time they were questioned. Many girls who did not need to reduce for health reasons wished to reduce for purposes of appearance and were trying to do so. In contrast to these findings in adolescent girls, among the adolescent boys who were studied 19% were found to be obese, but only 24% of the boys interviewed had ever been on diets and only 6% were on diets at the time of the survey. From these findings we concluded that adolescent boys' weight standards seem to be more in line with medical standards while those of girls are not.

We also found that methods of attempting to lose weight vary by sex. Girls who have real or imaginary weight problems go on diets to lose weight, while boys prefer increased exercise and activity as a means of losing excess poundage.

In another study (7), we found that reporting of weight was more accurate among boys than girls. The girls, with the exception of the leanest subjects, tended to under-report their weights, while boys did not. Perhaps this is indicative of how highly charged the whole subject of weight is among adolescent girls.

SEX DIFFERENCES—BOYS

In sharp contrast to adolescent girls, who continually worry about being fat, adolescent boys rarely worry about obesity unless it is very marked. Overweight, whether it is due to massiveness of frame, muscularity, or fat, may be a definite advantage in some sports such as football or wrestling in which sheer crushing power is important. Male fashions do not encourage weight control, since they are shapeless enough to hide fairly large amounts of excess weight. Unless the obesity is very marked, those disturbances which do exist over body weight and fatness in adolescence generally occur in early puberty and concern body fat laid down in what the boys consider to be a sex-inappropriate manner. The girdle-like type of fat distribution around the hips, buttocks, thighs, and occasionally the chest may embarrass a boy who has this growth pattern, but for most boys this type of fat distribution is only a transient stage and most of them grow out of it.

Several other differences between adolescent boys' and adolescent girls' attitudes toward obesity have already been mentioned in this paper. It seems that boys are not concerned enough about obesity, while girls are perhaps overconcerned.

Concluding remarks

Adolescent attitudes toward weight and obesity probably do not change drastically in later life. It seems that men continue to exhibit the lack of concern about weight which they did as adolescents, unless they become very obese or are told to reduce for medical reasons. Adult women continue to worry about their weights and periodically go on diets to stave off weight gain. This carry-over of adolescent attitudes may account for the tendency, more marked in men than in women, to increase in weight with age during the early twenties, which was first observed by Hathaway and Foard (9). Data from the National Health Survey (18) show that women appear to achieve maximum weights about two decades later than do men. Maximum average weights for men occur between ages 35 and 54, while maximum average weights for women come between the ages of 53 to 64. The lower weights for women probably arise partially from their dieting efforts, as well as from differences in activity between men and women.

The findings discussed in this paper suggest that there is a great deal of misinformation about obesity and other developmental variations among adolescents. A practical approach to remedy this might be to include in the life sciences curriculum of junior high schools an explanation by a physician of the broad range of normal individual variation in adolescent growth and appearance.

REFERENCES

1. Adams, J. F. "Adolescents' Identification of Personal and National Problems," *Adolescence*, 1966, 1, pp. 240–250.
2. Angelino, H. and Mech, E. V. "Fears and Worries Concerning Physical Changes: A Preliminary Survey of 32 Females," *J. Psychol.*, 1955, 39, pp. 195–198.
3. Bullen, B. A., Monello, L. F., Cohen, H., and Mayer, J. "Attitudes toward Physical Activity, Food, and Family in Obese and Nonobese Adolescent Girls," *Am. J. Clin. Nutr.*, 1963, 12, pp. 1–11.
4. Canning, H. and Mayer, J. "Obesity: Its Possible Effect on College Acceptance," *New Engl. J. Med.*, 1966, 275, pp. 1172–1174.
5. Deisher, R. W. and Mills, C. A. "The Adolescent Looks at his Health and Medical Care," *Am. J. Public Health*, 1963, 53, pp. 1928–1936.
6. Dwyer, J. T., Feldman, J. J., and Mayer, J. "Adolescent Dieters: Who are They? Physical Characteristics, Attitudes, and Dieting Practices of Adolescent Girls," *Am. J. Clin. Nutr.* 1967, 20, pp. 1045–1056.
7. Dwyer, J. T., Seltzer, C. C., Feldman, J. J., and Mayer, J. "Body Image in Adolescents: Attitudes Toward Weight and Perception of Appearance in Adolescents," in press.
8. Harms, E. "Puberty—Physical and Mental," 1966, 1, pp. 293–296.
9. Hathaway, M. L. and Foard, E. D. *Heights and Weights of Adults in the United States. Home Economics Research Report No. 10.* Washington, D.C.: Agricultural Research Service, U.S. Department of Agriculture, 1960.
10. Hinton, M. A., Eppright, E. S., Chadderdon, H., and Wolins, L. "Eating Behavior and Dietary Intake of Girls 12–14 Years Old," *J. Am. Dietet. Assoc.*, 1963, 43, pp. 223–227.
11. Huenemann, R. L., Shaping, L. R., Hampton, M. C. and Mitchell, B. W. "A Longitudinal Study of Gross Body Composition and Body Conformation and Association with Food and Activity in a Teen-age Population: Views of Teen-age Subjects on Body Conformation, Food, and Activity," *Am. J. Clin. Nutr.*, 1966, 18, pp. 323–338.
12. Jones, M. C. "The Later Careers of Boys who were Early or Late Maturing," *Child Development*, 1957, 28, pp. 113–128.
13. Jones, M. C., and Bayley, N. "Physical Maturing among Boys as Related to Behavior," *J. Educ. Psychol.*, 1950, 41, pp. 129–147.
14. Latham, A. J. "The Relationship Between Pubertal Status and Leadership in Junior High School Boys," *J. Genetic Psych.*, 1951, 78, pp. 185–194.
15. Monello, L. F., and Mayer, J. "Obese Adolescent Girls: An Unrecognized Minority Group?", *Am. J. Clin. Nutr.*, 1963, 13, pp. 35–39.
16. More, D. M. "Developmental Concordance and Discordance during Puberty and Early Adolescence," *Child Development Monographs*, 1953, vol. 18, no. 56.

17. Mussen, P. H. and Jones, M. C. "Self Conceptions, Motivations, and Interpersonal Attitudes of Late and Early Maturing Boys," *Child Development,* 1957, 28, pp. 243–256.
18. National Center for Health Statistics. *Weight by Height and Age of Adults. United States 1960–62.* Washington, D.C.: U.S. Government Printing Office, 1966. Vital and Health Statistics, Public Health Service Pub. No. 1000, Series 11, No. 14.
19. Seltzer, C. C., and Mayer, J. "Body Build and Obesity: Who are the Obese?", *J. Am. Med. Assoc.,* 1964, 189, pp. 677–684.
20. Seltzer, C. C., and Mayer, J. "A Simple Criterion of Obesity," *Postgrad. Med.,* 1965, 38 (2), pp. A-101–A-107.
21. Stolz, H. R., and Stolz, L. M. "Adolescent Related to Somatic Variation," in: Henry, N. B. (Editor), *Adolescence: 43rd Yearbook of the National Committee for the study of Education.* Chicago: University of Chicago Press, 1944, pp. 80–99.
22. Stone, G. P. and Barker, R. "Attitudes and Interests of Pre- and Post-Menstrual Females of the Same Chronologic Age," *J. Comp. Physiol. Psych.,* 1937, 23, pp. 439–455.
23. Stone, G. P., and Barker, R. "Attitudes and Interests of Pre- and Post-Menstrual Females," *J. Genetic Psychol.,* 1939, 54, pp. 27–71.
24. Stuart, H. C. "Obesity in Childhood," *Quart. Rev. Pediatrics,* 1955, 10, No. 3, pp. 131–145.
25. Stunkard, A. J. and Burt, V. "Obesity and the Body Image. II: Age at Onset of Disturbances in the Body Image," *Am. J. Psychiat.,* 1967, 123, pp. 1443–1447.
26. Stunkard, A. J. and Mendelson, M. "Disturbances in Body Image of Some Obese Persons," *J. Am. Dietet. Assoc.,* 1961, 38, pp. 328–331.
27. Stunkard, A. J. and Mendelson, M. "Obesity and the Body Image I. Characteristics of Disturbances in the Body Image of Some Obese Persons," *Am. J. Psychiat.,* 1967, 123 (10), pp. 1296–1300.

[7]   *Franklyn N. Arnhoff & Ernest N. Damianopoulos*

SELF-BODY RECOGNITION: AN EMPIRICAL

APPROACH TO THE BODY IMAGE

The concept of *body image* is almost as old as psychology itself. It was used to organize and explain various clinical observations and empirical phenomena relating to both normal and disturbed body functioning. The concept has never

FROM *Merrill-Palmer Quarterly,* 1962, 8, 143–148. REPRINTED BY PERMISSION OF THE AUTHORS AND THE PUBLISHER.

been precisely defined with clear operational referents, and a number of other terms are subsumed under its aegis and often used interchangeably. Head (8) referred to *body schema,* and Schilder (12) used both body image and body schema interchangeably. Recent years have seen the introduction of further terminology such as *body percept* and *body concept* (9, 14) in an attempt to separate the difference types of events and empirical phenomena usually encompassed by the term body image, and to attempt to make them logically, and psychologically related. The empirical data subsumed under the body image term include quite diverse phenomena such as, depersonalization (6), phantom limb (7), psychosomatic illness (4), as well as a wide variety of anomalies of sensation and distorted body perceptions (2, 11, 12).

From a theoretical standpoint, the role of the body in personality development and function has long been noted and has been stated as being the basic structure from which the "ego" or "self" develops. Hence, Freud (5), Federn (3) and Szasz (15) have noted that the ego or self is first and foremost a body ego. From the increments in knowledge derived from body experience and exploration, self-body boundaries are formed and the personality begins to develop. From this point of view, the body image has been seen as a primary issue in developmental psychopathology, particularly the schizophrenias, with frequent mention of the faulty body perceptions of the schizophrenic (3, 9, 12, 15). While most writers view these perceptual distortions as indications of faulty ego-body integration, Szasz (15) has further indicated that the body itself, is still another perceptual object for the ego to perceive and deal with as it does any other object.

The theoretical and conceptual analysis of the body image concept by Smythies (14) distinguished a number of different components to the gross term, and restricted the meaning of body image *per se* to the primarily visual memory image one has of one's own body. Following this restricted meaning of the term, we have attempted to give it an experimentally amenable, empirical referent, utilizing a self-body recognition task. In the present study, base-rate data on the performance of young, *normal* subjects (Ss) in such a recognition situation was obtained as a preliminary step towards investigating schizophrenic performance in dealing with their own bodies.

If the question is asked, can a person recognize his own body, devoid of clothing, facial, or situational clues to identity, the tendency is towards an affirmative answer. However, basing the expectations of success or failure of such a task on the most pertinent and comparable experimental literature, the prediction of success becomes equivocal. When Wolff (16) presented his Ss with surreptitiously taken photographs of their own hands, self-recognition was far from unanimous, despite the fact that from the standpoint of familiarity (experience), the hands are almost constantly in the visual and perceptual field and thus are almost constantly seen. Other experimental findings dealing with other body parts, point to similar conclusions in that many Ss failed to recognize themselves (Lindzey, *et al.,* 10; Bellof and Bellof, 1). To the writers' knowledge, no studies exist which deal with recognition of one's own nude body. The present study posed the task for S to recognize his own body, devoid of clothing, facial or situational identifications, from a series of other body photographs ranging in similarity from *most* similar to *least* similar, and to then state his degree of certainty as to his final choice.

Method

SUBJECTS AND DESIGN

A total of 90 male college students served as paid Ss to establish the initial photographic pool from which, eventually, the experimental Ss were chosen. Ss who had scars, moles, tattoos, blemishes or other identifying characteristics on the ventral body surfaces were not considered. Each S was photographed individually against a black background, clad only in a pair of white jockey shorts, posed in a standard position, viz. legs slightly spread, head facing front, with arms slightly spread away from the body. The photographs were taken with a Rolleiflex camera, Plus-X Pan film, at a standard distance of ten feet. Four photoflood lamps provided almost shadowless lighting. The negatives were enlarged to 4 × 10 inches. The image of each S was enlarged to the same size so that there would be no comparative height cues when viewing the series of photographs in the later experimental sessions.

The complete head on each photograph was blacked out with India ink, eliminating not only the facial features, but also the shape of the head and the outline of the hair. The area of the body covered by the shorts was chemically bleached out to give a detailess area since it had been observed that under the strong lights the shorts were translucent and the outline of the penis was often discernible, giving a clue as to circumcision.

The design of the study required that seven degrees of similarity be presented to each S, ranging from highest similarity (in terms of visual appearance), to least similarity. The seven degrees of similarity included a photo of S, and six other photos, one matched for maximum similarity to S, and five other photos in decreasing degrees of similarity to S. Consequently, those Ss finally chosen from the total photographic pool to serve as experimental Ss in the recognition task, were those for whom an identical (maximum similarity) match was available.

On the basis of height, weight and age data obtained at the time of photographing, a somatotype was computed for each S following the Sheldon (13) method. The resulting somatotypes served as rough indices for grouping the bodies for the matching for similarity. Since our interest, and the experimental task, dealt with the visual appearance of the body, additional factors such as skin color, hair color, and hair distribution had to be taken into consideration as factors making for similarity-dissimilarity. Therefore, following the somatotyping, all photographs were spread out on the floor in columns and rows, according to somatotype to make them available for simultaneous visual inspection and comparison.

The first step in the selection procedure was to obtain those photos from the total group for which a near-identical match was available, in terms of identical somatotype, as well as similarity on the additional criteria of hair distribution, etc. Although most of the chosen pairs were of identical somatotype, a few differed by one somatotype component. From the total group of 90 Ss, 21 Ss were chosen for the experimental groups on the basis of having a near-identity match. An additional five photos, representing the five degrees of decreasing similarity were then selected for each S, following the rule of choosing photos one somatotype component removed in both endomorphy and mesomorphy (ectomorphy was not well represented in the total group), for each additional degree of decreasing similarity. For each of the somatotype components, the extremes were not well represented so that the choices for most dissimilar were made on the basis of what was available. Both experimenters worked together on this task, making judgments jointly rather than independently. After choosing each pair for near-identity, and then the five other photos for decreasing similarity, the selected photos were placed back in their original positions and the process repeated for each of the 21 Ss selected as experimental Ss.

For the 21 Ss thus chosen, the mean age was 21.67 years, SD 3.58 years, and all with at least two years of college. At the time of the initial photographing, all Ss were informed that they might be called back at a later date to serve in further work, with additional remuneration.

PROCEDURE

For the recognition task, each individual S was presented with a series of seven photographs (including one of his own body). The photos were presented in random order on a picture stand, painted flat black, and placed about 24 inches in front of S on a table near eye level for his visual inspection. E read the following instructions to each S:

As you recall, a short time ago we took your picture. I am now going to show you seven pictures to look at carefully. Please tell me if you believe that your picture is among them. As you look at the pictures, please tell me which ones you are considering as possibly being you. Refer to the pictures by the letter on the board above each picture. As you make your decision, I want you to tell me what you are thinking about. Sort of think out loud. If and when you finally decide that one of the pictures is your own, tell me which one it is and why.

After the instructions were read, the pictures were exposed by turning the picture stand upright and E started his stop watch to time the performance. Following completion of the recognition task, S was asked to give his degree of certainty as to the correctness of his choice and was briefly interviewed regarding attitudes towards his body, attitudes towards nudity and frequency of exploration of body parts.

Results and discussion

On the basis of the comparable literature discussed previously, it was assumed that at least some of the Ss would fail to recognize themselves and that clues as to the differences in performance might be found from the interview material. However, the entire group of 21 Ss was able to correctly identify their own pictures from the series presented to each of them. Each S, however, was not certain as to the correctness of his choice to the same degree. When asked to express their degree of certainty as to the correctness of their choice, 52.4 per cent were positive, 33.3 per cent were fairly sure, and 14.3 per cent were uncertain. Despite the fact that their identification was correct, two Ss denied that their pictures were among those presented to them, stating that their choice was of photographs that they felt were most similar to themselves. Although we attempted to minimize cues from posture and position, it is quite possible that these cues did come through in at least some cases to some extent and served as orientation cues with or without Ss' awareness.

While the results are quite clear cut as far as overt recognition is concerned, the question has barely been approached rather than answered. On the one hand, the degree of uncertainty as to their own bodies by a number of our Ss and the denial that their bodies were represented in the photos by two Ss needs further investigation and exploration. Since there was no attempt to investigate personality integration or adjustment, such factors may well relate to the differential performance. Furthermore, our experiences prior to the experiment proper, during the preliminary structuring of the task also indicate the need for further investigation. While collecting photos, determining poses, lighting, etc., we utilized some of our colleagues as Ss. After a number of photos had been collected, our curiosity got the better of us, and roughly matching six photos on the similarity-dissimilarity continuum to the photos of a few of our colleagues, we presented the series to each of them for recognition. Not all of them were able to recognize themselves, and some only with extreme difficulty. After the results of the study proper were available, we began to question the discrepancy between these preliminary findings and the performance of the experimental Ss. One fact in particular, in fact the only single clue we were able to come up with was the matter of the difference in age between these preliminary Ss and those in the experimental group; where the experimental Ss were all in their early 20's, the preliminary Ss were in their early forties. While this is only the barest sort of rough data, it seems consistent with the observation of clinicians that at or about middle age, there seems to be a lag in keeping the body image up to date and the person tends to report his physical body in terms appropriate to an earlier period in his life.

For our younger Ss, however, the overt recognition was quite accurate, and unexpected, in view of the findings of Wolff (16), Bellof and Bellof (1), and Lindzey, et al. (10) who dealt with body parts and views which are more frequently seen and less threatening and subject to taboos than the body *per se*. While the study does establish base-rate performance for *normals* as a preliminary to comparison with schizophrenics it has raised many questions for further research and understanding.

Summary

For the purposes of the study, the term "body image" was defined as the largely visual memory-image one has of his own body. A body recognition task was devised to ascertain the ability of a group of young, *normal* college students to recognize their own bodies, devoid of clothing, facial and situational cues, from among a series of seven photographs matched to each photograph and ranging from maximal to minimal similarity. On the basis of the literature dealing with recognition of one's own hands or face, it was expected that some Ss would not be able to recognize their own bodies. On the contrary, however, recognition was 100 per cent correct for the group of 21 Ss. The theoretical implications, as well as limitations, and future projections of this approach to the body image problem were discussed.

REFERENCES

1. Bellof, H. & Bellof, J. Unconscious self-evaluation using a stereoscope. *J. abnorm. soc. Psychol.*, 1959, **59**, 275–278.
2. Brain, W. R. *Mind, perception and science.* Oxford: Blackwell, 1951.
3. Federn, P. *Ego psychology and the psychoses.* New York: Basic Books, 1952.
4. Fisher, S. & Cleveland, S. E. *Body image and personality.* New York: Van Nostrand, 1958.
5. Freud, S. *Collected papers.* London: Hogarth Press, 1949.
6. Galdston, I. On the etiology of depersonalization. *J. nerv. ment. Dis.*, 1947, **105**, 25–39.
7. Haber, W. B. Reactions to loss of limb: Physiological and psychological aspects. *Ann. N.Y. Acad. Sci.*, 1958, **75**, Article 1, 14–24.
8. Head, H. *Studies in neurology.* London: Oxford Univ. Press, 1920, 605–608.
9. Kolb, L. C. The body image in the schizophrenic reaction. In Auerback, A. (Ed.) *Schizophrenia: An integrated approach.* New York: Ronald Press, 1959, 87–97.
10. Lindzey, G., Prince Blanche, and Wright, H. K. A study of facial asymmetry. *J. Person.*, 1952, **21**, 68–84.
11. Riddoch, G. Phantom limbs and body shape. *Brain*, 1941, **64**, 197–222.
12. Schilder, P. *The image and appearance of the human body.* New York: Int. Univ. Press, 1950 (original, 1935).
13. Sheldon, W. *Atlas of Men.* New York: Harper and Bros., 1954.
14. Smythies, J. R. The experience and description of the human body. *Brain*, 1953, **76**, 132–145.

15. Szasz, T. S. *Pain and pleasure.* New York: Basic Books, 1957.
16. Wolff, W. *The expression of personality.* New York: Harper and Bros., 1943.

[8]   *Alexander Frazier & Lorenzo K. Lisonbee*   ADOLESCENT

CONCERNS WITH PHYSIQUE

A major task of adolescence is to adjust to the dramatic physical changes which mark the development of the child into the adult.[1] In addition, the adolescent has, somewhere along the line, the problem of accepting his emerging shape and size as the physique with which he will have to proceed through life. Knowledge of the nature of adolescent physical changes is considerable; however, knowledge about the feelings of the adolescent seems less well documented. In searching for such evidence, the present writers were struck by the frequency with which the small, but intensively analyzed, sample represented in a California study is cited.[2] In order to prepare materials for helping adolescents toward adjustment, it was felt desirable to collect local evidence that might be somewhat broader in its possible implications.

The Present Study

A QUESTIONNAIRE

The present report covers the responses of all tenth-graders at North Phoenix High School for the year 1949–50. These 580 students, 309 girls and 271 boys, were enrolled in the required biology course. A questionnaire was drawn up to discover how these children saw themselves physically and how they felt about their conceptions of themselves. The major sections of the questionnaire dealt with weight, height and proportions, rate of development, facial appearance, and desire for self-improvement. All students answered anonymously.

For the first three sections, self-description was based on five choices. For example, in the section on height these choices were (1) short, (2) rather short, (3) about average, (4) rather tall, and (5) tall. In Section 4, facial appearance, the student was simply to check those of 59 items that he felt

FROM *School Review,* 1950, *58,* 397–405. REPRINTED BY PERMISSION OF THE SENIOR AUTHOR AND THE UNIVERSITY OF CHICAGO PRESS. COPYRIGHT 1950 BY THE UNIVERSITY OF CHICAGO.

applied to him; items were grouped under "nose," "mouth," "skin," etc. Section 5, dealing with self-improvement, was designed to elicit a free written response. After each item of self-description in Sections 1 through 4, there followed a five-point scale for expression of worry or concern: (1) "Never think about it," (2) "Think about it now and then," (3) "Worry about it a little," (4) "Worry a good deal," and (5) "Worry a lot." To simplify reporting, the responses on this scale from 3 through 5 are combined and considered to represent what we will call *concern*.

LIMITATIONS OF THE STUDY

In reporting the findings of this survey, the writers acknowledge that whatever generalizations may be drawn must be regarded as highly tentative. The sample is not large. It represents only tenth-graders. The school population is largely middle-class. The attempt to measure concern is undoubtedly ambitious. Yet the need for studies of this kind is so great that the writers wish to offer their results to other persons who are working to collect evidence on the same problem.

SECTION I: WEIGHT

How do these tenth-grade boys and girls see themselves in terms of weight? If they think of themselves as heavy or thin, how do they feel about it? Students were asked to rate themselves both for their entire body and for various sections on a five-point scale: (1) too thin, (2) rather thin, (3) about right, (4) rather heavy, and (5) too heavy. They were also to indicate their degree of concern on the scale described above.

As shown in Table 1, almost a third of the girls see themselves as heavy (combining "rather heavy" and "too heavy"), with more than half of them expressing some degree of concern. Only 13 per cent of the boys describe themselves in this manner, and little concern is expressed by them. Two-thirds of the boys describe themselves as "about right" compared to 54 per cent of the girls. Boys are more inclined than girls to rate themselves thin, although the girls express more concern over thinness. However, boys show more than seven times as much concern about being thin as about being heavy. Throughout this study, boys are found less expressive of concern than girls.

Boys and girls were also asked to describe themselves in terms of weight of body sections (face, neck, shoulders, chest, abdominal section, hips, upper arm, forearm, upper leg, lower leg, and ankles). When the two positions for heaviness and thinness at either end of the scale were combined, items checked as heavy or thin by as many as 25 per cent of the boys or girls served to reinforce the picture given above. Nearly half the girls (46 per cent) think they have heavy hips. Heavy abdominal sections (43 per cent) and upper legs (38 per cent) rank next. The forearm is the only section marked thin by any sizable number of girls (28 per cent). Supposed heaviness of these parts of the body greatly concerns the girls, just as it does in reference to the entire body. Of the girls who consider their hips heavy, 64 per cent express concern. Heavy upper legs bother half the girls so describing themselves; heavy mid-regions, a third.

Thinness of body sections is self-assigned by a considerable per cent of the boys, bearing out the inclination noted in the description of the entire body. One-third of the boys consider their upper arms thin; 30 per cent mark themselves as having thin forearms; 27 per cent, thin chests. One section, the mid-region, is marked heavy by a sizable number (28 per cent). Here again, concern is less pronounced for boys than for girls. Heaviness of abdominal sections concerns one-third of the boys so describing themselves; thinness of upper arm, 27 per cent; thinness of chest, 21 per cent; and thinness of forearm, 20 per cent.

The tenth-grade girls in this study tend to think of themselves as heavy, particularly in certain sections of the body. Girls express a high degree of concern about their weight. Boys tend to think they are "about right," with some inclination toward thinness, particularly in upper arms, forearms, and chests. Boys are less expressive of concern about weight than are girls.

SECTION 2: HEIGHT AND PROPORTIONS

How do these students see themselves in terms of height and proportions, and how do they feel about their self-conceptions? The questionnaire asked the tenth-graders to describe themselves in terms of a five-point scale for height, width of hips and shoulders, and length of arms, legs, trunk, and feet. The "worry" scale was the same for this section as for the others.

Most of the boys and girls saw themselves as "about average" in height. However, as shown in Table 1, girls were a little more inclined to think of themselves as short, boys as tall. As far as concern was expressed, it centered rather dramatically in tallness for girls (49 per cent of the girls who thought of themselves as tall expressed concern) and in shortness for boys (39 per cent concern). Tall boys felt little concern, not much more than did heavy boys.

The items which attempted to get at possible concerns over proportions revealed little, except that a rather large number of girls (37 per cent) consider themselves to have wide hips and express a high degree of concern (60 per cent) about it. Such a self-conception and concern with width of hips is undoubtedly related to their consciousness of heaviness in that region, as revealed under weight. Large feet are accepted as their lot by 28 per cent of the girls, with an expressed concern of 37 per cent. Although 35 per cent of the boys think their feet are large, only 10 per cent of these express concern.

Half the tall girls among these tenth-graders are concerned about their height. Nearly 40 per cent of the short boys express concern. These findings are the most significant in this section of the questionnaire.

TABLE 1 Per Cents of 580 Tenth-Grade Boys and Girls Giving Certain Descriptions of Their Physiques and Per Cents Expressing Concern about the Characteristics Described*

DESCRIPTION	PER CENT SO DESCRIBING THEMSELVES		PER CENT EXPRESSING CONCERN	
	Boys	Girls	Boys	Girls
Thin	21	16	22	48
Heavy	13	30	3	55
Short	26	27	39	22
Tall	28	22	4	49
Development early	19	24	6	15
Development slow	17	13	40	36

* The table is read as follows: 21 per cent of the boys and 16 per cent of the girls described themselves as thin; 22 per cent of the boys and 48 per cent of the girls so describing themselves expressed concern about this characteristic.

SECTION 3: RATE OF DEVELOPMENT

How many of these boys and girls think of themselves as slow or fast in development? How concerned are they? Both sexes were asked to describe themselves in terms of total growth. Boys were also asked to rate themselves as to growth of beard, muscular development, and voice change.

Most of these tenth-graders consider themselves average, as will be seen from the percentages for early and slow development given in Table 1. A larger percentage of girls than of boys think their rate early; more boys than girls see themselves as slow-developing. Concern over early development is not too large with either boys or girls, although more than twice as much for girls.

The most significant fact emerging from this section of the study is that 40 per cent of the boys who consider themselves slow-maturing express concern. This is the highest amount of concern expressed by boys, except that over blackheads and pimples. While the slow-developing girls express 36 per cent concern, the fact that boys of this group are even more expressive is highly indicative of the insecurity that faces slow-developing boys, even at the tenth-grade level. In actual per cents of total boys and girls, those who express concern over what they consider their slow rate of development is only 6 per cent. The number is not large, but the concern is great, particularly for boys.

SECTION 4: FACIAL APPEARANCE

How do these boys and girls describe themselves in terms of facial appearance, and how much concerned are they? For each of the 59 items that might be checked, students were asked to mark also the usual five-point scale of concern.

As shown in Table 2, only 17 of the items were marked by as many as 10 per cent of the girls; 18 items by 10 per cent of the boys. In addition to the nine items common to both sexes (blackheads or pimples; heavy eyebrows; freckles; oily skin; scars, birthmarks, moles; glasses; irregular teeth; too long nose; and receding chin), the girls included high forehead, too round face, too homely, dry skin, thin lips, low forehead, too big nose, and odd-shaped nose. The boys listed lack of beard, heavy lips, protruding chin, ears stick out, heavy beard, dark skin, gaps in teeth, too thin face, and too large ears.

That 57 per cent of both sexes testify to having blackheads and pimples and that both boys and girls are more concerned about the problem than about any other item in the entire questionnaire is the outstanding fact revealed by this section. Both boys and girls express considerable concern also about oily skin, irregular teeth, and glasses. Concern is heavy for girls who think they have a nose that is too big, skin that is too dry, or that they are just too homely.

A few other facts are of interest. We note that nearly twice as many girls as boys wear glasses. Boys express no concern about freckles; girls, 24 per cent. Lack of beard, which a third of the boys acknowledge, causes little "worry," reinforcing what we had found on this item under rate of development.

Apparently, complexion problems form the chief physical worry of these tenth-grade boys and girls. Nothing else, in either this or other sections, looms as large in affecting so many and in "worrying" a majority of both boys and girls who are affected.

SECTION 5: DESIRE FOR SELF-IMPROVEMENT

The fifth part of the questionnaire was designed to find out what tenth-grade boys and girls thought of the desirability of changing themselves. This question was asked: "Would you change your physical self in some way if you could?" As shown in Table 3, two-thirds of this group said they would.

What kinds of changes are desired? In a second question, students were asked, if they desired change, to specify in what ways. As shown in Table 4, the responses have been broken down and classified for both boys and girls by areas, number of items for each area, percentages, and rank order. However, before examining the total picture, it may be of interest to look at the desires of each sex separately.

TABLE 2 Items of Self-Description Checked by 10 Per Cent or More of 580 Tenth-Grade Boys and Girls, with Amount of Expressed Concern

| | BOYS | | | GIRLS | |
Item of Description	Per Cent Checking	Per Cent of Concern	Item of Description	Per Cent Checking	Per Cent of Concern
Blackheads or pimples	57	51	Blackheads or pimples	57	82
Lack of beard	34	2	Heavy eyebrows	24	11
Heavy eyebrows	27	1	Freckles	23	24
Scars, birthmarks, moles	20	13	Oily skin	22	52
Irregular teeth	17	39	Scars, birthmarks, moles	22	30
Heavy lips	14	5	Glasses	21	31
Protruding chin	13	6	High forehead	19	8
Ears stick out	13	6	Too round face	19	21
Oily skin	12	27	Too homely	18	42
Freckles	12	—	Dry skin	16	43
Heavy beard	11	13	Irregular teeth	16	42
Glasses	11	23	Thin lips	15	13
Dark skin	10	4	Low forehead	13	3
Receding chin	10	4	Too long nose	11	23
Gaps in teeth	10	26	Too big nose	11	44
Too long nose	10	8	Receding chin	10	13
Too thin face	10	15	Odd-shaped nose	10	23
Too large ears	10	8			

THE CHANGES GIRLS WANT

Girls are highly specific about the ways in which they would like to change themselves, as the following samples indicate:

My hips and legs are too large and fat. If I could have smaller hips and legs, I'd have a much better figure. I'd also like to be a *little* more developed above the waist than I am, but I am not flat. I wish I didn't have so many pimples or had to wear glasses.

(1) I would make myself thinner. (2) I would make my ears lie back. (3) I would make my forehead lower. (4) I would take away my pimples and make my complexion clear and soft. (5) I would make my eyes just a little bigger. (6) I would make my feet smaller.

TABLE 3 Number and Per Cents of 580 Tenth-Grade Boys and Girls Desiring Some Change in Physical Selves

	YES		NO		NO ANSWER		TOTAL	
SEX	No.	Per Cent	No.	Per Cent	No.	Per Cent	No.	Per Cent
Boys	164	61	92	34	15	5	271	100
Girls	222	72	60	19	27	9	309	100
Both	386	67	152	26	42	7	580	100

TABLE 4 Areas in Which 222 Girls and 164 Boys in Grade X Specify Desire for Self-Improvement

CATEGORY	GIRLS			BOYS		
	Number of Items	Per Cent of Items	Rank Order	Number of Items	Per Cent of Items	Rank Order
Proportions	122	20.6	1	81	24.4	1
Complexion	109	18.4	2	38	11.4	5
Weight	74	12.5	3	50	15.1	3
Hair	62	10.5	4	14	4.2	7
Height	59	10.0	5	55	16.6	2
Features	55	9.3	6	16	4.8	6
Eyes	52	8.8	7	10	3.0	9
Teeth	21	3.6	8	11	3.3	8
Daintiness	13	2.2	9	—	—	—
Strength	—	—	—	46	13.9	4
Personal qualities	9	1.5	10	3	0.9	11
Freedom from disease or deformity	1	0.2	11	5	1.5	10
Unclassified	15	2.5	—	3	0.9	—
Total	592	100.1	—	332	100.0	—

I would first of all change my nose, as it is huge. I think someday I will go to a plastic surgeon and get my nose changed. I would not be so tall. I would like a wider jaw. I thought when I got my teeth straightened my jaw would be wider, but it is still sharp and pointed. I would like a clear, unscarred complexion. I have blackheads and pimples. I may go to a dermatologist. My eyes are small with short lashes. I have many moles which I saw a doctor about, but they cannot be removed without scars or pits.

I'd have cute legs, a cute figure, and a shorter forehead. I'd also be three inches shorter and have smaller feet. I'd have blue eyes and blond hair fixed in page-boy.

I would weigh 101 pounds.

I would rather not wear glasses. I would lose ten pounds. I would like a complexion that stays nice all the time.

When these responses had been itemized and classified, it was plain that the desires of the girls to change were distributed through most of the categories. Since lack of space prohibits the listing of all the items grouped under each category, only the largest clusters can be mentioned.

Under the category Proportions in Table 4, with 122 items, these clusters were slimmer hips (31), smaller feet (24), smaller waist (17), and good shape (16). The major clusters under the category Complexion (109 items) were clear complexion (42), no pimples (21), and no freckles (16). The category Weight (74 items) lent itself to simple subdivision, more slender (50) and fatter (24). Most of the items under the category Hair (62) were contributed by girls, who wanted to have hair that was dark (15), blond (12), longer (12), or naturally curly (10). Under the category Height (59 items), the girls were chiefly desirous of being shorter (38), although some wished to be taller (17). The chief desire under the category Features (55 items) was to have a nice nose (16) or a pretty face (13). The desires under the category Eyes (52 items) centered in no glasses and better vision (21) and blue eyes (12).

THE CHANGES BOYS WANT

The questionnaire results consistently revealed that the boys were less expressive than the girls. The boys responded with answers that were analyzed into 332 items, as compared with the 592 of the girls. A few of these statements in their entirety follow:

I would make my chest bigger than it is now and also my shoulders. I would like to weigh a little bit more, say about twenty to twenty-five pounds more than

I do now.

Be bigger and have more muscular development. Be taller and get rid of skin blemishes.

I would make myself look handsomer and not fat. I would have wavy black hair. I would change my whole physical appearance so that I would be handsome, with a good build.

Well, I would start off by putting on some meat, next would be to get rid of my pimples, then to get some muscles, then to get rid of my glasses.

I would build up my upper arm, forearm, chest, shoulder, and abdomen muscles.

I would be taller, more muscular, slimmer, have better posture, lighter and more slowly-growing head of hair, big, broad shoulders, and heavier calves.

Categories of major importance for boys are shown in Table 4 as being Proportions, Height, Weight, Strength, and Complexion. The clusters of items under each of these reveal the chief concerns. Under Proportions (81 items), the chief clusters are better build (17), broader shoulders (17), and larger chest (11). The category Height (55 items) is singularly centered in becoming taller (51). The items under the category Weight (50) are chiefly for heavier (36). The category Strength (46 items), perhaps poorly balanced by what we have termed "Daintiness" for girls, has two chief clusters, better muscular development (28) and stronger (10). For the boys, only one cluster emerges under the category Complexion (38 items), and that is no pimples (16).

These tenth-graders of both sexes are most conscious of a desire to conform to their conceptions of the ideal physical appearance in the areas of proportions, weight, height, and complexion, with a somewhat different rank order for each sex, chiefly notable for a switch in emphasis on complexion and height. Girls are more aware of complexion problems, boys of stature. In addition, a major category, which is plainly sex-determined, appears for both girls and boys among the top five categories. These categories are hair for girls; strength for boys.

Agreement in categories is not borne out, of course, in the clusters of items under weight and height. Girls desire to be thinner, boys heavier; girls want to be shorter, boys taller. In part, these differences may reflect the fact that girls of this age will be more mature than boys. Probably, the differences are largely differences in the ideal physique held in mind by each sex. An interesting check upon another section of the questionnaire is provided by the fact that proportions here rank first, whereas we had failed to elicit much response from the students for that aspect of Section 2. Our items there were apparently not the right ones.

Summary

In order to collect more information about how adolescents think of themselves physically and how concerned they are over their self-conceptions, the writers questioned one tenth-grade group of 580 students in terms of weight, height and proportions, rate of development, facial appearance, and desire for change. As reported here, the findings seem to justify the following generalizations:

1. The girls in this study are inclined to think of themselves as heavy and to express a high amount of concern about their supposed heaviness. Boys think of themselves as about right in weight but incline toward describing themselves as thin, with considerable concern about thinness in the upper arms and chest.

2. Height concerns chiefly the girls who think of themselves as tall, the boys who consider themselves short. Short boys express what is, for their sex, a high degree of concern.

3. Fewer of these boys and girls consider themselves slow in maturing than think themselves early. Most of them see themselves as average in this respect. However, among both boys and girls, the slow-maturing children express high concern. This is particularly outstanding among the boys in comparison with other expressions of male concern.

4. Blackheads and pimples are self-ascribed by a majority of the group. The concern of both sexes is higher for this item than for any other item in the entire questionnaire.

5. Two-thirds of these tenth-graders express a desire for some change in themselves physically, with items relating to proportions leading the categories for both sexes. Weight, height, and complexion are the other top areas in which desired change is common to both boys and girls.

Implications

As an aid toward more effective teaching and counseling, these chief generalizations and some of the other findings seem to suggest a number of guidelines to the writers and to other persons working in biology, health, guidance, and over-all curriculum development in this particular high school. Perhaps some of these tentative proposals for action will interest other educational workers.

1. What is being taught about the normality of weight and height range should be reviewed to find out whether it is sufficiently helpful. Attention needs to be given particularly to nutrition instruction for girls in this age group, who may be attempting to do something on their own about their supposed overweight.

2. Present instruction in the process of maturation needs to be reviewed to see whether it begins early enough to give fullest guidance and continues long enough to deal with the fears of slow-maturing children, particularly boys.

3. More attention needs to be given in Grade X to complexion disorders—their causes and treatment. This problem looms as a major concern of this age group. Ways in which to help need to be studied broadly by the school.

4. Tenth-graders may profit from help in looking at the ways in which they have gained their conceptions of the ideal physique—as revealed by their statements of changes that they would like to make in themselves. Advertising, as well as movies and novels, may come under discussion.

5. Autobiographical documents, in which younger and older adults report methods they have used to adjust to concerns about physique, are being collected in evening classes of adults by Mrs. Lillian Whitney, director of the psychology department of Phoenix College. These documents promise to provide a rich resource for helping tenth-graders gain perspective.

6. The possibility of devising from this study an instrument for self-assessment of the physique should be explored. Perhaps the health-counseling of biology teachers would be better directed if each student were provided with a form on which he could describe himself physically and tell how he feels about what he thinks he is.

NOTES

1. This task, along with others, is well defined in the following publication: Robert J. Havighurst, *Developmental Tasks and Education*. Chicago: University of Chicago Press, 1948.

2. Herbert R. Stolz and Lois Meek Stolz, "Adolescent Problems Related to Somatic Variations," *Adolescence*, pp. 81–99. Forty-third Yearbook of the National Society for the Study of Education, Part I. Chicago: Distributed by the University of Chicago Press, 1944.

THREE COGNITION, THOUGHTS, CONCEPTS, AND CREATIVITY IN ADOLESCENTS

Much of the early research on intellectual development focused on the intellectual and conceptual development of children. It is only recently that psychologists have emphasized that a qualitative change in cognitive structure takes place during adolescence and, consequently, that adult thought processes, conceptualizations, and intellectual capacities are different from those of children. Contrary to the earlier belief that adult intellectual capacity is reached by age sixteen—an assumption underlying early standardization of intelligence tests which used young subjects—educational psychologists now propose that intellectual ability increases through the late teens and early twenties. Increased mental age scores and reduced test-retest fluctuations in late adolescence combine to convince researchers that intellectual ability improves throughout the teenage years, gradually stabilizing at its adult level. Recent studies in adolescent cognitive development focus on a broad range of subjects, including cognitive change, mental structure, conceptual development, intellectual development, and creativity.

Two basic developmental insights emerge from the article by Neal W. Dye and Philip S. Very (9) concerning age changes and sex differences in intellectual structure. First, human intellectual ability, which in early childhood consists of one general, undifferentiated cognitive ability—the "g" of Stern's one-factor theory of intelligence—organizes into patterns of specific, highly differentiated intellectual factors in late adolescence. Second, between ninth and eleventh grade, intellectual abilities differentiate earlier and more specifically in boys than in girls. The hypothesis that women remain generalists after men begin to specialize offers a basis on which to revise tests of intelligence that minimize sex differences, such as the Stanford Binet. The Dye and Very hypothesis is indirectly supported by a study by R. Amthauer (1963) which demonstrates that men achieve on the basis of specific intellectual abilities while women draw more heavily on what Amthauer calls "compensatory factors of intelligence," such as memory, attention, concentration, organization, and industriousness.

J. P. Guilford's presidential address, "Creativity," delivered before the American Psychological Association in 1950, stirred professional interest in an area of intellectual development previously neglected by teachers, parents, college admission officers, and psychologists oriented to behaviorism. The article by

Jacob W. Getzels and Philip W. Jackson (10) explores this area and provides valuable data on adolescent creativity by systematically comparing "highly intelligent" and "highly creative" adolescents. The study reveals that although the "highly intelligent" students average twenty-three IQ points higher than the "highly creative" students, and although teachers consistently favor the "highly intelligent" over other students, both groups exhibit high motivation to succeed in school and both produce superior work. The "highly intelligent" student, however, shows a preference for the personality traits and goals supported by the school and adult society. The "highly creative" individual, on the other hand, tends to cultivate personality traits and to choose goals that are neither those that he believes to be preferred by the teacher nor those that are believed to predict adult success. In general, therefore, the "highly intelligent" adolescent is more conventional and convergent in his thinking than the "highly creative" adolescent, whose answers show "incongruities, playfulness, humor, and unexpected endings."

E. Paul Torrance and Dean C. Dauw (11) provide additional information concerning attitudinal and personality correlates of high creativity in adolescents. In contrast to the control group of unselected students, the creative seniors showed a significantly greater degree of "freedom orientation" and a correspondingly low degree of "control orientation." The creative seniors in this study shared three important characteristics with the subjects in the Getzels and Jackson study: desire for recognition, high "achievement orientation," and evidence of anxiety or conflict.

Robert J. Havighurst (12), more explicitly than the previous researchers, assumes the extreme environmentalist position that the influence of the social environment is the primary factor in mental superiority. Havighurst chooses to "ignore the biological elements in the production of superior children." In doing so he takes a position concerning the nature of human intelligence that has been challenged by educational psychologists with a genetic orientation. Havighurst presents convincing evidence for the well-supported observation that intelligence is closely linked to socio-economic conditions. A large proportion of intellectually superior students, for example, come from families with high socioeconomic standings. Social class differences in adolescent development are considered in more detail by Kobrin (38) later. Havighurst's article also discusses the psychological dilemma of the underachiever, a student with superior intellectual ability who, through lack of motivation or insufficient challenge in the classroom, does not fully utilize his learning potential.

REFERENCES

Amthauer, R. Über das "Spezifische" und das "Kompensatorische" beim Zustande-kommen von Leistungen, aufgezeigt an Ergebnissen einer Untersuchung zur Frage der Leistungsunterschiede der Geschlechter. *Psychologische Rundschau,* 1963, 14, 151–170.

[9] *Neal W. Dye & Philip S. Very* DEVELOPMENTAL

CHANGES IN ADOLESCENT MENTAL STRUCTURE

Introduction

Since the introduction of multiple factor analytic techniques to the study of human abilities, one of the major areas of research to which psychologists have devoted themselves has been clarification of the number and types of factors underlying human intellective ability. With the increase in volume and scope of this kind of research and the subsequent increase in empirically derived knowledge, periodic attempts have been made to design a theoretical framework which would satisfactorily explain the factorial structure of intelligence. One aspect of theory that has received considerable attention has been the development of factorial abilities, which some authors (6, 15) have attempted to explain by proposing an Age Differentiation Hypothesis, the basis of which is the differentiation of intellective ability from one general ability to a complex pattern of very specific abilities. None of these attempts, however, has been successful, and experts in the field remain about equally divided on this question, as do studies purporting to validate or repudiate the age differentiation hypothesis.

The purpose of this study is (a) to test the Age Differentiation Hypothesis by comparing factorial structure in a battery of reasoning tests at three chronological ages, and (b) to investigate sex differences in the development of reasoning abilities by comparison of the factorial structure of sexes at each age level. The use of college students, in addition, provides an opportunity to replicate some recent research in sex differences in ability at the college level (29).

Study of the age differentiation of ability is of primary significance in determining the ages at which various abilities are present. This research can be directly applied to the field of Education, and more specifically to curriculum planning. Even more pertinent than the above, however, is substantiation of the Age Differentiation Hypothesis, which would be of major importance in the development of an empirically valuable information in this intellective ability. A further area of potentially valuable information in this respect is the accumulation of research findings regarding what kinds of tests

FROM *Genetic Psychology Monographs*, 1968, 78, 55–88 (ABRIDGED). REPRINTED BY PERMISSION OF THE SENIOR AUTHOR AND THE JOURNAL PRESS.

are best utilized in investigating age and sex differences in the development of abilities in groups other than college students.

A. THE AGE DIFFERENTIATION HYPOTHESIS

The process by which human intellective ability differentiates from one global, undifferentiated ability—g—in early childhood to still general verbal and quantitative factors, and ultimately to the complex pattern of abilities repeatedly found in college students, has been proposed for many years (6, 13, 14, 15, 16). Restated, the Age Differentiation Hypothesis postulates (a) the emergence of abilities at particular points in maturation which become increasingly specific and refined with age, (b) that certain abilities present at one age level should not be present at some earlier age, and (c) that it is possible to demonstrate this process through factor analysis of performance on a particular battery of tests.

B. FACTORS AND ABILITIES

Another topic about which considerable disagreement exists is the question of exactly what factors are or what they represent. Definitions of factors range from "primary mental abilities" (26) to "descriptive categories" or "expression(s) of correlation among behavior measures" (3). In fact, the terms "factor" and "ability" are often used synonymously. Statistically, a factor refers to a group of performances which are highly interrelated, but separate and distinct from other such groups of interrelated performances (10). Whether factors actually represent the abilities they purport to measure, or whether factors are underlying genetically determined aspects of intelligence is not at issue in this study. Rather, the focus here is directed at differences between the factorial structures of the sexes at several age levels. Both terms are used interchangeably in this study and refer to statistical entities indicating distinct groups of highly interrelated performances.

II. Review of the literature

After more than 10 years of research into the age factor in mental organization, Garrett proposed a developmental theory of inelligence, based on the differentiation of ability with age, "from a fairly unified and general ability to a loosely organized group of abilities or factors" (15, p. 373). Garrett's own research (13, 14, 16) and the work of others, such as Anastasi (1), Bryan (5), Clark (7), Reichard (22), Schiller (23), Schneck (24), Thorndike (25), and Thurstone and Thurstone (27), had revealed a consistent decrease in correlations among verbal, memory, numerical, and spatial abilities from childhood to maturity, suggesting that intelligence becomes increasingly differentiated with age.

Correlations between verbal and number factors were high enough (.83) in 9-year-olds to be considered a homogeneous general factor [see Schiller (23)], while in college students correlations between these two factors decreased to .26. Similarly, Bryan (5) found a group of memory tests to be as closely related to vocabulary as they were to each other in 5-year-olds, while Anastasi (1) and Schneck (24) had found near-zero correlations between verbal and memory factors in college women. Garrett *et al.* (16) found progressive decreases in intercorrelations among verbal, memory, and numerical abilities in 9-, 12- and 15-year-olds. Intercorrelation of factors in this study and that of the Thurstones (27) revealed lower correlations among factors with increased age, which Garrett interpreted as a loss of generality of intelligence with maturity or age differentiation of ability.

Other studies, however, have yielded results apparently inconsistent with the Age Differentiation Hypothesis [see Balinski (4), Cohen (8, 9), Doppelt (11), and McNemar (21)]. These studies have utilized only tests of general ability, such as the Wechsler or Stanford-Binet Scales, and have shown either an increase or relative constancy of general factor variance—g—from early childhood through adulthood. Cohen (8, 9), for example, has shown that the proportion of total test variance attributable to general factor variance increases from 35 to 52 per cent from age 7 through adulthood, a finding which is flatly contradictory to age differentiation of ability. Yet Cohen (9) notes that individual subtests of the Wechsler Scales cannot be considered measures of different abilities because of their generally high relationship to the general intelligence factor. Further, McNemar has concluded that the Stanford-Binet Scale satisfies the conditions necessary for the measurement of general intelligence because of the absence of group factors (21, p. 122). It seems clear, then, that these studies have been limited to measurement of one general intelligence factor that is highly verbal in nature, and thus the increase in general factor variance with age reflects greater verbal ability with age and not necessarily a trend towards increased generality of intelligence.

Burt (6) has pointed out additional methodological weaknesses in these studies, noting that the limited range of tests, failure to include sufficient numbers of tests to allow for clear emergence of factors, and use of factor analytic techniques designed for identification of a single general factor have precluded demonstration of anything but increased general factor variance with age. Another reviewer of research in age differences in ability, Anastasi, states that "despite apparently conflicting results, the differentiation hypothesis appears to offer the most promising account of the age changes in trait organization from infancy to adolescence" (2, p. 371).

Studies of sex differences in ability have generally indicated male superiority in reasoning and mathematics and female superiority in verbal ability and perceptual speed [see Anastasi (2) and Tyler (28)]. Recent research in sex differences in ability at the college level (29), however, has demonstrated marked differences between the sexes in factorial patterns of reasoning ability, with males possessing more and better defined abilities than females. Five reasoning factors were isolated in this study in males, while of the four factors found in females only one, general reasoning, was interpretable. In addition, the factor structure of the total group was unlike that of either sex, suggesting that important differences may have been obscured in previous studies through neglect of the sex factor. While separate analyses for sex have been performed in earlier studies, as in those by Garrett *et al.* (16) and Reichard (22), with some evidence for both age and sex differences in ability, the few abilities studied appear to have been insufficient to allow for clear demonstration of differential patterns of abilities for the sexes, and it should be noted that age and not sex was the major variable under investigation. Studies of sex differences in the organization of abilities agree that different factorial compositions for sex may exist in at least some abilities (1).

It would seem, then, that failure to control for sex differences in ability patterns in previous studies may be responsible for the less than conclusive evidence in support of the age differentiation hypothesis. By controlling for both sex and age in this study, the present authors predict that age differentiation of ability does in fact occur and further predict that this differentiation process is greater and more specific in males than in females. Age differentiation of ability, if present, will be demonstrated operationally by an increase in the number of factors present at successive ages and by the concurrent increased clarity or specificity of such factors. The presence of sex differences in the differentiation process will be demonstrated by a greater number of factors in males than in females at each age level.

III. Method

A. SUBJECTS

A total of 556 subjects was used in this study. The entire ninth- and eleventh-grade classes at an "urban-fringe" New England high school were utilized for the two lower age levels, and volunteers from introductory psychology courses at a New England state university provided the sample college students. The ninth-grade sample consisted of 77 males and 88 females, for a total of 165 subjects; the eleventh-grade of 94 males and 99 females, for a total of 193; and the college group of 87 males and 111 females, for a total of 198. Mean ages were 14.0 years for the ninth-grade group, 16.2 years for the eleventh-grade, and 19.8 years for the college group. . . .

B. THE INSTRUMENT

A battery of 20 tests developed by Very[1] was used in this study. Item analysis and revision of this battery are currently in progress. The majority of tests in the battery, however, were selected on the basis of demonstrated factorial validity in Very's study (29).

The battery includes several tests of each of the five reasoning abilities found in Very's study, in addition to tests of verbal ability, perceptual speed, numerical facility, and mathematics achievement. These were included to control for the possible effects of item difficulty, time limits, and achievement at lower age levels. A pilot study conducted with college students in the summer of 1966 had provided the basis for time limits. In addition, one aspect of the first revision of this battery included the incorporation of upper- and lower-limit items so as to insure adequate measurement of abilities at the lower ages. Since it could not be determined beforehand what the precise effects of item difficulty, the speeded nature of tests, and achievement would be, the numerical facility, perceptual speed, verbal ability, and mathematics achievement tests were included. If these variables appreciably affected performance, this would be reflected in the relationship of the control tests to the experimental measures. For example, if speed were a major variable in performance on the battery, this would be indicated in the resultant factorial patterns by the clustering of tests on a factor defined primarily by tests of perceptual speed.

Each of the factors predicted to underlie performance, with the tests included to measure it, is described below. . . .

1. Numerical facility A control factor, numerical facility, is measured by five short tests of Addition, Subtraction, Multiplication, Division, and Arithmetic Computation. These tests commonly require rapid performance of basic numerical operations, although the Arithmetic Computation test requires use of decimals in addition. Numerical Facility has repeatedly been isolated as a highly distinct factor [see French (12)].

2. Perceptual speed Two tests, Number Comparisons and Perceptual Velocity, require rapid scanning of groups of numbers to select similar or different numbers within these groups. Also included as a control test, a perceptual speed factor has been found consistently in factor analytic studies of ability (12).

3. Verbal ability A vocabulary test was included as a test of this ability, as vocabulary has repeatedly been demonstrated as the best single measure of verbal ability [see Cronbach (10)]. This test requires no production of language, but rather selecting the one word best defining the test word from a group of choices.

4. Mathematics achievement One test of mathematics achievement was incorporated in the battery to determine whether performance on the tests of arithmetic reasoning and mathematical aptitude was related to mathematics achievement.

5. Inductive reasoning Two tests of this ability, Inductive Reasoning and Induction, were included. Each test has previously loaded highly on an inductive reasoning factor. The Inductive Reasoning test is a series of verbal items which require discovery of a general rule among a series of concepts and application of that rule to specific instances. Induction is similarly constructed, but consists solely of series of symbols. Also included with these tests was Matrices, a nonverbal reasoning test thought to involve primarily inductive reasoning.

6. Deductive reasoning   Nonsense Syllogisms, consisting of syllogistic or formal reasoning items stated in illogical terms to eliminate a technical knowledge factor, and Deductive Reasoning, with deductive reasoning items stated in a more general fashion were the tests employed to measure the Deductive Reasoning factor. As noted previously, considerable difficulty has been encountered in isolating this factor in the past, yet in Very's study (29) these tests defined the factor clearly.

7. Arithmetic reasoning   The Arithmetic Reasoning and Mathematics Aptitude tests are analogous to those best defining Very's Arithmetic Reasoning factor. These tests require mathematical solution to verbally stated questions. While tests of this variety have loaded on a General Reasoning factor in previous studies, care was taken to use only items of a strictly arithmetic nature in these tests so as to maximize the distinction between the Arithmetic Reasoning and General Reasoning factors.

8. General reasoning   As defined by Guilford (18), general reasoning appears to be a combination of some arithmetic ability and reasoning of a more general type than inductive or deductive. Since Guilford has most clearly and consistently demonstrated this ability, attempts were made via the Reasoning and Logical Relationships test to use items requiring a reasoning approach neither wholly inductive, arithmetic, or deductive in nature. The Reasoning test, however, requires more arithmetic reasoning ability than does Logical Relationships, which consists solely of verbal reasoning items neither inductive nor deductive in nature. Combination of these two tests on a single factor would seem to satisfy Guilford's criteria for a general reasoning factor.

9. Estimative ability   The Judgment and Mathematical Puzzles tests require an estimative approach and the ability to generate and evaluate hypotheses where strictly mathematical or reasoning solutions are not immediately apparent. These tests defined the Estimative factor in Very's study, yet such a factor has not generally been isolated in previous research.

C. PROCEDURE

Administration of the battery, including completion of the personal data sheet, required 100 minutes. College students were administered the battery in one session, from 7 to 9 PM, with a 10-minute rest period approximately halfway through the battery. Two consecutive evening sessions were required to accommodate the entire college group, which was arbitrarily split into two subgroups because of limited space.

Because of difficulties imposed by testing during the school day, the battery was broken into three approximately equal parts for the high school subjects and administered in three 40-minute sessions on alternate days. These groups were divided into four sections, and tests were administered by four examiners. Ninth-grade subjects were tested in the last week of October 1966, and eleventh-grade students in the first week of November 1966.

IV. Results

A. QUANTITATIVE SEX DIFFERENCES

Quantitative sex differences, determined by performing t-tests on the scores of males and females for each of the 20 tests in the battery at each age level, are presented in Table 1. Results of this analysis indicated a gradual

TABLE 1 Means, Standard Deviations, and t-Values

| TEST | MALES | | FEMALES | | |
	$\overline{X}$	SD	$\overline{X}$	SD	t
	College (N = 198)				
	(n = 87)		(n = 111)		
No Comp	31.64	7.58	34.70	6.64	3.00**
Add	39.05	8.28	41.38	8.83	1.89
Mult	45.28	10.56	46.26	11.81	0.63
Subtr	50.71	14.17	52.64	11.53	0.97
Div	30.77	9.58	31.41	9.00	0.48
Per Vel	12.30	3.70	20.70	3.38	2.79**
Ar Comp	7.53	2.54	7.80	3.09	0.66
Ar Reas	6.02	2.15	5.34	1.50	2.61*
Matr	6.48	2.19	6.11	2.11	1.21
Vocab	14.11	5.72	15.43	4.37	1.83
Non Syl	14.74	3.24	13.87	2.99	1.93
Math Ach	7.05	2.20	6.05	2.15	3.70**
Induct'n	6.00	2.26	6.25	1.88	0.85
Judgt	5.01	1.66	4.77	1.75	0.96
Math Apt	6.78	2.07	5.51	1.95	4.40**
Ded Reas	6.48	1.66	6.68	1.47	0.86
Math Puz	2.57	1.28	2.61	1.23	0.21
Ind Reas	6.57	1.93	6.90	1.88	1.19
Reasng	7.57	2.17	6.60	1.97	3.28**
Log Rel	7.54	1.93	7.68	1.57	0.58

TABLE 1 (*continued*)

| TEST | MALES | | FEMALES | | |
	$\overline{X}$	SD	$\overline{X}$	SD	t

Eleventh Grade (N = 193)

| TEST | MALES ($n = 94$) | | FEMALES ($n = 99$) | | |
	$\overline{X}$	SD	$\overline{X}$	SD	t
No Comp	35.02	8.56	36.72	8.37	1.38
Add	30.87	7.82	32.02	6.81	1.09
Mult	35.67	12.23	37.19	13.37	0.82
Subtr	35.57	12.42	37.54	12.91	1.07
Div	24.39	8.66	23.29	10.26	0.80
Per Vel	20.45	4.32	22.39	4.02	3.23**
Ar Comp	5.49	2.22	5.48	2.51	0.01
Ar Reas	4.46	2.03	3.84	2.06	2.09*
Matr	5.93	2.18	5.57	2.02	1.18
Vocab	6.59	3.44	8.51	4.74	3.19**
Non Syl	13.15	3.96	14.26	3.83	1.98*
Math Ach	4.97	2.05	4.65	2.03	1.09
Induct'n	4.66	2.08	5.57	2.31	2.84**
Judgt	3.71	1.75	3.81	1.75	0.38
Math Apt	5.05	2.23	4.43	2.04	2.00*
Ded Reas	4.74	1.81	5.02	1.88	1.03
Math Puz	3.05	1.45	3.03	1.63	0.10
Ind Reas	4.90	1.92	5.59	2.02	2.39*
Reasng	5.76	2.03	5.21	1.97	1.88
Log Rel	5.79	2.07	5.62	2.05	0.57

decrease in sex differences with increasing age. At the ninth-grade level female performance was generally superior to that of males, particularly with respect to tests of numerical facility and perceptual speed. At the eleventh-grade level this difference was somewhat modified. Females retained superiority in perceptual speed, but also gained superiority in verbal ability and several tests of verbal reasoning. At the college level, however, females retained superiority only in tests of perceptual speed, while male performance was superior in every test of arithmetic reasoning and mathematics aptitude in the battery. Few statistically significant sex differences occurred in the various

TABLE 1 (*continued*)

TEST	MALES		FEMALES		
	$\overline{X}$	SD	$\overline{X}$	SD	t
		Ninth Grade (N $= 165$)			
		($n = 77$)		($n = 88$)	
No Comp	35.79	7.98	40.35	7.23	3.85**
Add	25.45	7.70	29.31	7.90	3.14**
Mult	28.49	11.05	33.98	11.52	3.08**
Subtr	28.75	10.47	34.41	11.55	3.26**
Div	18.03	10.17	22.20	9.83	2.66**
Per Vel	20.57	4.28	24.11	3.23	6.01**
Ar Comp	3.81	2.22	4.32	2.17	1.49
Ar Reas	3.57	1.77	3.16	1.77	1.48
Matr	5.95	2.14	5.82	1.20	0.40
Vocab	4.86	2.41	5.38	2.88	1.26
Non Syl	12.68	4.02	13.07	3.65	0.65
Math Ach	4.34	2.04	4.19	1.70	0.49
Induct'n	4.60	2.16	5.34	2.32	2.11**
Judgt	3.48	1.61	2.97	1.32	2.24**
Math Apt	4.16	2.48	3.72	2.07	1.23
Ded Reas	3.77	1.83	4.43	1.49	2.60**
Math Puz	2.36	1.30	2.32	1.38	0.22
Ind Reas	4.52	2.31	4.64	1.86	0.36
Reasng	4.60	2.15	4.68	1.82	0.27
Log Rel	4.51	1.83	4.82	2.11	1.00

* $p < .05$.
** $p < .01$.

tests of reasoning ability, and in most of the cases where differences did occur these were so small as to be of little practical significance.

Results of this analysis of importance to developmental and sex differences in ability are (*a*) the increasing superiority of males in arithmetic ability, and (*b*) the maintenance of female superiority in perceptual speed. In addition, differences between means at the college level which *approached* statistical significance suggested a tentatively interpreted female superiority in verbal ability for this age group. These findings are in general agreement with the large body of research in quantitative sex differences in ability, in which female superiority in verbal ability and perceptual speed, and male superiority in mathematical ability have been consistently demonstrated (28).

B. FACTOR ANALYTIC RESULTS

Rotated matrices[2] of factor loadings are presented in summary fashion in Table 2, and in detail with factor loadings in Table 3. Each factor isolated in this study is discussed below in terms of the tests which define it, sex differences, and differences among the three age groups.

TABLE 2 Summary of Comparative Factorial Structure[a]

NINTH GRADE		ELEVENTH GRADE		COLLEGE	
Males	Females	Males	Females	Males	Females
Numerical Facility	Numerical Facility	Numerical Facility	Numerical Facility	Numerical Facility	Numerical Facility
		Perceptual Speed	Perceptual Speed	Perceptual Speed	Perceptual Speed
Arithmetic Reasoning	Arithmetic Reasoning	Arithmetic Reasoning	Arithmetic Reasoning	Arithmetic Reasoning	Arithmetic Reasoning
		Inductive Reasoning	Inductive Reasoning	Inductive Reasoning	Inductive Reasoning
Symbolic-Inductive Reasoning		Symbolic-Inductive Reasoning		Symbolic-Inductive Reasoning	
Verbal Reasoning	Verbal Reasoning	Verbal Reasoning	Verbal Reasoning	Verbal Ability	Verbal Ability
Reasoning	Reasoning	Reasoning	Reasoning	General Reasoning	Reasoning
Estimative Ability		Estimative Ability		Estimative Ability	Estimative Ability
"Deductive" Reasoning			"Deductive" Reasoning	"Deductive" Reasoning	"Deductive" Reasoning
				Mathematics Achievement	

[a] Where a particular factor was found for some groups but not for others, a blank space has been left to make differences in factorial structure more evident.

TABLE 3 Comparative Factorial Structure with Factor Loadings of Tests[a]

	Ninth Grade		Eleventh Grade		College	
	Males	**Females**	**Males**	**Females**	**Males**	**Females**
Numerical Facility	Mult .89 Add .85 Subtr .81 Div .71 No Comp .65 Per Vel .61 Ar Comp .49 Ind Reas .34	Mult .86 Subtr .85 Add .82 Div .75 No Comp .70 Per Vel .57 Ar Comp .40	Mult .90 Add .85 Div .78 Subtr .75 Ar Comp .53 Math Ach .35	Add .90 Mult .88 Subtr .86 Div .77 Ar Comp .61	Subtr .87 Mult .87 Add .81 Div .74 Ar Comp .63 Per Vel .35	Add .87 Subtr .87 Mult .87 Div .76 Ar Comp .64 No Comp .38 Per Vel .32
Perceptual Speed			No Comp .89 Per Vel .86	No Comp .92 Per Vel .85	No Comp .85 Per Vel .79	No Comp .73 Per Vel .71 Induct'n .68 Ind Reas .35
"Deductive" Reasoning	Non Syl .91		Non Syl	Non Syl .77 Math Ach −.41	Non Syl .93	Non Syl .95
Arithmetic Reasoning	Ar Comp .64 Reasng .58 Ar Reas .56 Math Apt .50	Math Apt .72 Ar Reas .57 Matr .50 Ar Comp .49	Reasng .86 Math Apt .68 Ar Reas .49 Math Ach .48	Math Puz .86 Reasng .68 Math Ach .49 Induct'n .48	Ar Reas .80 Reasng .76 Math Apt .75 Ded Reas .64	Ar Reas .79 Reasng .64 Math Apt .56 Math Ach .54

TABLE 3 (continued)

	NINTH GRADE		ELEVENTH GRADE		COLLEGE	
	MALES	**FEMALES**	**MALES**	**FEMALES**	**MALES**	**FEMALES**
Arithmetic Reasoning	Subtr .33 Per Vel −.33	Induct'n .49 Reasng .42 Ded Reas .36 Ind Reas .31	Ar Comp .40	Ar Reas .34	Ind Reas .63 Ar Comp .42 Div .32	Div. .30
Inductive Reasoning			Log Rel .80 Judgt .71 Ind Reas .46 Ar Reas .46 Subtr .37 Non Syl .30	Matr .82 Ind Reas .63 Ar Reas .43 Math Ach .32 Math Apt .31 Non Syl .30	Judgt .85 Ind Reas .49 Induct'n .35	Matr .77 Judgt .61 Ind Reas .46 Vocab .42 Reasng .36
Symbolic-Inductive Reasoning	Matr .81 Math Ach .53 Ar Reas .38		Matr .87 Ind Reas .48 Induct'n .47 Ded Reas .37		Matr .95 Induct'n .31	
Verbal Reasoning	Vocab .75 Judgt .74 No Comp .38 Log Rel .38	Judgt .75 Log Rel .66 Ind Reas .54 Ded Reas .53	Vocab .80 Math Ach .47 Ded Reas .46	Vocab .79 Judgt .74 Log Rel .62 Induct'n .56	Vocab .84 Math Puz .49	
Verbal Ability						Log Rel .78 Vocab .54 Ded Reas .40 Ind Reas .34

Induct'n	.82	Vocab	.49	Math Apt	.44
Ind Reas	.62	Ar Reas	.48	Ar Reas	.37
Ded Reas	.54	Math Ach	.46	Reasng	.35
Log Rel	.53			Div	.34
Math Apt	.41			Ded Reas	.33
Reasng	.36			Ind Reas	.31
Judgt	.35				
Per Vel	.34				

Reasoning[b]

Non Syl	.64	Non Syl	.75	Ded Reas	.72	Log Rel	.87
Reasng	.60	Induct'n	.65	Ar Comp	.58	Reasng	.32
Math Puz	.54	Judgt	.40	Ar Reas	.48		
Ar Comp	.53			Math Apt	.31	Ded Reas	.68
Matr	.41			Judgt	.30	Judgt	.58
						Math Apt	.56

Estimative Ability

Math Puz	.92	Math Puz	.93	Math Puz	.85
		Ind Reas	−.36	Vocab	.48

Mathematics Achievement

Math Puz	.81	Math Ach	.71		
Math Ach	.57	Induct'n	−.50		
Ded Reas	.46				
Math Apt	.34				

[a] Where both negative and positive loading occurred on a factor, these have been multiplied by a constant (−1) for ease of interpretation.
[b] Of all the Reasoning factors, only that of the College Males could be classified as General Reasoning and is so identified in the text.

1. Numerical facility   Skill in performing basic numerical operations is defined by the Addition, Subtraction, Multiplication, Division, and Arithmetic Computation tests. A highly specific factor, Numerical Facility, was present in both sexes at each age level. This factor was related to the Arithmetic Reasoning factor in all groups except college and eleventh-grade females. In fact, only the Arithmetic Computation test was meaningfully related to the Arithmetic Reasoning factor, and this relationship decreased directly with increased age.

A rather unique result of this study is the absence of separate factors for Numerical Facility and Perceptual Speed in the ninth-grade group. In this group, the two tests of Perceptual Speed were highly loaded on the factor best defined by tests of numerical facility and did not emerge as a separate factor until the eleventh-grade level. The loading of numerical facility and perceptual speed tests on one factor at this lowest age level suggests the presence of a more general factor in this group and at lower ages, which becomes differentiated into the two distinct Numerical Facility and Perceptual Speed factors by the eleventh grade. The increased specificity of these abilities with age is highly consistent with predictions of the Age Differentiation Hypothesis and has not been demonstrated in previous research.

2. Perceptual speed   As noted above, a Perceptual Speed factor, defined by the Number Comparisons and Perceptual Velocity tests, was not present in the ninth-grade group, but emerged as a clear, highly distinct factor in both sexes in the eleventh-grade and college groups. These tests require rapid scanning of large amounts of information in order to make comparisons for similarities or differences. Perceptual Speed was most meaningfully related to performance of college females on two tests of inductive reasoning. It appears, then, that this group relied somewhat on perceptual speed rather than pure inductive reasoning in the solution of these items.

The Perceptual Speed factor was extremely distinct and generally unrelated to performance on other tests in the battery, except the inductive reasoning tests in college females. As a control factor, then, the absence of loadings of other tests on the Perceptual Speed factor indicates that speed was not an important aspect in performance on this battery.

3. Arithmetic reasoning   This factor is defined by the Arithmetic Reasoning, Reasoning, Mathematics Aptitude, Mathematics Achievement, and Arithmetic Computation tests, although several reasoning tests were meaningfully loaded on the factor in college males and ninth-grade females. These tests commonly require mathematical solution of verbally-stated problems, and the Arithmetic Reasoning factor was present in all groups.

Sex differences in the tests defining Arithmetic Reasoning diminished as age increased, resulting in virtually identical test loadings for males and females in the college group. The major sex and developmental differences occurring in this factor were the decrease in loadings of the Arithmetic Computation test as age increased, and the introduction of a Mathematics Achievement factor distinct from Arithmetic Reasoning in college males. The Mathematics Achievement test did not load at all on the factor in the ninth-grade group, showed moderate loadings in the eleventh-grade and college female groups, and separated completely from Arithmetic Reasoning in college males. In addition, the slight loadings of the Inductive and Deductive Reasoning tests on this factor in college males suggest the application of other types of reasoning to solution of these items, or somewhat greater flexibility in arithmetic reasoning exercises by college males. The Arithmetic Reasoning factor thus becomes increasingly independent from numerical facility with age, to a point where it is basically unrelated to the numerical operations from which it appears to originate. Arithmetic Reasoning was most undifferentiated in ninth-grade females and most specific in college males and females.

4. Mathematics achievement This factor was found only in college males, and is defined primarily by the Mathematics Achievement test. Emergence of a Mathematics Achievement factor in this particular group suggests that achievement in mathematics becomes independent of actual arithmetic reasoning ability in college males. The moderately high but negative loading of the Induction test on this factor may be an artifact, but it is possible that Mathematics Achievement and Inductive Reasoning exist at opposite ends of the same factorial dimension or continuum. There is not sufficient evidence here, however, to justify further evaluation of this possible relationship.

5. Verbal ability A verbal ability factor independent of reasoning abilities was present in all groups and is best measured by the Vocabulary test. Since only one test of verbal ability was included in this battery as a control test, this factor appears to be a combination of verbal ability and the verbal element of other tests. A greater number of tests of verbal ability would be necessary to obtain a purely verbal factor.

The Verbal Ability factor was clearest and most purely verbal in college males. For all female groups and for eleventh- and ninth grade males, Verbal Ability was additionally defined by the Judgment, Logical Relationships, Deductive Reasoning, and Inductive Reasoning tests. The Verbal Ability factor was most specific in male groups, and at the college level no reasoning test loaded on this factor. In addition, the increasing specificity of this factor with age for both sexes, and the obvious verbal element of those reasoning tests meaningfully loaded on this factor, suggest that Verbal Ability might better be designated Verbal Reasoning and considered as a factor intermediate between Verbal Ability and higher level reasoning factors.

6. Inductive reasoning The ability to reason from specifics to a general principle emerged as a distinct factor only in the eleventh-grade and college groups, with major age and sex differences in specificity and composition. This factor became clearer with age in both sexes and was most specific in college males, being defined by precisely those tests which were intended to measure it—Judgment, Inductive Reasoning, and Induction. The most significant sex difference in addition to the specificity of the factor was the high loading of the Matrices test on the Inductive Reasoning factor of females. In males, Matrices separated into another factor which is defined below. Although Inductive

Reasoning became somewhat clearer with age in females, even at the college level it remained a less specific factor than that of college males.

7. Symbolic-inductive reasoning An additional inductive reasoning factor, defined by two nonverbal tests of inductive reasoning, Induction and Matrices, was found at each age level in males only. Again, this factor was clearest in college males, but its emergence was observable even in ninth-grade males, in spite of the absence of an Inductive Reasoning factor in this group. As of this writing, no factor similar to Symbolic-Inductive Reasoning is to be found in the literature; yet the nature of the items in these tests strongly suggests that ability to reason with symbols in a strictly nonverbal fashion is its basis.

It appears, then, that a major sex difference exists with respect to inductive reasoning. That is, inductive reasoning is more specific and clearly defined in males, even becoming differentiated into verbal and nonverbal factors, while in females inductive reasoning is a more general factor even at maturity.

8. Reasoning This factor is defined by tests of inductive, deductive, and arithmetic reasoning in all groups except college males. Only in college males did Reasoning resemble the General Reasoning factor described by Guilford et al. (18); that is, a factor requiring application of general reasoning approach. In all other groups it was defined by such differing combinations of reasoning tests that it could not be defined more specifically than simply Reasoning. Developmentally, Reasoning appears to be a relatively undifferentiated reasoning factor with a quantitative emphasis, and it does become more specific, though not more meaningful, with increasing age. The General Reasoning factor in college males seems to be reasoning ability which involves both quantitative and verbal types of reasoning, but which is not as specific as other reasoning abilities. Thus, Reasoning seems to develop into General Reasoning, but only in males at maturity. In females, it remains a composite factor involving diverse types of reasoning.

9. "Deductive" reasoning This factor is tentatively designated Deductive Reasoning in light of the high loading of the Nonsense Syllogisms test. However, a Deductive Reasoning factor did not emerge as had been predicted, and reasons for the failure of the Deductive Reasoning test to load on this factor are not clear. In addition, there was no discernible developmental trend in the emergence or definition of this factor, and thus it cannot be considered a reliable measure of deductive reasoning. Both tests appear to be measuring deductive reasoning ability: the Nonsense Syllogisms test was designed to test ability in formal logic, and Deductive Reasoning to measure deductive ability in more general items. Deductive Reasoning, though, has never been clearly and consistently isolated (3), although why it emerged in Very's (29) college group and not this group cannot be determined without further factor analytic study of the deductive reasoning area.

10. Estimative ability Estimative Ability is defined primarily by the Mathematical Puzzles test, which requires ingenuity and the ability to generate and evaluate new hypotheses in the solution of quantitative problems where a mathematical method is not immediately apparent. Estimative Ability appears to be a higher order factor than Arithmetic Reasoning. It was found in both sexes at the college level, not only in males in the eleventh- and ninth-grade groups. The loading of the vocabulary test on the Estimative factor in college females indicates the emphasis of verbal ability by that group rather than reasoning or quantitative ability in solution of these problems. Males appeared to use a more mathematical or quantitative reasoning approach on this test than females, as is suggested by the structure of the factor at earlier ages.

V. *Summary and discussion*

The greater number of factors at each successive age level and the increased specificity of factors with age are consistent with predictions based on the Age Differentiation Hypothesis. The greater number of factors in males in each age group supports the hypothesized sex differences in the differentiation process.

It is seen that in the ages studied those abilities surveyed become increasingly specific with age and are most specific in males. The greatest differentiation of ability was found in college males, with college females having fewer and less well-defined factors. This trend is similar in the eleventh- and ninth-grade groups, with female factorial structures consistently less differentiated and more difficult to interpret than those of males. Major sex differences appeared in the development of reasoning and arithmetic abilities. In males, the development of inductive reasoning ability can be observed even in the ninth grade, where tests of inductive reasoning loaded highest on the Reasoning factor, while in ninth-grade females this factor combined tests of diverse reasoning abilities in no discernible pattern. Further, in both the eleventh-grade and college groups the Inductive Reasoning factor was clearer and more specific in males than in females. Males also develop a nonverbal, or Symbolic-Inductive Reasoning, ability, whereas the tests defining this factor loaded on the Inductive Reasoning, Reasoning, or Verbal Reasoning factors in females and did not emerge as a separate factor. Thus a distinct inductive reasoning ability not only develops in accordance with the Age Differentiation Hypothesis, but the process of differentiation is greatest in males.

The increased independence of Arithmetic Reasoning from Numerical Facility is a further example of age differentiation of ability. Arithmetic reasoning at maturity becomes independent of the numerical operations that are its basis at earlier ages. The small loadings of numerical facility tests which are present in the ninth grade decrease directly with increased age. The emergence of a separate Mathematics Achievement factor in college males is contrasted with the moderate loadings of the Mathematics Achievement test on the Arithmetic Reasoning factor in college females.

The clearest evidence of age differentiation of ability, however, is seen in the differentiation of a single, general factor combining tests of numerical facility and perceptual speed in the ninth-grade groups into two separate factors, Numerical Facility and Perceptual Speed, in the eleventh-grade and college groups. This kind of differentiation is exactly that which proponents of the

Age Differentiation Hypothesis have described, but as yet have failed to demonstrate clearly (15). The differentiation process seen here suggests that ninth-grade students applied one ability to both types of tests, while eleventh-grade and college students applied a distinct ability to each area.

Further support for the Age Differentiation Hypothesis is suggested by the presence of a factor in college males consistent with the description by Guilford *et al.* (18) of General Reasoning Ability, while comparable factors in the other groups were not clear enough to be interpreted beyond a Reasoning factor. Also, an Estimative Ability factor, present in both sexes in the college group but only in males in the lower age groups, showed slightly different composition between sexes, with females relying more on verbal ability than estimation in this area. Generally speaking, females utilized verbal ability to a greater extent than males throughout the battery, as witnessed by the greater number of loadings of the Vocabulary test for females.

Reasons for the failure of the Judgment and Mathematical Puzzles tests to load on a single factor are not clear. While these tests had been highly related in Very's study, Judgment seems clearly an inductive reasoning test and Mathematical Puzzles cannot be legitimately interpreted at the college level because of the lack of other loadings on this factor. Reasons also for the lack of relationship between the Nonsense Syllogisms and Deductive Reasoning tests are not apparent. Further investigation of these tests is necessary before either the Deductive Reasoning or Estimative Ability factors are confirmed.

Loadings of the control tests tend to refute the effects of speed and verbal ability on performance in the ninth-grade and eleventh-grade groups. Loading of the Mathematics Achievement test on several reasoning factors in these groups, however, suggests that achievement may be related to such abilities as Inductive and Arithmetic Reasoning.

A further problem of the battery is the low reliability of the tests at the ninth-grade level, as indicated by the communalities [see Harman (19) and Kerlinger (20)]. This finding suggests that a major change in ability patterns occurs at or near this age, at least in females (2). As the study of abilities is extended to lower ages, comparison of this age group on that form of the battery developed for lower ages may clarify the problem.

In summary, the results of this investigation can be considered as evidence in support of the Age Differentiation Hypothesis and sex differences in ability patterns. Reasoning factors, or abilities, are more numerous and better defined in males than in females at each age level studied. The greater specificity of factors is particularly evident in the areas of inductive, arithmetic, and general reasoning, and in the presence of a mathematics achievement factor in college males and not in college females. It is interesting to note that the relatively few and less-differentiated reasoning abilities in college females are seemingly compensated for by greater use of verbal ability, which may explain females' frequently demonstrated superiority in verbal skills.

With respect to the Age Differentiation Hypothesis and the results of this study, it should be noted that grade in school and not chronological age was the independent variable employed for each group. Since age in school is undoubtedly related to educational, social, and cultural experiences, differences in factor structure among the three groups may well have been influenced by these factors and not by age alone as Burt (6) has proposed. Further, although previous factor analytic research has indicated that geographical location of subjects has had little influence on results, it must be stated that the subjects used in this study were drawn from an "urban-fringe" area—that is, an area not truly urban, suburban, or rural in nature.

IMPLICATIONS FOR FUTHER RESEARCH

Further study of the Age Differentiation Hypothesis and sex differences in ability patterns would seem to be essential in constructing a theoretical model for the development of intelligence in man. Such research might be based on a developmental approach to the structure of adult intelligence model proposed by Guilford (17). Primary considerations in this area of research, however, are extension of the methodology employed in this study to younger ages and expansion of the number of abilities measured. Comparison of the factorial structure of college students with unselected adults, and the patterns of normal children and adolescents with retardates, would be helpful in determining the effects, if any, of level of general intelligence and educational experience on factorial patterns.

A more immediate need than this is clarification of the deductive reasoning and estimative ability factors. Reliable, factor-pure measures of these abilities are necessary, particularly in further clarification of the reasoning abilities, since there is evidence supporting the existence of these abilities, and yet they have not been consistently isolated with any degree of certainty.

Once factorial structure at various ages has been sufficiently clarified and verified, orthogonal rotation of the factors at each age level should be followed by rotation to oblique simple structure, so that relationships among factors at different ages could then be directly compared. This information would provide further evidence for or against the Age Differentiation Hypothesis, and separate analyses for the sexes should yield further differences in the differentiation process for males and females.

NOTES

1. The Very Developmental Battery is presently being constructed as part of Public Health Service Grant No. 9–R01–HD–03270–01.

2. Intercorrelation matrices and principal components factor matrices have been deposited as Document number 9966 with the ADI Auxiliary Publications Project, Photo-duplication Service, Library of Congress, Washington, D.C. 20540. A copy may be secured by citing the Document number and by remitting $2.50 for photoprints, or $1.75 for 35-mm. microfilm. Advance payment is required. Make checks or money orders payable to Chief, Photoduplication Service, Library of Congress.

REFERENCES

1. Anastasi, A. Further studies on the memory factor. *Arch. Psychol.*, 1932, No. 142.
2. ———. Differential Psychology (4th ed.). New York: Macmillan, 1958.
3. ———. Psychological Testing (2d ed.). New York: Macmillan, 1961.
4. Balinski, B. An analysis of the mental factors of various age groups from nine to sixty. *Genet. Psychol. Monog.*, 1941, **23**, 191–234.
5. Bryan, A. I. Organization of memory in young children. *Arch. Psychol.*, 1934, No. 162.
6. Burt, C. The differentiation of intellectual ability. *Brit. J. Educ. Psychol.*, 1954, **47**, 76–90.
7. Clark, M. P. Changes in primary abilities with age. *Arch. Psychol.*, 1944, No. 291.
8. Cohen, J. The factorial structure of the WAIS between early adulthood and old age. *J. Consult. Psychol.*, 1957, **21**, 238–290.
9. ———. Factorial structure of the WISC. *J. Consult. Psychol.*, 1959, **23**, 285–299.
10. Cronbach, L. J. Essentials of Psychological Testing (2d ed.). New York: Harper, 1960.
11. Doppelt, J. E. The organization of mental abilities in the age ranges 13 to 17. *Teach. Coll. Contr. Educ.*, 1950, No. 962.
12. French, J. W. The description of aptitude and achievement factors in terms of rotated factors. *Psychomet. Monog.*, 1951, No. 5.
13. Garrett, H. E. A study of the CAVD intelligence examination. *J. Educ. Res.*, 1930, **21**, 103–108.
14. ———. Differentiable mental traits. *Psychol. Rec.*, 1938, **2**, 259–298.
15. ———. A developmental theory of intelligence. *Amer. Psychologist*, 1946, **1**, 372–378.
16. Garrett, H. E., Bryan, A. I., & Perl, R. The age factor in mental organization. *Arch. Psychol.*, 1935, No. 176.
17. Guilford, J. P. The structure of intellect. *Psychol. Bull.*, 1956, **53**, 267–293.
18. Guilford, J. P., et al. A factor analytic investigation of the factor called general reasoning. Studies of aptitudes of high-level personnel. *Rep. Psychol. Lab.* No. 14, Univ. So. Calif., Los Angeles, 1955.
19. Harman, H. Modern Factor Analysis. Chicago: Univ. Chicago Press, 1962.
20. Kerlinger, F. N. Foundations of Behavioral Research. New York: Holt, Rinehart & Winston, 1964.
21. McNemar, Q. The Revision of the Stanford-Binet Scale. New York: Houghton Mifflin, 1942.
22. Reichard, S. Mental organization and age level. *Arch. Psychol.*, 1944, No. 295.
23. Schiller, B. Verbal, numerical and spatial abilities in young children. *Arch. Psychol.*, 1934, No. 161.
24. Schneck, M. R. The measurement of verbal and numerical abilities. *Arch. Psychol.*, 1929, No. 107.

25. Thorndike, E. L. The Measurement of Intelligence. New York: Columbia Univ. Press, 1926.
26. Thurstone, L. L. Primary mental abilities. *Psychomet. Monog.*, 1938, No. 1.
27. Thurstone, L. L., & Thurstone, T. G. Factorial studies of intelligence. *Psychomet. Monog.*, 1941, No. 2.
28. Tyler, L. E. The Psychology of Human Differences. New York: Appleton-Century-Crofts, 1956.
29. Very, P. S. Differential factor structures in mathematical ability. *Genet. Psychol. Monog.*, 1967, 75, 169–207.

[10] *Jacob W. Getzels & Philip W. Jackson* THE HIGHLY INTELLIGENT AND THE HIGHLY CREATIVE ADOLESCENT: A SUMMARY OF SOME RESEARCH FINDINGS

Introduction

"Giftedness" as related to children has most often been defined as a score on an intelligence test, and typically the study of the so-called gifted child has been equated with the study of the single I.Q. variable. Implicit in this unidimensional definition of giftedness, it seems to us, are several types of confusion, if not outright error.

First, there is the limitation of the I.Q. metric itself, which not only restricts our perspective of the more general phenomenon but places on the one concept a greater theoretical and predictive burden than it was intended to carry. For all practical purposes, the term "gifted child" has become synonymous with the expression "child with a high I.Q.," thus blinding us to other forms of potential excellence. Second, within the universe of intellectual functions we have frequently behaved as if the intelligence test represented an adequate sampling of *all* these functions. For example, despite the recent work on cognition and creativity, the latter concept is still generally treated as if it applied

FROM C. W. TAYLOR (ED.), *The Third (1959) University of Utah Research Conference on the Identification of Creative Scientific Talent*, SALT LAKE CITY: UNIVERSITY OF UTAH PRESS, 1959. THE ARTICLE ALSO APPEARED IN C. W. TAYLOR AND F. BARRON (EDS.) *Scientific Creativity: Its Recognition and Development*, NEW YORK: JOHN WILEY AND SONS, 1963. REPRINTED BY PERMISSION OF THE SENIOR AUTHOR AND THE UNIVERSITY OF UTAH PRESS.

only to performance in one or more of the arts. In effect, the term "creative child" has become synonymous with the expression, "child with artistic talents," thus limiting our attempts to identify and foster cognitive abilities related to creative functioning in areas other than the arts.

And finally, third, there has been a failure to attend sufficiently to the difference between the *definition* of giftedness as given by the I.Q. and the variations in the *value* placed upon giftedness as so defined. It is often taken for granted, for example, that the gifted child is equally valued by teachers and by parents, in the classroom and at home; that he is considered an equally good prospect by teachers and by parents to succeed as an adult; and that children themselves *want* to be gifted. It is demonstrable that none of these assumptions can be held without question. Empirical data indicates that the gifted child is *not* equally valued by teachers and by parents, in the classroom and at home; he is not held to be an equally good prospect to succeed as an adult; and children themselves do *not* necessarily want to be gifted, at least not in the traditional sense of the term.

Despite its longevity, there is nothing inevitable about the use of the I.Q. in defining giftedness. Indeed, it may be argued that in many ways this definition is only an historical happenstance—a consequence of the fact that early inquiries in this field had the classroom as their context and academic achievement as their major concern. If we moved the focus of inquiry from the classroom setting, we might identify qualities defining giftedness for other situations just as the I.Q. did for the classroom. Indeed, even *without* shifting our focus of inquiry, if we only modified the conventional criteria of achievement, we might change the qualities defining giftedness even in the classroom. For example, if we recognized that learning involves the production of novelty as well as the remembrance of course content, then measures of creativity as well as the I.Q. might become appropriate in defining characteristics of giftedness.

The series of studies we are now conducting is based on the foregoing consideration. Broadly speaking, these studies attempt to deal not only with intelligence as the quality defining giftedness but with such other qualities as creativity, psychological health, morality, and the like. Comparisons between groups of adolescents who are outstanding in these qualities serve as the basic analytic procedure of the research.

Problem

The central task we set ourselves in the specific part of the research we are presenting here was to differentiate two groups of adolescents—one group representing individuals very high in measures of intelligence, but *not* high in measures of creativity, the other group representing individuals very high in measures of creativity, but *not* high in measures of intelligence—and to compare the two groups with respect to the following questions: (See Getzels and Jackson, 1958a, b, c, and 1959).

1. What is the relative achievement—achievement as defined by learning in school—of the two groups?
2. Which of the two groups is preferred by teachers?
3. What is the relative need for achievement—as defined by McClelland's measures—of the two groups?
4. What are the personal qualities the two groups prefer for themselves?
5. What is the relationship between the personal qualities preferred by the two groups for themselves and the personal qualities they believe teachers would like to see in children?
6. What is the relationship between the personal qualities preferred by the two groups for themselves and the personal qualities they believe lead to "success" in adult life?
7. What is the nature of the fantasy productions of the two groups?
8. What are the career aspirations of the two groups?

Identifying the experimental groups: subjects, instruments, procedures

The experimental groups were drawn from 449 adolescents comprising the total population of a Midwestern private secondary school on the basis of performance on the following instruments:

1. Standard I.Q. tests. Either a Binet, a WISC, or a Henmon-Nelson score was available for each adolescent. The scores obtained from the WISC and the Henmon-Nelson were converted by regression equation to comparable Binet I.Q.'s.
2. Five creativity measures. These were taken or adapted from Guilford and Cattell, or constructed especially for the study, as follows:
   a. Word Association. The subject was asked to give as many definitions as possible to fairly common stimulus words, e.g., "bolt," "bark," "sack." His score depended upon the absolute number of definitions and the number of different categories into which these definitions could be put.
   b. Uses for Things. The subject was required to give as many uses as he could for objects that customarily have a stereotyped function attached to them, e.g., "brick," "paper-clip." His score depended upon both the number and originality of the uses which he mentioned.
   c. Hidden Shapes. The subject was required to find a given geometric form that was hidden in more complex geometric forms or patterns.
   d. Fables. The subject was presented with four fables in which the last lines were missing. He was required to compose three different endings for each fable: a "moralistic," a "humorous," and a "sad" ending. His score depended upon the number, appropriateness, and originality of the endings.
   e. Make-Up Problems. The subject was presented with four complex paragraphs each of which contained a number of numerical statements, e.g.,

"the costs involved in building a house." He was required to make up as many mathematical problems as he could that might be solved with the information given. His score depended upon the number, appropriateness, and originality of the problems.

On the basis of the I.Q. measure and a summated score on the five creativity instruments, the two experimental groups were formed as follows:

1. The High Creativity Group. These were subjects in the top 20% on the creativity measures when compared with like-sexed age peers, but *below* the top 20% in I.Q. (N = 26).
2. The High Intelligence Group. These were subjects in the top 20% in I.Q. when compared with like-sexed age peers, but *below* the top 20% on the creativity measures. (N = 28).

With the experimental groups thus defined it is possible to approach each of the research questions in turn.*

QUESTION 1: What is the relative school achievement of the two groups?

As the data in Table 1 indicate, the results were clear and striking. Despite the similarity in I.Q. between the high Creative and the school population, and the twenty-three point difference in mean I.Q. between the high Creatives and the high I.Q.'s, the achievement scores of the two experimental groups were *equally superior* to the achievement scores of the school population as a whole.

It was evident at this point that the cognitive functions by our creativity battery accounted for a significant portion of the variance in school achievement. Moreover, since our creative students were not in the top of their class by I.Q. standards their superiority in scholastic performance places them in the rather suspect category of so-called "over-achievers." This dubious classification often implies that the observed I.Q.–Achievement discrepancy is a function of motivational (as opposed to cognitive) variables. It is assumed that the motivational elements pushing the student to out-do himself, as it were, are linked in varying degree to pathological conditions. We could raise the issue, at least for our present group, whether it is motivational pathology or intellectual creativity that accounts for their superior scholastic achievement. Indeed, we wonder whether the current studies of cognitive functions other than those assessed by standard I.Q. tests do not underscore the need for reexamining the entire concept of "over-achievement."

QUESTION 2: Which of the two groups was preferred by teachers? To answer this question we asked the teachers to rate all students in the school on the degree to which they would enjoy having them in class. The ratings of the two groups were then compared with those of the entire school population.

* As might be expected, the Creativity measures and I.Q. were not independent, the correlation between the two ranging from 0 to .56. Adolescents high in both Creativity and I.Q. are the focus of an investigation now in progress.

TABLE 1 Means and Standard Deviations of Highly Creative and Highly Intelligent Groups on Experimental Variables

		TOTAL POPULATION[a]	HIGH I.Q.	HIGH CREATIVE
		(N = 449)	(N = 28)	(N = 24)
I.Q.	$\overline{X}$	132.00	150.00**	127.00
		15.07	6.64	10.58
School	$\overline{X}$	49.91	55.00**	56.27**
Achievement		7.36	5.95	7.90
Teacher	$\overline{X}$	10.23	11.20*	10.54
Preference		3.64	1.56	1.95
Ratings				
Need	$\overline{X}$	49.81	49.00	50.04
Achievement		9.49	7.97	8.39
(T-scores)				

[a] For purposes of comparison the scores of each experimental group were extracted from the total population before the tests were computed.
* Significant at the .01 level.
** Significant at the .001 level.

The results, which are shown in Table 1, were again quite clearcut. The high I.Q. group stands out as being more desirable than the average student, the high creative group does not. It is apparent that an adolescent's desirability as a student is not a simple function of his academic standing. Even though their academic performance, as measured by achievement tests, is equal, the high I.Q. student is preferred to the high Creative student.

This finding leads one to suspect either that there are important variables, in addition to the purely cognitive ones, that distinguish the experimental groups, or that the discriminating cognitive functions are themselves differentially preferable in the classroom. Actually, these alternatives should not be posed as either-or since, as we shall demonstrate, evidence can be adduced which tends to support both points of view.

QUESTION 3: What is the relative need for achievement of the two groups?

In effect, we wanted to know here whether the superior school achievement of the high Creatives—by I.Q. standards, their so-called "over-achievement"— could be accounted for by differences in motivation to achieve. To answer this question we administered six of the McClelland n:Achievement stimulus-pictures. Each picture was shown on a screen for 30 seconds and the subjects were given four minutes in which to write their responses. The results are presented in Table 1 and show no differences in n:Achievement between the high Creatives, the high I.Q.'s, and the total school population.

This failure to find differences does not, of course, mean that differences in motives do not exist. We could, and did, use other assessment procedures aimed at identifying motivational and attitudinal differences between the experimental groups. The next group of three questions deals with our efforts in this direction.

QUESTION 4: What are the personal qualities that the two groups prefer for themselves?

QUESTION 5: What is the relationship between the personal qualities preferred by the two groups for themselves and the personal qualities they believe teachers prefer for them?

QUESTION 6: What is the relationship between the personal qualities preferred by the two groups for themselves and the personal qualities they believe lead to "success" in adult life?

Answers to these questions were obtained from data provided by an instrument called the Outstanding Traits Test. The instrument contained descriptions of 13 children, each of the 13 exemplifying some desirable personal quality or trait. For example, one child is described as having the highest I.Q. in the entire school, another as being the best athlete, another as having the best sense of humor, another as being the best-looking, another as being the most creative person in the school, and so on.

Our subjects ranked these 13 children in three ways: (1) on the degree to which they would like to be like them; (2) on the degree to which they believed teachers would like them; (3) on the degree to which they believed people with these various qualities would succeed in adult life.

The entire population of the school almost without exception ranked "social skills" first as the quality in which they would like to be outstanding, and "athletics," "good-looks," "high energy level," and "health" last. In view of this very high agreement, we re-ranked the responses omitting the uniformly-ranked qualities. The findings we are reporting here are on the re-ranked data.

The high I.Q.'s ranked the qualities in which they would like to be outstanding in the following order: (1) character, (2) emotional stability, (3) goal directedness, (4) creativity, (5) wide range of interests, (6) high marks, (7) I.Q., (8) sense of humor. The high Creatives ranked the qualities in the following order: (1) emotional stability, (2) sense of humor, (3) character, (4.5) wide range of interests, (4.5) goal directedness, (6) creativity, (7) high marks, (8) I.Q. Most noteworthy here is the extraordinarily high ranking given by the Creative group to "sense of humor," a ranking which not only distinguishes them from the high I.Q. group (who ranked it last) but from all other groups we have studied.

Perhaps the most striking and suggestive of the differences between the two groups are observed in the relationship of the qualities they want for themselves and the qualities they believe lead to adult success and the qualities they believe teachers favor.

For the high I.Q. group, the rank-order correlation between the qualities they would like to have themselves and the qualities making for adult success was .81; for the high Creativity group it was .10. For the high I.Q. group, the correlation between the qualities they would like to have themselves and the qualities they believe teachers favor was .67; for the high Creativity group it was (minus) −.25. The data are presented in Table 2.

TABLE 2 Rank Order Correlations Among Sub-sections of the Outstanding Traits Test

COMPONENTS OF CORRELATIONS	SUBJECTS	
	I.Q. (N = 28)	Creative (N = 26)
"Personal traits believed predictive of success" and "Personal traits believed favored by teachers"	.62	.59
"Personal traits preferred for oneself" and "Personal traits believed predictive of adult success"	.81	.10
"Personal traits preferred for oneself" and "Personal traits believed favored by teachers"	.67	−.25

In effect, where the high I.Q. adolescent wants the qualities he believes make for adult success and the qualities that are similar to those he believes his teachers like, the high Creative adolescent favors personal qualities having no relationship to those he believes make for adult success and are in some ways the reverse of those he believes his teachers favor.

These findings reflect directly on the answers to two earlier questions—the one on teacher ratings and the one on the relationship between creativity and school achievement. If the desirability of students in the classroom is related to the congruence or discrepancy between their values and their teacher's values, then in the light of the above data it is hardly surprising that our high I.Q. students are favored by teachers more than are our creative students. Furthermore, if the motivational impetus represented by a concern with adult success and a desire to emulate the teacher is absent or weak among creative students, the observed relationship between creativity and school achievement becomes all the more significant.

QUESTION 7: What is the nature of the fantasies of the two groups?

In addition to scoring the n:Achievement protocols conventionally for the single achievement theme, we analyzed the *total content* of the stories. We first sorted "blind" 47 protocols written by matched creative and non-creative subjects. This blind sorting resulted in only seven misplacements. Using the categories suggested by this sorting, we then systematically analyzed the protocols of the two experimental groups. The analysis showed striking differences in the fantasy productions of the high I.Q.'s and the high Creatives. The Creatives made significantly greater use of *stimulus-free themes, unexpected endings, humor, incongruities,* and *playfulness.* The data are presented in Table 3.

Here, for example, in response to the picture-stimulus perceived most often as a man sitting in an airplane reclining seat returning from a business trip or professional conference, are case-type stories given by a high I.Q. subject and a high Creative subject.

THE HIGH I.Q. SUBJECT: "Mr. Smith is on his way home from a successful business trip. He is very happy and he is thinking about his wonderful family and

TABLE 3   Categorization of Fantasy Productions of Highly Creative and Highly Intelligent Group

CONTENT ANALYSIS CATEGORIES	HIGH CREATIVITY (N = 24)		HIGH I.Q. (N = 28)		
	Frequency[a] %		Frequency[a] %		χ^2
Stimulus-free theme	18	.75	11	.39	5.31**[b]
Unexpected ending	22	.92	17	.61	5.05*
Presence of humor	17	.71	7	.25	9.16**
Presence of incongruity	17	.71	10	.36	5.06*
Presence of violence	18	.75	13	.46	3.27
Playful attitude toward theme	21	.89	9	.32	14.04**

[a] Numbers in the frequency column represent the subjects whose fantasy productions fit the corresponding categories.
[b] Yates correction was applied in the computation of chi-squares.
* Significant at the .05 level.
** Significant at the .01 level.

how glad he will be to see them again. He can picture it, about an hour from now, his plane landing at the airport and Mrs. Smith and their three children all there welcoming him home again."

THE HIGH CREATIVE SUBJECT: "This man is flying back from Reno where he has just won a divorce from his wife. He couldn't stand to live with her anymore, he told the judge, because she wore so much cold cream on her face at night that her head would skid across the pillow and hit him in the head. He is now contemplating a new skid-proof face cream."

Or one more, this in response to the stimulus-picture most often perceived as a man working late (or very early) in an office.

THE HIGH I.Q. SUBJECT: "There's ambitious Bob, down at the office at 6:30 in the morning. Every morning it's the same. He's trying to show his boss how energetic he is. Now, thinks Bob, maybe the boss will give me a raise for all my extra work. The trouble is that Bob has been doing this for the last three years, and the boss still hasn't given him a raise. He'll come in at 9:00, not even noticing that Bob had been there so long, and poor Bob won't get his raise."

THE HIGH CREATIVE SUBJECT: "This man has just broken into this office of a new cereal company. He is a private-eye employed by a competitor firm to find out the formula that makes the cereal bend, sag, and sway. After a thorough search of the office he comes upon what he thinks is the current formula. He is now copying it. It turns out that it is the wrong formula and the competitor's factory blows up. Poetic justice!"

Recall that these stories are written in group sessions, often more than a hundred adolescents in the same room, with the maximum writing time four minutes per story. "Skid-proof face cream!" "Cereal that will bend, sag, and sway!" It seems to us that it is this ability to restructure stereotyped objects with ease and rapidity—almost "naturally"—that is the characteristic mark of our high Creatives as against our high I.Q. subjects.

There is one other characteristic that is well illustrated by a number of the stories. This is a certain mocking attitude on the part of the Creatives toward what they call the All-American Boy—a theme that is almost never mentioned by the high I.Q.'s. Here, for example, are two responses to the stimulus-picture most often perceived as a high school student doing his homework.

THE HIGH I.Q. SUBJECT: "John is a college student who posed for the picture while doing his homework. It is an average day with the usual amount of work to do. John took a short break from his studies to pose for the pictures, but he will get back to his work immediately after. He has been working for an hour already and he has an hour's more work to go. After he finishes he will read a book and then go to bed. This work which he is doing is not especially hard but it has to be done."

THE HIGH CREATIVE SUBJECT: "The boy's name is Jack Evans and he is a senior in school who gets C's and B's, hates soccer, does not revolt against convention, and has a girl friend named Lois, who is a typical sorority fake. He is studying when someone entered the room whom he likes. He has a dull life in terms of anything that is not average. His parents are pleased because they have a red-blooded American boy. Actually, he is horribly average. He will go to college, take over his dad's business, marry a girl, and do absolutely nothing in the long run."

This "anti-red-blooded-boy" theme is also quite consistent with the Creatives' rejection of "success" which was mentioned earlier.

QUESTION 8: What are the career aspirations of the two groups?

We have just begun the analysis of the data in this area. But this much is already clear—the two groups do indeed give different occupational choices and career aspirations. The data are presented in Table 4.

When the two groups were asked, on sentence-completion type question-

TABLE 4   Quantity and Quality of Occupations Mentioned by the Experimental Groups on Direct and Indirect Sentence Completion Tests[a]

| TEST | GROUP | NUMBER OF OCCUPATIONS MENTIONED | | | UNUSUAL OCCUPATIONS | |
		Total	$\overline{X}$	σ	Number Mentioned	Number of S's Mentioning
Direct	I.Q. (N = 28)	51	1.82*	1.09	6	5**
	Creative (N = 26)	68	2.61*	1.41	24	16**
Indirect	I.Q. (N = 28)	100	3.57**	1.81	12	10*
	Creative (N = 26)	130	5.00**	1.80	29	17*

[a] t was used to test differences between means in the fourth column. χ^2 was used to test differences between frequencies in the seventh column.
   * Significant at .05 level.
   ** Significant at .01 level.

naires, to report the kinds of occupations they would like to have, the high Creatives mentioned a significantly greater variety of occupations than did the high I.Q.'s. When the types of occupations mentioned are divided into conventional and unconventional career categories—e.g., doctor, engineer, businessman, were classified as conventional; inventor, artist, spaceman, disc jockey, as unconventional—18% of the high I.Q.'s give unconventional career aspirations; 67% of the high Creatives give such aspirations.

Discussion

Several conceptual formulations may be adduced to account for the present data. In the context of this conference, however, we suggest that Guilford's factors of convergent and divergent thinking are highly relevant. Discussing the production of tests to assess these factors, he states:

In tests of convergent thinking there is almost always one conclusion or answer that is regarded as unique, and thinking is to be channeled or controlled in the direction of that answer . . . In divergent thinking, on the other hand, there is much searching about or going off in various directions. This is most easily seen when there is no unique conclusion. Divergent thinking . . . (is) characterized . . . as being less goal-bound. There is freedom to go off in different directions . . . Rejecting the old solution and striking out in some new direction is necessary, and the resourceful organism will more probably succeed. (See Guilford, 1957.)

It seems to us that the essence of the performance of our Creative adolescents lay in their ability to produce new forms, to risk conjoining elements that are customarily thought of as independent and dissimilar, to "go off in new directions." The creative adolescent seemed to possess the ability to free himself from the usual, to "diverge" from the customary. He seemed to enjoy the risk and uncertainty of the unknown. In contrast the high I.Q. adolescent seemed to possess to a high degree the ability and the need to focus on the usual, to be "channelled and controlled" in the direction of the right answer—the customary. He appeared to shy away from the risk and the uncertainty of the unknown and to seek out the safety and security of the known.

Furthermore, and most important, these differences do not seem to be restricted to the cognitive functioning of these two groups. The data with respect to both intellectually-oriented and socially-oriented behavior are of a piece, and the findings with regard to each of the eight questions can be put into the same conceptual formulation. The high I.Q.'s tend to converge upon stereotyped meanings, to perceive personal success by conventional standards, to move toward the model provided by teachers, to seek out careers that conform to what is expected of them. The high Creatives tend to diverge from stereotyped meanings, to produce original fantasies, to perceive personal success by unconventional standards, to seek out careers that do not conform to what is expected of them.

Turning to the social implications of this research, and, indeed, of the great bulk of research dealing with creativity, there seems to be little doubt as to which of these two personal orientations receives the greater welcome in the majority of our social institutions. Guilford, who quite clearly perceived this social bias, states, "(Education) has emphasized abilities in the areas of convergent thinking and evaluation, often at the expense of development in the area of divergent thinking. We have attempted to teach students how to arrive at 'correct' answers that our civilization has taught us are correct. This is convergent thinking . . . Outside the arts we have generally discouraged the development of divergent-thinking abilities, unintentionally but effectively." (See Guilford, 1957.)

It is, we believe no less than a tragedy that in American education at all levels we fail to distinguish between our convergent and divergent talents—or, even worse, that we try to convert our divergent students into convergent students. Divergent fantasy is called "rebellious" rather than *germinal;* unconventional career choice is called "unrealistic" rather than *courageous.*

It is our hope that the present emphasis upon research in creativity will enlarge our understanding of cognitive functioning in both the laboratory and the classroom.

REFERENCES

1. Getzels, J. W. & Jackson, P. W. The social context of giftedness: A multidimensional approach to definition and method. Paper read at the American Sociological Society Meetings, Seattle, Wn., August 1958. (a)
2. ———. The highly creative and the highly intelligent adolescent: An attempt at differentiation. Paper read at the A.P.A. Meeting, Washington, September, 1958. (b)
3. ———. The meaning of "giftedness": An examination of an expanding concept. *Phi Delta Kappan,* 1958, *40,* 75–77. (c)
4. ———. Occupational choice and cognitive functioning: A study of the career aspirations of highly intelligent and of highly creative adolescents. Paper read at the A.P.A. Meeting, Cincinnati, Ohio, September, 1959.
5. Guilford, J. P. A revised structure of intellect. *Rep. Psychol. Lab.,* No. *19,* Los Angeles: Univer. of Southern Calif., 1957.

[11]   E. Paul Torrance & Dean C. Dauw   ATTITUDE

PATTERNS OF CREATIVELY GIFTED

HIGH SCHOOL SENIORS

In two previous articles . . . Torrance and Dauw (1965ab) have discussed the mental health problems, aspirations, and dreams of creatively gifted high school seniors as identified by tests of creative thinking ability. In other sources, Dauw (1966ab) has reported findings concerning the personality self-descriptions and life experiences of these highly creative young people. We believe that such information has contributed to a deeper understanding of creative development and of the problems and aspirations of these young people. It has also increased our understanding of and confidence in the potentiality of tests of creative thinking ability to help identify a kind of giftedness that makes a great deal of difference in the lives of people. The present study is an attempt to extend our understandings of the dynamics of the mental and personality functioning tapped by the tests of creative thinking in the direction of attitude patterns and orientations to life.

In what is perhaps thus far the most important study of the personality dynamics of high school seniors, Parloff and Datta (1965) of the National Institute of Mental Health studied the males who competed in the 1963 Westinghouse Science Talent Search. This highly competitive program attempts to discover young people whose scientific achievements, skills, and abilities indicate potential creative originality. From the over 2,500 male applicants who completed successfully all entry requirements, Parloff and Datta selected the 573 who scored in the upper one-fifth on a science aptitude examination. Each of these subjects had also submitted a report describing his independently conducted research project. This project had been initiated and conducted by the contestant over as long a period as he felt necessary, ranging from a few weeks to three years. The judges scored the entries for "creativity and potential creativity."

Parloff and Datta (1965) regard this product criterion as a valid predictor because it is quite comparable to the criterion used to assess the creative contributions of adult scientists. They identified three groups on the basis of their criteria: Group I, High Potential Creativity, including 112 men; Group II,

FROM Gifted Child Quarterly, SUMMER 1966, 53–57. REPRINTED BY PERMISSION OF THE SENIOR AUTHOR AND THE PUBLISHER.

Moderate Potential Creativity, including 140; and Group III, Low Potential Creativity, including 285. These groups were then compared on a variety of life experience and personality test variables.

The investigators found no meaningful differences among these three groups of young men on age, intelligence, measured scientific aptitude, vocations of fathers, socioeconomic status, and intactness of family. There were statistically significant differences, however, on the California Psychological Inventory when the members of Group I were compared with those in Group III. Those in Group I were more ambitious and driving; more independent, autonomous, self-reliant; more efficient and perceptive; more rebellious toward rules and constraints; and more imaginative.

Parloff and Datta's subjects were not administered a test of creative thinking ability. Thus, one of the purposes of the present study is to determine whether or not high school seniors identified as creatively gifted solely on the basis of a battery of tests of creative thinking ability possess characteristics similar to the subjects of Parloff and Datta's study. The subjects of our study were not administered the California Psychological Inventory, but the Runner Studies of Attitude Patterns used in this study attempts to assess many of the same variables. Furthermore, the Runner instrument (Runner and Runner, 1965) is of interest to us because of its attempt to assess many of the orientations or attitudes patterns that directly help understand the dynamics of creative functioning.

Procedures

The 115 creatively gifted high school seniors studied herein were selected from a population of 712 seniors in a single metropolitan high school on the basis of the Abbreviated Form of the Torrance Tests of Creative Thinking (1962, 1966). This battery includes two verbal tasks (Product Improvement and Unusual Uses of Tin Cans) and two figural tasks (Incomplete Figures and Circles), each requiring ten minutes. All tasks were scored on both originality and elaboration, using a standardized scoring guide.

The test of creative thinking ability was administered in September, 1964, to all 712 seniors. The Runner Studies of Attitude Patterns (Interview Form III) was administered to the 115 creatively gifted students in May, 1965. The inventory section of this instrument consists of 118 questions that are answered "Yes" or "No." The following are sample items:

Do you enjoy trying out a hunch just to see what will happen?
Do you prefer a life of dependable regularity?
Are you careful to follow the rules of proper social behavior at all times?

Responses are scored for each of the following attitudes or orientations: Experimental, Rules, Intuitive, Planfulness, Power, Passive Compliance, Extraversiveness, Hostility, Resistance to Social Pressure, Social Anxiety, Pleasure in Tool-Implemented Hand Skills, and Performance Anxiety.

On the basis of factor analysis procedures, five orientations or clusters of scales have been identified. Experimental Orientation, Intuitive Orientation, Resistance to Social Pressure, and Tool Interests make up the Freedom Orienta- tion. The Control Orientation cluster includes Rules Orientation, Plans and Structure, Hostility, and Passive Compliance. The Achievement Oriented scales are Resistance to Social Pressure, Experimental Orientation, and Power Drive. The Recognition Orientation scales are Extraversion and Power Drive. The Anxiety Oriented scales are Social Anxiety and Performance Anxiety.

The scores of the 115 creatively gifted seniors (56 girls and 59 boys) were compared with those of a sample of 100 records of unselected job applicants. As indicated in a previous article (Torrance and Dauw, 1965b), the age distribu- tion, distribution of parental occupations, and the like of these 100 subjects are quite similar to those of the population from which our 115 creatively gifted seniors came.

Results

Each of the records of the 115 creatively gifted seniors and 100 unselected job applicants was analyzed for high patterns on the Runner Studies of Atti- tude Patterns. A high pattern was defined as a score that places one in the upper 25 per cent of the Runners' adult norm group. The comparison of the occurrence of high patterns among the highly creative seniors and the compari- son group is presented in Table 1. It will be noted that the differences are quite impressive. A far greater proportion of the creative seniors than the members of the comparison group have high Experimental, Intuitive, and Resistance to Social Pressure orientations. Far more of the members of the comparison group have high patterns on Rules and Tradition, Planfulness (Need for Structure), and Passive Compliance. There is also a statistically significant tendency for the unselected subjects to have high scores on Hostility and Blame.

On most of the scales, the proportion of high patterns was almost identical for the creative boys and the creative girls. A larger proportion of the creative girls than the creative boys had high patterns on Passive Compliance (46 per cent compared with 20 per cent) and a larger proportion of the boys than the girls have high patterns on Power Orientation (25 per cent compared with 5 per cent). Compared with the norm population, however, few of the young people in this study have high patterns on Power Orientation. The orientations of the seniors high on Originality did not significantly differ from those on Elaboration.

Next, each set of profiles was analyzed according to the clusters of scales or orientations. Again, a high pattern was defined as one that placed the subject in the upper 25 per cent of the adult norm group. To qualify as having a high

TABLE 1 Comparison of High Patterns of Highly Creative High School Seniors and a Similar Unselected Group on the Runner Studies of Attitude Patterns

ATTITUDE OR ORIENTATION	CREATIVE SENIORS ($N = 115$)		UNSELECTED ($N = 100$)	
	Number	Per cent	Number	Per cent
Experimental	94	82	23	23°
Intuitive	105	91	56	56°
Rules and Tradition	22	19	40	40°
Planfulness (Structure)	17	15	44	44°
Power and Authority	18	17	18	18
Passive Compliance	38	33	56	56°
Extraversiveness	51	44	44	44
Hostility and Blame	47	41	59	59°°
Resistance to Social Pressure	76	66	35	35°
Social Anxiety	91	79	70	70
Pleasure in Tool-Implemented Hand Skills	66	57	78	78
Performance Anxiety	88	76	70	70

° Difference in percentages is significant at better than .01 level.
°° Difference in percentages is significant at better than .05 level.

pattern, the subject was required to have high patterns on all of the scales composing a cluster. An exception was made on the Freedom and Control Orientations when three of the four scales met the criteria and the fourth fell only one point short of this standard. The data comparing the creative seniors with the comparison sample are shown in Table 2. The differences shown here are even more impressive than those shown in Table 1. The high Freedom and low Control Orientations of the creative seniors stands out in even bolder relief. Perhaps more impressive, however, is the difference in Achievement Orientation. Almost one-half of the creative subjects compared with only four per cent of the unselected young people have high patterns on Achievement Orientation. The differences on the Recognition and Anxiety Orientations are less impressive but again reflect the strong drive, ambitiousness, and conflicts of the highly creative young person.

There are no statistically significant differences in the distribution of high orientations among the creative boys and the creative girls. The high Elaborators tend more frequently than the high Originals to have Freedom patterns (79 per cent compared with 53 per cent). The high Originals tend more fre-

TABLE 2   Comparison of Orientations of Highly Creative High School Seniors and a Similar Unselected Group on the Runner Studies of Attitude Patterns

ORIENTATION	CREATIVE SENIORS (N = 115)		UNSELECTED (N = 100)	
	Number	Per cent	Number	Per cent
Freedom Orientation	68	59	15	15*
Control Orientation	10	9	36	36*
Achievement Orientation	51	44	4	4*
Recognition Orientation	47	41	21	21*
Anxiety Orientation	77	67	55	55**

*Difference in percentages is significant at better than .01 level.
** Difference in percentages is significant at better than .05 level.

quently than the high Elaborators to have strong Achievement orientations (53 per cent compared with 41 per cent). These differences approach the .05 level of significance.

Discussion

The attitude patterns and orientations to life that characterize the highly creative high school seniors studied by the authors are quite compatible with the results of the Parloff and Datta study of the most promising of the participants in the Westinghouse Science Talent Search and with those of studies of eminent creative persons. This is of special interest, since many of our subjects express their creative abilities and needs outside of the sciences (art, music, writing, dancing, politics, and the like). As a group, our creatively gifted seniors can be described as high in Freedom Orientation, low in Control Orientation, high in Achievement Orientation, high in Recognition Orientation, and high in Anxiety Orientation. These findings are rich in clues for parents, teachers, and counselors in finding more productive ways of working with creative young people. From them, it is easy to understand why they react more favorably, learn more, produce more, and behave more constructively to a responsive environment than to a control or authority oriented one.

The relatively large proportion of high patterns among the creative seniors is of special interest in the light of the Runners' (1965) rationale concerning the meaning of high and low patterns. The Runners maintain that high patterns indicate that the person feels intensely about things and tries to resolve his inner conflicts by committing himself vigorously to activities that permit him to discharge his feelings. Such a person has a desire to lose himself in intense absorbing, emotionally expressive activity. A person having generally low patterns, according to the Runners, usually dislikes all forms of uncontrolled emotional expression. The finding here is consistent with those of studies of eminent creative adults who are usually described as strongly committed, seeming to be motivated by a sense of destiny. It is interesting that this indicator appears so strongly in the creative seniors identified by the tests of creative thinking ability employed in this investigation.

Summary

From a population of 712 seniors administered the Abbreviated form of the Torrance Tests of Creative Thinking, 115 highly creative high school seniors were identified and administered the *Runner Studies of Attitude Patterns*. These 115 creatively gifted seniors were compared with a similar group of unselected job applicants tested by the Runners. The creative seniors more frequently than the comparison group have high patterns on the Experimental, Intuitive, and Resistance to Social Pressures scales and less frequently have high patterns on Rules and Tradition, Planfulness (Structure), Passive Compliance, and Hostility and Blame. Using the clusters determined by factors analysis procedures, the creative seniors also more frequently have high Freedom, Achievement, Recognition, and Anxiety Orientations and less frequently have high Control Orientations. There were no highly significant differences between the creative boys and the creative girls and between the high Elaborators and the high Originals, as identified by the tests of creative thinking ability. These findings are rich in suggestiveness for more productive ways of teaching and guiding creatively gifted young people.

REFERENCES

Dauw, D. C. "Life Experiences of Original Thinkers and Good Elaborators." *Exceptional Children,* 1966, 32, 433–440. (a)
Dauw, D. C. "Personality Self-Descriptions of Original Thinkers and Good Elaborators." *Psychology in the Schools,* 1966, 3, 78–79.
Parloff, M. B. and Lois-Ellin Datta. "Personality Characteristics of the Potentially Creative Scientist." *Science and Psychoanalysis,* 1965, 8, 91–106.
Torrance, E. P. *Guiding Creative Talent.* Englewood Cliffs, N. J.: Prentice-Hall, Inc., 1962.
Torrance, E. P. *Torrance Tests of Creative Thinking.* Princeton, N. J.: Personnel Press, Inc., 1966.
Torrance, E. P. and D. C. Dauw. "Mental Health Problems of Three Groups of Highly Creative High School Seniors." *Gifted Child Quarterly,* 1965, 9, 123–127. (a).
Torrance, E. P. and D. C. Dauw. "Aspirations and Dreams of Three Groups of Creatively Gifted High School Seniors and a Comparable Unselected Group." *Gifted Child Quarterly,* 1965, 9, 177–182.

[12] *Robert J. Havighurst* CONDITIONS PRODUCTIVE OF SUPERIOR CHILDREN

Children become mentally superior through a combination of being born with superior potential and being raised in a superior environment. Nobody knows the relative importance of these two factors. Certainly, biological intelligence is too low in some children to permit them to develop even average mental ability. Probably a severe environmental handicap can prevent the potentially most able child from showing more than average mental ability.

It seems probable that our society actually discovers and develops no more than perhaps half its potential intellectual talent. Some evidence for this statement lies in the fact that former immigrant groups, which at one time did the heavy labor of America, at first produced very few mentally superior children; but after a sojourn in this country of two or three generations, they have produced large numbers of mentally superior people. They did this through bettering the environment in which they reared their children. The same process is now going on in the underprivileged groups of today—the Negroes, the Puerto Ricans, the rural southern whites—as they secure better economic conditions and then create a more favorable environment for the mental development of their children.

There is some validity to a view of the production of mentally superior people as a *processing* of human material. Some of this material is of better biological quality than other parts of it, but it all depends heavily on social processing for the quality of the final product.

In this paper we shall deliberately ignore the biological element in the production of mentally superior children and consider only the cultivation of mental superiority through the family, the school, and the community. We shall try to answer the question: What kind of social environment produces mentally superior children most efficiently, and how can we expand this environment and make it more effective?

Social class and cities

Mentally superior children come in relatively high proportions from upper and upper-middle class families and in relatively lower proportions from lower

FROM *Teachers College Record*, 1961, 62, 524–531. REPRINTED BY PERMISSION OF THE AUTHOR AND THE PUBLISHER.

working class families. This fact has been affirmed in dozens of studies of the relations between IQ and socio-economic status.

Some idea of the relative efficiencies of the various social classes in processing their children for mental ability is given in Table 1, which comes from a

TABLE 1   Efficiencies of the Various Social Classes in Producing Children in Top and Bottom Quarters of IQ Distribution

Sixth Grade in River City

SOCIAL CLASS	Percentage Distribution of Children	EFFICIENCY RATIO[1] IN PRODUCING CHILDREN IN	
		Top Quarter	Bottom Quarter
Upper and Upper Middle	10	1.8	.4
Lower Middle	27	1.5	.6
Upper Lower	39	.8	1.1
Lower Lower	24	.4	1.6

[1] These ratios indicate the relative efficiencies of the various social classes. If all classes were equally efficient in producing children of a given quartile in IQ, the ratios would all be 1.

study of all the children in the sixth grade of the public schools of a medium-sized midwestern city. The upper and upper-middle classes, combined, produced 1.8 times as many children in the upper quarter of the IQ distribution as they would if all social classes had been equally efficient at this, and only .4 times as many children in the lowest quarter. The lower working class showed a reversal of these efficiency ratios.

If all four socio-economic groups had been as efficient as the upper and upper-middle class groups in providing children with IQ's in the top quarter (above about 110), there would have been 180 children with IQ's over 110 in this community for every 100 such children today. In other words, the numbers of mentally superior children would have been almost doubled, and the intelligence level of the child population would have been lifted enormously.

Similar conclusions arise from a study of high school seniors in a city of 500,000. Roughly 5 per cent of the seniors were selected by a systematic screening program as being "academically superior." As can be seen in Table 2, the various high schools contributed to this total in rough proportion to the socio-economic status of the parents. The school with highest socio-economic status contributed 19 per cent of its seniors to the select group. Within this group, 92

TABLE 2 Efficiencies of Schools of Various Socio-Economic Levels in Producing Academically Superior High School Seniors

Data from an American city of 500,000 population.

| | HIGH SCHOOL | | | | | | |
	A	B	C	D	E	FGH	Total
No. of graduates	412	392	325	71	400	1,203	2,803
No. of superior students in graduating class	77	45	30	5	17	20	194
Per cent of superior students	19	12	9	7	4	1.5	5.1
Rank in Socio-economic status	1	2	3	4	5	7	
No. of superior students if A ratio prevailed	77	74	62	14	76	229	532

per cent of the fathers were high school graduates; 65 per cent were college graduates. The three schools with lowest socio-economic status contributed 1.5 per cent of their seniors to the select group. Less than 40 per cent of the fathers of the superior students in these three schools were high school graduates. If all schools had contributed as efficiently as School A to the production of superior students, there would have been 532 instead of 194, or almost three times as many. Probably the reason this proportion is higher than the proportion reported in Table 1 is that Table 1 refers to sixth graders, Table 2 to twelfth graders. The cultural advantages of the higher status children probably cumulated between the sixth and twelfth grades to give them even greater superiority over their less privileged age-mates.

Granted the assumption we are making in this paper—that mental superiority is largely a product of social environment—the mental level of the population would be raised very greatly if we could give all children the kinds of social environment which upper middle class children have today.

Mentally superior children also tend to come from urban and suburban communities, rather than from rural communities. This is not as pronounced an effect as the social class effect, but it seems to indicate that the urban-suburban environment is more stimulating mentally than the rural environment.

Within the families lower on the socio-economic scale, there is enough production of mentally superior youth to indicate that socio-economic status alone is not what makes the difference between a good and poor environment for mental growth. It is probably certain cultural and motivational deprivations that often go with low socio-economic status that reduce the efficiency of lower status families. Whenever a very bright boy or girl is discovered in a family of low economic status, it turns out that this family has unusual characteristics which give the youth an advantage. These characteristics may consist of thrift and ambition or of an interest on the part of the mother or father in literature, art, or science.

Summing up the argument thus far, it seems that boys and girls who are mentally superior have become so because of (1) a home and school environment which stimulated them to learn and to enjoy learning; (2) parents and other significant persons who set examples of interest and attainment in education which the children unconsciously imitated, and (3) early family training which produced a desire for achievement in the child. When these influences act upon a child with average or better biological equipment for learning, the child will become mentally superior. They are sometimes found in unexpected places.

For instance, Paul is a very good student in high school. His mother has worked as a waitress for years, since her husband deserted her, to support herself and Paul. She placed Paul in a boys' home sponsored by a church, and he has lived there from the age of 8 until his present age of 18. He says, "My father and mother never went to college. I thought I'd like to do better in life than they did." At the boys' home, the superintendent and the teachers were demanding but warm. Under them, Paul performed well in the elementary school until time for senior high, when he went to the local public school. Here he had some difficulty at first. He says, "English was about my worst subject. The teacher helped me though, and I improved a lot. I consider her an important person in my life." A careers unit in civics helped him to decide on engineering or mathematics, and he will go to college with scholarship help. Two of his closest friends have college plans. The superintendent of the home has urged him to go. "He told me to go to college. He said I was a good student, and I ought to go to college."

Divergent thinkers

Among the mentally superior part of the population some people are creative and some are not. Much attention has been paid recently to the quality or qualities of creativity on the assumptions that our society needs not only intellectually facile people but, more especially, creative people, and that a high IQ does not guarantee creativity.

Guilford and others have made a distinction between "convergent thinking" and "divergent thinking." The person with "convergent" intellectual ability is retentive and docile. He tends to seek the single, predetermined "correct" answer to an intellectual problem. On the other hand, the "divergent" thinker is constructive and creative. He tends to seek the novel, experimental, and multiple answer to an intellectual problem.

Guilford has devised a number of tests of creative intelligence which have only a low positive correlation with the usual intelligence tests. Getzels and Jackson (3),* using these tests, picked out a group of high school pupils who were high in IQ (average 150) but not especially high in creative thinking for comparison with a group high in creative thinking but lower in IQ (average 127). The two groups did equally well in achievement tests, but the high intelligence, noncreative group were preferred by their teachers as the kind of students they liked to have in their classes. The high creative group, in freely-written stories, showed more humor, more unexpected endings, more incongruities, and generally a freer play of fantasy. Similarly, Cattell and Drevdahl (2) compared outstanding research scientists with outstanding teachers and administrators in the same fields on the 16 P.F. Personality Inventory. They found the researchers to be more self-sufficient and schizophrenic (introverted), to have a greater drive for mastery, and to entertain more radical ideas.

We know relatively little, as yet, about creative people and even less about what makes them creative. If it proves to be true that some or all of the qualities of creativity can be taught, this will become another goal in the society's processing of mentally superior children.

The under-achievers

In the study of intellectually superior children, attention has been called to a substantial group whose educational performance falls below what might reasonably be expected from their performance on intelligence tests. These mentally superior under-achievers are people with biological or environmental superiority who have not put their superiority to use in school. They may be regarded as products of an inadequate processing in the home, the community, or the school. This conclusion emerges from . . . studies of . . . under-achievers.

Thus, Terman and Oden, in their study of adults whom they had followed from childhood as gifted children (9), compared the 150 men in their sample who had been most successful in their occupations with the 150 least successful men. As children, these men had all had IQ's of 135 or higher. The more successful group had had an average IQ of 155 in 1922, while the less successful had had an average of 150. However, there were considerable differences in other respects between the two groups. Ninety per cent of the more successful had been graduated from college, compared with 37 per cent of the less successful. Fifty per cent of the fathers of the more successful group were college graduates, compared with only 16 per cent of the fathers of the less successful. In occupation, 38 per cent of the fathers of the more successful were professional men, compared with 19 per cent of the fathers of the less successful.

Terman concludes, "Where all are so intelligent, it follows necessarily that differences in success must be due largely to non-intellectual factors"; and "Everything considered, there is nothing in which the (more successful and

* The study is reprinted as Chapter 10 of this book.

less successful) groups present a greater contrast than in drive to achieve and in all-round social adjustment. . . . At any rate, we have seen that intellect and achievement are far from perfectly correlated."

Most of the studies of under-achievement have been made on boys rather than girls, because bright boys are under-achievers in school much more frequently than girls are. The many studies have produced substantially similar results and point to under-achievement as a form of personal and social maladjustment. In one or another of these studies, the following characteristics of underachieving able students appear:

1. They see themselves as inadequate persons.
2. They have lower aspirations than achievers.
3. They do not like school as well as achievers do.
4. They do not enjoy learning from books.
5. They have lower popularity and leadership status in the eyes of their age-mates.
6. They tend to come from homes that are broken or emotionally inadequate in other ways.
7. They tend to come from homes of low socio-economic status.
8. Their vocational goals are not as clearly defined as those of achievers.
9. Their study habits are not as good as those of achievers.
10. They have narrower interests than those of achievers.
11. They have poorer personal adjustment than that of achievers.

Haggard (6), comparing high with low achieving high IQ children, found that the high achievers had better mental health. In particular, the high achievers in arithmetic, "had by far the best-developed and healthiest egos, both in relation to their own emotions and mental processes and in their greater maturity in dealing with the outside world of people and things." Haggard concluded, "Our findings indicate that the best way to produce clear thinking is to help children develop into anxiety-free, emotionally healthy individuals who are also trained to master a variety of intellectual tasks."

Much the same conclusion is expressed by Gowan (4) after receiving a number of studies of underachievement. He says, "To summarize, achievement is an indication that the individual has successfully transferred a large enough portion of his basic libidinal drives to areas of cultural accomplishment so that he derives a significant portion of his gratification from them."

Although the general proposition seems justified that high IQ underachievers are people with inadequate socialization and poor personal-social adjustment, there are two major exceptions to this generalization. One exception refers to a group of high IQ boys with a limited horizon. They are well-adjusted within a small world which does not require more than average school achievement and does not require a college education. Take Kenny, for example. With an IQ of 145, Kenny found school work easy and more or less coasted through his studies, doing enough work to get fairly good grades, but falling down somewhat in high school, where he graduated at about the middle of his class. Kenny's parents were earnest people, good church members, with little formal education. They did not read very much and had no intellectual interests. They were satisfied with Kenny's report cards and pleased that he was going further in school than they had gone. They were especially pleased with Kenny's interest in earning money. He always had several jobs waiting for him and showed great enterprise as a salesman. During his later years in high school, he worked in a shoe store where his employer was so pleased with his work that he offered Kenny a full-time job and a chance to buy into his business when he was graduated from high school. This seemed good to Kenny, and he is now getting along well as junior partner in the store.

The other exception refers to a rather large group of girls with high intelligence who achieve very well up to the end of high school, when their grades fall off and they show little or no interest in going to college. These girls either get married as soon as they finish high school or they take a job in an office or a shop for a few years until they marry. Girls do not generally show as underachievers because their school grades are pretty well maintained until the end of high school. But they would be called underachievers if under-achievement were defined as failure to go as far in education as one's abilities would justify.

With this broad definition of under-achievement, one can say that the gifted underachievers have not been effectively processed by the society for maximal or optimal educational achievement for one or more of the following reasons:

Inadequate home environment leaves them personally maladjusted and unable to use their intellectual ability.

Inadequate home environment limits their horizon and fails to stimulate them to use education for vocational achievement, although they are personally well adjusted.

Inadequate home environment fails to instill in them a deep drive or need for achievement.

School and home together fail to instill in them an intrinsic love of learning.

The social role of wife and mother is seen by some girls as more important than that of student; and the home, school, and community have caused them to see a conflict between marriage and a home, on the one hand, and continued educational achievement on the other.

Increasing the supply

Holding to our tentative assumption that production of mentally superior people is more a matter of social engineering than of discovery and exploitation of a rare natural resource, we may essay an answer to the question of how to increase the supply of mentally superior children who are well motivated to achieve in school and college.

First, it must be remembered that our culturally deprived families, both in the big cities and in isolated rural areas, have always in the past improved themselves as producers of superior children when they had economic opportunity. The same process of improvement is evident today among working class Negroes, Puerto Ricans, and white emigrants from the rural South. It is to these groups that we may look for an increased supply of able youngsters, and the rate of increase is likely to be considerably facilitated by increasing their degree of economic opportunity and enriching their cultural environment. This point is a central one for those social policies related to our long-range needs for manpower and for school programs aimed at the underprivileged and academically impoverished. Within the schools, there is a grave need for greater attention to rewards for achievement within these groups, for a keener recognition of developing intellectual effort, and for a greater responsiveness to embryonic academic motives.

Second, counseling and guidance services could usefully focus on increasing educational motivation among superior pupils. The well adjusted child with limited horizons, like Kenny, represents a kind of national loss. If education is concerned with the actualizing of individual potentialities, then special attention to youngsters of this kind is more than warranted. A sound argument can be made for the school counselor's devoting more of his time to this sort of developmental enterprise than to the remediation of "problem cases" and to the support of the pathological, the delinquent, and the dull. Both kinds of service are desirable and necessary, of course; but we may have overemphasized the guidance workers' obligation to the educationally handicapped to the serious neglect, both in training and in on-the-job functionings of his potentialities for working productively with the superior child with low academic motivation.

Third, studies of the unconscious drive for achievement, like those by McClelland (7) and Rosen (8) indicate that the early training of boys in the home has a great deal to do with their motivation to use their mental ability for school achievement. Closer collaboration between school and home, especially with lower class parent groups, can be helpful here. Even more, an explicit and articulate concern with the development of intellectual motivations in the earliest school years could possibly harvest a more widespread drive for academic achievement and a deeper channeling of intellectual capacities into school work and the kinds of goals that our schools and colleges represent. It is not so much that boys lack a need to achieve, but they often find little reward in harnessing their motives to the activities of the conventional classroom or school.

Fourth, the demonstration that intellectually superior and "creative" abilities are not the same thing suggests that we could profitably expand our search for the gifted to include the "divergent thinker." More clarity and precision in our methods of identifying creative youngsters with above-average but not extremely high IQ's, and more imagination and effort in our attention to such children might yield a happy increment in the numbers of those able to think inventively about important problems. This approach requires, of course, that we reward the innovator, the person with new and deviant ways of dealing with the world; and while this requirement is one to which we all pay lip service, it is one that is likely to entail trouble and inconvenience if it is realistically met. That the trouble and inconvenience will be worth the result is highly probable, but the result hardly alters, although it may more than justify, the cost.

Finally, the most potent means of increasing the numbers of mentally superior children that lies at hand for teachers is to teach so that learning is made more attractive to children. This alone will cause children to increase their own mental abilities. For example, the experiment in Manhattanville Junior High School and the George Washington Senior High High School in New York City is having this effect (1). Boys and girls from culturally deprived families are getting an enriched program, combined with guidance and attempts to improve the home environment. This program has kept pupils in school longer, and there has been a measurable increase in IQ points for these children as they have progressed from the sixth to the ninth grades.

REFERENCES

1. Board of Education of the City of New York. Demonstration guidance project: Junior High School 43 Manhattan and George Washington High School. *Third Annu. Progr. Rep.*, 1958–59.
2. Cattell, R. B., & Drevdahl, J. E. A comparison of the Personality Profile (16 P.F.) of eminent researchers with that of eminent teachers and administrators, and of the general population. *British J. Psychol.*, 1955, 46, 248–261.
3. Getzels, J. W., & Jackson, P. W. The highly creative and the highly intelligent adolescent. In *Third University of Utah Research Conference on the Identification of Creative Scientific Talent*. Univer. of Utah Press, 1959. pp. 46–57.
4. Gowan, J. C. Factors of achievement in high school and college. *J. counsel. Psychol.*, 1960, 7, 91–95.
5. Guilford, J. P. The structure of intellect. *Psychol. Bull.*, 1956, 53, 267–293.
6. Haggard, E. A. Socialization, personality, and academic achievement in gifted children. *School Rev.*, 1957, 65, 388–414.
7. McClelland, D. C., Atkinson, J., Clark, R., & Lowell, E. L. The achievement motive. New York: Appleton-Century-Crofts, 1953.
8. Rosen, B. C., & D'Andrade, R. The psychosocial origins of achievement motivation. *Sociometry*, 1959, 22, 185–218.
9. Terman, L. M., & Oden, Melita. *The gifted child grows up*. Stanford, Calif.: Stanford Univer. Press, 1947.

FOUR ATTITUDES, INTERESTS, AND VALUES

The stability, social orientation, and independence from adult models of adolescent interests, attitudes, and values appear to be more influenced by physical maturation than are those of children. Whereas, in general, a child's interests are short-lived, situationally determined, and strongly susceptible to the influence of respected adults, an adolescent is capable of lasting attention directed toward a stable set of interests which are more allocentric than the egocentric and at times solitary concerns and pursuits of childhood. During this period, the adolescent also begins to develop his own value system based primarily on personal preference and individual conviction rather than on handed down parental values. Robert J. Havighurst (1951), who postulates the developmental task of "building conscious values in harmony with an adequate scientific world-picture" and Erik H. Erikson (21), who applies the construct of identity formation agree that adolescents are concerned with adjusting and integrating a system of values into the whole personality. In a classic study, C. P. Stone and R. G. Barker (1939) emphasized the interrelationship between physical maturation and the development of attitudes and interests. The Stone and Barker study of pre- and post-menarcheal girls revealed that postmenarcheal girls had stronger heterosexual interest, more concern for appearance, and less interest in sports than pre-menarcheal girls of the same age, a finding which substantiated their hypothesis that interest patterns are directly related to sexual maturation. Recognizing that values, attitudes, and interests are not only the results of maturation and environmental influences such as peer and other social pressure, but in turn also are contributing factors in an adolescent's behavior, educational psychologists find this area of study of major importance for the understanding of adolescent development.

Mary Cover Jones (13) explores in detail one aspect of the interrelationship between historical change and change in interests. Her study reveals that between 1933 and 1953, the attitudes and interests of ninth graders increased in social sophistication, heterosexual interest, general degree of tolerance, and sense of purpose, to the maturity level of eleventh graders in 1933. Supplementing a study by A. W. Boyne (1960), which established that girls mature not only physically but also intellectually before boys, the Jones study reveals that the maturational acceleration over a twenty year period was more pronounced for girls than for boys, and that girls exhibited a decided shift in sex role patterns. Although Jones discusses only the shift in female interest from passive to active physical pursuits, other psychological researchers have observed a more active female involvement in courtship, mate selection, and sexual activity. The findings of the Jones article are in substantial agreement with the broad acceleration of physical and social development among adolescents which was discussed in more detail in article 5.

The stabilization of choice during adolescence is the topic of a study by John P. McKinney (14) which expands on earlier work by J. E. Horrocks and M. E. A. Buker (1946) on the decline of friendship fluctuations and the stabilization of sociometric preferences with age. Investigating the influence of age and sex on interest patterns, attitudes, and long range goals, McKinney draws two major conclusions. First, he finds that the stabilization of choice occurs earlier in girls than in boys, a conclusion which agrees with the general findings that girls mature earlier than boys. See Dwyer and Mayer. Second, he finds that fluctuation scores decline more rapidly and steadily between second and fourth grades and between fourth and sixth grades than at later ages, because choices begin to stabilize during early adolescence. During adolescence, apparently, the capricious choices of children, influenced by momentary pressures or changes in situation, give way to a stable value system which guides the more mature choices of adolescents.

Joseph Adelson and Robert P. O'Neil (15) investigate changes in attitudes and values of adolescents from eleven to eighteen, as revealed by changes in political thought. The test questions assessed the subject's attitude toward the relationship between an individual's rights and those of the community. Findings indicate that before the age of thirteen, subjects have relatively little concern for the long range implications of political action, and that the younger subjects are more Hobbesian in their political views than the older adolescents, viewing the individual citizen as "willful and potentially dangerous" and society as "rightfully, needfully, coercive and authoritarian." With increasing age, the subjects exhibit an evolving "sense of community" and a growing awareness of the needs and responsibilities of citizenship. This transition from egocentric to allocentric political awareness during adolescence closely follows Jean Piaget's theory of cognitive development, which posits that with increasing age, the adolescent becomes more capable of solving social and abstract mental problems and of developing a personal ideology on the basis of abstract principles.

Part IV concludes with a review of "moral education," in an article by Lawrence Kohlberg (16) that summarizes previous findings on moral development. In opposition to the psychoanalytic theorists, Kohlberg maintains that moral character is not determined early in life as the result of deep-seated, highly emotionalized experiences; neither does he believe that moral behavior is determined purely situationally, dependent from moment to moment on reward and punishment. He suggests instead that moral development is a slow, continuous growth process, by which the child moves through a sequence of increasingly more sophisticated moral stages. These stages form a hierarchy, beginning with premoral, basically egoistic and egocentric orientation in early childhood, evolving to a level of conventional role conformity during the elementary school years, and finally reaching a mature level of personally evaluated moral principles. Like Piaget's developmental construct of "cognitive structure," Kohlberg's theory of "moral charatcer" is based on maturation and socialization rather than on traits fixed by birth or early childhood experiences. In Kohlberg's theory moral growth is the combined result of maturational forces and experience in moral judgment. The theory of an evolving morality is particularly enlightening for educators, because moral values, although never taught explicitly, are transmitted through the discipline methods in the school. Because attempts to influence character through education have had little success, Kohlberg's developmental theory offers a new approach for teachers concerned with molding adolescent morals and values.

REFERENCES

1. Boyne, A. W. "Secular changes in the stature of adults and the growth of children, with special reference to changes in intelligence of 11-year-olds." In *Human Growth*. J. M. Tanner (Ed.), Oxford: Pergamon, 1960.
2. Coleman, J. S. *The Adolescent Society*. New York: Free Press of Glencoe, 1961.
3. Havighurst, R. J. *Developmental Tasks and Education*. New York: Longmans, Green, 1951.
4. Horrocks, J. E. and M. E. A. Buker. "A study of the friendship fluctuations of rural boys and girls." *Journal of Genetic Psychology*, 1946, *69*, 189–198.
5. Jones, M. C. and N. Bayle, "Physical Maturing among Boys as related to Behavior in Adolescence and Adult Years." *Journal of Educational Psychology*, 1950, *41*, 129–148.
6. Stone, C. P. and R. G. Barker. "The Attitudes and Interests of Pre-Menarcheal and Post-Menarcheal Girls." *Journal of Genetic Psychology*, 1939, *54*, 27–71.

[13]   *Mary Cover Jones*   A COMPARISON OF THE
ATTITUDES AND INTERESTS OF NINTH-GRADE
STUDENTS OVER TWO DECADES

This paper compares the interests, activities and opinions of a sample of ninth graders in 1935 with those of ninth graders in the same junior high school in 1953[1] and again in 1959. The 1935 sample consists of members of the Oakland Growth Study (1932–1939). As adults, this group is now cooperating in a follow-up study in which records are being obtained of their contemporary interests and attitudes and their estimate of how they believe they answered similar items when they were adolescents. To evaluate the consistency of the records, it seems important to consider trends which may have occurred as a result of social changes. Tests of new groups of the same age as the adolescents in our original sample have provided the basis for this comparison survey.

Are teenagers today more serious or more frivolous, more conforming or more rebelling, more sophisticated or more naive, than teenagers of a generation ago? This is not a question which can have a general answer, since trends (if they occur) will not necessarily be in the same direction in different regions or in different social classes. However, where relevant data are available for known samples it seems desirable to report them and consider their implications in relation to other research in this field. What adolescents think, do, want is of interest from many different theoretical and practical points of view.

Comparison of samples

In a state growing as rapidly as California, the population composition of some neighborhoods has changed so greatly that temporal trends would be difficult to disentangle from differences in social groups. Fortunately for our purpose, the neighborhoods involved in this study have to a fairly high degree maintained the stability which was noted at the time this junior high school was chosen for the longitudinal study.

Table 1 compares the distribution of parents' occupations (Edwards, 1933) in 1935 and 1953, and Table 2 the census tract classifications for home ad-

FROM *Journal of Educational Psychology*, 1960, 51, 175–186. COPYRIGHT 1960 BY THE AMERICAN PSYCHOLOGICAL ASSOCIATION, AND REPRODUCED BY PERMISSION OF THE AUTHOR AND THE PUBLISHER.

TABLE 1 Socioeconomic Classification: Parents' Occupation (Edwards 6-Point Scale) (Expressed in Percentages)

	1935	1953
1. Professional	07	17
2. Managerial	18	29
3. Semiprofessional	38	25
4. Skilled	29	25
5. Semiskilled	06	04
6. Unskilled	02	00
Median	3.12	2.59
SD	1.04	1.12

TABLE 2 Census Tract Classification[a] (Expressed in Percentages)

	FAS	1935	1953
1. Exclusive[b]	768	21	25.6
2. Good neighborhood	666	38	41
3. New good neighborhood	576	00.6	14
4. Neighborhood of modest homes	466	29	17

[a] Tryon classification (8 is high):
F = Family life, i.e., detached owner occupied home
A = Assimilation, i.e., native white
S = Socioeconomic independence, i.e., managerial, professional males
[b] The four classifications listed account for the majority of the subjects in this study.

dresses of our two samples, based on Tryon's cluster analysis of the 1940 and 1950 census tract data for this area. An increase has occurred in professional and managerial occupations, and the total for white collar occupations has increased from 59 to 65%. Similarly, a slight upward shift has occurred in the neighborhood classifications; here the principal change has resulted from the opening of a neighborhood of new homes, and the diminished proportion remaining in an older neighborhood.[2]

To some extent these changes reflect the general upward mobility in living standards, income and education which has occurred over this 18-year period. An additional contributing factor was a change in the elementary school sources of this junior high school population. Before 1940 it drew from five elementary schools in the northern part of Oakland. By 1953 a new elementary school (mean occupational rating 2.59) had been added, and one school with an occupational rating of 3.9 had been displaced, its pupils being sent to a different junior high school. This change is in the direction of a more homogeneous middle class group, slightly above the former average.

If these changes had resulted in a very marked alteration of the social structure of the junior high school district, we would expect to find significant changes in the intelligence distribution. This has not occurred as is shown in Table 3.

TABLE 3 Intelligence Test (IQ) Classification (Expressed in Percentages)

	1935[a]	1953[b]
130–139	02	01
120–129	06	12
110–119	27	30
100–109	38	30
90–99	21	18
80–89	05	07
70–79	01	02
Mean	105.49	105.18
SD	10.75	12.28

[a] Terman Group Test, Form A and B.
[b] Kuhlmann-Anderson.

As a further control on the comparability of the two populations in socio-economic status, a subsample was selected of 40 cases for each sex and each period under study (1935 and 1953), carefully matched on the basis of parents' occupation. The responses for the subsamples on a 139 item comparison were in general agreement with those of the larger sample. A selection of these items, Things to be—Occupations is shown in Table 4. Because of the advantages of dealing with a larger sample, it was decided to use the total ninth grade population as the basis of this report.

Subjects and procedures

Results are discussed below for an inventory consisting of some 250 items pertaining to activities, interests, and attitudes. Levels of significance (Walker,

TABLE 4 Things to Be—Occupations (A Comparison of Responses for 40 Selected Cases and for the Total Sample)

	BOYS % POSITIVE RESPONSE			
	1935		1953	
	N = 40	N = 72	N = 40	N = 95
Architect	45	49	37.5	35
Athletic Coach	67.5	61	40	42
Artist	25	31	05	09
Aviator	67.5	68	42.5	44
Chemist	37.5	36	25	29
College Teacher	27.5	25	05	07
Dentist	15	17	27.5	21
Doctor	32.5	31	35	39
Engineer	52.5	53	60	55
Farmer	42.5	37	45	28
Lawyer	35	41	25	33
Policeman	27.5	28	17.5	23

	GIRLS % POSITIVE RESPONSE			
	1935		1953	
	N = 40	N = 70	N = 40	N = 78
Artist	35	48	22.5	22
Bookkeeper	35	36	20	19
Decorator	20	30	45	44
Doctor	30	22	25	22
Kindergarten Teacher	35	33	30	35
Librarian	22.5	23	20	18
Nurse	42.5	41	35	36
Secretary	60	62	70	60
Stenographer	47.5	59	40	32
Teacher	25	30	22.5	24
Telephone Operator	32.5	31	32.5	29
Waitress	20	19	22.5	20

1953) have been computed for the sexes separately in a comparison of earlier with later records. Sex differences within each temporal sample have been analyzed, as well as age trends over the seven-year period in the earlier, longitudinal sample.

Members of the Oakland Growth study, 72 boys and 70 girls, are represented in the 1935 testing, when they were in the ninth grade. For this group an interest record (Jones, 1940) was administered yearly for seven years, an activity schedule yearly from the 9th through the 12th grade, and an opinion ballot in the 8th, 9th, and 11th grades.

For the 1953 comparison, all ninth-grade students in the same junior high school were tested. The boys numbered 95 and the girls 78. The additional test program in 1959 included 134 boys and 123 girls. Nonwhite students, now numbering about 20, were eliminated to maintain comparability with the earlier samples.

The test used in 1953 and in 1959 included a representative selection of items from the three inventories used in the longitudinal study. It was administered in one class period of 50 min. Students were asked to check items organized on separate pages under such headings as Where I Went Last Week, and What I Read Last Week. They were asked to indicate whether they liked, disliked, or were indifferent to a number of items listed under titles such as Things to Own, or Things to Be: Occupations. Headings such as Things You Talk About were answered on a 5-point scale from Never to Very Often.[3] Attitudes were sampled under the heading My Opinion, which instructed the Ss to report whether they approved, disapproved, or sometimes approved the behavior or ideas listed.

The categories of items as presented were administrative rather than functional. Items belonging to a given functional classification (such as interest in sex-social activities) occurred under different phrasing in each of the nine parts of the test. Thus, preoccupation with mixed group activities and interest in the opposite sex might presumably be tapped by the Ss desire to own new party clothes, to go to a good dance hall, to want to stay out late, or to talk about dates. Similarly, a student might indicate that he or she went to a dance or read a love story last week, and approval of "permanents."

Results

One fact is outstanding in our results. In the more recent tests, boys and girls in the ninth grade marked items in such a way as to indicate greater maturity and greater social sophistication. This is demonstrated in their responses to items which show an age trend in adolescence for the earlier study group. Some of these items, representing "juvenile" interests or immature behavior, are, in the longitudinal sample, rejected increasingly as boys and girls grow older. At the same time, other items which represent greater maturity of interests and attitudes become more frequently selected. For example, members of the adolescent study group, as they grew older, no longer wanted to "own a stamp collection," to read "*Boy's Life*," to go to a "secret clubhouse" or to be "a detective." On the other hand, as they grew older, they more often checked such items as this week "I went to a dance"; I approve of "thinking about how I look"; I talk about "having dates" (Table 5).

On such age-relative items, we now find that ninth graders in the '50s are more comparable to the eleventh- or twelfth-grade students of 20 years earlier than to those of their own age (Table 5).

Interest, activity, and attitude items which illustrate this tendency to check the more mature response have been grouped under subheadings such as social-sex interests, sense of responsibility, tolerance, and antiaggression attitudes. For each of these categories, one item which illustrates the findings has been selected for discussion.

In the area of social-sex or heterosexual preoccupation, Fig. 1 shows the response for the item *I approve of the use of lipstick*. For boys and girls respectively, the solid and broken lines indicate age trends in the longitudinal sample, in the 1930s. The responses of ninth graders in 1953 and 1959 are also indicated; black circles represent the percentages for boys, open circles the percentages for girls. Lipstick symbolizes as well as any one specific item could, the sensitization in early adolescence toward a new sex role and toward being grown up. While its use is confined to girls, opinions about its use are not, as the figure indicates. The lag shown in the data for boys (as compared with girls) may indicate either less interest or active antagonism toward signs of maturing from members of the less mature sex who are being pressured into the heterosexual phase ahead of schedule. Recorded conversations in the 1930s suggest the latter:

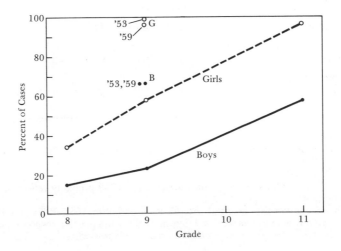

FIGURE 1   Approve of using lipstick

TABLE 5   Social-Sex Interests

	BOYS % POSITIVE RESPONSE			GIRLS % POSITIVE RESPONSE		
	1935	1953	1959	1935	1953	1959
	$N=72$	$N=70$	$N=134$	$N=70$	$N=78$	$N=123$
Activities						
I took care of my clothes[a]	9	21*	22	70	86	77*
I manicured my nails	0	7*	16	62	74*	63*
I went to a dance	25	27*	40	24	41	61
I read a love story	8	3*	5*	30	42	55
Interests						
Would like to own a phono- graph and dance records	55	60*	72	50	93	92
Conversations						
I talk about having dates[b]	46	56	63	58	92	84
I talk about clothes, things to wear	42	57	66	89	94*	91*
I talk about girl friends	55	71	74			
I talk about boy friends				65	94	96
Attitudes						
I approve of using lipstick[c]	23	66	66	58	99	96
I approve of "permanents"[d]	29	49	42*	62	72*	57*
I approve of thinking about how you look	27	51	65	40	77	72
I approve of love scenes in movies	26	29*	37*	39	59	53

[a] Check Yes.

[b] Never, Seldom, Sometimes, Often, Very often. Per cent equals sum of Sometimes, Often, Very often.

[c] Yes, No, Sometimes.

[d] The reduced positive response for both sexes in 1959 probably reflects a change in hairdress fashion.

* Comparisons *not* significant at the .05 level or better 1935–1953 and 1935–1959 are starred. Significance levels were not determined for the positive response percentages shown in the table, but from chi squares based on *all* responses (e.g., Yes, No, Sometimes).

Boy to Girl: Where's Jane?

Girl: Down at the beauty parlor getting ready for the dance.

Boy: They all look alike to me whether they get fixed up or not.

Or going down the hall the first day of school, Roy says to Bob: There goes Irene. And the reply is: All painted up and looks like a horse.

Adult observers of seventh graders in the Growth Study considered it worth a notation that Shirley had lipstick on. In the high eighth grade, however, they commented: The Foster sisters were the only ones at the party without lipstick.

The data show that by the 1950s (1953 and 1959), for both boys and girls, the percentage approving of the use of lipstick was higher in the 9th grade than in the 11th grade sample 20 years earlier. It is well known that there are social class and regional differences in attitudes toward the use of lipstick and other aspects of adolescent grooming. But here we find also a temporal difference in samples living in the same neighborhood and comparable in social status.

In a recent study comparing Minnesota junior and senior high school students' responses in 1957 to those of Symond's (1936) Tulsa and New York City youth in 1935, Harris (1959) interprets similar findings: "Today youth marry younger and show earlier interest in social relations, love and marriage." (p. 458) Our own evidence of interest in grooming activities among ninth graders shows how a temporal trend in heterosexual preoccupation may extend down into the middle period of adolescence.

Other items in the category of social-sex interest are shown in Table 5. For the most part (except for the few comparisons indicated by asterisks) differences are significant between 1935 and 1953 and between 1935 and 1959.

When we described the junior high school culture of our group in the 1930s, we interpreted their concern with social activities as in conflict with achievement motives of an academic nature. This preoccupation often seemed inconsistent with an interest in homework, in assuming responsibilities or in showing concern for any but their own narrow peer group activities (Stolz, 1937). Does a similar situation hold today? Is an increased social interest accompanied by a decreased commitment in other areas?

Quite the contrary. These 14 year olds in 1953 and 1959 can be described from their answers as more studious, more broadly interested in the contemporary scene, more tolerant in their social attitudes, more inclined to value controlled behavior and to disapprove of aggression or irresponsible behavior in others. Comparative results for the item *This week I studied* are shown in Fig. 2. A significantly higher percentage of boys and of girls in the 1950s reported studying. The actual percentages in the ninth grade were virtually the same as those of high school seniors in the 1930s. Other items indicating a greater sense of personal and social responsibility, as marked in the more recent sample, are shown in Table 6. There were more frequent reports of talking about their studies and talking about other school activities. They

TABLE 6   Responsible Behavior

	BOYS % POSITIVE RESPONSE			GIRLS % POSITIVE RESPONSE		
	1935	1953	1959	1935	1953	1959
Activities						
I studied	67	86	85	54	92	94
I took care of children	8	20	25	30	47	53
I earned some money	57	69*	69*	22	58	49
I read						
something about science	17	35	40	4	12*	17
The Bible	16	20*	21*	12	35	32
something about religion	8	19*	18*	11	28	30
I went to Sunday School	41	43*	40*	35	69	62
I went to Church	46	47*	56*	55	82	78
Conversations						
I talk about						
what you are going to be	58	77	69*	74	89	89
money and things you need	60	78	75	53	84	86
church and things about re-ligion	21	46	45	33	72	71
studies, classwork	63	83	80	82	93	91
school activities	49	59*	64*	58	89	82
things about the government, politics	38	67	48*	14	51	30
Attitudes						
I Approve of						
worrying about the future	12	27	31	5	17	32

*Comparisons with 1935 are starred for chi squares *not* significant at the .05 level or better.

liked to go to school assemblies. Such responses indicate a more school-centered orientation in the '50s than in the '30s.

A greater proportion said they earned money, took care of their clothes and their rooms, talked about what they were going to be when they grew up and thought it appropriate to worry about the future (Table 6). This, in

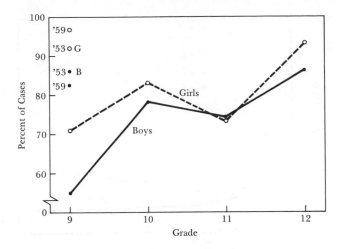

FIGURE 2 This week I studied

prosperous times as contrasted with depression years and (for the 1953 sample) before Sputnik!

The difference shown in Table 6 may be in part differences in the *Zeitgeist,* and in part a matter of situational changes. Thus, an increase in the number of young children, and the development of baby-sitting, may be largely responsible for the increase (especially among girls) in "taking care of children" and "earning money." The increased interest reported by both sexes in such items as "reading about science" and "talking about political matters" may define a generally higher level of intellectual-cultural maturity

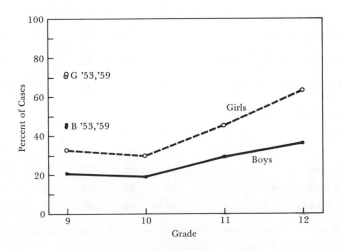

FIGURE 3 Talking about: religion

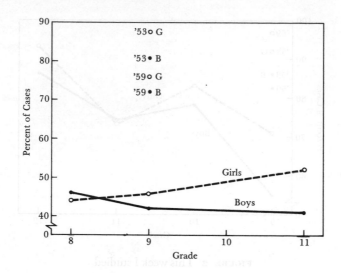

FIGURE 4   Approve of foreigners

prosperous times as contrasted with depression years and (for the 1953 sample) below-capacity.

The difference shown in Table 6 may be in part difference in the 7.0 past, and in part a more accurate reflection of changed how, an increase in the number of young children, and the development of baby-sitting, may be related to the increased leisure apparently available to the high-school girl of today. Though students in 1953 showed less interest . . . By with . . . , . . . talking about political interest, now define a generally higher level of . . . intellectual maturity

TABLE 7   Tolerant Attitudes

	BOYS % POSITIVE RESPONSE			GIRLS % POSITIVE RESPONSE		
	1935	**1953**	**1959**	**1935**	**1953**	**1959**
Approving of foreigners	42	81	72	46	88	76
Giving criminals another chance	9	34	40	6	22	39
Approving of women doctors	44	72	61	76	90	88*
Tolerance toward						
gambling	6	21	34	2	7*	5
betting on games	25	40	47	17	13*	23*
playing cards	64	86	77	66	72*	71*
playing cards for money	18	33	34	11	5*	12*
women smoking	18	35	31	26	35*	22

* Comparisons with 1935 are starred for chi squares *not* significant at the .05 level or better.

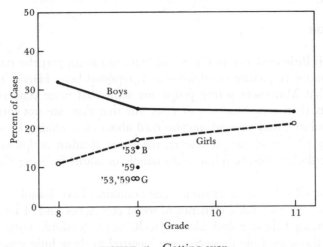

FIGURE 5   Getting even

in the more recent junior high school samples. The markedly significant increases especially among girls in religious interests may reflect an additional factor; the percentages reached in the '50s are higher than any we obtained even in the 12th grade in the '30s (Fig. 3).

Table 6 presents data for a number of items illustrating different aspects of tolerance. As shown in Figure 4, *I approve of foreigners* elicits a much more affirmative response in the '50s, from both boys and girls.

One group of items in Table 7 (approval of betting, gambling, etc.) suggests a more relaxed attitude which might be thought to be incompatible with the greater expressed interest in the church and its influences (as shown in the preceding table). However, this acquiescence does not extend to what might be classified as inconsiderate or aggressive behavior. The ninth graders of the '50s manifest more disapproval of antisocial behavior such as "*getting even*" or "doing what I want when I want to" (Fig. 5).

Some of the responses discussed above suggest a greater socialization and also a more conforming attitude. The latter characteristic is frequently attributed to our present generation of young people. But not all items which connote acquiescence are approved by the recent samples as compared with the '30s. More adolescents countenance "disagreeing with my parents," and "saying exactly what I think." "Always doing what is expected," is indicated as much less acceptable.

More in line with the findings of the present study is an early report by Pressey (1946) on attitude changes between 1923 and 1943. Pressey was encouraged by "the general freeing of young people over the past 20 years . . . from a great variety of borderland social taboos, inhibitions and restrictions . . ." (p. 186). A second trend which he applauded was "the growth of activities" (p. 187).

Discussion

There is little evidence in the recent literature to support the rather favorable contemporary picture of adolescents as reported here. Harris' 1957 study indicates that Minnesota young people are somewhat more concerned about study-habits than were students in 1935 but that they are not much 'interested." Similarly, they seemed unconcerned about civic affairs. Remmers and Radler (1957) lament that teenagers, rebellious of adult authority in many areas, nevertheless tend to follow the example of adults in being illiberal and conformist.

Other studies based on attitudes questionnaires have found (among college students) considerable evidence of social conscience and of toleration for nonconforming behavior and ideas (Jacob, 1957; Sanford, 1956; Webster, 1958). At the same time these Ss were reported to show little concern about social issues.

The data summarized here are for a small sample in a single geographic location representing a limited range of social status. But if we believe what our Ss tell us, all is not lost for youngsters growing up in the '50s.

Sex differences and sex role patterns

Check lists of children's interests, such as those employed in this study, have been used by a number of investigators to examine the development of sex role concepts and sex differences. For most of the items in the area of social-sex development (listed in Table 5) the indication of mature interest is more marked in girls than in boys. More girls than boys report "going to a dance." More girls than boys report that they talk about dates and opposite-sex friends.

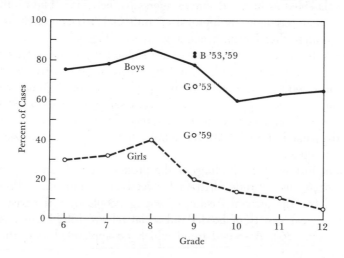

FIGURE 6 Experiment with chemistry

Earlier physiological maturing of girls (as compared with boys) would be expected to produce now, as formerly, an earlier maturing in social-sex development. However, it may be that the temporal trend in the direction of a generally earlier expression of heterosexual interest for both sexes, contributes to some blurring of sex role patterns as revealed in certain aspects of the data for the 1950s.

For example, this may account for the fact that in the 1950s boys' responses are more like those of girls on some items. More girls than boys checked that they manicured their nails, but between 1935 and 1959 the increase in percentage checking this item was significant only for boys.[4]

The boys' reduced interest in some aspects of scientific and mechanical manipulation (usually considered a masculine interest)[5] may be a temporary expression of earlier social maturing. To indicate interest in experimenting with a chemistry set or with electricity may at a certain age seem juvenile rather than socially mature. The percentages for the item *experimenting with chemistry* are shown in Fig. 6. The drop in interest for ninth-grade boys is significant at the .05 level in 1953 and in the same direction, though not significant at that level, in 1959. The data from both testings in the '50s indicate less interest in such matters than at any age in the '30s, even though the longitudinal sample maintained a downward trend with age in items of this nature.

Although greater social maturity in both boys and girls may be one factor which accounts for increased similarity of the sexes on some items, there is one area of interest in which results run counter to this observation. The girls seem to have made a striking shift from passive to active interest in sports and athletic activities.[6] In the earlier sample the percentage checking the positive response diminished from the 6th to the 12th grade. There was also a large sex difference in the 1935 sample, with boys showing more favorable attitudes.

Figure 7 gives the results for a representative item, showing the trend in percentage wishing *to own a baseball and bat*. Data are given for the 6th

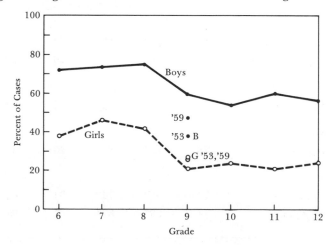

FIGURE 7   Own a baseball and bat

through the 12th grades in the '30s and also for the 9th grade in 1953 and 1959. Differences are significant for girls but not for boys (Table 8).

Recent studies by Rosenberg and Sutton-Smith (1960) and Rosenberg and Sutton-Smith (1959) of children's interests in games has compared the responses of boys and girls in this generation with the responses of each sex to similar questionnaire items in the 1920's (Terman, 1926, 1936). The authors report results for the fourth, fifth, and sixth grades which indicate that there has been a shift in the direction of increasing preferences of girls for what were formerly boys' games while boys tend to select fewer items which significantly differentiate their choices from those of girls. The authors interpret their findings as an indication that the female role perception is expanding in the direction of greater activity and increased masculinity. This tendency is shown in the present study for the responses listed in Table 8. Not only preferences but recent participation is reported (see also Table 9).

The question has been raised as to what the effect on the masculine role will be, if girls' interests are expanded to include traditionally masculine activities (Hartley, 1959a, 1959b). We might conjecture that, for this sample at least, boys may be staking out a new claim in the borderland of social respectability involving betting and gambling (Table 7). On the other hand, the increased heterosexual orientation of ninth-grade boys suggests that they may not be averse to sharing interests in some areas with girls.

TABLE 8 Interest in Athletics

	BOYS % POSITIVE RESPONSE			GIRLS % POSITIVE RESPONSE		
	1935	1953	1959	1935	1953	1959
Activities						
I watched athletic games	65	67*	62*	24	46	41
I played athletic games	77	80*	81*	28	79	57
Occupations						
Scout leader[a]	44	20	12	2	12	19
Things to Own						
Baseball and bat	78	82*	84*	20	67	43
Things to Do						
Be on a school team	74	75*	74*	34	63	41
Go to a playground	74	59*	57*	36	55	43*

* Differences are significant for the two sexes but in the opposite direction.

TABLE 9 Sex Differences: Significant Differences in Preferences, etc. 1935–53 (Test Items with Significant Differences)

TEST CATEGORY	NO. OF ITEMS IN TEST	BOYS		GIRLS	
		Acceptance Increased	Acceptance Decreased	Acceptance Increased	Acceptance Decreased
Things I did last week	20	1	1	8	9
Where I went	16	0	2	5	1
Things I read	18	2	3	6	1
Things to do	23	3	4	6	1
Occupations	47	0	28	2	9
Things you talk about	26	9	3	9	0
Places to go	23	1	14	3	6
Things to own	17	1	12	2	2
Magazines to read	17	0	10	1	6
My opinions	35	15	2	11	2
Totals	242	32	79	53	28
		12.5%	33%	21%	12%

Note.—For boys, 111 items (45% of total) showed significant differences; for girls, 81 items (33% of total) showed significant differences.

The overall picture indicates no striking changes in the number of items eliciting sex differences within each temporal sample. Comparing the significant changes for each sex for the two samples (1935–1953) we find boys' responses showing greater changes over time, with occupational rejections by the recent sample accounting for much of this disparity (Table 9). Girls give relatively more positive total responses in the later sample.

Tyler (1955) has suggested that awareness of role "enables the individual to rule out activities and goals not in keeping with it." In her longitudinal sample, Ss disliked more things as they grew older. Our own longitudinal results support her findings to some extent in the case of girls but not in the case of boys. In the area of vocational choices, for example, girls decreased their likes significantly on 20% of the items and increased them on 8%, from the 6th through the 12th grade. Boys, on the other hand, decreased their likes significantly on only 4% of the items, and increased them on 15%.

The maturity status of ninth-grade girls, higher than that of their male classmates, may be a factor in these findings. The nature of the items, the age of the Ss, and cultural differences, would also be determining factors in a comparison with other studies.

In relation to psychological sex-role development the data are not definitive. There is some blending of sex-role patterns but only as it is expressed concomitantly with earlier social maturing. There is some expansion of feminine interests into the male domain, but this is principally seen in sports activities. In the area of vocational preferences, girls' interests seem to be oriented toward supplementing the family income rather than toward a career. There is some constriction of the boys' vocational choices but this may be because we are comparing good times with the earlier depression era.

Members of the early growth study are now adults, some with adolescent offspring of their own. In interviews they often express their opinions about today's young people in contrast to their own remembered youth. They do not need to be told that adolescents now are more mature socially than in their day, though they may exaggerate the differences. In response to an interview question in this area, one of these young men said:

I was early-maturing but not by today's standards. I think part of it is the way they dress now. The girls wear lipstick and look older. If they had dressed that way when I was a kid, I would have been sure they would bite me.

There may be some relationship between the frequent complaint of these study members in interviews: "Why didn't someone make me study more when we were in school?" and our findings that ninth graders say they *do* study more now. Strange as it may seem, one young man's statement: "I didn't know that the reason I was getting poor grades was that I didn't study" is not an isolated remark. Having become aware of this sequential relationship, such individuals now apply parental pressures for "more studying."

So in a sense, the present attitudes of our original sample, and their contemporaries, now parents and citizens, are among the environmental factors affecting changes in the directions which we have seen. Parental influences, evidence of earlier maturing (Meleny, 1959; Tanner, 1955), altered school programs, historical events, all give direction to the secular trends in interests and attitudes recorded in this study.

Summary

This report compares the activities, interests and attitudes of three ninth-grade classes in the same school but separated in time by 18 and 24 years (1935, 1953, 1959). The samples are closely similar in age and IQ distributions, and fairly comparable in a number of social measures. The earlier group, members of the Oakland Growth Study, provided age-trend data through tests given at regular intervals over a seven-year period.

The more recent generations of ninth graders indicate greater maturity of heterosexual interests, more serious purpose and a more tolerant attitude toward social issues. They reject more "childish" activities.

Alterations over time in sex-role development are not striking. There is some blending of sex-role patterns in the more recent samples as expressed concomitantly with earlier social maturing. Currently, girls' interests have expanded in the area of sports activities. The responses of boys in the '50s indicate rejection of a greater number of occupations. Perhaps this is a reflection of occupational preferences as expressed during full employment as contrasted with the depression years. A greater verbal acceptance of "careers for women" is not accompanied by eagerness for a career among ninth-grade girls in the present generation. A variety of influences must be considered in accounting for the changes in interests and attitudes over the period of the study.

NOTES

1. The comparison of 1935 with 1953 data is more extensive, including sampling descriptions on the basis of census tract analysis of residence, intelligence test scores and ratings of parents' occupation. The 1959 testing was undertaken as a supplementary checking device for our 1953 interpretations and to bring the study up to date.
2. Tryon has compared eight social areas in his study of 1940 and 1950 census tract data in the San Francisco Bay Area, and has noted that ". . . in the year 1940, people who lived in these social areas differed greatly from each other." The differences (between these areas) in 1940 and in 1950 remain almost exactly the same (Tryon, 1955, 1959). In a personal communication Tryon has affirmed that the Oakland section from which our sample was drawn has remained highly stable by his method of analysis.
3. Some of the items were adaptations and extensions of material included in tests by Furfey (1928), Lehman and Witty (1927), Pressey (1933), and Symonds (1928).
4. The writer, who administered the tests on both occasions, can corroborate from observational notes the evidence of increased grooming activities in boys. Increased hair grooming was especially in evidence.
5. In 1958 Marshall used some of the items of the Interest Inventory to indicate awareness of appropriate or inappropriate sex-roles in fifth-grade boys and girls. Both boys and girls rated "experimenting with electricity" as something which boys would like and girls would dislike.
6. This is the only finding in the present investigation which is not supported by the school personnel from their observation and experience. The same teacher has been in charge of the girls' physical education program since the early thirties; she could offer no explanation of any results on the basis of curriculum

change or emphasis. However, several teachers and administrators cited the effective city recreational program which has been built up over this period, as a possible contributing factor.

A study by Meleny (1959) comparing the motor performance of eighth-grade girls now as compared to our longitudinal sample 24 years ago found no striking differences in these abilities. The more recent sample however was significantly taller and heavier.

REFERENCES

Edwards, A. M. A social reference: Economic grouping of the gainful workers of the United States. *J. Amer. Statist. Ass.*, 1933, **28**, 377–387.

Furfey, P. H. The measurement of development age. *Amer. Educ. Res. Bull.*, 1928, **2** (10), 40.

Harris, D. B. Sex differences in the life problems and interests of adolescents 1935–1957. *Child Develpm.*, 1959, **30**, 453–460.

Hartley, Ruth E. Sex role pressures and socialization of the male child. *Psychol. Rep.*, 1959, **5**, 457–468. (a)

Hartley, Ruth E. Some implications of current changes in sex-role patterns. Based on address, New York Society of Clinical Psychologists, 1959. (b) (Mimeo.)

Jacob, P. E. *Changing values in college: An exploratory study of the impact of college teaching.* New York: Harper, 1957.

Jones, M. C. *The I.C.W. Interest Record.* Inst. Child Welf., Univer. California, 1940.

Lehman, H. C., & Witty, P. A. *The psychology of play activities.* New York: A. B. Barnes, 1927.

Marshall, M. M. Awareness of sex-role and children's interest. Unpublished doctoral dissertation, Univer. California Education Library, 1958.

Meleny, H. E. Motor performance of adolescent girls today as compared with those of twenty-four years ago. MA thesis, Univer. California, 1959.

Pressey, S. L. Changes from 1923 to 1943 in the attitudes of public school and university students. *J. Psychol.*, 1946, **21**, 173–188.

Pressey, S. L., & Pressey, L. C. Development of the Interest-Attitude Tests. *J. appl. Psychol.*, 1933, **17**, 1–16.

Remmers, H. H., & Radler, D. H. *The American teen-ager.* Bobbs-Merrill, 1957.

Rosenberg, B. G., & Sutton-Smith, B. The measurement of masculinity and feminity in children. *Child Develpm.*, 1959, **30**, 373–380.

Rosenberg, B. G., & Sutton-Smith, B. A revised conception of masculine-feminine differences in play activities. *J. genet. Psychol.*, 1960, **51**, 175–186.

Sanford, N. (Ed.) Personality development during the college years. *J. soc. Issues*, 1956, **4**, 12.

Stolz, H. R., Jones, M. C., & Chaffey, J. The junior high school age. *Univer. High Sch. J.*, 1937, **2**, 15.

Symonds, P. S. A studiousness questionnaire. *J. educ. Psychol.* 1928, **19**, 152–167.

Symonds, P. S. Life interests and problems of adolescents. *Sch. Rev.*, 1936, **44**, 506–518.

Tanner, J. M. *Growth at adolescence.* Springfield, Illinois: Charles C. Thomas, 1955.

Terman, L. *Genetic studies of genius.* Vol. I. Palo Alto: Stanford Univer. Press, 1926.

Terman, L., & Miles, C. C. *Sex and personality.* New York: McGraw-Hill, 1936.

Tryon, R. C. *Identification of social areas by cluster analysis.* (A general method with an application to the San Francisco Bay area) Berkeley: Univer. California Press, 1955.

Tryon, R. C. Identity of attitude and demographic dimensions that distinguish social areas. *Amer. Psychologist* 1959, **14**, 371. (Abstract)

Tyler, Leona E. The organization of likes and dislikes in ten year old children. *J. genet. Psychol.* 1955, **86**, 33–44.

Walker, H. M., & Lev, J. *Statistical inferences.* New York: Holt, 1953.

Webster, H. Changes in attitudes during college. *J. educ. Psychol.* 1958, **49**, 109–117.

[14] *John Paul McKinney* THE DEVELOPMENT OF CHOICE STABILITY IN CHILDREN AND ADOLESCENTS

A. Introduction

A number of studies have demonstrated that friendship stability in childhood and adolescence increases with age. This finding has been reported with rural children (3), urban children (6), preadolescents (2), and college students (5). A recent study comparing retarded and normal children (4) indicates that this increased stability is related to mental level.

The subjects in these earlier studies listed their three best friends in the order of preference, and two weeks later listed them again. The amount of change over the two-week period was the index of friendship fluctuation.

The fact that friendship fluctuations decrease with age has been interpreted as an indication of increased social and mental maturity. The question asked in the present study is whether the stability of other choices might also show the same developmental trend. It is predicted that the decrease in friendship fluctuation is a special case of a general pattern of increasing stability of choices with age. Such a prediction does not contradict the earlier interpreta-

FROM *Journal of Genetic Psychology*, 1968, *113*, 79–83. REPRINTED BY PERMISSION OF THE AUTHOR AND THE JOURNAL PRESS.

tion based on social and mental maturity, but suggests a more general dimension of choice stability underlying the specific example of friendship stability.

B. Method

1. SUBJECTS

The subjects were 156 boys and girls in Grades 2, 4, 6, 8, 10, and 12, enrolled in a parochial elementary school and high school.

2. PROCEDURE

All the Ss were tested in their home classrooms with their teachers present. Each child answered a questionnaire which asked his name, age, sex, and grade, and the following nine questions:

1. What are your favorite colors?
2. What are your favorite television programs?
3. What are your favorite desserts?
4. What are your favorite animals?
5. Who are your favorite friends?
6. What are your favorite games?
7. What are your favorite subjects in school?
8. What things do you like to do when there's nothing else to do?
9. What profession or occupation would you like to have when you are thirty years old?

Three spaces were open at the end of each question for the Ss to write their answers in the preferential order of first, second, and third choice. The Ss were instructed to give each question careful consideration; and the younger Ss (second graders) were helped individually, as needed, with instructions, spelling, etc.

Two weeks later the Ss answered the same questionnaire under identical

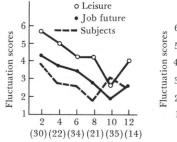
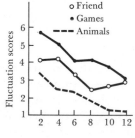
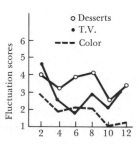

FIGURE 1   Mean choice fluctuation scores at each grade level. Numbers in parentheses refer to the number of subjects in each grade.

conditions. They were told that their choices may or may not be the same as their earlier choices, but that they should write their favorite current choices, regardless. In addition they were asked to estimate how long it had been since the first questionnaire.

A fluctuation score for each item was computed for each child by using the procedure described by Horrocks and Thompson (3). For any item, if the choices were the same and were given the same rank order on both occasions, the fluctuation score was zero. If the choices on the second occasion were identical to those given on the first occasion but differed in preferential order, a numerical value of 1 was given for each rank by which any choice had changed. If S gave new choices on the second testing, the following numerical values were assigned to the new choices: 2 for a new choice in third place, 3 for a new choice in second place, and 4 for a new choice in first place. The scores for each item for each child were then totaled.

C. Results

Means and standard deviations were obtained for each item for the males and females in each grade. The combined means are presented in Figure 1. Table 1 gives the results of analyses of variance of log unit transformations of these scores. The major variables in these analyses were grade level and sex of the child. For six of the nine items and for the total score there were significant differences between the grade levels. There were significant differences between the boys and the girls for three items and the total score, indicating greater fluctuation for males than for females. Finally, for the list of nine items reliability coefficients were computed. Since there were too few items to compute an odd-even correlation, Cronbach's alpha (1) was used: The alpha for each grade was as follows: =.41, grade two; = .15, grade four; = .53, grade 6; = .70, grade 8; = −.06, grade 10; = .60, grade 12.

TABLE 1   *F* Ratios on Choice Fluctuation Scores for Each Item for the Main Effects of Grade Level ($df = 5$, 144) and Sex ($df = 1$, 144)

ITEM	GRADE LEVEL[a]	SEX[b]
1. Color	2.52*	.01
2. TV program	1.33	5.13*
3. Dessert	3.28**	1.39
4. Animal	2.16	10.66**
5. Friend	1.16	1.89
6. Game	4.35**	.70
7. School subject	2.96*	1.96

TABLE 1
(continued)

ITEM	GRADE LEVEL[a]	SEX[b]
8. Leisure activity	6.24**	7.34**
9. Occupation	2.31*	2.01
10. Total of items 1 thru 9	8.83**	12.68**

[a] Fluctuation *decreases* with grade level (see Figure 1).
[b] For each item, the mean fluctuation score was higher for males than for females.
* $p < .05$.
** $p < .01$.

D. Conclusions

These results substantiate the view that choice stability increases with age. They also reveal that girls' choices are more stable than boys' (the proverbial feminine prerogative for changing one's mind notwithstanding). Since girls mature earlier than boys and since the phenomenon follows a developmental trend, this sex effect is understandable. It seems reasonable to conclude that friendship fluctuation is a special case of a more general trait—namely, choice fluctuation—and that the developmental trend applies to other choices, as well as friendship. Rather than contravening the earlier interpretation based on social and intellectual maturity, however, this finding would appear to give that interpretation added weight and wider significance.

While the alpha coefficients are not high, they are high enough at three of the upper grade levels to be suggestive of an underlying dimension of choice stability. The simplicity of the technique for measuring such a potential dimension would argue for lengthening the questionnaire and attempting to rule out other interpretations. For example, the dimension might be largely a memory factor, although this was guarded against in the present study by telling the subjects that their second choices may or may not be identical to their earlier choices. If such alternate interpretations could be ruled out, and a choice stability dimension could be measured reliably, one might look for correlates other than age, mental maturity, and sex. What antecedent conditions give rise to permanence of choice? Is this one aspect of a construct of commitment which may also include intensity of choice? Does environmental stability, including such things as changes in the family structure, frequent changes in geographic location, etc. affect the permanence with which a child will state a preference?

E. Summary

One hundred fifty-six boys and girls in Grades 2, 4, 6, 8, 10, and 12 were asked to respond to a questionnaire asking them to name their three favorite friends, games, animals, leisure activities, occupations, school subjects, TV programs, colors, and desserts. Two weeks later they were asked to complete an identical questionnaire. Results indicate a significant decrease in choice fluctuation with age and a significant sex difference, girls showing greater choice stability than boys. Moderate correlations (alpha) at three of the upper grade levels are suggestive of an underlying dimension of choice stability.

REFERENCES

1. Cronbach, L. J. Coefficient alpha and the internal structure of tests. *Psychometrika*, 1951, **16**, 297–334.
2. Horrocks, J. E., & Buker, M. E. A study of friendship fluctuations of preadolescents. *J. Genet. Psychol.*, 1951, **78**, 131–144.
3. Horrocks, J. E., & Thompson, G. G. A study of the friendship fluctuations of rural boys and girls. *J. Genet. Psychol.*, 1946, **69**, 189–198.
4. Kay, C. L., & McKinney, J. P. Friendship fluctuation in normal and retarded children. *J. Genet. Psychol.*, 1967, **110**, 233–241.
5. Skorepa, C. A., Horrocks, J. E., & Thompson, G. G. A study of friendship fluctuations of college students. *J. Genet. Psychol.*, 1963, **102**, 151–157.
6. Thompson, G. G., & Horrocks, J. E. A study of friendship fluctuations of urban boys and girls. *J. Genet. Psychol.*, 1947, **70**, 53–63.

[15]   *Joseph Adelson & Robert P. O'Neil*   GROWTH OF POLITICAL IDEAS IN ADOLESCENCE: THE SENSE OF COMMUNITY

During adolescence the youngster gropes, stumbles, and leaps towards political understanding. Prior to these years the child's sense of the political order is erratic and incomplete—a curious array of sentiments and dogmas, personalized ideas, randomly remembered names and party labels, half-understood platitudes. By the time adolescence has come to an end, the child's mind, much of the time, moves easily within and among the categories of political discourse. The aim of our research was to achieve some grasp of how this transition is made.

FROM *Journal of Personality and Social Psychology*, 1966, 4, 295–306. COPYRIGHT 1966 BY THE AMERICAN PSYCHOLOGICAL ASSOCIATION, AND REPRODUCED BY PERMISSION OF THE AUTHOR AND THE PUBLISHER.

We were interested in political ideas or concepts—in political philosophy —rather than political loyalties per se. Only during the last few years has research begun to appear on this topic. Earlier research on political socialization, so ably summarized by Hyman (1959), concentrated on the acquisition of affiliations and attitudes. More recently, political scientists and some psychologists have explored developmental trends in political knowledge and concepts, especially during childhood and the early years of adolescence; the studies of Greenstein (1965) and of Easton and Hess (1961, 1962) are particularly apposite.

Our early, informal conversations with adolescents suggested the importance of keeping our inquiry at some distance from current political issues; otherwise the underlying structure of the political is obscured by the clichés and catchphrases of partisan politics. To this end, we devised an interview schedule springing from the following premise: Imagine that a thousand men and women, dissatisfied with the way things are going in their country, decide to purchase and move to an island in the Pacific; once there, they must devise laws and modes of government.

Having established this premise, the interview schedule continued by offering questions on a number of hypothetical issues. For example, the subject was asked to choose among several forms of government and to argue the merits and difficulties of each. Proposed laws were suggested to him; he was asked to weigh their advantages and liabilities and answer arguments from opposing positions. The interview leaned heavily on dilemma items, wherein traditional issues in political theory are actualized in specific instances of political conflict, with the subject asked to choose and justify a solution. The content of our inquiry ranged widely to include, among others, the following topics: the scope and limits of political authority, the reciprocal obligations of citizens and state, utopian views of man and society, conceptions of law and justice, the nature of the political process.

This paper reports our findings on the development, in adolescence, of *the sense of community*. The term is deliberately comprehensive, for we mean to encompass not only government in its organized forms, but also the social and political collectivity more generally, as in "society" or "the people." This concept is of course central to the structure of political thought; few if any issues in political theory do not advert, however tacitly, to some of the community. Hence the quality of that conception, whether dim, incomplete, and primitive, or clear, complex, and articulated, cannot fail to dominate or temper the child's formulation of all things political.

The very ubiquity of the concept determined our strategy in exploring it. We felt that the dimensions of community would emerge indirectly, in the course of inquiry focused elsewhere. Our pretesting had taught us that direct questions on such large and solemn issues, though at times very useful, tended to evoke simple incoherence from the cognitively unready, and schoolboy stock responses from the facile. We also learned that (whatever the ostensible topic) most of our questions informed us of the child's view of the social order, not only through what he is prepared to tell us, but also through what he does not know, knows falsely, cannot state, fumbles in stating, or takes for granted. Consequently we approached this topic through a survey of questions from several different areas of the schedule, chosen to illuminate different sides of the sense of community.

Method

SAMPLE

The sample was comprised of 120 youngsters equally divided by sex, with 30 subjects at each of 4 age-grade levels—fifth grade (average age, 10.9), seventh (12.6), ninth (14.7), and twelfth (17.7). The sample was further divided by intelligence: At each grade level, two thirds of the subjects were of average intelligence (95–110) and one third of superior intelligence (125 and

TABLE 1 Distribution of Sample by Grade, Sex, and Intelligence

	BOYS		GIRLS	
	Average IQ	Superior IQ	Average IQ	Superior IQ
5th grade: *N*	10	5	10	5
Mean IQ	106.1	127.8	105.1	128.4
7th grade: *N*	10	5	10	5
Mean IQ	104.1	140.0	104.5	134.4
9th grade: *N*	10	5	10	5
Mean IQ	106.6	133.2	105.1	134.0
12th grade: *N*	10	5	10	5
Mean IQ	106.1	140.8	103.8	134.8

over), as measured by the California Test of Mental Maturity. Table 1 shows the distribution by grade, intelligence, and sex. For each grade, school records were used to establish a pool of subjects meeting our criteria for age, sex, and IQ; within each of the subgroups so selected, names were chosen randomly until the desired sample size was achieved. Children more than 6 months older or younger than the average for their grade were excluded, as were two otherwise eligible subjects reported by their counselor to have a history of severe psychological disturbance.

This paper will report findings by age alone (to the next nearest age) and without regard to sex or intelligence. We were unable to discover sex differences nor—to our continuing surprise—differences associated with intelligence. The brighter children were certainly more fluent, and there is some reason to feel that they use a drier, more impersonal, more intellectualized approach in dealing with certain questions, but up to this time we have not found that they attain political concepts earlier than subjects of average intelligence.

The interviews were taken in Ann Arbor, Michigan. We were able to use schools representative of the community, in the sense that they do not draw students from socioeconomically extreme neighborhoods. The children of average IQ were preponderantly lower-middle and working class in background; those of high intelligence were largely from professional and managerial families. Academic families made up 13% of the sample, concentrated in the high IQ group; 5% of the "average" children and somewhat over one quarter of the "brights" had fathers with a professional connection to the University of Michigan. In these respects—socioeconomic status and parental education—the sample, which combined both IQ groups, was by no means representative of the American adolescent population at large. Yet our inability to find differences between the IQ groups, who derive from sharply different social milieux, makes us hesitate to assume that social status is closely associated with the growth of political ideas as we have measured them, or that the findings deviate markedly from what we would find in other middle-class suburbs.

INTERVIEW

The aims, scope, and form of the interview schedule have already been described. In developing the schedule we were most concerned to find a tone and level of discourse sufficiently simple to allow our youngest subjects to understand and respond to the problems posed, yet sufficiently advanced to keep our older interviewees challenged and engaged. Another aim was to strike a balance between the focused interview—to ease scoring—and a looser, more discursive approach—to allow a greater depth of inquiry and spontaneity of response. Our interviewers were permitted, once they had covered the basic questions of a topic, to explore it more thoroughly.

The interviews were conducted at the school. There were six interviewers, all with at least some graduate training in clinical psychology. The interviews were tape-recorded and transcribed verbatim. Those conducted with younger subjects were completed in about 1 hour, with older students in about 1½ hours.

RELIABILITY

In order to appraise the lower limits of reliability, only the more difficult items were examined, those in which responses were complex or ambiguous. For five items of this type, intercoder reliabilities ranged from .79 to .84.

Results

When we examine the interviews of 11-year-olds, we are immediately struck by the common, pervasive incapacity to speak from a coherent view of the political order. Looking more closely, we find that this failure has two clear sources: First, these children are, in Piaget's sense, egocentric, in that they cannot transcend a purely personal approach to matters which require a sociocentric perspective. Second, they treat political issues in a concrete fashion and cannot manage the requisite abstractness of attitude. These tendencies, singly and together, dominate the discourse of the interview, so much so that a few sample sentences can often distinguish 11-year-old protocols from those given by only slightly older children.

The following are some interview excerpts to illustrate the differences: These are chosen randomly from the interviews of 11- and 13-year-old boys of average intelligence. They have been asked: "What is the purpose of government?"

11A. To handle the state or whatever it is so it won't get out of hand, because if it gets out of hand you might have to . . . people might get mad or something.
11B. Well . . . buildings, they have to look over buildings that would be . . . um, that wouldn't be any use of the land if they had crops on it or something like that. And when they have highways the government would have to inspect it, certain details. I guess that's about all.
11C. So everything won't go wrong in the country. They want to have a government because they respect him and they think he's a good man.

Now the 13-year-olds:

13A. So the people have rights and freedom of speech. Also so the civilization will balance.
13B. To keep law and order and talk to the people to make new ideas.
13C. Well, I think it is to keep the country happy or keep it going properly. If you didn't have it, then it would just be chaos with stealing and things like this. It runs the country better and more efficiently.

These extracts are sufficiently representative to direct us to some of the major developmental patterns in adolescent thinking on politics.

PERSONALISM

Under *personalism* we include two related tendencies: first, the child's disposition to treat institutions and social processes upon the model of persons and personal relationships; second, his inability to achieve a sociocentric orientation, that is, his failure to understand that political decisions have social as well as personal consequences, and that the political realm encompasses not merely the individual citizen, but the community as a whole.

1. "Government," "community," "society" are abstract ideas; they connote those invisible networks of obligation and purpose which link people to each other in organized social interaction. These concepts are beyond the effective

reach of 11-year-olds; in failing to grasp them they fall back to persons and actions of persons, which are the nearest equivalent of the intangible agencies and ephemeral processes they are trying to imagine. Hence, Subject 11A seems to glimpse that an abstract answer is needed, tries to find it, then despairs and retreats to the personalized "people might get mad or something." A more extreme example is found in 11C's statement, which refers to government as a "he," apparently confusing it with "governor." Gross personalizations of "government" and similar terms are not uncommon at 11 and diminish markedly after that. We counted the number of times the personal pronouns "he" and "she" were used in three questions dealing with government. There were instances involving six subjects among the 11-year-olds (or 20% of the sample) and none among 13-year-olds. (The most striking example is the following sentence by an 11: "Well, I don't think she should forbid it, but if they, if he did, well most people would want to put up an argument about it.")

Although personalizations as bald as these diminish sharply after 11, more subtle or tacit ones continue well into adolescence (and in all likelihood, into adulthood)—the use of "they," for example, when "it" is appropriate. It is our impression that we see a revival of personalization among older subjects under two conditions: when the topic being discussed is too advanced or difficult for the youngster to follow or when it exposes an area of ignorance or uncertainty, and when the subject's beliefs and resentments are engaged to the point of passion or bitterness. In both these cases the emergence of affects (anxiety, anger) seems to produce a momentary cognitive regression, expressing itself in a loss of abstractness and a reversion to personalized modes of discourse.

2. The second side of personalism is the failure to attain a sociocentric perspective. The preadolescent subject does not usually appraise political events in the light of their collective consequences. Since he finds it hard to conceive

TABLE 2   Purpose of Vaccination

| | AGE | | | |
	11	13	15	18
Social consequences (prevention of epidemics, etc.)	.23	.67	1.00	.90
Individual consequences (prevention of individual illness)	.70	.33	.00	.10

Note.—$\chi^2(3) = 46.53$, $p < .001$. In this table and all that follow $N = 30$ for each group. When proportions in a column do not total 1.00, certain responses are not included in the response categories shown. When proportions total more than 1.00, responses have been included in more than one category of the table. The p level refers to the total table except when asterisks indicate significance levels for a designated row.

the social order as a whole, he is frequently unable to understand those actions which aim to serve communal ends and so tends to interpret them parochially, as serving only the needs of individuals. We have an illustration of this in the data given in Table 2. Table 2 reports the answers to the following item: "Another law was suggested which required all children to be vaccinated against smallpox and polio. What would be the purpose of that law?"

A substantial majority—about three quarters—of the 11-year-olds see the law serving an individual end—personal protection from disease. By 13 there has been a decisive shift in emphasis, these children stressing the protection of the community. At 15 and after, an understanding of the wider purposes of vaccination has become nearly universal.

PARTS AND WHOLES

Another reflection of the concreteness of younger adolescents can be found in their tendency to treat the total functioning of institutions in terms of specific, discrete activities. If we return to the interview excerpts, we find a good example in the answer given by Subject 11B on the purpose of government. He can do no more than mention some specific governmental functions, in this case, the inspecting of buildings and highways. This answer exemplifies a pattern we find frequently among our younger subjects, one which appears in many content areas. Adolescents only gradually perceive institutions (and their processes) as wholes; until they can imagine the institution abstractly, as a total idea, they are limited to the concrete and the visible.

Table 3 is one of several which demonstrates this. The subjects were asked

TABLE 3   Purpose of Income Tax

	AGE			
	11	13	15	18
General support of government	.23	.33	.47	1.00*
Specific services only	.23	.17	.23	.00
Do not know	.53	.50	.30	.00

Note.—*p* level refers to row designated by asterisk.
* $\chi^2(3) = 9.54, p < .05$.

the purpose of the income tax. The responses were coded to distinguish those who answered in terms of general government support from those who mentioned only specific government services. (In most cases the services referred to are both local and visible—police, firefighting, etc.) We observe that the percentage of those referring to the government in a general sense rises slowly and steadily; all of the high school seniors do so.

NEGATIVES AND POSITIVES

Before we leave this set of interview excerpts, we want to note one more important difference between the 11- and 13-year-olds. Two of the former emphasize the negative or coercive functions of government ("To handle the state . . . so it won't get out of hand"; "So everything won't go wrong . . ."). The 13-year-olds, on the other hand, stress the positive functions of the government—keeping the country happy or working properly. This difference is so important and extensive that we will treat it in depth in a later publication, but it should be discussed at least briefly here. Younger subjects adhere to a Hobbesian view of political man. The citizenry is seen as willful and potentially dangerous, and society, therefore, as rightfully, needfully coercive and authoritarian. Although this view of the political never quite loses its appeal for a certain proportion of individuals at all ages, it nevertheless diminishes both in frequency and centrality, to be replaced, in time, by more complex views of political arrangements, views which stress the administrative sides of government (keeping the machinery oiled and in repair) or which emphasize melioristic ends (enhancing the human condition).

THE FUTURE

The adolescent years see a considerable extension of time perspective. On the one hand, a sense of history emerges, as the youngster is able to link past and present and to understand the present as having been influenced or determined by the past. On the other, the child begins to imagine the future and, what may be more important, to ponder alternative futures. Thus the present is connected to the future not merely because the future unfolds from the present, but also because the future is *tractable;* its shape depends upon choices made in the present.

This idea of the future asserts itself with increasing effect as the child advances through adolescence. In making political judgments, the youngster can anticipate the consequences of a choice taken here and now for the long-range future of the community and can weigh the probable effects of alternative choices on the future. The community is now seen to be temporal, that is, as an organism which persists beyond the life of its current members; thus judgments in the present must take into account the needs of the young and of the unborn. Further, the adolescent becomes able to envision not only the communal future, but himself (and others) in possible statuses in that future as well.

The items which most clearly expose the changing meaning of the future are those dealing with education. When we reflect on it, this is not surprising: Education is the public enterprise which most directly links the generations to each other; it is the communal activity through which one generation orients another toward the future. Several questions of public policy toward education were asked; in the answers to each the needs of the communal future weigh more heavily with increasing age. One item runs: "Some people suggested a law which would require children to go to school until they were sixteen years old. What would be the purpose of such a law?" One type of answer to this question was coded "Continuity of community"; these responses stress the community's need to sustain and perpetuate itself by educating a new generation of citizens and leaders. Typical answers were: "So children will grow up to be leaders," and "To educate people so they can carry on the government." Looking at this answer alone (analysis of the entire table would carry us beyond this topic), we find the following distribution by age (see Table 4).

Another item later in the interview poses this problem: "The people who did not have children thought it was unfair they would have to pay taxes to support the school system. What do you think of that argument?" Again the

TABLE 4   Purpose of Minimum Education Law

	AGE			
	11	13	15	18
Continuity of community	.00	.27	.33	.43

Note.—$\chi^2(3) = 11.95, p < .01$.

same category, which stresses the community's continuity and its future needs, rises sharply with age as shown in Table 5.

Finally, we want to examine another education item in some detail, since it offers a more complex view of the sense of the future in adolescent political thought, allowing us to observe changes in the child's view of the personal future. The question was the last of a series on the minimum education law. After the subject was asked to discuss its purpose (see above), he was asked whether he supports it. Almost all of our subjects did. He was then asked: "Suppose you have a parent who says 'My son is going to go into my business

TABLE 5   Should People Without Children Pay School Taxes?

	AGE			
	11	13	15	18
Continuity of community	.10	.10	.47	.60

Note.—$\chi^2(3) = 18.61, p < .001$.

anyway and he doesn't need much schooling for that.' Do you think his son should be required to go to school anyway? Why?"

Table 6 shows that as children advance into adolescence, they stress increasingly the communal function of education. Younger subjects respond more to the father's arbitrariness or to the economic consequences of the father's position. They are less likely to grasp the more remote, more general effects of a curtailed education—that it hinders the attainment of citizenship. Representative answers by 11-year-olds were: "Well, maybe he wants some other desire and if he does maybe his father is forcing him"; and ". . . let's say

TABLE 6   Should Son Be Required To Attend School Though Father Wants Him To Enter Business?

	AGE			
	11	13	15	18
Yes, education needed to function in community	.00	.23	.43	.77***
Yes, education good in itself	.03	.23	.20	.27
Yes, education needed in business	.40	.47	.23	.13
Yes, prevents parental coercion	.57	.47	.43	.23

Note.—p level refers to row designated by asterisk.
*** $\chi^2(3) = 25.54, p < .001$.

he doesn't like the business and maybe he'd want to start something new." These children stress the practical and familial aspects of the issue.

Older subjects, those 15 and 18, all but ignored both the struggle with the father and the purely pragmatic advantages of remaining in school. They discoursed, sometimes eloquently, on the child's need to know about society as a whole, to function as a citizen, and to understand the perspectives of others. Here is how one 18-year-old put it:

. . . a person should have a perspective and know a little bit about as much as he can rather than just one thing throughout his whole life and anything of others, because he'd have to know different things about different aspects of life and education and just how things are in order to get along with them, because if not then they'd be prejudiced toward their own feelings and what *they* wanted and they wouldn't be able to understand any people's needs.

Older subjects see education as the opportunity to become *cosmopolitan*, to transcend the insularities of job and kinship. For the older adolescent, leaving school early endangers the future in two ways. On the personal side, it threatens one's capacity to assume the perspective of the other and to attain an adequate breadth of outlook; thus, it imperils one's future place in the community. On the societal side, it endangers the integrity of the social order itself, by depriving the community of a cosmopolitan citizenry.

CLAIMS OF THE COMMUNITY

We have already seen that as adolescence advances the youngster is increasingly sensitive to the fact of community and its claims upon the citizen. What are the limits of these claims, the limits of political authority? To what point, and under what conditions can the state, acting in the common good, trespass upon the autonomy of the citizen? When do the community's demands violate the privacy and liberty of the individual? The clash of these principles —individual freedom versus the public welfare and safety—is one of the enduring themes of Western political theory. Many, perhaps most, discussions in political life in one way or another turn on this issue; indeed, the fact that these principles are so often used purely rhetorically (as when the cant of liberty or of the public good is employed to mask pecuniary and other motives) testifies to their salience in our political thinking.

A number of questions in the interview touched upon this topic tangentially, and some were designed to approach it directly. In these latter we asked the subject to adjudicate and comment upon a conflict between public and private interests, each of these supported by a general political principle— usually the individual's right to be free of compulsion, on the one hand, and the common good, on the other. We tried to find issues which would be tangled enough to engage the most complex modes of political reasoning. A major effort in this direction was made through a series of three connected questions on eminent domain. The series began with this question:

Here is another problem the Council faced. They decided to build a road to connect one side of the island to the other. For the most part they had no trouble buying the land on which to build the road, but one man refused to sell his land to the government. He was offered a fair price for his land but he refused, saying that he didn't want to move, that he was attached to his land, and that the Council could buy another piece of land and change the direction of the road. Many people thought he was selfish, but others thought he was in the right. What do you think?

Somewhat to our surprise, there are no strong developmental patterns visible, though we do see a moderate tendency (not significant statistically, however) for the younger subjects to side with the landowner (see Table 7). The next question in the series sharpened the issue somewhat between the Council and the reluctant landowner:

The Council met and after long discussion voted that if the landowner would not agree to give up his land for the road, he should be forced to, because the rights of all the people on the island were more important than his. Do you think this was a fair decision?

TABLE 7   Which Party Is Right in Eminent-Domain Conflict?

	AGE			
	11	13	15	18
Individual should sell; community needs come first	.30	.20	.30	.40
Detour should be made; individual rights come first	.60	.47	.27	.37
Emphasis on social responsibility; individual should be appealed to, but not forced	.10	.17	.17	.07
Ambivalence; individual is right in some ways, wrong in others	.00	.13	.27	.17

The phrasing of the second question does not alter the objective facts of the conflict; yet Table 8 shows decisive shifts in position. It is hard to be sure why: perhaps because the second question states that the Council has considered the matter at length, perhaps because the Council's decision is justified by advancing the idea of "the people's rights." Whatever the reason, we now see a marked polarization of attitude. The younger subjects—those 11 and 13—continue to side with the landowner; those 15 and 18 almost completely abandon him, although about one quarter of the latter want to avoid coercion and suggest an appeal to his sense of social responsibility.

The final question in the series tightened the screws:

TABLE 8   Should Landowner Be Forced To Sell His Land?

	AGE			
	11	13	15	18
Yes, rights of others come first	.40	.37	.63	.70
No, individual rights come first	.57	.50	.33	.07**
No, social responsibility should suffice	.03	.10	.00	.23

Note.—p level refers to row designated by asterisk.
** $\chi^2(3) = 12.17, p < .01$.

The landowner was very sure that he was right. He said that the law was unjust and he would not obey it. He had a shotgun and would shoot anyone who tried to make him get off his land. He seemed to mean business. What should the government do?

The landowner's threat startled some of the subjects, though in very different ways depending on age, as Table 9 shows: The younger subjects in these

TABLE 9   What Should Government Do If Landowner Threatens Violence?

	AGE			
	11	13	15	18
Detour	.60	.63	.37	.10
Government coercion justified	.23	.27	.57	.83

Note.—$\chi^2(3) = 29.21, p < .001$.

cases did not quite know what to do about it and suggested that he be mollified at all costs; the older subjects, if they were taken aback, were amused or disdainful, saw him as a lunatic or a hothead, and rather matter-of-factly suggested force or guile to deal with him. Nevertheless, this question did not produce any essential change in position for the sample as a whole. Those older subjects who had hoped to appeal to the landowner's social conscience despaired of this and sided with the Council. Otherwise, the earlier pattern persisted, the two younger groups continuing to support the citizen, the older ones favoring the government, and overwhelmingly so among the oldest subjects.

These findings seem to confirm the idea that older adolescents are more responsive to communal than to individual needs. Yet it would be incorrect to infer that these subjects favor the community willy-nilly. A close look at the interview protocols suggests that older adolescents choose differently because they reason differently.

Most younger children—those 13 and below—can offer no justification for their choices. Either they are content with a simple statement of preference, for example: "I think he was in the right"; or they do no more than paraphrase the question: "Well, there is really two sides to it. One is that he is attached and he shouldn't give it up, but again he should give it up for the country." These youngsters do not or cannot rationalize their decisions, neither through appeal to a determining principle, nor through a comparative analysis of each side's position. If there is an internal argument going on within the mind of the 11- or 13-year-old, he is unable to make it public; instead, he seems to choose by an intuitive ethical leap, averring that one or the other position is "fair," "in the right," or "selfish." He usually favors the landowner, because his side of the matter is concrete, personal, psychologically immediate, while the Council's position hinges on an idea of the public welfare which is too remote and abstract for these youngsters to absorb. Even those few children who try to reason from knowledge or experience more often than not flounder and end in confusion. A 13-year-old:

Like this girl in my class. Her uncle had a huge house in ——, and they tore it down and they put the new city hall there. I think they should have moved it to another place. I think they should have torn it down like they did, because they had a law that if there was something paid for, then they should give that man a different price. But then I would force him out, but I don't know how I'd do it.

What we miss in these interviews are two styles of reasoning which begin to make their appearance in 15-year-olds: first, the capacity to reason consequentially, to trace out the long-range implications of various courses of action; second, a readiness to deduce specific choices from general principles. The following excerpt from a 15-year-old's interview illustrates both of these approaches:

Well, maybe he owned only a little land if he was a farmer and even if they did give him a fair price maybe all the land was already bought on the island that was good for farming or something and he couldn't get another start in life if he did buy it. Then maybe in a sense he was selfish because if they had to buy other land and change the direction of the road why of course then maybe they'd raise taxes on things so they could get more money cause it would cost more to change directions from what they already have planned. [Fair to force him off?] Yes, really, just because one person doesn't want to sell his land that don't mean that, well the other 999 or the rest of the people on the island should go without this road because of one.

In the first part of the statement, the subject utilizes a cost-effectiveness approach; he estimates the costs (economic, social, moral) of one decision against another. He begins by examining the effects on the landowner. Can he obtain equivalent land elsewhere? He then considers the long-range economic consequences for the community. Will the purchase of other land be more expensive and thus entail a tax increase? Though he does not go on to solve these implicit equations—he could hardly do so, since he does not have sufficient information—he does state the variables he deems necessary to solve them.

The second common strategy at this age, seen in the last part of the statement, is to imply or formulate a general principle, usually ethico-political in nature, which subsumes the instance. Most adolescents using this approach will for this item advert to the community's total welfare, but some of our older adolescents suggest some other governing principle—the sanctity of property rights or the individual's right to privacy and autonomy. In either instance, the style of reasoning is the same; a general principle is sought which contains the specific issue.

Once a principle is accepted, the youngster attempts to apply it consistently. If the principle is valid, it should fall with equal weight on all; consequently, exceptions are resisted:

I think that the man should be forced to move with a good sum of money because I imagine it would be the people, it said the rights of the whole, the whole government and the whole community, why should one man change the whole idea?

And to the question of the landowner's threatening violence: "They shouldn't let him have his own way, because he would be an example. Other people would think that if they used his way, they could do what they wanted to." Even a child who bitterly opposes the Council's position on this issue agrees that once a policy has been established, exceptions should be resisted:

Well, if the government is going to back down when he offers armed resistance, it will offer ideas to people who don't like, say, the medical idea [see below]. They'll just haul out a shotgun if you come to study them. The government should go through with the action.

THE FORCE OF PRINCIPLE

Once principles and ideals are firmly established, the child's approach to political discourse is decisively altered. When he ponders a political choice, he takes into account not only *personal* consequences (What will this mean, practically speaking, for the individuals involved?) and pragmatic *social* consequences (What effect will this have on the community at large?), but also its consequences in the realm of *value* (Does this law or decision enhance or endanger such ideals as liberty, justice, and so on?). There is of course no sharp distinction among these types of consequences; values are contained, however tacitly, in the most "practical" of decisions. Nevertheless, these ideals, once they develop, have a life, an autonomy of their own. We reasoned that as the adolescent grew older, political principles and ideals would be increasingly significant, and indeed would loom large enough to overcome the appeal of personal and social utility in the narrow sense.

To test this belief we wanted an item which would pit a "good" against a "value." We devised a question proposing a law which, while achieving a personal and communal good, would at the same time violate a political ideal—in this case, the value of personal autonomy. The item ran: "One [proposed law] was a suggestion that men over 45 be required to have a yearly medical checkup. What do you think of that suggestion?" The answer was to be probed if necessary: "Would you be in favor of that? Why (or why not)?" Table 10 shows the distribution of responses.

The findings are interesting on several counts, aside from offering testimony on the degree to which good health is viewed as a summum bonum. The 11-year-olds, here as elsewhere, interpret the issue along familial and authoritarian lines. The government is seen in loco parentis; its function is to make its citizens do the sensible things they would otherwise neglect to do. But our primary interest is in the steady growth of opposition to the proposal. The basis for opposition, though it is phrased variously, is that the government has no business exercising compulsion in this domain. These youngsters look past the utilitarian appeal of the law and sense its conflict with a value that the question itself does not state. These data, then, offer some support to our suggestion that older adolescents can more easily bring abstract principles to bear in the

TABLE 10   Should Men over 45 Be Required To Have a Yearly Medical Checkup?

	AGE			
	11	13	15	18
Yes, otherwise they would not do it	.50	.07	.00	.03***
Yes, good for person and/or community	.50	.80	.70	.60
No, infringement on liberties	.00	.13	.27	.37**

Note.—p level refers to rows designated by asterisk.
** $\chi^2(3) = 11.95, p < .01$.
*** $\chi^2(3) = 33.10, p < .001$.

appraisal of political issues. Strictly speaking, the findings are not definitive, for we cannot infer that all of those supporting the law do so without respect to principle. Some of the older adolescents do, in fact, recognize the conflict implicit in the question, but argue that the public and personal benefits are so clear as to override the issue of personal liberties. But there are very few signs of this among the younger subjects. Even when pressed, as they were in a following question, they cannot grasp the meaning and significance of the conflict; they see only the tangible good.

Discussion

These findings suggest that the adolescent's sense of community is determined not by a single factor, but by the interaction of several related developmental parameters. We should now be in a position to consider what some of these are.

1. *The decline of authoritarianism.* Younger subjects are more likely to approve of coercion in public affairs. Themselves subject to the authority of adults, they more readily accept the fact of hierarchy. They find it hard to imagine that authority may be irrational, presumptuous, or whimsical; thus they bend easily to the collective will.

2. With advancing age there is an increasing grasp of the *nature and needs of the community.* As the youngster begins to understand the structure and functioning of the social order as a whole, he begins to understand too the specific social institutions within it and their relations to the whole. He comes to comprehend the autonomy of institutions, their need to remain viable, to sustain and enhance themselves. Thus the demands of the social order and its

constituent institutions, as well as the needs of the public, become matters to be appraised in formulating political choices.

3. *The absorption of knowledge and consensus.* This paper has taken for granted. and hence neglected, the adolescent's increasing knowingness. The adolescent years see a vast growth in the acquisition of political information, in which we include not only knowledge in the ordinary substantive sense, but also the apprehension of consensus, a feeling for the common and prevailing ways of looking at political issues. The child acquires these from formal teaching, as well as through a heightened cathexis of the political, which in turn reflects the generally amplified interest in the adult world. Thus, quite apart from the growth of cognitive capacity, the older adolescent's views are more "mature" in that they reflect internalization of adult perspectives.

4. We must remember that it is not enough to be exposed to mature knowledge and opinion; their absorption in turn depends on the growth of *cognitive capacities.* Some of the younger subjects knew the fact of eminent domain, knew it to be an accepted practice, yet, unable to grasp the principles involved, could not apply their knowledge effectively to the question. This paper has stressed the growth of those cognitive capacities which underlie the particular intellectual achievements of the period: the adolescent's increasing ability to weigh the relative consequences of actions, the attainment of deductive reasoning. The achievement of these capacities—the leap to "formal operations," in Piaget's term—allows him to escape that compulsion toward the immediate, the tangible, the narrowly pragmatic which so limits the political discourse of younger adolescents.

5. In turn the growth of cognitive capacity allows *the birth of ideology.* Ideology may not be quite the right word here, for it suggests a degree of coherence and articulation that few of our subjects, even the oldest and brightest, come close to achieving. Nevertheless there is an impressive difference between the younger and older adolescents in the orderliness and internal consistency of their political perspectives. What passes for ideology in the younger respondents is a raggle-taggle array of sentiments: "People ought to be nice to each other"; "There are a lot of wise guys around, so you have to have strict laws." In time these sentiments may mature (or harden) into ideologies or ideological dispositions, but they are still too erratic, too inconsistent. They are not yet principled or generalized and so tend to be self-contradictory, or loosely held and hence easily abandoned. When younger subjects are cross-questioned, however gently, they are ready to reverse themselves even on issues they seem to feel strongly about. When older subjects are challenged, however sharply, they refute, debate, and counterchallenge. In some part their resistance to easy change reflects a greater degree of poise and their greater experience in colloquy and argument, but it also bespeaks the fact that their views are more firmly founded. The older adolescents, most conspicuously those at 18, aim for an inner concordance of political belief.

These then are the variables our study has suggested as directing the growth of political concepts. We must not lean too heavily on any one of them: The development of political thoughts is not simply or even largely a function of cognitive maturation or of increased knowledge or of the growth of ideology when these are taken alone. This paper has stressed the cognitive parameters because they seem to be so influential at the younger ages. The early adolescent's political thought is constrained by personalized, concrete, present-oriented modes of approach. Once these limits are transcended, the adolescent is open to influence by knowledge, by the absorption of consensus, and by the principles he adopts from others or develops on his own.

A DEVELOPMENTAL SYNOPSIS

We are now in a position to summarize the developmental patterns which have emerged in this study. It is our impression that the most substantial advance is to be found in the period between 11 and 13 years, where we discern a marked shift in the cognitive basis of political discourse. Our observations support the Inhelder and Piaget (1958) findings on a change from concrete to formal operations at this stage. To overstate the case somewhat, we might say that the *11-year-old* has not achieved the capacity for formal operations. His thinking is concrete, egocentric, tied to the present; he is unable to envision long-range social consequences; he cannot comfortably reason from premises; he has not attained hypothetico-deductive modes of analysis. The 13-year-old has achieved these capacities some (much?) of the time, but is unable to display them with any consistent effectiveness. The *13-year-olds* seem to be the most labile of our subjects. Depending on the item, they may respond like those older or younger than themselves. In a sense they are on the threshold of mature modes of reasoning, just holding on, and capable of slipping back easily. Their answers are the most difficult to code, since they often involve an uneasy mixture of the concrete and the formal.

The *15-year-old* has an assured grasp of formal thought. He neither hesitates nor falters in dealing with the abstract; when he seems to falter, it is more likely due to a lack of information or from a weakness in knowing and using general principles. His failures are likely to be in content and in fluency, rather than in abstract quality per se. Taking our data as a whole we usually find only moderate differences between 15 and 18. We do find concepts that appear suddenly between 11 and 13, and between 13 and 15, but only rarely do we find an idea substantially represented at 18 which is not also available to a fair number of 15-year-olds.

The *18-year-old* is, in other words, the 15-year-old, only more so. He knows more; he speaks from a more extended apperceptive mass; he is more facile; he can elaborate his ideas more fluently. Above all, he is more philosophical, more ideological in his perspective on the political order. At times he is consciously, deliberately an ideologue. He holds forth.

REFERENCES

Easton, D., & Hess, R. D. Youth and the political system. In S. M. Lipset & L. Lowenthal (Eds.), *Culture and social character.* New York: Free Press of Glencoe, 1961. Pp. 226–251.

Easton, D., & Hess, R. D. The child's political world. *Midwest Journal of Political Science,* 1962, 6, 229–246.

Greenstein, F. *Children and politics.* New Haven: Yale University Press, 1965.

Hyman, H. H. *Political socialization.* Glencoe, Ill.: Free Press, 1959.

Inhelder, B., & Piaget, J. *The growth of logical thinking from childhood to adolescence.* New York: Basic Books, 1958.

[16] *Lawrence Kohlberg* MORAL EDUCATION IN THE SCHOOLS: A DEVELOPMENTAL VIEW

For many contemporary educators and social scientists, the term "moral education" has an archaic ring, the ring of the last vestiges of the Puritan tradition in the modern school. This archaic ring, however, does not arise from any intrinsic opposition between the statement of educational aims and methods in moral terms and their statement in psychological terms. In fact, it was just this opposition which the great pioneers of the social psychology of education denied in such works as John Dewey's *Moral Principles in Education*[1] and Emile Durkheim's *Moral Education.*[2] Both of these works attempted to define moral education in terms of a broader consideration of social development and social functions than was implied by conventional opinion on the topic, but both recognized that an ultimate statement of the social aims and processes of education must be a statement couched in moral terms.

Unfortunately, the educational psychologists and philosophers who followed Dewey's trail retained his concern about a broad phrasing of the goals of education in terms of the child's social traits and values (e.g., co-operation, social adjustment, "democraticness," mental health) without retaining Dewey's awareness that intelligent thought about these traits and values required the concepts dealt with by moral philosophers and psychologists. More recently, however, thoughtful educators and psychologists have become acutely aware

FROM R. E. GRINDER (ED.) *Studies in Adolescence.* (2ND ED.) NEW YORK: MACMILLAN, 1969, PP. 237–258. THE ORIGINAL VERSION OF THIS PAPER APPEARED IN *The School Review,* 1966, 74, 1–29. COPYRIGHT 1966 BY THE UNIVERSITY OF CHICAGO. REPRINTED BY PERMISSION OF THE AUTHOR, R. E. GRINDER, THE UNIVERSITY OF CHICAGO PRESS, AND THE MACMILLAN COMPANY.

of the inadequacies of dealing with moral issues under cover of mental health or group-adjustment labels. We have become aware, on the one hand, that these mental-health labels are not really scientific and value-neutral terms; they are ways of making value judgments about children in terms of social norms and acting accordingly. On the other hand, we have come to recognize that mental-health and social-adjustment terms do not really allow us to define the norms and values that are most basic as ideals for our children. The barbarities of the socially conforming members of the Nazi system and the other-directed hollow men growing up in our own affluent society have made us acutely aware of the fact that adjustment to the group is no substitute for moral maturity.

It is apparent, then, that the problems of moral education cannot be successfully considered in the "value-neutral" terms of personality development and adjustment. In this paper, I shall attempt to deal with some of the value issues involved in moral education but will approach these issues from the standpoint of research findings. I believe that a number of recent research facts offer some guide through the problems of moral education when these facts are considered from Dewey's general perspective as to the relationship between fact and value in education.

Research findings on the development of moral character relevant to moral education in the schools

One of the major reasons why the social functions of the school have not been phrased in moral-education terms has been the fact that conventional didactic ethical instruction in the school has little influence upon moral character as usually conceived. This conclusion seemed clearly indicated by Hartshorne and May's findings that character-education classes and religious-instruction programs had no influence on moral conduct, as the latter was objectively measured by experimental tests of "honesty" (cheating, lying, stealing) and "service" (giving up objects for others' welfare).[3] The small amount of recent research on conventional didactic moral education provides us with no reason to question these earlier findings. Almost every year a professional religious educator or community-service educator takes a course with me and attempts to evaluate the effect of his program upon moral character. While each starts by thinking his program is different from those evaluated by Hartshorne and May, none comes away with any more positive evidence than did these earlier workers.

While recent research does not lead us to question Hartshorne and May's findings as to the ineffectiveness of conventional, formal moral education, it does lead us to a more positive view as to the possibility of effective school moral education of some new sort. In particular, recent research leads us to question the two most common interpretations of the Hartshorne and May findings: the interpretation that moral behavior is purely a matter of immediate situational forces and rewards and the interpretation that moral character is a matter of deep emotions fixed in earliest childhood in the home. Instead, recent research suggests that the major consistencies of moral character represent the slowly developing formation of more or less cognitive principles of moral judgment and decision and of related ego abilities.

The first interpretation of the Hartshorne and May findings mentioned was essentially that of these authors themselves. Their conclusions were much more nihilistic than the mere conclusion that conventional moral-education classes were ineffective and essentially implied that there was no such thing as "moral character" or "conscience" to be educated anyway. Hartshorne and May found that the most influential factors determining resistance to temptation to cheat or disobey were situational factors rather than a fixed, individual moral-character trait of honesty. The first finding leading to this conclusion was that of the low predictability of cheating in one situation for cheating in another. A second finding was that children were not divisible into two groups, "cheaters" and "honest children." Children's cheating scores were distributed in bell-curve fashion around an average score of moderate cheating. A third finding was the importance of the expediency aspect of the decision to cheat, that is, the tendency to cheat depends upon the degree of risk of detection and the effort required to cheat. Children who cheated in more risky situations also cheated in less risky situations. Thus, non-cheaters appeared to be primarily more cautious rather than more honest than cheaters. A fourth finding was that even when honest behavior was not dictated by concern about punishment or detection, it was largely determined by immediate situational factors of group approval and example (as opposed to being determined by internal moral values). Some classrooms showed a high tendency to cheat, while other seemingly identically composed classrooms in the same school showed little tendency to cheat. A fifth finding was that moral knowledge had little apparent influence on moral conduct, since the correlations between verbal tests of moral knowledge and experimental tests of moral conduct were low ($r = .34$). A sixth apparent finding was that where moral values did seem to be related to conduct, these values were somewhat specific to the child's social class or group. Rather than being a universal ideal, honesty was more characteristic of the middle class and seemed less relevant to the lower-class child.

Taken at their face value, these findings suggested that moral education inside or outside the school could have no lasting effect. The moral educator, whether in the home or in the school, could create a situation in which the child would not cheat, but this would not lead to the formation of a general tendency not to cheat when the child entered a new situation. Carried to its logical conclusion, this interpretation of the findings suggested that "honesty" was just an external value judgment of the child's act which leads to no understanding or prediction of his character. It suggested that concepts of good or bad conduct were psychologically irrelevant and that moral conduct must be understood, like other conduct, in terms of the child's needs, his group's values, and the demands of the situation. "While from the standpoint of society, behavior is either 'good' or 'bad,' from the standpoint of the individual it always has some positive value. It represents the best solution for his conflicting drives that he has been able to formulate."[4] This line of thought was extended to the view that moral terms are sociologically as well as psychologically irrelevant. From the standpoint of society, behavior is not clearly good or bad either, since there are a multiplicity of standards that can be used in judging the morality of an action. As sociologists have pointed out, delinquent actions may be motivated by the need to "do right" or conform to standards, to both the standards of the delinquent gang and the great American standard of success.[5]

A second interpretation of the Hartshorne and May findings was somewhat less nihilistic. This interpretation was that suggested by psychoanalytic and neopsychoanalytic theories of personality.[6] In this interpretation, moral instruction in the school was ineffective because moral character is formed in the home by early parental influences. Moral character, so conceived, is not a matter of fixed moral virtues, like honesty, but of deep emotional tendencies and defenses—of love as opposed to hate for others, of guilt as opposed to fear, of self-esteem and trust as opposed to feelings of inadequacy and distrust. Because these tendencies are basically affective, they are not consistently displayed in verbal or behavioral test situations, but they do define personality types. These types, and their characteristic affective responses, can be defined at the deeper levels tapped by personality projective tests, but they are also related to other people's judgments of the child's moral character. This point of view toward moral character was most clearly developed and empirically supported in the writing and research of Robert Havighurst and his colleagues.[7]

While both the "situational" and the "psychoanalytic" interpretations of moral-character research have some validity, recent research findings support a different and more developmental conception of moral character with more positive implications for moral education.[8] While a specific act of "misconduct," such as cheating, is largely determined by situational factors, acts of misconduct are also clearly related to two general aspects of the child's personality development. The first general aspect of the child's development is often termed "ego strength" and represents a set of interrelated ego abilities, including the intelligent prediction of consequences, the tendency to choose the greater remote reward over the lesser immediate reward, the ability to maintain stable focused attention, and a number of other traits. All these abilities are found to predict (or correlate with) the child's behavior on experimental tests of honesty, teacher's ratings of moral character, and children's resistance to delinquent behavior.[9]

The second general aspect of personality that determines moral conduct is the level of development of the child's moral judgments or moral concepts. Level of moral judgment is quite a different matter from the knowledge of, and assent to, conventional moral clichés studied by Hartshorne and May. If one asks a child, "Is it very bad to cheat?" or "Would you ever cheat?" a child who cheats a lot in reality is somewhat more likely to give the conforming answer than is the child who does not cheat in reality.[10] This is because the same desire to "look good" on a spelling test by cheating impels him to "look good" on the moral-attitude test by lying. If, instead, one probes the reasons for the moral choices of the child, as Piaget and I have done,[11] one finds something quite different. As as example, we present the child with a series of moral dilemmas, such as whether a boy should tell his father a confidence about a brother's misdeed. In reply, Danny, age ten, said: "In one way, it would be right to tell on his brother or his father might get mad at him and spank him. In another way, it would be right to keep quiet or his brother might beat him up." Obviously, whether Danny decides it is right to maintain authority or right to maintain peer "loyalty" is of little interest compared to the fact that his decision will be based on his anticipation of who can hit harder. It seems likely that Danny will not cheat if he anticipates punishment but that he has no particular moral reasons for not cheating if he can get away with it. When asked, the only reason he gave for not cheating was that "you might get caught," and his teacher rated him high on a dishonesty rating form.

Danny's response, however, is not a unique aspect of a unique personality. It represents a major aspect of a consistent stage of development of moral judgment, a stage in which moral judgments are based on considerations of punishment and obedience. It is the first of the following six stages found in the development of moral judgment:[12]

Level I—premoral

Stage 1. Obedience and punishment orientation. Egocentric deference to superior power or prestige, or a trouble-avoiding set. Objective responsibility.

Stage 2. Naïvely egoistic orientation. Right action is that instrumentally satisfying the self's needs and occasionally others. Awareness of relativism of value to each actor's needs and perspectives. Naïve egalitarianism and orientation to exchange and reciprocity.

Level II—conventional role conformity

Stage 3. Good-boy orientation. Orientation to approval and to pleasing and helping others. Conformity to stereotypical images of majority or natural role behavior, and judgment of intentions.

Stage 4. Authority and social-order-maintaining orientation. Orientation to "doing duty" and to showing respect for authority and maintaining the given social order for its own sake. Regard for earned expectations of others.

Level III—self-accepted moral principles

Stage 5. Contractual legalistic orientation. Recognition of an arbitrary element or starting point in rules or expectations for the sake of agreement. Duty defined in terms of contract, general avoidance of violation of the will or rights of others, and majority will and welfare.

Stage 6. Conscience or principle orientation. Orientation not only to actually ordained social rules but to principles of choice involving appeal to logical universality and consistency. Orientation to conscience as a directing agent and to mutual respect and trust.

Each of these stages is defined by twenty-five basic aspects of moral values. Danny's responses primarily illustrated the motivation aspect of Stage 1, the fact that moral motives are defined in terms of punishment. The motivation for moral action at each stage, and examples illustrating them, are as follows:

Stage 1. Obey rules to avoid punishment. Danny, age ten: (Should Joe tell on his older brother to his father?) "In one way it would be right to tell on his brother or his father might get mad at him and spank him. In another way it would be right to keep quiet or his brother might beat him up."

Stage 2. Conform to obtain rewards, have favors returned, and so on. Jimmy, age thirteen: (Should Joe tell on his older brother to his father?) "I think he should keep quiet. He might want to go someplace like that, and if he squeals on Alex, Alex might squeal on him."

Stage 3. Conform to avoid disapproval, dislike by others. Andy, age sixteen: (Should Joe keep quiet about what his brother did?) "If my father finds out later, he won't trust me. My brother wouldn't either, but I wouldn't have a *conscience* that he (my brother) didn't." "I try to do things for my parents; they've always done things for me. I try to do everything my mother says; I try to please her. Like she wants me to be a doctor, and I want to, too, and she's helping me to get up there."

Stage 4. Conform to avoid censure by legitimate authorities and resultant guilt. Previous example also indicative of this.

Stage 5. Conform to maintain the respect of the impartial spectator judging in terms of community welfare or to maintain a relation of mutual respect. Bob, age sixteen: "His brother thought he could trust him. His brother wouldn't think much of him if he told like that."

Stage 6. Conform to avoid self-condemnation. Bill, age sixteen: (Should the husband steal the expensive black-market drug needed to save his wife's life?) "Lawfully no, but morally speaking I think I would have done it. It would be awfully hard to live with myself afterward, knowing that I could have done something which would have saved her life and yet didn't for fear of punishment to myself."

While motivation is one of the twenty-five aspects of morality defining the stages, many of the aspects are more cognitive. An example is the aspect of "The Basis of Moral Worth of Human Life," which is defined for each stage as follows:

Stage 1. The value of a human life is confused with the value of physical objects and is based on the social status or physical attributes of its possessor. Tommy, age ten: (Why should the druggist give the drug to the dying woman when her husband couldn't pay for it?) "If someone important is in a plane and is allergic to heights and the stewardess won't give him medicine because she's only got enough for one and she's got a sick one, a friend in back, they'd probably put the stewardess in a lady's jail because she didn't help the important one."

(Is it better to save the life of one important person or a lot of unimportant people?) "All the people that aren't important because one man just has one house, maybe a lot of furniture, but a whole bunch of people have an awful lot of furniture and some of these poor people might have a lot of money and it doesn't look it."

Stage 2. The value of a human life is seen as instrumental to the satisfaction of the needs of its possessor or of other persons. Tommy, age thirteen: (Should the doctor "mercy kill" a fatally ill woman requesting death because of her pain?) "Maybe it would be good to put her out of her pain, she'd be better off that way. But the husband wouldn't want it, not like an animal. If a pet dies you can get along without it—it isn't something you really need. Well, you can get a new wife, but it's not really the same."

Stage 3. The value of human life is based on the empathy and affection of family members and others toward its possessor. Andy, age sixteen: (Should the doctor "mercy kill" a fatally ill woman requesting death because of her pain?) "No, he shouldn't. The husband loves her and wants to see her. He wouldn't want her to die sooner, he loves her too much."

Stage 4. Life is conceived as sacred in terms of its place in a categorical moral or religious order of rights and duties. John, age sixteen: (Should the doctor "mercy kill" the woman?) "The doctor wouldn't have the right to take a life, no human has the right. He can't create life, he shouldn't destroy it."

Stage 5. Life is valued both in terms of its relation to community welfare and in terms of life being a universal human right.

Stage 6. Belief in the sacredness of human life as representing a universal human value of respect for the individual. Steve, age sixteen: (Should the husband steal the expensive drug to save his wife?) "By the law of society he was wrong but by the law of nature or of God the druggist was wrong and the husband was justified. Human life is above financial gain. Regardless of who was dying, if it was a total stranger, man has a duty to save him from dying."

We have spoken of our six types of moral judgment as stages. By this we mean more than the fact that they are age-related. First, a stage concept implies sequence, it implies that each child must go step by step through each of the kinds of moral judgment outlined. It is, of course, possible for a child to stop (become "fixated") at any level of development, but if he continues to move upward he must move in this stepwise fashion. While the findings are not completely analyzed on this issue, a longitudinal study of the same boys studied at ages ten, thirteen, sixteen, and nineteen suggests that this is the case. Second, a stage concept implies universality of sequence under varying cultural conditions. It implies that moral development is not merely a matter of learning the verbal values or rules of the child's culture but reflects something more universal in development which would occur in any culture. In order to examine this assumption, the same moral-judgment method was used with boys aged ten, thirteen, and sixteen in a Taiwanese city, in a Malaysian (Atayal) aboriginal tribal village, and in a Turkish village, as well as in America. The results for Taiwan and for America are presented in Figure 1.

Figure 1 indicates much the same age trends in both the Tiawanese and

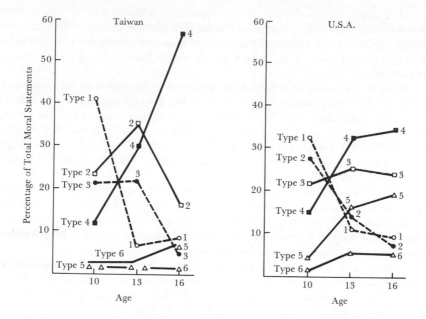

FIGURE 1   Mean per cent of use of each of six stages of moral judgment at three ages in Taiwan and the United States.

the American boys. It is evident that in both groups the first two types decrease with age, the next two increase until age thirteen and then stabilize, and the last two continue to increase from age thirteen to age sixteen. In general, the cross-cultural studies suggest a similar sequence of development in all cultures, although they suggest that the last two stages of moral thought do not develop clearly in preliterate village or tribal communities.

In the third place, the stage concept implies personality consistency. We said that there was little consistency to honest behavior as such. There is, however, a high degree of consistency, a "g-factor" of moral stage, from one verbal moral situation to the next.[13]

In order to consider the relevance of these moral-judgment stages for our conceptions of moral character, we must consider a little further their relationship to moral conduct. We have already noted that verbal agreement to moral conventions does not generally predict to moral behavior. We noted that when Hartshorne and May measured the child's "knowledge" of the society's moral conventions (as opposed to his response to moral-attitude tests, assessing strength of verbal assent to these convictions), slightly better predictions were obtained; tests of moral knowledge correlated with experimental tests of cheating in the low 30's, about as well as a single cheating test correlates with another. These tests of moral knowledge require somewhat more cognitive understanding of cultural moral prescriptions than do verbal moral-attitude tests, and they are somewhat more age developmental. Our tests of moral judgment, which are more genuinely developmental and reflective of basic cognitive structuring of values than moral-knowledge tests, are still better predictors of moral conduct, however, if moral conduct is conceived in developmental terms.

In referring to a definition of moral conduct, in developmental terms, we refer to the implications of the fact found by Hartshorne and May and corroborated by more recent investigations[14]—the fact that such behaviors as honesty (resistance to cheating) do not increase with age during the elementary school years.[15] In contrast, we saw that moral judgment and values were developing in sequential fashion during these years. For the majority of these elementary school years, however, the child has not developed any clear or internal moral values or principles that condemn cheating, so it is not surprising that cheating behavior does not decline in these years. While most elementary school children are aware of, and concerned about, the harm done others by acts of aggression or theft,[16] their only reason for not cheating is their fear of being caught and punished. Even at older ages, teachers give children few moral or mature reasons to think cheating is bad. Sixth-grade children tell us their teachers tell them not to cheat because they will get punished (Stage 1) "or because the person you copied from might have it wrong and so it won't do you any good" (Stage 2, expediency). In these years, then, resistance to cheating is not so much a matter of internal moral principles as of the situational and expediency factors stressed by Hartshorne and May. With regard to the type of cheating test situation used by Hartshorne and May, the critical issue for the subject's moral judgment is that of trust, what the experimenter or the teacher expects and what he has the right to expect. The experimenter explicitly leaves the subject unsupervised in a situation where he ordinarily expects supervision. This abandonment of control or authority is interpreted in varying ways. A very high degree of cheating in such a situation seems to primarily reflect a naïve abandon to the surface impression that the experimenter doesn't care. A lesser degree of cheating seems to reflect the child's belief that the experimenter doesn't care very much about his not cheating or he wouldn't leave him unsupervised and that a little cheating isn't too bad anyhow, so long as it is not too obvious and excessive or more than the others do.

In one study of sixth graders[17] almost all (80 per cent) of the children cheated somewhat. The majority of children at the premoral level of moral judgment (Stages 1 and 2) cheated a great deal, and the majority of the children at the conventional level of moral judgment (Stages 3 and 4) cheated a slight or moderate amount.[18] In contrast, adolescents at the level of moral principle (Stages 5 and 6) do interpret the opportunity to cheat as involving issues of maintaining trust, contract, social agreement, and equality of reward for equal effort and ability. The one sixth grader in the Kohlberg study at this level did not cheat at all.[19] Among a group of college students also studied, only one of nine principled-level subjects cheated on an experimental test while about one half of the twenty-six conventional-level subjects did so. (There were no premoral-level subjects in this group.)

Cheating, then, is not a good indicator of moral character until the child has developed in adolescence a set of inner moral principles that prohibit it. By that time, cheating behavior may reflect a lack of full development of moral values (i.e., a failure to reach the level of moral principles) or a discrepancy between action and moral values (a discrepancy due to a variety of possible deficits in ego strength or ego abilities).

More generally, then, there is some meaning to "moral character" as an aim of moral education if moral character is conceived of in developmental terms rather than as a set of fixed conventional traits of honesty, responsibility, etc.

Hartshorne and May's critique is justified insofar as it is a critique of a tendency of teachers to respond to isolated acts of deviance as indicating the child's bad or dishonest character. Specific acts of conformity or deviance in themselves reflect primarily situational wishes and fears rather than the presence or absence of conscience or moral character. Nevertheless, there is evidence that repeated misconduct tends to indicate general deficits or retardation of general moral-judgment capacities, or related guilt capacities, and the lack of internal ego control rather than simply situational values or emotional conflicts. While everyday judgments of moral character and worth are often psychologically erroneous, they do correlate with important consistencies in personality and development, which are positive from almost any viewpoint.

In addition to giving new meaning to notions of moral character, recent research also suggests that it may be possible to stimulate the development of moral character in the school. We said that there has been no recent research evidence to suggest revision of Hartshorne and May's finding that conention moral- and religious-education classes had no direct influence on moral conduct as usually conceived. (More recently, ongoing research by Jacob Kounin also suggests that the teacher's use of various techniques of punishment and reward for misconduct has no relationship to the amount and type of misconduct that occurs in the classroom.) These negative results have usually been interpreted as indicating that only the home can have any real effect in moral teaching, because only the home teaching involves the intense and continuing emotional relationships necessary for moral teaching or for induction of potential guilt feelings for wrongdoing. In fact, the failure of conventional moral education in the school is probably not the result of the powerlessness of the school to influence the child's character but the result of the inadequacy of prevalent American conceptions of character education. These conceptions usually center on the training of good "habits" of honesty, responsibility, etc., through preaching, example, punishment, and reward. This conception of character education appears to be just as ineffective in the home as it is in the school. Extensive research on parental practices has found no positive or consistent relationships between earliness and amount of parental demands or training in good habits (obedience, caring for property, performing chores, neatness, or avoidance of cheating) and their children's actual obedience, responsibility and honesty. Amount of use of praise, of deprivation of physical rewards, or of physical punishment is also not found to relate consistently or positively to measures of moral character.[20]

There are, of course, a number of unique influences of the home on the development of character which the school cannot reproduce. These are not matters of specific moral training, however, but of the emotional climate in which the child develops. The only parent-attitude variables consistently found to relate to children's moral character are not "moral training" variables but variables of parental warmth.[21] These emotional-climate variables, however, only account for a very small percentage of the differences between children in moral development or moral character. Many of the environmental influences important in moral development are more cognitive in nature than either the "good habits" or the "early emotions" views have suggested. In part, this cognitive influence is meant in a relatively conventional mental-age or I.Q. sense. Intelligence quotient correlates well with maturity of moral judgment (31 to 53 at varying ages) and almost equally well with behavioral measures of honesty. At the kindergarten level, the capacity to make judgments of good or bad in terms of standards rather than in terms of punishment and egoistic interests is a capacity almost completely determined by cognitive development on Piaget tests of cognition.[22]

We have discussed the influence of general intellectual advance upon the development of moral judgment. In addition, advances in a number of aspects of social concepts customarily thought of as part of the social-studies curriculum are correlated with advance in moral judgment. Children in the original Kohlberg study were asked to say how much and why various occupations (such as judge, policeman, soldier, artist, senator) were respected by most people, an apparent question of comprehension of social fact and function. Responses to this task could be scored in a fashion similar to the moral-judgment questions, and individual children's levels were similar on the two tasks.

This task pointed up the fact that some of the difficulties in moral development of lower-class children are largely cognitive in nature. Sociologists and social critics like Paul Goodman and Edgar Friedenberg have stressed the notion that the school not only transmits middle-class moral values at the expense of lower-class moral values but that there is a certain fundamental "immorality" or "inauthenticity" about these middle-class values to the lower-class child in comparison with lower-class values. While sociologists are correct in stressing class-linked value systems, they are not correct in postulating class-based differences in *basic moral* values. The lower-class parent and the middle-class parent show little difference in the rank order of moral values desired for their children; for example, both put honesty at the top of the list.[23] In the Kohlberg studies of moral ideology middle-class and working-class children (matched for I.Q.) differed considerably. These differences, however, were developmental in nature. At one age, middle-class and working-class children differed in one way, at another in a different way. At all ages, however, the middle-class children tended to be somewhat in advance of the working-class children. The differences, then, were not due to the fact that the middle-class children heavily favored some one type of thought, which could be seen as corresponding to the prevailing middle-class pattern. Instead, middle-class and working-class children seemed to move faster and farther.

This finding becomes intelligible when it is recalled that the institutions with moral authority (law, government, family, the work order) and the basic moral rules are the same regardless of the individual's particular position in society. The child's position in society does to a large extent, however, determine his interpretation of these institutions and rules. Law and the government are perceived quite differently by the child if he feels a sense of understanding and potential participation in the social order than if he does not.[24]

The slower development of moral judgment of the working-class boys seemed largely accountable for by two factors, lesser understanding of the broader social order and lesser sense of participation in it. Both factors showed up especially in the social-concept task conceiving occupations but were apparent in their moral judgments as well. It seems likely that social-studies programs in the school could have considerably more positive effect upon these class-differentiating aspects of moral development than is true at present.

Our discussion of social class stressed opportunities for social participation and role-taking as factors stimulating moral development. Perhaps a clearer example of the importance of social participation in moral development is the finding that children with extensive peer-group participation advance considerably more quickly through the Kohlberg stages of moral judgment than children who are isolated from such participation (with both groups equated for social class and I.Q.). This clearly suggests the relevance and potential of the classroom peer group for moral education. In pointing to the effects of extra-familial determinants upon moral development, we have focused primarily on their influence upon development of moral judgment. However, these same determinants lead to more mature moral behavior as well, as indicated by teachers' ratings and experimental measures of honesty and of moral autonomy.[25]

A development conception of the aims and nature of moral education

The facts, then, suggest the possibilities of useful planning of the moral-education component of schooling. Such planning raises more fundamental value issues, however, the issues as to the legitimate aims and methods of moral education in the American public schools. The writer would start by arguing that there are no basic value problems raised by the assertion that the school *should* be consciously concerned about moral education, since all schools necessarily are constantly involved in moral education. The teacher is constantly and unavoidably moralizing to children, about rules and values and about his students' behavior toward each other. Since such moralizing is unavoidable, it seems logical that it be done in terms of conscious formulated goals of moral development. As it stands, liberal teachers do not want to indoctrinate children with their own private moral values. Since the classroom social situation requires moralizing by the teacher, he ordinarily tends to limit and focus his moralizing toward the necessities of classroom management, that is, upon the immediate and relatively trivial behaviors that are disrupting to him or to the other children. Exposure to the diversity of moral views of teachers is undoubtedly one of the enlightening experiences of growing up, but the present system of thoughtlessness as to which of the teacher's moral attitudes or views he communicates to children and which he does not leaves much to be desired. Many teachers would be most mortified and surprised to know what their students perceive to be their moral values and concerns. My seven-year-old son told me one day that he was one of the good boys in school, but he didn't know whether he really wanted to be. I asked him what the differences between the good and bad boys were, and he said the bad boys talked in class and didn't put books away neatly, so they got yelled at. Not only is it highly dubious that his teacher's moralizing was stimulating his or any of the children's moral development, but it is almost inevitable that this be the case in an educational system in which teachers have no explicit or thought-out conception of the aims and methods of moral education and simply focus upon immediate classroom-management concerns in their moralizing.

The value problems of moral education, then, do not arise concerning the necessity of engaging in moral education in the school, since this is already being done every day. The value problems arise, however, concerning the formulation of the aims and content of such education. At its extreme, such a formulation of aims suggests a conception of moral education as the imposition of a state-determined set of values, first by the bureaucrats upon the teachers, and then by the teachers upon the children. This is the system of "character education" employed in Russia, as described by U. Bronfenbrenner.[26] In Russia, the entire classroom process is explicitly defined as "character education," that is, as making good socialist citizens, and the teacher appears to have an extremely strong influence upon children's moral standards. This influence rests in part upon the fact that the teacher is perceived as "the priest of society," as the agent of the all-powerful state, and can readily enlist the parents as agents of discipline to enforce school values and demands. In part, however, it rests upon the fact that the teacher systematically uses the peer group as an agent of moral indoctrination and moral sanction. The classroom is divided into co-operating groups in competition with one another. If a member of one of the groups is guilty of misconduct, the teacher downgrades or sanctions the whole group, and the group in turn punishes the individual miscreant. This is, of course, an extremely effective form of social control if not of moral development.

In our view, there is a third alternative to a state moral-indoctrination system and to the current American system of moralizing by individual teachers and principals when children deviate from minor administrative regulations or engage in behavior personally annoying to the teacher. This alternative is to take the stimulation of the development of the individual child's moral judgment and character as a goal of moral education, rather than taking as its goal either administrative convenience or state-defined values. The attractiveness of defining the goal of moral education as the stimulation of development rather than as teaching fixed virtues is that it means aiding the child to take the next step in a direction toward which he is already tending, rather than imposing an alien pattern upon him. An example of the difference may be given in terms of the use of the peer group. In Russia the peer-group structure is created by the teacher (i.e., he divides the classroom into groups), and the peer group is then manipulated by punishments and rewards so as to impose the teacher's or the school's values upon its deviant members. If one took the stimulation of the moral development of the individual child as a goal, one would consider the role of the peer group in quite a different way. In the previous section we discussed the fact that classroom isolates were slower in development of moral judgment than were integrates. This suggests that inclusion of the social isolates in the classroom peer group might have considerable influence on their moral development, though not necessarily an influence of immediate conformity to teacher or school demands.

The implementation of this goal would involve various methods to encourage inclusion of isolates such as are under investigation in a research project at the University of Michigan conducted by Ronald Lippett. Some of these methods involve creating a classroom atmosphere encouraging participation rather than attempting to directly influence sociometric integrates to include isolates. Some of these methods involve more direct appeal to integrated members of sociometric groups, but an appeal to the implementation of already existing social and moral values held by these children rather than an effort to impose the teacher's values upon them by reward or punishment. The process raises many valuable issues potentially stimulating the moral development of the integrates as well, since they must cope with the fact that, "Well, we were finally nice to him and look what he did." These issues involve the opportunity for the teacher to play a different and perhaps more stimulating and open role as a "moral guide" than that involved in supporting conformity to school rules and teacher demands.

A definition of the aims of moral education as the stimulation of natural development is most clear-cut in the area of moral judgment, where there appears to be considerable regularity of sequence and direction in development in various cultures. Because of this regularity, it is possible to define the maturity of a child's moral judgment without considering its content (the particular action judged) and without considering whether it agrees with our own particular moral judgments or values or those of the American middle-class culture as a whole. In fact, the sign of the child's moral maturity is his ability to make moral judgments and formulate moral principles of his own, rather than his ability to conform to moral judgments of the adults around him.[27]

How in general, then, may moral maturity as an aim of education be defined? One general answer starts from the conception of maturity in moral judgment and then considers conduct in terms of its correspondence to such judgment. Maturity levels are most clearly apparent in moral judgment. Furthermore, the general direction of maturity of moral judgment is a direction of greater morality. Each of the Kohlberg stages of moral judgment represents a step toward a more genuinely or distinctly moral judgment. We do not mean by this that a more mature judgment is more moral in the sense of showing closer conformity to the conventional standards of a given community. We mean that a more mature judgment more closely corresponds to genuine moral judgments as these have been defined by philosophers. While philosophers have been unable to agree upon any ultimate principle of the good that would define "correct" moral judgments, most philosophers agree upon the characteristics that make a judgment a genuine moral judgment.[28] Moral judgments are judgments about the good and the right of action. Not all judgments of "good" or "right" are moral judgments, however; many are judgments of esthetic, technological, or prudential goodness or rightness. Unlike judgments of prudence or esthetics, moral judgments tend to be universal, inclusive, consistent, and to be grounded on objective, impersonal, or ideal grounds.[29] "She's really great, she's beautiful and a good dancer"; "the right way to make a Martini is five to one"—these are statements about the good and right that are not moral judgments since they lack these characteristics: If we say, "Martinis should be made five to one," we are making an esthetic judgment, and we are not prepared to say that we want everyone to make them that way, that they are good in terms of some impersonal ideal standard shared by others, and that we and others should make five-to-one Martinis whether they wish to or not. In a similar fashion, when Danny answered our "moral should" question, "Should Joe tell on his older brother?" in Stage 1 terms of the probabilities of getting beaten up by his father and by his brother, he did not answer with a moral judgment that is universal (applies to all brothers in that situation and ought to be agreed upon by all people thinking about the situation) or that has any impersonal or ideal grounds. In contrast, the Stage 6 statements quoted earlier not only specifically use moral words, such as "morally right" and "duty," but use them in a moral way; for example, "regardless of who it was" and "by the law of nature or of God" imply universality; "morally, I would do it in spite of fear of punishment" implies impersonality and ideality of obligation, etc. Thus the value of judgments of lower-level subjects about moral matters are not moral responses in the same sense in which the value judgments of high-level subjects about esthetic or morally neutral matters are not moral. The genuinely moral judgment just discussed is what we mean by "judgments of principle" and "to become morally adult is to learn to make decisions of principle; it is to learn to use 'ought' sentences verified by reference to a standard or set of principles which we have by our own decision accepted and made our own."[30]

How can the teacher go about stimulating the development of moral judgment? We have already rejected the notion of a set curriculum of instruction and exhortation in the conventional moral virtues, a conception killed by Hartshorne and May's demonstration of ineffectiveness. Dewey[31] pointed to the inadequacy of such a conception long ago and traced it to the fact that it assumed a divorce between moral education and inellectual education on the one side, and a divorce between education and real life on the other. To put Dewey's critique more bluntly, both conventional character-education classes or preaching and conventional moralizing by teachers about petty school routines are essentially "Mickey Mouse" stuff in relationship to the real need for moral stimulation of the child. To be more than "Mickey Mouse," a teacher's moralizings must be cognitively novel and challenging to the child, and they must be related to matters of obvious, real importance and seriousness.

It is not always necessary that these matters be ones of the immediate and real-life issues of the classroom. I have found that my hypothetical and remote but obviously morally real and challenging conflict situations are of intense interest to almost all adolescents and lead to lengthy debate among them. They are involving because the adult right answer is not obviously at hand to discourage the child's own moral thought, as so often is the case. The child will listen to what the teacher says about moral matters only if the child first feels a genuine sense of uncertainty as to the right answer to the situation in question. The pat little stories in school readers in which virtue always triumphs or in which everyone is really nice are unlikely to have any value in the stimulation of moral development. Only the presentation of genuine and difficult moral conflicts can have this effect.

We have mentioned that the stimulation of moral communication by the teacher should involve issues of genuine moral conflict to the child and represent new cognitive elements. There is also an important problem of match between the teacher's level and the child's involved in effective moral communication. Conventional moral education never has had much influence on children's moral judgment because it has disregarded this problem of developmental match. It has usually involved a set of adult moral clichés that are meaningless to the child because they are too abstract, mixed up with a patronizing "talking down" to the child in concrete terms beneath his level. In fact, the developmental level of moral-education verbalizations must be matched to the developmental level of the child if they are to have an effect. Ideally, such education should aim at communicating primarily at a level one stage above the child's own and secondarily at the child's own level. Experimental demonstration of this principle is provided in a study by E. Turiel.[32] Turiel ascertained the moral level of sixth graders on the Kohlberg stages, matched them for I.Q., and divided them into three experimental groups (and a fourth control group). All the groups (except the controls) were then exposed to short role-playing and discussion sessions with the experimenter centered on hypothetical conflict situations similar to those used in the Kohlberg tests. For one experimental group, the experimenter presented a discussion using moral judgments and reasons *one level above* the child's own. For a second group, the experimenter used moral judgments *two levels above* the child's own. For the third group, the experimenter used moral judgments *one level below* the child's own. All the children were then retested on the original test situations as well as on the situations discussed with the experimenter. Only the children who were exposed to moral judgments one level above their own showed any appreciable absorption of the experimenter's moral judgments. The children exposed to judgments one level below their own showed some absorption (more than those exposed to judgments two levels above) but not nearly as much as those exposed to one level above. Thus, while children are able to understand moralizing that is talking down beneath their level, they do not seem to accept it nearly as much as if it is comprehensible but somewhat above their level. It is obvious that the teacher's implementation of this principle must start by his careful listening to the moral judgments and ideas actually expressed by individual children.

The two principles just mentioned were used by Blatt[33] to develop a four month program of once-weekly moral discussions for a class of twelve children aged 11 to 12. Children discussed and argued hypothetical dilemmas. The teacher supported and clarified the arguments of the children which were at an average (Stage 3) level as against those one step below that level (Stage 2). When these arguments seemed understood, using new situations, the teacher would challenge the level (Stage 3) previously supported, and support and clarify the arguments of those one stage above (Stage 4) the previous consensus. The children were given a pre- and post-test, using different stories than those involved in the classroom discussions (with some new stories given only for the post-test). Fifty per cent of the children moved up one stage, 10 per cent moved up two stages, the remainder staying the same. In contrast, 10 per cent of a control group moved up one stage during this period, the remainder staying the same. Blatt and others are continuing this experimental work in varying settings (e.g., ghetto schools) and at varying ages.[34] The potential value of such educational efforts appears in terms of some recent longitudinal findings (on a small sample of middle class males), which indicate that moral maturity at age 13 is an extremely good ($r = .78$ to $.92$) predictor of adult moral maturity (at age 24 to 27).[35] This is not because moral judgment development stops at age 13, it continues past college in most of this group. (As an example, while none of the 13-year-olds were primarily at the principled level, 36 per cent of the 24-year-olds in this sample were at the principled level (Stage 5 and 6).) Those who did not develop some (over 15 per cent) thinking by later high school, however, did not develop into the principled stage in young adulthood. In general, then, while moral development continues into adulthood, mature 13-year-olds retain their edge in development, presumably because development is stepwise and the advanced boys have less further steps to go through. Blatt is now conducting longitudinal follow-ups to see if those whose moral judgment was raised in his group retain this developmental advantage in subsequent years.

So far, we have talked about the development of moral judgment as an aim of moral education. The sheer ability to make genuinely moral judgments is only one portion of moral character, however. The remainder is the ability to apply these judgmental capacities to the actual guidance and criticism of action. We have pointed out that advance in moral judgment seems to produce more mature moral action. Principled subjects both cheat much less and resist pressures by authorities to inflict pain on others much more than do less mature subjects. We do not yet know whether educational stimulation of moral judgment advance would actually produce more mature conduct in conflict situations. In any case, in addition to stimulating the development of general moral judgment capacities, a developmental moral education would stimulate the child's application of his own moral judgments (not the teacher's) to his actions. The effort to force a child to agree that an act of cheating was very bad when he does not really believe it (as in the case of the author of the school-newspaper article) will only be effective in encouraging morally immature tendencies toward expedient outward compliance. In contrast, a more difficult but more valid approach involves getting the child to examine the pros and cons of his conduct in his own terms (as well as introducing more developmentally advanced considerations).[36]

In general, however, the problem of insuring correspondence between developing moral judgments and the child's action is not primarily a problem of eliciting moral self-criticism from the child. One aspect of the problem is the development of the ego abilities involved in the non-moral or cognitive tasks upon which the classroom centers. As an example, an experimental measure of high stability of attention (low reaction-time variability) in a simple monotonous task has been found to clearly predict to resistance to cheating in Hartshorne and May's tests ($r = .68$).[37] The encouragement of these attentional ego capacities is not a task of moral education as such but of general programming of classroom learning activities.

Another aspect of the encouragement of correspondence between the child's moral values and his behavior is more difficult and fundamental. In order to encourage the application of his values to his behavior, we need to make sure that the kinds of behavior demands we make have some match to his already existing moral values. Two major types of mismatch occur. One type, which we have already mentioned, occurs when teachers concentrate on trivial classroom routines, thus moralizing issues that have no moral meaning outside the classroom. If the teacher insists on behavioral conformity to these demands and shows no moral concerns for matters of greater relevance to the child's (and the society's) basic moral values, the child will simply assume that his moral values have no relevance to his conduct in the classroom. It is obvious that the teacher must exert some influence toward conformity to trivial classroom rules, but there are two things he can do to minimize this sort of mismatch. The first is to insure that he does communicate some of his values with regard to broader and more genuinely moral issues. The second is to treat administrative demands as such and to distinguish them from basic moral demands involving moral judgment of the child's worth and moral sanctions. This does not imply that no demands should be treated as moral demands but that the teacher should clearly distinguish his own attitudes and reactions toward moral demands from his more general conformity demands.

The most serious and vital value issues represented by school life are not moral values per se but are intellectual in nature. As Dewey points out in discussing moral education, the serious business of the school is, and should be, intellectual. The principal values and virtues the teacher attends to are intellectual. However, the teacher may attend to these values and virtues either with awareness of their broader place in moral development or without such awareness. If such awareness is not present, the teacher will simply transmit the competitive-achievement values that dominate our society. He will train the child to think that getting a good mark is an absolute good and then suddenly shift gears and denounce cheating without wondering why the child should think cheating is bad when getting a good mark is the most important value. If the teacher has a greater awareness of the moral dimensions of education, his teaching of the intellectual aspects of the curriculum will illustrate the values of truth integrity, and trust in intellectual affairs and intellectual learning in such a way as to carry over to behaviors like cheating.

The second form of mismatch between the teacher's moral demands and the child's moral values arises from the fact that the teacher feels that certain behavioral demands are genuine moral demands, but the child has not yet developed any moral values that require these behaviors. We gave as an example the fact that resistance to cheating on tests does not derive from anything like moral values in young children aged five to seven, whereas resistance to theft and aggression do correspond to more spontaneous and internal moral values at this age. Given this fact, it does not seem wise to treat cheating as a genuine moral issue among young children, while it may be with older children. In general, the teacher should encourage the child to develop moral values relevant to such behavior as cheating but should not treat the behavior as a moral demand in the absence of such values.

It is clear, then, that a developmental conception of moral education does not imply the imposition of a curriculum upon the teacher. It does demand that the individual teacher achieve some clarity in his general conceptions of the aims and nature of moral development. In addition, it implies that he achieves clarity as to the aspects of moral development he should encourage in children of a given developmental level and as to appropriate methods of moral communication with these children. Most important, it implies that the teacher starts to listen carefully to the child in moral communications. It implies that he becomes concerned about the child's moral judgments (and the relation of the child's behavior to these judgments) rather than about the conformity of the child's behavior or judgments to the teacher's own.

REFERENCES

1. J. Dewey, *Moral Principles in Education* (Boston: Houghton Mifflin Co., 1911).
2. E. Durkheim, *Moral Education* (Glencoe, Ill.: The Free Press, 1961; originally published in 1925).
3. H. Hartshorne and M. A. May, *Studies in the Nature of Character* (3 vols.; New York: Macmillan Co., 1928–30).
4. I. M. Josselyn, *Psychosocial Development of Children* (New York: Family Service Association, 1948).
5. It is evident that the cheating behavior so extensively studied by Hartshorne and May does not represent a conflict between unsocialized base instinctual impulses and moral norms. The motive to cheat is the motive to succeed and do well. The motive to resist cheating is also the motive to achieve and be approved of, but defined in more long-range or "internal" terms. Moral character, then, is not a matter of "good" and "bad" motives or a "good" or "bad" personality as such. These facts, found by Hartshorne and May, have not yet been fully absorbed by some clinical approaches to children's moral character. If a child deviates a little he is normal; if he deviates conspicuously, he is believed to be "emotionally disturbed," i.e., to have mixed good and bad motives; if he deviates regularly or wildly, he is all bad (a "psychopathic" or "sadistic" personality).
6. E.g., S. Freud, *Civilization and Its Discontents* (London: Hogarth Press, 1955; originally published in 1930); E. Fromm, *Man for Himself* (New York: Rinehart, 1949); and K. Horney, *The Neurotic Personality of Our Time* (New York: W. W. Norton & Co., 1937).
7. R. J. Havighurst and H. Taba, *Adolescent Character and Personality* (New York: John Wiley & Sons, 1949); and R. F. Peck and R. J. Havighurst, *The Psychology of Character Development* (New York: John Wiley & Sons, 1960).
8. L. Kohlberg, "Moral Development and Identification," in H. Stevenson, ed., *Child Psychology* (Chicago: University of Chicago Press, 1963): "The Development of Children's Orientations Toward a Moral Order: I. Sequence in the Development of Moral Thought," *Vita Humana*, VI (1963), 11–33; and "The Development of Moral Character and Ideology," in M. Hoffman and L. Hoffman, eds., *Review of Child Development Research* (New York: Russell Sage Foundation, 1964).
9. Kohlberg, "The Development of Moral Character and Ideology," *op. cit.* These factors are also stressed in the works of Peck and Havighurst, *op. cit.*, who found extremely high correlations between ratings of moral character and ratings of ego strength.

10. L. Kohlberg, *Stages in the Development of Moral Thought and Action* (New York: Holt, Rinehart and Winston, 1969 [in preparation]).

11. J. Piaget, *The Moral Judgment of the Child* (Glencoe, Ill.: The Free Press, 1948; originally published in 1932); Kohlberg, "The Development of Children's Orientations Toward a Moral Order: I," *op. cit.*

12. Kohlberg, "The Development of Children's Orientations Toward a Moral Order: I," *op. cit.*

13. L. Kohlberg, "Stage and Sequence: The Developmental Approach to Moralization," M. Hoffman, ed., *Moral Process* (Chicago: Aldine Press, 1966).

14. Kohlberg, "The Development of Moral Character and Ideology," *op. cit.*

15. This has sometimes been viewed as consistent with the psychoanalytic view that character is fixed at an early age in the home. In fact, this does not seem to be true, as there is little predictability from early moral conduct to later adolescent moral conduct (*ibid.*).

16. R. Krebs, "The Development of Moral Judgment in Young Children" (Master's thesis, Committee on Human Development, University of Chicago, 1965).

17. R. Krebs, "Relations between Attention, Moral Judgment and Conduct" (Unpublished Ph. D. dissertation, University of Chicago, 1966).

18. The attitude of this latter group is probably well expressed by the following anonymous student article in a British school paper written after a siege of experimental studies of honesty: "The next test reminded me of the eleven plus exam. I had great fun doing these but they are sure to think I am barmy. But then they made a fatal mistake; they actually gave us our own papers to mark. We saw our mistakes in time and saved the day by changing the answers."

19. Kohlberg, *Stages in the Development of Moral Thought and Action, op. cit.*

20. Findings reviewed in Kohlberg, "Moral Development and Identification," *op. cit.*, and "The Development of Moral Character and Ideology," *op. cit.*

21. See footnote 20.

22. Krebs, *op. cit.*

23. M. Kohn, "Social Class and Parental Values," *American Journal of Sociology,* LXIV (1959), 337–51.

24. The effect of such a sense of participation upon development of moral judgments related to the law is suggested by the following responses of sixteen-year-olds to the question, "Should someone obey a law if he doesn't think it is a good law?" A lower-class boy replies, "Yes, a law is a law and you can't do nothing about it. You have to obey it, you should. That's what it's there for." For him the law is simply a constraining thing that is there. The very fact that he has no hand in it, that "you can't do nothing about it," means that it should be obeyed (Stage 1).

A lower-middle-class boy replies, "Laws are made for people to obey and if everyone would start breaking them. . . . Well, if you owned a store and there were no laws, everybody would just come in and not have to pay." Here laws are seen not as arbitrary commands but as a unitary system, as the basis of the social order. The role or perspective taken is that of a storekeeper, of someone with a stake in the order (Stage 4).

An upper-middle-class boy replies, "The law's the law but I think people themselves can tell what's right or wrong. I suppose the laws are made by many different groups of people with different ideas. But if you don't believe in a law, you should try to get it changed, you shouldn't disobey it." Here the laws are seen as the product of various legitimate ideological and interest groups varying in their beliefs as to the best decision in policy matters. The role of law-obeyer is seen from the perspective of the democratic policy-maker (Stage 5).

25. Kohlberg, "The Development of Children's Orientation toward a Moral Order: II," *op. cit.*

26. U. Bronfenbrenner, "Soviet Methods of Character Education: Some Implications for Research," *American Psychologist,* XVII (1962), 550–565.

27. A research indication of this comes from the Kohlberg study. After individual moral-judgment interviews, the children in the study were subjected to pressure from an adult and from disagreeing peers to change their views on the questions. While maturity of moral judgment predicted to moral behaviors involving conformity to authority (e.g., cheating), it predicted better to behaviors involving maintaining one's own moral views in the face of pressure from authorities ($r = .44$). Among college students, not only were principled subjects much less likely to cheat, but they were much more likely to engage in an act of moral courage or resistance when an authoritative experimenter ordered them to inflict pain upon another subject (Kohlberg, *Stages in the Development of Moral Thought and Action, op. cit.*).

28. R. M. Hare, *The Language of Morals* (New York: Oxford University Press, 1952); I. Kant, *Fundamental Principles of the Metaphysics of Morals,* trans. T. K. Abbott (New York: Liberal Arts Press, 1949); and H. Sidgwick, *Methods of Ethics* (London: The Macmillan Co., 1901).

29. L. Kohlberg, "The Development of Modes of Moral Thinking and Choice in the Years Ten to Sixteen" (Ph.D. dissertation, University of Chicago, 1958).

30. Hare, *op. cit.*

31. J. Dewey, *Moral Principles in Education, op. cit.*

32. E. Turiel, "An Experimental Analysis of Developmental Stages in the Child's Moral Judgment," *Journal of Personality and Social Psychology,* 3 (1966), 611–618.

33. M. Blatt, and L. Kohlberg, "The Effects of Classroom Moral Discussion upon Children's Level of Moral Judgment," submitted to *Merrill Palmer Quarterly,* 1968.

34. M. Blatt, "Experimental Studies in Moral Education Using a Developmental Approach" (Unpublished Ph.D. dissertation, University of Chicago, 1959).

35. L. Kohlberg, *Stages in the Development of Moral Thought and Action, op. cit.*

36. This is actually more valuable for acts of good conduct than for acts of bad conduct. We expect children to justify defensively acts of misconduct. If we take the trouble to find out, however, we will often be surprised that the acts of good conduct we praise are valued by the child himself for immature reasons and that we are really rewarding "selfish" rather than moral values. In such cases it is relatively easy to foster the application of developmentally more advanced values in the child's repertoire to his own behavior.

37. P. Grim, L. Kohlberg, and S. White, "Some Relationships between Conscience and Attentional Processes," *J. Pers. So. Psychol.,* 8 (1968), 239–253.

FIVE PARENT AND PEER GROUP INFLUENCES ON ADOLESCENTS

". . . when I was seven my father knew everything, when I was fourteen my father knew nothing, but when I was twenty-one I was amazed how much the old man had learned in those seven years."

"When I think of my own junior-high experience and remember the necessity of obtaining peer acceptance . . . I would have preferred death to any action not totally acceptable to my peers."

These two quotes, by Mark Twain and by a student looking back on her early adolescent years, illustrate the dilemma of adolescents in modern Western society. During the transition period noted by Twain when children begin to break close parental ties in preparation for the emotional independence of adulthood, the peer group frequently moves into the vacuum, offering temporary psychological and social support at the price of demanding peer conformity. The influence of the peer group follows a pattern complementary to that of parental influence, having little significance to a child of seven, reaching its peak at about age fourteen, and evolving into a pattern of balanced friendships by twenty-one. Peer group affiliation and the questioning of parental values, which may manifest itself in open rebellion, allows the adolescent to begin shifting his orientation from the family of origin to the family of procreation, a major emotional prerequisite for a successful marriage. The articles in Part Five analyze the broad theoretical and empirical implications of this transition period, exploring in detail the relative influence of parents and peer group on the developing adolescent.

The first selection, a study by Robert E. Grinder and Judith C. Spector (17), examines the adolescent's perception of and identification with the parent who controls the "desirable resources" in the family. According to the "status-envy hypothesis" on which the Grinder and Spector study is based, "children will model their behavior after the parent who controls most of the goals and resources (e.g., both rewards and freedom from punishments) that they covet." The data from this study supports the initial hypothesis that girls perceive the mother as more powerful, while boys are more likely to perceive their father in control. By identifying with the more powerful parent, the adolescent consequently is aided in establishing proper sex-role identity.

While Grinder and Spector investigate the perceived power differences between father and mother, Clay V. Brittain (18) examines the relative importance of parents versus peers in adolescent decision-making. In the Brittain study, adolescent girls were exposed to hypothetical conflict situations in which the individual had to choose between parental and peer expectations. The study's major finding is that the tendency to conform either to parental or to peer group expectations is dependent upon the nature of the situation and the adolescent's perception of the relative competence of peers or parents as counselors. Choices that are likely to have immediate consequences, such as the choice of a dress or separation from school friends, or decisions concerning rapidly changing social values, are influenced more by the peer group than by parental pressures. Choices which have long range implications, on the other hand, are referred to parents more often than peers. Obviously, whenever communication between parents and adolescents breaks down, parent-peer pressure subsides and peer group influence becomes the major consideration in the decision-making process. This last conclusion may help to explain the prevailing belief that peer group conformity is the dominant influence on adolescent behavior.

The selection by Norman E. Gronlund and Loren Anderson (19) identifies personality characteristics related to social acceptance, neglect, and rejection. Using a sociometric test to determine how junior-high school students rate one another, Gronlund and Anderson establish that socially accepted girls and boys are "attractive, neat, and in general possessing aggressive and outgoing behavior," the boys, however, being more active in games than the girls. Socially rejected girls are "rated as being not good looking, untidy, not likeable, restless, and talkative," and, like the socially rejected boys, capable of aggressive behavior that attracts unfavorable attention. Socially neglected students are generally quiet, receiving little attention in terms of sociometric choices. The researchers observe that an adolescent who is not accepted by his peers is more peer-conforming than the aggressive, outgoing individual who is socially accepted.

In the last article in this part, Philip R. Constanzo and Marvin E. Shaw (20) demonstrate that conformity to peer group suggestions increases as a function of age up to thirteen, and declines afterward. Although the findings pertaining to sex differences in this study are not statistically significant, the data, substantiated by earlier studies, seem to indicate that girls conform more than boys at all age levels. A variable that probably affects the findings in this study is the type of stimulus that was used. The lack of ambiguity in this study may be one factor influencing the peak age of peer group conformity. In a study by E. Tuma and N. Livson (1966), for example, the use of an ambiguous stimulus results in the conclusion that peer group conformity increases to age sixteen for girls, and fifteen for boys, in contrast to thirteen as indicated by the Constanzo and Shaw study. Constanzo and Shaw conclude their article with the suggestion that "the development of conforming behavior patterns runs parallel with the socialization process. . . . With the onset of pubescence, the child becomes acutely aware of his social peers and relies upon them for many of his external behavior patterns. . . ."

REFERENCES

Tuma, E. & Livson, N. Family Socioeconomic Status and Adolescent Attitudes to Authority. *Child Development,* 1960, 31, 387–399.

[**17**]   *Robert E. Grinder & Judith C. Spector*   SEX

DIFFERENCES IN ADOLESCENTS' PERCEPTIONS

OF PARENTAL RESOURCE CONTROL

A. *Introduction*

Children's perceptions of their parents' power to direct and to control behavior have been described extensively. On the whole, the research literature (4, 7, 8, 9, 15) suggests that children of both sexes tend to see their mothers as in control of nurturance and see their fathers as "boss" or in control of granting autonomy. Further, there is empirical evidence that children's perception of the degree of their fathers' absolute power varies during middle childhood (4, 8) and that, during adolescence, the tendency to view the mother and the father as equal in power increases for both sexes (8).

Although in general children may look to their mothers for nurturance and to their fathers for authority (whereas adolescents may tend to equate their parents on these dimensions), adolescence, nonetheless, is a developmental stage during which sex-role differentiation and identity with adult standards and responsibilities are major cultural expectations. One would expect, therefore, adolescent girls to interact more frequently with their mothers and to be strongly oriented toward the feminine characteristics of their roles; also, analogously, one would expect adolescent boys to be oriented toward the masculine characteristics of their fathers. Bronfenbrenner (2) has observed that adolescent girls report their mothers and that adolescent boys report their fathers to be the principal decision-maker in the family. However, the classifications of family-authority structure were based on the adolescents' responses

FROM *Journal of Genetic Psychology,* 1965, 106, 337–344. REPRINTED BY PERMISSION OF THE SENIOR AUTHOR AND THE JOURNAL PRESS.

to a single question: "Who in your family really has had the final say about things concerning the children (discipline, staying out late, getting special privileges, etc.)?" As Bronfenbrenner (2) has noted, considerable subjectivity may be reflected in the adolescents' responses. Moreover, the exploratory nature of the data were such that statistical tests of significance were not applied.

Clarification of the issue as to whether adolescent girls tend to view their mothers and adolescent boys tend to view their fathers as exerting more influence upon them has important implications for analyses of parent-child relationships, for (presumably) the perceptions affect motivation to identify with parental behavior patterns, attitudes, and values. The present study was designed, therefore, to provide an empirical and reliable analysis of variation by sex in adolescents' perception of parental authority and status.

Two aspects of psychoanalytic theory furnish the rationale for most contemporary theories of children's and adolescents' motivation to identify with parental figures. Anna Freud's formulation of "identification with the aggressor" (6) suggests that children, being afraid to retaliate against parental punishments for fear of further punitive action, attempt to satisfy the parents by incorporating parental characteristics. A second viewpoint, referred to by Bronfenbrenner (1) as anaclitic identification, suggests that children strive to become like their parents because they fear loss of the parents' love. The former hypothesis states that identification depends upon aggression, threats, and hostility; the latter hypothesis states that it depends upon a positive, affectionate parent-child relationship.

In spite of the contradictory nature of these viewpoints, recent research (3, 12, 14) indicates that the motivational qualities of both the rewarding-nurturance and the threatening-punitive aspects of child-rearing may function together to create an efficient learning situation in which children may identify effectively with their parents. Apparently, parents strongly motivate children to identify with them when they make rewards contingent upon approved behavior and, at the same time, hold punishment up as a threat for disapproved behavior. For example, Mussen and Distler (12, p. 354) report that young boys who had made "substantial father-identifications . . . perceived their fathers as both more nurturant *and* more punitive." In a recent restatement of identification theory, Burton and Whiting (3) hypothesize that children will model their behavior after the parent who controls most of the goals and resources (e.g., both rewards and freedom from punishments) that they covet. This formulation, named the "status-envy hypothesis," implies that motivation for identification depends upon the perception of a discrepancy by the child or the adolescent between his control of desirable resources and that of his model and upon his envying the greater privileges, status, and power of the model. Thus he assimilates the behavior of the model feeling that in this way he, too, will have access to the latter's privileges.

The resources that parents control that might promote "status envy" are much narrower in scope for children than for adolescents. Sex-role differentiation is much less crucial. Children's aspirations and social needs are relatively more simple. In general, they are either rewarded with or deprived of novel objects (toys), foods (candy), praise, and affection. By contrast, adolescents' interests are more similar to those of adults; thus the range of resources that affect adolescents is far more extensive. On the one hand, parents may restrict an adolescent's use of the telephone, family car, and home; on the other, his finances, choice of friends, interests, activities, and freedom to keep his own hours. Children are punished relatively more than adolescents by deprivation of privileges and by arousal of physical pain; adolescents, however, experience more nonmaterial punishment: *e.g.*, ostracism, rejection of ambitions and aspirations, ridicule of attitudes and values, shame, etc.

As a consequence of these considerations, in the present study adolescent boys and girls are compared in terms of the degree to which they attribute control over certain resources either to their mother or to their father. The resources pertain to parental authority to grant autonomy to engage in activities, parental capacity to arouse a sense of well-being or despair through nonmaterial rewards and punishments, or parental control of desirable material incentives. According to the status-envy hypothesis, it is assumed that the parent who is perceived as having greater control of desirable resources and, by inference, as having higher status will be the parent with whom the adolescent is most likely to identify.

B. Method

1. SUBJECTS

Subjects were randomly drawn in groups of 19 girls and 19 boys from the ninth-, tenth-, and twelfth-grade of a community high school. None of the 114 Ss were from broken homes or lived with stepparents. The high school served a rural area comprised of approximately 3,500 middle-class families.

2. MEASURE AND PROCEDURE

In order to assess adolescents' perceptions of parental resource control, Ss were asked to name which of their parents held control over 28 resources generally desirable to teen-agers. Ss responded to each of the 28 items by choosing among four alternatives placed on an axis with "mother" choices at one pole and "father" choices at the other. On *a priori* grounds, the first alternative was labeled "most likely mother" and weighted one point; the second alternative, "possibly mother," two points; the third, "possibly father," three points; and the fourth, "most likely father," four points. Five of the situations are listed below:

1. Which parent would have more control over giving you permission to go out at night—for example to a party or to the movies?
2. Which parent would have more control over your choice of a career?

3. Which parent would you go to for consolation if you were unhappy?
4. Which parent would control the amount of privacy you could have—regarding your relations with friends, telephone conversations, etc.?
5. Which parent would be more influential in planning the use of the family's leisure time?

The situations involving resources and the multiple-choice alternatives for each were listed serially in a booklet and were administered to males and females together in groups of about 20. Ss were asked to mark only the alternative that they thought to be appropriate. Further, Ss were instructed not to put their names on the booklets and were assured that no one at the school would see their responses. The following general instructions were printed on the cover of each booklet:

Although there is generally a great difference in age between parents and high school students, they have many interests in common. Material things such as cars and money, and non-material items such as affection and independence are of concern to both groups. Generally parents have more control over these things though, and in order to obtain them younger people must get permission or approval from their parents.

This questionnaire deals with some of these things that high school students would like to have but which parents control. In answering these questions we would like you to tell us *which of your parents* would have more control over each item or situation if the problem arose in your family.

If you feel that some of the questions don't really apply to your family, please make a choice anyway by imagining what would happen if the situation *did* come up in your family.

If you feel that neither of your parents controls a particular item for you anymore, please make a choice based on your *best recollection* of who *did* control it when you were younger.

3. SCORING THE PARENTAL RESOURCE-CONTROL INVENTORY

On the basis of two pilot tests, items were modified for sake of clarity, brevity, and discrimination. In the absence of external criteria for evaluating the comparability of the score weights across situations, the responses of the experimental Ss were empirically scaled by the method of reciprocal averages (11, 13). The method maximizes the reliability of each item, the internal consistency of the overall instrument, and the correlation between items and the total score. These properties are acquired by an iterative procedure that decreases the weight of alternatives that bear little empirical relation to Ss' total scores and increases the weights of those alternatives that discriminate well between the scores of mother- and father-oriented Ss.

An empirical content analysis of the inventory conducted in accordance with the procedure noted yielded a reliability coefficient of .88 for internal consistency.

C. Results

The means and standard deviations of subjects' total weighted scores by sex and grade are shown in Table 1. The empirical weights assigned by the

TABLE 1   Mean Scores and Standard Deviations of Subject by Grade and Sex

| SEX | GRADE | | | | | |
| | 9 | | 10 | | 12 | |
	M	SD	M	SD	M	SD
Male	83.16	8.94	80.63	9.93	82.32	11.08
Female	78.32	6.05	81.95	8.39	73.58	10.06

method of reciprocal averages show that the optimum range of the inventory was from 57 to 105 points. The adolescents who scored at the low end of the scale are those who view their mothers as in control of resources; conversely, those at the high end of the scale see their fathers as in control. The empirically determined midpoint is 81, and the means presented in Table 1 suggest that adolescent girls and boys tended to perceive the relative power of their parents as nearly equal.

In spite of the similarity between girls' and boys' mean scores, the analyses of variance summarized in Table 2 reveal that during adolescence girls are

TABLE 2   Analysis of Variance of Scores by Grade and Sex

SOURCE	*df*	MS	F
Sex (A)	1	476.22	5.61*
Grade (B)	2	121.96	1.44
A x B	2	244.05	2.87
Error	108	84.91	
Total	113		

* $p < .05$.

more likely to view their mothers as holding more parental control and boys their fathers ($p < .05$). Differences between the sexes are not apparent through the ninth, tenth, and twelfth grades, and the interaction between sex and grade is nonsignificant.

D. Discussion

In terms of adolescents' perceptions of variation in their parents' control of desirable resources, the empirical data of the present study indicate that girls attribute relatively more power and status to their mothers; whereas boys attribute relatively more power and status to their fathers. The statistical analysis confirms Bronfenbrenner's finding (2) that adolescents view their same-sex parent as the principal decision maker in the family.

It is noteworthy that the present data refer only to the adolescents' perception of the *relative* distribution of resource control or power between their parents. Doubtless, a parent's effectiveness as a socializing agent also depends upon the kind of *absolute* family power the parent is perceived to hold. Researchers have noted that either too much affection or too little, too strict or too lax a discipline, may have deleterious effects upon socialization (2); but within the extreme positions, considerable latitude may exist. Conceivably, parental statuses within a given family may be structured rather loosely and neither parent may be viewed as being very influential. On the other hand, in another family, both parents may make attainment of desirable resources rigidly contingent upon conformity. From the standpoint of general socialization theory, the latter parents should be more facilitative than the former in motivating identification, even though the differential in relative power between the two parents of each set may be similar. Successful adult-role identification during adolescence is surely fostered by the same-sex parent being perceived as holding relatively more status in the family, but the logic of the foregoing discussion suggests that other factors (including optimal exercise of absolute parental power) are also crucially important antecedents of effective and efficient socialization.

The absence of meaningful grade or age differences in adolescents' perceptions of parental authority is partly a function of the measuring instrument used in the study. Subjects who felt particular situations involving their parents and resources were inapplicable to them (perhaps because the situations had not yet come up in their families) were asked to imagine what would happen if they should occur. In the instance of situations that were no longer applicable, subjects were asked to recall what happened on earlier occasions. Nevertheless, in spite of these limitations of the instrument, the appearance of age differences was unlikely—at least within the four-year age range of the subjects of this study. Throughout this period, adolescents would be expected to maintain a consistently strong interest in models of the same sex. By the ninth grade, femininity has become an attraction to girls and masculinity (particularly in athletic competition) has become conspicuously important to boys; moreover, in early adolescence, boys and girls tend rigidly to sex type their activities and interests. Later in adolescence, girls are likely to focus a measure of their feminine interests upon their potential roles as homemaker and mother, whereas boys are expected to shift to their potential roles as breadwinner and father.

The postulates of the status-envy hypothesis suggest that adolescent girls and boys should be strongly motivated to identify with models whom they see as powerful sources of rewards and punishments. Under circumstances in which adolescents see their same-sex rather than opposite-sex parents as occupying relatively high status roles, it follows that the adolescents should be more likely to assimilate these parents' interests, attitudes, and behavior patterns. The tendency for adolescents to view their same-sex parents as more powerful doubtless is a critical factor in adolescents' acquisition of appropriate sex-role identity. Certainly, it would be highly disruptive to the socialization process, especially from the standpoint of the acute dangers during this period of role diffusion (5) and of cross-sex identity conflicts (3, 10), if adolescents of both sexes indiscriminately chose either parent as their salient model.

E. Summary

In this investigation, an analysis is made of adolescents' perceptions of parental authority and status, as inferred from their view of parental control of certain desirable resources. Motivation for appropriate sex-role identification and for attainment of adult standards and responsibilities is presumed to be affected by whether or not adolescent girls and boys attribute relatively more resource control to their same-sex parents. The results show, as expected, that girls are likely to see their mothers and boys, their fathers, as more powerful.

REFERENCES

1. Bronfenbrenner, U. Freudian theories of identification and their derivatives. *Child. Devel.,* 1960, **31,** 15–40.
2. ———. Toward a theoretical model for the analysis of parent-child relationships in a social context. In J. C. Glidewell (Ed.), *Parental Attitudes and Child Behavior.* Springfield, Ill.: Thomas, 1961. Pp. 90–109.
3. Burton, R. V., & Whiting, J. W. M. The absent father and cross-sex identity. *Merrill-Palmer Quart.,* 1961, **7,** 85–95.
4. Emmerich, W. Family role concepts of children ages six to ten. *Child. Devel.,* 1961, **32,** 609–624.
5. Erikson, E. H. Childhood and Society. New York: Norton, 1950.
6. Freud, A. The Ego and the Mechanisms of Defense. New York: Internat. Univ. Press, 1946.

7. Hawkes, G., Burchinal, L., & Gardner, B. Pre-adolescents' views of some of their relations with their parents. *Child Devel.*, 1957, **28**, 393–399.

8. Hess, R. D., & Torney, J. V. Religion, age, and sex in children's perceptions of family authority. *Child Devel.*, 1962, **33**, 781–789.

9. Kagan, J. The child's perception of the parent. *J. Abn. & Soc. Psychol.*, 1956, **53**, 257–258.

10. McCord, J., McCord, W., & Thurber, E. Some effects of paternal absence on male children. *J. Abn & Soc. Psychol.*, 1962, **64**, 361–369.

11. Mosier, C. I. Machine methods in scaling by reciprocal averages. *Proceedings, Research Forum.* New York: IBM, 1946, Pp. 35–39.

12. Mussen, P., & Distler, L. Masculinity, identification, and father-son relationships. *J. Abn. & Soc. Psychol.*, 1959, **59**, 350–356.

13. Ragsdale, R., & Baker, F. The method of reciprocal averages for scaling of inventories and questionnaires: A computer program for the CDC 1604 Computer. Unpublished manuscript, Numerical Analysis Laboratory, University of Wisconsin, Madison, 1962.

14. Sears, R. R., Maccoby, E. E., & Levin, H. Patterns of Child-Rearing. Evanston, Ill.: Row, Peterson, 1957.

15. Stagner, R., & Drought, N. Measuring children's attitudes toward their parents. *J. Educ. Psychol.*, 1935, **26**, 169–176.

[18]   *Clay V. Brittain*   ADOLESCENT CHOICES AND PARENT-PEER CROSS-PRESSURES

As they are commonly portrayed, adolescents confronted with parent-peer cross-pressures tend to opt in favor of the peer-group. But to what extent and under what circumstances does this image square with reality?[1] Does the tendency toward peer-conformity vary as a function of the type of choice to be made by the adolescent?

The concept of reference group is useful in attacking this problem. Following Shibutani's[2] formulation that a reference group is one whose perspective constitutes the frame of reference of the actor, both peers and parents might be thought of as reference groups; i.e., as groups each provides perspectives in terms of which adolescents make choices. Does the extent to which adolescents tend to adopt these different perspectives vary systematically across situations? We hypothesized that in making certain kinds of choices, adoles-

FROM *American Sociological Review*, 1963, 28, 385–391. REPRINTED BY PERMISSION OF THE AUTHOR AND THE AMERICAN SOCIOLOGICAL ASSOCIATION.

cents are inclined to follow peers rather than parents; in making certain other types of choices, the opposite is true.

Procedure

Situations involving conflict between parent-peer expectations were described to the subjects—girls in grades 9 through 11. Each situation was structured around an adolescent girl who was trying to choose between two alternatives, one of which was favored by her parents and the other by her friends. The following item illustrates the procedure:

A large glass in the front door of the high school was broken. Jim broke the glass. But both he and Bill were seen at the school the afternoon the glass was broken and both are suspected. Bill and Jim are friends and they agree to deny that they know anything about the broken glass. As a result, the principal pins the blame on both of them. Nell is the only other person who knows who broke the glass. She was working in the typing room that afternoon. She didn't actually see the glass broken, but she heard the noise and saw Jim walking away from the door a few moments later. Nell is very much undecided what to do. The three girls she goes around with most of the time don't think Nell should tell the principal. These girls hate to see an innocent person punished. But they point out to Nell that this is a matter between Jim and Bill and between Jim and his conscience. Nell talks the matter over with her mother and father. They felt that Jim is unfairly using Bill in order to lighten his own punishment. Her parents think Nell should tell the principal who broke the glass. Can you guess what Nell did when the principal asked her if she saw who broke the glass?
— She told him that she didn't see it broken.
— She told him who broke the glass.[3]

Two versions of 12 items each were constructed to make up two forms (A and B) of the present instrument, which will be called the Cross-Pressures Test, or CPT. The two forms were identical in all respects except for the opinions and preferences attributed to parents and friends. These were reversed from one form to the other. The parent-favored alternatives on Form A were the peer-favored alternatives on Form B, and vice versa.[4] The instructions accompanying the CPT were:

The following stories are about young people like your friends and the people you know. These people are in situations where they are not sure what to do. We would like to have you read each story carefully and tell us which one of the two things the person in the story is more likely to do. Do *not* tell us what the person should do, but what she is *likely* to really do. We hope you will enjoy doing this.

The CPT was administered to an experimental group and a small control group. The experimental group responded to one form and then to the other;

the control responded twice to the same form. Both were divided into sub-groups and tested as follows:

EXPERIMENTAL GROUP	FIRST TESTING	SECOND TESTING
Group AB	Form A	Form B
Group BA	Form B	Form A

CONTROL GROUP		
Group A	Form A	Form A
Group B	Form B	Form B

One to two weeks intervened between the testing dates. The subjects were not told that they were to be tested a second time.

As can be seen from the specimen item, the dilemmas described on the CPT were double-barrelled (as well as double-horned). There is the dilemma embodied in the content of the alternatives (e.g., telling who broke the glass in the door of the high school versus not telling; or going steady with a boy having certain personal qualities versus going steady with a boy having other personal qualities), and, on top of this, the dilemma posed by the cross-pressures from parents and friends. The subjects could respond to either dilemma or to both. We anticipated that they would respond to both; i.e., the tendency to choose the parent-favored or the peer-favored alternative would depend upon what the dilemma was about. Hence, there would be marked inter-item variation in the frequency of parent-conforming and peer-conforming choices.

The experimental group data were analyzed for differential preferences for the parent-favored and peer-favored alternatives. In response to each item there were three possibilities: (1) The subject, responding to the content of the dilemma, chooses the same content alternative on both forms of the CPT. (2) The peer-favored alternative is selected on both forms. (3) The parent-favored alternative is selected on both forms. In event of 2 or 3, the choice of content alternative shifts from the first testing to the second. The data, then, were analyzed for shifts in choice of content alternatives from one form of the CPT to the other.[5] The control group was used to help establish that the shifts in the experimental group were due to differences in the forms of the test and not simply to the tendency to respond randomly.

Items on which peer-conforming response shifts were more frequent and those on which parent-conforming shifts were more frequent were identified. From the content of these items inferences were drawn about the bases of preferences for peer-favored and parent-favored alternatives.

Following the second testing, 42 girls in grades 9 and 10 were individually interviewed.[6] The interview data help to clarify the above analysis of responses to the CPT.[7]

Subjects

The subjects were girls[8] from high schools in Alabama and Georgia. The 280 girls in the experimental group came from an urban high school, a high school in a small city, and three small rural high schools. Analysis of the data did not reveal any rural-urban differences. The 58 control respondents were from a high school in a small town and a rural high school.

Results

Comparison of the experimental and control groups indicates that the findings reported below were not due to the tendency to respond randomly, but that changes in form did elicit changes in choice of content alternatives. The data are given in Table 1. On item one, for example, 23 per cent of the control subjects, who responded twice to the same form, shifted content alternatives from the first testing to the second as compared to 52 per cent in the experimental group. On each of the 12 items, shifts in choice of content alternative occur more frequently in the experimental group. On 11 of the items the experimental-control differences were significant at the .01 level or better.

An analysis of the experimental group data is given in Table 2. The responses to each item were first broken down in terms of the following two categories: (1) The choice of content alternatives did not shift from one form to the other. (2) The content choice did shift; i.e., the peer-favored or parent-favored alternative was consistently chosen. (See columns NS and S). The second category was then broken down into peer-conforming and parent-conforming choices. (See columns P and F.) As can be seen from this break-down, items 1, 6, and 8 tended more strongly to elicit peer-conforming choices; items 3, 4, 5, 7, 9, 11, and 12 tended to elicit parent-conforming choices. All of these differences except that for item 4 are significant at the .05 level or better. Parent-conforming and peer-conforming choices were distributed equally on item 2.

Before interpreting these findings, note the following observations. They suggest the results were not dictated simply by the method.
(1) The subjects responded naively. Of the 42 girls individually interviewed soon after the second testing, only two were able to tell how the two forms of the CPT differed.

TABLE 1 Proportion of Control Group and Experimental Group Shifting Responses

ITEM	EXPERIMENTAL GROUP N = 280	CONTROL GROUP N = 58	DIFFERENCE $P^E - P^C$	CHI SQUARE[1]
1. Which course to take in school	.52	.23	.29	15.60**
2. Which boy to go steady with	.50	.28	.22	12.71**
3. How to get selected for a school honor	.33	.28	.05	.94
4. Whether to report boy who damaged school property	.35	.14	.21	13.57**
5. Whether to enter beauty contest or be cheerleader	.44	.16	.28	22.52**
6. How to dress for football game and party	.51	.19	.32	26.42**
7. Whether to be beauty contestant or appear on TV program	.39	.14	.25	18.56**
8. Which dress to buy	.58	.19	.39	39.39**
9. Which one of two boys to date	.49	.16	.33	29.00**
10. Which part-time job to take	.34	.16	.18	10.66*
11. Whether to report adult who damaged public property	.38	.19	.19	10.23*
12. How to let boy know she is willing to date him	.36	.21	.15	6.66*

[1] Chi square computer from frequencies. df = 1, * $p < .1$, ** $p < .001$.

(2) Responding to the CPT seemed to be accompanied by anxiety. In informal group discussions immediately following the second testing there were expressions of irritability at having to make the choices called for. This suggests that the subjects did tend to become emotionally involved in the hypothetical situations themselves.

TABLE 2   Frequency of Shifts in Choice of Content Alternatives From One Form to the Other

ITEM	NOT SHIFTING CONTENT ALTERNATIVES (NS)	SHIFTING CONTENT ALTERNATIVES			CHI SQUARE[1]
		Total (S)	Alternative Selected		
			Parent(P)	Peer(F)	
1. Which course to take in school	135	145	48	97	16.56***
2. Which boy to go steady with	141	139	70	69	.01
3. How to get selected for a school honor	187	93	63	30	11.70***
4. Whether to report boy who damaged school property	182	98	58	40	3.30
5. Whether to enter beauty contest or be cheerleader	156	124	93	31	28.26***
6. How to dress for football game and party	138	142	47	95	16.22***
7. Whether to be beauty contestant or appear on TV program	170	110	83	27	31.00***
8. Which dress to buy	118	162	59	103	11.92***
9. Which one of two boys to date	143	137	81	56	4.56*
10. Which part-time job to take	184	96	69	27	18.37***
11. Whether to report adult who damaged public property	174	106	73	33	15.09***
12. How to let boy know she is willing to date him	180	100	64	36	(7.84)**
Column totals	1908	1452	808	644	—

[1] Chi square for differences between columns P and F computed on the basis of 50/50 assumption. df = 1. * $p < .05$; ** $p < .01$; *** $p < .001$.

(3) Groups of subjects differentiated on the basis of their responses to the CPT were also differentiated on the basis of sociometric data. For example, subjects who most frequently chose peer-favored alternatives tended not to be well accepted by their peers.

(4) At least some of the response trends were consistent with what informal observation of adolescent behavior would lead one to expect. For example, choices relating to dress were especially likely to be peer-conforming.

Discussion

The findings, as reported in Table 2, are consistent with the hypothesis that responses of adolescents to parent-peer cross-pressures are a function of the content of the alternatives and that peer-conformity in adolescence, rather than being diffuse, tends to vary systematically across situations. The response variation across items supports the hypothesis.

More specific interpretations of the response trends are now in order. Why were the peer-favored alternatives more commonly selected in response to some of the hypothetical situations and parent-favored alternatives in response to others? This question relates to the more general problem of understanding the processes involved in coming to terms with conflicting pressures, which, as Merton[9] has pointed out, is salient for reference group theory.

From the content of the hypothetical dilemmas, viewed against the response trends shown in Table 2, the following hypotheses are offered:

1. The responses reflect the adolescent's perception of peers and parents as competent guides in different areas of judgment.

    The general social orientation of adolescents is of a dual character. Choices tend to derive meaning from either of two general reference groups, or both: the peer society in which many status and identity needs are gratified, and the larger society in which the status positions which one can aspire to as an adult are found. When choices pertain to the latter, parents are perceived as the more competent guides. In response to the hypothetical situation involving choice of part-time jobs (item 10), for example, preferences commonly were for the parent-favored rather than the peer-favored alternatives.

2. The responses reflect concern to avoid being noticeably different from peers. Two of the items to which responses showed clearcut peer-conforming trends involved a choice of dress; i.e., item 6—how to dress for a football game and party, and item 8—which one of two dresses to buy.

3. The responses reflect concern about separation from friends. Peer-conforming choices were predominant in response to item 1—which one of two courses to take in school, where the consequence of a peer-defying choice would have been some degree of separation from friends.[10]

4. A fourth hypothesis overlapping but different from those above is that the choices reflect perceived similarities and differences between self and

peers and self and parents. Adolescents, for example, perceiving themselves to be more like peers in regard to tastes in clothes and in regard to feelings about school, find peer-favored alternatives in these areas psychologically closer and more acceptable. But in other areas the greater perceived similarity is between self and parents. For example, with respect to values involved in the difficult choice whether to report a person who has destroyed property (items 4 and 11), the parent-favored alternatives are closer and more acceptable.[11]

The interviews referred to above provided a source for further inferences. According to one hypothesis derived from the interview data, responses to the CPT were a function of the perceived difficulty of the content choices. Parent-conformity was more prevalent in response to dilemmas posing what were perceived to be the more difficult choices. The 42 subjects interviewed soon after the second testing were asked to rank the content choices according to difficulty. The items from the CPT, with the parent-versus-peer aspect deleted, were typed on small cards; the subjects were asked to select from among them, first the situation in which the girl would have the greatest difficulty making up her mind, then the situation in which she would have the least difficulty. This was repeated until the choices were ordered from most to least difficult. Median ranks were computed. The items eliciting predominantly peer-conforming trends fell at the least difficult end of the resulting rank order. Hence, the tendency toward parent-conformity was directly related to the perceived difficulty of the choice.

A second inference was suggested by a discrepancy between the interview data and CPT responses. Interviewees were asked to select from among the content dilemmas, as presented on the cards, the two about which a girl would most likely talk to her friends rather than her parents. Neither of the two items most frequently selected had elicited predominantly peer-conforming CPT response shifts. Choices in response to one of them (item 9—which one of two boys to date) were more frequently parent-conforming; while in response to the other (item 2—which one of two boys to go steady with) parent-conforming and peer-conforming choices were equally frequent. No such discrepancy was found when the girls were asked to select the two dilemmas about which a girl was most likely to talk to her parents rather than her friends. The three items most commonly selected (i.e., 4, 10, and 11) had all elicited predominantly parent-conforming response shifts.

This divergence of interview and test data may indicate that the latter lead to an over-estimate of parent-conformity. But it also suggests a device used by adolescents in coping with parent-peer cross-pressures, namely, avoiding communication with parents. This would be likely to occur in areas in which parent-peer conflict is most acute. If this is the case, such discrepancies as those reported here could be used to identify points at which adolescents tend to be most disturbed by cross-pressures from parents and peers.

Let me note one other aspect of the data. Despite the greater overall incidence of parent-conformity, there was greater convergence relative to peer-conforming choices. As shown in Table 2, a majority of the items elicited a preponderance of parent-conforming over peer-conforming choices. On each of the items where there was a reversal of this trend (i.e., items 1, 6, and 8) there were, however, more peer-conforming choices than parent-conforming choices on any single item. This suggests the following possibility: Analogous trends in the social behavior of adolescents create the impression that peer-conformity in adolescence is more diffuse than actually is the case. Lack of parent-adolescent communication about certain types of choices contributes to this impression.

Summary and further applications

The study explored the hypothesis, suggested by reference-group theory, that adolescent choices in response to parent-peer cross-pressures are dependent upon the character of the content alternatives presented. Hypothetical dilemmas were described to adolescent girls. In each dilemma a girl was confronted with a complex choice where one course of action was favored by parents and another by peers. The respondents were asked in each case to indicate what the girl would probably do. With the situations remaining otherwise unchanged, peer-favored and parent-favored alternatives were interchanged and the hypothetical dilemmas again presented to the respondents. Comparison of responses to the two forms of the test revealed that peer-conforming choices were more prevalent in response to certain of the dilemmas and parent-conforming choices in response to others. These results were taken to support the hypothesis.

The content of the items suggested additional specific hypotheses as partial explanations of the trends toward peer-conforming and parent-conforming responses: (1) The responses reflect the adolescent's perception of peers and parents as competent guides in different areas of judgement. (2) The responses reflect a concern to avoid being noticeably different from peers. (3) The responses reflect concern about separation from peers. (4) The choices reflect perceived similarities and differences between self and peers and self and parents.

Additional data were collected by interviewing a number of the respondents. From the interview data and from discrepancies between test and interview it was hypothesized that: (1) The tendency toward parent-conformity is directly related to the perceived difficulty of the choices. (2) Adolescents attempt to come to terms with parent-peer cross-pressures by simply not communicating with parents.

The present study argues the value of the approach exemplified here in exploring an important facet of adolescence. What considerations predispose adolescents toward peer-conformity in situations where they are confronted with parent-peer cross-pressures? What are the persisting cognitive schemata against which choices in such situations are made? We believe that through applications of the present method or adaptations of it, hypotheses relating to these questions could be investigated. For example:

1. Stability of social values: Adolescents are more strongly given to peer-conformity in making choices in areas in which social values are changing rapidly, than making choices in areas in which social values are relatively stable.

2. Time perspective: Adolescents are more strongly disposed toward peer-conformity in making choices where immediate consequences are anticipated than in making choices where the emphasis is on long term effects.

In addition, the present procedure might be used to assess individual differences in predispositions toward peer-versus parent-conformity. Although the study did not deal with the problem, the subjects were found to differ from one another in their tendencies to make parent-conforming or peer-conforming choices. At the extremes four groups were identified: (1) subjects manifesting relatively strong tendencies toward parent-conformity; (2) subjects manifesting relatively strong tendencies toward peer-conformity; (3) a mixed-conformity group composed of subjects making parent-conforming choices and peer-conforming choices with relatively great and about equal frequency; and (4) subjects making very few responses of either type; i.e., subjects whose responses were mostly consistent by content. The stability of these response biases and their possible correlates remain a problem for further study.

REFERENCES

1. There is controversy about the legitimacy of this image. For contrasting views see Frederick Elkin and William A. Westley, "The Myth of the Adolescent Peer Culture," *American Sociological Review,* 20 (December, 1955), pp. 680–684; and James S. Coleman, *The Adolescent Society,* New York: The Free Press, 1961, Ch. 1.

2. Tamotsu Shibutani, "Reference Groups as Perspectives," *American Journal of Sociology,* 60 (May, 1955), pp. 562–569.

3. Item number 4 on the instrument used in the study.

4. The alternate version of the item given above read as follows: "The three girls she goes around with most of the time feel that Jim is unfairly using Bill in order to lighten his own punishment. They think that Nell should tell the principal who broke the glass. Nell talks the matter over with her mother and father. They don't think Nell should tell the principal. Nell's parents hate to see an innocent person punished. But her father points out to Nell that this is a matter between Jim and Bill and between Jim and his conscience." There are obviously many situations for which this type of reversal would not be plausible.

5. Biases toward parent-favored or peer-favored alternatives showed up also as

differences in first test responses between experimental subgroups AB and
BA. A comparison of these groups, not reported here, reveals substantially
the same trends as shown in the present analysis.

6. Both the interviewing and the testing were done by the writer.

7. Sociometric data were collected in one of the schools included in the study,
but only brief reference is made to them in this paper.

8. This imposes an important qualification in generalizing the findings. If a
sample of adolescent boys were studied in similar manner, the findings would
undoubtedly diverge at some points from those presented here.

9. Robert K. Merton, *Social Theory and Social Structure*. Revised and Enlarged Edition, New York: The Free Press, 1957, p. 244.

10. An example identical on both forms concerned which one of two high schools
to attend. Responses to it were predominantly peer-conforming.

11. This hypothesis holds, in effect, that there is a close interrelationship between what Merton refers to as normative type and comparison type reference
groups. Merton, *op. cit.*, p. 283.

[19]   *Norman E. Gronlund & Loren Anderson*

PERSONALITY CHARACTERISTICS OF SOCIALLY

ACCEPTED, SOCIALLY NEGLECTED, AND SOCIALLY

REJECTED JUNIOR HIGH SCHOOL PUPILS

A recent study (4) has shown that the extent to which junior high school
pupils are accepted by their classmates is related to the degree to which they
are accepted throughout the school and in their neighborhoods. This pervasiveness of pupils' social status among their peers has increased the importance of
identifying factors related to their social acceptability. Why is it that some
pupils are highly accepted by their peers while others are neglected, or even
actively rejected by them? Are there distinct personality patterns that characterize the socially accepted, the socially neglected, and the socially rejected
pupils? Answers to such questions as these should enable teachers to better
understand their pupils' social relations. Even more important, a study of the
personality factors related to social acceptability should provide suggestions
for improving the status of those pupils who are socially neglected or socially
rejected.

FROM *Educational Administration and Supervision*, 1957, 43, 329–338. REPRINTED
BY PERMISSION OF THE SENIOR AUTHOR.

Several research studies (5, 6, 8) have been concerned with the aspects of personality pre-adolescent and adolescent pupils consider most desirable in each other. In general, high social acceptability was found to be associated with positive personality characteristics such as cheerfulness, enthusiasm, friendliness, and the like. Pupils with low social acceptability were characterized as lacking in positive personality traits and possessing some negative characteristics, such as restlessness, talkativeness, fighting, and so forth. These studies have made valuable contributions concerning the factors related to social acceptability. However, none of the investigators separated the characteristics of the socially neglected pupils from those of the socially rejected pupils. Although both groups of pupils have low social acceptability, it is expected that they would have quite different personality patterns. Northway's (7) clinical study of pupils with low social acceptability bears directly on this point. She found that some of the pupils who lacked social acceptance among peers were shy, withdrawing, socially uninterested persons, while others were noisy, boastful, socially ineffective individuals. Common sense would indicate that pupils in the first category would probably be socially neglected by their peers and those characterized as having undesirable, aggressive traits would in all probability be socially rejected. Testing this common-sense relationship between personality patterns and the two categories of pupils having low social acceptability is the main concern of this study. Specifically, the personality characteristics of the socially neglected and the socially rejected pupils will be compared and contrasted with those of the socially accepted pupils.

Method of investigation

The social acceptability of the pupils participating in this study was determined by means of a sociometric test. This test requested choices of pupils on three positive criteria and one negative criterion. Each pupil was asked to indicate the five classmates he *most* preferred as work companions, the five classmates he *most* preferred as play companions, and the five classmates he *most* preferred as seating companions. The negative criterion required the names of the five classmates the pupil *least* preferred as seating companions. This criterion was used as a measure of rejection. It was felt that one negative criterion was sufficient for the purpose and that a larger number might place unnecessary emphasis on the rejective aspects of the sociometric choosing.

This sociometric device was administered to all of the seventh- and eighth-grade pupils in a small city located in central Illinois. There were one hundred and fifty-eight pupils with approximately an even number of boys and girls. The six classroom groups ranged in size from twenty-five to twenty-eight pupils. The regular classroom teacher administered the sociometric test to each classroom group. All data were obtained during the second semester of the school year.

In addition to making choices on the sociometric test, each pupil responded to a social analysis form based on the "guess who" technique. This form presented brief positive and negative descriptions of eighteen personality traits and instructed the pupils to indicate which of their classmates best fitted each description. The following items illustrate the positive and negative descriptions for *friendliness*.[1]

1. "Here is someone who is very friendly, who has lots of friends, who is nice to everybody."

2. "Here is someone who does not care to make friends, who is bashful about being friendly, or who does not seem to have many friends."

Similar positive and negative items were included for each of the other personality traits. After each descriptive sketch, spaces for six names were provided. The pupils were encouraged to write as many names as they desired after each description and to use each classmate's name as often as needed. Thus they had complete freedom in assigning the behavior descriptions to their classmates.

Analysis of data and results

The sociometric results were analyzed by totaling the number of choices each pupil received on each of the sociometric criteria. In accord with the findings in a previous study (3), there was considerable overlap in the choosing on the three positive criteria. If a pupil was highly chosen as seating companion he also tended to be highly chosen as work companion and play companion. Consequently, choices on these three criteria were combined into a single measure of social acceptability. These scores ranged from 0 to 46 with a mean of 15. The social rejection scores, obtained on the single negative criterion, ranged from 0 to 21 with a mean of 5.

These sociometric results were used to select the socially accepted, the socially rejected, and the socially neglected groups. There were ten boys and ten girls in each category. The twenty pupils in the most *socially accepted* group received an average of 29 choices on the positive sociometric criteria. The twenty pupils in the most *socially rejected* group received an average of 12 rejection choices. The twenty most *socially neglected* pupils were those receiving the smallest number of choices on both the positive and the negative criteria. They had an average of 4 acceptance choices and 2 rejection choices. It should be noted that the larger number of acceptance choices received is due to the fact that these are based on three sociometric criteria while the rejection choices are based on one sociometric criterion.

The Social Analysis form was scored for each pupil by totaling the number of mentions he received on each item and then algebraically summing the positive and negative scores for each personality characteristic. Thus if a pupil received 10 mentions as being friendly (+) and 2 mentions as being unfriendly (−) his score for friendliness would be 8. Positive scores indicate socially desirable traits and negative scores indicate their opposites. The strength of the personality trait in the individual is assumed to be roughly equivalent to the number of mentions he receives on that trait.

SOCIAL ACCEPTABILITY AND PERSONALITY CHARACTERISTICS OF GIRLS

The personality characteristics most closely associated with the three social acceptability categories for girls are presented in Table 1. These characteristics

TABLE 1   Average Number of Mentions Received on Social Analysis Form by Most Accepted, Most Neglected, and Most Rejected Girls ($N = 30$)

CHARACTERISTIC	ACCEPTED	NEGLECTED	REJECTED
Good-looking	14		−8
Tidy	13		−4
Friendly	10		
Likable	8		−4
Enthusiastic	8		
Cheerful	7		
Quiet (not restless)	7	3	−4
Interest in dating	6		
Humor (self)	4		
Initiative	4		
Humor (jokes)	3		
Talkative	3	−3*	5

* Minus sign (−) means opposite of trait.

are self-explanatory, with the possible exception of those on humor. *Humor (self)* means she enjoys a joke on herself. *Humor (jokes)* means she enjoys hearing jokes. Only those traits receiving an average of 3 or more mentions are included in the analysis. The numbers of mentions received have been rounded off to the nearest whole number.

It will be noted that the socially accepted girls were characterized as being attractive, neat, and in general possessing aggressive and out-going behavior. These findings are similar to the results of other studies (1, 5). Our main interest here, however, is to contrast the socially neglected and the socially rejected groups with that of the socially accepted group.

The socially neglected girls received neither positive nor negative mention on most of the personality traits. They were characterized as being quiet and *not* talkative. In general then, they seemed to attract neither favorable nor unfavorable attention. They apparently were the neutral personalities who were overlooked, rather than disliked, by their classmates. This low social acceptability group appears to be similar to the quiet withdrawing pupils identified by Northway's (7) clinical analysis.

The socially rejected girls also received little mention on the positive traits. However they were not overlooked on the negative items. Since they were rated as being *not* good looking, untidy, *not* likable, restless, and talkative, it would appear that they were aggressive enough to attract attention. However the attention they attracted to themselves was generally unfavorable. The resemblance between this group and Northway's (7) "socially ineffective" category is quite obvious. Apparently these rejected girls were attempting to make social contact with their peers but lacked the necessary grooming and social skill.

The characteristic "talkative" deserves special attention. It will be noted that both the accepted and the rejected groups were characterized as being talkative, while the neglected group was rated as being *not* talkative. This seems to indicate that although talkative girls gain recognition they do not necessarily gain social acceptance. It is probably the nature of their conversation, as well as other personality characteristics, rather than the talking itself, that determines whether they will be accepted or rejected by their peers.

There were six personality traits omitted from the above analysis, since they did not receive sufficient mention in any of the three social acceptance categories. These traits are those of being bossy, fighting, seeking attention, being active in games, being a tomboy, and being daring. Apparently these characteristics are not related to social acceptability among these junior high school girls.

SOCIAL ACCEPTABILITY AND PERSONALITY CHARACTERISTICS OF BOYS

In order to make the analysis for boys comparable to that for the girls, the same twelve personality characteristics have been listed in the same order in Table 2. In addition, a thirteenth characteristic has been added to the list, since it has been shown to discriminate among the boys. As in the case of girls, only those traits receiving an average of 3 or more mentions are recorded in the table.

In general, the socially accepted boys were characterized as possessing personality traits similar to those of the socially accepted girls. However, there are some important differences. Four of the traits that were characteristic of the socially accepted girls, are not descriptive of the socially accepted boys. These are those of being quiet, having an interest in dating, showing initiative, and being talkative. In addition, one trait, not significant in the case of girls, was indicated as being the trait most closely related to boys' social acceptability, that is, being active in games. These differences between boys and girls seem

TABLE 2   Average Number of Mentions Received on Social Analysis Form by Most Accepted, Most Neglected, and Most Rejected Boys ($N = 30$)

CHARACTERISTIC	ACCEPTED	NEGLECTED	REJECTED
Good-looking	7		−7*
Tidy	7		−3
Friendly	5		
Likable	7		−3
Enthusiastic	4		
Cheerful	5		
Quiet (not restless)		3	−6
Interest in dating			
Humor (self)	4		
Initiative			
Humor (jokes)	5		
Talkative			6
Active in Games	12		

* Minus sign (−) means opposite of trait.

to reflect developmental differences characteristic of this age level. The boys' previous interests in active pursuits (8) are carried over into the junior high school, while the earlier-maturing girls' are concerned with quiet activities, dating, etc., which are characteristic of more advanced social adjustments.

The differences between the socially accepted boys and the socially accepted girls should not distract attention from the characteristics they had in common. The socially accepted pupils of both sexes were characterized as being good-looking, tidy, friendly, likable, enthusiastic, cheerful, and having a good sense of humor. These results are similar to those found for boys and girls at both the sixth and the twelfth grade levels by Kuhlen and Lee (5).

The socially neglected boys were overlooked on practically all of the personality traits. They received an average of 3 mentions as being quiet. Their lack of mention on both the positive and the negative items verifies the similar findings for girls. Apparently socially neglected pupils of both sexes lacked social stimulus value. They were members of the classroom group but in a sense were "social islands" unto themselves. Members of this low social acceptance group were truly socially *neglected* by their peers.

The characteristics of the socially rejected boys are identical to those of the socially rejected girls. Both groups had the reputation of being *not* good-looking, untidy, *not* likable, restless, and talkative. It should be pointed out that in addition to possessing these negative traits, they lacked the positive characteristics associated with social acceptability. Thus, the socially rejected pupils attracted attention among their peers, but it was primarily negative attention. This is in contrast to the positive attention directed toward the socially accepted pupils and the lack of attention rendered the socially neglected pupils.

The personality traits which did not receive sufficient mention to discriminate among the three social acceptability types for boys are, interest in dating, initiative, being bossy, fighting, seeking attention, being a sissy, and being daring. Apparently the undesirable aggressive behavior, indicated by several of these characteristics, loses its prestige value (2) by the time boys reach the junior high school age.

Implications for the classroom teacher

The results of this study clearly indicate that strong, positive personality characteristics are associated with social acceptability among junior high school pupils. Probably more important, the results suggest that pupils with low social acceptability cannot be placed in a single category. The socially neglected pupils appear to be ignored or overlooked by their classmates while the socially rejected pupils are actively disliked. These findings should provide implications for improving the social acceptability of pupils.

The emphasis placed on appearance and friendly, aggressive behavior seems to indicate the importance of good grooming and social skills at the junior high school level. Assisting pupils in these areas may help improve their social acceptability. A special unit could be included in the home-room program. This unit need not be restricted to grooming and social skills but could include other aspects of social acceptability. One effective method of beginning such a unit is to present to the pupils a list of the personality characteristics related to social acceptability. This list could be obtained from published studies, or, more effective for discussion purposes, it might be based on a study of the teacher's own classroom. Just making the pupils aware of the factors related to social acceptability is sometimes helpful. In addition, a discussion of such factors serves to motivate pupils to want to learn how to improve their grooming and social skills. This approach is, of course, most effective with pupils who lack the knowledge of what is important in social relations and are awkward in their use of social skills. It is not expected that such an approach, by itself, is sufficient to improve the peer acceptance of the socially neglected and the socially rejected pupils.

Somehow, the neglected pupils must be brought to the attention of their peers. Interaction with classmates may be facilitated through small group work, through minor positions of responsibility in the classroom, through working on class projects, and through other avenues of social contact with fellow pupils. It is important that the introduction to group activities be gradual and that the pupil's social skills are sufficient to cope with the new social activity. It should be noted that increased aggressiveness, on the part of the socially neglected pupil, can lead to social rejection as well as to social acceptability. If their social status is to be improved, rather than made worse, careful guidance is needed in developing socially effective aggressiveness.

Improving the social acceptability of the rejected pupil is a special problem. Before he can be helped to gain social status, it is first necessary to remove or modify the characteristics causing rejection. This cause may be as simple as being untidy or it may involve a complicated pattern of traits that is difficult, if not impossible, to modify. Where possible, the teacher should attempt to identify the causes of rejection and remove them. In some cases individual counseling, or other outside help, may be necessary to modify the behavior of the rejected pupil.

In addition to changing the behavior of the rejected pupil, the teacher must make a special effort to change the child's reputation among his classmates. Changes in behavior are not automatically accompanied by changes in reputation. The child who was once thought of as *not* likable remains *not* likable until experience proves otherwise. Since rejected children are generally avoided, these *new* experiences do not readily occur unless the teacher takes an active rôle. Seating the rejected child near those who reject him least and having him work with small groups of pupils will help him get reëstablished. From this vantage point he can gradually be integrated into the larger group. Casual comments by the teacher, concerning his improved behavior, may also help. However, it should be recognized that the classroom teacher cannot give the rejected child social acceptance among his peers. She can only help him develop the characteristics, and arrange for the necessary social interaction that leads to social acceptability.

In addition to providing implications for improving the social acceptability of individual pupils, the results of this study indicate the shortcomings of the "guess who" technique for obtaining the personality characteristics of pupils. Since the neglected pupils seldom receive either positive or negative mention on the behavior characteristics, a description of their personality is either very sketchy or completely lacking. In the present study the neglected pupils were characterized as being quiet, but even on this characteristic they received relatively few mentions. Thus, although the "guess who" technique may be a useful method for obtaining behavior descriptions of aggressive pupils, it is of little value in determining the characteristics of pupils who lack sufficient aggressiveness to attract the attention of their classmates.

NOTES

1. The complete form, entitled Social Analysis of the Classroom, may be found in bibliography item (6), pp. 80–85.

REFERENCES

1. Merle E. Bonney, "Personality Traits of Socially Successful and Socially Unsuccessful Children," *Journal of Educational Psychology,* 34: 449–72, November, 1943.
2. Merle E. Bonney, "Sex Differences in Social Success and Personality Traits," *Child Development,* 15: 63–79, March, 1944.
3. Norman E. Gronlund, "Generality of Sociometric Status over Criteria in the Measurement of Social Acceptability," *Elementary School Journal,* 56: 173–76, December, 1955.
4. Norman E. Gronlund and Algard P. Whitney, "Relation Between Pupils' Social Acceptability in the Classroom, in the School, and in the Neighborhood," *School Review,* 64: 267–71, September, 1956.
5. Raymond G. Kuhlen and Beatrice J. Lee, "Personality Characteristics and Social Acceptability in Adolescence," *Journal of Educational Psychology,* 34: 321–40, September, 1943.
6. Frances Laughlin, *The Peer Status of Sixth- and Seventh-Grade Children,* New York, Bureau of Publications, Teachers College, Columbia University, 1954.
7. Mary L. Northway, "A Study of the Personality Patterns of Children Least Acceptable to Their Age Mates," *Sociometry,* 7: 10–25, February, 1944.
8. Caroline M. Tryon, *Evaluations of Adolescent Personality by Adolescents,* Monographs of The Society for Research in Child Development, Vol. 4, No. 4 Washington, National Research Council, 1939.

[20]   *Philip R. Costanzo & Marvin E. Shaw*   CONFORMITY AS A FUNCTION OF AGE LEVEL

It is generally assumed that conformity behavior is the result of developmental processes (Berg & Bass, 1961). However, the nature and consequences of these developmental processes have not been fully explored, and the theories concerning the relation between ontogenetic level and conformity are often in disagreement. The stimulus for the present study is derived from the work of Piaget (1954). He proposed that social development progresses through an orderly sequence of stages. Implicit in his analysis of the way the child learns the "rules of the game" is the hypothesis that the relation between age and conformity to rules (norms) is curvilinear. That is, at an early age the child is

FROM *Child Development,* 1966, 37, 967–975. © 1966 BY THE SOCIETY FOR RESEARCH IN CHILD DEVELOPMENT, INC. REPRINTED BY PERMISSION OF THE SENIOR AUTHOR AND THE SOCIETY FOR RESEARCH IN CHILD DEVELOPMENT.

uninfluenced by rules but gradually begins to follow them until at about age 11–12 the rules are internalized and utilized completely. After this stage, the individual begins to express individual modes of response by creating and codifying certain of his own rules. Since conformity is the act of behaving in accordance with social rules or norms, it follows that conformity behavior should increase with increasing age until the child reaches the stage at which rules are internalized, and decrease thereafter.

Experimental studies of the relation between age and conformity typically have dealt with only limited age ranges. The evidence relative to the above hypothesis is therefore less than adequate, but, with a few exceptions, it appears to support the hypothesis. Marple (1933) found that high school students were more likely to conform to majority or expert opinion than either college students or adults. Similarly, Patel and Gordon (1960) found that conformity decreased from the tenth to the twelfth grade, although there were some reversals with high-prestige suggestions. These findings led Campbell (1961) to conclude that "The older a person is, the more established his dispositions, and therefore the less conformant he is" (Campbell, 1961, p. 114). However, both Marple (1933) and Patel and Gordon (1960) limited their sample to postadolescent age groups. Their results are therefore consistent with both Campbell's conclusion and our hypothesis.

Berenda (1950) reports evidence that appears to be contrary to our hypothesis. She conducted four experiments, two of which involved a single subject exposed to erroneous judgments of length of lines. In both studies, subjects in the 7–10 age group conformed more than did subjects in the 10–13 age group. However, there are some aspects of Berenda's study that may account for this seeming contradiction. In the first experiment, pressure was exerted by the eight brightest children in the class, whereas in the second experiment, pressure was exerted by the teacher. Thus in both experiments subjects were exposed to pressure from high-status persons. It may well be that age differences in conformity to prestige suggestions follow a different pattern than age differences in conformity to peer suggestions. In this connection, it might be worth noting that Berenda found statistically reliable differences between age groups only when social pressure was exerted by the teacher.

A more recent study (Iscoe, Williams, & Harvey, 1963) presents results that are consistent with our hypothesis for females but not for males. These investigators studied four age groups (7-, 9-, 12-, and 15-year-old subjects) in a simulated conformity situation in which the task was to count the number of metronome clicks in a series. Maximum conformity occurred in the 12-year group for females, but in the 15-year group for males, although the difference between the 12-year and the 15-year male groups was not significant.

Thus, despite some inconsistent data, the evidence generally supports the hypothesis. Theoretical arguments in support of the hypothesis are also compelling. Until the child has had an opportunity to learn both the norms of his group and that conformity brings rewards, there is no logical reason to expect him to conform. Therefore, one would expect at least an initial increase in conformity with age. With increased age, many additional variables come into play. For example, it has been shown that lesser conformity is associated with (*a*) higher education (Tuddenham, 1959), (*b*) higher status (Crutchfield, 1955; Kelley & Volkart, 1952; Tuddenham, 1959), and (*c*) greater competence (Crutchfield, 1955; Tuddenham, 1959). Since all of these variables covary with age, it follows that, after an initial increase in conformity as a result of learning, conformity will decrease with age. These arguments are consistent with the hypothesis, but the age at which the shift from increasing to decreasing conformity occurs is not specified.

The present research was designed to measure directly the relation between age level and conformity. Based upon the considerations outlined above, it was expected that conformity, defined as a response to social pressure from peers, can best be represented by a two-stage theory of development. It was hypothesized that conformity increases with age in the preadolescent period to an asymptotic level in adolescence and then decreases in postadolescence through early adulthood.

Method

SUBJECTS

The subjects were 72 students from the P. K. Yonge Laboratory School at the University of Florida and 24 undergraduates at the same university. The admissions policies at the laboratory school virtually insure that subjects in different age groups are similar with respect to general intelligence and socioeconomic level. Half of the subjects were male and half were female.

EXPERIMENTAL DESIGN

A 2 × 4 factorial design was utilized, involving sex and four age groups. Twenty-four subjects, 12 male and 12 female, were assigned to each age group. Group I subjects ranged in age from 7 to 9 years; Group II subjects ranged from 11 to 13 years; Group III subjects ranged from 15 to 17 years; and Group IV subjects ranged from 19 to 21 years.

MATERIALS AND
APPARATUS

The apparatus used was similar to that described by Crutchfield (1955). It consisted of five booths arranged in a semicircle. The center booth was occupied by the experimenter (*E*). It contained a Besseler opaque projector for projecting the stimuli on a screen in front of the booths, and master panels of lights and switches. The subjects (*Ss*) occupied the four side booths and faced the projection screen which was approximately 10 feet from each booth.

Each subject booth contained a panel of twenty lights arranged in four rows of five lights each, with five mercury switches placed below the fourth row of lights. Each of these switches, when turned on, activated the light immediately above it in the fourth row and a corresponding light on the master response panel in E's booth. The lights in the other three rows on the S's panel were controlled by master switches in E's booth, although the procedure was such that each S believed these lights reflected the responses of other Ss. In the present experiment, only three of the five lights in each row were utilized.

The stimulus materials were patterned after those used by Asch (1958). Twelve stimulus cards were prepared, each containing three comparison lines and a standard line. One of the three comparison lines was the same length as the standard, one was ¼-inch shorter than the standard, and the third was ¼-inch longer than the standard. The S's task was to choose the line which matched the standard in length.

PROCEDURE

The experimental sessions were conducted in a room located at the school from which the Ss were drawn. Four Ss, all from a given age group and of the same sex, were run in each experimental session. The order in which the groups were run was random within the limits imposed by scheduling difficulties.

When Ss reported at the scheduled time, they were asked to select one of the four subject booths and be seated. The nature of the task and the manner of responding were explained in detail. The Ss were told that the order of responding would be random and that each S was to respond when E called out the number in his cubicle. Talking was prohibited. After the general instructions were given, E went to each booth and answered any question that Ss posed concerning procedure. At this time, each person was assigned the number "4." When E was sure that everyone understood the instructions, five practice trials were administered to insure that Ss understood and were able to perform the task. Following the practice trials, each stimulus card was presented twice in a predetermined order. Erroneous responses were signaled by E for Ss 1, 2, and 3 on 16 of the 24 trials. The conformity score for each S was the number of times his response agreed with the erroneous responses on these 16 critical trials. Therefore, the score for any given subject could range from zero to 16.

At the end of the experimental session, each S was asked the following question: "Did you find that some of your answers were different from the others, and if so, what do you think the reason for this was?"

Results

Before reporting the main results, it may be noted that on the pre-experimental, nonpressure trials only two errors were made on a total of 480 judgments. This result indicates that the errors made under pressure conditions cannot be attributed to the difficulty of the task.

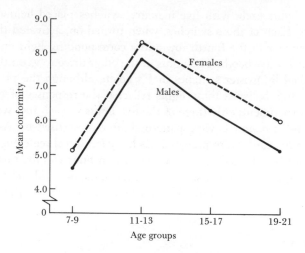

FIGURE 1   Mean conformity as a function of age.

The results of pressure on conformity behavior under the various experimental conditions are presented graphically in Figure 1, and a summary of the analysis of variance is given in Table 1. The only significant effect was that produced by the age variable ($p < .001$). As can be seen in Figure 1, conformity was least for Group I (ages 7–9), increased to a maximum for Group II (ages 11–13), and decreased again for Group III (ages 15–17) and Group IV (ages 19–21). Females conformed more than males at all age levels, although differences were not statistically significant.

It is perhaps worth noting that conformity as a function of age was also examined for each age level. The pattern of conformity was essentially the same as that shown in Figure 1, although the curve was not as smooth. Maximum conformity occurred at age 12.

The responses to the postexperimental question indicated that all Ss perceived some discrepancy between their responses and those of the other Ss in the group. The reasons given for these discrepancies were classified as either "internal" (that is, self-attributed reasons) or "external" (that is, other-attributed reasons). For example, "I must be going blind; I was wrong most of the time," was classified as internal, whereas "I think the other guys were crazy" was classified as external. These classifications were made by four graduate students in psychology who showed 100 per cent agreement. Since the two classes are reciprocally related, only the internally attributing responses were considered. The 7–9 age group gave 6 internally attributing responses, the 11–13 age group gave 17, the 15–17 age group gave 13, and the 19–21 age group gave 11. The distributions of internal-external responses among age groups differed significantly ($\chi^2 = 10.44$, $p < .02$). This pattern corresponds closely to the pattern of conformity behavior (Cf. Figs. 1 and 2), suggesting that Ss who blame themselves when their behavior is discrepant from that of their peers

TABLE 1   Summary of Analysis of Variance of Conformity Scores

SOURCE	*df*	*MS*	*F*	*P*
Age	3	49.37	10.37	< .001
Sex	1	12.76	2.68	n.s.
Age × Sex	3	0.15	.03	n.s.
Within subgroups	88	4.76	—	—
Total	95	—	—	—

are more likely to conform to group pressure than Ss who place the blame on others.

In order to test this suggestion more directly, a biserial r was computed between conformity and internal-external classification of subjects. This showed a highly significant relation ($r_b = .87$, $p < .01$). To clarify further the relations among age, blame attribution, and conformity, an index of correlation was computed between age and conformity. This yielded a value of .57 ($p < .01$), thus further supporting the results from the analysis of variance. The results indicate, therefore, that both the tendency to blame one's self and the tendency to conform to peers increase with age during the preadolescent period and decrease thereafter—at least through early adulthood.

Discussion

The results of this study lend decisive support to the hypothesis that conformity to pressure from peers is a nonlinear function of age. The developmental function (see Fig. 1) representing the mean number of conforming responses in each of the composite age groups supports the hypothesis that, from the preadolescent to the adolescent period of development, the amount of conformity to external social pressure increases, whereas conformity decreases after adolescence and through early adulthood.

Essentially, it appears that the development of conforming behavior patterns runs parallel with the socialization process. That is, the child in his early development is probably not fully aware of the social pressure to conform to certain standards adopted by his peers. Thus the effect of a unanimously wrong majority is not extremely threatening to the younger child, and hence the lower percentage of conformity in the 7–9 age group in this experiment. On the other hand, with the onset of pubescence, the child becomes acutely aware of his social peers and relies upon them for many of his external behavior patterns (that is, ways of dress, "code" between buddies, clubs, "gang age," etc.). There-

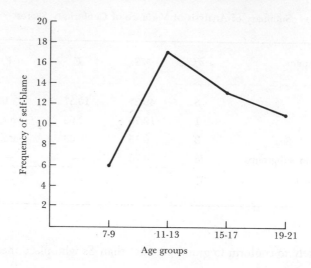

FIGURE 2   Frequency of self-blame responses as a function of age.

fore, the child at the pubescent stage displays much uncertainty with his own judgments and mirrors the behavior of his peers. By the postadolescent and early adulthood stages, the individual has learned that there are both situations which call for conformity and those which call for individual action. Thus, he becomes more confident about his own judgments despite the disagreement of a unanimous majority. However, since the individual in this postadolescent and young adult stage has experienced socialization, and since he has at some earlier time experienced the penalties of nonconformity, he does not attain the degree of individuality of judgment that is evident in the presocialization stage.

This interpretation is also consistent with the results of the analysis of the responses to the postexperimental question. It will be recalled that the pattern of internal attribution of responsibility for discrepant responses paralleled the conformity pattern.

Finally, it should be noted that the results of this experiment are generally consistent with those reported by Iscoe et al. (1963) but are in disagreement with Campbell's (1961) hypothesis concerning the relation of age and conformity and with results reported by Berenda (1950). The reasons for the failure to support Campbell's hypothesis are quite clear. His formulation was based upon the results of studies (Marple, 1933; Patel & Gordon, 1960) using high school students and adults as subjects, thus representing only the postadolescent period. The reasons for the discrepancy between our results and those reported by Berenda are not so obvious. As noted in the above, however, there were some significant differences in the experimental situations.

Probably the most important differences were in the nature of the social pressure. It will be recalled that in Berenda's experiments pressure was exerted by high-status persons: the eight brightest children in the class or the teacher. It was suggested that age differences in conformity might vary, depending upon whether the social pressure emanates from higher-status persons or from peers. One might suspect that younger children are relatively more influenced by high-status persons than by peers, whereas older children are relatively more influenced by peers. In fact, data concerning the typical adolescent reaction to authority figures are consistent with this hypothesis. If this line of reasoning is correct, the differences between the results of the present study and the results of the Berenda study can be accounted for by the differences in kind of social pressure. On the other hand, if this reasoning is correct, it means that our hypothesis of a bi-directional, two-stage relation between age and conformity is valid only for situations involving pressure from peers.

REFERENCES

Asch, S. E. Effects of group pressure on the modification and distortion of judgments. In E. E. Maccoby, T. M. Newcomb, & E. L. Hartley (Eds.), *Readings in social psychology.* New York: Holt, 1958. Pp. 174–183.

Berenda, Ruth W. *The influence of the group on the judgments of children.* New York: Kings Crown Pr., 1950.

Berg, I. A., & Bass, B. M. (Eds.) *Conformity and deviation.* New York: Harper, 1961.

Campbell, D. T. Conformity in psychology's theories of acquired behavioral dispositions. In I. A. Berg & B. M. Bass (Eds.), *Conformity and deviation.* New York: Harper, 1961. Pp. 101–142.

Crutchfield, R. S. Conformity and character. *Amer. Psychologist,* 1955, **10,** 191–198.

Iscoe, I., Williams, M., & Harvey J. Modification of children's judgments by a simulated group technique: a normative developmental study. *Child Develpm.,* 1963, **34,** 963–978.

Kelley, H., & Volkart, E. The resistance to change of group-anchored attitudes. *Amer. soc. Rev.,* 1952, **17,** 453–485.

Marple, C. H. The comparative susceptibility of three age levels to the suggestion of group versus expert opinion. *J. soc. Psychol.,* 1933, **10,** 3–40.

Patel, A. A., & Gordon, J. E. Some personal and situational determinants of yielding to influence. *J. abnorm. soc. Psychol.,* 1960, **61,** 411–418.

Piaget, J. *The moral judgment of the child.* New York: Basic Books, 1954.

Tuddenham, R. D. Correlates of yielding to a distorted group norm. *J. Pers.,* 1959, **27,** 272–284.

SIX THE DEVELOPMENT OF EGO IDENTITY

An individual who has found his "identity," according to Erik Erikson, "feels and acts predominantly in tune with himself, his capacities, and his opportunities. . . . He knows where he fits (or knowingly prefers not to fit) into present conditions and developments." During adolescence, more than any other period of life, an individual faces the crises of discovering and establishing a mature, personal identity; of evaluating the attitudes, beliefs, and goals acquired from his parents; and of answering the pressing questions, "Who am I?" "Where have I been?" "Where am I going?" As indicated in Part Five, during this period the adolescent often questions traditional beliefs in an attempt to test his new system of values through interaction with or imitation of peer group behavior. If an adolescent successfully establishes his identity, however, he becomes less dependent on both peers and parents and more prepared for the next stage of "intimacy" during young adulthood.

The concept of "identity" widely used in the current developmental literature originated in Erikson's psychosocial concept of the "eight stages of man." Erikson postulated a series of eight developmental tasks or crises which lead from the first social contacts after birth contributing to trust or mistrust to the last struggle for integrity in old age. The adolescent stage is characterized by the crisis of "identity versus role diffusion," in which the individual, confronted with fundamental physiological changes, becomes concerned with his self-concept and his social role. In "Youth and the Life Cycle" (21), a synopsis of and elaboration on the psychosocial theory of development, Erikson postulates that "every adolescent is apt to go through some serious struggle at one time or another" before he reaches his mature identity. Failure to resolve the adolescent crises may contribute to "identity diffusion," in which "a feeling of being (or, indeed, wanting to be) 'nobody' " may lead to withdrawal from reality and, in extreme cases, climax in mental illness or suicide. Failure to face adolescent crises, unwillingness to search for answers, and too much willingness to accept traditional values results in a cessation of growth called "foreclosure." The height of the adolescent crises is what Erikson calls "a psychosocial moratorium—a period of delay in the assumption of adult commitment." The moratorium implies a search for new answers and a new identity, and consequently offers greater potential for growth than either self-diffusion or foreclosure. A so-called delinquent youth who takes pride in his anti-social identity—may be engaging in a psychosocial moratorium that allows him to evaluate his capabilities and to experiment socially before making a decision about his future.

Commenting on the social and emotional instability of this life stage, Kurt

Lewin has characterized the adolescent as a "marginal man," a minority group member not fully accepted in society. Erikson (22) expands this definition in "A Memorandum on Identity and Negro Youth," which deals with the special identity problems of adolescents in a racial minority. Like the adolescent, the Negro in America is moving from a position of subordination and dependency to a position of autonomy. The identity crisis of the Negro youth, consequently, is twice as difficult as that of most adolescents, because he is engaged in a struggle to find both a personal and a racial identity. Faced with prejudice against his race as well as his age, the Negro adolescent is far more susceptible than his white counterpart to the dangers of over-identification with gangs, idols, and "negative heroes." The constant threat of loss of his individual identity enhances clannishness and intolerance. Erikson's exploration of "totalism" and "negative identity" provides one possible explanation for the high degree of juvenile delinquency in the ghetto.

While there can be no doubt that Erikson's psychological theory of development in general and his construct "identity versus role diffusion" in particular have had a great deal of influence on psychological thought, empirical studies to validate these theoretical formulations are limited. In "Development and Validation of Ego Identity Status" (23), James E. Marcia attempts to place Erikson's theoretical constructs in an empirical framework. He views the adolescent "identity versus role diffusion" crisis as four distinct, almost sequential, developmental steps, leading from role diffusion through foreclosure and moratorium to mature identity. Each of these four steps could be viewed as continuous growth toward mature identity, although not every individual experiences every status, and either role diffusion or foreclosure could become terminal if further search for identity is abandoned. Marcia defines these four steps toward maturity operationally, the important dimensions being the extent to which the individual has experienced or is experiencing crisis and the extent to which the individual is committed to a system of values or an ideology.

For Marcia, the identity diffusion subject is characterized by a lack of commitment to a system of values or beliefs; the foreclosure subject by commitment to a system of values accepted unquestioningly from others (frequently his family), by avoidance of crises, and by authoritarianism; the moratorium subject by confrontation with crisis, search for solutions, reluctance to accept explanations and values from others, and variability on concept-attainment tasks; and the achieved identity subject by personal commitment as an outgrowth of resolved crisis, realistic aspiration level, high self-esteem, and high scores on concept-attainment tests.

The Herbert A. Otto and Sandra L. Healy (24) article offers some positive balance to the wealth of literature that focuses on adolescent problems, maladjustment, delinquency, and social pathology. The study explores the nature of personality resources and the sources of strength that sustain the adolescent. By administering a "strength questionnaire" to two groups of high school students,

Otto and Healy were able to determine the general categories from which adolescents derive their personal strength. These include intellectual and emotional strength, social and spiritual strength, health, hobbies, sports, and educational strength. The questionnaire reveals that "the adolescent's self-perception of personality strengths are as limited as those of the adult and that the pattern of strength listings by male and female adolescents is more similar than dissimilar," the main difference between girls and boys being the former's greater emphasis on "social strength" and the boys' greater emphasis on "sports and activities." Both sexes illustrate the lack of communication between parent and adolescents reported by Brittain by refraining from listing "strengths through family and others" as a major factor in their development. Because the primary intent of the researchers is to create "a more positive image of the adolescent," and because the development of a positive, realistic self-concept is an important step toward identity formation, the article raises a disturbing question about the responsibility of the adult world to its adolescents: To what extent does society and its use of the mass media interfere with normal development by continuously drawing attention to the maladjustments and negative behavior of adolescents? How much easier would the years of adolescent crisis be if all adults assumed the positive attitude of Otto and Healy?

Gordon Allport (25) goes a step further than either Erikson or Marcia when he suggests that crisis is not only an intrinsic aspect of adolescence, but also a prerequisite for "normal" development. In his informal investigation, he identifies five main areas in which college students experience crisis: academic competition and failure; emotional threats, particularly the feeling of inferiority; religious and ideological conflicts; sexual stress; and family pressure. Allport's observations reinforce several stereotypes about the college years, including the belief that the sophomore year marks the peak of crisis for college students and that parent-adolescent relationships begin to normalize after the child reaches the age of twenty-three.

[21] *Erik H. Erikson* YOUTH AND THE LIFE CYCLE

QUESTION: Are there any points about your concepts of psychosocial development which you would now like to stress in the light of what you have heard about how they have been interpreted during the past decade in the training of professional persons and through them of parents and future parents?

FROM *Children*, 1960, 7, 43–49. REPRINTED BY PERMISSION OF THE AUTHOR AND THE CHILDREN'S BUREAU, U. S. DEPARTMENT OF HEALTH, EDUCATION, AND WELFARE.

Yes, I am grateful for the opportunity of making a few observations on the reception of these concepts. You emphasize their influence on teaching in various fields; let me pick out a few misunderstandings.

I should confess to you here how it all started. It was on a drive in the countryside with Mrs. Erikson that I became a bit expansive, telling her about a kind of ground plan in the human life cycle, which I seemed to discern in life histories. After a while she began to write, urging me just to go on; she had found my "plan" immediately convincing. Afterwards, a number of audiences of different professional backgrounds had that same sense of conviction —so much so that I (and others) became somewhat uneasy: after all, these psychosocial signposts are hardly *concepts* yet, even if the whole plan represents a valid *conception,* one which suggests a great deal of work.

What Mrs. Erikson and I subsequently offered to the White House Conference of 1950 was a kind of worksheet, which has, indeed, been used by others as well as myself in scientific investigation, and well integrated in a few textbooks.[3] But its "convincingness" has also led to oversimplification. Let me tell you about a few.

There has been a tendency here and there to turn the eight stages into a sort of rosary of achievement, a device for counting the fruits of each stage— trust, autonomy, initiative, and so forth—as though each were achieved as a permanent trait. People of this bent are apt to leave out the negative counterparts of each stage, as if the healthy personality had permanently conquered these hazards. The fact is that the healthy personality must reconquer them continuously in the same way that the body's metabolism resists decay. All that we learn are certain fundamental means and mechanisms for retaining and regaining mastery. Life is a sequence not only of developmental but also of accidental crises. It is hardest to take when both types of crisis coincide.

In each crisis, under favorable conditions, the positive is likely to outbalance the negative, and each reintegration builds strength for the next crisis. But the negative is always with us to some degree in the form of a measure of infantile anxiety, fear of abandonment—a residue of immaturity carried throughout life, which is perhaps the price man has to pay for a childhood long enough to permit him to be the learning and the teaching animal, and thus to achieve his particular mastery of reality.

You may be interested to know that further clinical research has indicated that our dream life often depicts a recovery of mastery along the lines of these stages. Moreover, nurses have observed that any adult who undergoes serious surgery has to repeat the battle with these nemeses in the process of recovery. A person moves up and down the scale of maturity, but if his ego has gained a positive balance during his developmental crises the downward movements will be less devastating than if the balance, at one stage or another, was in the negative.

Of all the positive aspects mentioned, trust seems to have been the most convincing—so convincing, in fact, that some discussions never reach a consideration of the other stages. I don't mean to detract from the obvious importance of trust as the foundation of the development of a healthy personality. A basic sense of trust in living as such, developed in infancy through the reciprocal relationship of child and mother, is essential to winning the positive fruits of all the succeeding crises in the life cycle: maybe this is what Christmas, with its Madonna images, conveys to us. Yet, it is the nature of human life that each succeeding crisis takes place within a widened social radius where an ever-larger number of significant persons have a bearing on the outcome. There is in childhood, first, the maternal person, then the parental combination, then the basic family and other instructing adults. Youth demands "confirmation" from strangers who hold to a design of life; and later, the adult needs challenges from mates and partners, and even from his growing children and expanding works, in order to continue to grow himself. And all of these relationships must be imbedded in an "ethos," a cultural order, to guide the individual's course.

In our one-family culture (supported by pediatricians and psychiatrists who exclusively emphasize the mother-child relationship) we tend to lose sight of the fact that other people besides parents are important to youth. Too often we ask only where a given youth came from and what he once was, and not also where he was going, and who was ready to receive him and his intentions and his specific gifts. Thus we have movements to punish parents for the transgressions of their children, ignoring all the other persons and environmental factors that entered into the production of a young person's unacceptable behavior and failed to offer support to his positive search.

Another way in which the life cycle theory has been oversimplified is in the omission of stages which do not fit into the preconceived ideas of the person who is adopting or adapting the theory. Thus a large organization devoted to parenthood distributed a list of the stages but omitted *integrity vs. despair*—the problem of senescence. This is too easy a way to dispose of grandparents; it robs life of an inescapable final step; and, of course, it defeats this whole conception of an intrinsic order in the life cycle.

This kind of omission ignores the "cogwheeling" of infantile and adult stages—the fact that each further stage of growth in a given individual is not only dependent upon the relatively successful completion of his own previous stages, but also on the completion of the subsequent stages in those other individuals with whom he interacts and whom he accepts as models.

Finally, I should point to the fact that what my psychoanalytic colleagues warned me of most energetically has, on occasion, come to pass: even sincere workers have chosen to ignore my emphasis on the intrinsic relation of the psychosocial to the psychosexual stages which form the basis of much of Freud's work.

All of these misuses, however, may be to a large extent the fault of my choice of words. The use of simple, familiar words like "trust" and "mistrust" apparently leads people to assume that they know "by feel" what the theory is all about. Perhaps this semantic problem would have been avoided if I had used Latin terms, which call for definitions.

I may point out, however, that I originally suggested my terms as a basis for discussions—discussions led by people who have an idea of the interrelated-

---

The Eight Stages in the Life Cycle of Man

"Personality," Erikson has written, "can be said to develop according to steps predetermined in the human organism's readiness to be driven toward, to be aware of, and to interact with a widening social radius, beginning with a dim image of a mother and ending with an image of mankind. . . ." Following are the steps he has identified in man's psychosocial development, and the special crises they bring. In presenting them, he has emphasized that while the struggle between the negatives and positives in each crisis must be fought through successfully if the next developmental stage is to be reached, no victory is completely or forever won.

I. Infancy: trust vs. mistrust

The first "task" of the infant is to develop "the cornerstone of a healthy personality," a basic sense of trust—in himself and in his environment. This comes from a feeling of inner goodness derived from "the mutual regulation of his receptive capacities with the maternal techniques of provision"[2]—a quality of care that transmits a sense of trustworthiness and meaning. The danger, most acute in the second half of the first year, is that discontinuities in care may increase a natural sense of loss, as the child gradually recognizes his separateness from his mother, to a basic sense of mistrust that may last through life.

II. Early childhood: autonomy vs. shame and doubt

With muscular maturation the child experiments with holding on and letting go and begins to attach enormous value to his autonomous will. The danger here is the development of a deep sense of shame and doubt if he is deprived of the opportunity to learn to develop his will as he learns his "duty," and therefore learns to expect defeat in any battle of wills with those who are bigger and stronger.

III. Play age: initiative vs. guilt

In this stage the child's imagination is greatly expanded because of his increased ability to move around freely and to communicate. It is an age of intrusive activity, avid curiosity, and consuming fantasies which lead to feelings of guilt and anxiety. It is also the stage of the establishment of conscience. If this tendency to feel guilty is "overburdened by all-too-eager adults" the child may develop a deep-seated conviction that he is essentially bad, with a resultant stifling of initiative or a conversion of his moralism to vindictiveness.

IV. School age: industry vs. inferiority

The long period of sexual latency before puberty is the age when the child wants to learn how to do and make things with others. In learning to accept instruction and to win recognition by producing "things" he opens the way for the capacity of work enjoyment. The danger in this period is the development of a sense of inadequacy and inferiority in a child who does not receive recognition for his efforts.

V. Adolescence: identity vs. identity diffusion

The physiological revolution that comes with puberty—rapid body growth and sexual maturity—forces the young person to question "all sameness and continuities relied on earlier" and to "refight many of the earlier battles." The developmental task is to integrate childhood identifications "with the basic biological drives, native endowment, and the opportunities offered in social roles." The danger is that identity diffusion, temporarily unavoidable in this period of physical and psychological upheaval, may result in a permanent inability to "take hold" or, because of youth's tendency to total commitment, in the fixation in the young person of a negative identity, a devoted attempt to become what parents, class, or community do not want him to be.

VI. Young adulthood: intimacy vs. isolation

Only as a young person begins to feel more secure in his identity is he able to establish intimacy with himself (with his inner life) and with others, both in friendships and eventually in a love-based mutually satisfying sexual relationship with a member of the opposite sex. A person who cannot enter wholly into an intimate relationship because of the fear of losing his identity may develop a deep sense of isolation.

VII. Adulthood: generativity vs. self-absorption

Out of the intimacies of adulthood grows generativity—the mature person's interest in establishing and guiding the next generation. The lack of this results in self-absorption and frequently in a "pervading sense of stagnation and interpersonal impoverishment."

VIII. Senescence: integrity vs. disgust

The person who has achieved a satisfying intimacy with other human beings and who has adapted to the triumphs and disappointments of his generative activities as parent and coworker reaches the end of life with a certain ego integrity—an acceptance of his own responsibility for what his life is and was and of its place in the flow of history. Without this "accrued ego integration" there is despair, usually marked by a display of displeasure and disgust.

---

ness of all aspects of human development. For the eight stages of psychosocial development are, in fact, inextricably entwined in and derived from the various stages of psychosexual development that were described by Freud, as well as from the child's stages of physical, motor, and cognitive development. Each type of development affects the other and is affected by it. Thus, I feel that discussants would do well to study each key word in its origins, in its usage in various periods and regions, and in other languages. Simple words that touch upon universal human values have their counterpart in every living language, and can become vehicles of understanding at international conferences.

Incidentally, I made up one new word because I thought it was needed. To me, "generativity" described the chief characteristic of the mature adult. It was turned into a comfortable, if inaccurate, homespun word before it ever left the Fact-Finding Committee of 1950. I had deliberately chosen "generativity" rather than "parenthood," or "creativity," because these narrowed the matter down to a biological and an artistic issue instead of describing the deep absorption in guiding the young or in helping to create a new world for the young, which is a mark of maturity in parents and nonparents, working people and "creative" people alike.

Enough of this fault-finding! But it *is* interesting to see what can happen to new ideas; and you *did* ask me.

QUESTION: During the past 10 years you have been treating and studying mentally ill young people at a public clinic in a low-income area in Pittsburgh and at a private, comparatively expensive, mental hospital in the Berkshires. Have you found any common denominator in the disturbances of these patients—from such opposite walks of life—that would seem to point to any special difficulty harassing the young people of our land today?

Since 1950, I have concentrated on the life histories of sick young people in late adolescence and early adulthood primarily in order to study one of the crises magnified, as it were, with the clinical microscope. I think that our initial formulations of the identity crisis have been clinically validated and much refined.[4]

Many of these sick young people in their late teens and early twenties had failed during their adolescence to win out in the struggle against identity confusion. They were suffering so seriously from a feeling of being (or, indeed, wanting to be) "nobody" that they were withdrawing from reality, and in some cases even attempting to withdraw from life itself: in other words, they were regressing to a position where trust had to be reinstated. Their malaise proved to be related to the same sense of diffuseness which drives other young adults to incessant and sometimes delinquent activity—an effort to show the world, including themselves, that they are "somebody" even if deep down they do not believe it.

In the meantime, of course, the identity issue has been taken up by many writers and by some magazines, almost in the form of a slogan. We are prone to think that we have cornered an issue when we have found a name for it, and to have resolved it when we have found something to blame. So now we blame "the changing world."

Actually, there is no reason why youth should not participate with enthusiasm in radical change; young people are freer for change than we are. The bewildering thing for them must be that we now complain about change, having eagerly caused it ourselves with inventions and discoveries; that we seem to have played at change rather than to have planned it. If we had the courage of our inventions, if we would grow into the world we have helped to create, and would give youth co-responsibility in it, I think that all the potential power of the identity crisis would serve a better world than we can now envisage.

Let me say a word about identity, or rather about what it is not. The young person seeking an identity does not go around saying, even to himself, "Who am I?" as an editorial in a national magazine suggested last year's college graduates were doing on their way home. Nor does the person with a secure sense of identity usually stop to think or to brag about the fact that he has this priceless possession, and of what it consists. He simply feels and acts predominantly in tune with himself, his capacities, and his opportunities; and he has the inner means and finds the outer ways to recover from experiences which impair this feeling. He knows where he fits (or knowingly prefers not to fit) into present conditions and developments.

This sense of a coincidence between inner resources, traditional values, and opportunities of action is derived from a fusion of slowly grown, unconscious personality processes—and contemporary social forces. It has its earliest beginnings in the infant's first feelings of affirmation by maternal recognition and is nurtured on the quality and consistency of the parental style of upbringing. Thus identity is in a sense an outgrowth of all the earlier stages; but the crucial period for its development to maturity comes with the adolescent crisis.

Every adolescent is apt to go through some serious struggle at one time or another. The crises of earlier stages may return in some form as he seeks to free himself from the alignments of childhood because of both his own eagerness for adulthood and the pressures of society. For a while he may distrust what he once trusted implicitly; may be ashamed of his body, and doubtful of his future. He experiments, looking for affirmation and recognition from his friends and from the adults who mean most to him. Unconsciously, he revamps his repertory of childhood identifications, reviving some and repudiating others. He goes in for extremes—total commitments and total repudiations. His struggle is to make sense out of what has gone before in relation to what he now perceives the world to be, in an effort to find a persistent sameness in himself and a persistent sharing of some kind of essential character with others.

Far from considering this process to be a kind of maturational malaise, a morbid egocentricity of which adolescents must be "cured," we must recognize in it the search for new values, the willingness to serve loyalties which prove to be "true" (in any number of spiritual, scientific, technical, political, philosophical, and personal meanings of "truth") and thus a prime force in cultural rejuvenation.

The strengths a young person finds in adults at this time—their willingness to let him experiment, their eagerness to confirm him at his best, their consistency in correcting his excesses, and the guidance they give him—will codetermine whether or not he eventually makes order out of necessary inner confusion and applies himself to the correction of disordered conditions. He needs freedom to choose, but not so much freedom that he cannot, in fact, make a choice.

In some adolescents, in some cultures, in some historical epochs this crisis is minimal; in others it holds real perils for both the individual and society. Some individuals, particularly those with a weak preparation in their preceding developmental crises, succumb to it with the formation of neuroses and psychoses. Others try to resolve it through adherence—often temporary—to radical kinds of religious, political, artistic, or criminal ideologies.

A few fight the battle alone and, after a prolonged period of agony characterized by erratic mood swings and unpredictable and apparently dangerous behavior, become the spokesmen of new directions. Their sense of impending danger forces them to mobilize their capacities to new ways of thinking and doing which have meaning, at the same time, for themselves and their times. In my book "Young Man Luther"[5] I have tried to show how identity is related to ideology and how the identity struggle of one intense young genius produced a new person, a new faith, a new kind of man, and a new era.

I think I chose to write about Luther and his time because there are many analogies between our time and his, although today the problems which beset all historical crises are global and, as it were, semifinal in character. Today, throughout the world, the increasing pace of technological change has encroached upon traditional group solidarities and on their ability to transmit a sense of cosmic wholeness and technological planfulness to the young.

To me one of the most disturbing aspects of our technological culture is the imbalance between passive stimulation and active outlet in the pleasures that are sanctioned for young people. With the passing of the western frontier and the accelerated appearance of automatic gadgets, young people have become increasingly occupied with passive pursuits which require little participation of mind or body—being conveyed rapidly through space by machines and watching violent fantasies at the movies or on television—without the possibility of matching the passive experience with active pursuits. When an adolescent substitutes passivity for the adventure and activity which his muscular development and sexual drives require, there is always the danger of explosion—and I think that this accounts for much of the explosive, unexpected, and delinquent acts on the part of even our "nice" young people.

This is probably why "Westerns," always on the borderline of the criminal and the lawful, capture the passive imagination of a youth which has traditionally substituted identification with the rugged individualist—the pioneer who ventures into the unknown—for commitment to a political ideology; and which now finds itself confronted with increasing demands for standardization, uniformity, and conformity to the rituals of a status-convention. While the national prototype has historically been based on readiness for change, the range of possibilities of what one might choose to be and of opportunities to make a change have narrowed. To this has been added most recently the rude shaking of the once "eternal" image of our Nation's superiority in productivity and technical ingenuity through the appearance of Sputnik and its successors.

Thus one might say the complexity of the adolescent state and the confusion of the times meet head on.

However, I believe that the "confusion" derives from a hypocritical denial of our true position, both in regard to obvious dangers and true resources. When youth is permitted to see its place in a crisis, it will, out of its very inner dangers, gain the strength to meet the demands of the time.

Clinical experience with young people has, it is true, verified that combination of inner and outer dangers which explains aggravated identity crises. On the other hand, it has convinced me and my colleagues, even in hospital work, of the surprising resources which young people can muster if their social responsibilities are called upon in a total environment of psychological understanding.

QUESTION: Does this kind of confusion have anything to do with juvenile delinquency?

I would not want to add here to the many claims concerning distinct and isolated causes of juvenile delinquency. But I would like to stress one contributing factor: the confused attitudes of adults—both laymen and professionals—towards the young people whom we, with a mixture of condescension and fear, call teenagers.

Except perhaps in some rare instances of congenital defects resulting in a low capacity to comprehend values, juvenile delinquents are made, not born; and we adults make them. Here, I am not referring to their parents exclusively. True, many parents, because of their own personalities and backgrounds, are not able to give their children a chance for a favorable resolution of the identity crisis. Nor am I referring to the failure of society at large to correct those blights on the social scene—such as overcrowded slums and inequality of opportunities for minority groups—which make it impossible for tens of thousands of young people to envisage an identity in line with the prevailing success-and-status ideology.

Rather I am referring to the attitudes of adults—in the press, in court, and in some professional and social institutions—which push the delinquent young person into a "negative identity," a prideful and stubborn acceptance of himself as a juvenile delinquent—and this at a time when his experimentation with available roles will make him exquisitely vulnerable (although he may not admit or even know it) to the opinions of the representatives of society. When a young person is adjudicated as a potential criminal because he has taken a girl for a ride in somebody else's car (which he intended to abandon, not to appropriate), he may well decide, half consciously, of course, but none the less with finality, that to have any real identity at all he must be what he obviously *can* be—a delinquent. The scolding of young people in public for the indiscretions they have committed, with the expectation that they show remorse, often ignores all the factors in their histories that force them into a delinquent kind of experimentation. It is certainly no help toward a positive identity formation.

In his insistence on holding on to an active identity, even if it is temporarily a "negative" one from the point of view of society, the delinquent is sometimes potentially healthier than the young person who withdraws into a neurotic or a psychotic state. Some delinquents, perhaps, in their determination to be themselves at all costs and under terrible conditions have more strength and a greater potential for contributing to the richness of the national life than do many excessively conforming or neurotically defeatist members of their generation, who have given up youth's prerogatives to dream and to dare. We must study this problem until we can overcome the kind of outraged bewilderment which makes the adult world seem untrustworthy to youth and hence may seem to justify the choice of a delinquent identity.

Actually, transitory delinquency, as well as other forms of antisocial or asocial behavior, often may be what I have called a *psychosocial moratorium*[4]— a period of delay in the assumption of adult commitment. Some youths need a period of relaxed expectations, of guidance to the various possibilities for positive identification through opportunities to participate in adult work, or even of introspection and experimentation—none of which can be replaced by either moralistic punishment or condescending forgiveness.

QUESTION: The theme of the 1960 White House Conference on Children and Youth charges the Conference with studying and understanding "the values and ideals of our society" in its efforts "to promote opportunities for children and youth to realize their full potential for a creative life in freedom and dignity." . . . Could you add a word about how these values, once identified, can be transmitted in a way that will insure their incorporation into the value systems of the young?

Like every other aspect of maturity the virtues which we expect in a civilized human being grow in stages as the child develops from an infant to an adult. What is expected of a child at any time must be related to his total maturation and level of ego-strength, which are related to his motor, cognitive, psychosexual, and psychosocial stages. You can't expect total obedience from a 2-year-old who must test a growing sense of autonomy, nor total truth from a 4-year-old involved in the creative but often guilt-ridden fantasies of the oedipal stage.

It would be in line with the course of other historical crises if in our Nation today a certain sense of moral weakness were producing a kind of frantic wish to enforce moral strength in our youth with punitive or purely exhortative measures.

Today, a sense of crisis has been aggravated by the long cold war and the sudden revelation of the technical strength of a supposedly "backward" rival. We are wondering whether we have made our children strong enough for living in such an unpredictably dangerous world. Some people, who suddenly realize that they have not been responsible guardians of all the Nation's young, now wonder whether they should have beaten moral strength into them or preached certain absolute values more adamantly.

No period, however, can afford to go back on its advances in values and in knowledge, and I trust that the . . . White House Conference will find a way to integrate our knowledge of personality development with our national values, necessities, and resources. What we need is not a plan whereby relatively irresponsible adults can enforce morality in their children, but rather national insistence on a more *responsible* morality on the part of adults, paired with an *informed* attitude toward the *development* of moral values in children. Values can only be fostered gradually by adults who have a clear conception of what to expect and what not to expect of the child as, at each stage, he comes to understand new segments of reality and of himself, and who are firm about what they are sure they *may* expect.

It must be admitted that psychiatry has added relatively little to the understanding of morality, except perhaps by delineating the great dangers of moralistic attitudes and measures which convince the child only of the adult's greater executive power, not of his actual moral power or true superiority. To this whole question, I can, on the basis of my own work, only indicate that the psychosocial stages . . . seem to open up the possibility of studying the way in which in each stage of growth the healthy child's developmental drives dispose him toward a certain set of qualities which are the necessary fundaments of a responsible character: in *infancy,* hope and drive; in *early childhood,* will and control; in the *play age,* purpose and direction; in the *school age,* skill and method; and in *adolescence,* devotion and fidelity. The development of these basic qualities in children, however, depends on the corresponding development in adults of qualities related to: in *young adulthood,* love, work, and affiliation; in *adulthood,* care, parenthood, and production; and in *old age,* "wisdom" and responsible renunciation.

Now I have given you another set of nice words, throwing to the winds my own warning regarding the way they can be misunderstood and misused. Let me point out, therefore, that I consider these basic virtues in line with our advancing psychoanalytic ego-psychology, on the one hand, and with our advancing knowledge of psychosocial evolution, on the other, and that the conception behind this list can only be studied in the context of advancing science. I will discuss this further in a forthcoming publication,[6] but I mention it now because I thought I owed you a reference to the way in which my contribution of 1950 has gradually led me in the direction of the great problem of the anchoring of virtue in human nature as it has evolved in our universe.

We ought to regard the breaking of a child's spirit—by cruel punishment, by senseless spoiling, by persistent hypocrisy—as a sin against humanity. Yet today we have back-to-the-woodshed movements. Last year in the legislature of one of our greatest States a bill was introduced to allow corporal punishment in the public schools and was lauded by part of the press. This gave the Soviets a chance to declare publicly against corporal punishment, implying that they are not sufficiently scared by their own youth to go back on certain considered principles in the rearing of the young. Actually, I think that we stand with the rest of the civilized world on the principle that if adult man reconsiders his moral position in the light of historical fact, and in the light of his most advanced knowledge of human nature, he can afford, in relation to his children, to rely on a forbearance which step by step will bring the best *out* of them. . . .

REFERENCES

1. Erikson, Erik H.: Childhood and society. W. W. Norton & Co., New York, 1950.
2. ———: Growth and crises of the "healthy personality." *In* Symposium on the healthy personality supplement II; Problems of infancy and childhood. M. J. E. Senn, ed. Josiah Macy, Jr., Foundation, New York, 1950.
3. Stone, L. Joseph; Church, Joseph: Childhood and adolescence; a psychology of the growing person. Random House, New York, 1957.
4. Erikson, Erik H.: The problem of ego identity. *Journal of American Psychoanalytic Association*, April 1956.
5. ———: Young man Luther. W. W. Norton & Co., New York, 1958.
6. ———: The roots of virtue. *In* The humanist frame, Sir Julian Huxley, ed. Harper & Bros., New York (in preparation).

[22]   *Erik H. Erikson*   A MEMORANDUM ON
IDENTITY AND NEGRO YOUTH

Introduction

A lack of familiarity with the problem of Negro youth and with the actions by which Negro youth hopes to solve these problems is a marked deficiency in my life and work which cannot be compensated for with theoretical speculation; and this least of all at a time when Negro writers are finding superb new ways of stating their and our predicament and when Negro youth finds itself involved in action which would have seemed unimaginable only a very few years ago. But since it is felt that some of my concepts might be helpful in further discussion, I will in the following recapitulate the pertinent ideas on identity contained in my writings.* This I do only in the hope that what is clear may prove helpful and what is not will become clearer in joint studies.

The fact that problems of Negro youth span the whole phenomenology of aggravated identity confusion and rapid new identity formation—cutting across phenomena judged antisocial and prosocial, violent and heroic, fanatic and ethically advanced—makes it advisable to include remarks concerning the origin of the concept of ego-identity in clinical observation in this review. However, the concept has come a long way since we first used it to define a syndrome in war—neurotics in World War II: I recently heard in India that Nehru had used the term "identity" to describe a new quality which, he felt, Gandhi had given India after offering her the equivalent of a "psychoanalysis of her past."

1. Childhood and identity

A

The growing child must derive a vitalizing sense of reality from the awareness that his individual way of mastering experience is a successful variant of

FROM *The Journal of Social Issues*, 1964, VOL. XX, NO. 4, PP. 29–42. REPRINTED BY PERMISSION OF THE AUTHOR AND THE SOCIETY FOR THE PSYCHOLOGICAL STUDY OF SOCIAL ISSUES.

* See: "*Childhood and Society*," W. W. Norton and Co., Inc., New York, 1950
"*Wholeness and Totality*," In *Totalitarianism*, Proceedings of a Conference held at the Am. Academy of Arts and Sciences, C. J. Friedrich, ed. Cambridge: Harvard University Press, 1954
"Identity and the Life Cycle," Monograph, *Psychological Issues*, Vol. I, No. 1, New York: Int'l Universities Press, 1959 with an intro. by D. Rapaport.
"Youth: Fidelity and Diversity" *Daedalus*, 91:5–27, 1962

a group identity and is in accord with its space-time and life plan. Minute displays of emotion such as affection, pride, anger, guilt, anxiety, sexual arousal (rather than the words used, the meanings intended, or the philosophy implied), transmit to the human child the outlines of what really counts in his world, i.e., the variables of his group's space-time and the perspectives of its life plan.

Here is the first observation I made (a decade and a half ago) on Negro children. I will quote it to characterize the point-of-view with which I started. The babies of our colored countrymen, I said, often receive sensual satisfactions which provide them with enough oral and sensory surplus for a lifetime, as clearly betrayed in the way they move, laugh, talk, sing. Their forced symbiosis with the feudal South capitalized on this oral sensory treasure and helped to build a slave's identity: mild, submissive, dependent, somewhat querulous, but always ready to serve, with occasional empathy and childlike wisdom. But underneath a dangerous split occurred. The Negro's unavoidable identification with the dominant race, and the need of the master race to protect its own identity against the very sensual and oral temptations emanating from the race held to be inferior (whence came their mammies), established in both groups an association: light—clean—clever—white, and dark—dirty—dumb—nigger. The result, especially in those Negroes who left the poor haven of their Southern homes, was often a violently sudden and cruel cleanliness training, as attested to in the autobiographies of Negro writers. It is as if by cleansing, a whiter identity could be achieved. The attending disillusionment transmits itself to the phallic-locomotor stage, when restrictions as to what shade of girl one may dream of interfere with the free transfer of the original narcissistic sensuality to the genital sphere. Three identities are formed: (1) mammy's oral-sensual "honey-child"—tender, expressive, rhythmical; (2) the evil identity of the dirty, anal-sadistic, phallic-rapist "nigger"; and (3) the clean, anal-compulsive, restrained, friendly, but always sad "white man's Negro."

So-called opportunities offered the migrating Negro often only turn out to be a more subtly restricted prison which endangers his only historically "successful" identity (that of the slave) and fails to provide a reintegration of the other identity fragments mentioned. These fragments, then, become dominant in the form of racial caricatures which are underscored and stereotyped by the entertainment industry. Tired of his own caricature, the colored individual often retires into hypochondriac invalidism as a condition which represents an analogy to the dependence and the relative safety of defined restriction in the South: a neurotic regression to the ego identity of the slave.

Mixed-blood Sioux Indians in areas where they hardly ever see Negroes refer to their full-blood brothers as "niggers," thus indicating the power of the dominant national imagery which serves to counterpoint the ideal and the evil images in the inventory of available prototypes. No individual can escape this opposition of images, which is all-pervasive in the men and in the women, in the majorities and in the minorities, and in all the classes of a given national or cultural unit. Psychoanalysis shows that the unconscious evil identity (the composite of everything which arouses negative identification—i.e., the wish not to resemble it) consists of the images of the violated (castrated) body, the "marked" outgroup, and the exploited minority. Thus a pronounced he-man may, in his dreams and prejudices, prove to be mortally afraid of ever displaying a woman's sentiments, a Negro's submissiveness, or a Jew's intellectuality. For the ego, in the course of its synthesizing efforts, attempts to subsume the most powerful evil and ideal prototypes (the final contestants, as it were) and with them the whole existing imagery of superior and inferior, good and bad, masculine and feminine, free and slave, potent and impotent, beautiful and ugly, fast and slow, tall and small, in a simple alternative, in order to make one battle and one strategy out of a bewildering number of skirmishes.

I knew a colored boy who, like our boys, listened every night to Red Rider. Then he sat up in bed, imagining that he was Red Rider. But the moment came when he saw himself galloping after some masked offender and suddenly noticed that in his fancy Red Rider was a colored man. He stopped his fantasy. While a small child, this boy was extremely expressive, both in his pleasures and in his sorrows. Today he is calm and always smiles; his language is soft and blurred; nobody can hurry him or worry him—or please him. White people like him.

As such boys and girls look around now, what other ideal (and evil) images are at their disposal? And how do they connect with the past? (Does non-violence connect totalistically or holistically with traditional patience and tolerance of pain?)

B

When children enter the stage of the adolescent Identity Crisis, a factor enters which characterizes the real kind of *crisis,* namely, a moment of decision between strong contending forces. "A moment" means that here something can happen very rapidly; "decision," that divergence becomes permanent; "strong and contending," that these are intense matters.

Developmentally speaking the sense of ego identity is the accrued confidence that one's ability to maintain inner sameness and continuity (one's ego in the psychoanalytic sense) is matched by the sameness and continuity of one's meaning for others. The growing child must, at every step, derive a vitalizing sense of reality from the awareness that his individual way of mastering experience is a successful variant of the way other people around him master experience and recognize such mastery.

In this, children cannot be fooled by empty praise and condescending encouragement. They may have to accept artificial bolstering of their self-esteem in lieu of something better, but what I call their accruing ego identity gains real strength only from wholehearted and consistent recognition of real accomplishment, that is, achievement that has meaning in their culture. On the other hand, should a child feel that the environment tries to deprive him too radically of all the forms of expression which permit him to develop and to integrate the next step in his ego identity, he will resist with the astonishing strength encountered in animals who are suddenly forced to defend their lives. Indeed, in the social jungle of human existence, there is no feeling of being alive without a sense of ego identity. Or else, there may be total self-abnegation (in more or less malignant forms) as illustrated in this observation. And here is an example of total denial of identity:

A four-year-old Negro girl in the Arsenal Nursery School in Pittsburgh used to stand in front of a mirror and scrub her skin with soap. When gently diverted from this she began to scrub the mirror. Finally, when induced to paint instead, she first angrily filled sheets of paper with the colors brown and black. But then she brought to the teacher what she called "a really *good* picture." The teacher first could see only a white sheet, until she looked closer and saw that the little girl had covered every inch of the white sheet with white paint. This playful episode of total self-eradication occurred and could only occur in a "desegregated" school: it illustrates the extent to which infantile drive control (cleanliness) and social self-esteem (color) are associated in childhood. But it also points to the extent of the crime which is perpetrated wherever, in the service of seemingly civilized values, groups of people are made to feel so inexorably "different" that legal dsegregation can only be the beginning of a long and painful inner reidentification.

Such crises come when their parents and teachers, losing trust in themselves and using sudden correctives in order to approach the vague but pervasive Anglo-Saxon ideal, create violent discontinuities; or where, indeed, the children themselves learn to disavow their sensual and overprotective mothers as temptations and a hindrance to the formation of a more "American" personality.

If we, then, speak of the community's response to the young individual's need to be "recognized" by those around him, we mean something beyond a mere recognition of achievement; for it is of great relevance to the young individual's identity formation that he be responded to, and be given function and status as a person whose gradual growth and transformation make sense to those who begin to make sense to him. Identity formation goes beyond the process of *identifying oneself* with ideal others in a one-way fashion; it is a process based on a heightened cognitive and emotional capacity to *let oneself be identified* by concrete persons as a circumscribed individual in relation to a predictable universe which transcends the family. Identity thus is not the sum of childhood identifications, but rather a new combination of old and new identification fragments. For this very reason societies *confirm* an individual at this time in all kinds of ideological frameworks and assign roles and tasks to him in which he can *recognize himself* and *feel recognized.* Ritual confirmations, initiations, and indoctrinations only sharpen an indispensable process of self-verification by which healthy societies bestow and receive the distilled strength of generations. By this process, societies, in turn, are themselves historically verified.

The danger of this stage is *identity diffusion;* as Biff puts it in Arthur Miller's *Death of a Salesman,* "I just can't take hold, Mom, I can't take hold of some kind of a life." Where such a dilemma is based on a strong previous doubt of one's ethnic and sexual identity, delinquent and outright psychotic incidents are not uncommon. Youth after youth, bewildered by some assumed role, a role forced on him by the inexorable standardization of American adolescence, runs away in one form or another; leaving schools and jobs, staying out all night, or withdrawing into bizarre and inaccessible moods. Once "delinquent," his greatest need and often his only salvation, is the refusal on the part of older friends, advisers, and judiciary personnel to type him further by pat diagnoses and social judgments which ignore the special dynamic conditions of adolescence. For if diagnosed and treated correctly, seemingly psychotic and criminal incidents do not in adolescence have the same fatal significance which they have at other ages. Yet many a youth, finding the authorities expect him to be "a nigger," "a bum," or "a queer," perversely obliges by becoming just that.

To keep themselves together, individuals and groups treated in this fashion temporarily overidentify, to the point of apparent complete loss of individual identity, with the heroes of cliques and crowds. On the other hand, they become remarkably clannish, intolerant, and cruel in their exclusion of others who are "different," in skin color or cultural background, in tastes and gifts, and often in entirely petty aspects of dress and gesture arbitrarily selected as *the* signs of an in-grouper or out-grouper. It is important to understand (which does not mean condone or participate in) such intolerance as the necessary *defense against a sense of identity diffusion,* which is unavoidable at a time of life when the body changes its proportions radically, when genital maturity floods body and imagination with all manners of drives, when intimacy with the other sex offers intense complications, and when life lies before one with a variety of conflicting possibilities and choices. Adolescents help one another temporarily through such discomfort by forming cliques and by stereotyping themselves, their ideals, and their enemies.

In general, one may say that we are apt to view the social play of adolescents as we once judged the play of children. We alternately consider such behavior irrelevant, unnecessary, or irrational, and ascribe to it purely delinquent or neurotic meanings. As in the past the study of children's spontaneous games was neglected in favor of that of solitary play, so now the mutual "joinedness" of adolescent clique behavior fails to be properly assessed in our concern for the individual adolescent. Children and adolescents in their presocieties provide for one another a sanctioned moratorium and joint support for free experimentation with inner and outer dangers (including those emanating from the adult world). Whether or not a given adolescent's newly acquired capacities are drawn back into infantile conflict depends to a significant extent on the quality of the opportunities and rewards available to him in his peer clique, as well as on the more formal ways in which society at large invites a transition from social play to work experimentation, and from rituals of transit to final commitments: all of which must be based on an implicit mutual contract between the individual and society.

2. Totalism and negative identity

If such contact is deficient, youth may seek perverse restoration in a negative identity, "totalistically" enforced. Here we must reconsider the proposition that the need for identity is experienced as a need for a certain wholeness in the experience of oneself within the community (and community here is as wide as one's social vision); and that, where such wholeness is impossible, such need turns to "totalism."

To be a bit didactic: *Wholeness* connotes an assembly of parts, even quite diversified parts, that enter into fruitful association and organization. This concept is most strikingly expressed in such terms as wholeheartedness, wholemindedness, and wholesomeness. In human development as well as in history, then, wholeness emphasizes a progressive coherence of diversified functions and parts. *Totality,* on the contrary, evokes a Gestalt in which an absolute boundary is emphasized: given a certain arbitrary delineation, nothing that belongs inside must be left outside; nothing that must be outside should be tolerated inside. A totality must be absolutely inclusive as it is absolutely exclusive. The word "utter" conveys the element of force, which overrides the question whether the category-to-be-made-absolute is an organic and a logical one, and whether the parts, so to speak, really have a natural affinity to one another.

To say it in one sentence: Where the human being despairs of an essential wholeness of experience, he restructures himself and the world by taking refuge in a totalistic world view. Thus there appears both in individuals and in groups a periodical need for a totality without further choice or alternation, even if it implies the abandonment of a much-needed wholeness. This can consist of a lone-wolf's negativism; of a delinquent group's seeming nihilism; or in the case of national or racial groups, in a defiant glorification of one's own caricature.

Thus, patients (and I think it is in this respect that patients can help us understand analogous group processes) choose a *negative identity,* i.e., an identity perversely based on all those identifications and roles which, at critical stages of development, had been presented to them as most undesirable or dangerous, and yet also as most real. For example, a mother having lost her first-born son may (because of complicated guilt feelings) be unable to attach to her later surviving children the same amount of religious devotion that she bestows on the memory of her dead child and may well arouse in one of her sons the conviction that to be sick or dead is a better assurance of being "recognized" than to be healthy and about. A mother who is filled with unconscious ambivalence toward a brother who disintegrated into alcoholism may again and again respond selectively only to those traits in her son which seem to point to a repetition of her brother's fate, in which case this "negative" identity may take on more reality for the son than all his natural attempts at being good: he may work hard on becoming a drunkard and, lacking the necessary ingredients, may end up in a state of stubborn paralysis of choice. The daughter of a man of brilliant showmanship may run away from college and be arrested as a prostitute in the Negro quarter of a Southern city; while the daughter of an influential Southern Negro preacher may be found among narcotic addicts in Chicago. In such cases it is of utmost importance to recognize the mockery and the vindictive pretense in such role playing; for the white girl may not have really prostituted herself, and the colored girl may not really have become an addict—yet. Needless to say, however, each of them could have placed herself in a marginal social area, leaving it to law-enforcement officers and to psychiatric agencies to decide what stamp to put on such behavior. A corresponding case is that of a boy presented to a psychiatric clinic as "the village homosexual" of a small town. On investigation, it appears that the boy had succeeded in assuming this fame without any actual acts of homosexuality, except that much earlier in his life he had been raped by some older boys.

Such vindictive choices of a negative identity represent, of course, a desperate attempt to regain some mastery in a situation in which the available positive identity elements cancel each other out. The history of such choice reveals a set of conditions in which it is easier to derive a sense of identity out of a *total* identification with that which one is *least* supposed to be than to struggle for a feeling of reality in acceptable roles which are unattainable with the patient's inner means.

There is a "lower lower" snobbism too, which is based on the pride of having achieved a semblance of nothingness. At any rate, many a late adolescent, if faced with continuing diffusion, would rather *be a total nobody, somebody totally bad, or indeed, dead—and all of this by free choice—than be not-quite-somebody.*

Thus, individuals, when caught up in the necessity to regroup an old identity or to gain a new and inescapable one, are subject to influences which offer them a way to wholeness. Obviously, revolutions do the first to gain the second. At any rate, the problem of totalism vs. wholeness seems to be represented in its organized form in the Black Muslims who insist on a totally "black" solution reinforced by historical and religious mysticism on the one hand; and the movement of non-violent and legal insistence on civil rights, on the other. Once such a polarization is established, it seems imperative to investigate what powerful self-images (traditional, revolutionary, and, as it were, evolutionary) have entered the picture, in mutually exclusive or mutually inclusive form, and what the corresponding symptoms are, in individuals and in the masses.

3. "Conversion" and more inclusive identity

In a little-known passage, Bernard Shaw relates the story of his "conversion": "I was *drawn into* the Socialist *revival* of the early eighties, among Englishmen *intensely serious* and *burning with indignation* at very *real* and *very fundamental evils* that affected *all the world*." The words here italicized convey to me the following implications. "Drawn into": an ideology has a compelling power. "Revival": it consists of a traditional force in a state of rejuvenation. "Intensely serious": it permits even the cynical to make an investment of sincerity. "Burning with indignation": it gives to the need for repudiation the sanction of righteousness. "Real": it projects a vague inner evil onto a circumscribed horror in reality. "Fundamental": it promises participation in an effort at basic reconstruction of society. "All the world": it gives structure to a totally defined world image. Here, then, are the elements by which a group identity harnesses the young individual's aggressive and discriminative energies, and encompasses, as it completes it, the individual's identity in the service of its ideology. Thus, identity and ideology are two aspects of the same process. Both provide the necessary condition for further individual maturation and, with it, for the next higher form of identification, namely, the *solidarity linking common identities*. For the need to bind irrational self-hate and irrational repudiation makes young people, on occasion, mortally compulsive and conservative even where and when they seem most anarchic and radical; the same need makes them potentially "ideological," i.e., more or less explicitly in search of a world image held together by what Shaw called "a clear comprehension of life in the light of an intelligible theory."

What are, then, the available ideological ingredients of the new Negro and the new American identity? For (such is the nature of a revolutionary movement) the new Negro cannot afford any longer just to become "equal" to the old white. As he becomes something new, he also forces the white man as well as the advanced Negro to become newer than they are.

4. Weakness and strength

A

In my clinical writings I have suggested that delinquent joining stands in the same dynamic relationship to schizoid isolation, as (according to Freud) perversion does to neurosis: negative *group* identities (gangs, cliques, rings, mobs) "save" the individual from the symptoms of a negative identity neurosis, to wit: a disintegration of the sense of time; morbid identity consciousness; work paralysis; bisexual confusion; and authority diffusion.

Unnecessary to say, however, a *transitory* "negative identity" is often the necessary pre condition for a truly positive and truly new one. In this respect,

I would think that American Negro writers may turn out to be as important for American literature as Irish expatriates were in the Europe of an earlier period.

On the other hand, there are certain strengths in the Negro which have evolved out of or at least along with his very submission. Such a statement will, I trust, not be misunderstood as an argument for continued submission. What I have in mind are strengths which one would hope, for the sake of all of us, could remain part of a future Negro identity. Here I have in mind such a traditional phenomenon as the power of the Negro mother. As pointed out, I must glean examples from experiences accessible to me; the following observation on Caribbean motherhood will, I hope, be put into its proper perspective by experts on the whole life-space of the Negro on the American continent.

B

Churchmen have had reason to deplore, and anthropologists to explore, the pattern of Caribbean family life, obviously an outgrowth of the slavery days of Plantation America, which extended from the Northeast Coast of Brazil in a half-circle into the Southeast of the United States. Plantations, of course, were agricultural factories, owned and operated by gentlemen, whose cultural and economic identity had its roots in a supra-regional upper class. They were worked by slaves, that is, men who, being mere equipment put to use when and where necessary, had to relinquish all chance of being the masters of their families and communities. Thus, the women were left with the offspring of a variety of men who could give no protection as they could provide no identity, except that of a subordinate species. The family system which ensued can be described in scientific terms only by circumscriptions dignifying what is not there: the rendering of "sexual services" between persons who cannot be called anything more definite than "lovers"; "maximum instability" in the sexual lives of young girls, whose pattern it is to relinquish the care of their offspring to their mothers; and mothers and grandmothers who determine that "standardized mode of co-activity" which is the minimum requirement for calling a group of individuals a family. They are, then, mostly called "household groups"— single dwellings, occupied by people sharing a common food supply. These households are "matrifocal," a word understating the grandiose role of the all-powerful mother-figure who will encourage her daughters to leave their infants with her, or, at any rate, to stay with her as long as they continue to bear children. Motherhood thus becomes community life; and where churchmen could find little or no morality, and casual observers, little or no order at all, the mothers and grandmothers in fact also became father and grandfathers,* in the sense that they exerted that authoritative influence which resulted in an ever newly improvised set of rules for the economic obligations of the men who fathered the children, and upheld the rules of incestuous avoidance. Above all,

* See the title "My Mother Who Fathered Me."

they provided the only super-identity which was left open after the enslavement of the men, namely, that of the mother who will nurture a human infant irrespective of his parentage. It is well known how many poor little rich and white gentlemen benefited from the extended fervor of the Negro women who nursed them as Southern mammies, as creole das, or as Brazilian babas. This cultural fact is, of course, being played down by the racists as mere servitude while the predominance of maternal warmth in Caribbean women is characterized as African sensualism, and vicariously enjoyed by refugees from "Continental" womanhood. One may, however, see at the root of this maternalism a grandiose gesture of human adaptation which has given the area of the Caribbean (now searching for a political and economic pattern to do justice to its cultural unity) both the promise of a positive (female) identity and the threat of a negative (male) one: for here, the fact that identity depended on the procreative worth of being born, has undoubtedly weakened the striving for becoming somebody by individual effort.

(This is an ancient pattern taking many forms in the modern Negro world. But—parenthetically speaking—it may give us one more access to a better understanding of the magnificently bearded group of men and boys who have taken over one of the islands and insist on proving that the Caribbean male can earn his worth in production as well as in procreation.)

My question is whether such maternal strength has survived not only in parts of our South but also in family patterns of Negro migrants; whether it is viewed as undesirable and treated as delinquent by Negroes as well as whites; and whether America can afford to lose it all at a time when women must help men more planfully not only to preserve the naked life of the human race but also some "inalienable" values.

C

This brings me, finally, to the issue of Fidelity, that virtue and quality of adolescent ego strength which belongs to man's evolutionary heritage, but which—like all the basic virtues—can arise only in the interplay of a stage of life with the social forces of a true community.

To be a *special kind* has been an important element in the human need for personal and collective identities. They have found a transitory fulfillment in man's greatest moments of cultural identity and civilized perfection, and each such tradition of identity and perfection has highlighted what man could be, could he fulfill all his potentials at one time. The utopia of our own era predicts that man will be one species in one world, with a universal identity to replace the illusory super-identities which have divided him, and with an international ethic replacing all moral systems of superstition, repression, and suppression. Whatever the political arrangement that will further this utopia, we can only point to the human strengths which potentially emerge with the stages of life and indicate their dependence on communal life. In youth, ego strength emerges from the mutual confirmation of individual and community, in the sense that society recognizes the young individual as a bearer of fresh energy and that the individual so confirmed recognizes society as a living process which inspires loyalty as it receives it, maintains allegiance as it attracts it, honors confidence as it demands it. All this I subsume under the term Fidelity.

Diversity and Fidelity are polarized: they make each other significant and keep each other alive. Fidelity without a sense of diversity can become an obsession and a bore; diversity without a sense of fidelity, an empty relativism.

But Fidelity also stands in a certain polarity to adolescent sexuality: both sexual fulfillment and "sublimation" depend on this polarity.

The various hindrances to a full consummation of adolescent genital maturation have many deep consequences for man which pose an important problem for future planning. Best studied is the regressive revival of that earlier stage of psychosexuality which preceded even the emotionally quiet first school years—that is, the infantile genital and locomotor stage, with its tendency toward auto-erotic manipulation, grandiose phantasy, and vigorous play. But in youth, auto-erotism, grandiosity, and playfulness are all immensely amplified by genital potency and locomotor maturation, and are vastly complicated by what we will presently describe as the youthful mind's historical perspective.

The most widespread expression of the discontented search of youth is the craving for locomotion, whether expressed in a general "being on the go," "tearing after something," or "running around"; or in locomotion proper, as in vigorous work, in absorbing sports, in rapt dancing, in shiftless *Wanderschaft,* and in the employment and misuse of speedy animals and machines. But it also finds expression through participation in the movements of the day (whether the riots of a local commotion or the parades and campaigns of major ideological forces); if they only appeal to the need for feeling "moved" and for feeling essential in moving something along toward an open future. It is clear that societies offer any number of ritual combinations of ideological perspective and vigorous movement (dance, sports, parades, demonstrations, riots) to harness youth in the service of their historical aims; and that where societies fail to do so, these patterns will seek their own combinations, in small groups occupied with serious games, good-natured foolishness, cruel prankishness, and delinquent warfare. In no other stage of the life cycle, then, are the promise of finding oneself and the threat of losing oneself so closely allied.

To summarize: Fidelity, when fully matured, is the strength of disciplined devotion. It is gained in the involvement of youth in such experiences as reveal the essence of the era they are to join—as the beneficiaries of its tradition, as the practitioners and innovators of its technology, as renewers of its ethical strength, as rebels bent on the destruction of the outlived, and as deviants with deviant commitments. This, at least, is the potential of youth in psychosocial evolution; and while this may sound like a rationalization endorsing any high-sounding self-delusion in youth, any self-indulgence masquerading as devotion, or any righteous excuse for blind destruction, it makes intelligible the tremendous waste attending this as any other mechanism of human adaptation, especially if its excesses meet with more moral condemnation than ethical guidance. On the other hand, our understanding of these processes is not furthered by the "clinical" reduction of adolescent phenomena to their infantile antecedents and to an underlying dichotomy of drive and conscience. Adolescent development comprises a new set of identification processes, both with significant persons and with ideological forces, which give importance to individual life by relating it to a living community and to ongoing history, and by counterpointing the newly won individual identity with some communal solidarity.

In youth, then, the life history intersects with history. Here individuals are confirmed in their identities, societies regenerated in their life style. This process also implies a fateful survival of adolescent modes of thinking in man's historical and ideological perspectives.

Historical processes, of course, have already entered the individual's core in childhood. Both ideal and evil images and the moral prototypes guiding parental administrations originate in the past struggles of contending cultural and national "species," which also color fairytale and family lore, superstition and gossip, and the simple lessons of early verbal training. Historians on the whole make little of this; they describe the visible emergence and the contest of autonomous historical ideas, unconcerned with the fact that these ideas reach down into the everyday lives of generations and re-emerge through the daily awakening and training of historical consciousness in young individuals.

It is youth that begins to develop that sense of historical irreversibility which can lead to what we may call acute historical estrangement. This lies behind the fervent quest for a sure meaning in individual life history and in collective history, and behind the questioning of the laws of relevancy which bind datum and principles, event and movement. But it is also, alas, behind the bland carelessness of that youth which denies its own vital need to develop and cultivate a historical consciousness—and conscience.

To enter history, each generation of young persons must find an identity consonant with its own childhood and consonant with an ideological promise in the perceptible historical process. But in youth the tables of childhood dependence begin slowly to turn: it is no longer exclusively for the old to teach the young the meaning of life, whether individual or collective. It is the young who, by their responses and actions, tell the old whether life as represented by their elders and as presented to the young has meaning, and it is the young who carry in them the power to confirm those who confirm them and, joining the issues, to renew and to regenerate, or to reform and to rebel.

I will not at this point review the institutions which participate in creating the retrospective and the prospective mythology offering historical orientation to youth. Obviously, the mythmakers of religion and politics, the arts and the sciences, the stage and fiction—all contribute to the historical logic presented to youth more or less consciously, more or less responsibly. And today we must add, at least in the United States, psychiatry; and all over the world, the press, which forces leaders to make history in the open and to accept reportorial distortion as a major historical factor.

Moralities sooner or later outlive themselves, ethics never: this is what the need for identity and for fidelity, reborn with each generation, seems to point to. Morality in the moralistic sense can be shown by modern means of inquiry to be predicated on superstitions and irrational inner mechanisms which ever again undermine the ethical fiber of generations; but morality is expendable only where ethics prevail. This is the wisdom that the words of many languages have tried to tell man. He has tenaciously clung to the words, even though he has understood them only vaguely, and in his actions has disregarded or perverted them completely. But there is much in ancient wisdom which can now become knowledge.

What, then, are the sources of a new ethical orientation which may have roots in Negro tradition and yet also reach into the heroic striving for a new identity within the universal ethics emanating from world-wide technology and communication? This question may sound strenuously inspirational or academic; yet, I have in mind the study of concrete sources of morale and strength, lying within the vitality of bodily experience, the identity of individual experience, and the fidelity developed in methods of work and cooperation, methods of solidarity and political action, and methods permitting a simple and direct manifestation of human values such as have survived centuries of suppression. As a clinician, I am probably more competent to judge the conditions which continue to *suppress* and attempt to *crush* such strengths; and yet I have also found that diagnosis and anamnesis can turn out to be of little help where one ignores sources of recovery often found in surprising and surprisingly powerful constellations.

[23]   *James E. Marcia*   DEVELOPMENT AND

VALIDATION OF EGO-IDENTITY STATUS

Ego identity and identity diffusion (Erikson, 1956, 1963) refer to polar outcomes of the hypothesized psychosocial crisis occurring in late adolescence. Erikson views this phase of the life cycle as a time of growing occupational and ideological commitment. Facing such imminent adult tasks as getting a job and becoming a citizen, the individual is required to synthesize childhood

FROM *Journal of Personality and Social Psychology*, 1966, 3, 551–558. COPYRIGHT 1966 BY THE AMERICAN PSYCHOLOGICAL ASSOCIATION, AND REPRODUCED BY PERMISSION OF THE AUTHOR AND THE PUBLISHER.

identifications in such a way that he can both establish a reciprocal relationship with his society and maintain a feeling of continuity within himself.

Previous studies have attempted to determine the extent of ego-identity achievement by means of an adjustment measure and the semantic differential technique (Bronson, 1959), a Q-sort measure of real-ideal-self discrepancy (Gruen, 1960), a measure of role variability based on adjective ranking (Block, 1961), and a questionnaire (Rasmussen, 1964). While these studies have investigated self-ratings on characteristics that should follow if ego identity has been achieved, they have not dealt explicitly with the psychosocial criteria for determining degree of ego identity, nor with testing hypotheses regarding direct behavioral consequences of ego identity.

To assess ego identity, the present study used measures and criteria congruent with Erikson's formulation of the identity crisis as a *psychosocial* task. Measures were a semi-structured interview and an incomplete-sentences blank. The interview (see Method section) was used to determine an individual's specific identity status; that is, which of four concentration points along a continuum of ego-identity achievement best characterized him. The incomplete-sentences blank served as an overall measure of identity achievement. The criteria used to establish identity status consisted of two variables, crisis and commitment, applied to occupational choice, religion, and political ideology. Crisis refers to the adolescent's period of engagement in choosing among meaningful alternatives; commitment refers to the degree of personal investment the individual exhibits.

"Identity achievement" and "identity diffusion" are polar alternatives of status inherent in Erikson's theory. According to the criteria employed in this study, an identity-achievement subject has experienced a crisis period and is committed to an occupation and ideology. He has seriously considered several occupational choices and has made a decision on his own terms, even though his ultimate choice may be a variation of parental wishes. With respect to ideology, he seems to have reevaluated past beliefs and achieved a resolution that leaves him free to act. In general, he does not appear as if he would be overwhelmed by sudden shifts in his environment or by unexpected responsibilities.

The identity-diffusion subject may or may not have experienced a crisis period; his hallmark is a lack of commitment. He has neither decided upon an occupation nor is much concerned about it. Although he may mention a preferred occupation, he seems to have little conception of its daily routine and gives the impression that the choice could be easily abandoned should opportunities arise elsewhere. He is either uninterested in ideological matters or takes a smorgasbord approach in which one outlook seems as good to him as another and he is not averse to sampling from all.

Two additional concentration points roughly intermediate in this distribution are the moratorium and foreclosure statuses. The moratorium subject is *in* the crisis period with commitments rather vague; he is distinguished from the identity-diffusion subject by the appearance of an active struggle to make commitments. Issues often described as adolescent preoccupy him. Although his parents' wishes are still important to him, he is attempting a compromise among them, society's demands, and his own capabilities. His sometimes bewildered appearance stems from his vital concern and internal preoccupation with what occasionally appear to him to be unresolvable questions.

A foreclosure subject is distinguished by not having experienced a crisis, yet expressing commitment. It is difficult to tell where his parents' goals for him leave off and where his begin. He is becoming what others have prepared or intended him to become as a child. His beliefs (or lack of them) are virtually "the faith of his fathers living still." College experiences serve only as a confirmation of childhood beliefs. A certain rigidity characterizes his personality; one feels that if he were faced with a situation in which parental values were nonfunctional, he would feel extremely threatened.

Previous studies have found ego identity to be related to "certainty of self-conception" and "temporal stability of self-rating" (Bronson, 1959), extent of a subject's acceptance of a false personality sketch of himself (Gruen, 1960), anxiety (Block, 1961), and sociometric ratings of adjustment (Rasmussen, 1964). Two themes predominate in the studies: a variability-stability dimension of self-concept, and overall adjustment. In general, subjects who have achieved ego identity seem less confused in self-definition and are freer from anxiety.

Four task variables were used to validate the newly constructed identity statuses: a concept-attainment task administered under stressful conditions, a level of aspiration measure yielding goal-setting patterns, a measure of authoritarianism, and a measure of stability of self-esteem in the face of invalidating information.

The hypotheses investigated were these:

1. Subjects high in ego identity (i.e., identity-achievement status) will receive significantly lower (better) scores on the stressful concept-attainment task than subjects lower in ego identity. Subjects who have achieved an ego identity, with the internal locus of self-definition which that implies, will be less vulnerable to the stress conditions of evaluation apprehension and oversolicitousness (see Method section).
2. Subjects high in ego identity will set goals more realistically than subjects all ego strength following identity achievement should be reflected in the low in ego identity on a level of aspiration measure. The increment to over-ego function of reality testing.
3. Subjects in the foreclosure status will endorse "authoritarian submission and conventionality" items to a greater extent than subjects in the other statuses.
4. There will be a significant positive relationship between ego identity measures and a measure of self-esteem.
5. Subjects high in ego identity will change less in self-esteem when given false information about their personalities than subjects low in ego identity.

6. There will be a significant relationship between the two measures of ego identity: the identity-status interview and the incomplete-sentences blank.

Method

SUBJECTS

Subjects were 86 males enrolled in psychology, religion, and history courses at Hiram College.

CONFEDERATE EXPERIMENTERS

Due to the possibility of contamination by subject intercommunication on a small campus, the study employed 10 confederate (task) experimenters who administered the concept-attainment task in one 12-hour period to all subjects. These task experimenters, 7 males and 3 females, were members of the author's class in psychological testing and had taken three or more courses in psychology. They had previously assisted in a pilot study and had been checked twice by the author on their experimental procedure. The use of a sample of experimenters, none of whom were aware of the subjects' standings on crucial independent variables, also has advantages in terms of minimizing the effects of experimenter bias (Rosenthal, 1964).

Identity status   Identity status was established by means of a 15–30 minute semistructured interview. All interviews followed the same outline, although deviations from the standard form were permitted in order to explore some areas more thoroughly. In most cases, the criteria for terminating an interview involved the completion of the prescribed question as well as some feeling of certainty on the interviewer's part that the individual had provided enough information to be categorized. Interviews were tape-recorded and then replayed for judging. Hence, each interview was heard at least twice, usually three or four times.

A scoring manual (Marcia, 1964) was constructed using both theoretical criteria from Erikson and empirical criteria from a pilot study. Each subject was evaluated in terms of presence or absence of crisis as well as degree of commitment for three areas: occupation, religion, and politics—the latter two combined in a general measure of ideology. The interview judge familiarized himself with the descriptions of the statuses provided in the manual and sorted each interview into that pattern which it most closely resembled. Analysis of interjudge reliability for the identity statuses of 20 randomly selected subjects among three judges yielded an average percentage of agreement of 75. One of the judges was essentially untrained, having been given only the scoring manual and the 20 taped interviews.

A sample question in the occupational area was:

How willing do you think you'd be to give up going into _____ if something better came along?

Examples of typical answers for the four statuses were:

[Identity achievement] Well, I might, but I doubt it. I can't see what "something better" would be for me.

[Moratorium] I guess if I knew for sure I could answer that better. It would have to be something in the general area—something related.

[Foreclosure] Not very willing. It's what I've always wanted to do. The folks are happy with it and so am I.

[Identity diffusion] Oh sure. If something better came along, I'd change just like that.

A sample question in the religious area was:

Have you ever had any doubts about your religious beliefs?

[Identity achievement] Yeah, I even started wondering whether or not there was a god. I've pretty much resolved that now, though. The way it seems to me is . . .

[Moratorium] Yes, I guess I'm going through that now. I just don't see how there can be a god and yet so much evil in the world or . . .

[Foreclosure] No, not really, our family is pretty much in agreement on these things.

[Identity diffusion] Oh, I don't know. I guess so. Everyone goes through some sort of stage like that. But it really doesn't bother me much. I figure one's about as good as the other!

Overall ego identity The Ego Identity Incomplete Sentences Blank (EI-ISB) is a 23-item semistructured projective test requiring the subject to complete a sentence "expressing his real feelings" having been given a leading phrase. Stems were selected and a scoring manual designed (Marcia, 1964) according to behaviors which Erikson (1956) relates to the achievement of ego identity. Empirical criteria were gathered during a pilot study. Each item was scored 3, 2, or 1, and item scores were summed to yield an overall ego-identity score. Two typical stems were: If one commits oneself ———, and, When I let myself go I ———. Scoring criteria for the latter stem are:

3—Nondisastrous self-abandonment. Luxuriating in physical release. For example, have a good time and do not worry about others' thoughts and standards, enjoy almost anything that has laughter and some physical activity involved, enjoy myself more.

2—Cautiousness, don't know quite what will happen, have to be careful. Defensive or trivial. For example, never know exactly what I will say or do, sleep, might be surprised since I don't remember letting myself go.

1—Goes all to pieces, dangerous, self-destructive, better not to. For example, think I talk too much about myself and my personal interests, tend to become too loud when sober and too melodramatic when drunk, sometimes say things I later regret.

Analysis of interscorer reliability for 20 protocols among three judges yielded an average item-by-item correlation of $r = .76$, an average total score correlation of $\bar{r} = .73$, and an average percentage of agreement of 74.

MEASURES OF TASK VARIABLES

Concept Attainment Task performance. The Concept Attainment Task (CAT) developed by Bruner, Goodnow, and Austin (1956) and modified by Weick (1964), requires the subject to arrive at a certain combination of attributes of cards. The subject may eliminate certain attributes by asking whether a card is positive or negative for the concept and he may guess the concept at any time. He is penalized 5 points for every request, 10 points for every guess, and 5 points for every 30 seconds that passes before he attains the concept. Level of aspiration was obtained by informing the subject of his previous time and asking him to estimate his time on the next problem.

Quality of performance on the CAT was assessed by the following measures: overall CAT scores (points for time plus points for requests and guesses), points for time alone, points for requests and guesses alone, number of "give-ups" (problems which the subject refused to complete). The main level of aspiration measure was attainment discrepancy or D score, the algebraic average of the differences between a subject's stated expectancy for a problem and his immediately preceding performance on a similar problem.

A combination of two stress conditions (stress defined here as externally imposed conditions which tend to impair performance) were used: evaluation apprehension and oversolicitousness. Evaluation apprehension refers to a subject's feeling that his standing on highly valued personal characteristics is to be exposed. The characteristic chosen for this study was intellectual competence, unquestionably salient for college students. Oversolicitousness was chosen as a logical complement to evaluation apprehension. It was assumed that unnecessary reassurance would validate and, hence, augment whatever anxiety the subject was experiencing.

Pilot study data indicated that the stress conditions were effective. Using the same task experimenters as in the final study, 56 subjects (27 males and 29 females) took the CAT under stress and nonstress (i.e., stress omitted) conditions. Each experimenter ran about 3 stress and 3 nonstress subjects. Stressed subjects performed significantly more poorly than nonstressed ones ($t = 2.61$, $df = 54, p < .02$).

Self-esteem change and authoritarianism   The Self-Esteem Questionnaire (SEQ-F) is a 20-item test developed by deCharms and Rosenbaum (1960) on which the subject indicates his degree of endorsement of statements concerning general feelings of self-confidence and worthiness.

In addition, statements reflecting authoritarian submission and conventionality, taken from the California F Scale (Adorno, Frenkel-Brunswik, Levinson, & Sanford, 1950), which were originally filler items, are used here as a dependent variable. The SEQ-F was administered twice, the first time in a classroom setting, the second, during the experimental situation following an invalidated self-definition.

The treatment condition of "invalidated self-definition" (ISD) followed the CAT and directly preceded the second administration of SEQ-F. It consisted of giving the subject false information concerning the relationship between his alleged self-evaluation and his actual personality.

PROCEDURE

Following is the experimental procedure: Subjects completed the EI-ISB and SEQ-F in class. Each subject was interviewed to determine his identity status. (This interviewing period lasted about 2 months.) On the day of the experiment, each subject went through the following conditions: (*a*) Administration of the CAT under stress by the task experimenter. *Evaluation apprehension* was created by the task experimenter's saying:

By the way, I thought you might be interested to know that this test is related to tests of intelligence[2] and that it's been found to be one of the best single predictors of success in college. So of course, you'll want to do your very best.

Oversolicitousness was created during CAT performance by the task experimenter's hovering over the subject, asking him if he were comfortable, advising him not to "tense up," not to "make it harder on yourself." (*b*) Following the CAT, the subject was seated in the author's office where he was given either a positive or negative (randomly assigned) invalidated self-definition. The subject found the experimenter intently scanning a data sheet and was told:

I've been looking over some of the data and it seems that while you consider yourself less [more] mature than other subjects, you actually come out as being more [less] mature. Is there any way you can account for this discrepancy? [Pause for the subject's response.] This seems to hold up also for self-confidence. It seems that you consider yourself as having less [more] self-confidence than other subjects, yet you actually come out having more [less].

(*c*) The subject was then sent to another room where he took the SEQ-F for the second time. The following day, each subject received a postcard from the experimenter explaining the false information.

Results

PERFORMANCE ON CAT

The relationship between the identity statuses and CAT performance was investigated by means of individual *t* tests. These are found in Table 1 and support the hypothesis of significant differences in CAT performance between subjects high and low in ego identity.

TABLE 1 Differences between Identity Statuses in CAT Performance

	N	M TIME	SD	M REQUESTS + GUESSES	SD	M OVERALL SCORE	SD	t
Identity status								
Identity achievement (A)	18	18.17	7.94	599.17	186.63	791.94	244.15	
Moratorium (B)	22	24.50	15.77	807.14	495.58	1024.82	612.04	
Foreclosure (C)	23	34.20	13.84	875.82	285.44	1147.83	407.98	
Identity diffusion (D)	21	29.73	18.52	767.38	266.43	1078.57	352.38	
Groups compared								
Time								
A versus D								2.39*
A versus B + C + D								2.41**
A versus C								2.90***
A + B + D versus C								2.24*
Requests + guesses								
A versus D								2.19*
A versus B + C + D								2.28*
A versus C								3.47***
A + B + D versus C								1.69
Overall score								
A versus D								3.47***
A versus B + C + D								2.45**
A versus C								3.19***
A + B + D versus C								1.63

* $p \leq .05$.
** $p \leq .02$.
*** $p \leq .01$.

For all three indices of CAT performance identity-achievement subjects perform significantly[3] better than identity-diffusion subjects (*p*'s ranging from .01 to .05), and identity-achievement subjects perform significantly better than the other three statuses combined (*p*'s ranging from .02 to .05).

Data involving the number of problems on which the subjects in the different identity statuses gave up are presented in Table 2.

TABLE 2 Number of CAT Problems on Which Subjects in Each Identity Status Gave Up

	Identity Achievement	Moratorium	Foreclosure	Identity Diffusion	All Other
			IDENTITY STATUS		
Give-ups	1	7	13	11	31
Completions	107	125	131	109	365
	$\chi^2 = 8.93^*$				$\chi^2 = 5.69^{**}$

* $p < .05.$
** $p < .02.$

Comparing identity-achievement subjects with other subjects, significantly fewer instances of giving up on CAT problems are found for the identity-achievement subjects. This, together with the previous findings concerning the relationship between identity status and CAT performance under stress, provides substantial confirmation of Hypothesis 1.

An interesting supplementary finding is that moratorium subjects were significantly more variable in overall CAT scores than subjects in the other three statuses combined ($F_{max} = 2.62$, $df = 21/61$, $p < .05$; see McNemar, 1955, pp. 244–247).

Correlations between all three CAT performance measures and the EI-ISB, while in the expected direction, failed to reach significance. The Pearson *r* between overall CAT performance and EI-ISB scores was $-.14$ ($df = 82$).

LEVEL OF ASPIRATION

The *D*, or attainment discrepancy score, reflects the difference between a subject's aspirations and his actual performance. An overall positive *D* score means that the subject tends to set his goals higher than his attainment; a negative *D* score means the opposite.

Inspection of original data revealed that no status obtained a negative average D score, the range being from 3.60 for identity achievement to 5.06 for foreclosure. Analysis of variance indicates a significant difference among statuses in D score ($F = 5.10$, $df = 3/80$, $p < .01$). The t tests presented in Table 3 show the foreclosure subjects exhibiting higher D scores than identity-achievement subjects ($t = 3.35$, $df = 38$, $p < .01$) and higher D scores than the other statuses combined ($t = 3.70$, $df = 82$, $p < .001$). It appears that foreclosure subjects tend to maintain high goals in spite of failure.

TABLE 3   Differences in D Score Between Identity Statuses

	N	M	SD	t
Identity status				
Identity achievement (A)	18	3.60	.80	
Moratorium (B)	22	4.11	.72	
Foreclosure (C)	23	5.06	1.65	
Identity diffusion (D)	21	3.91	1.49	
Groups compared				
C versus A				3.35*
C versus A + B + D				3.70**
B versus A				1.90
C + B + D versus A				.57

* $p \leq .01$.
** $p \leq .001$

AUTHORITARIAN SUBMISSION AND CONVENTIONALITY (F)

The t tests presented in Table 4 show that foreclosure subjects received significantly higher F scores than identity-achievement subjects ($t = 3.88$, $df = 38$, $p < .001$) and also significantly higher F scores than the other statuses combined ($t = 3.75$, $df = 82$, $p < .001$).

SELF-ESTEEM

The significant relationship found here was between EI-ISB scores and the initial SEQ ($r = .26$, $df = 84$, $p < .01$). No significant differences among identity statuses for SEQ were found ($F = .66$, $df = 3/82$, ns). In addition,

TABLE 4 Differences in F Scores Between Identity Statuses

	N	M	SD	t
Identity status				
Identity achievement (A)	18	34.28	8.99	
Moratorium (B)	23	37.57	8.05	
Foreclosure (C)	24	45.17	9.01	
Identity diffusion (D)	21	38.67	10.19	
Groups compared				
C versus A				3.88*
C versus A + B + D				3.75*
D versus A				.44
B versus A				1.20

* $p \leq .001$.

self-esteem appeared to be unrelated to authoritarian submission and conventionality ($r = - .03$, $df = 84$, ns) and to CAT performance ($r = - .03$, $df = 82$, ns).

CHANGE IN SEQ FOLLOWING ISD

Although differences in the expected direction were found (i.e., identity achievement changed less than identity diffusion), these were not significant ($t = 1.39$, $df = 37$, $p < .20$). Observer ratings of subjects' reactions to the invalidated self-definition indicated that this treatment condition was effective. The failure to obtain significant results may have been due to unreliability in the self-esteem measure engendered by the 2-month span between the first and second administration. There was a tendency for foreclosure subjects given negative information to show a greater decrease in self-esteem than identity-achievement subjects under similar conditions ($t = 2.60$, $df = 19$, $p < .02$). No relationship was found between EI-ISB scores and self-esteem change ($r = .001$, $df = 84$, ns).

EI-ISB SCORES AND IDENTITY STATUS

Two techniques were employed to assess the relationship between overall ego identity as measured by EI-ISB and identity status. These were an analysis of variance among the four statuses ($F = 5.42$, $df = 3/82$, $p < .01$), and t tests among the individual statuses. The latter are found in Table 5.

TABLE 5 Differences Between Identity Statuses in EI-ISB Scores

	N	M	SD	t
Identity status				
Identity achievement (A)	18	48.28	5.10	
Moratorium (B)	23	48.09	4.23	
Foreclosure (C)	24	46.17	4.62	
Identity diffusion (D)	21	43.33	3.52	
Groups compared				
A versus C				1.37
B versus C				1.41
B versus D				3.94*
A versus D				3.89*
A + C + B versus D				3.61*

* $p \leq .001$.

Identity-achievement subjects received significantly higher EI-ISB scores than did identity-diffusion subjects ($t = 3.89$, $df = 37$, $p < .001$), and the first three identity statuses taken together received significantly higher EI-ISB scores than did identity diffusion ($t = 3.62$, $df = 84$, $p < .001$). Thus, the distinctive group with respect to EI-ISB scores appears to be identity diffusion. These findings lend some support to the hypothesized relationship between overall ego identity and identity status.

Discussion

Of the two approaches to the measurement of ego identity, the interview, based on individual styles, was more successful than the incomplete-sentences test, which treated ego identity as a simple linear quality.

Particularly interesting was the relationship between such apparently diverse areas as performance in a cognitive task and commitment to an occupation and ideology. The interview and the CAT tapped two prime spheres of ego function: the intrapsychic, seen on the CAT, which required the individual to moderate between pressing internal stimuli (stress-produced anxiety) and external demands (completion of the task), and the psychosocial, seen in the interview, which evaluated the meshing of the individual's needs and capabilities with society's rewards and demands. The relationship between these two spheres contributes validity to both the identity statuses and to the generality of the construct, ego.

No confirmation of the hypothesis relating ego identity to resistance to change in self-esteem was obtained, possibly because the length of time between the first and second SEQ administration was 2 months. The variability in subjects' self-esteem over this period of time may have obscured differences due to treatment alone.

Following are experimentally derived profiles of each status:

1. Identity achievement. This group scored highest on an independent measure of ego identity and performed better than other statuses on a stressful concept attainment task—persevering longer on problems and maintaining a realistic level of aspiration. They subscribed somewhat less than other statuses to authoritarian values and their self-esteem was a little less vulnerable to negative information.

2. Moratorium. The distinguishing features of this group were its variability in CAT performance and its resemblance on other measures to identity achievement.

3. Foreclosure. This status' most outstanding characteristic was its endorsement of authoritarian values such as obedience, strong leadership, and respect for authority. Self-esteem was vulnerable to negative information, and foreclosure subjects performed more poorly on a stressful concept-attainment task than did identity-achievement subjects. In addition, their response to failure on this task was unrealistic, maintaining, rather than moderating, unattained high goals. This behavior pattern is referred to by Rotter (1954) as "low freedom of movement [and is associated with] the achievement of superiority through identification [pp. 196–197]"—an apt description for one who is becoming his parents' alter ego.

4. Identity diffusion. While this status was originally considered the anchor point for high-low comparisons with identity achievement, it occupied this position only in terms of EI-ISB scores. CAT performance was uniformly poorer than that of identity achievement, although not the lowest among the statuses. The identity-diffuse individuals to which Erikson refers and identity-diffusion subjects in this study may be rather different with respect to extent of psychopathology. A "playboy" type of identity diffusion may exist at one end of a continuum and a schizoid personality type at the other end. The former would more often be found functioning reasonably well on a college campus. While having tapped a rather complete range of adjustment in the other statuses, the extent of disturbance of an extreme identity diffusion would have precluded his inclusion in our sample. Hence, it is the foreclosure, and not the identity-diffusion, subject who occupies the lowest position on most task variables.

In conclusion, the main contribution of this study lies in the development, measurement, and partial validation of the identity statuses as individual styles of coping with the psychosocial task of forming an ego identity.

REFERENCES

Adorno, T. W., Frenkel-Brunswik, E., Levinson, D. J., & Sanford, R. N. *The authoritarian personality.* New York: Harper, 1950.

Block, J. Ego identity, role variability, and adjustment. *Journal of Consulting Psychology,* 1961, **25,** 392–397.

Bronson, G. W. Identity diffusion in late adolescents. *Journal of Abnormal and Social Psychology,* 1959, **59,** 414–417.

Bruner, J. S., Goodnow, I. J., & Austin, G. A. *A study of thinking.* New York: Wiley, 1956.

deCharms, R., & Rosenbaum, M. E. Status variables and matching behavior. *Journal of Personality,* 1960, **28,** 492–502.

Erikson, E. H. The problem of ego identity. *Journal of the American Psychoanalytic Association,* 1956, **4,** 56–121.

Erikson, E. H. *Childhood and society.* (2nd ed.) New York: Norton, 1963.

Gruen, W. Rejection of false information about oneself as an indication of ego identity. *Journal of Consulting Psychology,* 1960, **24,** 231–233.

Marcia, J. E. Determination and construct validity of ego identity status. Unpublished doctoral dissertation, Ohio State University, 1964.

McNemar, Q. *Psychological statistics.* (2nd ed.) New York: Wiley, 1955.

Rasmussen, J. E. The relationship of ego identity to psychosocial effectiveness. *Psychological Reports,* 1964, **15,** 815–825.

Rosenthal, R. Experimenter outcome-orientation and the results of the psychological experiment. *Psychological Bulletin,* 1964, **61,** 405–412.

Rotter, J. B. *Social learning and clinical psychology.* Englewood Cliffs, N. J.: Prentice-Hall, 1954.

Weick, K. E. Reduction of cognitive dissonance through task enhancement and effort expenditure. *Journal of Abnormal and Social Psychology,* 1964, **68,** 533–539.

[24]   *Herbert A. Otto & Sandra L. Healy*

ADOLESCENTS' SELF-PERCEPTION OF PERSONALITY STRENGTHS

As part of the Human Potentialities Research Project at the University of Utah, a number of studies have been conducted to determine the nature of adolescent strengths and personality resources.[1,2,3] Although the professional literature shows a preoccupation with adolescent problems and dysfunctional aspects of teen-age living, research into the strengths of the adolescent is minimal, and to the best of the writers' knowledge, no studies of this nature have been conducted. The formulation of a framework of adolescent strengths based on research also appears not to have been undertaken. One outcome of studies under the auspices of the Human Potentialities Research Project was an initial framework of adolescent strengths, which will be presented in the concluding section of this paper.

The study had a number of purposes: (1) to explore what adolescents consider to be their personality strengths, (2) to formulate an initial framework of the personality resources of the adolescent, (3) based on this, to develop an instrument designed to help the adolescent obtain an overview of his personality resources, and (4) to gather self-perceptions of personality strengths in order to develop group methods consonant with the needs of "strength-centered" experimental groups.

Methodology

The data for the study were collected over a one-year period. Early in 1964–65 an open-ended instrument titled "Strength Questionnaire" was administered to two groups of high school students. The first group, numbering 38 adolescents, attended East High School, Salt Lake City, Utah; the second group, numbering 62 adolescents, were students at Bountiful High School, Bountiful, Utah. The cooperation of the principals of both schools was obtained in securing a sample which they considered to be "a fair cross-section" representative of the student bodies of these schools.

The questionnaire which was used is open-ended and has spaces for the

REPRINTED FROM *Journal of Human Relations*, XIV, NO. 3 (THIRD QUARTER, 1966), PP. 483–490, WITH PERMISSION OF THE SENIOR AUTHOR AND OF THE PUBLISHER, CENTRAL STATE UNIVERSITY. COPYRIGHT 1966.

respondent's name and date in the upper right-hand corner. The centered heading is "Strength Questionnaire," while directly beneath the heading is a subhead—"The following are what I see as my strengths:"—with the remainder of the page blank. At the bottom of the page is the notation "Turn sheet over for additional space."

Standard procedures for administering the questionnaire were followed. The groups were told that (1) filled-out questionnaires would be treated as confidential and no names of students would be used, as the questionnaire was to be used for research purposes; and (2) to maintain confidentiality, instructions were given the students to write only their age and sex on the cover page of the schedule; (3) students were asked to complete the schedule within a time limit of eight minutes; (4) it was explained that they could use the reverse side of the questionnaire, if necessary; (5) no definition of "strengths" was given, and any question as to the meaning of strengths was referred back to the questionnaire by the following comment: "We are interested in finding out what you consider to be your strengths—put down anything you consider to be a strength."

Findings and discussion

A total of 100 adolescents participated in this study. Of this number, 51 were female and 49 were males, with ages ranging from sixteen to eighteen years. Mean age of the groups was seventeen, with all students participating in the study enrolled in the eleventh and twelfth grades.

An analysis was undertaken of all strength items listed by adolescents. On the basis of this analysis, it was found that the personal strengths listed by participants could be classified in certain categories. The following strength categories were distinguished:

1. *Health*—this includes being in general good health, promoting and maintaining health, and having energy and vitality.
2. *Aesthetic strengths*—included here are the ability to enjoy and recognize beauty in nature, objects, or people.
3. *Special aptitudes or resources*—this includes special abilities or capacities such as having special skills to repair things, ability to make things grow, or "green thumb," having ability in mathematics or music, etc.
4. *Employment satisfaction*—enjoyment of work or duties, ability to get along with co-workers, pride in work, superior satisfaction with work.
5. *Social strengths*—having sufficient friends of both sexes, use of humor in social relations, and the ability to entertain others were included here.
6. *Spectator sports*—attendance or interest in football, baseball games, the reading of books, fiction, plays, etc., were listed under this category.
7. *Strengths through family and others*—included here were getting along with brothers and sisters and parents, ability to talk over problems with father or mother, feelings of closeness or loyalty to family, etc.

8. *Imaginative and creative strengths*—use of creativity and imagination in relation to school, home or family, expression of creative capacity through writing, etc.

9. *Dependability and responsibility strengths*—listed here were ability to keep appointments, trust placed in respondent by other people, keeping promises, and perseverance in bringing a task to conclusion.

10. *Spiritual strengths*—attendance at church activities and meetings, church membership, reliance on religious beliefs, feeling close to God, using prayer, meditation, etc.

11. *Organizational strengths*—ability to lead clubs, teams, or organizations, capacity to give or carry out orders, having long- or short-range plans, etc.

12. *Intellectual strengths*—included here were an interest in new ideas from people, books or other sources, enjoyment of learning, interest in the continuing development of the mind, etc.

13. *Other strengths*—listed here were such items as ability to risk oneself, liking to adventure or pioneer, the ability to grow through defeat or crisis, etc.

14. *Emotional strengths*—ability to give and receive warmth, affection, or love, capacity to "take" anger from others, being aware of the feelings of others, etc., capacity for empathy, etc.

15. *Expressive arts*—included here were participation in dramatic plays, ballroom and other types of dancing, sculpting, playing a musical instrument, etc.

16. *Relationship strengths*—this category includes such items as getting along well with most of the teachers, being patient and understanding with people, helping others, accepting people as individuals regardless of sex, beliefs, or race; other people confiding in respondent, etc.

17. *Education, training, and related areas*—this included good grades received, the acquisition of special skills, such as typing, selling, or mechanical drawing, etc.

18. *Hobbies, crafts, etc.*—listing of any hobbies or interests such as stamp or coin collecting, sewing or knitting, hairstyling, etc.

19. *Sports and activities*—participation in swimming, football, tennis, basketball, etc., and enjoyment or skill in the foregoing activities or outdoor activities such as camping, hiking, etc., were listed here.

Six per cent of the total number of strengths listed, including such items as "I don't fear speed," "I can hold my liquor," were not included in the above categories.

The average number of personality strengths listed by adolescents was seven. This indicates a limited self-perception of personality strengths not too markedly different from that of adults. In similar studies which have been conducted, adults have listed an average of six strengths but at the same time were able to fill one or more pages with listings of their "problems" or "weaknesses."

Distribution of the self-perceptions of personality strength as listed by male

TABLE 1 Number and Percentage of Male Adolescents Listing Strengths as Grouped in Strength Categories

STRENGTH CATEGORY	NUMBER OF MALES RESPONDING	PER CENT
Relationship	37	74
Intellectual	25	50
Emotional	25	50
Hobbies, Crafts, etc.	15	30
Sports and Activities	15	30
Social	15	30
Health	15	30
Expressive Arts	12	24
Dependability	12	24
Education, Training, etc.	10	20
Spiritual	9	18
Organizational	8	16
Spectator Sports	7	14
Imaginative and Creative	6	12
Other	5	10
Special Aptitudes	5	10
Aesthetic	3	6
Employment Satisfaction	0	0
Family and Others	0	0

and female adolescents is illustrated by Tables 1 and 2. It is of interest that the largest number from both sexes listed Relationship Strengths. Of the girls, the next largest number listed Emotional Strengths, with boys designating Intellectual Strengths. Actually, there is a fairly close agreement here between adolescents of both sexes, most of whom listed relationship, emotional, and intellectual strengths as they filled out the questionnaire. *One of the surprising findings is the low number of adolescents listing Strengths from Family and Others.* None of the forty-nine boys listed such items; whereas, of the fifty-one girls, only six put down items in this category. It is probable this reflects the adolescent striving to free himself from family ties and to gain independence.

As could be expected, Social Strengths were listed by 49 per cent of the female respondents and only 15 per cent of the males. The comparatively small

TABLE 2 Number and Percentage of Female Adolescents Listing Strengths as Grouped in Strength Categories

STRENGTH CATEGORY	NUMBER OF FEMALES RESPONDING	PER CENT
Relationship	48	94
Emotional	38	74
Intellectual	28	55
Social	25	49
Dependability	19	37
Hobbies, Crafts, etc.	16	31
Spiritual	13	25
Other	15	29
Organizational	15	29
Health	14	27
Expressive Arts	14	27
Sports and Activities	10	20
Education, Training, etc.	7	14
Imaginative and Creative	6	12
Family and Others	6	12
Aesthetic	4	8
Special Aptitudes	4	8
Spectator Sports	3	6
Employment Satisfaction	1	2

percentage (12 per cent of boys and girls) listing Imaginative and Creative Strengths seems to reflect the emphasis of our educational system, which places a low value on the development of creativity and imagination. The same can be said for Aesthetic Strengths listed by even fewer adolescents (6 per cent of the boys and 8 per cent of the girls). This is another area where strengths are apparently not being fostered by the educational experiences provided. Or, to put it differently, if such experiences are provided, students are not helped to develop an awareness that aesthetic capacities are a part of an individual's personality resources. If the percentile distribution of the males and females listing strengths in the various categories is examined, it is found that the pattern of strength listings by both sexes is fairly close and that boys and girls show greater similarities than dissimilarities in their listing of strengths.

An additional outcome of the studies concerned with the strengths of adolescents, conducted at the University of Utah, has been the development of an initial framework of adolescent strengths. It has been a consistent observation that adolescents have personality resources or strengths *which differ qualitatively from those of adults, and that the distribution or pattern of their personality resources is both unique and distinctive.* The development of a framework of adolescent strengths would therefore seem desirable.

The following outline of adolescent strengths (as compared to those of adults) is offered as an initial and pilot construct:

Strengths of Adolescents (as compared to those of adults)

1. Considerable energy or drive and vitality.
2. Idealistic, and have a real concern for the future of this country and the world.
3. More often exercise their ability to question contemporary values, philosophies, theologies, and institutions.
4. Have heightened sensory awareness and perceptivity.
5. Courageous, able to risk themselves or stick their necks out.
6. Have a feeling of independence.
7. Possess a strong sense of fairness and dislike intolerance.
8. More often than not they are responsible and can be relied on.
9. Flexible and adapt to change more readily.
10. Usually open, frank, and honest.
11. An above average sense of loyalty to organizations, causes, etc.
12. Have a sense of humor which (more) often finds expression.
13. Have an optimistic and positive outlook on life more often than not.
14. Often think seriously and deeply.
15. Greater sensitivity and awareness of other person's feelings.
16. They are engaged in a sincere and on-going research for identity.

The foregoing pilot framework of adolescent strengths supports the point of view stressed by Maier that *adolescence is a distinct entity rather than a period of transition.* As Maier puts it, "as long as adolescence is conceptualized as an in-between stage, the adolescent has no status in his own right."[4] A clear recognition by the adult of the adolescent's differential strength pattern should contribute to the establishment of adolescence as a distinct entity while at the same time underlining that the adolescent can make a unique contribution both to the adult world and to society.

It is one of the major findings of this study that the adolescent's self-perception of personality strengths are as limited as those of the adult and that the pattern of strength listings by male and female adolescents is more similar than dissimilar. It has been a finding from previous studies that the process of identifying personality strengths is experienced as strengthening by the person engaged in this process.[5,6,7] Research has shown there is a positive correlation between the self-image of the adolescent and school achievement.[8] There is considerable evidence that members of the contemporary United States culture are more aware of their weaknesses and problems than their personality assets and resources. Experts are in general agreement that a positive self-image and self-concept is desirable, especially during adolescence. This suggests that during this important and formative period an assessment of his personality resources by the adolescent would provide him with an ego-strengthening experience leading to increased self-understanding and awareness. As a part of the Human Potentialities Research Project, an Inventory of Personal Resources, Form "A" has been developed, designed to give the adolescent an overview of his personality assets. This instrument is now in the process of being field-tested and is available for research purposes.

The development of an initial framework of adolescent strengths, here published for the first time, might constitute a beginning step toward developing a more positive image of the adolescent. The devaluing and negative attitudes of adults toward adolescents unquestionably are much more pervasively destructive and inimical to the personality development of the teen-ager than we would like to recognize. There is some evidence that these attitudes are particularly deeply entrenched among teachers. *The question must be raised whether it is not the responsibility of the educational system to give the student greater self-understanding and self-awareness which, in turn, is directly related to the development of his potentialities.* It would also seem both logical and necessary that during a period of maximal growth and stress such as adolescence, a series of strongly ego-supportive experiences be built into the educational sequence. As a preventive measure and to foster realization of the child's potential, such a program is urgently needed.

It is hoped that this initial exploration will stimulate further research into the strengths of the adolescent as well as investigations designed to clarify further the adolescent's vital role and contribution vis-à-vis the culture and society in which he is functioning.

REFERENCES

1. S. L. Healy, "Adolescent Strengths" (Master's Thesis, University of Utah, 1965).
2. C. E. Souba, "Revision of Inventory of Personal Resources, Form 'A' " (Unpublished manuscript, University of Utah).
3. Mary C. Nicholson, "Abstracts and Excerpts from the Professional Literature Related to the Strengths, Resources or Capacities of Adolescents" (Unpublished manuscript, University of Utah).
4. H. W. Maier, "Adolescenthood," *Social Casework,* XLVI, No. 1 (January, 1965), 3–6.
5. Herbert A. Otto, "The Personal and Family Resource Development Programs

—A Preliminary Report," *International Journal of Social Psychiatry,* VIII, No. 3 (Summer, 1962), 185–95.

6. Herbert A. Otto and Kenneth Griffiths, "A New Approach to Developing the Student's Strengths," *Social Casework,* XLV, No. 3 (March, 1963), 119–24.

7. Herbert A. Otto, "The Personal and Family Strength Research Projects— Some Implications for the Therapist," *Mental Hygiene,* XLVIII, No. 3 (July, 1964), 439–50.

8. Wilbur B. Brookover, Ann Paterson, and Sheiler Thomas, *The Relationship of Self-Image to Achievement in Junior High School Subjects* (East Lansing: Michigan State University, Office of Research and Publications, March, 1962).

[25] Gordon W. Allport CRISES IN NORMAL PERSONALITY DEVELOPMENT

There is one trick every teacher knows: When trapped in a state of ignorance throw the question back to the class. Without suspecting the teacher's predicament, bright students will often rescue him.

This is the strategy I employed to learn something about crises in normal personality development. I passed along the assignment to my class of 100 captive undergraduates, and they obligingly provided me, through their own autobiographical writing, with the insights that I articulate now. Parenthetically, let me say that in my opinion no teacher or counselor has the right to require intimate autobiographical documents from students. Yet when given a completely free choice, the large majority will choose to write in the autobiographical vein. For the few who would find the experience too threatening, it should not be prescribed.

Influence of teachers

First I shall report a minor investigation related to our main topic. I asked the hundred students, mostly sophomores and juniors, four questions with the results reported here. My first question was "Approximately how many different teachers at school and college have you had up to the present stage of your education?" The 100 respondents mentioned a total of 4,632 teachers. The

FROM *Teachers College Record,* 1964, 66, 235–241. REPRINTED BY PERMISSION OF THE PUBLISHER.

three remaining queries were concerned with varying degrees of influence exercised by the teachers on the development of these students. With the percentages indicated as having played formative roles in student lives, the questions and their answers were as follows:

How many teachers had a very strong or powerful influence on your intellectual or personal development? (8.5 per cent) How many others would you say had a reasonably strong, well-remembered influence? (14.8 per cent)
How many do you remember only vaguely, or who seem to have had no substantial influence on your development? (76.7 per cent)

We are immediately struck by the fact that more than three-quarters of the teachers are remembered only vaguely and are credited with no appreciable influence, whether intellectual or personal. As teachers, we all know the shock of discovering how little impact we have had. A former student of mine brightened my day by remarking, "Years ago I took a couse with you, but all I can remember about it is that the textbook had a blue cover." He grinned pleasantly while I shuddered inwardly.

Only about eight per cent of teachers are reported as having a very strong influence, and about 15 per cent are credited with a less strong but well-remembered influence. Another way of stating this finding is to say that the average teacher (assuming all teachers are equally effective) "gets through" to less than a quarter of the class, and exerts a really strong influence on not more than one student in ten.

Varieties of influence

Asked to tell when and in what way they were influenced the students give us three facts of special interest. First, about half of all their examples deal with experiences of intellectual awakening. For example,

She encouraged me to read poetry and drama beyond the class assignment.
In chemistry the instructor asked us why bubbles appeared overnight in a water glass. When we said we had never wondered about that, he told us that everyone must question even the most common and seemingly trivial things.

And about half of the examples deal with personal development:

She made me see that others did not judge me as harshly as I was judging myself.
He had so much warmth and humanity that I wanted to be like him.
She seemed tough and disagreeable, but was so kind and helpful to me that I realized I must think twice before passing judgment on anyone.

A second insight, based on the large array of illustrative incidents, reveals the remarkably *casual* nature of the influence. In hardly any case could the teacher or counselor have known that what he was saying at a given moment would make a lasting impression upon the growing mind and character of the student. Elsewhere (1) I have argued that in teaching values and attitudes it is not the deliberately adopted curriculum that is effective; it is rather the *obiter dicta*, the parenthetical remark, the "little true things," and above all the example of the teacher that count. And what holds for teachers no doubt holds for the counselor, too.

Finally, and most relevant to my topic, is the finding that in elementary school there are few remembered influences of special strength. Apparently development is gradual at this time, and the teacher does not often bring a sudden and traumatic experience of "dawn" to the pupil. Only 12 per cent report any strong or even appreciable teacher influence in elementary school. Fully 88 per cent of the reports date the occurrences in high school (58 per cent) or in college (30 per cent, with the college years still incomplete.)

So it is in middle and late adolescence where the role of the teacher is most vivid to the student. It is in this period, according to Erikson (4), that the identity crisis is in the ascendance. The young person seems to be moving from past childhood into present adulthood in a jerky manner. Development is not continuous like a hill; rather, it is episodic like a flight of stairs. It is this episodic or crisis character of development that brings both challenge and opportunity to the guidance officer.

Nature of crisis

What precisely is a "crisis"? It is a situation of emotional and mental stress requiring significant alterations of outlook within a short period of time. These alterations of outlook frequently involve changes in the structure of personality. The resulting changes may be progressive in the life or they may be regressive. By definition, a person in crisis cannot stand still; that is to say, he cannot redact his present traumatic experience into familiar and routine categories or employ simple habitual modes of adjustment. He must either separate himself further from childhood and move toward adulthood, or else move backward to earlier levels of adjustment, which may mean becoming disorganized, dropping out of school, escaping from the field, developing hostilities and defenses, and in general becoming a thorn in the flesh of the teacher, the parent, the counselor, the dean, and occasionally of the police. Sometimes, following a crisis, the adolescent will become stabilized anew after four or five weeks of severe disorganization; but in many cases the trauma retards development for a year or more, and may even leave a life-long scar.

Turning now to my data, drawn from college undergraduates, we ask first about the phenomenology of crisis. What does it "feel" like to the student? Common is a sense of numbness and apathy. Upon entering college, the youth finds fewer strict role-prescriptions than at home. He is no longer tied to his domestic filial role, to the highly structured routine of high school, to his siblings, to his church connections, to his teen-age subcultures. He has left his possessions behind—his stamp collection, his television, his girl friends, his boy friends. All his familiar roles are in suspension. As one student writes,

The complete freedom of college is itself a crisis. For the first time I live in close contact with people who are not members of my family. They don't even resemble people I have known before. They have different opinions, different origins, and different emotions. I feel numbed by it all.

Interestingly enough, this sense of hollowness does not necessarily have its maximum effect during the freshman year. The excitement of new scenes and especially frequent correspondence with and visits back to the home town keep the silver cord intact. The student feels that he should prove to his parents, teachers, friends, that he can master the college environment and thus please them and win their approval as he has done in the past. The impending crisis has not yet overwhelmed him (or her—for what I am saying is as true for college girls as for boys).

It is the sophomore year that seems (from my data) to be the year of crisis *par excellence.* Suddenly it becomes no longer tolerable to live one's life for the edification of people "back home." The time has come for the child of the past to be separated once and for all from the adult of the present. Here are typical phenomenological statements of this stage of the crisis:

I feel I have been dragged into something against my will.
I feel like a rat in a maze.
I want to be a law unto myself, but cannot.
It seems suddenly that the decisions I make must be valid for the rest of my life.
To shake off parental norms and values seems to me the most important thing I must do.

The life of the past and the life of the future seem suddenly to be at cross purposes. There is often an intolerable feeling of suspended animation. Re-crystallization is not yet possible. The youth is waiting still to make a choice of careers, a suitable marriage, and to find an integrative philosophy of life which his diverse college courses are too discordant to supply.

Apathy and anxiety

It is small wonder that apathy and a paralysis of will often occur. But apathy is only a mask for anxiety. The whole framework of life is disturbed. Whereas the majority of students contrive gradually to build a new framework in spite of, or perhaps because of, the goals of anxiety, yet a large minority cannot cope with the situation unaided.

From my data, I would estimate that three-quarters are able to take the progressive road in creating their new frame of existence. About one-quarter cannot immediately do so. Proof of this point is that the dropout rate during undergraduate years is surprisingly high—over 20 per cent at Harvard, about three-quarters of the cases representing voluntary withdrawals (3). The dropouts present a special problem of guidance. Blaine and McArthur (3) write,

The drop-outs as a group ultimately do quite well if properly handled. We attempt to establish a relationship, however brief or tenuous, with these students, not so much to prevent their leaving school, but rather in the hope of giving them some insight into the determinants of their difficulties so that their dropping out can be ultimately converted into a meaningful constructive experience instead of mere failure.

After a year or two of constructive work elsewhere, the majority of voluntary dropouts return to college and graduate. But they could not have met their crisis by remaining in the environment that was the context of their conflict.

The regressive road is surprisingly common. Among eventual dropouts, but also among other students, we find such self-destroying behavior as quitting classes, a compulsion to do trivial things, playing bride until four A.M., drinking bouts, feelings of unreality, fugues, and general debauchery. The candid documents received startle me a bit by the extent of plain juvenile delinquency among my innocent-appearing students:

One student finding himself unable to handle conflicts over choice of career and over friction with his roommate, indulged in plagiarism on a term paper in such a way that he would be caught and forcibly separated from college. In this case a wise instructor, catching him in the transgression, turned the occasion into constructive counseling, forgave the deed, and put the lad onto the progressive rather than regressive road.

Here I venture a theoretical digression. The problem, as I see it, is one of interiorizing motivation. To put it in a student's words: "I am fed up with having everybody else cheer me on. I want to work to please myself rather than others, but I don't know how to do it." This plaintive statement points to a serious dilemma in our educational process. In school, the child is rewarded and punished by good grades and bad grades. Even in college, As and Bs are pats on the back, Ds and Fs are punishments. To gain love, the student must read books and toe the academic line. Finally, he obtains his degree (which is a symbol of academic love) and is freed from this external form of motivation. What then happens?

We know that a shockingly high percentage of college graduates rarely or never read another book after receiving their bachelor's degree. Why should they? Their love now comes from their employer, their wife, their children, not from the approval of parents and teachers. For them, intellectual curiosity never became a motive in its own right. External rewards are appropriate props in early childhood. But we educators, being limited by current inadequate theories of learning, do not know how to help the student free himself from the props of reward and develop a functionally autonmous zeal for learning. With our slavish dependence on reinforcement theory, I think it surprising that we arouse as much internal motivation as we do. In any event, we cannot be proud of the many educational cripples who after graduation, lacking the routine incentive of college, sink into intellectual apathy.

Crisis areas

The counselor or teacher, of course, cannot wait for better theories of learning. He is confronted here and now with crises in the concrete. Four areas of conflict, judging from my data, are especially common.

Intellectual crises. First, there are students whose problem is one of intellectual malplacement. Among my cases, a large number report that in primary and secondary school they were too bright for their class. The penalty is one of boredom lasting down into college work, which they still do not find challenging enough for their abilities. At the same time, double promotions in elementary and high school are not a solution. To be placed with older children often creates social difficulties far more serious than boredom. In fact, the evil consequences reported from double promotion are so numerous that we should challenge this particular solution of the bright child's dilemma.

The opposite type of intellectual crisis is also common. It is the deep disturbance that often results in college from intensified competition. It is statistically impossible for most students to maintain the same relative superiority in college that they enjoyed in high school. While this fact does not trouble the majority, it is a critical experience for those who depend on scholarship aid or who frame their self-image almost entirely in terms of scholarly pre-eminence. They are suffering a severe narcissistic wound.

Specific inferiorities. A second area of crisis is the old, familiar "inferiority complex." Besides the sense of intellectual inferiority just described, we encounter deep disturbance due to physical handicaps or to plain physical appearance, with resulting shyness, loneliness, and misery. To be poor at athletics creates a crisis for males, probably more acute in high school than in college. To be a member of a minority group likewise creates an inevitable crisis somewhere along the line. Here again I suspect the major adjustments and defenses are prepared before the college age. Occasionally, the inferiority concerns guilt due to moral lapses. One student is still haunted by her dishonesty which enabled her to pass a certain course three years ago. She has felt miserable ever since about this critical experience and badly needs a means of expiation.

In this connection we may speak of religious crises. While they are uncommon in my sample, Havens (6) estimates that at any given time 12 per cent of college students have a critical concern, and sometimes acute crises, due to their religious conflicts. I suspect the concern is even more widespread, but since it pertains to one's whole ground of being, it is seldom configurated as a specific crisis at a given moment of time.

Another area, seldom mentioned but surely important, is the ideological crisis of modern society as a whole. Youth is inevitably worried, as are adults, by our uncertain future. Elsewhere I have discussed the withdrawal of American youth from their social and political context (5). Both the earlier and present data show an almost exclusive concern among American youth with their own lives. Compared with autobiographies of youth in other cultures, the American documents are far more self-centered, more privatistic. They are too baffled to articulate their distress, and so take refuge in their private concerns.

Sex and family

SEX CONFLICTS

Needless to say, our candid discussions of crises frequently, in fact usually, report acute sex conflicts. Extremely common are breakups in boy-girl relationships which are usually taken as a disaster only slightly less fatal than the end of the world. Such breakups are so recently experienced that college students do not realize that they will, in spite of their present feelings, eventually make a good recovery.

We should face the fact that at least in the early years of college life crises in the sexual sphere are for the most part frankly genital in their reference. The biological drive is so powerful that the youth is concerned with it almost by itself. Its integration into mature love, into marriage, into career plans, into an embracing philosophy of life, exceeds his present capacity. He is likely to think that genitality by itself is maturity. Sexual gratification is frankly the aim, often with devastating consequences. At this stage of development, the students have much to say about sex and little to say about mature love.

Family conflicts. I have left until last the most pervasive area of conflict and crisis. I am referring, of course, to the situation that exists between every adolescent and his parents. It is not enough to say that adolescent rebellion against the parents is the rule. Of course it is; but my documents show that the whole history of the relationships from the time of earliest memories is important. Almost any irregularity in normal family life is felt bitterly and may trouble a student even into adulthood. A mother who is neglectful or self-centered, or perhaps overpossessive and neurotic, leaves traumatic traces in the child's life. A father who is ineffectual and weak, or cruel, or absent (if only for wartime service) leaves the child with a lasting feeling of protest.

One document of unusual maturity notes that many college students seem to need their parents as scapegoats. They find it comfortable to blame parents for their own shortcomings. Perceiving that their parents are not all-powerful, all-wise, and all-perfect, they can say, "Well, no wonder I am having a hard time growing up; they didn't raise me right." Thus, an adolescent, having no genuine ground for complaint, may yet soak himself in self-pity, not being mature enough to relate his restricted image of his parents to the totality of human nature—not yet ready to appreciate the fact that his parents, considering human limitations, may have done a good job. Even if the job was not especially good, the adolescent seems not yet able to appreciate his parents' good intentions as an important value in their own right. From talking with many parents, I hazard the hypothesis that normally it is not until the age of twenty-three that a child encounters his parents on a mature, adult-to-adult basis.

This brief account of crises emanating from the parent-child relationship leads me to a final point. My students were required to discuss their crises from the point of view of personality theory. They were free to employ any of the theories they were studying in my course. Most of them took Freud. (I may add that the reason was not because Freud was their instructor's favorite author.)

The conditions of theory

Now my observation is this: Their Freudian interpretations seemed to fit well if and when the family situation in early life was disturbed. When the father was absent or ineffectual, when the mother was notably aggressive, when there was deliberate sex stimulation within the family—in such cases, it seems that the Oedipal formula provides a good fit, together with all its theoretical accoutrements of identification, superego conflict, defense mechanisms, castration threats, and all the rest.

When, on the other hand, the family life is reasonably normal and secure, a Freudian conceptualization seems forced and artificial. If we say, by way of rough estimate, that 60 percent of the students try a Freudian conceptualization of their own cases, about 10 per cent turn out to be wholly convincing and theoretically appropriate. The remaining 50 per cent appear to be somehow contrived and badly strained.

I am wondering whether the same ratio might be applicable to cases that come to counselors. If a counselor or a therapist approaches every client or patient with the preconceived belief that his life must fit a Freudian frame of conceptualization, he may win a minority of the cases, but lose in the majority.

Even where a Freudian approach is clearly justified, exclusive adherence to it may distract the counselor from many significant developments within the life—for example, from the present functional significance of religious and aesthetic values, from the competence and interests that extend beyond the neurotic core, from the client's conscious plans for the future, and from his "will to meaning" and existential concern with life as a whole.

Every person concerned with guidance, or for that matter with teaching, needs as background some general theory of the nature of human personality (2). Our tendency, I fear, is to draw our theories from the realm of illness and deviance. It is somehow tempting to apply psychiatric rubrics to all personalities, for psychiatric rubrics are vivid, incisive, dramatic, and easy. Our conceptual banners bear such sloganized concepts as Oedipal complex, character disorder, identity diffusion, schizoid, acting out, and maybe an array of dimensions drawn from the Minnesota Multiphasic Personality Inventory. All such concepts, of course, have their proper place. But personality theory for guidance and teaching needs also to be woven of less lurid fabrics.

Youth, whatever neurotic threads may lie in his nature, is busy with his realistic perceptions, with his gradual learning and quiet coping, with the slow extension of selfhood, with noncritical failures and successes, with developing a generic conscience and a personal style of life. Even in the throes of crisis, he seeks in undramatic ways to consolidate his gains and continue on the path of becoming. A theory of personality adequate to undergird the art of guidance will keep such nondramatic facts in mind. Crises in normal personality development are important, but so too is the slow growth of each youth's unique style of life.

REFERENCES

1. Allport, G. W. Values and our youth. *Teach. Coll. Rec.*, 1961, 63, 211–219.
2. Allport, G. W. Psychological models for guidance. *Harvard educ. Rev.*, 1962, 32, 373–381.
3. Blaine, G. B., & McArthur, C. C. *Emotional problems of the student.* New York: Appleton-Century-Crofts, 1961.
4. Erikson, E. *Childhood and society.* New York: Norton, 1950.
5. Gillespie, J. M., & Allport, G. W. *Youth's outlook on the future.* New York: Doubleday, 1955.
6. Havens, J. A study of religious conflict in college students. *J. sci. Stud. Relig.*, 1963, 3, 52–69.

SEVEN SEX DIFFERENCES, SEX ROLES, AND SEXUAL DEVELOPMENT

The period of pubescence, when the secondary sex characteristics develop and the primary sex organs reach reproductive maturity, magnifies the problems of the adolescent's social and emotional adjustment. The adolescent in Western society is faced with four major problems of sexual adjustment, each of which causes anxiety and frustration. First, the individual must learn to adjust to his own changing body, and begin to see himself sexually as an adult male or female. Although this process begins in early childhood, it becomes urgent only upon the attainment of reproductive maturity. Second, the adolescent must begin to understand the nature of physiological and psychological sex differences, and learn to establish new affectional relationships with members of the opposite sex. Successful dating relationships and marriage are founded on the awareness gained during adolescence of sex differences in perception, emotion, social awareness, and sensitivity. Third, the adolescent must incorporate his newly matured sexual drive into his personality, a psychological task requiring a redefinition of sexuality in relation to social values and the demands of the ego and the superego. Fourth, the adolescent must reconcile the conflict between his imperative sexual drive and society's repressive function in regard to sexual expression. Confronted on one hand with the physiological capacity to reproduce and on the other hand by both the social stricture against premarital sex and the financial inability to support a family, the adolescent male in particular faces a period either of sexual repression and inactivity or of clandestine sexual activity and the sense of guilt that often accompanies it. In summary, the adolescent faces an important developmental challenge in accepting his sex role, controlling his sex drive, relating to the opposite sex, and achieving the kind of sexual adjustment that is necessary for mature heterosexual relationships.

Elizabeth Douvan (26) provides empirical evidence, based on psychoanalytic constructs, concerning sex differences in the timing and the nature of personality development during adolescence. Boys who have resolved the Oedipal conflict and have internalized parental values and social mores in their superegos will be more concerned during adolescence than girls with developing integrated and independent behavior controls. Boys, consequently, see a greater difference between their own standards and those of their parents than do girls. The boy, by the time he reaches adolescence, has attained more autonomy in questioning and opposing external authority and values than has his female counterpart. Girls rely heavily on externally imposed standards and "maintain a compliant-dependent relationship with their parents" for a longer period of time. Since the girl's need for love is more central to her personality, she tends to resolve crises by searching for support and love from important people, and, consequently, develops sensitivity and skill in interpersonal relationships. Apparently, character development is accelerated in boys due to the intensity of the sexual impulses that the male must learn to control during adolescence. In contrast, the slower character formation in the female makes adjustment to her future husband possible.

David B. Lynn's (27) theoretical paper deals with the process of sex-role identification, that is, the internalization of sex-appropriate behavior according to both "the unconscious reactions characteristic of that role" and the prevailing social definition of the sex role. Lynn hypothesizes that the fundamental sex-role difference between male and female in Western society derives from the fact that the male identifies with a general cultural model of "maleness," while the female identifies with her mother. In the process of sex-role identification, male and female acquire different methods of learning. As a child the boy is less firmly identified with the male sex role than the girl is with the female sex role, because the young boy, like the young girl, identifies initially with the mother. With increasing age, and under the influence of socal attitudes directed toward the male, the boy eventually becomes more firmly identified with the male role than the girl with the female role.

Recognizing the adolescent's struggle to adjust to his sex role and to cope with his developing body, educators and psychologists feel that adequate sex education is a vital responsibility of one generation to the next. Few critics, however, have been able to establish conclusively whether the responsibility for sex education lies with the parents or the school. In Gordon Shipman's (28) article, significant data and a provocative psychodynamic interpretation are offered to question the appropriateness of the family as the primary source of sex information. According to Shipman's data, the transmittal of information concerning human sexuality is negligible either from father to son, father to daughter, or mother to son. Some mothers manage to educate their daughters, but even in this relationship, wide individual variations exist, the information being far more adequate for menstruation than for reproduction or other aspects of sexuality. This poor communication between adolescents and their parents, complicated by the misinformation from other sources, accounts for much of the adolescent's anxiety and embarrassment about sex. Having ascertained the general trend in familial sex education, Shipman suggests that the failure of parents to communicate sexual information to their offspring is not a matter simply of parental unwillingness or inability to discuss sexual issues, but rather the result of a symbolic incest taboo that precludes the sharing of sexual knowledge. In support of his incest taboo theory, Shipman offers the fact that sex communication declines as the child grows older, decreasing during the period when the adolescent's interest in and potential for mature sexual activity is increasing rapidly. To meet this problem, Shipman suggests that parents and teachers should modify their roles, the parent's role being "supportive and ritualistic while the teacher's role should be educative."

Moving from sex education to the "sexual revolution," Seymour L. Halleck (29) provides evidence indicating that it has had less effect on overt sexual activity than on expressed attitudes toward sex. Collating studies from random samples of college women, Halleck reveals that although in the last generation "there have been important changes in students' attitudes toward premarital sexual intercourse" and toward the frank discussion of sex, "there is nevertheless little evidence that the actual rate of premarital intercourse has radically changed." The danger in changing mores, as Halleck views it, is that "the stresses associated with choosing or sustaining sexual relationships before marriage . . . have been critical factors in precipitating severe emotional disorders." To substantiate this position, Halleck cites his studies with college-age psychiatric patients, which show that the degree of sexual permissiveness in the patient population is considerably higher than in the general population. Halleck's dominant concern, as a psychiatrist, is less with promiscuity or lack of it among college students, than with the mental health of a generation engaged actively or passively in the "sexual revolution."

The concluding article in this part compares the patterns of social hetero- sexuality of male and female Negro and white adolescents. Studying subjects between the ages of ten and seventeen, Carlfred B. Broderick (30) finds that the heterosexual orientation of white girls increases steadily with age, and is significantly greater than that of boys at all ages. The differences between the sexes is so great that the mean for girls is always higher than that of boys two years older, a finding related in part to the fact that girls mature an average of two years earlier than boys. Such an interpretation, however, does not fit the data on Negroes, for whom there is no gap between the heterosexual interest of males and females. The scores are similar for both sexes, except at the twelve to thirteen years level, when Negro boys actually show more heterosexual interest than the Negro girls. Negro boys, in addition, become involved in social-heterosexual activities at an earlier age than white boys. The only area in which white boys show greater interest than their Negro counterparts is in answer to the question, "Would you like to get married some day?" Among Negro boys, the affirmative response to this question declines noticeably as a function of age, while interest in the three other groups increases with age. Possibly as a result of the predominantly matrifocal family structure among lower-class Negroes, the Negro boy's interest in the prospect of marriage decreases as he approaches manhood.

[26]   *Elizabeth Douvan*   SEX DIFFERENCES IN

ADOLESCENT CHARACTER PROCESSES

According to psychoanalytic theory, adolescence represents a recapitulation of the Oedipus conflict. The relative calm and control achieved during latency suffer a disruption at this point because of the re-emergence of intense sexual impulses, and the child is plunged once more into Oedipal conflict.

Several critical new features mark this re-enactment of the Oedipal drama, however, and distinguish it from its earlier counterpart. The ego of the puberal child, enriched and articulated during latency, is in a more advantageous position in relation to the impulses than it was in the Oedipal phase. For during its struggle with impulses the ego has gained an ally in the agency of the super-ego. And the fact of genital capability opens for the child new possibilities for resolving conflict. The male child need not simply repress his love for the mother and gain mastery of his ambivalence and fears through identification. He may now seek substitutes for the mother, substitutes who are suitable love objects. Though he may identify with the father in a more or less differentiated fashion, he need not use identification as a global defense against overpowering fear of the rival father, since the father is no longer his rival in the same crucial way.

Part of the outcome of the adolescent struggle is the renegotiation of the ego–super-ego compact: that is, a change in character. As part of the process of remodeling his original identifications, the child establishes a set of values and controls which are more internal and personal than earlier ones and which reflect his new reality situation as an adult.

This is the developmental task and context facing the adolescent boy. But what of the task confronting the girl at this period? With what resources and what history does she enter adolescence? Analytic theory, though wanting in specificity, gives us some broad clues about this development, its unique characteristics, and the ways in which it differs from development in the male child.

First, we expect that super-ego is less developed in women (and in adolescent girls). Since the little girl has no decisive motive force comparable to the boy's castration anxiety, she does not turn peremptorily against her own instinctual wishes nor form the same critical and definite identification with the like-sexed parent. Her motives for internalizing the wishes of important adults are fear of loss of love and a sense of shame. According to Deutsch (1), an important step in the socialization of girls occurs when the father enters an agree-

FROM *Merrill-Palmer Quarterly*, 1960, 6, 203–211. REPRINTED BY PERMISSION OF THE AUTHOR AND THE PUBLISHER.

ment with the little girl whereby he exchanges a promise of love for her for-feiture of any direct expression of aggressive impulses.

A significant difference may be noted at this point: the boy who has accomplished the Oedipal resolution now has an *internal* representative of the parents which he must placate and which serves as a source of reinforce-ous super-ego. And in reworking the relation between the ego and the impulses, parents as the source of reward and punishment since her identifications are only partial and primitive.

At adolescence this difference has a critical significance: the boy enters the adolescent contest with an ego that is reinforced by a strong ally, a vigor-ous superego. And in reworking the relation between the ego and the impulses, there is an internal criterion by which the boy judges the new arrangement. His new values and controls are an individual accomplishment and are judged, at least in part, by individual standards. The girl meets the rearoused instincts of adolescence with an ego only poorly supported by partial identifications and introjects. She still needs to rely heavily on externally imposed standards to help in her struggle with impulses.

With this formulation as a starting point, we made a number of predic-tions about sex differences in character development and looked at data from two national sample surveys of boys and girls in the 14-to 16-year age group for tests of our predictions.[1] Specifically, we explored the following concep-tions:

1. Adolescent girls will show less concern with values and with developing behavior controls than will boys; that is, character will show rapid develop-ment in boys during adolescence, while girls will be less preoccupied with establishing personal, individual standards and values.
2. Personal integration around moral values, though crucial in the adjustment of adolescent boys, will not predict adjustment in girls. Rather, sensitivity and skill in interpersonal relationships will be critical integrative variables in adolescent girls and will predict their personal adjustment.

Our studies yield substantial support for the first speculation. Girls are consciously less concerned about developing independent controls than boys are. They are more likely to show an unquestioned identification with, and acceptance of, parental regulation. They less often distinguish parents' stand-ards from their own, and they do not view the parents' rules as external or inhibiting as often as boys do. Boys more often tell us they worry about con-trols—particularly controls on aggression; when we ask them what they would like to change about themselves, the issue of controls again emerges as an important source of concern. More important, perhaps, as evidence of their greater involvement in building controls, we find that boys tend to conceive parental rules as distinctly external, and, to some extent, opposed to their own interests. So when we ask why parents make rules, boys underscore the need to control children (e.g., to keep them out of trouble). Girls reveal an identi-fication with the parents when they say that parents make rules to teach their children how to behave, to give them standards to live by, to let children know what is expected of them. Boys think of rules as a means of restricting areas of negative behavior, while girls more often see them as a means of directing and channeling energy.

In answer to all of our questions about parental rules, boys repeatedly reveal greater differentiation between their own and their parents' standards.[2]

One of the most impressive indications of the difference between boys and girls in their stance toward authority comes from a series of projective picture-story questions. At one point in this series a boy or girl is shown with his parents, and the parents are setting a limit for the child. We asked respondents to tell what the child would say. A quarter of the boys questioned the parental restriction—not with hostility or any sign of real conflict, but with a freedom that implies a right to question—while only 4 per cent of the girls in the same age group responded in this way. On the other hand, a third of the girls reassured the parents with phrases like "don't worry," or "you know I'll behave, I'll act like a lady"; the boys almost never gave answers comparable to these.

Both of these response types reveal a respect for one's own opinions. They both indicate autonomy, but very different attitudes toward parental rules: the boy openly opposes; the girl not only acquiesces to, but reinforces the parents' regulation.

Girls are more authority reliant than boys in their attitudes toward adults other than their parents. And we find lower correlations among internalization items for girls, indicating less coherence in internalization for them than for boys.

These are examples of differences that support the claim that boys are actively struggling with the issue of controls, that they are moving in a process of thrust and counterthrust toward the construction of personal, individuated control systems more conscious and rational than previous global identifications; and that girls, on the other hand, are relatively uninvolved in this struggle and maintain a compliant-dependent relationship with their parents.

The second hypothesis suggested at the beginning of this paper deals with the significance of progress in internalization for the personal integration and adjustment of boys and girls. Having found that girls are less urgently struggling for independent character, we wonder what this means about their general ego development and integration. Are girls relatively undeveloped in these areas as well as in independence of character?

The analysis we have done to date indicates that the second alternative is at least a viable hypothesis. In an analysis of extreme groups, we find that the well-internalized boy is characterized by active achievement strivings, independence of judgment, a high level of energy for use in work and play, and self-confidence combined with realistic self-criticism. He is well developed in the more subtle ego qualities of organization of thought and time-binding. The boy who has not achieved internal, personal controls and who responds only to external authority is poorly integrated, demoralized, and deficient in all areas of advanced ego functioning (Table 1).

Again, we ask, what does girls' relatively common reliance on external controls mean about their ego integration? We find when we analyze extreme groups of girls that internalization of individual controls is no guarantee of ego development, and that girls who are dependent on external controls do not show the disintegration and demoralization that mark the noninternalized boy. In short, internalization of independent standards is not an efficient predictor of ego organization or ego strength in girls.

There are several possible explanations for this absence of significant association in girls. High internalization in girls may not reflect independence of standards. Deutsch (1) has observed girls' greater capacity for intense identification, compared to boys; and we may have in the girls' apparently well-internalized controls a product of fusion with parental standards rather than a differentiated and independent character. Moreover, dependence on external standards is the norm for girls in adolescence. Parents are permitted and encouraged to maintain close supervision of the growing girl's actions. Under these circumstances, compliance with external authority is less likely to reflect personal pathology or a pathological family structure.

To this point, then, we have seen that girls are less absorbed with the issue of controls, and that the successful internalization of controls is less crucial for their integration at this age than it is for boys.

We speculated that the critical integrating variable for the girl is her progress in developing interpersonal skill and sensitivity. A striking continuity in feminine psychology lies in the means of meeting developmental crises. In childhood, adolescence, and adulthood the female's central motive is a desire for love, and her means of handling crises is to appeal for support and love from important persons in her environment. This contrasts with the greater variety of methods—of mastery and withdrawal—that the male uses in meeting developmental stresses. The girl's skill in pleading her cause with others, in attracting and holding affection, is more critical to her successful adaptation.

We designed a test of the importance of interpersonal development in boys and girls. Again, taking extreme groups, those who reveal relatively mature attitudes and skills in the area of friendship and those who are impressively immature, we compared performance in other areas of ego development. With girls we found clear relationships between interpersonal development and the following ego variables: energy level, self-confidence, time-perspective and organization of ideas, and positive feminine identification (Table 2).

Interpersonal skill in boys is not significantly related to activity level, time-binding, self-confidence, or self-acceptance. In short, it does not assert the same key influence in the ego integration of boys that it does in feminine development.

What significance do these findings have? What are the sources of the

TABLE 1   Extreme Groups on an Internalization Index Compared on Measures of Other Ego Variables (Boy Sample)

SELECTED MEASURES OF EGO VARIABLES	INTERNALIZATION INDEX			
	High	Low	Chi Square	P Level
I. ACHIEVEMENT				
a. prefer success to security	.64	.47	8.140	< .01
b. choose job aspiration on achievement criteria	.78	.62	9.331	< .01
c. choose job aspiration because of ease of acquiring job, minimum demands	.01	.13	13.758	< .001
d. upward mobile aspirations	.70	.53	7.158	< .01
II. ENERGY LEVEL				
a. high on index of leisure engagements	.49	.40	2.729	< .10 > .05
b. belong to some organized group	.77	.65	5.50	< .05
c. hold jobs	.63	.42	12.576	< .01
d. date	.66	.52	6.007	< .05
III. AUTONOMY				
a. rely on own judgment in issues of taste and behavior	.40	.20	12.786	< .01
b. have some disagreements with parents	.67	.49	12.804	< .01
c. choose adult ideal outside family	.23	.14	4.547	< .05
d. have no adult ideal	.07	.16	8.621	< .01
e. authority reliant in relation to adult leaders	.23	.54	28.544	< .001
IV. SELF-CONFIDENCE				
a. high on interviewer rating of confidence	.43	.22	11.213	< .01
b. low on interviewer rating of confidence	.16	.35	14.205	< .001
c. high on rating for organization of ideas	.65	.43	9.861	< .01
d. low on rating for organization of ideas	.08	.28	19.006	< .001
V. SELF-CRITICISM				
a. wish for changes that can be effected by individual effort	.36	.12	16.22	< .001
b. wish for changes that cannot be effected by indiviual effort	.14	.30	12.613	< .01
c. no self-change desired	.27	.42	7.498	< .05

TABLE 1   (continued)

SELECTED MEASURES OF EGO VARIABLES	INTERNALIZATION INDEX			
	High	Low	Chi Square	P Level
VI. TIME PERSPECTIVE				
a. extended	.44	.28	7.604	< .05
b. restricted	.14	.33	15.721	< .01

Note.—The Internalization Index is based on responses to three questions: (a) What would happen if parents didn't make rules? (b) When might a boy (girl) break a rule? (c) one of the picture-story items: What does the boy (girl) do (when pressed by peers to ignore a promise to parents)? External responses are those which see children obeying only out of fear, breaking rules when they think they will not be caught, relying exclusively on externally imposed guides. Internal responses, in contrast, reveal a sense of obligation or trust about promises given, consider rules unbreakable except in emergencies or when they are for some other reason less critical than other circumstances, and think that children would rely on their own judgment were parental authority no longer available. Subjects who gave internal responses to two or three questions are included in the High category; those who gave two or more external responses are grouped in the Low Internalization category.

differences we have observed, and what do they mean about the later settlement of character issues in the two sexes in adulthood?

Differences in character processes in boys and girls probably reflect both basic constitutional and developmental differences between the sexes and also variation in the culture's statement of character crises for boys and girls.

Perhaps the most crucial factor leading to boys' precocity in moral development is the more intense and imperious nature of the impulses they must handle. The sexual impulses aroused in the boy at puberty are specific and demanding and push to the forefront the need for personal controls which accommodate his sexual needs. Acceptance of parental standards or maintenance of the early identification-based control would require denial of sexual impulses, and this is simply not possible for the boy after puberty.

The girl's impulses, on the other hand, are both more ambiguous and more subject to primitive repressive defenses. She has abandoned aggressive impulses at an earlier phase of development and may continue to deny them. Her sexual impulses are more diffuse than the boy's and can also more readily submit to the control of parents and to the denial this submission may imply.

The ambiguity of female sexual impulses permits adherence to earlier forms of control and also makes this a comfortable course since their diffusion and mystery implies a greater danger of overwhelming the incompletely formed ego adolescence. Freud noted the wave of repression that occurs in females at puberty and contrasted it to the psychic situation of the boy (5).

TABLE 2 Extreme Groups on an Interpersonal Development Index Compared on Measures of Other Ego Variables (Girl Sample)

SELECTED MEASURES OF EGO VARIABLES	INTERPERSONAL DEVELOPMENT INDEX			
	High	Low	Chi Square	P Level
I. ENERGY LEVEL				
a. high on index of leisure engagements	.41	.27	9.335	< .01
b. belong to some organized group	.97	.75	37.012	< .001
c. hold jobs	.60	.51	2.444	< .10 > .05
d. date	.81	.66	10.98	< .01
II. SELF-CONFIDENCE				
a. high on interviewer rating of confidence	.47	.32	9.071	< .01
b. low on interviewer rating of confidence	.17	.30	11.522	< .01
c. high on interviewer rating for poise	.38	.14	29.613	< .001
d. low on interviewer rating for poise	.14	.29	15.072	< .001
III. TIME PERSPECTIVE				
a. extended	.50	.37	8.621	< .01
b. restricted	.04	.13	12.714	< .01
IV. ORGANIZATION OF IDEAS				
a. high on interviewer rating	.51	.34	12.401	< .01
b. low on interviewer rating	.14	.28	13.168	< .001
V. FEMININE IDENTIFICATION				
a. high on index of traditional feminine orientation	.37	.11	37.93	< .001
b. choose own mother as an ideal	.48	.30	14.14	< .001

Note.—The Interpersonal Development Index is based on responses to three questions: (a) Can a friend ever be as close as a family member? (b) What should a friend be or be like? (c) What makes a girl (boy) popular with other girls (boys)? Answers counted highly developed are those that stress intimacy, mutuality, and appreciation of individuality and individual differences. Our High category consists of subjects who gave such answers to all three questions. The Low group comprises youngsters who gave no such answers to any of the three critical items.

Additional factors leading to postponement of character issues in girls are their greater general passivity and their more common tendency toward intensive identifications in adolescence and toward fantasy gratification of impulses.

I would like to mention one final point which, I think, has critical implications for character development in girls. Building independent standards and controls (i.e., settling an independent character) is part of the broader crisis of defining personal identity. In our culture there is not nearly as much pressure on girls as on boys to meet the identity challenge during the adolescent years. In fact, there is a real pressure on the girl *not* to make any clear settlement in her identity until considerably later. We are all familiar with the neurotic woman who, even in adulthood, staunchly resists any commitment that might lead to self-definition and investment in a personal identity, for fear of restricting the range of men for whom she is a potential marriage choice. This pattern, it seems, reflects forces that are felt more or less by most girls in our culture. They are to remain fluid and malleable in personal identity in order to adapt to the needs of the men they marry. Too clear a self-definition during adolescence may be maladaptive. But when broader identity issues are postponed, the issues that might lead to differentiation of standards and values are also postponed. . . . I do think that in all likelihood feminine character develops later than masculine character, and that adolescence— the period we ordinarily consider *par excellence* the time for consolidation of character—is a more dramatic time for boys than for girls.

NOTES

1. The studies were conducted at the Survey Research Center of the University of Michigan. Respondents were selected in a multistage probability sampling design, and represent youngsters of the appropriate age in school. Each subject was interviewed at school by a member of the Center's Field Staff; interviews followed a fixed schedule and lasted from one to four hours. For details about the studies, and copies of the complete questionnaire, readers may refer to the basic reports (2, 3).
2. In the full series, we asked respondents why parents make rules, what would happen if they didn't, when a boy might break a rule, whether the respondent himself had ever broken a rule, and what kind of rule he would never break. For exact phrasing and order of questions, the reader may refer to the basic study reports (2, 3).

REFERENCES

1. Deutsch, Helene. *The psychology of women.* New York: Grune and Stratton, 1944. 2 vols.
2. Douvan, Elizabeth, and Kaye, Carol. *Adolescent girls.* Ann Arbor, Mich.: Survey Research Center, University of Michigan, 1956.

3. Douvan, Elizabeth, and Withey, S. B. *A study of adolescent boys.* Ann Arbor, Mich.: Survey Research Center, University of Michigan, 1955.
4. Fenichel, O. The pregenital antecedents of the Oedipus complex. *Int. J. Psychoanal.*, 1931, **12**, 141–166.
5. Freud, S. Female sexuality. *Int. J. Psychoanal.*, 1932, **13**, 281–297.

[27] *David B. Lynn* THE PROCESS OF LEARNING PARENTAL AND SEX-ROLE IDENTIFICATION

The purpose of this paper is to summarize the writer's theoretical formulation concerning identification, much of which has been published piecemeal in various journals. Research relevant to new hypotheses is cited, and references are given to previous publications of this writer in which the reader can find evidence concerning the earlier hypotheses. Some of the previously published hypotheses are considerably revised in this paper and, it is hoped, placed in a more comprehensive and coherent framework.

Theoretical formulation

Before developing specific hypotheses, one must briefly define identification as it is used here. *Parental identification* refers to the internalization of personality characteristics of one's own parent and to unconscious reactions similar to that parent. This is to be contrasted with *sex-role identification*, which refers to the internalization of the role typical of a given sex in a particular culture and to the unconscious reactions characteristic of that role. Thus, theoretically, an individual might be thoroughly identified with the role typical of his own sex generally and yet poorly identified with his same-sex parent specifically. This differentiation also allows for the converse circumstances wherein a person is well identified with his same-sex parent specifically and yet poorly identified with the typical same-sex role generally. In such an instance the parent with whom the individual is well identified is himself poorly identified with the typical sex role. An example might be a girl who is closely identified with her mother, who herself is more strongly identified with the masculine than with the feminine role. Therefore, such a girl, through her identification with her mother, is poorly identified with the feminine role.[1]

FROM *Journal of Marriage and the Family*, 1966, 28, 466–470. REPRINTED BY PERMISSION OF THE AUTHOR AND THE NATIONAL COUNCIL ON FAMILY RELATIONS.

FORMULATION OF HYPOTHESES

It is postulated that the initial parental identification of both male and female infants is with the mother. Boys, but not girls, must shift from this initial mother identification and establish masculine-role identification. Typically in this culture the girl has the same-sex parental model for identification (the mother) with her more hours per day than the boy has his same-sex model (the father) with him. Moreover, even when home, the father does not usually participate in as many intimate activities with the child as does the mother, e.g., preparation for bed, toileting. The time spent with the child and the intimacy and intensity of the contact are thought to be pertinent to the process of learning parental identification.[2] The boy is seldom if ever with the father as he engages in his daily vocational activities, although both boy and girl are often with the mother as she goes through her household activities. Consequently, the father, as a model for the boy, is analogous to a map showing the major outline but lacking most details, whereas the mother, as a model for the girl, might be thought of as a detailed map.

However, despite the shortage of male models, a somewhat stereotyped and conventional masculine role is nonetheless spelled out for the boy, often by his mother and women teachers in the absence of his father and male models. Through the reinforcement of the culture's highly developed system of rewards for typical masculine-role behavior and punishment for signs of femininity, the boy's early learned identification with the mother weakens. Upon this weakened mother identification is welded the later learned identification with a culturally defined, stereotyped masculine role.

(1)* *Consequently, males tend to identify with a culturally defined masculine role, whereas females tend to identify with their mothers.*[3]

Although one must recognize the contribution of the father in the identification of males and the general cultural influences in the identification of females, it nevertheless seems meaningful, for simplicity in developing this formulation, to refer frequently to *masculine-role identification* in males as distinguished from *mother identification* in females.

Some evidence is accumulating suggesting that (2) *both males and females identify more closely with the mother than with the father.* Evidence is found in support of this hypothesis in a study by Lazowick[4] in which the subjects were 30 college students. These subjects and their mothers and fathers were required to rate concepts, e.g., "myself," "father," "mother," etc. The degree of semantic similarity as rated by the subjects and their parents was determined. The degree of similarity between fathers and their own children was not significantly greater than that found between fathers and children randomly matched. However, children did share a greater semantic similarity with their own mothers than they did when matched at random with other maternal

---

* Specific hypotheses are numbered and in italics.

figures. Mothers and daughters did not share a significantly greater semantic similarity than did mothers and sons.

Evidence is also found in support of Hypothesis 2 in a study by Adams and Sarason[5] using anxiety scales with male and female high school students and their mothers and fathers. They found that anxiety scores of both boys and girls were much more related to mothers' than to fathers' anxiety scores.

Support for this hypothesis comes from a study in which Aldous and Kell[6] interviewed 50 middle-class college students and their mothers concerning childrearing values. They found, contrary to their expectations, that a slightly higher proportion of boys than girls shared their mothers' childrearing values.

Partial support for Hypothesis 2 is provided in a study by Gray and Klaus[7] using the Allport-Vernon-Lindzey Study of Values completed by 34 female and 28 male college students and by their parents. They found that the men were not significantly closer to their fathers than to their mothers and also that the men were not significantly closer to their fathers than were the women. However, the women were closer to their mothers than were the men and closer to their mothers than to their fathers.

Note that, in reporting research relevant to Hypothesis 2, only studies of *tested similarity,* not *perceived similarity,* were reviewed. To test this hypothesis, one must measure tested similarity, i.e., measure both the child and the parent on the same variable and compare the similarity between these two measures. This paper is not concerned with perceived similarity, i.e., testing the child on a given variable and then comparing that finding with a measure taken as to how the child thinks his parent would respond. It is this writer's opinion that much confusion has arisen by considering perceived similarity as a measure of parental identification. It seems obvious that, especially for the male, perceived similarity between father and son would usually be closer than tested similarity, in that it is socially desirable for a man to be similar to his father, especially as contrasted to his similarity to his mother. Indeed, Gray and Klaus[8] found the males' perceived similarity with the father to be closer than tested similarity.

It is hypothesized that the closer identification of males with the mother than with the father will be revealed more clearly on some measures than on others. (3) *The closer identification of males with their mothers than with their fathers will be revealed most frequently in personality variables which are not clearly sex-typed.* In other words, males are more likely to be more similar to their mothers than to their fathers in variables in which masculine and feminine role behavior is not especially relevant in the culture.

There has been too little research on tested similarity between males and their parents to presume an adequate test of Hypothesis 3. In order to test it, one would first have to judge personality variables as to how typically masculine or feminine they seem. One could then test to determine whether a higher proportion of males are more similar to their mothers than to their fathers on those variables which are not clearly sex-typed, rather than on those which are judged clearly to be either masculine or feminine. To this writer's knowledge, this has not been done.

It is postulated that the task of achieving these separate kinds of identification (masculine role for males and mother identification for females) requires separate methods of learning for each sex. These separate methods of learning to identify seem to be problem-solving for boys and lesson-learning for girls. Woodworth and Schlosberg differentiate between the task of solving problems and that of learning lessons in the following way:

With a problem to master the learner must explore the situation and find the goal before his task is fully presented. In the case of a lesson, the problem-solving phase is omitted or at least minimized, as we see when the human subject is instructed to memorize this poem or that list of nonsense syllables, to examine these pictures with a view to recognizing them later.[9]

Since the girl is not required to shift from the mother in learning her identification, she is expected mainly to learn the mother-identification lesson as it is presented to her, partly through imitation and through the mother's selective reinforcement of mother-similar behavior. She need not abstract principles defining the feminine role to the extent that the boy must in defining the masculine role. Any bit of behavior on the mother's part may be modeled by the girl in learning the mother-identification lesson.

However, finding the appropriate identification goal does constitute a major problem for the boy in solving the masculine-role identification problem. When the boy discovers that he does not belong in the same sex category as the mother, he must then find the proper sex-role identification goal. Masculine-role behavior is defined for him through admonishments, often negatively given, e.g., the mother's and teachers' telling him that he should not be a sissy without precisely indicating what he *should* be. Moreover, these negative admonishments are made in the early grades in the absence of male teachers to serve as models and with the father himself often unavailable as a model. The boy must restructure these admonishments in order to abstract principles defining the masculine role. It is this process of defining the masculine-role goal that is involved in solving the masculine-role identification problem.

One of the basic steps in this formulation can now be taken. (4) *In learning the sex-typical identification, each sex is thereby acquiring separate methods of learning which are subsequently applied to learning tasks generally.*[10]

The little girl acquires a learning method which primarily involves (a) a personal relationship and (b) imitation rather than restructuring the field and abstracting principles. On the other hand, the little boy acquires a different learning method which primarily involves (a) defining the goal (b) restructuring the field, and (c) abstracting principles. There are a number of findings which are consistent with Hypothesis 4, such as the frequently reported greater problem-solving skill of males and the greater field dependence of females.[11]

The shift of the little boy from mother identification to masculine-role identification is assumed to be frequently a crisis. It has been observed that demands for typical sex-role behavior come at an earlier age for boys than for girls. These demands are made at an age when boys are least able to understand them. As was pointed out above, demands for masculine sex-role behavior are often made by women in the absence of readily available male models to demonstrate typical sex-role behavior. Such demands are often presented in the form of punishing, *negative* admonishments, i.e., telling the boy what not to do rather than what to do and backing up the demands with punishment. These are thought to be very different conditions from those in which the girl learns her mother-identification lesson. Such methods of demanding typical sex-role behavior of boys are very poor methods for inducing learning.

(5) *Therefore, males tend to have greater difficulty in achieving same-sex identification than females.*[12]

(6) *Furthermore, more males than females fail more or less completely in achieving same-sex identification, but they rather make an opposite-sex identification.*[13]

Negative admonishments given at an age when the child is least able to understand them and supported by punishment are thought to produce anxiety concerning sex-role behavior. In Hartley's words:

This situation gives us practically a perfect combination for inducing anxiety—the demand that the child do something which is not clearly defined to him, based on reasons he cannot possibly appreciate, and enforced with threats, punishments and anger by those who are close to him.[14]

(7) *Consequently, males are more anxious regarding sex-role identification than females.*[15] It is postulated that punishment often leads to dislike of the activity that led to punishment.[16] Since it is "girl-like" activities that provoked the punishment administered in an effort to induce sex-typical behavior in boys, then, in developing dislike for the activity which led to such punishment, boys should develop hostility toward "girl-like" activities. Also, boys should be expected to generalize and consequently develop hostility toward all females as representatives of this disliked role. There is not thought to be as much pressure on girls as on boys to avoid opposite-sex activities. It is assumed that girls are punished neither so early nor so severely for adopting masculine sex-role behavior.

(8) *Therefore, males tend to hold stronger feelings of hostility toward females than females toward males*[17] The young boy's same-sex identification is at first not very firm because of the shift from mother to masculine identification. On the other hand, the young girl, because she need make no shift in identification, remains relatively firm in her mother identification. However, the culture, which is male-dominant in orientation, reinforces the boy's developing masculine-role identification much more thoroughly than it does the girl's developing feminine identification. He is rewarded simply for having

been masculine through countless privileges accorded males but not females. As Brown pointed out:

The superior position and privileged status of the male permeates nearly every aspect, minor and major, of our social life. The gadgets and prizes in boxes of breakfast cereal, for example, commonly have a strong masculine rather than feminine appeal. And the most basic social institutions perpetuate this pattern of masculine aggrandizement. Thus, the Judeo-Christian faiths involve worshipping God, a "Father," rather than a "Mother," and Christ, a "Son," rather than a "Daughter."[18]

(9) *Consequently, with increasing age, males become relatively more firmly identified with the masculine role.*[19]

Since psychological disturbances should, theoretically, be associated with inadequate same-sex identification and since males are postulated to be gaining in masculine identification, the following is predicted: (10) *With increasing age males develop psychological disturbances at a more slowly accelerating rate than females.*[20]

It is postulated that as girls grow older, they become increasingly disenchanted with the feminine role because of the prejudices against their sex and the privileges and prestige offered the male rather than the female. Even the women with whom they come in contact are likely to share the prejudices prevailing in this culture against their own sex.[21] Smith[22] found that with increasing age girls have a progressively better opinion of boys and a progressively poorer opinion of themselves. (11) *Consequently, a larger proportion of females than males show preference for the role of the opposite sex.*[23]

Note that in Hypothesis 11 the term "preference" rather than "identification" was used. It is *not* hypothesized that a larger proportion of females than males *identify* with the opposite sex (Hypothesis 6 predicted the reverse) but rather that they will show *preference* for the role of the opposite sex. *Sex-role preference* refers to the desire to adopt the behavior associated with one sex or the other or the perception of such behavior as preferable or more desirable. *Sex-role preference* should be contrasted with *sex-role identification*, which, as stated previously, refers to the actual incorporation of the role of a given sex and to the unconscious reactions characteristic of that role.

Punishment may suppress behavior without causing its unlearning.[24] Because of the postulated punishment administered to males for adopting opposite-sex role behavior, it is predicted that males will repress atypical sex-role behavior rather than unlearn it. One might predict, then, a discrepancy between the underlying sex-role identification and the overt sex-role behavior of males. For females, on the other hand, no comparable punishment for adopting many aspects of the opposite-sex role is postulated. (12) *Consequently, where a discrepancy exists between sex-role preference and identification, it will tend to be as follows: Males will tend to show same-sex role preference with underlying opposite-sex identification. Females will tend to show opposite-*

sex role preference with underlying same-sex identification.[25] Stated in another way, where a discrepancy occurs both males and females will tend to show masculine-role preference with underlying feminine identification.

Not only is the masculine role accorded more prestige than the feminine role, but males are more likely than females to be ridiculed or punished for adopting aspects of the opposite-sex role. For a girl to be a tomboy does not involve the censure that results when a boy is a sissy. Girls may wear masculine clothing (shirts and trousers), but boys may not wear feminine clothing (skirts and dresses). Girls may play with toys typically associated with boys (cars, trucks, erector sets, and guns), but boys are discouraged from playing with feminine toys (dolls and tea sets). (13) *Therefore, a higher proportion of females than males adopt aspects of the role of the opposite sex.*[26]

Note that Hypothesis 13 refers to *sex-role adoption* rather than *sex-role identification* or *preference. Sex-role adoption* refers to the overt behavior characteristic of a given sex. An example contrasting sex-role adoption with preference and identification is an individual who *adopts* behavior characteristic of his own sex because it is expedient, not because he *prefers* it nor because he is so *identified.*

Summary

The purpose of this paper has been to summarize the writer's theoretical formulation and to place it in a more comprehensive and coherent framework. The following hypotheses were presented and discussed:

1. Males tend to identify with a culturally defined masculine role, whereas females tend to identify with their mothers.
2. Both males and females identify more closely with the mother than with the father.
3. The closer identification of males with their mothers than with their fathers will be revealed most frequently in personality variables that are not clearly sex-typed.
4. In learning the sex-typical identification, each sex is thereby acquiring separate methods of learning which are subsequently applied to learning tasks generally.
5. Males tend to have greater difficulty in achieving same-sex identification than females.
6. More males than females fail more or less completely in achieving same-sex identification but rather make an opposite-sex identification.
7. Males are more anxious regarding sex-role identification than females.
8. Males tend to hold stronger feelings of hostility toward females than females toward males.
9. With increasing age, males become relatively more firmly identified with the masculine role.
10. With increasing age, males develop psychological disturbances at a more slowly accelerating rate than females.

11. A larger proportion of females than males show preference for the role of the opposite sex.
12. Where a discrepancy exists between sex-role preference and identification, it will tend to be as follows: Males will tend to show same-sex role preference with underlying opposite-sex identification. Females will tend to show opposite-sex role preference with underlying same-sex identification.
13. A higher proportion of females than males adopt aspects of the role of the opposite sex.

NOTES

1. D. B. Lynn, "Sex-Role and Parental Identification." *Child Development,* 33:3 (1962), pp. 555–564.
2. B. A. Goodfield, "A Preliminary Paper on the Development of the Time Intensity Compensation Hypothesis in Masculine Identification," paper read at the San Francisco State Psychological Convention, April, 1965.
3. D. B. Lynn, "A Note on Sex Differences in the Development of Masculine and Feminine Identification," *Psychological Review,* 66:2 (1959), pp. 126–135.
4. L. M. Lazowick, "On the Nature of Identification," *Journal of Abnormal and Social Psychology,* 51 (1955), pp. 175–183.
5. E. B. Adams and I. G. Sarason, "Relation Between Anxiety in Children and Their Parents," *Child Development,* 34:1 (1963), pp. 237–246.
6. J. Aldous and L. Kell, "A Partial Test of Some Theories of Identification," *Marriage and Family Living,* 23:1 (1961), pp. 15–19.
7. S. W. Gray and R. Klaus, "The Assessment of Parental Identification," *Genetic Psychology Monographs,* 54 (1956), pp. 87–114.
8. *Ibid.*
9. R. S. Woodworth and H. Schlosberg, *Experimental Psychology,* New York: Holt, 1954, p. 529.
10. D. B. Lynn, "Sex-Role and Parental Identification," *op. cit.*
11. *Ibid.*
12. D. B. Lynn, "Divergent Feedback and Sex-Role Identification in Boys and Men," *Merrill-Palmer Quarterly,* 10:1 (1964), pp. 17–23.
13. D. B. Lynn, "Sex Differences in Identification Development," *Sociometry,* 24:4 (1961), pp. 372–383.
14. R. E. Hartley, "Sex-Role Pressures and the Socialization of the Male Child," *Psychological Reports,* 5 (1959), p. 458.
15. D. B. Lynn, "Divergent Feedback and Sex-Role Identification in Boys and Men," *op. cit.*
16. E. R. Hilgard, *Introduction to Psychology,* New York: Harcourt, Brace, and World, 1962.
17. D. B. Lynn, "Divergent Feedback and Sex-Role Identification in Boys and Men," *op. cit.*
18. D. G. Brown, "Sex-Role Development in a Changing Culture," *Psychological Bulletin,* 55 (1958), p. 235.

19. D. B. Lynn, "A Note on Sex Differences in the Development of Masculine and Feminine Identification," *op. cit.*

20. D. B. Lynn, "Sex Differences in Identification Development," *op. cit.*

21. P. M. Kitay, "A Comparison of the Sexes in Their Attitudes and Beliefs About Women: A Study of Prestige Groups," *Sociometry*, 3 (1940) pp. 399–407.

22. S. Smith, "Age and Sex Differences in Children's Opinion Concerning Sex Differences," *Journal of Genetic Psychology*, 54 (1939), pp. 17–25.

23. D. B. Lynn, "A Note on Sex Differences in the Development of Masculine and Feminine Identification," *op. cit.*

24. Hilgard, *op. cit.*

25. D. B. Lynn, "Divergent Feedback and Sex-Role Identification in Boys and Men," *op. cit.*

26. D. B. Lynn. "A Note on Sex Differences in the Development of Masculine and Feminine Identification," *op. cit.*

[28] *Gordon Shipman* THE PSYCHODYNAMICS OF SEX EDUCATION

For a period of years students in a university marriage course were assigned to write a family analysis in which they analyzed the internal dynamics of their own family of orientation. One item in the outline guide was "psychosexual development." In student autobiographical writing under this heading certain recurring themes appeared which should be of interest to anyone responsible for developing a curriculum in sex education. These themes focused around such things as the crisis of puberty, learning about procreation, learning about sexual deviations, suffering sexual anxieties associated with misconceptions, sexual experiences in courtship, and frightening sexual encounters with strangers.

This material suggested a number of questions: How prevalent are traumata for boys and girls at puberty? What kinds and what sources of sex training were associated with shock or with exuberance at puberty? How did mothers who did very well in sex education differ from those who did very poorly? How extensive and how acute were the sex anxieties of youth from the prepubertal period to early adulthood? What were their emotional reactions to learning about procreation and to their various sex experiences? How did such experiences as well as the nature of their training affect their later sex behavior and their orientation toward marriage?

With such questions in mind an eight-page questionnaire was prepared and

FROM *Family Coordinator*, 1968, 17, 3–12. REPRINTED BY PERMISSION OF THE AUTHOR AND THE NATIONAL COUNCIL ON FAMILY RELATIONS.

given to some 400 university students in marriage classes during 1965–66. Although these data have been transfered to data cards they have not been processed to discover relationships. Many of the data, however, have been descriptively treated to give some understanding of those behavioral realities concomitant with the psychosexual development of youth. This presentation, therefore, is exploratory and descriptive.

The data suggest one striking fact regarding the nature of American sex education. That is: It appears to be negligible for three of the parent-child relationships, i.e., father-son, father-daughter, and mother-son. It is significant only in the mother-daughter relationship wherein the range is from excellent to very poor. The general pattern is for some 70 percent of the mothers to do reasonably well in handling the questions of small children and for some 60 percent in preparing their daughters for the menarche, but they accomplish little else. This study, like those of previous years, confirms the absence of general sex training by parents. According to student evaluations, only 5 percent of the boys and 14 percent of the girls received what they considered to be adequate sex training from one or both parents. An examination of questionnaire data in all the studies since the Davis study in 1929 fails to reveal any appreciable improvement in the quality of parental sex education in spite of the current suppositions about increasing societal sophistication in this area.

This study has some relevance to the riddle of such persistence in poor communication between parents and children on sexual subjects in time perspective. David Mace has found this reluctance to be pervasive in all the countries he has visited and has speculated that it is related in some way to the incest taboo. This question has both theoretical and practical significance and should be resolved for sex educators forthwith.

A superficial examination of ethnographic literature suggests the hypothesis that there is no society in which there is an institutionalized pattern of verbal sex training between parent and child within the nuclear family unit. Sex training seems to be relegated either to kinfolk in the extended family or to adults with specialized training functions. The taboo on parent-child sex behavior may be so strong that any verbalization about sex in this relationship becomes symbolic incest. Psychoanalytic literature has dealt with symbolic incest in connection with the Oedipal situation, father-son rivalry and jealousy, and confusions over identity.

Yehudi Cohen has postulated a universal gene-carried "need for privacy," and that incest taboos are designed to satisfy this need; that the wellsprings for personal identity are personal and social and they require an emotional anchorage within primary social groups; that children tend to identify emotional anchorage with "those who instruct them in the ways of their society. Who teaches the young is more important than what is taught them. Seduction of a child by a parent has a devastating effect upon his identity and his ego. An orgastic state is a potentially overwhelming experience in which there is a temporary loss of personal boundaries and of self . . . . It is only as young people emerge from their identity struggles that their egos can master . . . intimacy.

The child's ego and modes of insularity are too weak to tolerate seduction by adults without severe pathological consequences . . . . It is for this reason that it is rare for societies to permit marriage before late adolescence." (Cohen, 1964, p. 172, ff.)

This need for privacy may have a special component reminiscent of man as a territorial animal. Is the crib of the child a territorial space in which he nurtures his identity and his need for privacy? In summarizing his impressions after studying sleeping arrangements in many cultures Whiting said, ". . . . the persons with whom a child shares the intimacy of a bed seem to have a profound effect on the development of his personality. It is our view that the nature and resolution of the Oedipus complex is determined by the social arrangements at night rather than during the day. It is then that intimate and intensive interpersonal feelings within the family are expressed rather than during the casual busy day when adults are concerned with making a living." (Whiting, 1960, p. 937)

However confused a child may be about sexual knowledge he may correctly associate sexual activity with sleeping arrangements in a nocturnal context. For an adult to approach his bed at night and abruptly confront him with a sexual lecture doubly violates his self-identity, his need for privacy, and the sanctity of his territorial space. David Mace reports the case of a man who said that his father did approach his bed at night when he was a boy to discuss sexual subjects and thereafter he suffered nightmares which endured throughout his life. Dickinson has 40 notations on 172 cases in which sex knowledge acquired from within the family led to fears, shock, and nightmares. As children acquire boundaries within which to nurture their privacy, so do parents. Cohen says, "One of the functions of parent-child incest taboos is to keep children out of the marital boundary-maintaining system so that their parents can maintain necessary identifications with each other." (Cohen, p. 184) It is possible that secrecy patterns associated with puberty rites may have relevancy to such boundary-maintaining systems. In all cultures both marriage and sexuality have sacred connotations. Perhaps they are profaned by any verbalization which violates the boundary-maintaining systems of both the child and his parents.

Implicit in ethnological literature is the idea that as the family situation increases the likelihood of incest, institutional defenses rise up against it in direct proportion. In psychiatric literature social psychological pressures toward and psychological defenses against it have been treated in similar fashion.* Again it is suggested that one of the most common of such defenses is reluctance to discuss sexual matters between parent and child. Other defenses, especially in nonliterate societies, may be the extrusion of children from the parental hut and certain avoidance patterns.

---

* Factors such as absence of the conjugal partner or sexual disharmony with the conjugal partner may impel a parent toward a child during his adolescence.

If we were to plot a curve representing the likelihood for parent-child incest in the life cycle it would begin at the zero point for infancy and rise to a peak at the bloom of adolescence; then decline as sons and daughters become oriented toward courtship, marriage, and departure from home.

In our society the spontaneous exhibitionism of young children is treated indulgently by adults, but as the children grow older the defenses of separate cribs, isolation of the sexes, separate bedrooms, locked doors, prudish behavior, and taboos on sexual communication set in. In young adulthood, however, children return from college with betrothed or marital partners and then may exchange both sex jokes and sex information with their parents.

In order to ascertain whether there was indeed a difference in the extent of sex communication on an age basis, the questions on sex training by parents were separated in the questionnaire under two headings: *Childhood Period* and *Puberty and Adolescence*. Forty-five percent of the females estimated that their childhood inquiries on sexual subjects were answered casually and truthfully by mothers, while only 20 percent of them indicated that similar inquiries during puberty and adolescence were answered fully by mothers. Males indicated a similar drop in adequate sex communication with their fathers from 15 percent to 4 percent; and with their mothers from 21 percent to 10 percent. The significance of this drop is enhanced when we consider that sexual curiosity and sexual anxieties reach their peak in adolescence.

The incest taboo and its defenses together with the associated concept of a need for privacy are not the only concepts to explain reluctance of parents to verbalize on sexual subjects. In several Western cultures there is a strong tradition of denying childhood sexuality. The counterpart of this is the refusal of children to recognize the personal sexuality of their parents.

In this connection John Gagnon has said, ". . . there is little doubt that most children and most adults are unable to consciously conceive of their parents as sexual creatures . . . . It is very difficult for children to believe that their parents even existed prior to their birth, and this primacy of mother as only mother, and father as only father, continues long into adolescence. Even after the experience of coitus, it is extremely difficult for a young man or woman to conceive of his parents in the same roles. It is of great significance that the original organization of sexual learning and attitude is never challenged in any major way, and it is not easily possible for the growing child to revise these early conceptions . . . . This phenomenon of nonlabeling or ignoring sexuality may not always have deleterious results for children. Since many parents have intense anxiety about their own sexuality, the manner and content of their direct instruction about sexual matters might be more damaging to the child than the nonfamilial and informal structures that actually supply the information." (Gagnon, 1965, p. 220, ff.)

Occasionally a case history suggests that a child has an unconscious resistance to grasping or absorbing the nature of the sex act even when subjected to a verbal or literal explanation. Such explanations, to be sure, are usually vague, but such resistance seems not uncommon. When young adults tell their parents how they learned about intercourse from peers or when they admonish their parents for not giving them better sex training, the parent will say, "But don't you remember that I told you?" It seems almost as if the taboo on communicating with parents on sexual subjects carries over to filling out questionnaires, for inconsistencies in evaluating such training on questionnaires have been common to more than one investigator.

Is the mutual denial of personal sexuality on the part of parent and child a latent manifestation of incest? This investigator is inclined to believe it is, but we need a new theoretical formulation of incest in all its manifestations. Any such formulation will have to explain why a few parents are able to overcome the verbal taboo and communicate adequately with their children on sexual subjects. The case history material suggests that some physicians and nurses are able to do well in sex training within the family because their professional experience gives them an advantage in treating physiological processes in an impersonal manner, but it is not necessary to have medical training in order to depersonalize sex discussion with children. In one sample of 163 questionnaires we selected 44 cases in which the mothers rated highest in sex training and 44 cases in which the mothers rated poorest. There was no appreciable difference in the background of the two groups with respect to religiosity, public versus parochial school attendance, religion, ethnic backgrounds, or mother's occupation. Only a third of the proficient mothers had some college training, although both parents in the more proficient group had more college education.

The crisis of puberty

We now turn to sex learning at the crisis of puberty. The first learning about menstruation for 263 female respondents is as follows: Mother and sisters 58 percent, school and reading 23 percent, and peers 18 percent. The quality of this instruction on a three-point scale regardless of the order of learning is given for each source on Table 1. It will be observed that the quality of this training in the order from best to poorest is: reading, school, mother, and peers. A slight majority of the mothers were first in talking to daughters and most of these did reasonably well in their explanation of menstruation.

How young girls are prepared for the menarche will influence the nature of their anticipation for it and determine how they react to it upon occurrence. From a sample of 239 respondents, 45 percent looked forward to its occurrence, another 45 percent accepted the idea with indifference or resignation and 10 percent developed negative feelings toward its occurrence. Reaction to the first menstrual period may be summarized as follows: about a quarter were elated or thrilled; another quarter were gratified; 30 percent accepted the experience with indifference and 10 percent were shocked or frightened. About 17 percent of these girls experienced the onset of their first period without understanding its nature, but the presence of supportive adults prevented undue concern in

TABLE 1 Evaluation by 263 Females of Adequacy of Education Re Menstruation from Several Selected Sources. Order of Learning Disregarded.

GROUP	VERY ADEQUATE		ADEQUATE		POOR	
(263)	Number	Percent	Number	Percent	Number	Percent
Mother	64	24	105	40	58	22
Sister	4	2	28	11	11	4
Peers	8	3	77	29	92	35
Reading	103	39	103	39	9	3
Church	2	1	8	3	9	3
School	75	29	81	31	31	12
Agency	4	2	3	1	5	2

some cases. However, 19 percent of the respondents suffered substantial fright. Typical expressions describing their shock follow: "I was scared to death"; "When I first saw the blood I was scared out of my wits"; "I thought I had cancer"; "I was very scared"; "I thought I had something wrong with me"; "I thought I was stabbed and was bleeding to death"; "I was completely shocked, I felt alone and afraid." In some cases the relationship with the mother was so poor that the daughter delayed her approach for help, which increased the length of her anxiety.

The opposite extreme is illustrated by the following account: "Thanks to my mother's good explanation of menstruation and the facts of life when I was 8 years old, I was not frightened in the least. Mother got books from the library and explained any questions we had. Because of this education, when my sister and I started to menstruate, we both were happy and excited that we were entering a new phase of life. I am not afraid of sex and, in fact, I am really looking forward to the time when I get married. I think of sex not only as love but also as excitement. I think sex is mutual and I hope to enjoy it as much as my husband."

The following case seems indicative of a new trend in American family life. After describing how well her mother had explained the approaching menarche the girl went on to say, "When I discovered it, I called my mother and she showed me what to do. Then she did something I'll never forget. She told me to come with her and we went to the living room to tell my father. She just looked at me and then at him and said, 'Well, your little girl is a young lady now!' My Dad gave me a hug and congratulated me and I felt grown-up and proud that I was really a lady at last. That was one of the most exciting days of my life . . . . I was so excited and happy."

The latter case illustrates a growing tendency to ritualize the menarche in middle-class families. There seems to be increasing reference to this occasion as a time for the family to celebrate the event as a rite of passage. The star in this family drama may be excused from washing dishes, served her favorite dessert, presented with her first high-heeled slippers, and congratulated by her father.

The examination of one sample of 162 questionnaires relative to learning about menstruation in contrast to learning about reproduction revealed a striking inconsistency. Nearly 40 percent of the respondents indicated their mothers did well in explaining the approaching menarche but said nothing about reproduction. In answer to another question, a third of these girls insisted that "there was no verbal communication between self and parent on sex matters." For them, apparently, menstruation was not a sex matter; it had only to do with becoming a woman and eventually having a baby. Could this inconsistency be additional evidence of inhibitions arising from the denial of the personal aspects of parental sexuality? It reinforces the idea that many girls will accept from mothers information about the menarche but not about reproduction.

There are some reasons why mothers should prepare their daughters for the menarche and not depend upon the school. In our sample the onset of the menarche ranged in age from 9 to 17. For obvious reasons mothers can time their instruction better than teachers. In their written class work a few girls whose mothers said nothing about menstruation indicated that even though they received excellent first instruction at school they wished their mothers had played a part in such teaching. It is not so much the information as the affective support they receive from mothers. In this connection the pattern of mother-daughter sessions on menstruation in a school or church setting seems to be satisfying.

The menarche is important in the socialization of tomboys or for girls who have some ambiguity about their sex identification. The autobiographical accounts suggest that it is the one overwhelming evidence of femininity and marks the final crystallization of sex identity. In this context a supportive mother plays an important role in the socialization of her daughter in appropriate adult sex roles.

Puberty for boys in American society is something quite different! The cultural assumption is that there is no need to explain anything prior to puberty; that its first evidence will be a pleasurable dream which the boys will come to understand and that later they will learn from peers whatever they need to know about sexual matters. For those adhering to such ideas this study should be a jolt. From a sample of 146 male respondents about 90 percent indicated that they received no information about nocturnal emissions from either parent and that what they learned from peers was most inadequate. The most adequate source of knowledge about nocturnal emissions was reading material which the boys sought out largely on their own initiative.

One gets the impression from the autobiographical materials that the first ejaculation in life is a profound experience for many boys. The outlet for its first occurrence is not necessarily the nocturnal dream; slightly over half arise from this source and the remainder from masturbation. If the first ejaculation is from a dream the incidence of fright is 15 percent; if the first ejaculation is from masturbation the incidence of fright is 20 percent. Typical expressions describing such reactions follow: "It scared the hell out of me"; "It was frustrating and shocking to me"; "I thought I was ill"; ". . . my first nocturnal emission came as a total shock"; ". . . it frightened me"; "I thought I had hurt myself"; ". . . a very fearful experience"; ". . . I thought I had regressed to the age of four and had wet the bed"; "After the second or third time I became alarmed."

The incidence of fright at puberty is not only greater for boys but wholesome anticipation of puberty is very much less. For girls positive anticipation characterized responses of 44 percent of the girls. Only 15 percent of the boys understood the phenomenon at time of occurrence. Whereas about half the girls reacted to the menarche with feelings of gratification or elation, only 6 percent of the boys estimated that they had feelings of satisfaction at the time of their first ejaculation which they associated with the beginning of manhood. Also, only 6 percent of our male respondents felt that they had been adequately prepared for this event by parents. The fright of the boys at their first ejaculation was also associated with embarrassment. Many of them tried to hide the stains on sheets and pajamas; they were consumed with wonder and curiosity but dared not ask about it.

One indication that our society has an absence of concern for the dramatic event of the first ejaculation is that we have no term for it. Puberty is a general term for a *period* of growth for both sexes, and menarche is a term for the first dramatic event in feminine growth; but there is no comparable term for the first dramatic event in masculine growth. For this milestone in male maturation I suggest one of two terms: we might call it *primus ejaculatus* from the Latin or *spermarche* from the Greek. I prefer the latter, which means "the beginning of sperm."

The lack of such a term seems the more remarkable in the light of the contrast between the two phenomena. The girl becomes aware of the event from visual evidence; the boy may experience erotic feelings which are suddenly discharged in overwhelming physical ecstasy—an ecstasy, unfortunately, quite ruined by fear arising from ignorance. In spite of the fact that the menarche involves no physical pleasure (and indeed any physical complications may be negative) the girl usually is oriented with psychological satisfaction toward her appropriate sex roles. The boy experiences his spermarche in a psychological and cultural void. Gagnon may have an important point when he says, "If the sexual domain is left relatively empty and undefined by processes of non-labeling, there seems to be a flow of aggression into this area." (Gagnon, 1965, p. 220) We shall have a bit of evidence about the incidence of such aggression below in the discussion of the sexual encounters of females.

We have alluded to the ritualization of the menarche in American family life which gives the girl so much satisfaction. Imagine an American boy coming to the breakfast table exclaiming, "Mom, guess what! I had my first wet dream last night. Now I'm a man." It is not without significance that such an imaginary episode is greeted in American culture with laughter. The incongruity lies in the fact that while the girl can deny the sexuality of her menarche and thus relate half-way to her mother's explanation, the boy and his parents know full well that the first ejaculation of life *is sexual* and thus all of them must abide by the verbal taboo.

Learning about intercourse

Learning about sexual information has two dimensions that are difficult to disentangle. Source of first knowledge has special impact no matter what its quality, but poor first knowledge may be corrected and implemented later by other sources of learning having differential quality. The time element between exposure to poor first sources and excellent later sources will have relevance to the intervals during which children suffer from misconceptions and anxieties.

Although a majority of girls learn first about menstruation from mothers and sisters, they tend to learn first about intercourse from peers. When asked to indicate the source which corrected the first impressions with respect to coition, conception and birth, reading was most frequent (65 percent) while parents and peers were equally negligible (8 percent). In similar fashion boys learn first from peers and have their ideas corrected by reading.

Prior to learning about human reproduction a fifth of the boys and a fourth of the girls confessed they had not thought about how it occurred. About three-fourths of both sexes indicated that prior to this learning they had entertained misconceptions about it—some of them quite fantastic. Girls reacted to this first knowledge with more surprise and disbelief than the boys. More of them also considered it vulgar and shocking. For the boys it seemed more natural and acceptable and they were gratified to have satisfied their curiosity.

Figure 1 shows the percentage incidence according to age for the menarche, learning about intercourse, and the time when first impressions about the latter are clarified. The peak year for consensual validation of such ideas is about six years later than the peak year for first learning about reproduction. During this interval our respondents suffered from all manner of sexual misconceptions and anxieties.

The increase in sexual worries as reported by 261 females from pre-puberty, puberty, and during adolescence respectively is 16 percent, 45 percent, and 78 percent. Similar percentages for a sample of 66 males were 21 percent, 44 percent, and 71 percent. In another sample of 108 males in which there was an elaborate chart listing seven different areas for checking both mild and severe anxiety, the percentages were higher. The severest anxieties focused on masturbation, which reached a peak in adolescence and declined somewhat in

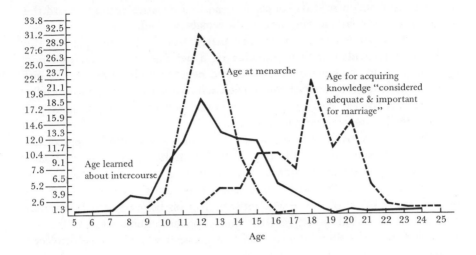

FIGURE 1 Percentage incidence of age at menarche and age for acquiring two types of sex knowledge.

early adulthood. Severe anxieties also revolved around petting, intercourse, and the possibility of impregnating one's girl friend. They rose to a peak in young adulthood. Anxieties about venereal disease rose steadily with age. Notions about being physically different from other males and anxieties about sexual deviations held steadily throughout all periods.

The general assumption that youth in the absence of parental sex instruction learn from peers is only partly true. They do indeed learn some things badly from peers, but not enough to allay their anxieties. They learn very much more from reading and learn it more accurately. Until such time as we can develop a sufficient number of sex educators we might well emphasize the distribution of appropriate reading materials for all age groups.

Petting behavior

One problem about petting that seems to be neglected relates to the incidence of neuromuscular reactions engendered by petting and how this affects the relationship between courting couples. If such physical frustration leads to negative physical or nervous reactions which come to be associated repeatedly with the courting partner until negative conditioning is established, then the very sight of the beloved triggers off a painful response. How many young couples who are well suited to each other break up because of such conditioning is an important question for those in premarital counseling.

In order to get at this problem the following questions were listed in the male questionnaire: Did you have considerable physical frustration from petting over a period of time? If so, did it: a. Produce pain in the testicles? b. Lead to a nervous reaction next day or so? c. Lead to a negative feeling toward the girl involved? Similar question were on the female questionnaire.

Forty-four percent of the men who petted heavily suffered pain in the testicles; about a fifth of them experienced a nervous reaction after petting episodes, and the same percentage developed negative feelings toward the girl involved. About 38 percent of the women who petted heavily experienced a nervous reaction after petting episodes and over 18 percent of them developed negative feelings toward the man involved.

The processes involved in the above conditioning may also be approached from the standpoint of role theory and the frustration-aggression syndrome. The male in the petting situation has two conflicting roles: (1) that of a virile male whose psychobiological being is oriented toward the completion of the sex act and (2) that of a male who must protect his beloved against violation and who must uphold the conventional norms of the community. The frustration inherent in the situation may lead to aggression which may be displaced onto the partner, himself, or other women.

To what extent is the breaking of relationships between steadies or fiancées influenced by the consequences of frustration in heavy petting? Do such frustrations and their aftermath affect marital adjustment in any way? Perhaps these questions deserve more attention.

Sexual encounters of females

The female respondents were asked whether they had ever had an encounter with nine different kinds of males who approached them with sexual aggressiveness or sexual deviancy. The results are indicated in Table 2 and Figure 2. Of 261 respondents, 196 indicated they had suffered from one or more such encounters, while 65 respondents had none. The 196 girls, however, had a total of 448 such encounters, averaging 2.28 per female. The respondents were asked to record their reactions in terms of terror, fright, and anxiety. Roughly about a quarter of the encounters involved terror, nearly half involved fright, and the remainder involved anxiety or disgust. Data from a sample of 146 males elicited the following: 45 percent reported an encounter with a homosexual but of these only 16 percent reported a physical contact; 8 percent said they had been seduced by an older female while in their early teens; 3.4 percent of the women had been raped and 3.7 percent of the men admitted to rape. Twenty-five percent of the women had encountered males who were over-aggressive in suggesting intercourse and 20 percent of the men admitted persuading a girl to have intercourse against "her moral convictions." After this question one respondent wrote, "I don't really know if it was a case of 'moral conviction' or 'playing hard to get.'" Another wrote: "There is a question as to just how deep these 'moral convictions' go. Are they her convictions or society's stamp?"

Such remarks tend to confirm what many have said about confusion of ex-

TABLE 2 Sexual Encounters and Reactions as Reported by 263 Females in Nine Categories

TYPE OF SEXUAL ENCOUNTER	NATURE OF REACTION			TOTAL	
	Terror	Fright	Anxiety Disgust	Number	Percent*
An exhibitionist	19	38	18	75	29
A voyeurist (defined as a man who has extreme urge to view sex objects)	5	8	6	19	7
A homosexual (another female)	3	16	13	32	12
Male who followed you making obscene gestures or remarks	21	41	8	70	27
Male who said obscene things to you over the phone	11	25	25	61	23
Male over-aggressive in suggesting intercourse	6	34	41	81	31
Male whose sexual aggressiveness you resisted by force	28	39	24	91	35
Male who forced you to intercourse	6	3	0	9	3
Older male who enticed or forced you into a sex act when you were a child	5	5	0	10	4
TOTAL	104	209	135	448	

* N = 263.

pectations in petting situations. It also appears more difficult to separate petting that is integrated with courtship from petting segregated from serious courtship. In Table 2 males listed in categories 6, 7, and 8 are aggressive sexually while the others represent cases of sexual inadequacy and arrested development. To what extent are these aggressive patterns associated with changing norms of a youth culture or with aggressive reactions arising from increasing sexual frustration in petting? When a girl has been subjected to trauma from sex deviants, she develops negative attitudes toward males and their sexuality. When she is then courted by a normal male who is premature in physical advances she may repel him and ruin a relationship that is potentially satisfactory. On the other hand we have case history material to indicate that when a male courts a traumatized girl carefully and gently she responds adequately.

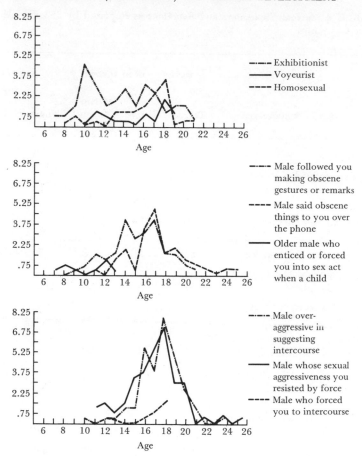

FIGURE 2 Percentage incidence of sexual encounters of various types involving 263 females of which 65 had no encounter.

Since the incidence of sexual deviations and the incidence of criminal sexual aggressiveness is poorly estimated from criminal statistics perhaps we should develop standardized instruments for sampling the incidence of such behavior using both male and female respondents so as to gauge such changes as to time and place.

In conclusion it is hoped that discussion of the incest taboo and its defenses, the need for privacy, the mutual denial of the personal sexuality of parents and children, and prolonged parataxic sexual fantasies of children which cannot be validated by forbidding parents will stimulate an attempt to unify such concepts into a theoretical formulation that will not only explain the poor communication which persists between parents and children on sexual matters but also delineate the appropriate roles of parents and teachers in sex education. Tentatively we suggest that the parental role should be supportive and ritualistic while the teacher role should be educative.

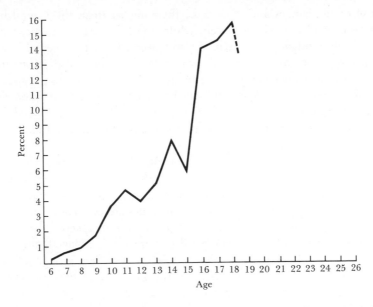

FIGURE 3   Percentage incidence of total number of sexual encounters by age for 263 females.

REFERENCES

Cohen, Y. A. *The Transition From Childhood to Adolescence.* Chicago: Aldine, 1964.
Dickinson, R. L. *The Single Woman.* Baltimore: Williams & Wilkins, 1934.
Gagnon, J. H. Sexuality and Sexual Learning in the Child. *Psychiatry*, 1965, **28**, 212–228.
Whiting, J. W. M., and Whiting, B. *Handbook of Research Methods in Child Development.* P. H. Mussen, Ed. New York: Wiley, 1960.

[29]   *Seymour L. Halleck*   SEX AND MENTAL HEALTH

ON THE CAMPUS

There is general agreement that sexual attitudes and sexual practices in American society are undergoing radical changes. I propose to examine the

FROM *Journal of the American Medical Association*, 1967, 200, 684–690. RE-PRINTED BY PERMISSION OF THE AUTHOR AND THE AMERICAN MEDICAL ASSOCIATION.

extent of these changes and to describe their impact upon the mental health of university students. My approach, while hopefully not moralistic, will not be free of value judgments. Like most psychiatrists I consider mental health to be something more than mere adjustment to the needs of the community. Mental health is defined according to certain values, values such as psychological comfort, intimacy, compassion, social responsibility, and self-knowledge. Once the psychiatrist begins to ask if a given sexual behavior is good or bad for a person's mental health he is no longer in a position to avoid making ethical judgments.

How much change has there been in sexual attitudes and behaviors among university students? Recent surveys suggest that there have been important changes in students' attitudes toward premarital sexual intercourse. These changes are most apparent when student attitudes are compared with those of their parents' generation. In one study when adults were asked if they believed sexual intercourse would be acceptable if a couple were engaged, only 20% of adult males and 17% of adult females said yes. In a student group, 52% of the males and 66% of the females answered the same question affirmatively. In another study, mothers and their co-ed daughters were asked to respond to the question, "How important do you think it is that a girl be a virgin when she marries?" Of the mothers, 88% answered very important; 12%, generally important, and 0%, not important. Of their daughters, 55% answered very important; 34%, generally important; and 13%, not important.[1] In a preliminary study of sexual attitudes of freshman and sophomore girls at the University of Wisconsin, Dr. Richard Sternbach and I found that only 30% felt that premarital intercourse was definitely wrong.

In judging the rightness or wrongness of premarital intercourse, today's student is confronted with alternative value systems which he can either accept or reject. Most students feel free to search for a morality which suits their own needs. They are not necessarily contemptuous nor rebellious toward older generations. Rather they have a live-and-let-live attitude. Students often say, "I wouldn't feel bad if I participated in premarital intercourse, but I wouldn't want my parents to know about it because they would feel my behavior was wrong. What they don't know won't hurt them."

Attitudes toward discussing sex have also changed. In the past two years, members of the University of Wisconsin Department of Psychiatry have had many requests to speak to student groups about sex. We have all noted an amazing openness and frankness on the part of both male and female groups. Seventeen- and 18-year-old girls for example have little shyness in a group setting in asking speakers about such previously taboo subjects as masturbation, orgasm, techniques of intercourse, oral-genital relations, and homosexuality. All students seem to be eager to create a dialogue with older generations as to the pros and cons of premarital intercourse.

Although there is undoubtedly a revolution in attitudes toward sex, accompanied by a refreshing frankness, there is nevertheless little evidence that the actual rate of premarital intercourse has radically changed. It may be true that more and more young people are engaging in heavy petting before marriage. But the physical state of virginity still seems to be the norm. Kinsey, studying volunteers, found that from 1910 to the 1950's there was no appreciable increase in the proportion of girls having intercourse before marriage.[2] More recent depth interview and questionnaire studies of randomly selected populations at major universities suggest that approximately 4/5 of undergraduate girls have *not* had coital experience.[3,4] At the University of Wisconsin, for example, a 1966 survey of 300 freshman through senior girls indicated that only 22% had experienced sexual intercourse.[5]

We might assume that some day the actual behavior of students will more closely approximate their expressed attitudes. Nevertheless, as of this date there is no evidence of a radical increase in premarital intercourse among university students. It may be reassuring in this regard to note that the great majority of students do not condone promiscuity. When they insist that premarital relations are morally justified, they are most frequently referring to intercourse between those who are engaged or deeply in love. Very few girls can envision themselves having relations with more than one partner. Of the 90 girls Dr. Sternbach and I surveyed, only four defended sex as something to be casually enjoyed with several partners. Some behavioral scientists believe that our culture is moving towards the Scandinavian model of sexual behavior which condones premarital sexual relations between people in love.[6] The expressed attitudes and actual behavior of our students reinforce this notion. In other words, it is unlikely that we will become a promiscuous society, but it is quite likely that we are on the way to becoming a nation in which couples who intend to marry begin sexual activity before marriage.

A trend toward sexual permissiveness based on affection and love should not alarm psychiatrists. After all, we believe in the values of intimacy and compassion, and the new sexuality seems to be moving in that direction. Unfortunately, the problem is not that simple. If a girl accepts the new attitudes and wishes to have sexual relations with a boy on the basis of mutual affection and love, she must still define the strength of their commitment. Inevitably she must struggle with the question of how close two people can be when not bound to one another by the responsibilities of a marital contract. Any relationship out of wedlock is plagued with certain ambiguities. The girl must struggle with questions such as, "Will the first argument or sign of incompatibility lead to a dissolution of the relationship and a search for a new partner?" If this does happen, will she simply deceive herself into promiscuity under the rationalization that each new relationship is meaningful? Will she "kid herself" into believing that she is in love when in actuality she is only succumbing to social and sexual pressures? It is my belief that these ambiguities have been heightened by changes in attitudes toward sex. The stresses associated with choosing or sustaining sexual relationships before marriage have had an especially intense effect upon female students. For some students such stresses have been critical factors in precipitating severe emotional disorders. In this sense a significant number of students are casualties of the sexual revolution.

Mental health and sexual permissiveness

If it is true that rates of sexual intercourse before marriage have not changed appreciably in the general student population, this trend is not apparent in those students who are psychiatric patients. In a recent survey of 24 Madison psychiatrists who were treating University of Wisconsin students, I found that of their 107 unmarried female patients 86% had had sexual relationships with at least one person and 72% had had relations with more than one person. Permissive sexual activity seems to be highly correlated with mental illness, or at least with a willingness to accept a mental illness role. This data raises some disturbing thoughts. Psychiatrists and other physicians have been in the vanguard of either praising or deploring new trends toward permissive sexuality. Judging from their publications, it appears that psychiatrists have gained the impression that promiscuity is rampant in our youth. However, if we compare the incidence of virginity among nonpatients with that among patients (remember that only 22% of the nonpatient students had had sexual intercourse) it appears that psychiatrists err when they generalize from experiences with a somewhat atypical clientele. Patients may be promiscuous, but most of the population is not.

How can we understand the relationship between mental health and permissive sexual behavior? Is it possible that casual sexual behavior can cause girls to be mentally ill? Or does being mentally ill make one more susceptible to free and easy sex? Or does some third factor have a causative influence upon both permissive sexuality and mental illness?

There is certainly a great deal of support for the latter two hypotheses, particularly for the proposition that poor mental health makes one more susceptible to frequent sexual contacts of a promiscuous nature. Martin Loeb has noted that teen-agers who trust themselves, who can contribute to others, and who can rely on others tend to have the least number of sexual relationships before marriage.[7] Maslow has described the sexual behavior of very healthy "self-actualized" people and notes that they have fewer premarital sexual contacts than less successful people. Their attitude seems to be, "We don't need sex but we enjoy it when we have it." Maslow points out that self-actualized people enjoy sex more than others but consider it less essential in their total frame of reference.[8] My own observations of highly disturbed delinquent girls suggest that their promiscuity is determined by primitive neurotic needs and is only one symptom of a pervasive emotional disturbance.[9] These girls seek multiple sexual experiences because they have despaired of finding any other means of obtaining nurturance and affection.

It is also possible that a high concordance of sexual permissiveness and mental illness is related to a third factor such as urban sophistication. Conceivably those who are most willing to accept psychiatric treatment are part of an avant-garde who are also willing to enjoy an unrestrained sexual life. Still another possibility is that a willingness to be a mental patient and a willingness to be a casual sexual partner are related to a general sense of alienation. An increasing number of students have rejected the prevailing norms of their own cultures and have not found substitute moralities with which to identify. Such students may be exceptioanlly casual about sex, and the painful effects of their identity diffusion may then be likely to bring them to psychiatrists.

Granted that mental illness may lead to promiscuity or that a third factor may be related to both, to what extent is it possible that liberal sexual behavior might be a *cause* of mental illness? Here we must be wary of circular thinking. The lower classes of society are willing to define promiscuity as "badness," but many members of the middle and upper classes automatically define it as "illness." The social conditioning of an upper- or middle-class girl leads her quickly to accept the patient role once she begins to think of herself as promiscuous. Sociologists and anthropologists might argue that there is no causative relationship between permissive sexual behavior and mental illness but that society simply equates promiscuity with mental illness as a means of enforcing chastity. They would insist that if permissiveness were the norm, promiscuous girls would not be patients.

The sociological argument is partially correct. I believe, however, that promiscuity can still produce emotional problems and that its causative influence is in practical terms relatively independent of current social definitions of normative behavior. The experiences associated with being promiscuous are in themselves stressful and are not conducive to the development of those personality traits generally considered to be characteristic of the "healthy" individual. Furthermore, whether society is right or wrong, it does impose social stresses upon the promiscuous girl which are sufficiently painful to drive her to the mental illness role.

I have noted that those students who are patients have a greater tendency towards promiscuity than the average student. It must be acknowledged of course that not every female patient who has had one or several affairs should be considered promiscuous. However, the kinds of stresses such students experience and the manner in which these stresses drive them towards a patient role will be clarified if we consider the case of one highly promiscuous girl.

Joan, an 18-year-old girl, made a psychiatric appointment the morning after she had slept with the tenth different boy in the space of a year. Sensing something self-destructive about her behavior, she made a pledge to seek help after her tenth affair. She had been depressed and unable to study. Her school performance had deteriorated to the point where she was contemplating leaving school. Joan initially had doubts about accepting the role of patient. She defended her sexual behavior, insisting that it was correct and moral. Although she assumed her parents would not approve of her conduct if they knew about it, she derided their values as "phony" and insincere. She maintained that she had experienced orgasm in every sexual encounter and that each new affair was more exciting than the last.

During the first month of treatment, Joan added two more lovers. When the therapist asked what these affairs meant to her, she stated, "It's just fun, like eating a good meal or seeing a good movie. The boys mean nothing to me; they just enjoy me, and I enjoy them." During this time her school performance continued to deteriorate. She smoked marijuana, drank heavily, and increasingly talked about the meaninglessness of life. As she became more depressed, she began to voice thoughts about suicide.

In the 12th hour of therapy, the patient reported that she had recently slept with a boy whom she actually despised. She was agitated and remorseful. At this point she began seriously to review her sexual history. She had had her initial affair one year earlier with a boy she had thought she loved. When he broke up with her, she had three new experiences in rapid succession. In each case Joan tried to convince herself that she was in love with her boyfriend, and in each case her relationship terminated in less than a month. Joan then decided that she would never sleep with another boy unless their relationship was meaningful. The next three relationships however did not last more than a week. Two of the boys did not even bother to call back after the first date. As Joan related the rest of her history she tearfully stated, "The last few months I've just been kidding myself. I try to convince myself that I really love these boys, but really I'm just scared that if I don't sleep with them no one will even ask me out. I begin to hate myself, but I can't stand the loneliness."

Joan was fortunate in having a successful therapy experience. Eventually she was able to feel better, to improve her school work, and to find a boy whom she married. One interesting aspect of her therapy was that after a year of treatment and after she had found a boy who loved her she admitted that she had previously never experienced orgasm during coitus. At this point she wondered how she could ever enjoy sex with anyone but her fiance and admitted to considerable remorse over earlier sexual experiences.

While I was convinced that Joan's personality problems had made her susceptible to promiscuity, it also seemed clear that her promiscuity had contributed to a state of chronic despair. As with so many girls, Joan's initial intention to associate sex only with love was subverted after the first few affairs. Eventually, sex became for her a remedy for loneliness. Her belief that she was finding intimacy and meaningfulness through sex was painfully recognized as a self-deception. It is difficult to see how Joan could have found intimacy or love. Her relationships were simply too transitory. There was no opportunity to get acquainted with her lovers. At the first argument, the first feeling of disgust or the first incompatibility, separation loomed as the most seductive alternative.

Joan's misery was at least in part related to a pervasive sense of guilt about her sexual activities. A sociologist might argue that Joan's guilt was caused by her restrictive upbringing and society's puritanical attitude toward sex. Indeed, Joan accepted this argument and insisted that her guilt was extraneous to her, a foreign body imposed upon her by a malevolent and self-righteous society. I would contend however that such an argument is a simplistic one insofar as it fails to comprehend the manner in which sex is intimately related to interpersonal processes. I do not believe that sex completely free of guilt is possible in modern society. As an interpersonal act, sex is a vehicle for expressing any type of emotional need humans can experience. In addition to being a source of physical pleasure, the sexual act also fulfills dependent needs, status needs, and aggressive needs. Psychoanalysts (particularly Bergler,[10] Brenman,[11] and Reik[12]) have pointed out how the quest for gratification of such needs comes to be associated with feelings of guilt. The girl who uses sex to combat loneliness, to gain status, or to exploit others cannot avoid a certain amount of guilt. Even if she is able to free herself from religious or moralistic scruples, she must deal with those guilt feelings which are associated with the selfish or aggressive uses of sex.

Furthermore, any dishonesty in the sex act, such as pretending to love while not loving, pretending to be someone else, pretending that her partner is someone else, or even pretending to enjoy the act while not enjoying it, can lead a normal person to feel guilty. The partner who constantly feels that she takes more than she gives will also be uneasy. So will the person who uses a moderately deviant fantasy to stimulate her sexual interest. In this day and age we have even invented new guilts, namely guilt for being unattractive or guilt for not having orgasm. It is unlikely that even the marriage contract does much more than attenuate these feelings. It would seem that all of the kinds of guilty feelings I have described are more likely to occur in a promiscuous relationship. To the extent that a girl such as Joan accepts the new sexual attitudes and actively seeks sex without guilt, she deceives herself and runs the additional risk of feeling more guilt simply because she knows she *is* guilty.

Another adverse effect of promiscuity, which is apparent in Joan's case, is that more sexual freedom for women has not been accompanied by an elevation of their status as women. The double standard is still with us. I have never heard a single phrase from any student, male or female, which suggests that girls were more esteemed as important and worthwhile persons because of their enlightened sexual attitudes. At the same time, I have seen many patients who abandoned career aspirations once they began to be involved with multiple partners. Unfortunately the sexually permissive girl comes to see herself as more of an object and less of an equal partner. At the same time, she is given more responsibility than ever before for prevention of pregnancy and is probably less able than girls of previous generations to count on the help of her boyfriend if she is impregnated. In effect, she is valued by men for her sexual capacities and for these alone. Social conditions may of course change, but the present trends toward sexual permissiveness have not liberated women; they have only strengthened the feminine mystique.

We might also note that a repetitive break with the rules of society pushes the promiscuous girl closer and closer to alienation from society. As her self-esteem declines and as she becomes more accustomed to rule-breaking behavior, she desperately seeks rationalization for her conduct. These are most easily found in attacks upon the entire social code. An overdetermined attack on the beliefs of the older generation moves the promiscuous girl further and further away from her own past. She begins to lose perspective on that part of her own history which identifies her with her society. Such alienation is highly correlated with feelings of powerlessness, with abdication of responsibility and, ultimately, with a willingness to identify oneself as a patient. Some of these problems are closely related to an increasing tendency of our youth to live in the present, to deny fidelity to past values, and to despair of hope in the future. Promiscuous sex contributes to such tendencies by its immediacy. It calls for gratification "now" and denies the possibility of better days ahead. Very few promiscuous girls look forward to a better sexual relationship after marriage. While it is difficult to determine which causes which, promiscuity is usually linked with alienation and seems to encourage withdrawal from social responsibility.

May[13] has defined Puritanism as a separation of passion and sexuality. May believes that the old puritans were passionate but not sexual and that many of our students are new puritans in the sense that they are sexual but not passionate. Certainly in the case of Joan and other promiscuous girls it is difficult to find the kind of passion and commitment that is characteristic of deeply involved people. The new sexuality does seem to be frighteningly sterile. An emphasis on orgasm pervades all age groups in our society. Among university students, the search for the ultimate orgasm has become almost a competitive matter. In Joan's case, it took over a year of therapy before she could admit her relative virginity. In our age, this has become the ultimate confession. I have seen other girls who admitted cheating, stealing, masturbating, and promiscuity with little shame but who wept violently when they confessed that they could not have orgasms.

While promiscuous girls emphasize the importance of orgasm, they are often too immature to actively desire or enjoy sexual intercourse. They are ahead of themselves in the sense that they could enjoy intensive petting, but actual coitus is perceived as alien and frustrating. One of my promiscuous patients stopped taking her birth control pills because of medical problems. Knowing that she could not have intercourse without risking pregnancy she settled for heavy petting on her next date. During an intense petting period she experienced an extremely satisfying orgasm, the first she had ever had outside of masturbation.

The stresses of promiscuity are indeed intense. Not only is the promiscuous girl denied intimacy and plagued with guilt and alienation, but she is often limited in her capacity to feel physical pleasure. Furthermore, she feels obligated to convince herself that she does experience pleasure and is likely to be guilty if she does not. If she feigns orgasm, her guilt is even greater.

The borderline girl

Let us now leave the problems of the promiscuous girl and consider the girl who believes that intercourse before marriage is morally justified only if it is always associated with love and commitment. What pressures does such a girl wrestle with, and how are these pressures related to her mental health?

In lengthy question and answer sessions following informal talks to female students, I have become convinced that the new sexual attitudes are having a significant influence upon all female students. More girls may not be indulging in premarital intercourse, but more girls feel pressured to do so.

The mass communication media in our country have a tendency to emphasize the most extreme forms of social behavior and to present them as the norm. Our students receive a heavy bombardment of *Playboy* philosophies which argue for the enjoyment of sex for the sake of physical pleasure alone. There are few social forces counteracting these philosophies. Even our religious leaders are modifying their pleas for rigid adherence to premarital chastity. Our youths seem to have accepted a number of questionable beliefs which serve to perpetuate these pressures. For example, many of the girls I have spoken to believe that physical frustration per se is psychologically unhealthy. They are convinced that petting without orgasm will be unhealthy for them and their partners. They continue to believe that there is an erotic health-producing quality to orgasm during intercourse which is not available through masturbation. While this belief is not supported by any current research, it nevertheless continues to exert a powerful influence.

Many girls also fear that denying their sexual charms to boys is a sign of selfishness. In an age where students are deeply concerned with communicating and cutting through one another's defensiveness, the act of intercourse is valued as an easy means to such goals. Not infrequently, the girl who retains chastity is accused of emotional coldness, of not trying to be an open person. Finally, most girls believe that there is more sexual activity taking place than is actually the case. If they do not participate, they see themselves as atypical and strange.

There are other highly varied pressures which produce conflict in the girl who wishes to make a rational decision as to premarital intercourse. Many girls simply feel that they will lose their boyfriends if they do not sleep with them. Others have convinced themselves that technical "know-how" is important for a successful sex life and that experience before marriage will make them better wives. Finally, the Vietnam conflict has had a deep impact upon people of draft age. Some girls out of guilt, compassion, or love feel obligated to give themselves to those who could lose their lives. The phrase, "Make love; not war" is a political slogan, but in this day and age it is also an effective argument for sexual permissiveness. All of these pressures produce conflict in the girl who wavers between chastity or fidelity and greater sexual freedom. Sometimes the conflict is directly related to the development of psychiatric difficulties.

Barbara, an 18-year-old freshman student, came to the clinic because of nervousness, depression, and inability to study. She was unable to sleep, had lost weight, and was becoming increasingly preoccupied with the meaninglessness of life. Barbara had received a Fundamentalist Protestant upbringing with strict sanctions against premarital sex. In spite of this, she had engaged in one prolonged and satisfying affair with her high school sweetheart. She had hoped to marry the boy, but he eventually rejected her.

In the course of her first interview, Barbara revealed that she had been assigned to a dormitory with girls who took a decidedly casual attitude toward sex. Her closest friends, including her roommate, were all promiscuous. She suspected that her friends were emotionally disturbed people, but she liked them and she was deeply impressed by them. As the semester progressed and Barbara learned more about her friends' sexual activities, she began to question her own values. She had always had a strong need for group identifications and a wish to be an "in" person. When her friends chided her as prudish, old-fashioned, and selfish she felt despondent. She was tempted to sleep with boys, but her early upbringing made it impossible to adopt a liberal attitude towards sex without experiencing enormous guilt. Faced with such conflicts, she became increasingly anxious and depressed. By the time she came to the psychiatrist, she was beginning to move toward withdrawal and alienation.[11]

It can be argued that Barbara was an immature girl who would have had difficulties irrespective of the social climate or her fortuitous association with promiscuous dormitory mates. I am not convinced. In a different era, or even in a different dormitory, Barbara's conflict would have been less intense. She had been exposed to a social climate in which the pressures for liberal sexuality were as great as or greater than the pressures for chastity. She was not experienced enough nor had she developed a sufficiently stable identity that she could resolve her conflict by selecting a value system which was congruent with her own sense of self.

Not all girls, of course, are as intensively exposed to subcultures of promiscuity as Barbara. Nevertheless, this subculture does exist on our campuses, and its influence is greater than would be anticipated from the size of its membership. Promiscuous girls are often seen as representing the vanguard of a new and better morality. They are not looked down upon by chaste girls (although interestingly enough, they themselves are quite contemptuous of those who are not promiscuous). Newspapers, periodicals and television describe them as the "new breed," as the "now people," and impressionable youngsters take these images seriously. In such a climate premarital intercourse can be enforced upon a girl in a manner not too dissimilar from that in which chastity was enforced upon girls in an earlier generation. Under such pressures, many girls like Barbara experience intense conflict which cannot be resolved without psychiatric assistance.

The problems of virginity

Psychiatric problems associated with efforts to retain virginity until marriage are not too different from those seen in the past. Psychiatrists still see patients whose depression and psychosomatic disorders appear to be directly related to repression of sexual drives. Of course the pressures against virginity are greater today, and a girl may have to develop rigid and highly maladaptive defenses if she wishes to remain chaste. Virginal girls are also tempted to exploit men into committing themselves to a more permanent relationship. This is especially true among those girls who espouse an "everything but" philosophy, who engage in heavy petting but stop at the point of intercourse.

Perhaps a new trend is indicated by a few girls who come to psychiatrists and present virginity as a problem. Such girls accept a moral code which condones pre-marital intercourse but find that they are unable to go through with the act when partners are available. It does seem in this day and age that girls who remain virgins (unless they have strong backing in religious beliefs) are likely to worry about their normality. The questions I hear in discussion sessions indicate some shame over virginity. It is as though the virginal girl fears that in remaining chaste she fails to prepare herself for the responsibility of love and marriage.

The problems of boys

I have said little about the impact of changes in sexual attitudes upon the mental health of boys. From a moral standpoint there has been little concern about boys. Neither those who advocate liberalism nor those who favor a double standard worry much when boys have abundant opportunities for sex. Yet there are a few aspects of the new sexuality that seem to have an adverse effect upon male students.

One problem is again created by the mass communication media which suggests that sex is everywhere available. There are dozens of sources telling boys that girls are more promiscuous than ever. The boy who chooses to abstain or who has difficulty in finding a partner feels more freakish than ever. When boys do have an opportunity for sex they sometimes take a desperately exploitative attitude toward their partners. Some of the competitive aspects of the new sexuality are manifested in a mechanical striving for perfection. Our clinic sees an increasing number of unmarried men who complain of impotence, premature ejaculation, and inability to have an ejaculation. My impression is that male patients feel under more pressure than ever before to prove themselves through the sex act. Many experience difficulty simply because they are more interested in the statusful than in the tender aspects of lovemaking.

Efforts to prove masculinity through multiple conquests are still common.

Those boys who are able to become part of the promiscuous subculture find it convenient to pursue sex as a kind of aggressive game. Many male students are tempted to postpone commitment to one person. Instead they lead the kind of life advocated by the *Playboy* philosophy. In earlier years some of these men might have been seduced into marriage in order to gain sexual gratification. While this old-fashioned resolution was unhealthy for some, it may have been quite healthy for others. Today, a man who fears closeness to or intimacy with a woman has fewer opportunities to resolve his problems. The casualness of his sexual encounters precludes his desiring or becoming entrapped in a relationship which might have eventually resolved his fears of intimacy.

Conclusions

It is far too early to evaluate the psychological consequences of our sexual revolution. I would, however, like to make a few observations.

First, it seems clear that changes in sexual attitudes and practices do have an influence upon the mental health of some students. The nature of this influence however is too complex to allow for generalizations as to whether a given practice is either good or bad for people. Psychiatrists at one time impugned Victorian sexual attitudes and considered them an important cause of mental illness. They advocated more permissiveness and our society has moved toward more permissiveness. And what has happened? Our patient load has not decreased, yet the majority of our youthful patients are not repressed nor inhibited people. Rather, today's patient is characterized by a high degree of sexual freedom and self-indulgence. The proposition that gratification of sexual needs is highly correlated with mental health seems to be at least questionable.

While I have pointed out the manner in which permissive sexual practices can potentiate mental illness, it would be equally dangerous to conclude that permissive sexual behavior is universally unhealthy. It may be true that our promiscuous patients are unhealthy, but there may be many promiscuous girls who never visit psychiatrists who are quite happy. The psychiatrist simply lacks information about the population as a whole. Until we know much more than we do now, we would be wise to stop generalizing about the relationship of sex to mental health.

At the same time that a psychiatrist must be wary of generalization, once he confronts a patient as an individual he does have some responsibility to help that person decide what is right or wrong. How does he do this? If we were to try to describe an ethical principle by which psychiatrists operate, we would have to include the psychiatrist's commitment to help the patient do what is best for himself, that is, to help the patient lead the most gratifying and most useful life without inflicting pain upon himself or others. Confronted with new sexual attitudes and practices which impose new stresses upon his patients, the psychiatrist finds that he often must interpose himself between a "thou shalt not" and an "anything goes" philosophy. He does this by repeatedly asking his patient, "Are you being honest with yourself? Will this behavior hurt you or those you love? Will it be good for you? Is it really what you want?"

A final consideration is whether psychiatrists or other physicians can help prevent mental illness which is associated with the sexual revolution. Certainly, providing sexual information which is not sensationalized, exaggerated, or contaminated by myth will help many young people make rational decisions about their future conduct. There may also be more specific preventative measures which discourage aimless and unsatisfying promiscuity.

A girl is most vulnerable to promiscuity shortly after she terminates a sexual relationship with her first lover. She has usually elected to give up her virginity because of a commitment to a boy she eventually hopes to marry. When she discovers that their relationship will not be permanent, she experiences a sense of depression over her loss and a sense of freedom from conventional restraints. Both factors militate towards promiscuous sexuality. It would be desirable for every young person who has just terminated an intense sexual relationship to have some opportunity for professional counseling. Perhaps an even more important need is to help our youth understand those conditions which favor and those conditions which interfere with a permanent relationship. If students were more capable of gauging the depth of commitment in their relationships, they would be in a better position to make the initial decisions as to their premarital sexual behavior.

REFERENCES

1. Reiss, I.: The Sexual Renaissance: A Survey and Analysis. *J Soc Issues* **22**: 123–137 (April) 1966.
2. Kinsey, A. C., et al: *Sexual Behavior in the Human Female.* Philadelphia: W. B. Saunders Co., 1953.
3. Ehrmann, W.: *Premarital Dating Behavior.* New York: Henry Holt & Co., Inc., 1959.
4. Freedman, M. B.: The Sexual Behavior of American College Women, *Merrill Palmer Quart* **11**:33–48 (Jan) 1965.
5. Grinder, R. E., and Schmidt, S. S.: Coeds and Contraceptive Information, *J Marriage Family*, **28**:471–479 (Nov) 1966.
6. Christensen, H. T.: Scandinavian and American Sex Norms: Some Comparisons With Sociological Implications, *J Social Issues* **22**:60–75 (April) 1966.
7. Loeb, M. B.: *Social Roles and Sexual Identity in Adolescent Males.* Casework Papers. National Association of Social Workers, New York, 1959.
8. Maslow, A.: *Motivation and Personality.* New York: Harper & Bros., 1954.
9. Halleck, S. L.: *Psychiatry and the Dilemmas of Crime,* New York: Harper & & Row, Publishers, Inc., 1967.

10. Bergler, E.: *The Basic Neurosis.* New York: Grune & Stratton, Inc., 1949.
11. Brenman, M.: On Teasing and Being Teased, *Psychoanal Stud Child* 7: 264–285, 1952.
12. Reik, T.: *Masochism in Modern Man,* New York: Farrar Straus & Co., 1941.
13. May, R.: Antidotes for the New Puritanism, *Saturday Rev.* March 26, 1966, pp. 19–20.

[30] *Carlfred B. Broderick* SOCIAL HETEROSEXUAL DEVELOPMENT AMONG URBAN NEGROES AND WHITES

Most research on the development of heterosexuality is concerned either with the earliest or the latest stages in the process. The focus is either on the problem of sex role learning and identification among young children, or on the sexual and social dilemmas of later adolescence and early adulthood. The purpose of this paper is to compare patterns of social heterosexuality of Negroes and whites during the relatively uncharted middle period from ten through 17 years of age.

In the larger study from which these data were drawn, four major components of social heterosexual development have emerged. The first component of heterosexual orientation is a positive attitude toward the general subject of romantic interaction with the opposite sex. This diffuse approval is reflected, for example, in one's enjoyment of romantic movies or in one's positive attitude toward marriage. The second component builds upon the first and involves an emotional attachment to some particular member of the opposite sex. Items on whether a boy has a girlfriend or has been in love get at this factor. At the earlier ages, these items most often index emotional rather than social involvement, since the level of reciprocation is typically very low. At the later ages, they more often are associated with reciprocal social behavior as well as feelings. The third component might be negativelyl defined as the absence of social prejudice toward the opposite sex as a class of persons. This social openness is expressed primarily in sociometric items, although items on playing games at parties also bear on it since this would necessarily involve mixed parties. The

FROM *Journal of Marriage and the Family,* 1965, 27, 200–203. REPRINTED BY PERMISSION OF THE AUTHOR AND THE NATIONAL COUNCIL ON FAMILY RELATIONS.

fourth and most advanced component of social heterosexuality during this age span involves actual social interaction on a romantic pair basis. This component of heterosexuality is tapped by questions on such interactions as serious kissing, dating, and going steady.

For the purpose of comparing the two racial groups, a simple index of social heterosexuality was developed from the nine questionnaire items used as examples above. These nine were chosen from a much larger number of items on a self-administered questionnaire to represent all of the four basic components of heterosexuality and to show evidence of construct validity; that is, each item differentiated between the sexes or among ages or communities in a meaningful way and related consistently to other variables. The exact wording and derivation of each item is given in Table 1.

Based on his responses to these items, each individual was assigned a social heterosexuality score. These scores ranged from zero to nine depending on how many of his responses were positive (heterosexual). A score of nine would indi-

TABLE 1 Nine Items Contributing to the Social Heterosexuality Score

---

1. "Would you like to get married someday?" *Yes* response was scored as positive, *No* and *Don't Know* were scored as negative.

2. Under a cartoon showing a group of boys and girls watching a love scene (a couple embracing) on the screen of a movie theater, the questions: "How do the boys feel about what they are seeing?" and "How do the girls feel about what they are seeing?" The responses concerning one's own sex group were considered a measure of one's own attitude. They were coded as *positive* (they enjoy it; they wish they were doing that) or *other,* which included a range of negative, neutral, and conditional responses.

3. "Do you have a girlfriend now?" (Or "Do you have a boyfriend now?" for the girls.) *Yes* or *No.*

4. "Have you ever been in love?" *Yes* or *No.*

5. "Name your best friend" and "List any others you like almost as well." (Five spaces were provided in all.) This item was scored positively if one or more members of the opposite sex were listed among the friends.

6. "Sometimes people play kissing games at some of their parties. Have you ever played kissing games?" *Yes* or *No.*

7. "Kissing in kissing games is usually just for fun. At other times a kiss may mean something special. Have you ever seriously kissed a girl?" ("A boy," if the respondent was a girl.) *Yes* or *No.*

8. "Have you ever had a date?" *Yes* or *No.*

9. "How many times have you gone steady?" *Once* or *more often* were counted as positive responses.

---

cate that the individual definitely wanted to get married someday, he liked the love scenes in movies, he had a girlfriend, he had been in love, he had named at least one member of the opposite sex among his five closest friends, he had played kissing games at parties, he had seriously kissed a girl on his own initiative, he had begun to date, and he had gone steady at least once. Someone with a score of zero, on the other hand, would have felt or experienced none of these things.

Sample

The sample consisted of 1,262 young people. It included all the fifth through twelfth graders attending school within the district on the day the study was made. The area in which these young people lived is part of the industrial complex of a middle-sized Pennsylvania city. Its economy is dominated by heavy industry and by a nearby military installation of some size.

Just over one quarter of the sample were Negroes. The primary ethnic origins of the white families were Eastern European. Although they lived in the same community, sent their children to the same schools, and derived their income from the same employers, there were several important differences between the circumstances of the Negro and white families in the sample.

Most fathers of both races were blue-collar workers, and although there were members of both races in each occupational category, Negroes were underrepresented among the foreman, skilled, and semi-skilled and overrepresented among the unskilled. The difference in occupational distribution of the two groups was significant at the .001 level.

In addition to these occupational differences, there were important differences in the family composition of Negroes and whites in the sample. Thirty-five percent of the Negro families had been broken by either death, divorce, or separation, whereas only 13 percent of the white families had been disrupted (the difference is significant at the .001 level). The sibling constellations of the two groups were also quite different. The proportion of only children among the white subjects was almost twice as great as among the Negro subjects (17 percent compared to nine percent). On the other hand, nearly twice as many Negro as white subjects reported having both brothers and sisters (60 percent compared to 36 percent). These figures indicated that the Negro subjects came from large families far more often than the white subjects.

Since there were these substantial socioeconomic and familial in addition to racial differences between the two groups to be compared, it might be argued that any difference in the pattern of social heterosexual development of Negroes and whites might be explained solely on the basis of these uncontrolled background factors. Unfortunately, with the present sample it was not possible to control on these factors (occupation, family stability, and family size) because the numbers in some cells would have become too small. It was possible, however, to test for the independent influence of these factors within one race (the white race) by examining the relationship of each background variable to each of the nine items of the social heterosexuality score. Only one item, attitude toward marriage, was significantly related to these background factors. Children from white-collar homes and from stable families were significantly more positive in their attitudes toward marriage than were children from blue-collar or broken homes. This relationship probably helps to explain why Negroes had a substantially lower percentage of postive responses than whites on this item and on no other item. This cannot, however, account for the results reported below since its effect is to reduce rather than to exaggerate the overall relationship between race and heterosexuality reported in this paper.

For purposes of comparison, each of the races was subdivided by age groupings (10–11, 12–13-, 14–15-, and 16–17-year-olds) and by sex. Table 2 indicates the manner in which the 1,262 subjects were distributed among the resulting 16 groups. Ten-year-olds were underrepresented since any below the fifth grade level were not included in the sample. Sixteen- and 17-year-olds were also underrepresented due to substantial school dropouts at these ages.

TABLE 2 Total Number in Each Analytical Cell

AGE	WHITE		NEGRO	
	Boys	Girls	Boys	Girls
10–11	79	77	25	37
12–13	143	104	49	47
14–15	166	154	52	50
16–17	100	98	46	35
Total	488	433	172	169

All significance statements for the remainder of the paper are based on simple t-tests or Chi-square tests, whichever is appropriate. The .05 level of significance is accepted throughout.

Findings

The mean social-heterosexuality scores for each of the 16 groups described above are presented graphically in Figure 1. It can be seen that among the whites, girls were significantly more heterosexual in their social orientation than boys at every age. In fact, at every age the mean score for white girls is higher than the mean score for boys two years older than themselves. An

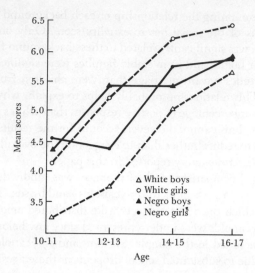

FIGURE 1. Mean Social Heterosexual Scores of Negroes and Whites by Sex and Age.

Differences between means are significant at or beyond the .05 level as follows: (a) between white boys and white girls at every age, (b) between Negro boys and Negro girls at ages 12–13, and (c) between Negro boys and white boys at age 12–13.

analysis of the particular items which contribute to this overall sex difference (Table 3) shows that girls gave more heterosexual responses than boys on wanting to get married (significant at every age), claiming a boyfriend/girlfriend (significant at every age), having been in love (significant at 10–11 and 12–13), and having kissed "when it meant something special" (significant at 12–13 and 14–15). Except for the kissing item, these items all involve romantic attitudes rather than social behavior; and it is worth noting that despite the striking sex differences on these items, there were no corresponding differences on involvement in kissing games, cross-sex friends, dating, or going steady.

This same sex differential was observed among Pennsylvania rural and suburban white youth involved in other phases of the larger project, and was observed also in a middle-class white Southern sample reported earlier.[1] As can be seen in Figure 1, however, urban Negro subjects did not conform to the usual pattern. Negro boys did not trail Negro girls in their heterosexual orientation or involvement. In fact, the only significant difference between the sexes was at 12–13, when the boys' mean score exceeded the girls'. At that age, the Negro boys, significantly more often than the girls, reported having a girlfriend/boyfriend, having begun to date, and having gone steady (Table 3). The latter two in particular involve heterosexual social interaction rather than romantic fantasy. The Negro boys also are significantly more heterosexually oriented than white boys at ages 12–13. (The difference approaches significance

TABLE 3 Percent of Positive Responses to Each Item by Age, Sex, and Race

ITEM—AGE	WHITE		NEGRO	
	Boys	Girls	Boys	Girls
1. Marriage				
10–11	57	87a	71	76
12–13	63	89ab	60	74
14–15	61	90a	67	85
16–17	77bc	90a	58	84a
2. Romantic Movie				
10–11	45	80a	68b	70
12–13	53	82a	75b	73
14–15	62	83a	83b	78
16–17	62	88a	62	79
3. Girlfriend/Boyfriend				
10–11	49	68a	65	64
12–13	49	66a	71ab	51
14–15	45	76a	58	72c
16–17	46	78a	62b	71
4. Love				
10–11	39	60a	46	57
12–13	47	62a	60	48
14–15	60c	72b	57	67
16–17	61	69	67	67
5. Cross-Sex Friend				
10–11	31	29	52	54b
12–13	30	38	48b	45
14–15	54c	59c	49	58
16–17	60	71	81bc	75
6. Kissing Games				
10–11	49	53	68	62
12–13	61c	81ac	92bc	72
14–15	80c	83	87	84
16–17	83	78	85	86

TABLE 3 Continued

ITEM—AGE	WHITE		NEGRO	
	Boys	Girls	Boys	Girls
7. Serious Kiss				
10–11	22	21	38	39b
12–13	28	41ac	51b	48
14–15	50c	62a	62	65
16–17	72c	73	79a	59
8. Date				
10–11	20	18	16	20
12–13	30	29	49abc	21
14–15	69c	70bc	69ac	48c
16–17	89c	82c	93c	88c
9. Steady				
10–11	27	17	40	27
12–13	34	46ac	59ab	34
14–15	49c	57	58	44
16–17	59	66	63	51

a Significant difference between the sexes ($p < .05$).
b Significant difference between the races ($p < .05$).
c Significant difference from previous age ($p < .05$).

at ages 10–11 also.) The items differentiating them are the same as those setting the Negro boys apart from the Negro girls at that age, with the addition of the romantic movie, cross-sex friends, and the two kissing items. These differences may reflect the fact that Negro boys tend to be sexually involved at an earlier age than white boys. The difference effectively disappears at ages 14–15, by which age it may be assumed that the white boy has caught up with his Negro counterpart.

One additional observation might be made about the item on attitude toward marriage. It was mentioned earlier that lower-class status and unstable home life tended to be associated with negative feelings about the desirability of getting married someday. Nevertheless, among white subjects of every class, attitude toward marriage tended to become more positive at each age. This pattern held not only in his community, but in all of the other communities studied in the larger project. It held for the Negro girls in the present sample. Among the

Negro boys, however, the reverse held true. As can be seen in Table 3, at 10–11, 71 percent of these boys felt sure that they wanted to get married some day; at 12–13, the percentage had dropped to 60 percent; and, after a brief rally at 14–15 (back to 67 percent), it dropped finally to 58 percent at 16–17. This suggests a process of progressive disillusionment with marriage among teen-age Negro boys in this community. It seems probable that high levels of unemployment among Negro males help to make the acceptance of family responsibility unattractive. The prominence of matrifocal family patterns among lower-class Negro families might also contribute to the negative attitude toward marriage which these data reveal. If longitudinal research confirms the reality and universality of this progressive disillusionment, it may help to clarify the dynamics of marital instability among Negroes.

Summary and conclusions

Questionnaire data were collected from 341 Negro and 921 white 10–17-year-olds living in the same urban industrial community. An index of social heterosexuality was developed which permitted interracial comparisons by sex and by age. The most striking difference between the races occurred during the pre-adolescent and pubescent ages of 10–13 years. At these ages, the white children showed the traditional pattern, with girls far more romantically oriented than boys although at about the same level in terms of actual heterosexual interaction. Negro boys, however, showed none of the heterosexual reserve of the white boys. They did not trail the Negro girls on any item except attitude toward marriage and, in fact, showed a higher level of heterosexual interaction at 12–13 than the girls did. This high level of preadolescent heterosexual interest and involvement among Negro boys, together with an apparent progressive disenchantment with marriage, suggests that the pattern of sociosexual development in the Negro subculture may differ markedly from that of the dominant culture.

The present study, depending on cross-section analysis and self-administered questionnaires, has been able to indicate only the broad outline of developmental patterns in the two races over the span of the important "middle" years. Further explication of the process must await longitudinal data and depth interviews.

REFERENCES

1. C. B. Broderick and S. E. Fowler, "New Patterns of Relationships between the Sexes Among Preadolescents," *Marriage and Family Living*, 23 (February 1961), pp. 27–30. See also C. B. Broderick, "Socio-Sexual Development in a Suburban Community," *Journal of Sex Research* 2 (April 1966), pp. 1–24.

EIGHT THE ADOLESCENT'S
ADJUSTMENT TO SCHOOL

For years, many concerned parents, educators, and psychologists have recognized that the secondary schools, rather than easing the problems of intellectual, emotional, social, and physical development, often complicate the normal course of adolescent development due to such factors as: pressure to achieve, competitiveness, overemphasis on cognitive development, and conflict between the individual and outdated educational methods and school goals. Adolescence and the secondary school are closely interrelated because an increasingly larger proportion of youth today spends more years than ever before in schools ill-equipped to handle the physical and psychological needs of adolescents. School laws keep the adolescent in school until he is at least sixteen. Some states have attempted to raise the minimum compulsory attendance age; other states extend the public school system upward into junior college. In addition, social custom, which demands high school and college diplomas as preparation for most employment opportunities and as a prerequisite for social mobility, forces adolescents to remain in school long past the age of physical maturity. At the same time, peer-group pressures to excel in areas exclusive of academics, such as sports, extracurricular activities, and dating, tend to alienate many adolescents from the entire realm of scholarship. The status and prestige accorded to the boy by his peers is based much less on his academic accomplishments than on his athletic prowess, physical strength, courage, and leadership qualities; for the girl it is influenced by her good looks, personality, and ability to socialize. Consequently the behavior valued and reinforced by the peer group may be quite different, if not in conflict with, the behavior valued and reinforced in the classroom by the teacher. Edgar Z. Friedenberg and Paul Goodman, two critics of the contemporary high school, condemn especially the rigid structure and the traditional curriculum as inadequate for the adolescent's need for self-control, responsibility, freedom, and relevancy. It is to this dilemma, and to the related problems of academic achievement, parental pressure, outmoded curricula, racial integration, and adolescent mental health, that the researchers and theorists represented in this section address themselves.

The Thomas A. Ringness (31) article, replicating in part an earlier study, compares the adolescent's identification with the father, the teacher, the school, and the peer group with the subject's level of achievement, rated on a scale of high, average, or low. Basing his study on the assumption that "identification is closely related to motivation," Ringness discovers that, although students realize that teachers who demand conformity prefer acquiescent students, most subjects identify with the father and a generalized conception of the school, deriving their motivation from these sources. The study concludes that high achievers perceive the school as significant in helping them develop their talent, while average and low achievers view the school more as a source of vocational preparation. High achievers are independent, admire scholarship, show achievement motivation, and see themselves as close approximations of the ideal of a "good student," while low achievers, who conform strongly to antiacademic peer-group values, often accept a philosophy of mediocrity that aims merely at "getting by." The divergent goals of high and low achievers pose a challenging problem for educators: How can the schools effectively reverse the direction of peer-group values, shifting the emphasis among low achievers from rejection or passive acceptance of academic pursuits to active achievement motivation?

Philip W. Jackson and Jacob W. Getzels (32) pursue further the problem of pupil adjustment by analyzing the factors responsible for satisfaction and dissatisfaction with the academic institution. Studying two groups of students in a Midwestern private school, they find that dissatisfied students do not differ from satisfied students either in school achievement or intelligence test scores. The satisfied students, however, exhibit better mental health as indicated by their responses to various measures of personality adjustment. The dissatisfied group describe themselves as bored, angry, restrained, and dull. Jackson and Getzels draw a distinction between the dynamics of dissatisfaction for girls and for boys. The satisfied students receive more favorable ratings by their teachers than the dissatisfied boys, but not more favorable than the dissatisfied girls. Girls, apparently, handle their dissatisfaction and frustration with school intrapunitively, viewing it as an indication of personal inadequacy, while boys handle their dissatisfaction extrapunitively by criticizing the school and the system and by alienating the teacher. These findings are consistent with the nature of adolescent sex differences as reported by Douvan (26). The finding that psychological rather than academic variables are primarily responsible for an adolescent's dissatisfaction with school suggests that dissatisfied students both in public high school and on college campuses need psychological as well as academic guidance in making their adjustment to their respective institutions.

David Gottlieb and Warren D. TenHouten (33) study the social segregation of Negro and white high school students in three schools of different racial composition. School A has a Negro population of 4.3 percent, school B of 47 percent, and school C of 99 percent. Except in highly structured activities, such as athletics and band-orchestra, which involve little interpersonal contact, the Negro and white students maintain segregation in extracurricular and social activities. The second major finding of the study is that criteria employed for filling leadership positions differ depending on the racial composition of the school. The criterion that students consider important for leadership position in school B, for example, is athletics, especially among the Negro students, whereas in schools A and C participation in the student council is the main route to social status and recognition. Third, although all students agree that the "ability to get along with all types of people" is the major criterion for popularity, there is little racial mixing in informal peer groups. Fourth, in terms of interracial sociometric choices,

Negro students show a higher self-preference than do whites. Fifth, in all three schools, Negroes place greater emphasis on dress and money than do whites. The findings from these three Northern urban high schools demonstrate that the legal integration of a school system does not automatically result in social integration. Gottlieb and TenHouten further point to the fact that the widely neglected field of social organization within the school needs broad and intensive study.

Recognizing that the emotional problems of adolescents are as much the result of the psychological make-up of the individual and pressures in the home and peer group as well as the result of the school, Richard H. Seiden (34) nonetheless maintains that suicide in particular is more prevalent among college students than among young adults who do not attend college. After comparing the subject of student suicides with the total student body population, Seiden concludes that a high proportion of suicidal students are over twenty-five, graduate students, and enrolled in languages and literature, especially English. The undergraduate who is suicidal has a higher grade-point average than the university mean, but is concerned about his own adequacy and his inability to meet the excessively high standards he has set for himself. Clinical diagnoses of suicidal students indicate frequent insomnia, depression, extreme moodiness, despondency, and reports of unusual physical complaints. Contrary to common belief, however, these incidents of suicide increase during the first week of the term rather than during examinations. Seiden relates suicide to factors such as competitive pressure, increasing age of college students, and the changing ratio between graduate and undergraduate students, and predicts "that future increase of student suicides may be expected."

[31]   *Thomas A. Ringness*   IDENTIFICATION PATTERNS, MOTIVATION, AND SCHOOL ACHIEVEMENT OF BRIGHT JUNIOR HIGH SCHOOL BOYS

Identification may be defined as the process of affiliation with one or more other persons, groups, or institutions, which tend to become models. Attitudes, values, and other behavior are imitated, and may be internalized by the imitator.

Identification is closely related to motivation, since one tends to identify

FROM *Journal of Educational Psychology*, 1967, 58, 93–102. COPYRIGHT 1967 BY THE AMERICAN PSYCHOLOGICAL ASSOCIATION, AND REPRODUCED BY PERMISSION OF THE AUTHOR AND THE PUBLISHER.

with those who provide him suitable reinforcers, and, on the other hand, reinforcers become so partly because they are dispensed by those with whom one identifies.

An extended discussion of identification and imitation is provided by Bandura and Walters (1963). Germane to the present study is the generally accepted belief that, in early childhood, both boys and girls tend to identify most closely with the mother. After early childhood, however, the small boy tends to identify with the father and to accept him as a role model; this transition usually takes place by the time the boy reaches school age.

In developing his system of values, attitudes, and motives, the child is exposed to other adult models (such as teachers), and to models in the peer group. He rarely reproduces all of the attributes of any given model, but selects certain ones from each. Accordingly, if identifying figures have many common attributes, there will be a corresponding reinforcing effect and the child's behavior should strongly reflect the consensual elements. If, however, identifying figures portray diverse behaviors, the child's own attributes may vary with the influence of the identifying figures.

In relation to motives to achieve in school, a number of possibilities exist. The boy may or may not identify closely with his father, or with both parents. The parents may or may not value school achievement and reinforce achievement striving. The boy may or may not identify with his teachers. The peer group with which he identifies may or may not value school achievement. Depending, therefore, on the identification patterns of the boy, the values of his models, those he has internalized, and his perception of school, motivation to achieve will vary. It is expected that these variables will be related to differences in academic achievement of children whose abilities and cultural backgrounds are such as to permit above-average school achievement.

In the present study no formal hypotheses were proposed, but questions were raised concerning the extent of the subjects' (Ss') identification with fathers, teachers, and peers, and with acceptance of school values, as these variables related to school achievement.

The research reported here is part of a larger study (Ringness, 1965c). It partially replicates an earlier study (Ringness, 1963, 1965a, 1965b) and is an attempt to confirm or refute previous findings. Certain differences in sampling and instrumentation were introduced so that the two studies are not entirely comparable.

The earlier research employed matched pairs of ninth-grade boys, half of whom attained a grade-point average (GPA) of 3.00 or above (based on a system where A = 4.00) and half of whom attained a GPA of 2.00 or below. The remarks of Thorndike (1963), among others, suggest that failure to include the middle range of achievement might neglect possible curvilinear relationships among data; the present study attempts to compensate for that omission.

Further, the earlier research employed a sample of Ss from an upper-middle socioeconomic status (SES) population. Since parents and youth from this SES may be more oriented toward school achievement than those from other SES classes, there may have been a bias in the earlier data; the present study embodies Ss from all SES classes.

Girls were not studied in either research, primarily because boys show poor school achievement approximately four times as frequently as girls, hence seem to constitute a more pressing problem. In addition, various studies (e.g., McGuire, Hindsman, King, & Jennings, 1961) have shown sex-specific factors related to school achievement.

Related literature

This study does not assume generalized motives to achieve (e.g., McClelland's, 1953, achievement motive). Rather, it is considered that behavior related to school achievement is related to values possessed and reinforcements offered by identifying figures. These may vary among themselves, with resultant influences on motives to achieve in school.

A number of studies have been concerned with the relationships of academic achievement to parent-child relationships. Taylor (1964) surveyed studies of personality traits related to discrepant school achievement. Employing the terms "overachiever" and "underachiever," he found general support for the belief that the overachiever accepts authority and has a good relationship with his parents. The parents tend to be supportive of their children's academic efforts and the children try to please them by doing well academically. Morrow and Wilson (1961) and the Portland Public Schools (1969) found that families of high achievers were more supportive, less authoritarian, and more permissive than families of low achievers; presumably such relationships encourage children's independence and striving behaviors.

However, the dynamics are not entirely clear, for Drews and Teahan (1957) found that domineering mothers tend to foster high achievement in their children, and Taylor notes that some studies suggest that overachievers may be compensating for a lack of love, warmth, or understanding at home. In the latter event, identification with the home might be lacking, but identification with the school might be present.

In contrast to high or overachievers, low or underachievers tend to react against the home and school, and provide more problem behavior for authorities (Frankel, 1960; Gowan, 1955; Ringness, 1963). Taylor found underachievers to be usually regarded as hostile and aggressive toward authorities, and conflict with parents seemed to be carried over to authority figures outside the home. Bandura and Walters' (1959) work on adolescent aggression tends to confirm this belief, and supports the notion that for boys, the father-son relationship may be the most important determiner. The weight of evidence suggests that identification with the home, especially with the father, may be closely related to the school achievement of boys.

Motive to affiliate with peers has been studied extensively. Ringness (1963) found that low achievers were more motivated to affiliate with peers than were high achievers, in contrast to the family orientation and engagement in family activities characterisitc of high achievers. Taylor's review found that over-achievers were more independent, leaderlike, responsible, and dependable than underachievers; the latter tended to identify with a peer group, from which they gained support. Peer group affiliation was seen as a means of gaining some emotional security and as a way of reducing anxiety for underachievers.

McGuire et al. (1961) tend to confirm the notion that low achievers are more dependent on peer-group support, but there is an implication that low achievers are not well accepted by the peer group at large. In a factor-analytic and multiple-regression study of predictors of talent, two independent peer-related factors were isolated. "Peer Stimulus Value" (PSV) was defined as a positive response to pressures imposed by age-mates. Children high in this factor were regarded as models by their peers; they were active, accepted, self-confident, and effective. A person high in the second peer-related factor, "Age-Mate Avoidance," (AMA) was regarded by age-mates as one who dislikes school, gets by, has to be told what to do, does what he feels, yet depends on peers for approval. Impulsivity and avoidance by peers were characteristics of Ss who were deviant and lacked "model value."

A factor of "Socially Oriented Achievement Motivation" (SOAM) was also found. This factor was defined by acceptance of school and cultural stand-ards and by scholastic motivation. Stability, restraint, relatively little criticism of education, and a tendency to be sociable were characteristic of Ss high in this factor.

Finally, there is widespread support in the literature for the idea that high achievers are more motivated to achieve in school than are low achievers (Tay-lor, 1964).

In summary, high achievers tend to identify more with parents, authority figures, and with cultural norms, and they employ socially-accepted behavior. They are motivated to achieve highly in school and gain satisfaction from their school activities. They are independent and leaderlike, and enjoy peer relations without being dependent on peer group support. Low achievers, in contrast, tend to reject parental and school values, resent authority, employ less socially-accepted behavior, are seen as deviant from the peer group, yet tend to lean on the peer group for support.

Procedure

THE SAMPLE

Two Midwestern cities cooperated in this study. The larger city (popula-tion 175,000) includes a state university, is the seat of state government, is a tourist and trade center, and is the home of both heavy and light industry; all

SES classes are present, although the majority of families would be considered of upper-middle or lower-middle SES. The smaller city (population 40,000) is primarily industrial in character; the population tends to lower-middle SES.

An initial sample of 310 eighth-grade junior high school boys was randomly drawn from 18 junior high schools. The Ss met the criterion of California Test of Mental Maturity IQ 120 or above, normal eighth-grade age, normal and comparable class loads, and absence of incapacitating physical defects or gross emotional disturbance. The sample was tested with the WISC, and Ss of IQ 116 or above were retained. Attrition reduced the final sample to 261 Ss.

The final sample was divided into three equal groups of high, average, and low achievers, on the basis of an equal-weight composite ranking of GPAs in the 7th and 8th grades and total score on the Iowa Test of Basic Skills. Complete data were obtained for 88 high, 85 average, and 88 low achievers.

INSTRUMENTATION

Germane to this part of the study are the student interview and card sort. A structured interview with allowance for elaboration by Ss was administered individually. Based on Ringness' (1963) previous study, the interview consisted of 55 questions tapping areas of occupational ambitions, identification with father, identification with teacher, acceptance of school values, peer relations, attitude toward school marks received, out-of-school activities, and attitude toward heterosexual relationships.

A rectangular card sort assessed dimensions of pupil self-report concerning independent behavior, nonconforming behavior, motive to affiliate with peers, and motive to achieve academically. Based on the earlier study, additional items were added to differentiate more clearly between nonconforming and independent behavior, validity of new items being judged by trainees in School Psychology. Eighty items were provided, 20 relating to each dimension. Eight cards were sorted into each of 10 compartments, and represented scores from 1 to 10; low scores represented "most like me" and high scores represented "least like me." Coefficients of internal consistency were .51 for the dimension of independence, .71 for motive to affiliate with peers, .85 for motive to achieve academically, and .93 for nonconforming behavior, as stepped up the Spearman-Brown formula.

Results

THE INTERVIEW

Table 1 presents only the relevant interview data, together with chi-square tests of significance. It should be noted that because responses were sometimes elaborated, a given S's responses might be included in two or more categories so that total responses to an item did not always equal 261.

For many of the data the total responses may be more interesting than the

TABLE 1   Interview Responses of Bright Eighth-Grade Boys ($N = 88$ high, 85 average, and 88 low achievers)

INTERVIEW AREA	NUMBER OF RESPONSES		
	HA	AA	LA
Identification with father			
Frequency of father-son activities:			
Week-ends or oftener	66	66	71
2 or 3 times per month	10	9	8
Once a month	7	3	1*a
Never	1	2	3
Don't know	4	6	5
Attitude toward father:			
Strong admiration	47	42	49
Admire with reservations	29	27	24
Not close	5	9	7
Desire to be different	1	0	1
Strong negative	0	2	1
Don't know	6	6	6
Identification with school			
Values of school:			
Not important	5	3	2
For occupational preparation only	58	75**a	82**a
To develop one's talents	17	2**a	1**a
Only for interest in subjects	8	8	3
Don't know	1	1	0
Values of school for future occupation:			
Very important	51	52	53
Somewhat important	18	14	11
Little or no importance	12	11	10
Don't know	6	9	14
Identification with teacher's values			
Perceived teacher norms for model pupil role:			
Conformity	79	66*a	77
Social competence	2	14**a	9*a
Academic competence	22	14	14

INTERVIEW AREA	NUMBER OF RESPONSES		
	HA	AA	LA
Intellectual liveliness	1	12**a	9*a
Don't know	1	1	3
Attitude toward perceived norms:			
Approve	76	72	75
Indifferent	3	9	9
Dislike	2	3	3
Don't know	7	2	1
Characterization of self like the perceived model:			
Much like model	81	54**a	61**a
A little like model	0	9**a	6*a
Try to be like model	0	10**a	3**b
Unlike model	6	11	11
Don't know	1	1	7
Perceived teacher opinion of S:			
Good, S cares	55	40*a	33**a
So-so, S cares	19	22	29
Poor, S cares	6	8	11
Good, S doesn't care	0	1	2
So-so, S doesn't care	2	2	2
Poor, S doesn't care	0	2	3
Don't know	8	11	7
Peer relationships			
Characteristics of popular peers:			
Athletic	14	7	8
Scholarly	5	0*a	3
Good personality	36	21*a	21*a
Athletic, good personality	20	25	17
Scholarly, good personality	6	9	18*a
Athletic, scholarly	2	5	5
All three	9	18	16
Don't know	4	0*a	4**a
Peer attitude toward good students:			
Admire	49	41	43

TABLE 1 Continued

INTERVIEW AREA	NUMBER OF RESPONSES		
	HA	AA	LA
Indifferent	8	12	8
Depends on personality	15	8	12
Square (negative attitude)	13	22	23
Don't know	3	4	3
Characteristics of S's most admired peer:			
Athletic	6	8	10
Scholarly	26	12*	20
Personality	31	20	25
Athletic, personality	3	3	5
Scholarly, personality	15	10	12
Athletic, scholarly	0	0	0
All three	29	22	20
Social status	0	1	0
No admired peer	2	6	4
Don't know	5	5	6
Peer attitude toward school tasks:			
Work hard as possible	12	13	9
Work little more than is necessary	18	21	15
Work enough to get by	55	47	61**b
Don't know	3	5	3

Note.—All chi-square tests of significance.
a Comparison with high achievers.
b Comparison with average achievers.
* $p < .05$.
** $p < .01$.

differences between groups. For example, Ss in this study enjoy a high frequency of activities with their fathers, and strongly admire them or admire them with some reservation. Ss do not tend to admit to poor father-son relationships and there are no significant differences among achievement groups in this regard.

Although significantly more high than average or low achievers state that school is valuable for helping them develop their talents, and although significantly more average and low than high achievers stress the value of school for vocational preparation, the majority of Ss view school as primarily useful for vocational preparation. Since "vocational preparation" at the eighth-grade level is primarily that of gaining general educational tools, it would seem that (with the exception of a few high achievers) school is more of a routinely-accepted environment than a place which is viewed as important to self-development or which provides interesting content and activities. This, in turn, may be related to the perceived teacher norms for model pupil behavior.

Most Ss state that teachers view the "model pupil" as conforming. For the sample as a whole, academic and social competence and intellectual liveliness fare less well. Although there are statistically significant differences in the ways high achievers differ from average and low achievers as to perceived norms of social competency and intellectual liveliness, it is noteworthy that there is high agreement concerning conformity. By implication, achievers must be conformers, a finding which agrees with those of studies cited earlier.

Differences in achievement are not related to differences in pupil perceptions of teacher expectations, but they are related to attainment of the model pupil role. Although most Ss state that they approve the conformity role, high achievers feel that they are like the model more than do average or low achievers; average and low achievers state significantly more often that they are a little like the model, and average achievers mention that they "try to be" like the model. There are no significant differences in the extent to which achievement groups state that they are unlike the model. Most Ss say that they care how they are perceived by the teacher.

Taken as a whole, these data suggest that most Ss identify well with their fathers and with teachers. They perceive school as a place one attends for vocational purposes, and where conformity is demanded. At this point in their lives they are generally willing to accept the conformity role, and care how they are regarded by their teachers.

In regard to peer relationships it is patent that having a "nice personality" is the most important factor in popularity. Good students are admired by about half the sample, but 35 Ss mention that a good student is popular primarily if he has appropriate personality attributes. Fifty-eight Ss, or about one-fifth of the sample, describe good students as "square" and another 28 are indifferent to scholarship attributes. These findings are also borne out in responses to questions concerning characteristics of most-admired peers. The majority of Ss feel that the effort norm of the peer group is that of doing just enough to "get by," although 54 think most peers do a little more than necessary.

Thus although school norms are perceived as those of conformity and Ss accept this norm and attempt to be like the perceived model, the model is not viewed by the majority as that of intellectual development so much as that of "good behavior." This seems related to the responses which indicate that peer achievement norms are essentially those of "getting by" or doing "just a little more than necessary." Popularity seems to result from possession of a pleasing personality; athletic prowess, scholarship, and other attributes may supplement such personal qualities, but are in themselves not conducive to peer acceptance.

THE CARD SORT

Table 2 presents card sort data, together with two-tailed tests of significance of differences. It will be recalled that scores might range from 1 to 10, with lower scores being "most like me."

It is seen that high and average achievers are less nonconforming or less rebellious than low achievers. On the other hand, high achievers are more independent and autonomous than low achievers.

· High achievers are significantly more oriented toward academic achievement than average achievers, who are significantly more oriented toward achievement than are low achievers. But average and low achievers are significantly more oriented to affiliate with peers than are high achievers.

TABLE 2   Card Sort Data for Bright Eighth-Grade Boys ($N = 88$ high, 85 average, and 88 low achievers)

DIMENSION	SCORES		MEAN DIFFERENCES		
	$\overline{X}$	SD	Groups	Difference	t
Nonconformity:					
High achievers	7.30	.74	H–A	− .02	.17
Average achievers	7.32	.82	H–L	.40	3.64*
Low achievers	6.90	.73	A–L	.42	3.50*
Independence:					
High achievers	4.98	.64	H–A	− .08	.80
Average achievers	5.06	.68	H–L	− .26	2.60*
Low achievers	5.24	.69	A–L	− .18	1.80
Achievement motivation:					
High achievers	4.17	.77	H–A	− .32	2.67*
Average achievers	4.49	.80	H–L	− .81	6.23*
Low achievers	4.98	.90	A–L	− .49	3.77*
Affiliation motivation:					
High achievers	5.15	.96	H–A	.46	3.07*
Average achievers	4.69	1.04	H–L	.60	3.33*
Low achievers	4.55	.87	A–L	.14	.93

* $p < .01$.

Discussion

This study was undertaken partly to confirm or refute findings of an earlier study. In most respects, but not all, confirmation was found. Within the limits of changes in sampling and instrumentation mentioned earlier, some comparison of findings may be made.

In both studies the father was admired, or admired with some reservations, by a majority of Ss; however, the 1963 findings showed that fathers of high achievers spent more time with their sons than did fathers of low achievers, suggesting closer father identification, but this was not found in the present study. It cannot be concluded from the present (and larger) study that father identification differentiates between high-, average-, and low-achieving Ss. There is one possibility, which was not attacked in either study, which might account for the differential findings. It was noted earlier that the prior study dealt with a sample from the upper-middle SES population whereas the present sample dealt with all SES groups. If, as was suggested, upper-middle SES fathers are more oriented toward high scholastic achievement than fathers of other SES groups, differences in the two studies may simply represent differences in parental value-orientations. This tends to confirm McGuire's notion that talent factors are possibly community-bound. At the moment this must be regarded as an area for future research.

In regard to identification with the teacher or with school values, both studies showed Ss to perceive the teacher's concept of the model pupil as one who conforms, or poses no problems in the classroom. In the 1963 study high achievers approved this role concept but low achievers did not; the present data show no significant differences among groups. However, both studies show that high achievers feel that they are more like the role model than are other groups; although most Ss desire to be viewed as like the role model.

Data in both investigations showed that school is viewed by most students as valuable for vocational preparation; however, high achievers more than others saw school as a place to develop one's talents. "Good students" were accepted by about half the Ss in each study; the 1963 data showed that high achievers admired scholars more than did low achievers, but this difference was not found in present data. Good students are characterized as "squares" by about one-fifth of the present sample; in previous data low achievers were more likely to make this statement. In both studies the peer norm for academic achievement was that of doing just enough to "get by."

Both studies showed that high achievers are motivated to achieve academically more than other groups, whereas low achievers are more motivated to affiliate with peers. High achievers are presently found to be independent, whereas low achievers are somewhat nonconforming; this finding appears to document statements of Taylor (1964).

The work of McGuire et al. isolated certain predictors of talent which were noncognitive. Among these were Peer Stimulus Value, Age-Mate Avoidance, and Socially Oriented Motivation. (They also found male-specific factors of Anxious Emotionality and Antisocial Wariness, but these were less clearly specified.) PSV suggests that the talented are likely to be leaderlike, independent, and effective. This is similar to present findings in the card sort that high achievers are more independent than other Ss. PSV, however, suggests that possessors are models for peers. Interview findings of the two studies by Ringness attacked the questions of popularity and "most-admired peers" and it was found that models for these samples were chosen more for "personality" than any other reason.

The AMA factor is similar to card sort findings that low achievers are more nonconforming, yet more affiliation-oriented than high achievers. The SOAM factor is essentially confirmed by both card sort and interview findings that high achievers are motivated to conform to school and adult values, they identify well with home and school, and are academically motivated.

The main difference in the findings of the McGuire and the present study is in the implications in the former that peers tend to admire the talented, whereas in present findings popularity and admiration are associated with achievement primarily by high achievers, when so associated at all. In other respects, although the factors combined attributes of achievers in a somewhat different fashion from the present study, essentially the same characteristics were found; these are also similar to those summarized in Taylor's review.

There seems sufficient evidence to support the conclusion that low achievers identify more with the peer group and are governed more by the peer group than are high achievers. Since the peer norm for achievement is seen as that of mediocrity, and since low achievers state less motivation for academic achievement, it would follow that an important problem to schools is that of finding ways to foster high achievement values in the peer group at large. The image of the scholar as "square" must be erased. It is possible that this image is fostered partly by the fact that a certain percentage of high achievers are not well-rounded persons, lack desirable personality attributes, and are not popular.

The image of the teacher needs revision. He is viewed as demanding conforming behavior, but is not seen as fostering intellectual development or liveliness. Schools are seen as places to prepare for future vocations, but are seen by relatively few as places to develop talents, pursue interest, or to improve social adjustment.

The present study refutes the notion that high achievers identify more with their fathers than do low achievers. However, at junior high school age, parent identification apparently does not provide reinforcements for academic achievement to low achievers to the same extent it does for high achievers. It is possible that differential parent values are operating, and it would seem desirable for school counselors to discuss such matters with fathers of low achievers when the attainments of the latter are of sufficient concern.

One other comment may be justified. It is apparent that the stereotype of school tasks as being necessary evils seems still to exist. Social reinforcements such as teacher praise and blame, grades and marks, and other typical reinforcements provided by the school are not as effective with low achievers as could be wished. The implication is that much more effort needs to be spent on finding other kinds of reinforcers for academic achievement. Efforts to employ concrete reinforcers may provide some clues; efforts to make the curriculum more meaningful to boys like those in these samples may also bear fruit.

REFERENCES

Bandura, A. & Walters, R. H. *Adolescent aggression*. New York: Ronald Press, 1959.

Bandura, A., & Walters, R. H. *Social learning and personality development*. New York: Holt, Rinehart and Winston, 1963.

Drews, E., & Teahan, J. Parental attitudes and academic achievement. *Journal of Clinical Psychology*, 1957, **13**, 328–332.

Frankel, E. A comparative study of achieving and underachieving high school boys of high intellectual ability. *Journal of Educational Research*, 1960, **53**, 172–179.

Gowan, J. C. The underachieving gifted child. *Exceptional Children*, 1955, **21**, 247–249.

McClelland, D. C., Atkinson, J. W., Clark, R. A., & Lowell, E. L. *The achievement motive*. New York: Appleton-Century-Crofts, 1953.

McGuire, C., Hindsman, E., King, F. J., & Jennings, E. Dimensions of talented behavior. *Educational and Psychological Measurement*, 1961, **21**, 3–38.

Morrow, W. R., & Wilson, R. R. Family relations of bright high-achieving and under-achieving high school boys. *Child Development*, 1961, **32**, 501–510.

Portland Public Schools. *The gifted child in Portland*. Portland, Oregon, 1959.

Ringness, T. A. Differences in attitudes toward self and others of academically successful and non-successful ninth-grade boys of superior intelligence. Final report, post-doctoral research fellowship sponsored by National Institute of Mental Health. University of Wisconsin, Madison, 1963. (Mimeo)

Ringness, T. A. Affective differences between successful and non-successful bright ninth-grade boys. *Personnel and Guidance Journal*, 1965, **43**, 600–606. (a)

Ringness, T. A. Emotional adjustment of academically successful and non-successful bright ninth-grade boys. *Journal of Educational Research*, 1965, **59**, 88–91. (b)

Ringness, T. A. Non-intellective variables related to academic achievement of bright junior high school boys. Final report, Cooperative Research Project S–036, United States Office of Education. Madison, Wisconsin, 1965. (c) (Mimeo)

Taylor, R. G. Personality traits and discrepant achievement: A review. *Journal of Counseling Psychology,* 1964, **11,** 76–82.

Thorndike, R. L. *The concepts of over- and underachievement.* New York: Bureau of Publications, Teachers College, Columbia University, 1963.

[32] *Philip W. Jackson & Jacob W. Getzels*

PSYCHOLOGICAL HEALTH AND CLASSROOM FUNCTIONING: A STUDY OF DISSATISFACTION WITH SCHOOL AMONG ADOLESCENTS

The problem of dissatisfaction with school among children is of theoretical and practical significance to both psychologists and educators. At the theoretical level dissatisfaction with school becomes part of a broader area of inquiry which aims at an understanding of the individual's functioning in an institutional setting and which includes studies of staff morale, role conflict, productivity, and the like. At a practical level the question of why children like or dislike school is directly related to the immediate problems of school dropouts, grouping procedures, planning for the gifted child, and the like.

As might be expected, a social phenomenon as important as dissatisfaction with school is not without its explanatory hypothesis. Some of these spring from empirical findings, while others appear to be part of our cultural ethos. Educational studies that point to an empirical linkage between school failure and school dropouts, and industrial studies that demonstrate a relationship between low morale and decreased output, lead one to suspect that reduced effectiveness in school (i.e., low scholastic achievement) would be a natural concomitant of dissatisfaction with the institution. Thus one would expect to find heightened dissatisfaction among students who have low ability or who are unable for one reason or another to deal adequately with scholastic material.

More recently it has been suggested (although never adequately demonstrated) that many successful students with high ability are dissatisfied with their school experiences; the term "boredom" is often linked with the term "gifted child" in current expositions by educators. The boredom problem

FROM *Journal of Educational Psychology,* 1959, *50,* 295–300. COPYRIGHT 1959 BY THE AMERICAN PSYCHOLOGICAL ASSOCIATION, AND REPRODUCED BY PERMISSION OF THE SENIOR AUTHOR AND THE PUBLISHER.

among "gifted" combined with the failure experiences of the low ability child suggests that the greatest number of dissatisfied students is to be found among extreme ability groups. Those who are low in ability and achievement would be expected to show dissatisfaction because of the numerous frustrations they experience in the classroom. Those who are high in ability and achievement would be expected to show dissatisfaction because of the relative lack of stimulation which they experience in the classroom.

Both of these explanations (or, more accurately, hypotheses) contain the implication that dissatisfaction with an institution arises out of the individual's interaction with that institution. An alternative explanation might be that the individual brings a set toward satisfaction or dissatisfaction *to* the institution—that it is a reflection of a more pervasive personal orientation and that success or failure experiences within the institution have a limited influence upon it. This hypothesis obviously places more emphasis than do the earlier ones upon psychological variables, as opposed to environmental variables, in understanding dissatisfaction with school. The research described here was designed to test the relative merit of these alternative views.

Problem

The purpose of this investigation is to examine the differences in psychological functioning and classroom effectiveness between two groups of adolescents—those who are satisfied with their recent school experiences and those who are dissatisfied.

Subjects and procedure

The Ss of this investigation were two groups of adolescents identified from among 531 students enrolled in a Midwestern private school. These students were divided into five class groups ranging from the prefreshmen to the senior year of high school. In this institution a single grade, the prefreshmen, is substituted for the usual seventh and eighth grades. The instrument used to select the experimental groups, called the Student Opinion Poll, was a 60-item opinionnaire designed to elicit responses concerning general satisfaction or dissatisfaction with various aspects of school—viz., the teachers, the curriculum, the student body, and classroom procedures. The following are sample items, one in each of the four areas.

3. While there are some differences among them, most teachers in this school are:
    a. Very inspiring
    b. Quite inspiring
    c. Somewhat inspiring
    d. Not inspiring

16. Most of the subjects taught in the school are:
    a. Interesting and challenging
    b. Somewhat above average in interest
    c. Somewhat below average in interest
    d. Dull and routine
14. From the standpoint of intellectual ability, students in this school are:
    a. Too bright—it is difficult to keep up with them
    b. Just bright enough
    c. Not bright enough—they do not provide enough intellectual stimulation
 5. The freedom to contribute something in class without being called upon by
    the teacher is:
    a. Discouraged more than it should be—students do not have enough op-
    portunity to have their say
    b. Encouraged more than it should be—students seem to be rewarded just
    for speaking even when they have little to say
    c. Handled about right

The instrument was scored by giving one point each time the S chose the
"most satisfied" response to a multiple-choice item. Thus, the possible range of
scores was from 0 to 60. For the total school population the mean score on
the Student Opinion Poll was 37.30; the standard deviation was 9.57. The
experimental groups were chosen as follows:

Group I—the "dissatisfied" group—consisted of all students whose score on
the opinionnaire was at least one and a half standard deviations *below* the mean
of the entire student body. This group contained 27 boys and 20 girls. Group II
—the "satisfied" group—consisted of all students whose score on the opinionnaire
was at least one and a half standard deviations *above* the mean of the entire
student body. This group contained 25 boys and 20 girls.

The experimental groups were compared on the following variables:

 1. *Individual intelligence tests.* In most cases this was the Binet. A small number
    of children were given the Henmon-Nelson, the scores of which were converted
    by regression equation into equivalent Binet scores.
 2. *Standardized verbal achievement test.* The Cooperative Reading Test was used.
    Prefreshmen and freshmen were given Test C_1, Form Y; older students were
    given C_2, Form T.
 3. *Standardized numerical achievement tests.* Because of the differences in the
    curricula of the various grade groups it was not possible to administer the same
    test of numerical achievement to all Ss. The following tests were given according
    to grade placement:
    Prefreshman—Iowa Everypupil Arithmetic Test, Advanced Form O.
    Freshmen—Snader General Mathematics Test.
    Sophomores—Cooperative Elementary Algebra Test, Form T.
    Juniors—Cooperative Intermediate Algebra Test.
    Seniors—Cooperative Geometry Test, Form 2.

4. *California Personality Test.* Two forms of this instrument were used. The intermediate form was given to prefreshmen; the secondary form was given to all of the older groups. Two subscores were obtained, "personal adjustment" and "social adjustment."

5. *Direct Sentence Completion Test.* Ss were asked to complete 27 sentences of the type: "When I saw I was going to fail I . . . . ," or, "I think my father is . . . ." Each sentence was given a plus or minus score depending upon the presence or absence of morbid fantasy, defeatism, overt aggression, and the like. The total score was the summation of the individual sentence scores.

6. *Indirect Sentence Completion Test.* This instrument was identical with the Direct Sentence Completion Test except that proper names were inserted for the pronoun "I," thus changing it from a "self-report" to a "projective" instrument. Boys' names were used in the male form of the instrument and girls' names in the female form. The instrument was presented as a "thinking speed" test. To reinforce this notion Ss were asked to raise their hands when they were finished and the elapsed time was written on their test booklet. This instrument was administered approximately two weeks prior to the administration of the Direct Sentence Completion Test.

7. *Group Rorschach.* Cards III, IV, IX, and X were projected on a screen. For each picture the S was presented with 10 responses and was asked to choose the three which he thought to be most appropriate. Each list of 10 contained four "pathological" responses. The S's score was the number of nonpathologic responses among his 12 choices. This group technique follows that described by Harrower-Erikson and Steiner (1945).

8. *Teacher ratings.* Each student was given three ratings by his present teachers. These ratings included: (a) his general desirability as a student; (b) his ability to become involved in learning activities and (c) his possession of leadership qualities. Teachers were required to place all of their students on a five-point scale so that Categories 1–5 each contained one-twelfth of the students; Categories 2 and 4 each contained one-fourth of the students; and Category 3 contained one third of the students. The values 5, 8, 10, 12, and 15 were assigned to categories and were used in quantifying the ratings.

9. *Adjective Check List.* From a list of 24 adjectives each student was asked to choose the 6 which best described his characteristic feelings while attending classes in particular school subjects. The list contained 12 "positive" (e.g., confident, happy, eager, relaxed) and 12 "negative" adjectives (e.g., bored, restless, misunderstood, angry). The use of the negative adjectives by the experimental groups was analyzed both quantitatively and qualitatively.

Results

With the exception of the adjective check list the results of all comparisons are shown in Table 1. Contrary to popular expectations the "satisfied" and "dissatisfied" students did *not* differ from each other in either general intellectual ability or in scholastic achievement. Those differences which did appear were linked to psychological rather than scholastic variables. More

TABLE 1 Mean Scores, Standard Deviations, and t Statistics for Satisfied and Dissatisfied Adolescents on Dependent Variables[a]

| | BOYS | | | | | GIRLS | | | | |
| | Dissatisfied (N = 27) | | Satisfied (N = 25) | | | Dissatisfied (N = 20) | | Satisfied (N = 20) | | |
	x̄	s	x̄	s	t	x̄	s	x̄	s	t
IQ	134.85	14.58	136.44	14.59	ns	128.45	15.06	128.00	11.45	ns
Verbal Achievement	49.96	8.69	50.68	7.87	ns	50.63	9.11	52.28	6.76	ns
Numerical Achievement	50.35	9.75	52.17	10.52	ns	47.78	8.61	48.50	10.26	ns
Calif. Personal Adjust.	45.58	9.82	53.40	7.63	3.18**	47.90	13.03	54.76	9.25	1.86*
Calif. Social Adjust.	44.85	11.37	51.84	8.93	2.45**	47.00	13.15	55.76	7.89	2.50**
Direct Sentence Comp.	46.93	10.58	49.25	10.02	ns	46.65	12.01	54.00	5.73	2.53**
Indirect Sentence Comp.	47.19	9.61	51.29	6.95	1.75*	49.60	10.35	53.47	7.97	ns
Group Rorschach	48.35	10.66	47.44	10.30	ns	47.35	11.35	54.16	8.32	2.15**
Teacher Rating I: Desirability as a student	8.94	1.83	10.35	1.70	2.85**	9.84	1.91	10.05	1.59	ns
Teacher Rating II: Leadership qualities	9.01	2.08	10.13	1.96	2.00*	9.91	2.37	10.04	1.24	ns
Teacher Rating III: Involvement in learning	9.09	2.14	10.23	1.69	2.14**	9.67	2.32	10.33	2.11	ns

* Significant at the .05 level.
** Significant at the .01 level.

[a] With the exception of IQ, all scores were based upon parameters of the total student body from which the experimental groups were drawn. The scores of all tests were transformed to T scores with a mean of 50 and a standard deviation of 10. For the total population the teacher ratings have a mean of 10 and a standard deviation of 2. The mean IQs for the total school population are: boys, 132, and girls, 128.

specifically, each of the test instruments designed to assess psychological health or "adjustment" was effective in distinguishing "satisfied" from "dissatisfied" students within one or both sex groups.

For both sexes the experimental groups were differentiated by their scores on the California Test of Personality. The experimental groups of boys were further differentiated by their responses to the Indirect Sentence Completion Test. For girls additional differences appeared in their responses to the Direct Sentence Completion Test and the Group Rorschach.

On all of these test variables the "satisfied" group attained the "better" score—i.e., the score signifying a more adequate level of psychological functioning. It is also worthy of note that whenever a significant difference appeared, the mean score of the total student population fell between the mean scores of the experimental groups. Thus, the variables that differentiate the experimental groups tend also to distinguish them from the total population of students.

In addition to showing differences on psychological health variables, "satisfied" and "dissatisfied" boys were perceived differently by their teachers. On all three of the teachers' ratings the "satisfied" boys received more favorable judgments than did "dissatisfied" boys. The fact that this result does not appear to be true for girls lends support to the popular expectation that boys are more likely to express their negative feelings publicly than are girls. This hypothesis receives some confirmation from the results of the adjective check list which are described below.

In Table 2 are shown the number of Ss who chose negative adjectives when asked to describe their typical classroom feelings. As they are arranged in Table 2 the adjectives reflect the rankings of four judges who were asked to rank the words on the degree to which they involved an implicit or explicit criticism of others. The 12 adjectives were typed on separate cards and were accompanied by the following directions:

On the following cards are a number of negative adjectives which a person might use to describe himself. Rank these adjectives on the degree to which they involve an implicit or explicit criticism of others. For each adjective ask the question: If a person used this adjective *to describe himself* would he also be implicitly or explicitly criticizing others? Give a rank of 1 to the adjective which would be *least* critical of others and a rank of 12 to the adjective which would be *most* critical of others.

Four psychologists served as judges. The average rank order correlation among the four sets of judgments was .84. The adjectives are presented in Table 2 according to the ranked sum-of-ranks of the judges. The adjective "inadequate" was judged as being most free of criticism of others, while the adjective "restrained" was judged as involving the greatest amount of criticism of others.

As might be expected, the use of negative adjectives was far more frequent among dissatisfied students than among satisfied students. Four adjectives seemed to discriminate equally well between the experimental groups for both sexes; these were: "bored," "angry," "restrained," and "dull."

An examination of Table 2 also suggests the existence of sex differences in the students' description of their typical classroom feelings. Remembering the classificatory scheme by which the adjectives are ranked in Table 2, it appears that dissatisfied girls are somewhat less likely than dissatisfied boys to use negative adjectives involving implicit criticism of others. Dissatisfied boys, on the other hand, are less likely than dissatisfied girls to be distinguished from their satisfied counterparts by the use of adjectives *not* involving implicit criticism of others. If one thinks of criticism directed towards others within Rosenzweig's schema of "intropunitiveness" and "extrapunitiveness" (Murray, 1945), then the observed sex differences may be conceptualized by saying that dissatisfied girls are more *intropunitive* than satisfied girls; dissatisfied boys are more *extrapunitive* than satisfied boys.

This difference in the direction of aggression may provide a context for the obtained differences in teacher ratings discussed earlier. If the dissatisfied boy is more likely than his female counterpart to lay the blame for his dissatisfaction upon others in his environment, particularly school authorities, it is reasonable to expect that he would be viewed as somewhat less than completely desirable by the classroom teacher. The dissatisfied girl, on the other hand, seems more willing to direct her negative feelings inward, thus avoiding the additional risk of counter-aggression by school authorities or by other adults.

Discussion

Two major conclusions are suggested by the findings of this study. First, dissatisfaction with school appears to be part of a larger picture of psychological discontent rather than a direct reflection of inefficient functioning in the classroom. It is almost as if dissatisfaction were a product of a pervasive perceptual set that colors the student's view of himself and his world. Second, it appears that the "dynamics" of dissatisfaction operate differently for boys and girls. Boys seem to project the causes of their discontent upon the world around them so that adults are seen as rejecting and lacking in understanding. This tendency to blame adults may be one reason why these boys are seen as less attractive by teachers than are satisfied boys. Girls, on the other hand, are more likely to be self-critical, turning blame for their dissatisfaction inward. Feelings of inadequacy, ignorance, and restlessness more sharply differentiate satisfied and dissatisfied girls than is the case with boys. This tendency to be intropunitive may partially explain why teacher ratings fail to distinguish between our two experimental groups of girls.

The atypicality of the same population used in this research places a number of limitations upon the inferential statements which can be made on the basis of these findings. Fortunately, however, the major portion of the investigation has recently been replicated using seventh and eighth grade lower-class Negro adolescents as Ss (Spillman, 1959). The findings of the latter study are essentially the same as those reported here. Again the psychological rather than the intellectual or scholastic variables discriminated between satisfied and dissatisfied students. The findings with respect to the use of negative adjectives were not as clear-cut but, again, every intropunitive adjective was used more frequently by dissatisfied girls as compared with dissatisfied boys, while the latter exceeded the girls in their use of extrapunitive adjectives.

It should be noted that even the most satisfied students made some use of negative adjectives when asked to describe their typical feelings in the classroom. Also, the average member of the satisfied group expressed some dissatisfaction on one-sixth of the questions in the Student Opinion Poll. These two observations should serve as ample cautions against the danger of interpreting any sign of dissatisfaction with school as symptomatic of deeper psychological difficulties. Apparently, some degree of dissatisfaction is the rule rather than the exception. Nonetheless, the responses of the extremely disgruntled group of students leaves little doubt that dissatisfaction with school, like beauty, is frequently in the eye of the beholder.

Summary

This investigation examines the differences in psychological functioning and classroom effectiveness between two groups of adolescents—those who are satisfied with their recent school experiences and those who are dissatisfied. The major findings point to: (a) the relevance of psychological health data rather than scholastic achievement data in understanding dissatisfaction with school; (b) the importance of differentiating the attitudes of dissatisfied girls from those of dissatisfied boys, the former being characterized by feelings of personal inadequacy, the latter by feelings critical of school authorities. Rosenzweig's concepts of intropunitiveness and extrapunitiveness are applied to these findings and a relevant theoretical framework is proposed.

REFERENCES

Harrower-Erikson, M. R., & Steiner, M. E. Large scale Rorschach techniques. Springfield, Ill.: Charles C Thomas, 1945.

Murray, H. A. *Explorations in personality.* New York: Oxford Univer. Press, 1938.

Spillman, R. J. Psychological and scholastic correlates of dissatisfaction with school among adolescents. Unpublished master's thesis. Univer. of Chicago, 1959.

[33]   *David Gottlieb & Warren D. TenHouten*   RACIAL
COMPOSITION AND THE SOCIAL SYSTEMS OF
THREE HIGH SCHOOLS

In recent years, social scientists have shown a growing concern with youth
socialization and the emergence of youth subcultures. In pursuit of explanations of these phenomena, the social scientist has looked to what has become
a traditional set of independent variables. Generally, these are family organization, social class, religion, parental education, and community structure and
size. It is interesting to note that race, as an independent variable, is rarely
utilized in any systematic way. This is not to suggest that race has been
totally neglected, but rather that a type of methodological segregation has
been practiced. In studies of youths within the formal setting of the high
school, Negroes tend to be either "lumped" together with other students or
excluded from the analysis with the explanation that their presence would
distort the findings. It is primarily in the area of social problems that Negro
youths are given some research consideration. In these instances, however, the
race variable is merely a marginal showing what percent of all delinquents,
dropouts, gang members, and so forth are Negroes.

The failure to look at Negro youths within the school setting is all the
more difficult to understand, given our awareness of the importance of race
in interpersonal relations, the development of self-concept, aspirations as well
as goal attainment, and the perceptions one holds of his society.

This paper deals with differences and similarities in the social systems of
Negro and white youths as observed in three American high schools. The
research instrument used was a paper-and-pencil questionnaire completed by
all students in attendance on a midweek school day. The schools are located
in a large Midwestern metropolis. In selecting sample schools, the following
factors were considered:

First of all, schools were selected in the inner city in order to minimize
the social class differences between Negroes and whites. As indicated by Table
1, this effort was fairly successful. School A, the school with the large majority of white students, has the greatest proportion of fathers who are working
and fathers who are at the top of the working-class ladder. Moving toward

FROM *Journal of Marriage and the Family*, 1965, 27, 204–212. REPRINTED BY
PERMISSION OF THE SENIOR AUTHOR AND THE NATIONAL COUNCIL ON FAMILY RELA-
TIONS.

TABLE 1   Selected Family Background Characteristics of Students, by Race and School

FAMILY BACKGROUND CHARACTERISTICS	SCHOOL A		SCHOOL B		SCHOOL C	
	Negro	White	Negro	White	Negro	White
Regular Home						
Both parents	73.0	84.5	58.1	75.0	55.0	35.3
Mother only	13.5	8.5	22.4	14.9	24.6	11.8
Father only	1.8	1.2	3.0	2.2	2.4	5.8
Other	11.7	5.9	16.4	7.9	18.0	47.0
Total percent	100.0	100.1	99.9	100.0	100.0	99.9
Total number	111	2484	841	966	1649	17
Father's Education						
Average years of schooling	11.7	10.8	10.9	9.8	9.8	10.9
Standard deviation	2.8	2.7	2.7	2.7	2.8	3.2
Total number	87	2291	642	798	1450	15
Percent of Fathers Working	91.3	94.7	90.9	92.3	83.8	80.0
Total number	103	2352	751	887	1508	15
Percent of Mothers Working	45.1	36.8	36.4	38.7	34.6	23.5
Total number	113	2519	866	980	1700	17
Father's Occupation						
Professional	5.7	7.7	5.2	4.3	5.1	—
Proprietors, managers	11.5	12.0	6.7	6.0	6.6	10.0
Clerical, sales	2.3	7.6	3.7	4.8	25.2	20.0
Craftsmen, foremen	13.8	29.9	23.7	34.5	20.1	20.0
Operatives	24.1	20.2	37.1	35.2	26.3	40.0
Service, incl. private house	12.6	11.7	13.4	8.4	8.7	10.0
Laborers	29.9	10.9	10.2	6.8	8.0	—
Total percent	99.9	100.0	100.0	100.0	100.0	100.0
Total number	87	2276	598	807	930	10

TABLE 1   Continued

FAMILY BACKGROUND CHARACTERISTICS	SCHOOL A		SCHOOL B		SCHOOL C	
	Negro	White	Negro	White	Negro	White
Mother's Occupation						
Professional	3.9	8.3	15.9	1.8	6.2	33.3
Proprietors, managers	7.8	5.6	3.2	4.2	28.8	—
Clerical, sales	25.5	44.7	19.7	27.4	10.6	—
Craftsmen, foremen	9.8	2.0	1.0	2.9	0.9	—
Operatives	17.6	8.2	6.0	18.2	11.1	33.3
Service, incl. private house	29.4	23.9	51.7	41.4	36.0	33.3
Laborers	5.9	7.3	2.5	4.0	6.4	—
Total percent	99.9	100.0	100.0	99.9	100.0	99.9
Total number	51	928	315	379	577	3

schools with larger populations of Negro students, the proportion of working fathers decreases, as does the number of fathers employed in occupations within the skilled worker category. In each case, when compared to white, Negro students have a lesser proportion of fathers employed or in elite work positions and, with one small exception in School B, a greater proportion of mothers working. There are also relationships between race, school attended by the respondent, and parental work history. These findings would be anticipated given (1) that Negroes hold the lower occupational positions in American society and (2) that among working-class whites, those who would be last to leave a neighborhood undergoing racial change would be those who could least afford to make the move. Thus, although there is some variation between the different school populations with respect to socio-economic background, there is little difference between the Negro and white students within each of the schools.

A second concern in the design of this research was to select schools at different stages of racial change. Since the natural process of racial integration into most social institutions in the United States is Negro in-migration and white out-migration, differences can be expected in the social systems of high schools as the proportion of Negroes increases. Within the social system of the high school, selecting one school predominantly white, one racially balanced, and one predominantly Negro, enables examination of what processes occur when the "student establishment" is confronted by an incoming group. In addition, examination can be made of how the newcomers establish themselves and how they are absorbed within the ongoing structure. Although this approach does not offer the analytical opportunities provided by a longitudinal examination, it does allow for the making of comparisons between systems at various stages of racial change. The race and sex distributions for each of the three sample schools are presented in Table 2.

TABLE 2   Percentage of Negroes in Schools and School Populations, by Race and Sex

SEX	SCHOOL A	SCHOOL B	SCHOOL C
	% Negro (N)	% Negro (N)	% Negro (N)
Male	4.3 (1285)	44.4 (957)	98.9 (816)
Female	4.3 (1347)	49.6 (889)	99.1 (902)
Total number	4.3 (2632)	46.9 (1846)	99.0 (1718)

Involvement in school activities

The degree to which students are integrated within the social setting of the school can be determined in part by their involvement in the various extracurricular activities offered by the school. Table 3 deals with the proportion of Negro and white, male and female students in each school who participate in available activities. From Table 3, it can be seen that only in School A are Negro students less likely to be involved in extracurricular activities than their white peers. In addition, School A shows the least variation between the proportion of students in each racial group involved in these activities. As there is a progression from a small minority of Negro students, School A, to a growing Negro student population, Schools B and C, there is a decline in the activity participation of white students. This decline reaches its lowest point in School C, where white students are only one percent of the student population. These data reflect a departure on the part of the white population and an increased involvement on the part of the Negro population; this finding evinces the importance of examining in greater detail the social processes by which Negro adolescents begin, maintain, and enhance their involvement in the social system of the high school. These data were sought to determine whether (1) there is an undifferentiated mass exodus on the part of white students who have already been in the system, or whether (2) there is a gradual giving up and taking on of certain roles and functions by both racial groups in the school. It will be shown that as the racial change takes place, the withdrawal of whites from the system is hardly undifferentiated

TABLE 3   Percentage of Students Involved in Some Extracurricular Activity, by Race, Sex, and School

SCHOOL	MALE	FEMALE
Race	% (N)	% (N)
School A		
Negro	54.5 (55)	51.7 (58)
White	64.2 (1196)	61.1 (1164)
School B		
Negro	73.8 (401)	71.4 (420)
White	43.5 (531)	49.0 (440)
School C		
Negro	72.3 (800)	71.4 (876)
White	33.0 (8)	20.0 (9)

mass exodus; on the contrary, definite structure appears in the changes in roles and functions of Negro and white students in the high school social system. It will be shown that Negro and white students develop distinct social systems, which result in both racial groups maintaining their own forms of racial segregation.

In terms of increasing Negro participation in the high school, the following findings were anticipated:

A. In situations where there is an already established social system of white students, the incoming Negro group will enter first into those activities which call for a minimum of social or unstructured interpersonal contact between the races. That initial participation within the school will be limited to those activities which are not perceived as prestige-giving by the white majority or the Negro minority.

B. As the proportion of Negro youth within a school increases and they become a sizable segment of the population, two separate social systems will emerge. In this case, clearer distinctions will appear between the races with respect to the type of activity in which the student is involved and the prestige attributed to those engaged in the activity.

C. When there has been a total changeover in population and the Negro youths constitute the social system, their concentration in certain activities will decline. In addition, they will show greater variation in the kinds of activities which they perceive as giving one prestige with his peers. In this

TABLE 4 Type of Activity in which the Student Participates, by Race, Sex, and School*

ACTIVITY	SCHOOL A				SCHOOL B				SCHOOL C			
	NM	WM	NF	WF	NM	WM	NF	WF	NM	WM	NF	WF
Band or Orchestra	17.5	17.1	10.0	9.4	16.9	16.0	10.0	11.8	19.4	66.7	5.6	—
Chorus, Vocal	15.0	8.5	36.7	25.0	15.5	7.8	40.7	25.9	13.7	—	37.2	100.0
Dramatics	5.0	4.8	6.7	9.6	5.7	6.5	19.0	8.8	6.7	33.3	11.8	—
School Paper and Yearbook	5.0	14.1	6.7	13.8	6.1	13.5	9.3	16.1	3.4	33.3	7.8	—
Debate Club	6.7	3.3	4.5	3.2	8.1	14.7	8.0	8.8	9.5	—	7.2	—
Student Government	7.5	17.2	6.7	14.9	6.1	13.1	6.0	13.9	10.8	66.7	18.4	—
Language Clubs	5.0	5.1	—	3.6	3.4	11.7	4.7	13.7	9.8	—	25.4	—
Hobby Clubs	5.5	15.0	33.3	11.0	8.1	18.6	14.3	13.4	14.8	—	11.9	—
Athletics (Varsity Club)	70.0	62.1	62.1	36.6	70.9	53.7	58.0	35.6	52.4	66.7	35.3	—
Vocational Clubs	15.0	7.9	16.7	12.1	9.4	7.4	18.0	10.6	15.5	—	18.2	50.0
Total number	30	768	30	712	296	231	300	216	579	3	626	2

* Percentages may total over 100.0 since this is a multiple choice item.

case, their behavior within the school will not be too different from any other groups of adolescents of similar backgrounds and high schools.

Table 4 deals with the type of school activity engaged in by the students in each of the sample schools. From this table, it can be seen that while some variation occurs between students of the same race in different schools, the more frequent pattern is for variation among Negro and white youths in the same school. In school A, comparison of both males and females from both racial groups shows that there are five out of ten activities in which the differential of involvement exceeds five percent. Of particular interest are the activities in which both groups of students are more likely to be involved. For the Negro males in School A, Athletics, Band or Orchestra, Vocational Clubs, and Chorus are the primary areas for involvement. For the white males, the five activities most frequently noted are Athletics, Student Government, Band or Orchestra, Hobby Clubs, and School Newspaper. The two activities in which both groups have a high rate of involvement are Athletics and Band-Orchestra, which are highly structured activities requiring little interpersonal contact. Student Government, School Newspaper, and Hobby Clubs, on the other hand, demand a closer and more consistent contact which frequently takes place in a relatively informal setting.

The pattern among females in School A is not too different from that observed among the males. The one exception is the Negro female involvement in Hobby Clubs. This high level of involvement can be explained, however, by the fact that the club to which the Negro girls are referring is a school-sponsored popular music group organized by the Negro girls.

In School B, there are seven groups among the males and eight among the females where differences in activity involvement exceed five percent. In addition, it will be noted that there are similarities between Schools A and B in the types of activities in which both racial groups are involved. Finally, the findings for School B lend support to the proposition that with an increase in the Negro population, there will be indications of the emergence of two separate social systems.

For School C, the school with few white students, the Negro students show a greater spread in activity involvement. As suggested earlier, in a school where the process of racial change is completed and the Negro student body does in fact become the social system, there will be less concentration in specific activities and a more even diffusion in all activities within the school. Although the white group in School C is quite small, it is interesting to note that it is very much like the minority Negro group in School A in that these white students cluster within but a few activities.

Among the various consequences of change in racial composition, it was expected that in addition to variations in activity involvement, there would be differences in the prestige attributed to various roles held by students within the system.

TABLE 5 Percentages of Students Giving Various Answers to "Who Are the Leaders" in Their School, by Race, Sex and School

LEADING GROUP	SCHOOL A				SCHOOL B				SCHOOL C			
	NM	WM	NF	WF	NM	WM	NF	WF	NM	WM	NF	WF
Athletes	12.8	22.3	14.3	14.3	42.3	19.7	43.6	16.0	36.1	12.5	35.0	20.0
Fraternity, Sorority	4.2	5.1	4.1	22.3	3.1	4.3	2.3	1.7	2.0	—	1.5	—
Delinquents	2.1	6.8	4.1	1.9	7.3	11.1	4.1	4.7	4.1	—	3.1	—
Good Students	34.0	14.7	24.5	14.9	20.4	30.2	20.4	39.2	21.1	50.0	21.8	40.0
Party-Goers	6.4	16.1	6.1	11.2	11.7	5.1	16.1	8.5	8.1	—	10.9	—
Student Government	40.4	32.0	44.9	33.1	11.7	26.1	8.9	26.2	27.0	25.0	25.7	40.0
Clubs	—	—	2.0	2.3	0.3	—	—	—	0.3	—	0.8	—
Other	—	3.0	—	—	3.1	3.4	4.6	3.7	1.3	12.5	1.2	—
Total percent	99.9	100.0	100.0	100.0	99.9	99.9	100.0	100.0	100.0	100.0	100.0	100.0
Total number	47	1001	49	1164	383	467	392	401	701	8	778	5

Leadership in the social system of the high school

Table 5 deals with the responses of students in each school to the question, "Who, in your estimation, are the real leaders in your school?"

Beginning with School A, among both the Negro males and females a contradiction appears between the activities in which they are involved and the activities which they see as important to leadership. Student Council, for example, was an activity in which Negro students showed limited participation, yet they perceived it as important to student leadership. Athletics, on the other hand, attracts Negro students but is given little weight as a means to student status. Finally, Negroes place greater emphasis on being a "Good Student" than white students. This would be anticipated, given the initial position that Negroes in a minority situation will seek entrance into the system through more formal activities. In this case, Negro students show stronger dependency on the formal system by seeking rewards from adults in the system through taking on the role of the "Good Student."

In School B, where the emergence of two separate social systems was predicted, greater consensus was found between both Negroes and whites as to what leads to leadership and activity involvement. Negroes are more likely than whites to be involved in athletics, and they see this activity as important to leadership. Conversely, whites are lower on athletic activities and give athletics less status. Student government involvement is higher for whites, and they are more likely to see it as a means of leadership than are the Negro students. Finally, unlike School A, where "Party Going" was more likely to be perceived by whites than by Negroes as important to leadership, the opposite occurs in School B. Here, Negro students appear to be in the process of developing their own informal networks, quite apart from the white student body.

In School C, the situation among Negro students resembles that noted among the white students in School A where whites are a clear majority. There is a more even spread in the kinds of activities identified with leadership, as there is in activity participation. Here the total system is in the hands of the Negro students, and there is little reason to concentrate one's involvement in any one activity or group of activities. The small white minority in School C has little involvement in school-centered activities and tends—not unlike the Negro minority in School A—to turn to the formal system for rewards.

Criteria for popularity within the peer group

The preceding section demonstrated that a racial minority in a high school sought status in formal activities requiring a minimum of cross-race interaction. Racial composition was seen to be an important determinant of the kinds of activities students of a given race see as important to status. Here, examination is made of different race-sex group characteristics in each school that are perceived as status-giving, not in the total system, but in the student's own informal peer group. Students were presented a set of alternatives to the following question: "In the group you go around with, which of the things below are important to be popular with the group?" The distribution of responses to this question is presented in Table 6.

"Ability to get along with all types of people" was mentioned as important to popularity in the peer group more than twice as frequently as any other choice by every race-sex group in every school.

In all three schools, Negroes tend to place higher status value on dress and the possession of money.

Negroes in all schools place a higher value of being informed about the popular heroes of teen-age mass culture. In both race groups, girls give this response more frequently than boys. The School A Negroes are in general more apt to value instrumental attributes that are rewarded by the formal system—being higher than whites on talent, and slightly lower on good grades.

In School B, all groups place more emphasis on talent and grades. The Negro boys, compared to the white boys, place even more emphasis than in School A on dress, driving a car, and having money. Negro and white girls, on the other hand, both place less emphasis on these attributes than in School A. School B Negroes, having a better-developed interpersonal system than School A Negroes, place much greater emphasis on getting along with people and less emphasis than in School A on emulating middle-class morality.

There is very little difference between the Negroes in Schools B and C. In school C, talent and grades are given slightly more emphasis. Talent and grades, however, increase for every group, from Schools A to B to C, with the one exception of the white boys in School C.

In summary, considerable variation of responses occurs between race-sex groups *within* each school, but very little variation occurs for race-sex groups *between* schools. The small differences found between schools are more readily explained by class differences than by racial composition. For a given race-sex group, the racial composition of their school is not highly related to the frequency with which they respond to various criteria for popularity in the peer group. This is in contradistinction to responses for leadership activities for the whole school. Though Negroes and whites participate to some extent in the same formal school activities, they are far less apt to belong to the same *informal* peer groups. Racial composition of a school is unimportant to popularity in the peer group because, in all three schools, peer groups are racially segregated, i.e., they are racially homogeneous. A high level of racial cleavage in friendship patterns was observed in seating arrangements, in the lunchrooms, and in the halls of the schools. In addition, sociometric data was obtained from each student, to measure the amount of cross-race friendship choices of students in each school. These data are examined in the following section.

TABLE 6 Percentages of Students Giving Selected Criteria as Important to Being Popular in Their Peer Group, by Race, Sex, and School*

CRITERIA	SCHOOL A				SCHOOL B				SCHOOL C			
	NM	WM	NF	WF	NM	WM	NF	WF	NM	WM	NF	WF
Having some special talent	18.9	14.8	7.7	4.1	20.3	18.4	11.8	5.2	22.7	11.1	12.1	—
Being a sharp dresser	30.2	26.5	28.8	25.5	35.6	27.1	13.5	19.6	33.0	—	17.9	—
Have easy moral standards	17.0	17.5	21.2	12.1	19.3	18.8	21.4	10.0	20.4	44.4	18.8	—
Have high moral standards	17.0	14.4	23.1	33.9	15.3	11.9	16.3	27.4	15.5	11.1	20.3	12.5
Good grades	11.3	13.8	13.5	17.1	18.3	17.0	15.9	12.2	22.2	11.1	23.3	37.5
Drive a car	17.0	28.5	13.5	12.0	27.1	28.7	7.2	8.8	23.9	11.1	9.0	—
Know what's going on in the world of popular singers and movie stars	15.1	8.6	25.0	14.9	12.5	8.5	20.7	15.5	16.1	—	21.8	37.5
Drinking or smoking	11.3	15.9	1.9	5.2	12.5	15.6	4.3	3.6	8.1	—	4.3	—
Have money	18.9	21.1	15.4	7.4	22.0	22.5	9.6	8.8	25.3	11.1	10.3	—
Ability to get along with all types of people	75.5	70.8	82.7	90.1	77.2	70.8	91.1	87.6	75.2	88.9	88.7	100.0
Total number	53	1178	52	1264	399	494	416	419	786	9	860	8

* Percentages may total over 100.0 since this is a multiple choice item.

The racial composition of informal peer groups

Lundberg and Dickson have shown that Negro high school students show greater self-preference than whites, and that this greater self-preference is most marked for friendship choices, is intermediate for work, and is least for leadership.[1]

In this study, sociometric data were collected only for friendship choices. All students were asked to name their three best friends. From this data, the self-preference levels of each race-sex group in each school was determined, using Criswell's double-ratio index of self-preference:[2]

$$\frac{\text{number of same-race choices} \div \text{number of cross-race choices}}{\text{number of students in same-race} \div \text{number of students in other race}}$$

The self-preference scores for Schools A and B are presented in Table 7. Since there were so few whites in School C, and since they made so few within-

TABLE 7   Indices of Self-Preference of All Race-Sex Groups in School A and School B

RACE-SEX GROUP	SCHOOL A	SCHOOL B
Negro Boys	58.0	74.9
Negro Girls	104.2	94.1
White Boys	4.7	17.7
White Girls	60.4	21.9

sample choices, the indices for that school are virtually meaningless and are not presented.

As expected, Negroes show higher self-preference than whites. Within each racial group, girls show higher racial self-preference than boys.

It was stated earlier that, in a minority situation where there is an already established social system of white students, the incoming Negro group will enter first into those activities which call for a minimum of social contact with whites. The Negro minority in School A does show a high level of self-preference in their choices of friends. In this situation, their participation in the school, in activities, and so forth, is largely limited to those activities which require a minimum of cross-race interaction. This high level of self-preference persists in the situation where the Negro population is greater, in School B, with the emergence of two separate social systems. In addition, analysis of School B's sociometric choices shows a decline in the proportion of cross-race choices made by white students. This is further evidence that there are two separate social systems in School B, one Negro and one white.

The Negro minority at School A and the white minority at School C both showed a marked tendency to choose as their three best friends persons not in the school. The percent of choices made within the school shows the increasing alienation of whites from the school as the proportion of Negroes increases. In School A, the whites are about twice as apt to choose within the school as are the Negroes. In School B, there is no marked difference in in-school choices among Negroes and whites. In School C, the Negroes become most committed to the school, and the whites highly alienated. This leads to the following

TABLE 8   Total Sociometric Choices, Percentage of Choices Made Within School, Total In-School Choices, and Percentage of In-School Choices Given to Other Race, by Race, Sex, and School

SCHOOL RACE, SEX	TOTAL NUMBER OF CHOICES MADE	PERCENT OF CHOICES IN-SCHOOL	TOTAL NUMBER OF IN-SCHOOL CHOICES	PERCENT OF IN-SCHOOL CHOICES CROSS-RACE
School A				
Negro Boys	113	15.9	18	27.7
Negro Girls	136	25.0	34	17.6
White Boys	2594	33.8	877	0.9
White Girls	3306	40.2	1331	0.1
School B				
Negro Boys	946	32.6	605	1.4
Negro Girls	1095	38.4	421	1.1
White Boys	1095	34.6	379	4.7
White Girls	1081	37.9	410	3.4
School C				
Negro Boys	1870	37.6	703	0.4
Negro Girls	2308	38.2	881	—
White Boys	16	6.2	1	100.0
White Girls	11	18.2	2	50.0

proposition: the level of commitment of students to their high school varies directly with the proportion of students in the school who are of their own race.

Racial composition is seen to be a strong determinant of cross-race interaction. Since the Negroes in School A are so few, by chance alone, i.e., in the absence of social forces, it can be expected that they will choose whites much more often than themselves. Table 8 shows that 17.6 percent of the Negro girls' choices and 27.7 percent of the Negro boys' choices were given to whites, whereas less than one percent of the whites' choices went to Negroes. Clearly, the proportion of cross-race choices is heavily influenced by the racial composition of the school, since "control" for racial composition by the use of Criswell's self-preference index shows that Negroes have higher self-preference scores than whites.

In School B, the percent of cross-race choices is low for both Negroes and whites. This is additional evidence for the conceptualization that there are two social systems in this school. Finally, in School C, the Negroes choose almost entirely among themselves, as they constitute 99 percent of the student body, and the whites direct friendship choices outside of the school.

Satisfaction with school

One final set of data indicate how students feel about their high school.

In response to the question, "If you could attend any high school in your community, which one would you choose?" Major differences appeared between the races both within and among high schools. Table 9 shows that for the white students, preference for some other school is lowest in School A, highest in School C, with School B falling in the middle. The least discrepancy between Negro and white students in the same school is found in School B. Again, this lack of difference might be explained by the existence of two social systems, with both groups feeling less racial pressure than in the other two

TABLE 9 Percentages of Students that Would Prefer to Attend a Different High School, by Race, Sex, and School

RACE-SEX GROUP	SCHOOL A	SCHOOL B	SCHOOL C
	% Diff. (N)	% Diff. (N)	% Diff. (N)
Negro Boys	35.6 (45)	28.0 (308)	38.4 (487)
Negro Girls	41.1 (56)	22.3 (378)	45.6 (698)
White Boys	6.3 (1016)	25.3 (468)	75.0 (3)
White Girls	13.0 (1234)	28.8 (411)	83.3 (6)

schools. In both Schools A and C, the minority groups express the stronger preference for some other high school. The one case which does not seem to fit into the analytical scheme is the Negro students in School C, the school with the largest proportion of Negro students. The question can be raised as to why these students, who are a majority, would be so different from the majority white group in School A. In part, the answer is supplied by comments from respondents in each school who chose to explain why they preferred another school. Here again, race is an important factor, but it operates differently for Negro and white students in different schools.

For the Negro students in School C, preference for some other school was stimulated by a desire for better school facilities and more extensive educational programs. It was not the result of feeling uncomfortable within the system, but rather a reasonable request for the better things that are found in other high schools within the community. That is, Negro students who are a majority in a high school perceive that they are still a minority in the larger context of the community and that predominantly white school systems are allocated a greater proportion of community resources. The comments of one Negro girl in School C express this sentiment:

It's an old school and it just does not have the same kinds of things that you can find at C. . . . The classrooms are dark and the place is crowded. At C. . . . they have all kinds of special programs for students in my field. Here there is nothing like that.

For the small group of white students in School C, preferences for some other school were clearly related to race and to feelings of alienation. As one white male in this school noted:

I can't go anywhere else because I live in this district. I don't like it here. It is a school for colored kids and I don't like the way they push me around. I just go to class and then go home. I don't want any part of this place.

The Negro minority group in School A mentions race as an important factor in explaining why they would prefer to go somewhere else. The comments of two Negro students in School A provide some insight as to what the Negro minority might feel within the social setting of a school:

O . . . has too many race problems in my opinion. N . . . is mostly made up of my race. It doesn't have conflict the way O . . . has.

In some schools people are not friendly. This is one of the schools that are not friendly. I don't mean everyone, but the majority of them.

The white majority in School A was the most satisfied group of all, with only ten percent responding that they would rather go to another school. The

School A whites frequently mentioned the newness and high quality of their physical plant, and that their school is relatively free of Negroes. As one white student responded:

It's new and I did not want to go to school with Negroes, and I heard a lot of good things about it.

Conclusion

This paper represents an attempt to deal with the variable of race in a study of adolescents. More particularly, the concern has been with the problem of racial composition as a factor in the kinds of social systems which develop among Negro and white high school students. The initial proposition was that with changes in the proportion of Negroes entering a school, significant alterations would occur in the kinds of relationships that developed between and among both Negro and white students. The data presented here would appear to support this initial proposition. On the other hand, it should be kept in mind that the sample consisted of three schools within a single city. Obviously, other factors within a school could produce different kinds of results. Certainly the location of the school would be important. The history of the school system and the community in matters of race could be a salient factor. The role played by school personnel would be yet another variable that might influence the kinds of relationships that exist between students.

The authors hope that this paper will stimulate a greater research involvement on the part of behavioral scientists in contemporary matters of race, education, and the socialization of youth.

REFERENCES

1. George A. Lundberg and Lenore Dickson, "Interethnic Relations in a High School Population," *American Journal of Sociology*, 58 (1952), pp. 1–10; George A. Lundberg and Lenore Dickson, "Selective Association Among Ethnic Groups in a High School Population," *American Sociological Review*, 17 (1952), pp. 23–35. A recent study confirms this result: see Nancy Hoyt St. John, "De Facto Segregation and Interracial Association in High School," *Sociology of Education*, 37 (1964), pp. 334–338.
2. Joan H. Criswell, "Racial Cleavage in Negro-White Groups," *Sociometry*, 1 (1937), pp. 81–89. Joan H. Criswell, "A Sociometric Study of Race Cleavage in the Classroom," *Archives of Psychology*, No. 235 (1939), p. 19.

[34]   *Richard H. Seiden*   CAMPUS TRAGEDY: A
STUDY OF STUDENT SUICIDE

The act of self-destruction rudely challenges our supposed love for life and fear of death. It is always a puzzlement, but in no case is suicide more shocking or bewildering than it is in the college student. For here are a relatively privileged group of persons enjoying valued advantages of youth, intelligence, and educational opportunity. Why should persons, seemingly so rewarded, seek to kill themselves, and, indeed, to commit suicide at a rate significantly in excess of their noncollege peers (Bruyn & Seiden, 1965, p. 76)?

This perplexing question—"Why do students suicide?"—has motivated a great deal of concern among college health authorities leading to several studies and evaluations of the problem in American universities (Braaten & Darling, 1962; Jensen, 1955; Parrish, 1957; Raphael, Power, & Berridge, 1937; Temby, 1961). Unfortunately, these studies have all had an exclusively descriptive approach. They have drawn conclusions about certain characteristics of suicidal students but, seemingly, without appreciation for the degree to which these same characteristics are shared by the entire student body population. What has been conspicuously omitted is a baseline—a standard of comparison against which the diagnostic value of their findings might be judged. One is reminded of the gentleman who, when asked, "How is your wife?" astutely responded, "Compared to what?" This very question of relative comparison must also be asked in the study of student suicides.

The present study attempted to remedy this situation by applying a reasonable standard of comparison, namely, the great majority of fellow college students who do not commit suicide. By investigating what characteristics significantly differentiate suicidal students from their classmates plus examining those situational-temporal conditions associated with campus suicides, it was hoped to achieve a clearer diagnostic picture. Once the high-risk, suicide-prone student can be identified, a large and necessary step will have been taken toward the ultimate objective of effective prophylaxis.

Method

The approach used in the present study was one of analytic epidemiology, that is, comparing for particular characteristics the subset of student suicides

FROM *Journal of Abnormal Psychology,* 1966, 71, 389–399. COPYRIGHT 1966 BY THE AMERICAN PSYCHOLOGICAL ASSOCIATION, AND REPRODUCED BY PERMISSION OF THE AUTHOR AND PUBLISHER.

with the total student body population from which they were drawn. This particular procedure meets the methodological criteria for selection of comparison groups, as stated by MacMahon, Pugh, and Ipsen (1960):

A comparison group is a group of unaffected individuals believed to reflect the characteristics of the population from which the affected group was drawn. Ideally the comparison group should not differ from the affected group in any respect (other than not being affected) which might be likely to influence the frequency of the variable or variables suspected of being causally connected. This means either that both the patient and comparison groups must be representative of the same population or that if selective factors enter into the choice of the patterns, the same factors ought to enter into the patterns, the selection of the comparison group [p. 235].

The method of the present study involved a comparison of the sample of 23 University of California at Berkeley (UCB) students who committed suicide during the 10-year period 1952 through 1961, with the entire UCB student body population during this same decade. The objective of this comparison was to determine what special characteristics differentiated the suicide-prone student from his classmates. Within this framework the following working definitions were employed: (a) *Student*—the definition of a student was established by registration on the Berkeley campus of the University of California, in either graduate or undergraduate status, during the regular college semester periods. Summer sessions were not included because of the unreliability of data for these periods and changes in the usual composition of the student body population during summer sessions. (b) *Suicide*—refers to a completed suicide, established by a death certificate stating suicide as the legal cause of death. In one instance, involving a jump from the Golden Gate bridge, this was not possible. Since the body was never recovered, a certificate was not issued; however, the case was well-documented in police and newspaper files. By keeping to this legalistic definition of suicide, one runs the very likely probability that the true number of suicides will be underenumerated. For example, cases of equivocal student deaths, such as by falls or drowning, were regarded as accidental, in keeping with the coroner's findings, even though these deaths, listed as accidents, could have been suicides which were covered up to avoid the social stigma related to suicide. Indeed, it has been estimated that only about 70% of successful suicides are ever recorded as such (Dublin, 1963, p. 3). The advantage in using this definition is that one can be quite certain that deaths recorded as suicide are bona-fide cases since the error is, almost always, in the direction of underreporting. (c) *Exposure to risk*—the period of exposure to risk comprised the 10-year span 1952–1961 inclusive, a total of 10 academic or 7½ calendar years. This important variable, the length of exposure, was to some degree controlled since both the suicidal and nonsuicidal students were exposed to the same period of risk. (d) *Population at risk*—population at risk was the total student body of UCB during the 10-year period cited. Case finding procedures were extremely painstaking, requiring several months of effort to detect and verify 23 bona-fide study cases. Numerous sources of information were used, but for the suicidal students the primary source was the standard death certificate, obtained from the state health department. Secondary sources consisted of newspaper clippings, police files, and University records. The source of materials for the baseline data for the total student body population was the UCB Office of the Registrar. Their publication, *A Ten-Year Survey of Certain Demographic Characteristics of the Student Population* (Suslow, 1963), was indispensable.

In terms of research design, the procedures consisted of collecting and analyzing data regarding selected attributes of the total student population. These data were then used as a baseline to which the sample of suicidal UCB students could be compared. Since suicide may also involve a strong volitional component, further analyses were made with respect to certain situational-temporal features of the academic environment.

Results and discussion

Results are presented in tabular and graphic form and discussed in the text by order of their appearance. The various comparisons were statistically analyzed by testing the significance of the difference between two proportions (Hill, 1961, pp. 122–132), specifically, the significance of proportional differences between the suicidal sample and expected population values as based upon knowledge of the student universe. All probability statements are two-tailed probabilities.

INCIDENCE AND PREVALENCE

Previous research on the UCB population (Bruyn & Seiden, 1965) investigated by general question of student suicide risk. By comparing the student suicide experience with the suicide incidence among a comparable group of non-college-age cohorts, it was established that the incidence of suicide among students was significantly greater than for non-student-age peers ($p = .004$). Conversely, the general mortality experience from all causes was significantly more favorable for students when compared to their non-academic-age peers ($p < .001$). In terms of total mortality, suicides accounted for 23 of the 68 student deaths which occurred during the 10-year study period. Proportionally, it ranked as the second leading cause of death (34%), exceeded only by accidents (37%).

AGE

For the United States as a whole, there is a well-documented positive correlation between age and suicide (Dublin, 1963, p. 22). This same relationship holds for the student population. If the student body is divided on the basis

TABLE 1 Selected Demographic Characteristics of Suicidal and Nonsuicidal Students, UCB, 1952–61

DEMOGRAPHIC CHARACTERISTICS	SUICIDAL STUDENTS		TOTAL STUDENT BODY POPULATION	
	Frequency distribution ($n = 23$)	% distribution	% distribution	p
Age				
Under 25	9	39	70	.001
25 and above	14	61	30	
Class standing				
Undergraduate	12	52	72	.033
Graduate	11	48	28	
Sex				
Male	17	74	67	ns
Female	6	26	33	
Marital status[a]				
Married	3	14	23	ns
Never married	19	86	77	
Race				
White	20	87	89	ns
Nonwhite	3	13	11	
Religion				
Protestant	15	65	60	ns
Jewish	5	22	18	
Catholic	3	13	22	
Nationality				
U.S.A.	19	83	96	.002
Foreign	4	17	04	
Major subject[b]				
Mechanical-mathematic	10	50	64	ns
Aesthetic-social	10	50	36	
Grade-point average[c]				
Above average	14	67	50	ns
Below average	7	33	50	
Mental health service				
Psychiatric patient	8	34	10	$< .001$
Nonpatient	15	66	90	

[a] Excludes one divorced student.
[b] Excludes three students who had not declared majors.
[c] Excludes two students who did not complete a semester.

of those who are above and below age 25, one finds that the percentage of suicides in the older age group is approximately twice their proportional percentage in the population (see Table 1). This distinction is graphically portrayed in Figure 1 which presents the relative frequency of suicidal and nonsuicidal students by 5-year age groups. It is notable that only about 6% of all students fall in the 30- to 34-year age category while more than 26% of the

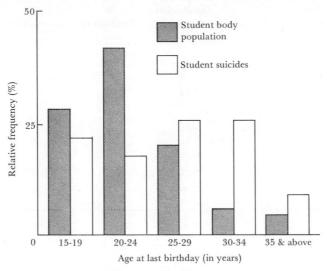

FIGURE 1   Age distributions of student suicides and total student body population, UCB, 1952–61.

suicidal students are found in this interval. In fact, the median age for the student body population is 22 years, 6 months, while the median age for the suicidal students, 26 years, 5 months, is greater by almost 4 years.

CLASS STANDING

Directly correlated with, and, indeed, almost identical to, chronological age, is the class standing of individual students. Median class standing for the entire student population was the junior year, for the suicidal sub-set it was the senior year. When the groups are divided on the basis of graduate or undergraduate standing, one finds that graduate students committed suicide in numbers significantly greater than could be expected from their proportions in the student body at large (see Table 1).

SEX

Of the 23 student suicides, 17 were male, 6 female, a sex ratio approximating 3:1 (see Table 1). This finding accords with those sex ratios reported in previous studies of completed suicide (Dublin, 1963, p. 23). However, an adjustment is necessary to correctly relate this information to the college population. Whereas the sexes are about equally distributed in the general United States population, they are not equally distributed on campus. For the years under study, males outnumbered females in the student body population by approximately 2:1. Accordingly, the obtained sex ratio of 3:1 must be halved to yield an adjusted student ratio of about 1.5 male suicides for each female suicide. This student sex ratio is considerably narrower than the sex ratio for the country at large. It seems to indicate a heightened risk of suicide among female students as compared to the general female population. However, this indication must remain somewhat speculative since the female suicides were considerably older (median age 30 years, 1 month) than were male suicides (median age 26 years, 1 month). As a consequence one cannot be entirely sure that the constricted ratio is not an effect of confounding between age and sex. Should further research confirm that there is, in fact, a greater risk of suicide among female students as opposed to female nonstudents, it would follow the predictions of Gibbs and Martin (1964). They proposed a rise in female suicides due to increasing social pressures. According to their status-integration theory, as more women enter the labor force they encounter cross-pressures from conflicting social roles. They postulate that these stresses will lead to increasing numbers of female suicides.

MARITAL STATUS

Of the 23 student suicides, it was possible to classify 22 persons into the categories of "married" or "never married," which corresponded to the available student population data. One divorced student was thereby excluded from the analysis. There were no remarkable disparity between the suicidal and nonsuicidal students on the basis of marital status (see Table 1). For the entire United States population, suicide is less common among married persons (Dublin, 1963, p. 26), but this was not the case for campus suicides. Only three of the student suicides were married, and only one of those married had children. The remaining two cases, both females, committed suicide shortly after their marriages.

RACE

Of the 23 known suicides, only three were nonwhite and all three of these nonwhite students were Chinese. There were no suicides among Negro, East Indian, or American Indian students who, at any event, comprised only about 3% of the student body population. The distribution of suicides by race corresponded closely to the racial proportions found in the student population (see Table 1). It should be mentioned, however, that there is good reason to question the adequacy of these racial data. Since University records do not ask for nor indicate students' race, these breakdowns, furnished by the University Dean of Students Office, were presumably obtained from simple headcounts with all the imprecision that this method implies.

RELIGION

Religion was not a significant factor in differentiating suicidal students from the general campus population (see Table 1). As was the case with racial statistics, the religious data, likewise, must be regarded with great skepticism. The University does not conduct a religious census of its students. Consequently, the religious population figures were estimated from student residence information cards on which "religious affiliation" is an optional item. Very frequently it is left unanswered.

NATIONALITY

Only 4 of the 23 student suicides were foreign students. Nonetheless, their representation in the student body was so negligible (only 4%) that they appear among the suicides in approximately four times the magnitude one would expect from their proportions in the student population (see Table 1). As a group, these four "international student" suicides were characterized by some striking similarities. As youngsters, all of the four had known and suffered from the ravages of war, and three of them were forced to flee from their childhood homes. Two of the students, natives of mainland China, had been dispossessed by the Communist revolution; another student, born in Austria, lost his family in the horrors of the Nazi concentration camps and subsequently migrated to Israel. The fourth student, a native Israeli, had grown up amidst the Arab-Jewish war of the Palestine partition.

Moreover, they shared a similar pattern of conflicts, centering to a large degree around strong feelings of shame. These feelings were reflected in a deep dread that they would not meet expectations that others had set for them. There was some reality to these fears, in that other persons had sent them abroad, were paying their expenses, and probably did expect from them some measure of academic achievement. Still, their excessive concern about "what others would think" was unduly frenetic. All four of them were known to the Student Mental Health Service where they had been seen for psychiatric treatment. These findings, however, must be interpreted with some caution since the median age of foreign students (26 years, 1 month), exceeded the median age of American students (24 years), raising the possibility that the differences were due in some degree to age rather than nationality.

MAJOR SUBJECT

For this comparison, the suicidal subjects were divided into two categories, corresponding somewhat to William James' distinction between the "tough" and "tender minded." Of the 20 suicidal students who had declared majors, the breakdown was 10 students in the "tough-minded" or mechanical-mathematics group (Engineering, Professional, Physical Sciences, Biological Sciences, Agricultural majors) and 10 students in the "tender-minded" or esthetic-social group (Arts, Social Sciences, Language and Literature majors). Relative to their population proportions, there was a greater incidence of suicides in the tender-minded group, but not a large enough imbalance to achieve statistical significance. Further analysis, by individual subject groups, revealed that suicides were significantly more frequent among students majoring in languages and literature (five cases), especially English majors, who comprised three of the five cases (see Table 2).

TABLE 2 Suicides among Language and Literature Majors *vs.* All Other Subject Majors

MAJOR SUBJECT GROUP	SUICIDAL STUDENTS		TOTAL STUDENT BODY POPULATION	p
	n	%	%	
Language and literature	5	25	9	.012
All other majors	15	75	91	

Note.—Excludes three students who had not declared major subjects.

GRADE-POINT AVERAGE

Grade-point analysis required some basic adjustments since graduate and undergraduate grading systems are not directly comparable. In practice, an undergraduate "C" is approximately equivalent to a graduate "B." For the student population, the grade-point average (GPA) for undergraduates was 2.50, while for graduates it was 3.35 (calculated to the scale: A = 4, B = 3, C = 2, D = 1, F = 0). Given this discrepancy, it is obviously necessary to separately compare undergraduate and graduate students with reference to their respective grade-point distributions. When the suicidal students (excluding two who did not complete a full semester at UCB) are ranked by means of achievement above or below their population GPA, we find that two-thirds of them were above average while, by definition, only half of the general student body achieved this mark. Although suggestive of a tendency toward higher grades among suicidal students, the difference, in fact, did not achieve statistical significance. However, further analysis, distributing GPA by class standing, revealed a marked discrepancy between graduate and undergraduate students. The breakdown is detailed in Table 3 and reveals that of the 11 undergraduate students who committed suicide (after one complete semester at the University), 10 of them had surpassed the undergraduate GPA. For graduate student suicides, only 4 of the 10 who had completed a semester ex-

TABLE 3   Grade-Point Averages for Graduate and Undergraduate Student Suicides

GPA	SUICIDAL STUDENTS		STUDENT POPULATION	
	n	%	%	p
Class standing				
Undergraduate				
Above mean	10	91	50	
Below mean	1	09	50	.006
Graduate				
Above mean	4	40	50	
Below mean	6	60	50	ns

Note.—Excludes two students; one graduate, one undergraduate, who suicided during their first semester.

ceeded the graduate GPA. Despite the differential grading system that rewards the graduate student with more grade points for a similar level of work, the suicidal undergraduate students received a higher overall GPA than the graduate student suicides (see Table 4).

This finding seems to indicate that undergraduate and graduate suicides differ markedly from one another in terms of academic achievement. The undergraduate suicides performed on a level well above their fellow classmates and performed considerably better than did graduate suicides. Looking at the personal histories of these undergraduate students one discovers an interesting paradox. To an external observer, say someone viewing their transcripts, these students achieved splendidly in their academic pursuits. They

TABLE 4   Observed and Expected GPA of Student Suicides by Class Standing

CLASS STANDING	GPA	
	Observed	Expected
Undergraduate	3.18	2.50
Graduate	2.90	3.35

had all been A or B students in high school since a B or better average is required for undergraduate admission, a policy which is estimated to limit entrance to the top 10–12% of graduating high school seniors. Reports from family and friends, however, reveal that self-satisfaction was not the case with these students. Rather, they seemed filled with doubts of their adequacy, dissatisfied with their grades, and despondent over their general academic aptitude. This exacerbated fear of failure was tempered somewhat by the fact that in every case of undergraduate suicide the final semester's GPA was lower ($x = 2.53$) than the previous cumulative GPA ($x = 3.34$). Another consideration is whether these students aspired to graduate school which requires a higher than average GPA (2.5–3.0 at UCB). Unfortunately, these exact data are not available; however, a check of those students in major subjects which definitely indicated future graduate work, for example, premedicine, revealed academic achievement in excess of grade requirements. Nevertheless, on balance, they were still achieving loftily above the average of their classmates. How can one explain their deep self-dissatisfaction despite contrary and objective indications of their competence? Two possible explanations suggest themselves: (*a*) The internal standards these students applied to themselves were so Olympian, the demands they imposed upon themselves so exacting, that they were destined to suffer frustration and disappointment no matter how well they fared; and/or (*b*) Whereas they had previously been crackerjack students in high school or junior college, excelling without much difficulty, the precipitous drop in grade points over the final semester threatened their feelings of self-esteem. Thus, faced by a sudden loss of status, they may have suicided as a response to this egoistic conflict. In any case, the discrepancy between perceived self-concept and objective reality indicates that a purely objective approach often obscures more than it reveals. What one needs to try and understand is the phenomenological response of the individual student. What is necessary to know is what inner standards, what idealized fantasy he uses to judge himself and his own personal worth. For the graduate student suicides as a group, there was no discrepancy between their academic achievements and what might be expected on the basis of the general population of graduate students. While they produced slightly below their population mean, the variation in this instance was primarily due to two students who were in considerable scholastic straits. Contrary to the undergraduates, graduate suicides showed no pattern of decline in their terminal semester GPA. Confirmation of the scholastic disparity between graduate and undergraduate suicides is further revealed by the irregular distribution of academic awards. Inspection of Table 5 indicates that undergraduate students garnered scholarship honors at a rate well beyond the general undergraduate population, while the graduate student suicides did not differ significantly from their classmates in earning academic awards. Even though graduate student awards were far more plentiful, the great majority of awards (10 of 11) were held by undergraduate student suicides.

TABLE 5   Scholastic Awards by Class Standing

| | SUICIDAL STUDENTS | | STUDENT POPULATION | |
CLASS STANDING	n	%	%	p
Undergraduate				
Scholarship	7	58	05	
Nonscholarship	5	42	95	< .001
Graduate				
Scholarship	1	10	23	
Nonscholarship	10	90	77	ns

MENTAL HEALTH

Of the 23 student suicides, 8 had been referred to the student mental health service for psychiatric treatment (of the 8 students, apparently only 2 were diagnosed as psychotic reactions). These 8 cases comprised better than one-third of the student suicides, significantly exceeding the approximately 10% of the total student body population seen at the mental health facilities (see Table 1). Besides the 8 students known to the student psychiatric service, an additional 3 students were in private psychiatric treatment, making a total of almost 50% of the suicidal group who gave this particular indication of prior mental disturbance.

TEMPORAL-SITUATIONAL RELATIONSHIPS

Among all causes of death, suicide allows for the greatest degree of violition. The suicidal person is in a position to choose the date, place, and method of his death, and it has long been speculated that there may be a special psychological significance to these choices. Through tracing the time, place, and method of student suicides, the following particular patterns were observed:

Time   When student suicides were charted by calendar months they formed a bimodal curve with peaks occurring during February and October. A more meaningful comparison obtained when the academic semester was used as the time interval. This distribution, as illustrated in Figure 2, challenges a frequently held belief about campus suicides. Academic folklore often explains student suicides as a response to the anxieties and stresses of final examinations. Yet, surprisingly, the data showed that almost the reverse relationship held. Only 1 of the 23 student suicides was committed during finals. (Even that single instance may be dubiously related to final exams since this student was

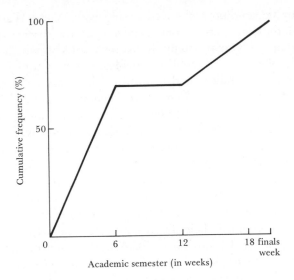

FIGURE 2 Time distribution of student suicides, UCB, 1952–61.

doing well in school and had expressed satisfaction with his "finals" performance.) Most of the suicides occurred at the beginning of the semester. When
the semester is divided into three equivalent parts, the vast majority of cases,
16 out of 23, are found to occur during the first 6-week segment. (Actually, the
period is only 5 weeks from when instruction begins; the first week is confined
to registration procedures.) No cases were found during the second 6-week
period which includes the mid-term examinations. Over the remaining third of
the semester there were seven cases, just one of which occurred during finals
week itself (always the last week of the semester). This irregular time distribution of student suicides departed significantly from uniform expectation ($x^2_2 =$
16.8, $p < .001$). Clearly, the old saw about suicides and finals was not supported. Instead, the danger period for student suicide was found to be the
start, not the finish, of the school semester. Incidentally, the day of the week
departed significantly from the null hypothesis of uniformity ($x^2_1 = 4.18$,
$p < .05$) with almost one-half the cases occurring on Monday or Friday,
terminals of the school week. Unfortunately, the data were none too precise
since some cases were based on coroner's estimates as to the date of death.

The unexpectedly low correspondence between final examinations and the
commission of student suicide bears some resemblance to a parallel phenomenon involving student mental health during the recent free speech activities
on the UCB campus. In the course of these supposedly stressful times, there
was a striking drop in admissions to the student mental health service (20%
below average) and no recorded student suicides during the 1965 academic
year. (Such behavior corresponds to the drop in suicides, psychosomatic ill-

ness, and neurotic conditions observed during both World Wars.) Why, in the midst of all the controversy, turmoil, and tempest was student mental health apparently enhanced? One possibility is that some students who had previously been grappling with internal problems now had the opportunity to act out, to ventilate their inner conflicts, and to displace their intrapunitive anger and hostility by redirecting it toward an external symbol, namely, the University. Perhaps it was the galvanized and heightened sense of community that facilitated mental well-being. Certainly many students felt involved in a common cause; probably, for some it imparted meaning to their lives where previously they had felt alienated and purposeless. If so, it was also a perfect antidote to the kinds of feelings that often drive people to self-destruction.

Place   Most of the students, 12 of 23, committed suicide at their residences. The next most frequent location was the University itself, upon whose grounds 4 students ended their lives. Three students were found dead in parked autos on isolated suburban roads. Another 3 suicided in out-of-town hotel rooms, and 1 student leaped from the San Francisco Golden Gate bridge. It is difficult to determine any significance to the site of these suicides, except for the 4 cases who killed themselves on the university grounds. Of these, the most symbolic suicide was the one student who jumped from the Campanile, an architectural landmark of the Berkeley campus.

Method   The most frequent agent of choice was firearms, followed by ingestions and asphyxiations. A comparison with the methods used by Yale student suicides (see Table 6) revealed considerable similarity in the methods employed by the two groups of students. The relatively larger number of

TABLE 6   Methods of Suicide Used by UCB and Yale Students

METHOD	UCB (1952–1961)		YALE (1920–1955)[a]	
	n	%	n	%
Firearms	8	35	10	40
Poisonings	6	26	3	12
Asphyxiation	4	17	5	20
Hanging	2	09	6	24
Jumping from high place	2	09	1	04
Cutting instruments	1	04	—	—
Total	23	100	25	100

[a] Source: Parrish, 1957, p. 589.

poisonings among UCB students is most likely due to the more recent availability of tranquilizers and barbiturates.

For only two of the Berkeley cases was there the least equivocation about assigning suicide as the cause of death. These two cases, both involving ingestions of poisonous substances, were qualified as "probably suicide" but routinely coded as "deaths due to suicide." In at least 10 instances, suicide notes were left by the decedents. These notes ranged from simple instructions concerning the disposal of personal belongings to lengthy, literary dissertations, one of which finished by tersely quoting Camus: "Life as a human being is absurd."

PSYCHOLOGICAL FACTORS

A statistical approach, per se, can go just so far in describing the suicide-prone student. The additional use of case history materials provides a fuller, more clinically oriented dimension to the portrayal. As such, the following inferences were derived from anecdotal reports of friends and acquaintances of the students, along with those members of the University community whose lives they touched. From a preventive standpoint, the most pertinent questions which might be asked are, "What prodromal signs, what clues to suicide could be discerned from the personal lives of these students? Specifically, were there any indications or harbingers of their ultimate destinies?" Lastly, "Was there a characteristic conflict which precipitated their self-destructive actions?" The question of prodromal indications can be flatly answered "yes." There were numerous warnings in almost every case. At least five of the students had made past suicide attempts. Warnings of a more subtle nature could be discovered in the histories of the remaining students. For example, the pupil who went out of his way to modify an item on the medical history form. Where it had requested, "Whom shall we notify in case of emergency?" he crossed out the word "emergency" and substituted "death." Or the student who confided that he sometimes takes 10 or so nembutals because "I am an adventurer." Other students evidenced a long-standing infatuation with death, often initiating "bull sessions" about the futility of life, or making wry jokes about killing themselves. Prior to their suicides a disproportionately large number of these students were involved in psychiatric treatment. As a group, they presented similar symptomatic patterns featuring symptoms of insomnia, anorexia, and extreme moodiness, especially moods of despondency; in all, it was a psychological picture compatible with the general diagnosis of agitated depression.

Although their prodromal response to stress was very similar, the particular crises that precipitated their suicides were not. Bearing in mind that each individual case was unique, for purposes of description, the main prodromal conflicts could be classified into the following three categories:

1. **Concern over studies** In many cases acquaintances of the students made such judgments as "he pushed himself too hard," "worried over grades," "felt his grades were not as good as he thought they should be," or similar

scholastic anxieties which, they felt, triggered the suicidal crisis. It is difficult to evaluate these inferences since "worry over grades" is often seen by informants as a most likely explanation. At any event, if true, their exaggerated concern over studies contrasted vividly with generally excellent academic grades.

2. Unusual physical complaints   A number of the students complained of inability to eat or sleep, one student warranting a diagnosis of "avitaminosis." Others worried about possible deterioration such as the student who feared that his "failing sight" might ruin a prospective medical career. A few pupils, however, presented physical complaints of a bizarre semidelusional quality, for instance, the young man whose stomach literally persecuted him. From childhood on he had suffered from anorexia and "stomach ache." Although an exploratory laparotomy did not disclose anything, by the time he entered the University he was at least 50 pounds underweight, still wracked by chronic stomach pains. He then moved from his fraternity house, in the hope of gaining weight by selecting his own food. This plan proved to no avail, nor did extensive medical testing at the student health service, all of which proved negative. He finally ended his torment, perhaps symbolically, by ingesting cyanide.

3. Difficulties with interpersonal relationships   Combined under this heading were two different types of conflicts, both reflecting problems in personal relationships. First were the students involved in stormy love affairs. Here the critical stresses were feelings of rejection which had been engendered by broken romances. In the one recorded instance of double suicide, the precipitating event was parental opposition to the youngsters' marriage. Much more typical, however, was the essentially asocial, withdrawn student. These particular students were uniformly described as terribly shy, virtually friendless individuals, alienated from all but the most minimal social interactions. Frequently they had compensated for their personal solitude by increased study and almost total absorption in schoolwork. The most calamitous example of such human isolation was the student, dead for 18 days before he was found in his lonely room. It is a tragic commentary to his existence, and perhaps a cause for his suicide, that there were no friends, no people involved enough in his life to know, or to care, that he had been missing for well over 2 weeks.

INTERPRETATION

Reviewing the results of the present study, one can reasonably conclude that significant associations between student suicide and numerous variables, both personal and environmental, have been demonstrated. Nonetheless, one cannot, with certitude, infer that these relationships are causal ones. This type of inference would require procedures more exacting than the limited epidemiological methods herein employed. For instance, the total student body population, used as a matched control or comparison group, included a number of students who had unsuccessfully attempted suicide. Quite possibly their inclusion diluted the significance of the obtained differences between suicidal and presumably nonsuicidal students. This is a relatively minor concern, compared to other more cautionary limitations. A primary concern is to what degree the observed relationships were spuriously increased by a common variable. For example, the correlation between student suicide and declining terminal GPA may very well be due to a third factor—emotional disturbance —which both depressed scholastic grades and led to self-destruction. As a corollary, it should be recognized that not all of the selected variables were independent of one another. It is known for one that age and class standing are highly dependent, and it was observed, also, that the variable of age probably confounded to some degree the comparisons by sex and by nationality. Another area of uncertainty concerns the time-order sequence of student suicide. One is unable to state, with certainty, which comes first, the disturbed student or the stresses of student life. Are the suicides due to selection into colleges of mentally unstable individuals or are they due to competitive pressures of the academic environment? The fullest answer to these questions will only come from further research. Toward this goal some salient lines of inquiry could include: the investigation of student suicide attempters and student accident cases, postcollegiate follow-up studies, and the use of "pschological autopsy" procedures, as described by Shneidman and Farberow (1961).

Within the expressed limits of the study design, what predictions about the future suicide problem are warranted? Extrapolating from results of the present study, it appears that a future increase of student suicides may be expected. This increase should occur as a function of two variables, that is, age and academic competition, both of which are directly correlated to student suicides, and both of which are slated to increase in future student body populations. Average student age is already rising as a result of ever-increasing proportions of graduate students in the American university system. For example, architects of the UCB educational master plan are considering an ultimate 50:50 graduate-undergraduate ratio. The second variable, academic competition, will likely increase as a result of mounting public demands for quasiuniversal college education. As a case in point, the enrollment demands at UCB have already exceeded the available academic supply. Consequently, it has been necessary to restrict enrollment to the uppermost fraction of high school graduating classes. If accepted, the pressure on the student to achieve and maintain very high GPAs gives no indication of abatement. In fact, the situation ominously resembles a suicidal problem which prevails among the youth of Japan. In the Japanese case there are tremendous pressures to attend college, and those students who fail to gain entrance frequently turn to suicide as a solution to their dilemmas. Such conflicts, in addition to a more accepting cultural attitude, have probably helped to make Japan "a country of youthful suicides where suicide has become the number one cause of death in individuals under 30 [DeVos, 1964, p. 6]."

Summary

The purpose of this study was to identify distinctive attributes of the suicidal student, and to determine those environmental conditions which heighten his susceptibility to suicide.

Using an epidemiological approach, demographic comparisons were made between the sample of 23 UCB students who committed suicide during the years 1952–1961 inclusive, and the total student body population for those years. As an additional procedure, the temporal-situational characteristics of student suicides were described and analyzed.

The main findings of the research were:

1. Suicidal students could be significantly differentiated from their classmates on the variables of age, class standing, major subject, nationality, emotional condition, and academic achievement. Compared to the student population at large, the suicidal group was older, contained greater proportions of graduates, language majors, and foreign students, and gave more indications of emotional disturbance. In addition, the undergraduate suicides fared much better than their fellow students in matters of academic achievement.

2. Contrary to the popular belief that suicides frequently occur during final examinations week, time relationships indicated that the peak danger period for student suicides was the beginning (first 6 weeks), not the midterm, nor end of the semester.

3. Most of the students gave recurrent warnings of their suicidal intent. Many of them presented a similar prodromal pattern marked by anorexia, insomnia, and periods of despondency.

4. Major precipitating factors were: Worry over schoolwork, chronic concerns about physical health (sometimes of a decidedly bizarre nature), and difficulties with interpersonal relationships. This last category contained some students who had reacted to romantic rejections but, for the most part, comprised the emotionally withdrawn and socially isolated student.

5. A future increase of student suicides was predicted on the basis of changes taking place in the age structure of college populations and in the competitive pressures of student life.

REFERENCES

Braaten, J., & Darling, C. Suicidal tendencies among college students. *Psychiatric Quarterly*, 1962, **36**, 665–692.

Bruyn, H. B., & Seiden, R. H. Student suicide: Fact or fancy? *Journal of the American College Health Association*, 1965, **14**, 69–77.

DeVos, G. Role narcissism and the etiology of Japanese suicide. Berkeley, Calif.: Institute of International Studies, University of California, 1964. (Mimeo)

Dublin, L. I. *Suicide: A sociological and statistical study.* New York: Ronald, 1963.

Gibbs, J. P., & Martin, W. T. *Status integration and suicide.* Eugene: Oregon University Press, 1964.

Hill, A. B. *Principles of medical statistics.* New York: Oxford University Press, 1961.

Jensen, V. W. Evaluating the suicidal impulse in the university setting. *Journal Lancet,* 1955, **75**, 441–444.

MacMahon, B., Pugh, T. F., & Ipsen, J. *Epidemiological methods.* Boston: Little, Brown, 1960.

Parrish, H. M. Epidemiology of suicide among college students. *Yale Journal of Biology and Medicine,* 1957, **29**, 585–595.

Raphael, T., Power, S. H., & Berridge, W. L. The question of suicide as a problem in college mental hygiene. *American Journal of Orthopsychiatry,* 1937, **7**, 1–14.

Shneidman, E. S., & Farberow, N. L. Sample investigations of equivocal deaths. In N. L. Farberow & E. S. Shneidman (Eds.), *The cry for help.* New York: McGraw-Hill, 1961. Pp. 118–128.

Suslow, S. *A ten-year survey of certain demographic characteristics of the student population.* Berkeley: Office of the Registrar, University of California, 1963. (Mimeo)

Temby, W. D. Suicide. In G. B. Blaine & C. C. McArthur (Eds.), *Emotional problems of the student.* New York: Appleton-Century-Crofts, 1961. Pp. 133–152.

NINE SOCIO-CULTURAL BASIS OF ADOLESCENT BEHAVIOR

Adolescence is not a universal phenomenon; the nature of the adolescent experience, the degree of crisis, and the amount of sexual repression experienced are highly dependent on sociocultural factors. The cultural relativity in the adolescent experience is dramatically illustrated in Margaret Mead's *Coming of Age in Samoa,* which demonstrates that the *sturm und drang* quality of adolescence in Western society is not part of the pattern of growing up in Samoa. Since the publication of Mead's study, considerable evidence has been presented showing that the specific adjustment problems of the adolescent and the nature and social meaning of the transition from childhood to adulthood varies greatly according to social expectations and cultural forces. This transition period may be very short, as in many primitive societies, or may last more than a decade, as in modern Western society, where the prolongation of adolescence increases the period of emotional and economic dependence and the consequent struggle by the adolescent for autonomy. Sociocultural and socioeconomic milieus determine not only the length but also the quality of the adolescent experience. The most obvious example of this influence may be seen by contrasting primitive and advanced societies, but even within a multiplistic society such as the United States, considerable differences exist in the adolescent experiences of youths in religious, racial, and national subgroups. The socialization process varies further according to socioeconomic class, region, and urban or rural residence. Finally, in the transition process, the influence of peers versus parents, sex role concepts, sexual adjustments, patterns of dating, courtship, marriage, education, and employment are all significant in the timing of adolescence and in the manner in which adult status is attained and recognized by society. The primary conclusion emerging from the articles in Part Nine is that adolescence, in contrast to pubescence, is not a physiological event, but rather is defined by social and cultural factors.

The first selection, by Rolf E. Muuss (35), considers the psychological and social significance of puberty rites and the cultural variation in their timing, meaning, and severity. The article emphasizes the wide social variations that exist in the length of the adolescent period and in the social recognition of menarche and the other physiological changes of puberty. In Western societies, where the period of adolescence is prolonged, no single experience, initiation, or graduation takes the place of the formal puberty rites in primitive societies, although many have been suggested. The problems young people face in modern society due to the prolongation of the adolescent period and the absence of clearly defined status roles are reflected in the adolescent's search for what

Erik H. Erikson calls an "individual identity." The individual has to find and define for himself the status or role that society does not bestow on him formally.

Cultural differences manifest themselves not only in the physiological area of sexual adjustment and preparation for marriage, but also in the subtle social area of peer and adult pressure. Urie Bronfenbrenner (36) demonstrates that the divergence of peer group and adult values is greater in the United States than in Russia, where peer group and adult values seem to converge around a core of socially-accepted values. In Russia, the peer group utilizes its influence on the individual to further the values and objectives held by society. The article by Bronfenbrenner offers additional perspectives on the articles by Clay V. Brittain (18), Philip R. Constanzo (20), and James S. Coleman (40), which deal respectively with the parent-peer cross-pressure, the tendency of adolescents in the United States to conform to peer-group behavior, and the autonomy of the adolescent peer group. The adolescent in Russia, apparently, experiences less of this cross-pressure between peer and adults than youths either in England or the United States because the goals and values of peers and adults in Russia are congruent. In agreement with Elizabeth Douvan's (26) observations concerning sex differences in adolescent character development, Bronfenbrenner notes that "boys are more inclined to engage in socially undesirable activity than girls," a sex difference that exists in Russia as well as in the United States.

Contrasting the late adolescent's perception of social sex roles in the United States, the West German Federal Republic, and the East German Democratic Republic, Georgene H. Seward and William R. Larson (37) uncover "reflections of cultural history, remote and recent." The study includes the findings that American boys view men as more competitive than do German boys; that American boys and East German boys view men as braver than do West German boys; that women in East Germany appear to be more active in politics than they do in West Germany or the United States; that women appear to be less brave in West Germany and the United States than in East Germany; that the father is not considered to be as strong a leader in East Germany as he is in West Germany and the United States, but is considered more active in both Germanies than in America; that American adolescents rate themselves as more passive, possibly as a result of their relative affluence in contrast to the German boys; and, finally, that all groups indicate a generation gap by rating themselves wiser, more cooperative, and better able to lead than their elders. The authors conclude that "the American emphasis on competitiveness and courage in the male image fits the individualism of a pioneer tradition," while in West Germany, "the relatively lower ratings on the cowardly-brave continuum for *men* seems to point to a socially castrating carry-over of military defeat from which the East under the strong impetus to build and identify with a new society has recovered more rapidly." The interested reader may find a more detailed and technical account of the material summarized here under the same title in *Human Development*, 1968, ii, 217-248.

Solomon Kobrin (38) looks at the sociocultural and socioeconomic bases of variations in adolescent socialization. While the middle class parent fosters his child's struggles for achievement, providing impulse control and adult supervision, the lower-class parent provides less specific goals for socialization. Lower-class children consequently must find models in the next older age group of peers, with the result that "impulse expression, aggressivity, and independence from authority" are much more prevalent than among middle-class children. In relation to two major developmental problems of adolescence—integration of dependency needs and the achievement of autonomy—middle-class parents willingly accept their responsibility for control and protection during the dependency phase, while lower-class parents eagerly grant autonomy. These different socialization patterns suggest that middle class youth have more difficulty in establishing their independence, whereas lower-class youth, who encounter more difficulty in accepting adult authority, maintain a "defensive expression of dependency hunger" that manifests itself in unswerving loyalty to the peer group, in the formation of gangs, and in their frequent intense involvement in lower-class crowd activities.

[35] *Rolf E. Muuss* PUBERTY RITES IN PRIMITIVE AND MODERN SOCIETIES

The transition from child to adult status

The period of adolescence may be long or short, depending on social expectations and on society's definition as to what constitutes maturity and adulthood. In primitive societies adolescence is frequently a relatively short period of time, while in industrial societies with patterns of prolonged education coupled with laws against child labor, the period of adolescence is much longer and may include most of the second decade of one's life. Furthermore, the length of the adolescent period and the definition of adulthood status may change in a given society as social and economic conditions change. Examples of this type of change are the disappearance of the frontier in the latter part of the nineteenth century in the United States, and, more universally, the industrialization of an agricultural society.

In modern society, puberty rites have lost their formal recognition and symbolic significance and there no longer is consensus as to what constitutes an initiation ritual. Social ceremonies have been replaced by a sequence of steps that lead to increased recognition and social status. For example: grade school

FROM *Adolescence*, 1970, 5, 109–128. REPRINTED BY PERMISSION OF LIBRA PUBLISHERS, INC.

graduation, high school graduation and college graduation constitute such a sequence, and while each step implies certain behavioral changes and social recognition, the significance of each depends on the socioeconomic status and the educational aspirations of the individual. Puberty rites have also been replaced by legal definitions of status roles, rights, privileges and responsibilities. It is during the nine years from the twelfth birthday to the twenty-first that the protective and restrictive aspects of childhood and minor status are removed and adult privileges and responsibilities are granted. (While there are significant variations in the laws from state to state, the ages discussed here are intended to represent a general pattern.) The twelve-year-old is no longer considered a child and has to pay full fare for train, airplane, theater and movie tickets. Basically, the individual at this age loses childhood privileges without gaining significant adult rights. At the age of sixteen the adolescent is granted certain adult rights which increase his social status by providing him with more freedom and choices. He now can obtain a driver's license; he can leave public schools; and he can work without the restrictions of child labor laws. At the age of eighteen the law provides adult responsibilities as well as rights; the young man can now be drafted, but he also can marry without parental consent. A girl can agree to have sexual intercourse, which prior to the age of eighteen would legally be considered rape. At the age of twenty-one the individual obtains his full legal rights as an adult. He now can vote, he can buy liquor, he can enter into financial contracts, and he is eligible to run for public office. No additional basic rights are acquired as a function of age after majority status has been attained. None of these legal provisions determine at what point adulthood has been reached but they do point to the prolonged period of adolescence in modern society.

Adolescence is frequently defined as a period of transition, that is, the transition from childhood status and dependency on parents to adulthood status and full membership in society. According to Lewin (7) adolescence is the process of changing basic membership in social groups. Both the role of the child and the role of the adult are fairly clearly defined by society and generally understood and accepted. The adolescent, in contrast—especially in modern society—has a less clearly defined role concept, since he belongs partly to the child group and partly to the adult group without really belonging to either. This situation has also been referred to as the "not quite" stage—not quite an adult, not quite a child, and not quite sure of himself. This marginal standing produces role ambiguity: the adolescent at times feels like a child, wants to be a child, and acts childish; at other times he feels like an adult, wants to be an adult, and attempts to act grown-up and adultlike. He may experience being left out, since he neither has the protection of the child nor the rights of the adult. The same role ambiguity is evident among the significant adults with whom he comes in contact. Consequently, at certain times he is treated like a child by parents, teachers, and other adults; at other times he is treated like an adult. The ambiguity that results in modern society is clarified in many primitive societies through the *rites de passage* which serve to define social status role.

If the childhood group and the adult group are clearly separated in their role status, as is the case in many primitive societies, the adolescent transition period may be relatively short and clearly marked by puberty rites which require evidence of pain tolerance, endurance, courage and strength, after which the elders or the chief bestow upon the young man or woman adulthood status. The young man and woman by passing these tests give evidence that they are ready to be accepted as members of the adult community. The rituals and the ceremonies make the change in status visible to the community. In addition, these puberty ordeals—which may involve circumcision, mutilation of body and tattooing—frequently leave body scars as proud documents of adulthood status, just as in a few German fraternities the dueling scar on one's cheek is viewed as a more visible and more treasured symbol of academic status than the actual diploma.

In technologically advanced cultures the boundaries between the children's group and the adult group are not as clearly defined. The adolescent thus moves through a psychological no-man's-land in which the routes to goals are not clear and frequently even the goals themselves are not yet determined. The individual experiences conflicts in attitudes, values, and patterns of behavior, since he is shifting from the habits established during childhood to the new perspective of what he thinks adulthood is like. Furthermore, the transition period is prolonged by increased educational demands and legal restrictions on employment and marriage. Society no longer bestows adulthood status at any one point. Confirmation, Bar Mitzvah, and the coming-out party have lost their significance as puberty rites, therefore the adolescent must struggle on his own to attain the desired adulthood status. For the adolescent himself, the first shave, or acquisition of a driver's license and access to a car, seems to constitute a modern *rite de passage,* but is rarely recognized as such by society in general. In literature, hunting and killing one's first animal is sometimes interpreted as the initiation of the boy into male maturity. Faulkner in *Go Down, Moses* describes Ike McCaslin shooting his first buck and having his face marked "with the hot blood which he has spilled and he ceased to be a child and became a hunter and man" (6, p. 178). However, such experiences, even though symbolically significant to the individual, constitute an exception rather than a common adolescent initiation experience. Some of the ordeals to which boys are exposed before being accepted in gangs, and some of the hazing in college fraternities—such as fencing with sharp sabers and without the fencing mask in German university fraternities—are not at all unlike the tests of endurance and courage that are part of the initiation ceremonies in primitive societies.

Some of the adolescent difficulties in Western society may be better understood if one considers the adolescent as the marginal man who stands in a psychological no-man's-land without clear understanding of what is expected of him, struggling to attain adult status. Consequently, he reaches for the more obvious but not necessarily the most essential characteristics of adulthood: smoking, drinking, using drugs, having the feeling of freedom and power that a car can give, sexual conquests, and the defiance of authority.

Social variations in the nature of puberty rites

Pubescence, the process of attaining reproductive maturity, is a universal phenomenon that is found among all human species and even among mammals. Human beings have the same biological characteristics and the sequence of body changes that accompany pubescence appears to be more or less universal (13). However, whether or not social recognition is given to the attainment of sexual maturity and what the nature of such recognition is, is socially defined and results in considerable variations of patterns, just as there are wide variations in the social interpretation of menstruation. The menstruating girl has been considered by her society as dangerous (Northern California Indians); as good and contributing to the growth of crops (Yuki Indians); as prone to enemy magic (Gilbert Islands); as capable of performing magic (Thompson Indians); as experiencing supernatural blessings (Apache Indians); or menstruation may be seen as unrelated to taboos and rituals (Samoa) (13). Similarly, the nature of the initiation ceremony, the emphasis on maleness and femaleness in a given culture, the age level at which one's social status changes, are all predominantly functions of social customs and cultural norms. Physiological changes are not casually related to psychological adolescence, but they do seem to provide a range of restrictions within which social adolescence takes place, since initiation ceremonies coincide or follow puberty but never precede it (1). What constitutes psychological adolescence, and how the transition from childhood to adulthood is accomplished and is socially recognized, is not the result of biological changes but is defined by social customs and traditions. However, all known societies recognize a difference in the status of the child as distinguished from the status of the adult. "The development of heterosexual interest and activity at puberty does serve to distinguish this period from the periods preceding it and from maturity." (11, p. 537). A clearer understanding of the different patterns found in various societies may provide a better appreciation of the way our own cultural environment contributes to adolescent development and personality structure.

SEVERITY OF PUBERTY RITES

Initiation rituals may vary in the emotional intensity and the amount of physical discomfort which they produce, ranging from rituals which appear to us as sadistic tortures to ceremonies which are pleasurable feasts with little or no emotional or physical discomfort. For the Apache Indians, initiating the boy is like breaking a colt. "They force him to make holes in the ice and bathe, run with water in his mouth, humiliate him on his trial war parties and generally bully him." (2, p. 94). The Nandi of East India invent ingenious tortures which accompany the circumcision of the boy, and he is rewarded if he does not show signs of pain (2). During the pubertal ceremonies of the Tukuna Indian girl, her hair is plucked from her head and the pain may be so intense that the initiate faints (14).

In contrast, the Samoan girl, even though she passes through well-marked periods of increased responsibility, does not experience any formalized rituals which delineate childhood from adulthood. Puberty is pleasant and enjoyable and free of conflict. There are no ceremonies or taboos related to menstruation, and the menstruating girl is even allowed to prepare most foods. It is not the menarche that is celebrated but the recognition of defloration (10). The hostility between preadolescent children of the opposite sex slowly disappears when they reach puberty, and a few years later clandestine, casual love affairs under the palm trees are commonplace (9).

Whiting, Kluckhohn and Anthony (15) found support for their psychoanalytic hypothesis that the severity of the initiation ritual at puberty is a function of the mother-child relationship in infancy. If the infant and the mother share the same bed for a year while the father is excluded, and if society has a taboo against sexual relations between husband and wife for at least one year after childbirth, initiation rituals are severe. They frequently include painful hazing, genital operations, seclusion from women and tests of manliness. They are believed to make up for the lack of father's discipline during childhood. The severe initiation rituals symbolically terminate the boy's desire to return to the lap of his mother, they prevent him from revolting against his father, and they help him to learn to identify with maleness in his society. In societies in which there is no exclusive mother-infant sleeping arrangement and no post-partum sex taboo, initiation rituals are less severe or completely lacking. Apparently, societies that indulge infants are more demanding on their adolescents and those that place greater restrictions on the infant are more indulgent of their adolescents. The relationship is not universal and the interpretation has been challenged by Brown (4, 5) and Young (17).

SEX DIFFERENCES IN PUBERTY RITES

The sex of the child is a significant consideration in the cultural variation of the *rite de passage*. Benedict (2) argues that sexual maturity is of greater significance in the life cycle of the female than of the male. Furthermore, if the cultural importance attached to puberty were to follow the significance of physiological changes in the individual, puberty rites would be more marked and more frequent for girls than for boys. But since man's role in most societies is defined as the more dominating and the one that has more prerogatives, more cultures actually emphasize the initiation ceremony of the adolescent male rather than the female. Mead (10) interprets differently the greater emphasis on the pubertal ceremonies of the boy. Since for the girl puberty, especially menarche, is dramatic and unmistakable, there is no reason for her or for anyone else to question her new status as a woman. Menarche constitutes a definite dividing line between childhood and adulthood. For the boy, pubertal changes are many and occur slowly over an extended period of time; there is no one specific developmental event that gives him the assurance to say "I am a man now." Consequently, society steps in and provides him with a sexual identity and a new definition of himself by way of *rites de passage,* which make his new status known to the tribe or to the village. In addition, his new social status is frequently documented by visible body scars as evidence: circumcision, incision, subcision, pierced ears, teeth filling, teeth excision, as well as changed names, special gifts and tattooing. The initiation ceremonies of the female are usually less painful and harsh, but may include any one or several of these activities: "bathing, beautification such as new hair arrangement, isolation in a special place, dietary restrictions, and announcement of the initiate's changed status and instruction in such matters as womanly tasks, etiquette, behavior toward in-laws, menstrual observances, contraceptive devices and observances during pregnancy." (4, p. 81). The ceremony is at times related to other significant events in the development of the girl, such as her first menstruation, betrothal or marriage. In other instances, menarche is a "prerequisite for initiation, and initiation in turn is often prerequisite for betrothal and marriage." (4, p. 82).

Puberty rites may take place for only one sex, or they may be more elaborate for one sex than the other; they may be quite different for both sexes and they may be identical for boys and girls. The latter is less common, since most societies make different provisions for the initiation of both sexes. The Sepik people of New Guinea have developed elaborate male initiation ceremonies which assume that men can become men only by "ritualizing birth and taking over—as a collective group—the function that women perform naturally." (10, p. 98). The Sepik do not express as much concern with women's fertility and menstrual ceremonies. In Central Africa (2), where emphasis is placed on promoting the marriageability of the pubescent girl and obesity is a sign of beauty and attractiveness, the emphasis falls on the girl. At puberty she is separated from her family and fed sweets and fatty foods for several years, and at the same time allowed no physical activities. When, after several years, society's beauty ideal of obesity is achieved, she is brought forth to be married. While elaborate ceremonies are held for the male in most of Australia, the female moves into adulthood without formal ceremony. The initiation rituals of the Mundugumor have different meanings for the sexes. To the girl it is a privilege granted to the extent that she is aggressive; to the boy it is a penalty consisting of blows, curses and being scared by a crocodile skull, from which he cannot escape (8). Among the Indians of the interior of British Columbia the puberty rites are identical for boys and for girls; they are rites of magical training for their future occupations (2).

According to Brown (5) initiation ceremonies for girls are more likely to be emphasized in those societies in which (a) the young woman stays, even after marriage, in her mother's household; (b) ambiguity about sex role exists [the ceremony itself—through painful genital operations—facilitates proper sex role identity]; (c) women make a definite contribution to subsistence. To the extent that these three characteristics are lacking—as in our own and in Samoan society—formalized female pubertal ceremonies are also absent.

RELATIONSHIP OF INITIATION CEREMONIES TO PHYSIOLOGICAL PUBERTY

Puberty rites may be quite independent of physiological puberty. To the extent that they are unrelated to biological changes, the term "puberty rites" is a misnomer. It would be more appropriate to speak of initiation ceremonies, *rites de passage* and adolescent rites. Such rites may be directly related to the attainment of sexual maturity, as is frequently the case in the menstrual ceremonies that are associated with menarche. Among the Tukuna Indians of the upper Amazon River, immediately upon onset of menarche the young girl hides from men by going into the seclusion hut, where she stays for three months in complete isolation. In preparation for the festivities the girl's body is painted. During the three days of ceremonies, dancing and merrymaking the girl's hair is plucked from her head. Immediately after the ceremony the young woman is permitted to marry, but there is no wedding feast. The puberty ritual is the most significant public ceremony in her lifetime, changing her status from that of a child to a marriageable young woman. (14).

For the Manus girl, menarche also determines the timing of the ceremonies and the public observances. When the girl has her first menstruation, the father throws a great number of coconuts into the sea, to the enjoyment of the village children. There is no embarrassment associated with the public announcement of menstruation, even though Manus society is rather puritanical and henceforth menstruation is kept secret until marriage. The girls of the village come to sleep with the initiate, large exchanges of food take place, and several feasts and ceremonies are held. For the girl the ceremony signifies that the carefree play activities of her childhood have come to an end; she is expected to passively and submissively settle down and wait until she is married. In spite of the fact that menstruation and puberty rites are closely associated events and receive thorough cultural recognition among the Manus, it has relatively little psychological importance in the life of the girl, in sharp contrast to the Tukuna. Real change in the status of the Manus girl had already occurred several years earlier when she was betrothed and when she moved into her future husband's hut.

Since such a specific physiological event is missing in the development of the male, the timing of the ceremonies may be quite unrelated to physiological changes. For example, the male initiation ceremonies of the Arapesh are quite divorced from physiological or developmental criteria. The large public initiation takes place only every six or seven years, so that inevitably some of the boys are overaged and oversized and know already some of the "revelations" that are to be made to the initiate during the ceremony; they might already have seen some of the "marvelous sights" they are to be shown (8, p. 61).

The symbolic interaction hypothesis of puberty rites advanced by Young (17) states that the reason for initiation is the stabilization of the boy's sex role. Puberty rites give the boy a sexual identity as a male and demand a high degree of male solidarity which requires loyalty to all males. In some societies the boy himself determines when he is ready to undertake the strenuous tests, submit to ceremonies, and take on adult responsibility.

THE LENGTH OF THE TRANSITION PERIOD

The transition from childhood to adulthood may be as brief as one ritual that serves to "punctuate a growth sequence that is inherently unpunctuated" (10, p. 175), or it may be a period of marginal standing full of ambiguity lasting a decade or more. To the extent that the child has been made into an adult almost overnight, adolescence has been reduced to a ceremony, and in such a situation it is inappropriate to think of adolescence as a prolonged transition period, which is the common pattern in modern technological societies. For the Nandi of East Africa the initiation ceremonies of both the boys and the girls determine a sudden change from childhood to adulthood by providing the initiate with a new sex status. The young man has become a warrior and may seek a sweetheart; for the girl the ceremony makes her marriageable (2). The Arapesh boys and girls at the first sign of puberty must obey eating and drinking taboos for a year. However, as societies become industrialized and as technological sophistication increases, the period of adolescence becomes prolonged, because increased training in the form of apprenticeships and schooling is required before adult roles can be assumed. Among graduate students in the United States, with its demand for highly specialized professional training, adolescence may last twelve to fourteen years.

THE PERSONAL MEANING OF PUBERTY RITES

The personal significance of the ceremony also varies greatly from one society to another. On the one extreme the initiate is provided with new revelations, new knowledge, and an understanding of heavily guarded secret rituals. On the other extreme the ceremony may serve a purely decorative and pleasurable purpose. The Zuni Indian boy, after being whipped by the "scare kachina" —the punitive masked god unto whom he has ascribed supernatural powers up to this point—becomes terrified when the kachina mask is lifted from the "god" and placed on the initiate's head, and when he is also given the yucca whip and ordered to strike the kachina himself. "It is the first object lesson in the truth that they, as mortals, must exercise all the functions which the uninitiated ascribes to the supernaturals themselves." (2, p. 63). In contrast, among the Manus a feast is held to celebrate the initiation of the boys between the ages of twelve and sixteen who, as part of the ceremonies, have their ears pierced in public, but apparently only for decorative purposes, since no new social or economic duties and responsibilities are demanded, nor are any new rights granted (12). In its simplest form the ceremony may not be much more than a haircut or a change in clothing.

CONTINUITIES AND DISCONTINUITIES
IN PUBERTY RITES

Puberty rites and physiological puberty may constitute a well-marked cultural discontinuity in that the self-concept and social status, as well as duties, responsibilities, and privileges drastically change. Or it may be an event that is continuous with previous experiences without any basic change in self-concept, duties and status. Cultural continuity means that the child learns nothing which at a later age he must unlearn. Continuity of cultural conditioning is most apparent in the case of the Samoan girl whose responsibilities to the family and obligations toward siblings increase slowly and continuously. Physiological puberty does not give her a new status nor is it celebrated publicly, but is described as a peaceful and pleasant period of life. As the girl matures, her attitude toward the opposite sex changes slowly from initial preadolescent antagonism to an enjoyment of sex adventures in the bushes a few years later. Her attitude toward sex is continuous; even as a child she has observed sexual activities of adults, masturbation is prevalent, no sex repression is practiced and premarital sex has no social stigma associated with it. For the Dobuans too, cultural continuity rather than discontinuity marks the preadolescent period. The sex life of the girl has begun long before puberty and there are no rituals to give her a new status when she actually reaches puberty. There are no cultural fears or taboos associated with menstruation (11). The Arapesh girl upon first menstruation goes through elaborate ceremonies, e.g., she feasts while in her menstrual hut and afterwards receives decorative cuts on shoulders and buttocks. However, since she already has lived for four years in her future husband's household, "her puberty ceremony is not a ritual admission to an order of life, but merely a bridging of a physiological crisis that is important to her health and her growth." (8, p. 76). The ritual neither makes the girl available for marriage—since she has already been betrothed—nor is it a marriage ceremony. While the ceremony symbolizes the end of the girl's childhood, it does not constitute a basic discontinuity to her self-concept or her social role. The most impressive illustration of cultural discontinuity becoming apparent in the *rites de passage* is reported by Benedict (3). The initiation ceremonies of Australian and Papuan cultures symbolize the "Making of the Man." Since men and women are considered to possess opposing and conflicting status roles, and since the child's status is undefined, the ceremony itself serves to initiate the boy into the male role. During the ceremony of the Arunta, the boy is literally snatched away from his mother, and in the final stage of the ceremony, which is taboo to women, he emerges out of the men's ceremonial "baby pouch," reborn as a man. The drawing of blood from each other's veins which follows, symbolizes masculine solidarity, and the boy is now admitted to the man's house. The cultural discontinuity between child and man has been bridged by the ritual.

SOCIETAL PROVISION FOR SEX EDUCATION AND SEX EXPERIENCES DURING PUBERTY

The onset of puberty increases sexual tensions and sexual curiosity. These sexual needs eventually lead to courtship and mate selection. However, the social pressures that inhibit, facilitate or even encourage the expression of these psychosexual needs differ greatly from one society to another and foster quite different patterns of behavior, even though the underlying biological pressures are similar. Social provision for sex education and social tolerance for or restriction of premarital sexual experimentation are in some societies closely interrelated to puberty ceremonies which may give the initiate the status of marriageability, as in the case of the Nandi. The interrelationship between puberty rites and the sexual status of the initiate is also implied in such practices as circumcision, genital operations and the ritual deflowering of girls. Societies may provide youth with sexual knowledge and, in rare cases, even sexual experiences. On the other hand, puberty may not change the sexual status of the individual at all, since this occurs several years later, or the status may not change because sexual activities have preceded physiological puberty.

Sexual activities precede puberty among the Dobuans living on the eastern shores of New Guinea. The Dobuans are considered dangerous and treacherous and are feared by their neighbors. Their society is one of anarchy where every man is against every other man. The sex life of the girl begins long before puberty (11), and since following puberty the boy's home is closed to him, he sleeps every night in the house of available young girls and leaves before dawn. If he leaves too late he is trapped into marriage by a hostile act of his mother-in-law to be, who blocks the exit of the house. As the villagers gather around the doorway the couple is formally betrothed. Later in marriage, adultery becomes a favorite pastime.

In Samoan society, puberty goes unnoticed and does not change the social or the sexual status of the individual. Samoan children have an early understanding of sex, gathered from occasional glimpses of sexual activities of adults and also from the fact that children go without clothes and that adults are barely clothed. Masturbation begins at the age of six or seven. Puberty itself does not produce a significant change in sex attitudes. Menstruation is experienced without pain and without change in status role. No puberty rites mark the beginning of adolescence, and the common practice of premarital intercourse does not being until two or three years after physiological maturity has been attained (9).

The Cagaban society takes an extreme position, since the boy when he reaches puberty is not only given specific instruction about sexual intercourse but in addition he is sent to live with a widow in a specially built hut until he has mastered his newly-acquired knowledge. The boy is reported to be terrified but he is not permitted to leave the hut until he succeeds (15).

For the Arapesh of New Guinea, sexual life and physical growth are antithetical. Sex is considered good for those who have finished their physical growth, but dangerous for children who have not yet completed their growth. When the boy reaches puberty he is made aware of the physiology of sex. But taboos are placed upon experimenting with sex because it is believed that this would endanger his physical growth and would prevent him from having children when he is a man. The social taboos are not so much concerned with morality and punishment as with the consequences which the act is believed to have (8). Therefore, after puberty the parents-in-law increase the chaperonage of their son's bride.

The Manus in contrast have prudish and puritanical attitudes toward sex; it is bad, shameful, and relegated to the darkness of the night. Children are not supposed to know about it or witness it and consequently feel ashamed about the knowledge which they inevitably acquire. They feel ashamed of their body, about excretion, and about their sex organs. The secrecy about sexual knowledge goes so far that the Manus men have no knowledge of the fact that unmarried girls menstruate. When they are told that this is a fact, Manus men shrug their shoulders and deny it: "Manus women are different" (12, p. 98). Wives are supposed to be virtuous; actually, in spite of childhood masturbation, Manus women are quite frigid. Illegitimate premarital sex affairs place her, her partner-in-sin, and even her kin in danger of death by the ever-observant spirits. The unmarried man over 20 is a threat to the sex mores of the community, which are not based on love and respect but upon exchange of property and fear of the supernatural.

Among Western societies, sexual behavior is more complex and variations within a given culture are much greater. However, a cross-cultural comparison between French and American youth is of relevance in this context. According to Wylie (16), French children learn to accept externally set limits, including the limitations of nature, more readily than American children. American parents set fewer limits and want their children to discover for themselves the rules that govern reality. Consequently, the Frenchman sees less of a discrepancy between the ideal and the reality, since he has learned at an early age to accept reality as it is, while the American is more oriented toward the ideal and continuously wants to improve reality and come closer to the ideal. Since sex is a basic force of nature which cannot be denied, Frenchmen are more likely to accept it as part of reality; in addition, they have learned more self-control in accepting limits earlier. The American has learned more idealistic standards of behavior as far as sex is concerned, but he is continuously bombarded with sexual stimuli from the newspaper stands in the drug store, TV, movies, magazines, comic strips, advertisements and locker room jokes. Consequently, he is pulled into a personal conflict between the ideal and reality.

"The American adolescent must choose between observing the standards and feeling frustrated and cheated, or violating the standards, feeling guilty and risking social sanction." (16, p. 296). In certain ways the French come closer to the pattern of the Cagaban society described earlier. The French boy is frequently initiated into sexual matters by an older experienced woman, and only after he has become experienced himself does he initiate his girl friend—who ideally is a virgin and becomes his future wife. This pattern of sexual learning is also a common theme in French novels and movies.

The American adolescent finds the idea of sexual relations with a woman the age of his mother revolting. He receives his initial sex training—just as much other learning—by trial and error. His first sexual experience may be with a slightly older and slightly more experienced girl in the back seat of his car after a couple of beers. "This is not a very satisfactory experience for either one of the couple, and it has been suggested that the whole clumsy operation may help account for the feeling of inadequacy by many American adults." (16, p. 297).

REFERENCES

 1. Ausubel, D. P. *Theory and Problems of Adolescent Development.* New York: Grune & Stratton, 1954.
 2. Benedict, R. *Patterns of Culture.* New York: Mentor Book, 1934.
 3. ———. Continuities and Discontinuities in Cultural Conditioning. *Psychiatry,* 1938, 1, 161–167.
 4. Brown, J. K. Adolescent Initiation Rites Among Preliterate Peoples. In R. E. Grinder (Ed.), *Studies in Adolescence.* New York: Macmillan, 1963. pp. 75–85.
 5. ———. Female Initiation Rites: A Review of the Current Literature. In D. Rogers (Ed.), *Issues in Adolescent Psychology.* New York: Appleton-Century-Crofts, 1969, pp. 74–86.
 6. Faulkner, W. *Go Down, Moses.* New York: Random House, 1942.
 7. Lewin, K. Field Theory and Experiment in Social Psychology: Concepts and Methods. *American Journal of Sociology,* 1939, 44, 868–897.
 8. Mead, M. *Sex and Temperament in Three Primitive Societies.* New York: Mentor Book, 1935.
 9. ———. *Coming of Age in Samoa.* New York: Mentor Book, 1949.
10. ———. *Male and Female.* New York: William Morrow, 1950.
11. ———. Adolescence in Primitive and in Modern Society. In G. E. Swanson, T. M. Newcomb & E. L. Hartley (Eds.), *Readings in Social Psychology.* (Rev. ed.) New York: Henry Holt, 1952, pp. 531–538.
12. ———. *Growing Up in New Guinea.* New York: Mentor Book, 1953.
13. Muuss, R. E. *Theories of Adolescence.* (2nd ed.) New York: Random House, 1968.
14. Schultz, H. Tukuna Maidens Come of Age. *National Geographic Magazine,* 1959, 116, 629–649.

15. Whiting, J. W. M., Kluckhohn, R. & Anthony, A. The Function of Male Initiation Ceremonies at Puberty. In E. E. Maccoby, T. M. Newcomb & E. L. Hartley (Eds.) *Readings in Social Psychology.* (3rd ed.) New York: Henry Holt, 1958, pp. 359–370.
16. Wylie, L. Youth in France and the United States. In E. H. Erikson (Ed.) *The Challenge of Youth.* New York: Doubleday Anchor Book, 1965, pp. 291–311.
17. Young, F. W. The Function of Male Initiation Ceremonies: A Cross-Cultural Test of an Alternate Hypothesis. *American Journal of Sociology,* 1962, 67, 379–396.

[36] *Urie Bronfenbrenner* RESPONSE TO PRESSURE

FROM PEERS VERSUS ADULTS AMONG SOVIET AND

AMERICAN SCHOOL CHILDREN

Problem

The experiment to be reported here is part of a more extensive research project investigating the differential impact of adults and peers on the behavior and personality development of children in different cultural contexts. Our earlier studies had pointed to important differences from culture to culture in the part taken by peers *vis-a-vis* adults in the socialization process. For example, in Germany the family appears to play a more central and exclusive role in upbringing than it does in the United States, where children spend a substantially greater proportion of their time outside the family in peer group settings (Devereux, Bronfenbrenner and Suci, 1960). The influence of peers emerged as even stronger, however, among English children, who were far more ready than their American age-mates to follow the lead of their companions in socially disapproved activities rather than adhere to values and behaviors approved by parents and other adults (Devereux, Bronfenbrenner and Rodgers, 1965). In other words, the evidence suggested that in both these Western countries, especially in England, peers often stood in opposition to adults in influencing the child to engage in anti-social behavior.

In contrast, field observations in the Soviet Union (Bronfenbrenner, 1963) indicated a rather different pattern. In that country, in keeping with the edu-

FROM *International Journal of Psychology-Journal International de psychology,* 1967, 2, 199–207. REPRINTED BY PERMISSION OF THE AUTHOR, THE INTERNATIONAL UNION OF PSYCHOLOGICAL SCIENCE, AND DUNOD, PUBLISHER, PARIS.

cational principles and methods developed by Makarenko (1952) and others, an explicit effort is made to utilize the peer group as an agent for socializing the child and bringing about an identification with the values of the adult society (Bronfenbrenner, 1962). Accordingly we were led to the hypothesis that in the Soviet Union, in contrast to America or England, children are less likely to experience peer pressure as conflicting with adult values and hence can identify more strongly with adult standards for behavior.

Research design and procedures

An opportunity to investigate this hypothesis was provided during the author's visits as an exchange scientist at the Institute of Psychology in Moscow in 1963 and 1964. With the cooperation of Soviet colleagues, it was possible to carry out a comparative study of reaction to pressure from peers *vs* adults in six American (N = 158) and six Soviet (N = 188) classrooms at comparable age and grade levels (average age of 12 years in both countries, 6th graders in US, 5th graders in USSR, where school entrance occurs one year later).

To measure the child's responsiveness to pressure from adult *vs* peers we employed the following experimental procedure.* Children were asked to respond to a series of conflict situations under three different conditions: 1) a *base* or *neutral* condition, in which they were told that no one would see their responses except the investigators conducting the research; 2) an *adult* condition in which they were informed that the responses of everyone in the class would be posted on a chart and shown to parents and teachers at a special meeting scheduled for the following week; and 3) a *peer* condition, in which the children were notified that the chart would be prepared and shown a week later to the class itself. The conflict situations consisted of 30 hypothetical dilemmas such as the following:

The Lost Test

You and your friends accidentally find a sheet of paper which the teacher must have lost. On this sheet are the questions and answers for a quiz that you are going to have tomorrow. Some of the kids suggest that you not say anything to the teacher about it, so that all of you can get better marks. What would you *really* do? Suppose your friends decide to go ahead. Would you go along with them or refuse?

REFUSE TO GO ALONG WITH MY FRIENDS			GO ALONG WITH MY FRIENDS		
absolutely certain	fairly certain	I guess so	I guess so	fairly certain	absolutely certain

* This procedure was developed by the author in collaboration with the other principal investigators for the project as a whole: E. C. Devereux, Jr., G. J. Suci, and R. R. Rodgers, who also carried out the American phase of the experiment.

Other items dealt with such situations as going to a movie recommended by friends but disapproved by parents, neglecting homework to join friends, standing guard while friends put a rubber snake in the teacher's desk, leaving a sick friend to go to a movie with the gang, joining friends in pilfering fruit from an orchard with a "no trespassing" sign, wearing styles approved by peers but not by parents, running away after breaking a window accidentally while playing ball, etc.

A Russian-language version of the same thirty items was prepared, with minor variations to adapt to the Soviet cultural context. Each response was scored on a scale from − 2.5 to + 2.5, a negative value being assigned to the behavior urged by age mates. To control for a positional response set, scale direction was reversed in half of the items. The situations were divided into three alternate forms of 10 items each, with a different form being used for each experimental condition. Thus under any one condition a child could obtain a score ranging from − 25 to + 25 with zero representing equal division between behavior urged by peers and adults. Split-half reliabilities for the ten-item forms ranged from .75 to .86 under different experimental conditions; the reliability of the total score (*i.e.*, sum across all three conditions) was .94. All reliability coefficients are corrected for length of test by the Spearman-Brown formula.

The basic research design involved a double Latin square with experimental treatments constituting the three rows, classrooms appearing in the columns, and forms distributed randomly, with the restriction that each form appear only once in each column and twice in each row. This basic pattern was repeated twice in each culture, once for boys and once for girls, for a total of four sets of double Latin squares (three conditions by six classrooms in four sex-culture combinations). In order to equate for varying numbers of boys and girls in each classroom, the individual cell entries used for the primary analysis of variance were the mean scores obtained by all boys or girls in a given classroom under a particular experimental condition. In this model, classrooms and forms were treated as random variables, and culture, experimental treatment, and sex of child as fixed effects. It is, of course, the latter three which constitute the primary focus of interest in the experiment.

Results

Mean values obtained by boys and girls in each culture under the three experimental conditions are shown in Table 1, relevant mean differences and corresponding significance levels in Table 2. Several findings emerge from this analysis. First of all, there is clear evidence that Soviet children are far less willing than their American age mates to say that they will engage in socially disapproved behavior. The mean scores for Russian boys and girls (Table 1, col. IV) average about 13 and 16 respectively, values that are clearly on the adult side of the continuum. The corresponding American averages of approximately 1 and 3.5 are barely over the dividing line, indicating that the children

TABLE 1 Mean Scores Obtained by Boys and Girls in the US and the USSR Under Three Experimental Conditions

SUBJECTS	I Base	II Adult	III Peer	IV *M* across Conditions
Boys				
Soviet	12.54	14.21	13.18	13.30
American	1.02	1.57	.16	.92
Difference	11.52	12.64	13.02	12.38
Girls				
Soviet	15.13	17.02	16.90	16.33
American	3.83	4.35	2.38	3.52
Difference	11.30	12.67	14.52	12.82
Both sexes				
Soviet	13.84	15.62	15.04	14.82
American	2.43	2.96	1.27	2.22

are almost as ready to follow the prompting of peers to deviant behavior as to adhere to adult-approved standards of conduct. The above cultural difference is highly significant across both sexes (Table 2, Line 1).

Second, the data indicate that both in the USSR and in the United States, boys are more inclined to engage in socially undesirable activity than girls. The absence of a reliable sex by culture interaction (Table 2, Col IV) indicates that the sex difference was no larger in one country than in the other. It is noteworthy that despite the differing conceptions of the role of women in the two societies, females in the Soviet Union as in the United States lay greater claim to virtuous behavior, at least up to the age of twelve!

Third, turning to the experimental effects, we learn (Table 2, Line 3) that in both countries children gave more socially approved responses when told that their answers would be seen by adults than when faced with the prospect of having their statements shown to classmates. Although American youngsters exhibited a greater shift than their Soviet counterparts, a fact which suggests stronger conflict between peer and adult influences in the United States, this cultural difference is not statistically significant (Table 2, Line 3, Col. IV). A reliable difference does appear, however, for the remaining independent degree of freedom which measures whether the two shifts from base condition differed from each other; that is, whether there was any difference in direction

TABLE 2 Differences in Total Score and Experimental Effects by Culture and Sex

	I SOVIET	II AMERICAN	III. EFFECT ACROSS BOTH CULTURES (SOV. + AMER.)	IV. CULTURAL DIFFERENCE (SOVIET − AMER.)
Total scores				
1. Both sexes (Girls + Boys)	14.82	2.22	—	12.60**
2. Sex differ. (Girls − Boys)	3.03	2.60	5.63**	.43 ns
Shift scores (Girls + Boys)[1]				
3. Ad[2]-peer conflict (Ad − Peer)	.58	1.69	2.27**	− 1.11 ns
4. Ad shift (Ad − Base)	1.78	.53	2.31	1.25
5. Peer shift (Base − Peer)	− 1.20	1.16	− .04	− 2.36
6. Ad shift − Peer shift	2.90	− .63	2.35 ns	3.61*

* significant at .05.
** significant at .01.
[1] None of the shift effects showed a significant interaction by sex.
[2] Ad = Adult.

or degree between the shift from base to adult condition and that from base to peer condition. As indicated in Table 2 (Line 6), Soviet children shifted more when subjected to pressure from grown-ups, whereas Americans were slightly more responsive to pressure from peers. The components entering into this difference are shown in Lines 4 and 5 of the same table. Although the cultural differences cannot be subjected to an independent statistical test, since they are incorporated in the single degree of freedom tested in Line 6, they do provide a more detailed picture of the differing reactions of children in the two countries to pressure from grown-ups *vs* age mates. Thus we see from Line 4 that although both Russian and American youngsters gave more socially acceptable responses in moving from the neutral to the adult condition, this shift was more pronounced for the Soviet children. Moreover, under pressure from peers (Line 5), there was a difference in direction as well as degree. When told that classmates would see their answers, American pupils indicated greater readiness to engage in socially-disapproved behavior, whereas Soviet children exhibited increased adherence to adult standards. In other words, in the USSR, as against the United States, the influence of peers operated in the same direction as that of adults.

Discussion

Our original hypothesis has been sustained in a number of respects. First, in contrast both to American and English children, Russian youngsters showed less inclination to engage in anti-social activity. Second, although pressure from adults induced greater commitment to socially approved behavior in both cultures, Soviet children were more responsive to the influence of grown-ups than of peers, whereas their American age-mates showed a trend in the opposite direction. Putting it another way, pressure from peers operated differently in the two countries. In the USSR, it strengthened commitment to adult-approved behavior; in the United States it increased deviance from adult standards of conduct.

If, as our data strongly suggest, the social context is a powerful determinant of behavior, then we should expect differences in responses to be associated not only with molar social structures like cultures but also smaller units such as classroom groups. This expectation can be tested from our data by determining whether, in each culture, there were significant classroom effects; the error term used for this comparison was the mean square for individual differences within classrooms. Table 3 shows the variance of classroom means in each country under each of the three experimental conditions. The accompanying significance levels reveal that there are reliable classroom differences in both countries, but only under base or peer conditions, never in the adult condition. It would appear that the tendency to conform to peer group norms operates only in the absence of monitoring by parents and teachers, and threat of exposure to adults has the effect of dissolving pressure to conform to peer standards. Although the pattern of classroom variances under the three experimental

TABLE 3   Variances Among Classroom Means Under Three Experimental Conditions

	AMERICAN	SOVIET
Base	36.01**	43.40**
Adult	13.43	9.25
Peer	45.77**	17.01

**F significant at .01.

conditions differs in the two countries—the highest mean square occurs under peer condition in the United States and base condition in the USSR—this cultural variation was not significant. Nor were there any reliable classroom differences associated with the sex of the child.

What about individual differences within classrooms? Is there a greater tendency for children to conform to classroom norms in one country than in the other? The data of Table 4 reveal that there is such a cultural difference, but for one sex only. Although American boys show slightly higher individual variation than either Soviet boys or American girls, these differences are not significant. Soviet girls, however, show a surprisingly strong tendency to respond as a classroom group, with little individual deviance. The variances are about half the size of those for any other group, and significantly smaller. Finally, individual differences for the Russian girls were smallest when exposed to pressure from adults. It will be recalled that the Soviet girls were the most adult-oriented of the four groups of subjects. Under all those conditions, including peer pressure, their mean scores were above 15, closer to the maximum possible 25 than to the borderline of anti-social behavior represented by zero on the scale. Given this combination of especially high means with extremely low variances, we may conclude that it is Soviet girls in particular who support adult standards of behavior and, both as individuals and as a classroom collective, experience and exert social pressure to conform to these standards.

TABLE 4   Average Variance of Individuals Within Classrooms

	AMERICAN	SOVIET	RATIO US/USSR
Boys	$df = 75$	$df = 103$	
Base	5.70	5.03	1.13
Adult	6.10	5.23	1.17
Peer	6.05	5.71	1.06
Total	14.07	11.55	1.22
Girls	$df = 71$	$df = 73$	
Base	4.28	2.08	2.06**
Adult	4.98	1.73	2.88**
Peer	5.36	2.03	2.64**
Total	11.31	3.02	3.74**

**F significant at .01.

The finding that in both societies adult pressure dissolved group solidarity suggests some opposition between adult values and peer interests in the Soviet Union as well as in the United States. The fact remains, however, that at least in our data, readiness to resist promptings to anti-social behavior, and responsiveness to adult influence, were greater among Russian than among American children. In addition, the results showed that in the USSR peer groups exerted some influence in support of adult standards, whereas in America they encouraged deviance from adult norms.

Although these results are in accord with our original hypothesis, and indeed perhaps for this very reason, it is important to stress the limitations of the study. To begin with, our samples were rather small, only six classrooms, comprising less than 200 cases, in each culture. Second, both samples were essentially accidental, the American classrooms being drawn from two schools in a small city in upstate New York, the Russian from three *internats* or boarding schools, in Moscow. The latter fact is especially important since one of the reasons for the widespread introduction of boarding schools in connection with the educational reform carried out in the Soviet Union during the past decade was to make possible more effective character education in the school environment. It is therefore possible that pupils in the internats are more strongly identified with adult values than those attending day schools. For this reason, the experiment here described is currently being carried out, through the collaboration of the Institute of Psychology, in six other Moscow classrooms in schools of the more conventional type where the students live at home. At the same time, the experiment is also being repeated in a series of classrooms in a large American city more comparable to Moscow.

Even if these further and more relevant replications confirm the trends revealed by the present data, two additional questions remain. First there is the matter of the generalizability of the results outside the experimental setting. Although carried out in school classrooms, the research remains in effect a laboratory study dealing with hypothetical situations rather than behavior in real life. What evidence is there that in fact American children are more likely than their Soviet age-mates to engage in anti-social behavior? None in the present study. The present investigator has reported elsewhere, however, some field observations of Soviet children which described a pattern quite in accord with the findings of the present research. For example, "In their external actions they are well-mannered, attentive, and industrious. In informal conversations, they reveal strong motivation to learn, a readiness to serve their society . . . Instances of aggressiveness, violation of rules, or other anti-social behavior appear to be genuinely rare" (Bronfenbrenner, 1963).

Finally, we must bear in mind that both the earlier observations and present experimental study were carried out with children at a particular age level, namely late childhood and early adolescence. We are therefore left with the all-important question, unanswered by our data, as to how these same youngsters will behave as adults. Do children who at the age of 12 or 13 yield to peer pressures toward anti-social behavior continue to show such reactions in later years? Does early commitment to the values of the adult society endure? Does the presence of such a commitment in adulthood require that the norms of behavior among children be fully compatible with those of grown-ups, or does some conflict of interest further the development of capacities for independent thought and responsible social action? Our results shed little light on these important questions.

Despite the acknowledged limitations of the study, it permits several inferences, both theoretical and practical. With respect to the former, the experiment demonstrates that social pressure has appreciable effects in such differing social systems as those of the Soviet Union and the United States. At the same time, the research indicates that these effects can vary significantly as a function of the larger social context. Where the peer group is to a large extent autonomous, as it often is in the United States, it can exert influence in opposition to values held by the adult society. In other types of social systems, such as the USSR, the peer group, and its power to affect the attitudes and actions of its members, can be harnessed by the adult society for the furtherance of its own values and objectives. This fact carries with it important educational and social implications. Thus it is clear that in the Soviet Union the role of the peer group is in large part the result of explicit policy and practice. This is hardly the case in the United States. In the light of the increasing evidence for the influence of the peer group on the behavior and psychological development of children and adolescents, it is questionable whether any society, whatever its social system, can afford to leave largely to chance the direction of this influence, and realization of its high potential for fostering constructive development both for the child and his society.

REFERENCES

Bronfenbrenner, U. Soviet methods of character education. *American Psychologist,* 1962, **17,** 550–564.

Bronfenbrenner, U. Upbringing in collective settings in Switzerland and the USSR. Paper presented at the XVIIth International Congress of Psychology, Washington, D.C., 1963.

Devereux, E. C., Jr., Bronfenbrenner, U. & Suci, G. J. Patterns of parent behavior in the United States of America and the Federal Republic of Germany: A cross-national comparison. *International Social Science Journal* (UNESCO), 1962, **14,** 488–506.

Devereux, E. C., Jr., Bronfenbrenner, U. & Rodgers, R. R. Child-rearing in England and the United States: A cross-national comparison. Unpublished manuscript.

Makarenko, A. S. *O Kommunisticheskom Vospitanii* (On Communist Upbringing). Moscow: Gosudarstvennoe Uchebno-pedagogicheskoye Izdatel'stvo, 1952.

[37]   *Georgene H. Seward & William R. Larson*

ADOLESCENT CONCEPTS OF SOCIAL SEX ROLES IN THE UNITED STATES AND THE TWO GERMANIES

Of the many problem areas in the changing world, one of the most challenging concerns the attitudes of youth toward the social roles they will be assuming as men and women. At the close of World War II, Seward (1946) attempted to delineate sex roles as they were at that time in the United States, Germany, and the Soviet Union. During the subsequent two decades these social orders have changed and a new generation has grown up under their differential influences.

Problem

The present study was an attempt to gauge the effects of living under diverse social climates on the ways social sex roles are conceptualized by contemporary youth. The specific comparisons concerned the United States, the Federal Republic of Germany, and the sovietized German Democratic Republic.

Subjects

The difficulty of getting representative samples of nations was compounded by the reality problem of availability. In an attempt to "neutralize" local differences, several samples were used where possible. In the United States, one group was obtained from Los Angeles, another from Muncie, Indiana, the original "Middletown," the Lynds' (1956) "typical" American city. In the West German Federal Republic, samples were drawn from Frankfurt and Hanover. For the East German Democratic Republic, however, Jena was the only representative.

Adolescence was selected as the period of identity crisis during which boys and girls are acutely concerned with the problem of sex roles (Erikson, 1956). All Ss were selected within the age range 16–19 yr.

In an attempt to match groups for educational level across the disparate

FROM *Proceedings of the 76th Annual Convention of the American Psychological Association,* 1968. COPYRIGHT 1968 BY THE AMERICAN PSYCHOLOGICAL ASSOCIATION, AND REPRODUCED BY PERMISSION OF THE AUTHOR AND THE PUBLISHER.

school systems involved, seniors from West German *Gymnasia,* seniors from East German *Oberschule,* and freshmen from American public colleges were compared. The five main groups were each represented by a population of approximately 100 boys and 100 girls.

Procedure

Osgood's (1964) Semantic Differential technique was adapted to the present research requirements. The following 12 bipolar 7-point scales were selected because of their relevance to social sex roles: *hard-soft; ugly-beautiful; insensitive-sensitive; cowardly-brave; competitive-cooperative; calm-excitable; leading-following; cautious-rash; active-passive; friendly-unfriendly; strong-weak; foolish-wise.* To preserve connotative constancy across the language barrier, double translation from English to German and back to English again was done by two bilinguals working independently.

Scale ratings were obtained anonymously from Ss for the concepts, *my father, my mother, men,* and *women. Myself* was included for comparison with the other concepts to determine points of identification and differentiation.

In preparing the test booklets, the order of the scales, as well as their polarity, was randomized for each concept to counteract the operation of response sets. The tests were administered according to standard instructions by the classroom teachers in the context of regular academic work.

Results

Multiple discriminant function analyses (Cooley & Lohnes, 1962) based on Fisher's (1936) discriminant function, *F,* made possible intercomparisons of national groups for each concept, with the 12 scales taken together as a profile. For the *F* ratios, *p* values were determined as indices of the significance of the obtained differences.

The *F* ratios for overall cross-national comparisons, which were uniformly significant at the .001 level, show that the American boys and girls differed significantly from their German age peers in the ways they conceptualized *men, women, father, mother,* and *self.* The results of the boys' concepts are summarized in Table 1.

The weights appearing in the conventionalized vector columns indicate the particular contributions of each scale to the group separations on the various concepts, with a loading of 1.00 as maximum. Thus, for *men* the greatest differential occurs on the competitive-cooperative dimension; for *women* on cowardly-brave, etc.

The girls' data (not shown) revealed analogous though not identical group differences.

Having demonstrated general cross-national differences, the next step was to locate their distribution and direction. Multivariate analyses of the samples

TABLE 1   Multiple Discriminant Function Analysis, *F*, by Geographic Areas: USA, GFR, and GDR. Conventionalized Vectors

SCALE	BOYS' CONCEPTS				
	M	W	F	M	S
Hard-soft	.15	.31	.02	.89	.38
Ugly-beautiful	.31	.38	.52	.69	.67
Insensitive-sensitive	.27	.17	.18	.86	.32
Cowardly-brave	.85	1.00	.42	.29	.16
Competitive-cooperative	1.00	.34	.49	.18	.21
Calm-excitable	.30	.41	.25	.59	.27
Leading-following	.66	.69	.77	.03	.15
Cautious-rash	.54	.09	.28	1.00	.07
Active-passive	.19	.74	1.00	.96	1.00
Friendly-unfriendly	.70	.09	.32	.26	.46
Strong-weak	.19	.15	.49	.26	.07
Foolish-wise	.34	.49	.31	.42	.14
F^*	8.91	4.74	5.44	4.39	9.47

* $F = 2.13$, $df = 24/764$, $p = .001$.

taken by pairs permitted within-nation as well as between-nation comparisons. These results, which unfortunately cannot be presented in this brief report, amply validated the expectation that cross-national differences would outweigh sample differences within nations. Specifically, American Ss viewed *men* as more competitive than did any of the German groups. Bravery was another attribute figuring importantly in the American boys' imagery of *men,* a view shared by East German boys but conspicuous by its absence from the West German records.

In the case of *women,* the most remarkable finding was their relatively low rating by the Americans on bravery, the very attribute on which *men* were evaluated so highly. Within Germany, a more active picture of *women* in the Democratic Republic contrasted with the traditionally passive role still in evidence in the West.

An interesting feature of international discrepancy was the lower degree of leadership ascribed to *father* in the Eastern sector than in either West Germany or the United States. Moreover, in the eyes of American boys, *father* appeared less active than he did to boys in either Germany.

For *mother* there were no pervasive differences in ratings among the main groups.

The most unequivocal trend appeared on the *self* concepts which American boys and girls consistently projected as less active than did the corresponding Ss from either Germany.

In addition to intercomparisons of groups on each concept, concepts were compared with one another within each group and the differences tested for significance by *t* ratios. While abundantly confirming the familiar social stereotypes of masculine aggressiveness and feminine sensitivity in their concepts of *men* vs. *women, father* vs. *mother,* the results also revealed a notable generation gap between the adolescents' self-concepts and the way they saw their elders. Boys and girls of all samples seem to have relinquished the old models and to share with each other, regardless of sex or nationality, a more action-oriented idea of themselves as surpassing previous generations in cooperation, leadership, and wisdom.

Conclusions

The cross-national differences demonstrated in the present study may be interpreted as reflections of cultural history, remote and recent. Thus, the American emphasis on competitiveness and courage in the male image fits the individualism of a pioneer tradition. In West Germany, the relatively lower ratings on the cowardly-brave continuum for *men* seems to point to a socially castrating carry-over of military defeat from which the East under the strong impetus to build and identify with a new society has recovered more rapidly. In the case of *women,* the German students, unlike the Americans, perceived them as equals in courage perhaps in recognition of their demonstrated valor in adversity.

For the German *father,* the greater activity ascribed to him than to the American *father* may be the last vestige of the patriarchal image which has already lost its leadership charisma in the Democratic Republic.

As regards the adolescents themselves, the tendency toward passivity in the American *self* concepts suggests a complacency in the "affluent society" in contrast with the more urgent demands for action in the two Germanies.

Whatever the meaning of the differences among the national samples compared, the outstanding finding of the present research was the generation gap separating youth from parents. Boys and girls of all groups studied shared a view of themselves as taking a more responsible part in the society of the future.

REFERENCES

Cooley, W., & Lohnes, P. *Multivariate procedures for the behavioral sciences.* New York: Wiley, 1962.

Erikson, E. H. The problem of ego identity. *Journal of the American Psychoanalytic Association*, 1956, **4**, 56–121.

Fisher, R. The use of multiple measurements in taxonomic problems. *Annals of Eugenics*, 1936, **7**, 179–188.

Lynd, R. S., & Lynd, H. M. *Middletown: A study in American culture.* New York: Harcourt, Brace, 1956.

Osgood, C. E. Semantic differential technique in the comparative study of cultures. *American Anthropologist*, 1964, **66**, 171–200.

Seward, G. H. *Sex and the social order.* New York: McGraw-Hill, 1946.

[38]   *Solomon Kobrin*   THE IMPACT OF CULTURAL

FACTORS ON SELECTED PROBLEMS OF

ADOLESCENT DEVELOPMENT IN THE MIDDLE

AND LOWER CLASS

Three common problems of adolescent development are here examined in relation to the differential cultural patterning of their resolution in the middle class and the lower class. In its ideal typical form each class exhibits a distinctive set of norms, values, and concerns generating different modes of response to the problems of adolescent development which occur uniformly in all social class groups. For the training of the young the social and cultural system of the middle class is organized to foster impulse control, planfulness, and achievement in the interest of maximizing status. Essential in the attainment of these goals is acceptance by the young of adult authority. In contrast, the social and cultural system of the lower class is uncommitted to a positive program of child training and by virtue of this fact fosters impulse expression, aggressivity, and independence from adult authority. These features define the elements of the two subcultural systems relevant for the present discussion (1).

Adult authority and the early adolescent period

THE DEVELOPMENTAL PROBLEM[1]

The period of early adolescence is relatively free of serious problems, and ordinarily exhibits an easy and stable accommodation across the generational

FROM *American Journal of Orthopsychiatry*, 1962, 33, 387–390. COPYRIGHT ©, THE AMERICAN ORTHOPSYCHIATRIC ASSOCIATION, INC. REPRODUCED BY PERMISSION OF THE AUTHOR AND THE PUBLISHER.

line. This period is commonly regarded as characterized by a minimum of parent-child conflict. There prevails, instead, a situation of mutual respect for each other's spheres of responsibility and values resulting from the rather sharp divergence of interests. This contrasts with the situation in later adolescence when the interests of the young person tend to parallel and ultimately to merge with those of the adult as the requirements of sexual and occupational adjustment come increasingly into focus. As this takes place, the accommodation of the earlier period is dissolved, and what had existed formerly as latent cross-generational hospitality then becomes explicit and calls for an effort at a new accommodation.

CULTURAL FACTORS IN ITS RESOLUTION

The cultural experiences of middle- and lower-class children during the period of early adolescence exhibit crucial differences affecting the readiness with which the accommodation required in the later phase of the adolescent period is accomplished. The middle-class mode of child rearing surrounds the child, during both the prepubertal and early adolescent period, with a wide network of adult supervised training and socializing institutions. The young person pursues the separate and independent interests of his juvenile world within these structures, which function, on the whole, under the relentless surveillance of adults. The freedom of the child is thus a qualified one in which he is subtly conditioned to accept the primacy of adult authority. In contrast, the freedom of the lower-class child, commonly expressed in the spontaneity of his street life, is unqualified by a similar omnipresent spirit of adult surveillance. Inescapably this results in his failure to acquire a similar conditioning to an implicit acceptance of adult authority. When, therefore, he moves into the struggle of later adolescence to come to terms with the more stringent demands of adult authority he tends to be distinctively handicapped in his task of assimilating the requisite elements of an adult identity, although he is not necessarily more rebellious than his middle-class counterpart. This feature of the differential impact of cultural conditioning is not unrelated to the relatively high rates of delinquents in the urban lower class.

The role of adult models in the resolution of ambivalence respecting dependence and independence

THE DEVELOPMENTAL PROBLEM

As is known, the adolescent comes in time to want independence with respect to the whole range of adult objects and interests, and will not readily accept dictation as to what he should value. However, in the very newness of his interests he needs, and senses his need for, guidance and advice. However, he can accept the dependency implicit in such guidance only by segregating the dependency of the new type from infantile dependency. For this reason parents are generally unacceptable (or only ambivalently acceptable) for this purpose. Consequently, he needs and will readily idealize a non-parental adult who meets this requirement.

CULTURAL FACTORS IN ITS RESOLUTION

Non-parental adults capable of filling the role described are everywhere in short supply, although they are relatively more available to middle-class youth. In the lower class such figures are notably in short supply. The cultural factors operating systematically to reduce the availability of such adult figures in the lower-class milieu are, first, the cultural strangeness of professional personnel provided in part for this purpose (teachers, group workers, recreation workers, etc.) based primarily on the divergence between middle-class and lower-class concerns, values and goals; and, second, the absence of a culturally based interest in the lower class with the problem of child rearing. Although age-graded segregation to some degree is a cultural universal, the definition of the problem of child training as a legitimate object of concern in a cultural system operates to reduce isolation on the basis of age grades. In the lower class there appears to be relatively little tendency on the part of adults to take a serious interest in child rearing as a distinctive problem area, due, probably, to the prevailing truncated view of the future. This results in a tendency in boys in lower-class communities to select their role models from the next oldest age group, with a consequent tendency for the traditions of street life, including its delinquent patterns, to be transmitted relatively intact.

Phase relations of dependency and autonomy

THE DEVELOPMENTAL PROBLEM

In meeting the problems of adolescent development all viable cultural systems must possess workable practices for meeting three types of contingencies: 1) the regression of the adolescent to dependent modes of response and behavior; 2) the thrust toward autonomy through independent modes of response and behavior; and 3) the alternate phasing of the two. The security of the person, at the deepest levels, is bound up with the availability of dependency relationships; his achievement of autonomy with opportunity for independent decision and action; and the progressive attainment of maturity with an appropriate phasing of the alternation of the two modes. Clinical observation suggests the hypothesis that each phase is intrinsically disorganizing for its alternate, and that systematic differential receptivity in parents and other adult figures to either dependency modes or autonomy modes tends to limit and in extreme cases to undermine an appropriate resolution of the phase relation problem.

CULTURAL FACTORS IN ITS RESOLUTION

Middle-class and lower-class subcultural systems may be differentiated in the distribution of their receptivity to dependency and autonomy in adolescents. Parents in both class subcultures are equally subject to the requirement of the general culture that they produce a new generation of competent and responsible adults. However, by virtue of the heavy investment in their children as a means of status maintenance and potential mobility, middle-class parents in contrast to lower-class parents are expectedly more protective and controlling in their relations with their children, and hence accept relatively more readily the dependency phases of adolescent development. Lower-class parents, being less invested in their children as instruments of status maintenance and mobility, are less protective and controlling in their relations with their children, and accept relatively more readily the autonomy phases of adolescent development. As a result, the dependency phases of adolescent experience are more protracted and prominent in the middle class, the autonomy phases in the lower class. This inference, based on observation of the two subcultural systems, is supported by the essentially psychological observation that the single most problematic aspect of adolescent development among middle-class adolescent youth centers on the establishment of their independence. The complementary observation with respect to lower-class adolescent youth, infrequently made, is that their developmental problem centers on the management of their dependency needs. As a consequence, their autonomy, so fully supported by their social and cultural system, has a qualitatively different character from that found in the psychologically mature middle-class adult.

Hypothetically, the autonomy of the lower-class adult may be expected to be compromised and tainted by an attraction to random forms of group support, expressive of what may be termed an unsatisfied psychological hunger for dependency relationships. This view would be supported by studies, for example, which have shown a correlation between educational level, an index of class affiliation, and susceptibility to nonrational types of crowd action. Another example is furnished by the observations of Walter Miller, a cultural anthropologist, who has noted a structured defensive expression of dependency hunger in the street boy's aversion to all forms of adult authority and control (2). The primacy of the peer group in the street life of lower-class youth offers further evidence on this point.

NOTES

1. The statement of the developmental problem concerned in the first two topics has been freely adapted from Irene Josselyn, *The Adolescent and His World* (New York: Family Service Association of America, 1952).

REFERENCES

1. Davis, Allison, and Robert J. Havighurst. *Social Class and Color Differences in Child Rearing.* Am. Sociol. Rev., 11: 698–710, 1946.
2. Miller, Walter. *Lower Class Culture as a Generating Milieu of Gang Delinquency.* J. Soc. Issues, 14, 3: 5–19, 1958.

TEN THE ADOLESCENT
SUBCULTURE

A recurring question in current developmental literature is whether psychologists and educators, on the basis of experimental data, are justified in hypothesizing a distinct, autonomous "adolescent subculture." If Urie Bronfenbrenner's comparison of Russian and American youth (36) is generalizable beyond the particular population sample and beyond the methodology employed, then the study implies that American adolescents, far more than Russians, have begun to develop a subculture which distinguishes itself from the larger culture on several important points. Although the behavior patterns, clothing styles, approaches to drugs and sex, modes of entertainment, heroes, and attitudes of adolescents, particularly their mistrust of adults and their disdain for money, success, and "the establishment," indicate that young people in America are consciously or unconsciously attempting to set themselves off from other segments of the community, several major questions remain to be answered before researchers can establish with certainty the existence of a subculture. How widespread, for example, are revolutionary youth groups such as the hippies, Yippies, drug culture advocates, and student activists? To what extent do members of these youth groups serve as admired and envied models for young people not actively involved in these groups? How much of the individual's life space is influenced and molded by the values of the adolescent subculture? Does loyalty to peer group involve only the more tangible and overt forms of behavior, such as clothing, hair style, language patterns, entertainment and music preferences, and the challenge of authority, or does the influence extend to fundamental attitudes toward sexual behavior, the socioeconomic structure, governmental organization, vocational goals, and other personal and social variables? In the former case, the adolescent once he graduates from school and from his peer group may readily absorb the value patterns of adult society. In the latter case, however, adult society may gradually give way to a new value structure based on the attitudes and goals of today's "adolescent subculture."

Robert C. Bealer, Fern K. Willits, and Peter R. Maida (39), while not denying the common occurrence of adolescent rebellion, consider such rebellion a temporary developmental phenomenon which does not justify the reference to a separate adolescent subculture. The authors further suggest that the existence of an adolescent subculture cannot be ascertained until sociologists agree on the definition of the concepts "culture" and "subculture." The reader may wish to contrast the assertions made by Bealer, Willits, and Maida and by Albert Bandura (2) and with those made by James S. Coleman (40) before drawing his own conclusions.

Coleman (40) provides evidence in support of the hypothesis that an adolescent subculture exists. After administering a questionnaire which asks, "How would you most like to be remembered in school: as an athletic star, a brilliant student, or most popular?" Coleman concludes that whatever activity receives social recognition by the peer group will attract the most capable students. The study reveals that most students want to be remembered as star athletes since this is a value held by members of the "leading crowd." Because the capable student, acquiescing to peer group values, often invests his energies in athletic rather than academic activities, mediocre students tend to receive the intellectual honors while their superiors struggle for social rewards. Lamenting the fact that "students with ability are led to achieve only when there are social rewards, primarily from their peers, for doing so," Coleman suggests that if interscholastic academic competition and achievement were stressed as much as athletic competition, peer group pressure might be used positively to reinforce values that might sustain the adolescent as an adult.

Joseph S. Himes's (41) "Negro Teen-Age Culture" explores the Negro adolescent's struggle to establish an identity in the face of racial prejudice and emotional and economic deprivation. Like the white adolescent subculture, the Negro youth culture is divided along two coordinates, high prestige versus low prestige groups, and Southern rural versus Northern urban residence. Himes dramatically emphasizes the interrelatedness of social class and Negro culture in the section entitled "The Street." Kobrin's (38) analysis of lower-class adolescents is of particular relevance to Himes' findings concerning lower-class Negro youth.

Recent social concern with adolescent problems has been directed not only to the dramatic problems of adolescents from low socioeconomic classes and the Negro minority, but also to the problems created by affluence among suburban, middle-class youth. William A. Schonfeld's (42) article questions why material abundance fails both to create a better environment than it does for the rearing of young people, and, more specifically, why affluence seems to contribute to the difficulties the adolescent faces in resolving his developmental crises. Paradoxically, Schonfeld finds that the affluent adolescents who are showered with material rewards and parental attention often remain emotionally deprived and grow up incapable of tolerating frustration. Schonfeld hypothesizes that the benefits of wide educational experience provided by affluence is outweighed by the "great expectation syndrome" of parents who demand the socially prestigious indications of academic success, such as high grades, scholastic honors, and diplomas, rather than any deep, essential conquest of the academic material. Finally, Schonfeld suggests that suburban adolescents turn to the peer-group for the support they lack in disordered, matrifocal families, and to drugs as an escape from frustration. "Socioeconomic Affluence as a Factor" stands as an effective summary of the "over-thirty" generation's interpretation of the adolescent crisis. As one of the editor's students notes,

"No other article is as valuable or as appropriate as this one, which is so characteristic of how an adult sees an adolescent—with a mixture of frustration, resentment, guilt, and even perhaps, jealousy."

Eli A. Rubenstein (43) analyzes the nature of student activism, and synthesizes various interpretations of student dissatisfaction. The article focuses on four paradoxes in the protest movement. First, although the student activist views himself as the defender of human liberties, he does not hesitate to infringe upon the freedom of others, disrupt college programs, and perform acts of violence. Second, the activist movement is characterized by "intellectual anti-intellectualism or the dogmatic anti-dogmatism." The attacks on the movement on the inflexibility and dogmatism of the academic institution, the "establishment," the capitalist system, and democracy, frequently reveal as high a degree of dogmatism as they attribute to their opponents. Third, the activists rebel against the "authoritarian and unresponsive politicized society," but in the process of organizing themselves, they become involved in political cabals, authoritarian tactics, and illiberal strategies. The fourth paradox is what Rubenstein terms the activist position of "no matter what you do, you can't win!" The student activist, through this position, manages to convince himself that he is misused and destined to defeat regardless of the opposition's response. Rubenstein's four paradoxes clearly indicate that in the process of protesting existing inequalities, students create variations on the situations they condemn. Finally, the author concludes that much of the vitality and force of the movement derives less from ideological tenets than from a sense of drama, "the feeling of participation, the excitement of being caught up in a group experience."

In the concluding article, Davis and Munoz (44) distinguish between two groups of hippie drug users, the "heads" and the "freaks," examining their patterns of drug use, ideologies, and life styles. The "head," as the term implies, is inwardly-directed, using drugs to discover "where his head is" through mind-expanding experiences. The heads are more likely than the freaks to include the regular users of LSD. As a group, the heads stay close to the middle-class orientation toward life, using the drug mainly as a means to self-realization and self-fulfillment, meditation, and religious experience. The term "head" further implies an openness to experience, a spontaneity and sensitivity to one's own emotions and the feelings of others. Heads are frequently found among the more established, less transient population of the hippie movement. In contrast, the "freaks" are basically hedonistic in their orientation and seek, instead of mind-expanding experiences, the sensual stimulation obtained by injecting Methedrine, or "speed." Speed is used for "kicks" and results in "freaking out," which accounts for the group's name. The basic life style of the freaks is close to the lower class, while within the hippie population itself the freaks are among the more transient elements. In a broad sense, the term "freak" is applied to any individual with the dominant characteristics of the freak—

aggression, violence, and emotional "hang ups." While the underground press raves about the virtues of "acid," its editors seldom condone the extreme, hedonistic "freak" pattern of drug use.

[39]   Robert C. Bealer, Fern K. Willits, & Peter R. Maida

THE REBELLIOUS YOUTH SUBCULTURE—A MYTH

Adolescence in American society is often described as a period of rebellion against parental norms and rejection of traditional attitudes and values. A social counterpart to individual discontent is said to be represented by a distinctive youth subculture which channels and reinforces the rebellion of the individual. However, there is a large body of research findings which does not support the rebellion image as the characteristic or most widespread pattern of adolescent behavior. It is the task of this article to present a small part of the relevant research and to then discuss first, why the rebellion image exists, and second, some detrimental consequences resulting from the persistence of the myth.

Research evidence

The degree to which adolescents see parents as significant in their lives can be a convenient starting point for examining the empirical findings against a rebellious youth subculture. In a study of 4 Minnesota rural high schools, 506 students were asked who was the most important reference point in their lives —family, school chums, or someone else. Somewhat over three-fourths indicated parents; school chums accounted for less than 10 percent of the answers.[1] The same high incidence of perceived importance of the family on personality development was reported by Oklahoma college freshmen.[2]

These studies are in accord with what has been found by outside observers who have noted the correlation of beliefs, attitudes, and practices between generations. For example, it has been found that nationally the political attitudes of lower income and upper income family teenagers closely follow the voting patterns of counterpart adults.[3, 4] Congruity also appears in more rigorous data comparing children and parents directly. In this regard, a study of 1,088 stu-

FROM *Children*, 1964, *11*, 43–48. REPRINTED BY PERMISSION OF THE SENIOR AUTHOR AND THE CHILDREN'S BUREAU, U.S. DEPARTMENT OF HEALTH, EDUCATION AND WELFARE.

dents in 13 different colleges found that most of these young people, particularly the females, conformed to the religious ideologies of their parents.[5] Investigations of participation in formal organizations by approximately 2,000 New York families found that if parents are active in organizations, their children will also tend to be participators. Where parents are nonparticipators, their children usually show the same pattern.[6]

The particular family situation can even override otherwise strong predisposing factors. In orientation to education, persons of lower socioeconomic status usually are unsympathetic to the school. But, in a study of high school dropouts in a midwestern city it was found that while only 13 percent of the lower class parents whose children dropped out of school opposed the adolescent's leaving, a group of students matched for social class and IQ who stayed in school showed 68 percent of the parents strongly insisting on attendance.[7]

Perception of parents

While parents may be vitally important in determining their children's behavior, it could be that this influence is coercive. The perceived importance of parents could indicate that rebellion, although tried, is unsuccessful. To examine this possibility, data are required which bear on the "favorableness" of the adolescent's perception of his parents, and by inference his felt need to rebel.

A study of 3,000 Minnesota adolescents and preadolescents centering on the descriptive terms supplied by them to a sentence completion test of the order, "My father is _____," found that both boys and girls expressed overwhelmingly more favorable than unfavorable attitudes toward their parents.[8] Another study revealed that youth were willing to ascribe even more favorable traits to adults than were their parents.[9]

Studies of rural Pennsylvania high school sophomores in 1947 and 1960 assessed the acceptability of such behaviors as drinking, smoking, school failure, use of makeup, card playing, divorce, dancing, dating, use of money, and church attendance. In both time periods it was found that the youth were most likely to evaluate their parents' points of view toward these actions as "sensible" rather than as "too critical" or "not critical enough." This appraisal of the family's orientation was by far the mode.[10, 11] Thus it would seem that the value positions of youth and adults are not in serious conflict. Indeed, the data imply value congruence between generations.

The similarity in points of view between peers and parents is particularly vital when interpreting the research which shows the characteristic "withdrawal" of adolescents from family-centered and family-attended activities. Participation in academic and extracurricular school activities usually means physical withdrawal from the family and high exposure to peer influence. However, this need not mean rejection of parental norms. The test of the importance of norms lies in the ability to direct behavior without the literal presence of others for enforcement; in other words, when they have been internalized by the individual. In the Pennsylvania study cited previously,[11] as youths increased their involvement in school functions, the proportion of "sensible" answers for the family's attitudes went up, not down, as would be expected if physical withdrawal decreased the saliency of parental norms.

The similarity in values between adults and youth should not imply that disagreements are lacking. On the contrary, in specific decision-making situations what an adolescent's parents believe he "ought" to do and what his peer group thinks would be appropriate behavior may differ. When this happens the question can be raised: Which group does the individual follow? Students in 10 midwestern high schools were asked which would be the hardest result "to take" if, in joining a school club, parents disapproved of it, the teachers were negative, or it required breaking with one's closest friend. Even though the nature of the question seems to carry a bias toward obtaining the last alternative, parents still receive a majority vote. About 53 percent of the boys and girls said parental disapproval would be the hardest to take while 43 percent said breaking the friendship would "count" most.[12]

Another study conducted among girls in 7 Georgia and Alabama high schools inquired into 12 specific situations, such as which of 2 dresses to buy and whether or not to report a boy whom one saw damaging school property. The stories which conveyed the situation also indicated what alternative the parents urged and what behavior the peer group desired. The students were then asked what they would do. The tests were readminstered after 2 weeks and the peer group and parent expectations were switched. Fifty-seven percent of the students' responses did not change between the first and second testing. Of the 43 percent which changed, a majority altered "what they would do" to the parental urging in 9 of the 12 situations. Two of the three situations where the shifts in answer went toward the peer group more often than parents involved matters of dress.[13]

This pattern of relative importance of peers and parents is certainly not always true. Perhaps the best generalization is that there is a flux in reference points depending on the situation.[14] However, the setting would seem rare where the parental wishes are totally ignored. Indeed, if there is to be continuity between generations, there must be some sharing of basic values between adults and youth. That such continuity exists is shown by the simple fact that American society has survived over time. Moreover, "there is remarkable agreement as to what American values are or have been and agreement upon their stability through more than 150 years."[15] Such stability could hardly be evidenced if adolescents rebelled and rejected the basic value tenets of the preceding generation.

In summary we can profitably recall a conclusion given elsewhere:

The failure to find evidence of parent-youth conflict regarding what constitutes proper patterns of behavior does not necessarily mean that parents and their offspring do not disagree in regard to some—and perhaps many—questions. The adolescent seeking to establish his identity in adult society may disagree with his parents regarding when recognition of his maturity should occur. He may wish to engage in activities which symbolize his adulthood while his parents feel that he is still too young. This type of 'rebellion' is as temporary as is the period of adolescence itself, and, rather than rejection of parental norms, it is perhaps better characterized as acceptance of and eagerness to participate in the larger society. Once the youth is accepted as a member of the adult society, this type of conflict ceases. It is this disagreement with parents concerning the adulthood of the adolescent which is probably responsible for the popular image of rebellious youth. However, this cannot accurately be described as a group rejection of societal norms. It constitutes an individual resistance to specific authority patterns.[10]

Of course, this kind of "rebellion" is important. It is often painfully experienced by both parent and child. It can lead to tragic results in some cases —neurosis, delinquency, even suicide or murder. It helps bring teenagers together in their cliques, friendship groups, and wider modes of affiliation and helps to hold them together as a unit. But, such conflict occurs *within a value framework* and not characteristically *over values*.

Why the myth?

In light of the foregoing review, the question arises: Why does the myth of a rebellious youth subculture exist? It may be that at least part of the explanation lies in the conceptual framework implicitly or explicitly used to understand "culture."

The meaning of culture, and in turn subculture, is not standardized in the social sciences. Among many professionals interested in the study of human behavior, culture is equated with *all* aspects of man's social actions. Wearing blue jeans and black leather jackets, listening to Elvis Presley or Pat Boone, drinking beer or chocolate milk shakes—all are taken as equally indicative of, and caused by, one's culture. It is implied that men, through their group affiliations, have defined for themselves correct or appropriate behavior for every phase of life and for all situations. Thus, whatever the individual does is due to his meanings, motives, and definitions of the situation—jointly summed as "his culture." If two persons in a similar setting behave differently, it is because "they have different cultures" stemming from different group affiliations.

This understanding of "culture" is one of preference in emphasis and it has considerable validity. Among other things, it underscores the idea that human behavior is socially conditioned. But, it comes close to substituting social determinism for other forms of single factor explanations. More specifically, we would suggest that this understanding of "culture" helps to explain the presence of the myth. To indicate the way this can occur requires setting out a contrasting conception of culture.

Instead of emphasizing all aspects of human behavior as "manifesting culture," the second understanding of the term is less inclusive. Thus, it is taken that: (1) culture is widely shared or held in common by the members of a society but, (2) those things which are shared are the ideals for behavior, the values or criteria by which both the ends and the means to them ought to be selected. Whether in fact actual behavior conforms to cultural standards or values is problematic. Characteristically, the ideal pattern is only approximated by actual behavior. This is so if for no other reason than that the values are *general* and action situations are *specific*.

While one can take honesty as a value, just what acts fulfill honesty are not always clear. Culture here is taken as a recipe calling for a dash of ground garlic (not ¼ teaspoon), a medium wedge of cheddar (not 8 ounces), salt to taste, and so on. The results of persons following such a recipe are variable, although the outcome is still identifiable as cheese sauce and not bouillon. This conception of culture assumes that expressed behavior is not a simple and direct reflection of cultural standards. Rather, it makes room for genetic and physiological differences in personality; allows that physical conditions influence behavior; and recognizes that factors such as the size of groups, their number, and heterogeneity all help to determine human action.

The distinction between these two conceptions and their outcomes can be clarified by taking science as an illustration of a culture. Under the first usage a cultural description of "science" would emphasize, for example, the total array of the physicist's behavior—his use of electron miscroscopes, his precise measurement techniques, rigorous experimental setups, and so on. Turning to sociology, the "culture" of science shows a vastly different set of behaviors and characteristics. For the sociologist there are no machines comparable to electron microscopes, he utilizes relatively imprecise measurement, and he has few laboratory experiment set-ups. Therefore, one is tempted to see two different and, indeed, even conflicting cultures.

Culture as values

In particular actions, the physicist and the sociologist are widely separated. Yet it can be shown that in basic principles they are in agreement. Both sociology and physics subscribe to the same canons for ascertaining truth, particularly the acceptance of the validity of sense data. The second conception of culture emphasizes this essential unity by seeing science *not in terms of particulars and specifics*—which can vary widely—but in terms of the basic values it adheres to in arriving at truth. These values clearly distinguish science from other types of "culture"; for instance, religion with its characteristic emphasis on revelation. The point is that people can vary in the details and particulars of their behavior without that difference necessarily signifying conflict over, or rejection of, underlying principles or values.

Similarly, the behavior of adolescents in American society differs from that of adults. Teenagers' mode of dress and grooming is sometimes radical and given to fads. They have their own magazines which cater to adolescent tastes and reflect their concerns. Among these are such problems as acne, incompetence in interpersonal relations, and knowledge of the opposite sex. Movies, popular music, and radio seem to be their virtual monopoly. The automobile has a crucial and, all too often, a deadly role to play in their lives. Dating provides a mechanism for heterosexual play and experimentation in erotic styles and is a dominant focus of attention and of time consumption. Their vocabulary is sometimes strange to adult ears.

However, the differences in adolescent and adult behavior, while real, are differences in degree rather than in kind. And the degree of dissimilarly has often been overstressed. Adult garb shows yearly change. Dale Carnegie has made a fortune through correcting adults' "shyness," and cosmetics have a tradition of hiding nature's "flaws." The fanfare given Detroit's latest models, the 5 or 6 million new cars sold annually, and the father's usual pride in showing off his new purchase to the neighbors are commonplace. Kinsey's reports, divorce court scandals, and the ever-present aura of sexuality in advertising aimed at adults suggest that cross-sex interest and variety in erotic play does not wither with youth. Adults, too, have their specialized "languages" stemming from their work.

If one ignores the basic similarities between adolescents and adults and emphasizes culture as the "particulars" of behavior, then disagreements and differences at the level of specific action may be misinterpreted and assumed to apply to the general value framework as well. As has been mentioned, however, research has pointed to the fact of congruity between generations. In stressing the similarity in values, in the second sense of culture, one does not say that knowing whether singer X or singer Y is currently in favor at a particular school or in a given town is unimportant. It may be crucial knowledge in gaining and keeping rapport with teenagers. By concentrating on the idiosyncratic aspects of adolescent behavior, however, one can miss the similarity in values between adults and youth. Failure on the part of many writers to distinguish between the two understandings of culture and the resulting tendency to see conflict between youth and their parents in *all* areas of behavior because differences exist in some activities may at least partially explain the presence of the rebellious adolescent subculture myth.

Moreover, viewing the period of adolescence primarily in terms of a distinctive, rebellious subculture can hinder understanding of many aspects of youth behavior. We shall take, as one example, the problem of school dropouts.

School dropouts

Focusing on the "rebellion" of the adolescent and implying as this does the discontinuity of values between generations tend to underestimate the difficulty of changing the potential dropout's orientation so as to keep him in school. By viewing the individual as "in rebellion" the image is cast that such a person is adrift. If the teenager has "rejected" his parents, then he will be looking for new anchorages. Thus, the task of keeping the potential dropout in school appears to be a matter of merely presenting and "selling" the values that will make him see the advantages of this course of action. But the notion of youth adrift through rebellion ignores the possibility that there may be stringent competition with the proposed values. By ignoring the fact of continuity in culture, one can be led to miss the simple fact that there is often parental support for the dropout adolescent's decision—support which may be tacit but nonetheless present. That is, some parents tend to see little utility in a secondary education and may openly encourage, or at least reinforce, the youth's choice to leave school. As a result, any attempt to change values must take into account the possible familial buttressing of teenage decisions.

We need to recognize that the adolescent who drops out of school may not be adrift in a rebellious youth subculture. He can, in fact, be closely tied to the relatively stable cultural background of his parents and may leave school prior to graduation because of this very fact. The problem of changing values and influencing these young people to stay in school is not, therefore, a short run task, nor is it an easy one. The matter is not as simple as throwing a life preserver to a drowning sailor, for the persistent fact remains that persons often reject such "help" when it is not supported by their social and cultural environment. The limited success of slum clearance projects, educational retraining programs, and efforts to rehabilitate criminals are cases in point. The problems of high school dropouts would seem to be similar. Any remedial program hoping for dramatic gains must be total, involving not just the individual, but his family and perhaps the general community as well. The rebellious youth myth can cause us to overlook this simple but vital fact.

The conception of a rebellious youth subculture emphasizes the generational split as the most important and, hence, directs attention primarily to the age-youth cleavage. It implies that all teenagers can be considered as members of a homogeneous unit standing in opposition to parents. Such a position tends to ignore the variability *among* young people—variability which is crucially important in understanding school dropouts.

Social class differences

One line of important differentiation is a distinction based on social class or socioeconomic status. Research has shown that there are many things involved in a student's leaving school prior to graduation, but the single factor most persistent and widespread in its relationship to early withdrawal is social class position or socioeconomic status.[16] These studies indicate that lower socioeconomic-class adults generally place less value on formal education than do middle-and upper-class persons. This devaluation of school attendance on the part of the adult population is often, in turn, reflected in the adolescent's own decision to withdraw prior to graduation. Such a person manifests a decision which is frequently anchored in the value system of his originating culture. Rather than some sort of rejection of the parentally sponsored norms, the act of dropping from school may represent an affirmation of them.

At the same time one ought to be aware that:

> . . . action oriented to the achievement and maintenance of the lower class system may violate norms of middle class culture and be perceived as deliberately non-conforming or malicious by an observer strongly cathected to middle class norms. This does not mean, however, that violation of the middle class norm is the dominant component of motivation; it is a by-product of action primarily oriented to the lower class system. . . . a distinctive tradition many centuries old with an integrity of its own.[17]

Such an idea, of course, runs counter to many persons' conception of lower-class culture. Indeed, until quite recently it was fashionable to picture lower-class society as unstable, disorganized, and hence exhibiting little continuity from generation to generation. To support this notion writers pointed to, among other things, the high incidence of "broken" homes composed of only mother and children. This is at variance with a normal middle-class family in which a father is present. It does not mean necessarily that the mother-child family lacks viability. The contrary is true. For example, the lower-class family form in which the father is absent has shown amazing persistence through time. One need not condone this type of family unit nor ignore the possible behavioral outcomes for the children involved, to see its vitality. The person who wishes to change social structure or the values substrating it must start with a recognition of reality and not from his own wishes about it or conclusions drawn from a middle-class sense of "correctness." In terms of the values of the potential dropout, the first step in this process is to appreciate the wide variation existing within the grouping, "adolescents."

While social class differences represent perhaps the most striking case of important variability, others also occur and need emphasis. We have stressed class because it is a vital element. However, our discussion should not be taken to mean that no lower-class youths finish high school. They do. "There is a sizeable proportion of the lower class group who do not incorporate this [a lower-class] value system."[18] We know that parents serve as mediators to the larger cultural milieu and thus particular familial considerations, such as parental encouragement to finish school or to aspire to high status positions, may overcome the effect of typical lower-class devaluations of education.[19] We do not know enough, however. What creates the situation for general parental support for high aspirations? The fact that there are some lower-class persons who highly value education represents a challenging problem. If the factors causing these persons to reject devaluation of education can be identified, we may be able better to direct other lower-class adolescents toward similar goals. In this cause a flexible conception is required which can not only allow for the variation that is lower-class culture, but which can see variability within the lower (or other) class itself. Unfortunately, the rebellious subculture idea does not foster recognition of any such differentiation.

The idea of varying and possibly competing values needs emphasis not only because of the stress which can result for the target of the change program, but also because it presents certain personal conflicts for the individual who is interested in bringing about change. Most change agents, reflecting the dominant middle-class values of American society, tend to see no problem as unyielding in the face of simple educational effort. But values represent basic criteria of worth, and, hence, are not easily changed nor readily amenable to compromise. Therefore, any action program designed to keep teenagers in school is potentially fraught with conflict, for it requires altering the potential dropout's values. Furthermore, this goal transgresses one of the basic value premises of the change agent's own cultural background—the belief that one ought to "live and let live." Since he may be unable or unwilling to accept the possibility of open conflict, it gives him some reassurance to believe that the dropout adolescent is adrift and desires his help. This is often not the case, but the idea of rebellious youth salves one's conscience, eases anxiety, and makes a difficult job appear easier than it is. Perhaps these functions of the myth also help to preserve its existence.

REFERENCES

1. Rose, Arnold M.: Reference groups of rural high school youth. *Child Development,* September 1956.
2. Ostlund, Leonard A.: Environment-personality relationships. *Rural Sociology,* March 1957.
3. Remmers, H. H.; Radler, D. H.: The American teenager. Bobbs-Merrill, Indianapolis, Ind. 1957.
4. Lipset, Seymour M.: Political man. Doubleday & Co., Garden City, N. Y. 1960.
5. Putney, Snell; Middleton, Russell: Rebellion, conformity, and parental religious ideologies. *Sociometry,* June 1961.
6. Anderson, W. A.: Types of participating families. *Rural Sociology,* December 1946.
7. Havighurst, Robert J.; Bowman, P. H.; Matthews, Gordon B.; Pierce, James V.: Growing Up in River City. John Wiley & Sons, New York. 1962.
8. Harris, Dale B.; Tseng, Sing Chu: Children's attitudes toward peers and parents as revealed by sentence completions. *Child Development,* December 1957.
9. Hess, Robert D.; Goldblatt, Irene: The status of adolescents in American society: a problem in social identity. *Child Development,* December 1957.
10. Bealer, Robert C.; Willits, Fern K.: Rural Youth: a case study in the rebellious

ness of adolescents. *The Annals of the American Academy of Political and Social Science,* November 1961.

11. Wilson, Paul B.; Buck, Roy C.: Pennsylvania's rural youth express their opinions. Pennsylvania Agricultural Experiment Station Progress Report No. 134. 1955.

12. Coleman, James S.: The adolescent society. The Free Press of Glencoe, New York. 1961.

13. Brittain, Clay V.: Adolescent choices and parent-peer cross-pressures. *American Sociological Review,* June 1963.

14. Solomon, Daniel: Adolescents' decisions: a comparison of influence from parents with that from other sources. *Marriage and Family Living,* November 1961.

15. Kluckhohn, Clyde: Have there been discernible shifts in American values during the past generation? *In* The American style. (Elting E. Morison, ed.) Harper & Bros., New York. 1958.

16. Blough, Telford B.: A critical analysis of selected research literature on the problem of school dropouts. Unpublished dissertation. University of Pittsburgh, Pennsylvania. 1956.

17. Miller, Walter B.: Lower class culture as a generating milieu of gang delinquency. *Journal of Social Issues,* Vol. XIV, No. 3, 1958.

18. Hyman, Herbert H.: The value systems of different classes: a social psychological contribution to the analysis of stratification. *In* Class, status and power. (Reinhard Bendix and Seymour M. Lipset, eds.) The Free Press, Glencoe, Ill. 1958.

19. Simpson, Richard L.: Parental influence, anticipatory socialization, and social mobility. *American Sociological Review,* August 1962.

[40] *James S. Coleman* THE ADOLESCENT

SUBCULTURE AND ACADEMIC ACHIEVEMENT

Industrial society has spawned a peculiar phenomenon, most evident in America but emerging also in other Western societies: adolescent subcultures, with values and activities quite distinct from those of the adult society—subcultures whose members have most of their important associations within and few with adult society. Industrialization, and the rapidity of change itself, has taken out of the hands of the parent the task of training his child, made the parent's skills obsolete, and put him out of touch with the times—unable

FROM *American Journal of Sociology,* 1960, 65, 337–347. COPYRIGHT 1960 BY THE UNIVERSITY OF CHICAGO PRESS, AND REPRODUCED BY PERMISSION OF THE AUTHOR AND THE PUBLISHER. COPYRIGHT 1960 BY THE UNIVERSITY OF CHICAGO.

to understand, much less inculcate, the standards of a social order which has changed since he was young.

By extending the period of training necessary for a child and by encompassing nearly the whole population, industrial society has made of high school a social system of adolescents. It includes, in the United States, almost all adolescents and more and more of the activities of the adolescent himself. A typical example is provided by an excerpt from a high-school newspaper in an upper-middle-class suburban school:

SOPHOMORE DANCING FEATURES CHA CHA

Sophomores, this is your chance to learn how to dance! The first day of sophomore dancing is Nov. 14 and it will begin at 8:30 A.M. in the Boys' Gym. . . . No one is required to take dancing but it is highly recommended for both boys and girls. . . . If you don't attend at this time except in case of absence from school, you may not attend at any other time. Absence excuses should be shown to Miss ———— or Mr.————.

In effect, then, what our society has done is to set apart, in an institution of their own, adolescents for whom home is little more than a dormitory and whose world is made up of activities peculiar to their fellows. They have been given as well many of the instruments which can make them a functioning community: cars, freedom in dating, continual contact with the opposite sex, money, and entertainment, like popular music and movies, designed especially for them. The international spread of "rock-and-roll" and of so-called American patterns of adolescent behavior is a consequence, I would suggest, of these economic changes which have set adolescents off in a world of their own.

Yet the fact that such a subsystem has sprung up in society has not been systematically recognized in the organization of secondary education. The theory and practice of education remains focused on *individuals*; teachers exhort individuals to concentrate their energies in scholarly directions, while the community of adolescents diverts these energies into other channels. The premise of the present research is that, if educational goals are to be realized in modern society, a fundamentally different approach to secondary education is necessary. Adults are in control of the institutions they have established for secondary education; traditionally, these institutions have been used to mold children as individuals toward ends which adults dictate. The fundamental change which must occur is to shift the focus: to mold social communities as communities, so that the norms of the communities themselves reinforce educational goals rather than inhibit them, as is at present the case.

The research being reported is an attempt to examine the status systems of the adolescent communities in ten high schools and to see the effects of these status systems upon the individuals within them. The ten high schools are all in the Midwest. They include five schools in small towns (labeled 0–4 in the figures which follow), one in a working-class suburb (6), one in a well-to-do suburb (9), and three schools in cities of varying sizes (5, 7, and 8). All but No. 5, a Catholic boys' school, are coeducational, and all but it are public schools.

The intention was to study schools which had quite different status systems, but the similarities were far more striking than the differences. In a questionnaire all boys were asked: "How would you most like to be remembered in school: as an athletic star, a brilliant student, or most popular? The results of the responses for each school are shown in Figure 1,[1] where the left corner of the triangle represents 100 per cent saying "star athlete"; the top corner represents 100 per cent saying "brilliant student"; and the right corner represents 100 per cent saying "most popular." Each school is represented by a point whose location relative to the three corners shows the proportion giving each response.

The schools are remarkably grouped somewhat off-center, showing a greater tendency to say "star athlete" than either of the other choices. From each school's point is a broken arrow connecting the school as a whole with its members who were named by their fellows as being "members of the leading crowd." In almost every case, the leading crowd tends in the direction of the athlete—in all cases *away* from the ideal of the brilliant student. Again, for the leading crowds as well as for the students as a whole, the uniformity is remarkably great, not so great in the absolute positions of the leading crowds but in the direction they deviate from the student bodies.

This trend toward the ideal of the athletic star on the part of the leading crowds is due in part to the fact that the leading crowds include a great number of athletes. Boys were asked in a questionnaire to name the best athlete in their grade, the best student, and the boy most popular with girls. In every school, without exception, the boys named as best athletes were named more often—on the average over twice as often—as members of the leading crowd than were those named as best students. Similarly, the boy most popular with girls was named as belonging to the leading crowd more often than the best student, though in all schools but the well-to-do suburb and the smallest rural town (schools 9 and 0 on Fig. 1) less often than the best athlete.

These and other data indicate the importance of athletic achievement as an avenue for gaining status in the schools. Indeed, in the predominantly middle-class schools, it is by far the most effective achievement for gaining a working-class boy entrée into the leading crowd.

Similarly, each girl was asked how she would like to be remembered: as a brilliant student, a leader in extracurricular activities, or most popular. The various schools are located on Figure 2, together with arrows connecting them to their leading crowd. The girls tend slightly less, on the average, than the

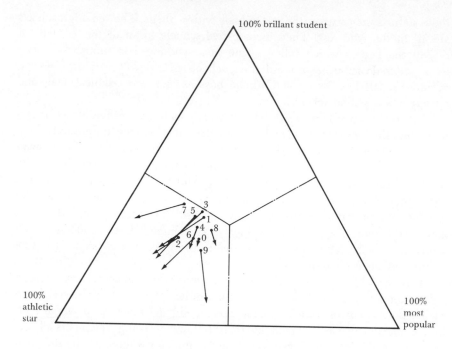

FIGURE 1   Positions of schools and leading crowds in boys' relative choice of brilliant student, athletic star, and most popular.

boys to want to be remembered as brilliant students. Although the alternatives are different, and thus cannot be directly compared, a great deal of other evidence indicates that the girls—although better students in every school—do not want to be considered "brilliant students." They have good reason not to, for the girl in each grade in each of the schools who was most often named as best student has fewer friends and is less often in the leading crowd than is the boy most often named as best student.

There is, however, diversity among the schools in the attractiveness of the images of "activities leader" and "popular girl" (Fig. 2). In five (9, 0, 3, 8, and 1), the leader in activities is more often chosen as an ideal than is the popular girl; in four (7, 6, 2, and 4) the most popular girl is the more attractive of the two. These differences correspond somewhat to class background differences among the schools: 2, 4, 6, and 7, where the activities leader is least attractive, have the highest proportion of students with working-class backgrounds. School 9 is by far the most upper-middle-class one and by far the most activities-oriented.

The differences among the schools correspond as well to differences among the leading crowds: in schools 2, 4, and 6, where the girls as a whole

The differences among the schools correspond as well to differences the school where the girls are most oriented to the ideal of the activities

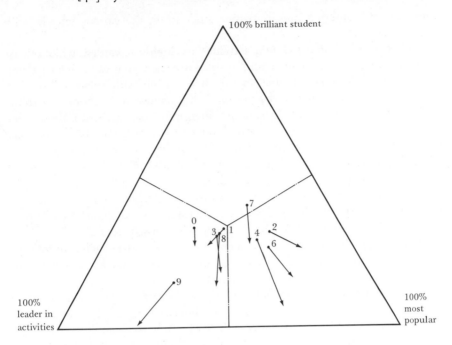

100% brilliant student

100%
leader in
activities

100%
most
popular

FIGURE 2   Titles as in fig. 6, but without last parentheses

leader, No. 9, the leading crowd goes even further in that direction.[2] In other words, it is as if a pull is exerted by the leading crowd, bringing the rest of the students toward one or the other of the polar extremes. In all cases, the leading crowd pulls away from the brilliant-student ideal.

Although these schools vary far less than one might wish when examining the effects of status systems, there are differences. All students were asked in a questionnaire: "What does it take to get into the leading crowd?" On the basis of the answers, the relative importance of various activities can be determined. Consider only a single activity, academic achievement. Its importance for status among the adolescents in each school can be measured simply by the proportion of responses which specify "good grades," or "brains" as adolescents often put it, as a means of entrée into the leading crowd. In all the schools, academic achievement was of less importance than other matters, such as being an athletic star among the boys, being a cheerleader or being good-looking among the girls, or other attributes. Other measures which were obtained of the importance of academic achievement in the adolescent status system correlate highly with this one.[3]

If, then, it is true that the status system of adolescents *does* affect educational goals, those schools which differ in the importance of academic achievement in the adolescent status system should differ in numerous other ways which are directly related to educational goals. Only one of those, which illustrates well the differing pressures upon students in the various schools, will be reported here.

In every social context certain activities are highly rewarded, while others are not. Those activities which are rewarded are the activities for which there is strong competition—activities in which everyone with some ability will compete.—In such activities the persons who achieve most should be those with most potential ability. In contrast, in unrewarded activities, those who have most ability may not be motivated to compete; consequently, the persons who achieve most will be persons of lesser ability. Thus in a high school where basketball is important, nearly every boy who might be a good basketball player will go out for the sport, and, as a result, basketball stars are likely to be the boys with the most ability. If in the same school volleyball does not bring the same status, few boys will go out for it, and those who end up as members of the team will not be the boys with most potential ability.

Similarly, with academic achievement: in a school where such achievement brings few social rewards, those who "go out" for scholarly achievement will be few. The high performers, those who receive good grades, will not be the boys whose ability is greatest but a more mediocre few. Thus the "intellectuals" of such a society, those defined by themselves and others as the best students, will not in fact be those with most intellectual ability. The latter, knowing where the social rewards lie, will be off cultivating other fields which bring social rewards.

To examine the effect of varying social pressures in the schools, academic achievement, as measured by grades in school, was related to I.Q. Since the I.Q. tests differ from school to school, and since each school had its own mean I.Q. and its own variation around it, the ability of high performers (boys who made A or A— average)[4] was measured by the number of standard deviations of their average I.Q.'s above the mean. In this way, it is possible to see where the high performers' ability lay, relative to the distribution of abilities in their school.[5]

The variations were great: in a small-town school, No. 1, the boys who made an A or A— average had I.Q.'s 1.53 standard deviations above the school average; in another small-town school, No. 0, their I.Q.'s were only about a third this distance above the mean, .59. Given this variation, the question can be asked: Do these variations in ability of the high performers correspond to variations in the social rewards for, or constraints against, being a good student?

Figure 3 shows the relation for the boys between the social rewards for academic excellence (i.e., the frequency with which "good grades" was mentioned as a means for getting into the leading crowd) and the ability of the high performers, measured by the number of standard deviations their average I.Q.'s exceed that of the rest of the boys in the school. The relation is extremely strong. Only one school, a parochial boys' school in the city's slums, deviates.

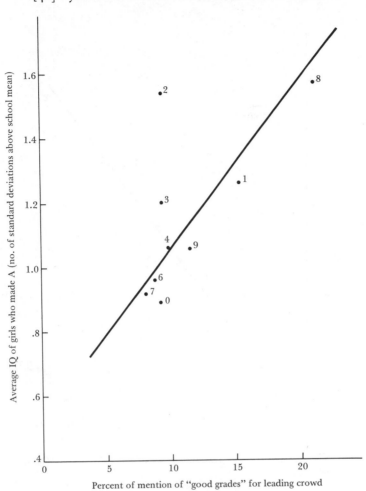

FIGURE 3 I.Q.'s of high achieving boys by importance of good grades among other boys

This is a school in which many boys had their most important associations outside the school rather than in it, so that its student body constituted far less of a social system, less able to dispense social rewards and punishments, than was true of the other schools.

Similarly, Figure 4 shows for the girls the I.Q.'s of the high performers.[6] Unfortunately, most of the schools are closely bunched in the degree to which good grades are important among the girls, so that there is too little variation among them to examine this effect as fully as would be desirable. School 2 is the one school whose girls deviate from the general relationship.

The effect of these value systems on the freedom for academic ability to

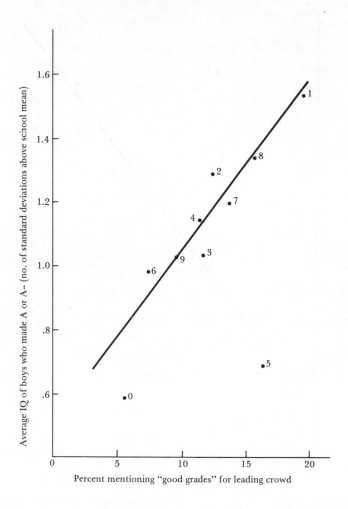

FIGURE 4   I.Q.'s of high achieving girls by importance of good grades among other girls

express itself in high achievement is evident among the girls as it is among the boys. This is not merely due to the school facilities, social composition of the school, or other variables: the two schools highest in the importance of scholastic achievement for boys and girls are *1* and *8*, the first a small-town school of 350 students and the second a city school of 2,000 students. In both there are fewer students with white-collar backgrounds than in schools *9* or *3*, which are somewhere in the middle as to value placed on academic achievement, but are more white-collar than in schools *7* or *4*, which are also somewhere in the middle. The highest expenditure per student was $695 per year in school 9, and the lowest was little more than half that, in school 4. These schools are close together on the graphs of Figures 3 and 4.

It should be mentioned in passing that an extensive unpublished study throughout Connecticut, using standard tests of achievement and ability, yielded consistent results. The study found no correlation between per pupil expenditure in a school and the achievement of its students relative to their ability. The effects shown in Figures 3 and 4 suggest why: that students with ability are led to achieve only when there are social rewards, primarily from their peers, for doing so—and these social rewards seem little correlated with per pupil expenditure.

So much for the effects as shown by the variation among schools. As mentioned earlier, the variation among schools was not nearly so striking in this research as the fact that, in all of them, academic achievement did not count for as much as other activities. In every school the boy named as best athlete and the boy named as most popular with girls was far more often mentioned as a member of the leading crowd, and as someone to "be like," than was the boy named as the best student. And the girl named as best dressed, and the one named as most popular with boys, was in every school far more often mentioned as being in the leading crowd and as someone "to be like," than was the girl named as the best student.

The relative unimportance of academic achievement, together with the effect shown earlier, suggests that these adolescent subcultures are generally deterrents to academic achievement. In other words, in these societies of adolescents those who come to be seen as the "intellectuals" and who come to think so of themselves are not really those of highest intelligence but are only the ones who are willing to work hard at a relatively unrewarded activity.

The implications for American society as a whole are clear. Because high schools allow the adolescent subcultures to divert energies into athletics, social activities, and the like, they recruit into adult intellectual activities people with a rather mediocre level of ability. In fact, the high school seems to do more than allow these subcultures to discourage academic achievement; it aids them in doing so. To indicate how it does and to indicate how it might do differently is another story, to be examined below.

Figures 1 and 2, which show the way boys and girls would like to be remembered in their high school, demonstrate a curious difference between the boys and the girls. Despite great variation in social background, in size of school (from 180 to 2,000), in size of town (from less than a thousand to over a million), and in style of life of their parents, the proportion of boys choosing each of the three images by which he wants to be remembered is very nearly the same in all schools. And in every school the leading crowd "pulls" in similar directions: at least partly toward the ideal of the star athlete. Yet the ideals of the girls in these schools are far more dispersed, and the leading crowds "pull" in varying directions, far less uniformly than among the boys. Why such a diversity in the same schools?

The question can best be answered by indirection. In two schools apart from those in the research, the questionnaire was administered primarily to answer a puzzling question: Why was academic achievement of so little importance among the adolescents in school *9*? Their parents were professionals and business executives, about 80 per cent were going to college (over twice as high a proportion as in any of the other schools), and yet academic excellence counted for little among them. In the two additional schools parental background was largely held constant, for they were private, coeducational day schools whose students had upper-middle-class backgrounds quite similar to those of school *9*. One (No. *10*) was in the city; the other (No. *11*), in a suburban setting almost identical to that of No. *9*. Although the two schools were added to the study to answer the question about school *9*, they will be used to help answer the puzzle set earlier: that of the clustering of schools for the boys and their greater spread for the girls. When we look at the responses of adolescents in these two schools to the question as to how they would like to be remembered, the picture becomes even more puzzling (Figs. 5 and 6). For the boys, they are extremely far from the cluster of the other schools; for the girls, they are intermingled with the other schools. Thus, though it was for the boys that the other schools clustered so closely, these

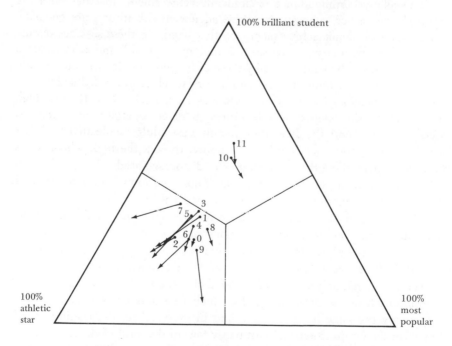

FIGURE 5   Title as in fig. *1*, but with added: (two private schools [*10, 11*] included)

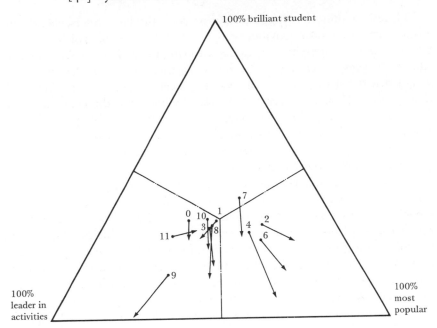

FIGURE 6   Positions of schools and leading crowds in girls' relative choice
of brilliant student, activities leader, and most popular (two private schools
[*10, 11*] included)

two deviate sharply from the cluster; and for the girls, where the schools
already varied, these two are not distinguishable. Furthermore, the leading
crowds of boys in these schools do not pull the ideal toward the star-athlete
ideal as do those in almost all the other schools. To be sure, they pull away
from the ideal of the brilliant student, but the pull is primarily toward a social
image, the most popular. Among the girls, the leading crowds pull in different
directions and are nearly indistinguishable from the other schools.

The answer to both puzzles—that is, first, the great cluster of the boys
and now, in these two additional schools, the greater deviation—seems to lie
in one fact: the boys' interscholastic athletics. The nine public schools are
all engaged in interscholastic leagues which themselves are knit together in
state tournaments. The other school of the first ten, the Catholic school, is in
a parochial league, where games are just as hotly contested as in the public
leagues, and is also knit together with them in tournaments.

Schools *10* and *11* are athletically in a world apart from this. Although
boys in both schools may go in for sports, and both schools have interscholastic
games, the opponents are scattered private schools, constituting a league in
name only. They take no part in state or city tournaments and have almost
no publicity.

There is nothing for the girls comparable to the boys' interscholastic athletics. There are school activities of one sort or another, in which most girls take part, but no interscholastic games involving them. Their absence and the lack of leagues which knit all schools together in systematic competition means that the status system can "wander" freely, depending on local conditions in the school. In athletics, however, a school, and the community surrounding it, cannot hold its head up if it continues to lose games. It *must* devote roughly the same attention to athletics as do the schools surrounding it, for athletic games are the only games in which it engages other schools and, by representation, other communities.

These games are almost the only means a school has of generating internal cohesion and identification, for they constitute the only activity in which the school participates as a school. (This is well indicated by the fact that a number of students in school *10*, the private school which engages in no interscholastic games, has been concerned by a "lack of school spirit.") It is as a consequence of this that the athlete gains so much status: he is doing something for the school and the community, not only for himself, in leading his team to victory, for it is a school victory.

The outstanding student, in contrast, has little or no way to bring glory to his school. His victories are always purely personal, often at the expense of his classmates, who are forced to work harder to keep up with him. It is no wonder that his accomplishments gain little reward and are often met by ridiculing remarks, such as "curve-raiser" or "grind," terms of disapprobation which have no analogues in athletics.

These results are particularly intriguing, for they suggest ways in which rather straightforward social theory could be used in organizing the activities of high schools in such a way that their adolescent subcultures would encourage, rather than discourage, the channeling of energies into directions of learning. One might speculate on the possible effects of city-wide or state-wide "scholastic fairs" composed of academic games and tournaments between schools and schools exhibits to be judged. It could be that the mere institution of such games would, just as do the state basketball tournaments in the midwestern United States, have a profound effect upon the educational climate in the participating schools. In fact, by an extension of this analysis, one would predict that an international fair of this sort, a "Scholastic Olympics," would generate interscholastic games and tournaments within the participating countries.

NOTES

1. I am grateful to James A. Davis and Jacob Feldman, of the University of Chicago, for suggesting such graphs for presenting responses to trichotomous items in a population.

2. This result could logically be a statistical artifact because the leaders were included among students as a whole and thus would boost the result in the direction they tend. However, it is not a statistical artifact, for the leading crowds are a small part of the total student body. When they are taken out for computing the position of the rest of the girls in each school, schools 2, 4, 6, and 7 are still the most popularity-oriented, and school 9 the most activities-oriented.

3. Parenthetically, it might be noted that these measures correlate on imperfectly with the proportion of boys or girls who want to be remembered as brilliant students. These responses depend on the relative attractiveness of other ideals, which varies from school to school, and upon other factors unrelated to the status system.

4. In each school but 3 and 8, those making A and A— constituted from 6 to 8 per cent of the student body. In order to provide a correct test of the hypothesis, it is necessary to have the same fraction of the student body in each case (since I.Q.'s of this group are being measured in terms of number of standard deviations above the student body). To adjust these groups, enough 6's were added (each being assigned the average I.Q. of the total group of 6's to bring the proportion up to 6 per cent (from 3 per cent in school 3, from 4 per cent in school 8).

5. The I.Q. tests used in the different schools were: (0) California Mental Maturity (taken seventh, eighth, or ninth grade); (1) California Mental Maturity (taken eighth grade); (2) SRA Primary Mental Abilities (taken tenth grade); (3) California Mental Maturity (taken ninth grade; seniors took SRA PMA, which was tabulated as a percentile, and they have been omitted from analysis reported above); (4) Otis (ninth and tenth grades; taken eighth grade); Kuhlman Finch (eleventh and twelfth grades, taken eighth grade); (5) Otis (taken ninth grade); (6) California Mental Maturity (taken eighth grade); (7) California Mental Maturity (taken eighth grade); (8) Otis (taken ninth or tenth grade); and (9) Otis (taken eighth grade).

6. For the girls, only girls with a straight-A average were included. Since girls get better grades than boys, this device is necessary in order to make the sizes of the "high-performer" group roughly comparable for boys and for girls. Schools differed somewhat in the proportion of A's, constituting about 6 per cent of the students in the small schools, only about 3 per cent in schools 6 and 7, 1 per cent in 8, and 2 per cent in 9. In 8 and 9, enough girls were added and assigned the average grade of the 7 (A—) group to bring the proportion to 3 per cent, comparable with the other large schools. The difference, however, between the large and small schools was left.

[41] *Joseph S. Himes* NEGRO TEEN-AGE CULTURE

Social situation

The quality of Negro teen-age culture is conditioned by four decisive factors: race, inferiority, deprivation, and youthfulness. Virtually every experience of the Negro teen-ager is filtered through this complex qualifying medium; every act is a response to a distorted perception of the world. His world is a kind of nightmare, the creation of a carnival reflection chamber. The Negro teen-ager's culture, his customary modes of behavior, constitute his response to the distorted, frightening, and cruel world that he perceives with the guileless realism of youth.[1]

A knowledgeable worker in Baltimore reported the life perceptions of poor Negro boys in the following manner.[2] "They feel rejected . . . say they cannot achieve but so much because they are Negroes. Say they have . . . less money . . . worse housing . . . and worse section of town."

Race, inferiority, deprivation, and youthfulness tend to trap Negro teen-agers by forces beyond their comprehension and control. School, the church, the mass media, city streets, and the other institutions of the pageant of American life serve to sharpen the sense of entrapment and deprivation. Oscar Handlin shows with clarity how the New York schools produce these results with Negro and Puerto Rican children.[3]

. . . A variety of factors prevent many of them from concentrating on their studies —the inability to use correct English, their own poverty and sometimes the necessity for part-time work, the lack of privacy at home, and the remoteness of the goals toward which education leads. The result is often a high rate of truancy. All too often, also, even those students who attend docilely merely sit out their lessons, without the incentive to pay attention to what transpires in the classroom.

Negro children learn early that only a part of the bright hope and glittering affluence of America is for them. A middle-class teen-ager from St. Paul put it this way:[4] "I have found . . . that as much as I wish to be completely equal, there is still a barrier which I have given up hope to break." Warren Miller notes that the sense of drab deprivation comes as early as the tenth or eleventh year to big-city children.[5]

FROM *The Annals of the American Academy of Political and Social Science,* 1961, 338, 92–101. (ABRIDGED) REPRINTED BY PERMISSION OF THE AUTHOR AND THE PUBLISHER.

Twin cultural heritage

In American society, a real void separates the better educated, the better off, the better situated Negro people from the great mass of poor, ill-educated, slum-dwelling individuals.[6] These two categories of individuals are the carriers of twin cultural heritages. The less numerous high-prestige category stresses moral conformity, good manners and taste, subordination of present gratifications to future achievements, and striving for social recognition and status. The heritage of the low-prestige masses emphasizes immediate material and creature gratifications, the tyranny of in-group standards, personal recognition, and insecurity and "egotouchiness."

Children enter teenhood from the two cultural streams. High-prestige and upwardly mobile low-prestige teen-agers pass into high-prestige adult roles through the college culture. Most low-prestige teen-agers, however, pass directly into the adult job and marriage roles of their original cultural rank. For both groups, the teen-age culture marks an interlude, a sort of cultural *rite de passage*.

What the teen-agers do

Teen-age culture is a variegated complex of behavior patterns. The teen-ager's speech is liberally sprinkled, often monopolized by slang expressions.[7] All reports indicate that profanity and obscenity are commonplace with low-prestige youths, especially boys,[8] although not around adults—parents, teachers, recreation leaders, and persons in similar capacities. With only minor local variations, the vogue is early and almost universal steady dating, a practice that leads to early marriage, sexual laxities, venereal infections, and unplanned pregnancies.[9] Eighty-four per cent of 295 students in a southern urban high school said they thought it was all right for teen-agers to go steady.[10] Some observers report intensive and random dating instead, while others mention steady dating among the younger teen-agers and random dating among the older ones.

The craving for things is intense—cars, clothes, stereo, records, transistors, cameras, and the like. It is widely reported that the teen-agers work, save, and even—especially among the low-prestige category—steal for them. The teen-agers favor such activities as car riding, vigorous dancing, competitive sports, animated "yackity-yacking," transistor toting, record listening, and the like. For example, current dance vogues in Durham, North Carolina, include the "pony," the "continental," the "twist," the "rocking Charlie," the "shimmy," the "watusi," the "booty green," the "jack-the-ripper," the "stran," and the "stupidity."

Field reports from all regions indicate that dress, grooming, and ornamentation are extreme and faddish. High-prestige boys and girls tend to follow the current national teen-age styles. Low-prestige teen-agers, however, are often slightly behind current vogues or distinguished by unique styles. Though there is much variety, some girls seem to favor colored sneakers, socks, flaring skirts, with crinoline petticoats, and sloppy Joe sweaters; others go for short tight skirts, burlap cloth being one current vogue, bulky sweaters with the ubiquitous sneakers and socks, and sometimes stockings. Older low-prestige boys feature caps or derbies, button-down collars, "continental" jackets, short tight-legged pants, and hard-heeled shoes. "Processed" (straightened and styled) or close-cropped hair for these boys and "shades" (sun glasses) for both sexes are popular. Girls feature heavy eye make-up, light matching shades of lipstick and nail polish, usually chosen to match some color of the outfit, which may include bright unharmonious colors.

The reports show a universal interest in music, which seems to work like a narcotic. The Negro musical heritage is a folk tradition compounded of spirituals, gospel hymns, blues, and jazz. The difference between high- and low-prestige teen-agers is less evident in musical taste than in most other areas.

The street

One unique feature of Negro teen-age behavior results from the relative lack of private facilities—bowling alleys, skating rinks, tennis courts, swimming pools—which forces Negro teen-agers into public recreational agencies, commercial hangouts, beer joints, and city streets.

The street as a social institution is an important factor in Negro culture, as it is in many European cultures. It is frequented by teen-agers as well as by adults and the following analysis is as accurate for them as for older persons.[11]

Whatever may be said in the way of explanation of the special significance that the street has for its habitues, the conclusion is unavoidable that it envelops a way of life defined not so much by those who participate in and share it, as by those who do not. The tendency on the part of the law enforcement agencies to permit a wide range of "shady" and illegal social and economic activity, the leniency on the part of the courts in disposing of many petty criminal cases involving Negroes only, and the more or less apathetic and indifferent attitudes of the larger [public] as well as a part of the Negro community help determine and define it. These factors designate the street area as one of special permission. Within this environment—relatively free from restrictions and taboos of the dominant moral order— the habitue receives a sense of belonging and a greater feeling of personal worth. This is evident in the self-assertiveness that characterizes much of his behavior. On the street, he is ready to laugh, play, and have fun. He is equally prepared to feud, fuss, and fight. This tendency to run the emotional gamut from sociability to aggression is definitive of many interpersonal relationships.

The function performed by the street for the total culture is, according to this reporter, to serve as a sluice for the aggressions resulting from frustration; without the permitted aggression, race relations would deteriorate. Thus:[12]

Within the public world of the street, as much the creation of the majority which lives outside it as the minority which shares it, the nature of the adjustment that the Negro makes depends very largely on the extent, at any particular time, that the larger controls are applied. To the degree that there are no controls, the Negro "problem" turns inward and "race relations" are accordingly "good." The street in this sense exhibits a sort of "organized disorganization" in which various elements of the Negro population find expression and adjustment and onto which the majority group "unloads" a potential "problem." "No control" for the one group becomes a form of social control for the other.

It is suggested that were the larger community to invoke the full weight of the legal and moral codes by which it governs its own conduct, without at the same time permitting the Negro a wider range and greater intensity of participation in the social and economic life, the "problem" would accordingly turn outward and "race relations" would in proportion become "bad."

Since the above analysis was made, the aggressions of high-prestige teen-agers have, in fact, been aimed outward rather than exclusively toward the ingroup, and, as predicted, race relations have become—at least transitionally —bad. We shall have more to say about the outward-aimed aggressions presently, but, at this point, it is interesting to note that, despite the large part that the street plays in the culture of the Negro teen-ager and despite—perhaps because of—the large amount of interpersonal aggression, fighting gangs are not characteristic of Negro teen-age culture.

No gangs

Thus, the field reports indicate that organized gang behavior is not a feature of general Negro teen-age culture. In Durham, North Carolina, only 11 out of 334 students who replied to the questionnaire admitted that they belonged to gangs.[13] Rather, the low-prestige youths tend to participate habitually in loose, fluid, shifting bands. Such bands appear to lack regular leaders, well-defined membership, and clear-cut organization. The comment of an observer in Syracuse is typical. "Leisure time activities seem to include . . . hanging around in large groups. I would not consider this a gang since the composition of the group is constantly changing though some few individuals are always the same."

A knowledgeable boys-worker in Baltimore wrote as follows about the situation in that city. "Have no gangs. Found clusters of individuals in and out of school. They just hang around. They are not fighting gangs." The observer in Buffalo stated: "Organized boys' gangs occasionally have fights. There are no girl gangs or auxiliaries. Gang activities are mild—usually consist of threatening clubs and groups from other parts of the city."

These bands hang out on street corners, soda shops, beer joints, dance halls, and frequently at recreational centers and playgrounds.

Sometimes they just wander about aimlessly, "looking for something to do." Idle, bored, and unsupervised, they are inclined to be touchy and resentful of such authorities as parents, teachers, ministers, recreation leaders, and policemen. At night, they crowd the dance floors of recreation centers, and, by day, they listen to records in the hangouts, play their transistors, and ride about in jalopies. But mostly they just "yackity-yack." The talk, too, is aimless, full of slang, profanity, and obscenity, and about their own doings, song hits, television shows (The Untouchables, Gunsmoke being favorites), clothes styles, Negro athletes, and so on. The talk, as well as the gregariousness, reveals their intense need to be accepted by peers. Almost always, also, a current of aggression runs just below the surface of this stream of talk— teasing, bantering, boasting, disparaging, blustering, threatening, cursing, playing the dozens. Occasionally, the aggression breaks through the veneer of talk into quick savage fights or delinquent acts.

The research suggests that organized gang behavior is part of the teen-age tradition only in specific slum areas of the great cities.[14] When Negro or Puerto Rican families invade these areas and succeed the prior populations, they tend to inherit the juvenile gang tradition along with the houses and institutions. Apparently, Negro teen-agers have not yet come into a tradition of organized gang behavior in the other urban centers. Dan Wakefield explains how Puerto Rican youths in New York acquired the pattern of gang behavior.[15]

Successive migrant groups have lived in similar conditions of poor housing and poverty, and followed similar patterns in forming gangs. The Puerto Rican teen-age gangs of today are not descended from any tradition of the streets of San Juan, but the streets of New York.

Aspiration levels

Aspiration patterns provide other keys to Negro teen-age culture. Significant models are compounded of traditional deprivations and the exciting new vistas of opportunity. Low-prestige teen-agers who can see no escape from the racial trap of deprivation tend to look forward to adult work and marriage roles of their social rank. But they have caught something of the spirit of the affluent society and so set great store by money and the things and immediate gratifications that money can buy. Moreover, many have sensed the spirit of quick, easy money through the ethical compromise, the confidence trick, the easy job, and "big shot" symbols. For example, when asked "Is it worse to cheat than to get caught cheating?" 122, or 37 per cent, of 328 students in a southern urban school said, "No."[16]

High-prestige teen-agers and, to a lesser degree, the upward mobile low-prestige ones, too, enjoy wider cultural communication, broader actual experiences, a tradition of long-range aspirations, and a less acute sense of racial entrapment. They are stirred by the ferment of social change and racial advancement that is abroad in the land.[17] The visible Negro success figures, the militant Negro press and organizations, expanding career opportunities, the new romance of engineering and science, and the increased affluence of the Negro middle classes all exert a powerful impact upon their levels and goals of aspiration. As will be shown below, one consequence is the Negro college-student protest movement. The romantic lure of Africa, thanks to stirring native nationalism and the strong pitch of the Peace Corps, is now bursting upon these teen-agers. In addition to Negro white-collar careers, today's teen-agers want to be engineers, scientists, aviators, technicians of all kinds, social workers, professional athletes, entertainers, radio and television workers, and so on.

Interlude of aggression

American teen-agers express aggression in the revolt against authority, bravado behavior, delinquency, gang activity, vandalism, and the like. . . . For most youngsters, teenhood comprises an interlude of aggression between childhood and adulthood. For Negro teen-agers, the interlude has at least two dimensions that merit examination. For them, it is the hiatus between the awareness of entrapment and the onset of compliance. For Negro teen-agers, too, the interlude is uniquely characterized by purposeful struggle.

Ultimately, most Negro teen-agers abandon the uneven struggle. The low-prestige ones tend to accept defeat in some version of the inferiority pattern. The high-prestige and upward mobile low-prestige teen-agers, however, tend to sublimate the struggle by adopting the middle-class pattern of respectability and formal protest.

Two patterns of aggression, namely, personal hostility and racial protest, comprise distinctive elements of the Negro teen-age culture. The former constitutes a carry-over into teenhood of low-prestige cultural patterns. Racial protest, on the other hand, is a cultural invention of Southern Negro teen-agers and represents a fusion of adolescent aggression, middle-class tradition, and college culture.

Personal hostility

For many of the big-city teen-agers, the sublimations of school, recreation center, church, job, and the like are both inadequate and inaccessible. Unexpended aggressions are turned inward upon themselves, their parents, their siblings, their friends, their schoolmates, and other teen-agers. The low-prestige tradition of their families and neighborhoods provides ready to hand the patterns and rationalizations of personal aggression.[18] The patterns range from use of derogatory words to deadly weapons, from talk to violence. Familiar examples include cursing, playing the dozens, blustering, threatening, fighting, and carrying knives or even pistols.

Personal aggression is reported from all sections of the country. For example, a perceptive Young Men's Christian Association (YMCA) worker in Baltimore reports that loose aggregations of low-prestige boys, sometimes numbering a hundred or more, roam about the city at night, crashing private parties, and making disturbances.[19] Occasionally, they precipitate fights in which knives and other weapons are flashed. An observer in Detroit wrote as follows:[20]

Boys who have been brought up in very scanty environment learn to fight for everything they want or need. Every new person is originally seen as trying to do the boy out of something. . . . They will pick fights with friends occasionally, but with just as much ferocity as if they had beer enemies.

As noted above, profane and obscene language is almost universal among low-prestige boys. The observers suggest that this language constitutes a mode of vicarious aggressive behavior. It is authoritatively reported that the carrying of knives is common among low-prestige individuals. Ninety-two, or 28 per cent, of 328 students in a southern urban high school said they thought it was all right to carry a knife.[21] Two-thirds of 318 students in the same school said they would "fight if someone messes with your money or food."

Racial protest

In the racial protest movement, southern Negro college-student teen-agers are creating a tradition of rational and disciplined aggression. The genius of this development is the fact that adolescent aggression against authority is fused with struggle for a cause.[22] Ruth Searles and J. Allen Williams, Jr., observe in this connection:[23] "The psychological functions of the movement would be to provide a 'legitimate' outlet for aggression and promote the loss of self through social devotion to a cause."

Although the sit-ins are the best known form of racial protest demonstration, there are at least three others:

(1) Applications by Negro children and their parents for public school transfers under the so-called "pupil assignment laws"; and applications of Negro college students for admission to southern state universities.[24]

(2) Boycott-picket efforts to promote hiring and/or upgrading of Negro workers in retail stores.

(3) Pickets, with supporting boycotts, to promote abandonment of racial segregation in motion picture theaters.

The sit-in protest

As seen by a spectator, a sit-in demonstration is a rather ordinary event.
A small group of Negro teen-agers, college and high school students of both
sexes, enter a place of business or public building, take seats intended for
customers, and ask to be served. The most usual places are lunch counters—
of dime and variety stores, department stores, drug stores, bus stations, and
public buildings—and public libraries. While waiting to be served, the students may study lessons, read newspapers, chat with one another, or just look
about. They make a conscious effort to avoid becoming involved in arguments
or altercations with persons looking on, store officials, and police officers. They
simply sit and act out the request for customer service.

Behind the public phase of the sit-in demonstration, however, there is a
great deal of planning and organization. Student leaders must arrange meetings to recruit demonstrators, make decisions, and prepare schedules and assignments. Sometimes, though not always, interested adults also participate
in the sessions where skills and disciplines are discussed, analyzed, and re-
hearsed. Negotiating conferences have to be arranged and conducted with the
establishments affected. Legal defense must be arranged for students who get
arrested and jailed, and public relations efforts must be kept going at all times.
Most of the sit-in demonstrations merged into long-time picket projects that
entailed a prodigious amount of organization and management.

The sit-in movement began in Greensboro, North Carolina, February 1,
1960, when four freshmen from the Agricultural and Technical College entered a dime store downtown and requested coffee at the lunch counter.[25]
Within a few weeks, college and high school students in at least sixteen other
North Carolina cities had initiated sit-ins or picket demonstrations at downtown chain drug and variety stores. Before the end of March 1960, the demonstrations had moved north into Virginia and West Virginia; south into South
Carolina, Georgia, and Florida; and west into Tennessee, Kentucky, Alabama,
Louisiana, Texas, and Arkansas. Sympathetic demonstrations developed in
university and college towns from New England to the West Coast. In June,
with the closing of schools, the movement subsided and, in August, several of
the variety and dime store chains desegregated their lunch counters in many
southern cities. In the fall and winter 1960–1961, the movement renewed or
turned its attention to movie houses and retail establishments.

During April and May 1960, in the height of the sit-in movement, 827
students in three of the Negro colleges in Greensboro and Raleigh, North
Carolina completed questionnaires regarding the demonstrations. Ruth Searles
and J. Allen Williams, Jr., reported the extent of participation of the 827 students in the following summary.[26]

In the "high participators" category (24 per cent of the total) were placed: those who said they had participated in the sit-in demonstrations and who had also walked in a picket line, distributed leaflets, acted on a committee of the movement, or helped in other ways such as making posters or telephoning. The "low participators" were those who did not participate at all (only 5 per cent . . .) or who only attended mass meetings and/or cooperated with the boycotts, a total of 44 per cent. The intermediate group comprised 31 per cent of the total.

When asked, "Were you glad the first time you heard about the sit-in demonstrations?" 318 of 332 students in a southern urban high school replied, "Yes."[27]

Conclusion

Bearing the inscription "Made in America," Negro teen-age culture comprises one submotif in the American cultural mosaic. It is compounded of typical adolescent behavior and unique group patterns, of earnest confidence in future promise and sullen resignation to present deprivation. A northern observer complains that the title "Negro Teen-Age Culture" begs the question, since he sees significant behavior differences as class-linked rather than racial. The southern spectator, however, is likely to be impressed by the Negro teen-age protest demonstrations.

Some thoughtful people believe that the teen-age racial protests have made a substantial impact on contemporary American life. They point to the new electric quality of interracial tension, the widespread response of the public opinion media, and recent changes of institutional structure. Yet, white teen-agers remain largely unresponsive to the challenge of organized serious social action. A few, both southern and northern, participated in the racial protest demonstrations. The majority, however, continues to be uninvolved with the serious issues of our times.

Two years ago almost no one could have predicted the dime-store sit-ins. It is equally difficult to predict today what Negro teen-agers may be doing two years hence. Some people seem to believe that protest activity is merely a teen-age fad. Some others see in it the wave of the future.

However, some of the trends which may condition Negro teen-age culture in the future are already evident. They include the following:
(1) Steadily improving levels of education and general cultural exposure.
(2) Widespread increase of the economic resources available to Negroes.
(3) Continuing expansion of opportunities for social participation and individual expression.
(4) Intensification of the stimulations and incentives to participate and achieve.
(5) Growing dissatisfaction with existing gulfs between aspirations and achievements.

It seems likely that Negro teen-agers may become more conscious of the squeeze placed on them by traditional institutions and patterns. One can only hope that the resultant aggressions will be imaginatively sublimated through such mechanisms as protest movements and the Peace Corps.

NOTES

1. See Warren Miller, *This Cool World* (Boston: Little, Brown, 1959).
2. Field document.
3. Oscar Handlin, *The Newcomers* (Cambridge: Harvard University Press, 1959), p. 78.
4. Personal document.
5. Warren Miller, *op. cit.*
6. In *Blackways of Kent* (Chapel Hill: University of North Carolina Press, 1955), pp. 233–256, Hylan G. Lewis differentiates the two traditions as "respectable" and "nonrespectable."
   See also Leonard H. Robinson, "Negro Street Society: A Study of Racial Adjustment in Two Southern Urban Communities" (unpublished doctoral dissertation, Ohio State University, 1950).
7. Theodore M. Bernstein examines some of the functions of slang in "Now It's Watch Your Slanguage," *New York Times Magazine*, February 28, 1960, pp. 31 and 94, ff.
8. Field documents from Syracuse, Buffalo, Baltimore, Washington, Durham, N.C., Columbus, Ohio, St. Paul, Detroit, St. Louis, and Houston.
9. James F. Donohue and Others "Veneral Diseases Among Teen-Agers," *Public Health Reports*, Vol. 70 (May 1955), p. 454, ff.
   Emily H. Mudd and Richard N. Hey, "When the Young Marry Too Young," *National Parent-Teacher*, Vol. 55 (September 1960), pp. 24–26.
10. Teen-Age Survey, Durham, North Carolina, April 1961.
11. Leonard Harrison Robinson, "Southern Urban Communities," *Journal of Human Relations*, Vol. 3 (Summer 1955), pp. 82–83.
12. *Ibid.*, p. 83.
13. Teen-Age Survey, Durham, North Carolina, April 1961.
14. Clifford R. Shaw and Henry D. McKay, *Juvenile Delinquency in Urban Areas* (Chicago: University of Chicago Press, 1942). Frederick M. Thrasher, *The Gang* (Chicago: University of Chicago Press, 1936). Albert K. Cohen, *Delinquent Boys* (Glencoe: Free Press, 1955).
15. Dan Wakefield, "The Other Puerto Ricans," *New York Times Magazine*, October 11, 1959, p. 24.
16. Teen-Age Survey, Durham, North Carolina, April 1961.
17. For a provocative comment on changing Negro teen-agers' aspirations, see Ernest Q. Campbell, "On Desegregation and Matters Sociological" (unpublished working paper, Institute for Research in Social Science, University of North Carolina), p. 9, ff.
18. See Lewis, *Blackways of Kent, op. cit.*, pp. 233–256 *passim*.
19. Field document.
20. Field document.

21. Teen-Age Survey, Durham, North Carolina, April 1961.
22. In the United States, general teen-age action appears to be typically non-serious, nonconstructive, noncause-linked, an expression of what Bernard calls "contraculture." Witness, for example, recent moblike demonstrations in Fort Lauderdale, Florida, Bowling Green State University, Ohio, and Galveston, Texas. Overt, often organized, sometimes violent politicosocial action, however, appears to be relatively characteristic of teen-agers and young adults in many European, Asian, and African countries.
23. Ruth Searles and J. Allen Williams, Jr., "Determinants of Negro College Students' Participation in Sit-ins" (unpublished working paper Institute for Research in Social Science, University of North Carolina, April 2, 1961).
24. There is a voluminous literature on school desegregation. Among the definitive studies of specific situations, see Wilson and Jane Cassels Record, *Little Rock, U.S.A.* (San Francisco: Chandler Publishing Company, 1960); Ernest Q. Campbell *et al., When a City Closes Its Schools* (Chapel Hill: University of North Carolina, Institute for Research in Social Science, 1960).
25. Daniel H. Pollitt, "Dime Store Demonstrations: Events and Legal Problems of First Sixty Days," *Duke Law Journal*, Summer 1960, pp. 317–337.
26. Ruth Searles and J. Allen Williams, Jr., *op. cit.*, p. 10.
27. Teen-Age Survey, Durham, North Carolina, April 1961.

[42]   *William A. Schonfeld*   ADOLESCENT TURMOIL:

SOCIOECONOMIC AFFLUENCE AS A FACTOR

Socioeconomic affluence has been found to play an important preparatory and determining role in how a youth copes with his adolescent crises.

In the past, studies of youths who are deviant from an adult viewpoint have been largely confined to disadvantaged socioeconomic groups. Recently, however, there have been many reports on deviant behavior and emotional disorders among affluent young people in high schools and colleges, with much sensational publicity focused on the suburbs and numerous books and articles published on the "up beat," the "new breed," or the "shook-up generation." I feel that we can learn a great deal about the attitudes and needs of all young people by studying the reaction of this "new species" of socioeconomically affluent adolescents.

The age-old contention that delinquency in youth is the prerogative of the poor is totally invalid. It is no more true than the notion that happiness is

FROM *New York State Journal of Medicine*, 1967, 67, 1981–1990. REPRINTED BY PERMISSION OF THE AUTHOR AND THE MEDICAL SOCIETY OF THE STATE OF NEW YORK.

synonymous with wealth and anxiety with poverty or that money and virtue reinforce each other. The point is that slum youths are more frequently arrested and forced to face the consequences of their acts, while those of affluent families are able to get away with it because of the consideration extended by law-enforcement agencies on the assumption that the affluent family will "do something about the youth," or charges are dropped because the affluent parent pays the cost of damages incurred.

The fact remains that progressively more adolescents in suburban areas and colleges are involved in a variety of antisocial and asocial acts. In this light it would be well to review some of the specific factors associated with affluence— in the family, the individual adolescent, and in the adolescent subculture— that are contributing to the confusion and the unfavorable outcome of the crises of adolescents.

Affluence of family

Early parent-child relationships and attitude "programming" play a vital role in the youth's concept of his own importance, the sources from which he desires status, his degree of independence, his method of assimilating new values, his concept of his own capacity for doing things for himself, his ability to withstand frustration, his need for pleasure and immediate gratification, his sense of responsibility, and the type of defenses he uses when his security or self-esteem is threatened. Security and abundance in the present and optimism for the future should create in affluent families ideal physical and emotional conditions for bringing up their children. Ironically, this is too often not the case.

Many of these privileged children are given too many material things but are deprived emotionally. Such youngsters do not know the joy of wanting for something or dreaming and anticipating. From birth they never had to wait for the fulfillment of any wish. They could have anything they wanted when they wanted it and often even before they knew they wanted it. They were deprived of the wholesome experience of learning to cope with reasonable frustrations. This often leads to a need for immediate gratification of all desires.

To be sure, affluence alone is not the single cause of this deprivation. The present confusion about values and standards contributes to the problem as well as a lazy abdication by parents from making demands for fear of incurring their children's anger. In other families it results from a projection of the emotional needs parents cannot satisfy in their own lives: They attempt to fulfill what they consider the needs of their offspring with material gifts. Many parents in our affluent society have an intense desire to avoid any anxiety or tension, which they convey to their children, and set an example for over self-indulgence.

Parents often project onto their children their own drives and needs. At times this may be constructive, but at other times it is a vicarious neurotic fulfillment which they may have successfully repressed in their climb to affluence. It often leads to acts of delinquency unconsciously sanctioned by the parents. All too often adolescent problems are a symptom of family disorder.

In the drive for material success, many a commuting father finds the demands of his working day time so great that he is prevented from being with his family, and this leads to paternal deprivation. Then, too, the drive for social participation in the suburban fun cult creates the weekend golf widow or the father lost to sailing or marathon viewing of TV sports events. We are concerned about the effect of the absentee father on the development of boys in the suburbs. The mother becomes the authority figure in the family, and the father often does not become involved until there is serious trouble.

Not only is there a reversal of parental role, but the mother often functions in a bisexual social capacity, which adds up to a blurring of sexual differences. This situation has created a matriarchal society and may account for unconscious feminine identification in many boys and confusion in girls as to what constitutes the feminine role.

Another overwhelming pressure on the adolescent is the "great expectation syndrome." Affluent parents cram all kinds of lessons and cultural and social experiences down the child's throat. This is done not so much to stimulate or satisfy a need in the child as to satisfy a need in the parent which the children are aware of. Parties, dating, dances, and the need to be popular are initiated too early, and so pressured is the child toward a social life that by the time he reaches high school he is bored with the usual. In short, affluent children get too much too soon.

Another "great expectation" is academic success with the goal of admission to the "right" college, starting in many affluent families when the child is first admitted to school. Often such ambitions are unrealistic and create a fear of inadequacy in a child. He soon comes to realize that his goals need not be learning but rather grades. Often this leads to cheating when the going gets tough, in the child who wants to please his parents, setting a pattern of behavior. In some instances the child deliberately or unconsciously uses academic failure as a weapon of retaliation against the parents.

Child-rearing attitudes in the last generation among affluent families have added pitfalls. Parents and educators have been permissive and shied away from "thwarting." Freedom of expression and action, regardless of others, has been encouraged. Then, too, the high value placed by democracies on liberty, political and social, has been translated into stressing freedom of expression and thought. Carried too far, this emphasis may entail rejection of authority. Just as in the political realm liberty without obligation is anarchy, so in the adolescent's world freedom without responsibility yields anarchy or what Wyle called pediarchy. Youth must learn to accept responsibility along with freedom.

Thus affluent families impose a multitude of pressures on their children; overpermissiveness, overstimulation, overgratification, hence overdeprivation.

Affluence of adolescent subculture

The social group to which a youth gravitates depends on his self concepts. There is the group whose values match those of the older generation. They want what the affluent society has to give and are optimistic about succeeding. They aspire to education and professional training and develop a sense of identity which resolves the discontinuity between childhood and adulthood and bridges the gap between generations. Although they are teen-agers, they are not truly a part of the teen-age subculture. They see themselves as well motivated and adjusted and in high school refer to themselves as "collegiates." Other teen-agers may refer to them as "squares." Many of these youths, however, may temporarily deviate from their parents' concepts in grappling with the adolescent tasks of achieving identity, heterosexual adjustment, and emancipation from parental control, but ultimately they revert to it. Others want the same things, but lack the intellect, talent, or culture, to attain them; they often become disillusioned because they cannot achieve ego identity.

Another heterogeneous group of youths are disenchanted with, and alienated from, the expressed standards of their families, adult society, and, in general, "The Establishment." Attractiveness and popularity are major concerns here. Happiness with absence of anxiety is a means and an end in itself. Group activities and group acceptance are of the utmost importance, often achieved at a cost to individuality. There is a rejection of adult roles and standards and authority figures. There is considerable restlessness, boredom, and a craving for excitement. It is this group which is growing, along with our society's affluence.

Today our young people are facing a "crisis of purpose" which is perhaps more difficult to deal with than the crisis of economics faced by those from economically and socially deprived homes. A surprisingly large number of these young people view our society as a "rat race." They see the adult world to which they are headed as a cold, mechanical arena where one simply goes through the motions of "playing the game." To them it is essential to stay "cool," detached, and uncommitted.

Some want to change the world and feel forced into detachment and premature cynicism because the affluent society seems to offer them so little that is relevant, stable, and meaningful. They are in search of values, goals, or institutions to which they could be genuinely committed. Many have learned the effectiveness of civil disobedience from the integration movement and are fighting for their own "rights" to have a say in the world in which they live: a "participating democracy." Given something like the Peace Corps, which promises challenge and genuine expression of idealism, an extraordinary number of young people are prepared to drop everything and join up.

Many of the alienated young people revert to special clothing, special hair styles, beards, footwear, bizarre behavior, and new-sound music in a calculated campaign for autonomy, to differentiate them from the adult world and to shock and alarm dissident adults.

The "beatniks" who are only one small part of this group may be characterized as persons of generally low energy level who regard a certain despairing look in clothes, personal appearance, and the way they live as essential to their status as deviant members of society. Many of them admire and aspire to artistic and intellectual expression, but reject academic and vocational achievement. They try to remain forever in the youth culture. Hippies, who are part of this subgroup, stress love, giving, and oriental philosophies and detach themselves from the realities of today.

Another subgroup of youth may be called "sickniks." They have lost their freedom of choice and act in a deviant manner because of the pressures of their emotional problems. Many of them never fitted into the society in which they lived from childhood. They alternate between feeling lonely and excluded from society and feeling superior to it. They band together on street corners, food shops, bars, at pot parties, on college campuses to gain support for the compensating convictions of superiority and allow a certain release from loneliness. Such youths have no fanatical zeal or any cause to fight. Because of their odd-ball self-image there is no externalization of aggression. Some are more seriously disturbed than others.

However, the subgroup with which we are particularly concerned includes the large number of young people from socioeconomic affluent society who fall into the category of "the new breed" or the "new species" of adolescents.

While adolescents have always wanted to be alike, because being different to them means being inferior, today's adolescents seem driven by a compulsion to follow the herd. The affluence of their families as well as their own affluence give them the opportunity to cater to their needs.

Adolescence, the time of fads and fancies where nonconformity seems the order of the day, is in fact the age of absolute conformity. The herd instinct is at its greatest, assuring anonymity in numbers. This accounts for the paradox of nonconforming conformity. In dealing with this age group we must be acutely aware of the unvoiced terror these youths have of being different. They may appear outlandishly dressed or behaved to adults, but their very nonconformation has identified them with themselves, allowing group assertiveness with individual self-effacement.

Naturally, not all affluent adolescents are driven by an equally strong compulsion to follow the herd, but few escape it. The ones most affected are those whose group status is somewhat precarious or those who want to improve their standing. The only adolescents who seem able to retain their indiviuality are the few whose position is so secure that nothing can shake it, those whose status is hopeless, and those who are not interested enough in peer activities to care.

There are two main reasons for the adolescent's willingness to relinquish his individuality for peer conformity besides the tasks inherent to adolescence. For one thing, the status-seeking "keeping up with the Joneses" culture has provided the adolescent with a model of conformity ever since he left his crib. He is confronted with conformists at home, in the neighborhood, and at school.

For another, there is the high value set on popularity. If it is necessary to follow the crowd to gain its acceptance, he will pay the price. If, on the other hand, being an individual means loneliness and, even worse, a derogatory attitude from his peers, he will do all within his power to avoid having this happen to him.

In our class-conscious culture of today, it would be surprising if the adolescent were not anxious to be identified with the leading crowds. He knows that the way to make this possible is to have the right status symbols as he understands them, which symbols often do not parallel his family's concepts of status. The less secure he is, the more preoccupied he becomes with these symbols.

The symbols change from year to year. Last year it was belonging, togetherness, going steady. In high school you went steady, in college you were pinned. This year it is no longer going steady, it is "steady going"—go, Go, GO. Having a date is unimportant. Status comes from "fitting in" with everyone. Date or no date, the thing is to be with people, to be going somewhere.

Similarly, not so long ago, to be able to drive the family car was the thing. Today, the big family car is out. Now it is a small sports car, preferably his own; and even that is rapidly changing into a motorcycle not only for boys but also for girls.

Involvement is in. Youth latches on to what tangible causes it can find: civil rights, anti-Vietnam, antidraft, and the many social hypocrisies and inconsistencies of our society. It is true that the largest number merely talk about involvement and only a small proportion are activists.

The new values come from the types adolescents are choosing as their heroes, mass media that glamorize extravagance and paint thrift as dowdy, bombard youth with erotic stimulation. Some of the new values arise within the peer group itself. If the group as a whole gives its stamp of approval to certain behavior, it is accepted as right. If it's okay to cheat, you cheat. If "everybody" is smoking pot, you join right in; if the thing to do is to be sexually promiscuous, you go right along, disregarding the consequences. Too often, the behavior is not motivated by convictions but merely by following the crowd.

The adolescent subculture is based on affluence and leisure. The mass media catering to youth foster the discretionary spending and unique buying habits of the young people who spent over 18 billion dollars last year and influenced the spending of another 35 billion dollars by adults. The teen-age market and the subculture that shapes its consumers' needs is now important to our economy. The affluence that created the adolescent subculture now leans on it quite heavily. Phenomena like the Beatles are the result of the economic affluence of youth.

Adults are overwhelmed by the large numbers of youth involved in any project to which they commit themselves. This is to be expected because of their uniform interests, their enjoyment of mass involvement, their mobility, the leisure time available to them, and the fact that they constitute a large part of our total population. Forty per cent of the population of the United

States is under twenty years of age, and adolescents have a tendency to congregate whether it be for a folk festival, a sporting event, a song fest, or to attend an open house. Adults become frightened because so little can change a crowd into a mob. We are concerned by the vengeful resentment that seems to underlie many of today's explosions. It indicates a boiling rage combined with a deep contempt for law and order.

Alliance has contributed to these problems in many ways, first by giving the youth the mobility to congregate and the financial resources to travel and to purchase tickets. But it has also created the attitude that money can pay for any damages. It may be said that boredom and righteous indignation seem to be ingredients that most often make for an explosive milieu. Riots usually occur at times when scheduled activities are at a minimum and a good deal of loose energy has been accumulated.

Affluence of individual adolescent

One thing to remember about adolescents is that gaining recognition and prestige, matters associated with sex, and acquiring independence are their chief preoccupations.

The youth's self-awareness and body image are based largely on how his parents, peers, and society see him and how he interprets their evaluation of him. Complicated and distorted communications from all about him impinge on the young person so that he has no clear signals to go by. Advertising media and purveyors of assorted ideologies tell him what he is, what he should be, and how he ought to act.

Seeking a way out, he first turns inward to mobilize his inner resources. But this may be inadequate to allow for personal assessment because abstract thinking has not developed sufficiently or has been distorted because of emotional conflicts. He also turns to an earlier trusted identification model, but often finds that he or she preaches one set of values and acts according to another. Feeling abandoned by their adult world, most teen-agers turn to their peer group as a model for their behavior.

The adolescent subculture is not static but ever changing, one trend being the earlier entrance of children into it. Among the factors accounting for this new precocity are earlier physiologic maturation, an indirect result of affluence with its better nutrition and good medical attention and increased outdoor activities; the widespread aping of the older adolescent by the younger one; and permissiveness and perhaps encouragement by parents.

Why do so many youths from affluent families revert to slum area behavior? Is it to escape from middle-class bounds? Is it basically the youth's desire to avoid the pressures, expectations, and demands of his affluent class and his belief that less is expected of the lower class in terms of education, vocational adjustment, living conditions, and moral values? There is a growing pattern of emotional uninvolvement. Many of the young people lack the drive to achieve affluence which motivated their parents because, unlike their parents, they know nothing but security. They want all that money can buy but resent the demands affluence may create.

Too many of today's affluent adolescents, however, tend to follow the philosophy of "let John do it." John may be parents, teachers, or Uncle Sam. They may be meticulous about maintaining their disheveled appearance, but school assignments are thrown together, home chores are neglected, they are constantly late for appointments, do not bother to answer party invitations but show up anyway, and raid the refrigerator without regard to whether food is intended for the next meal. They ask a girl to go steady and drop her if they find someone else who strikes their fancy. They come late for part-time jobs and drop them without notice, and they rush into marriage with no thought of how they are going to support the marriage.

This irresponsibility has often been cultivated in the individual since early childhood. Yet parents and teachers are surprised when it does not miraculously disappear with adolescence. Closely related to this lack of responsibility is the unfavorable attitude toward work. Having been waited on hand and foot, many develop the habit of putting forth as little as possible. They look on work as an evil. If they can get reasonably good grades by cheating, why study? If they can hold down a job by turning out a minimum of work, why "kill yourself for a slavedriver?" If they can get the gist of a classic by seeing the movie based on the book or reading a digest, why read the book?

The rise in family and national income has extended the period of youth by allowing longer periods of dependency, placing a premium on more and more formal education, and providing the means to educate a larger proportion of young people. In affluent families the adolescent's earnings from after school or vacation jobs are not needed. Those who do work are motivated by a wish for greater independence, to make a desired purchase, or to satisfy their need to achieve.

Affluence, too, means free time to get into mischief or do as one pleases. If the parents become too demanding, the adolescent has a powerful weapon over them. He will threaten to drop out of school, leave home and get a job, knowing that his parents and society want him to continue his education.

Despite the fact that more and more adolescents are going to college and professional schools, it is not always proof of intellectual interests. It may be merely the thing to do, a way of making a higher income in the future, or meeting the right people. Many girls who attend college do so not to "pursue learning but to learn pursuing," their objective being a husband.

There is also a tendency to stay in college as a way of avoiding vocational or life commitments and retaining their role as carefree students. Many continue their education to avoid military induction. Anti-intellectualism is also evident in the youth who cheats rather than study or who fails and drops out of school. Nevertheless, there are many who are highly motivated to study and learn.

Today's adolescent feels that all members of the older generation are out of tune with the times. He develops a derogatory attitude toward all people over thirty. This negative attitude is reinforced by what he sees and hears around him. Lack of respect and esteem for age and experience and adoration of youth are so much a part of the American scene that it would be unrealistic to expect the adolescent to feel otherwise.

As a result, the adolescent deprives himself of the guidance of anyone old enough and experienced enough to offer it. Since adolescents reject the values and opinions of older people, they turn to their peers for advice. Also, there is constant friction in the home. Expecting parents to pay their bills and assume many responsibilities for their daily life, they say hands off when it comes to doing what their parents expect of them. Family friction has always existed where adolescents were striving to gain independence, but this derogatory attitude toward the very people who are expected to do so much for them is a bitter pill for parents to swallow who pride themselves on the affluence they achieved and are so often motivated by a desire to make their children's lives easier and happier.

While adolescents have always been critical of their elders, it was never so fully and tactlessly expressed as today. A favorite indoor sport is debunking those in authority, whether it be parents, teacher, principal, or government.

Of course it is desirable that adolescents make a contribution to progress. It is not the criticism and suggestions for reform the adults resent. It is the rude and derogatory manner of presenting it. What the adolescent does is to sit in judgment on his parents and teachers rather than cooperate and work together for the improvement of the home or school. The adult in turn resents and rejects the youth's involvement, further complicating the situation. There is a greater than ever need for youth and adults to work together to resolve the problems of our society.

Every generation of adolescents has felt that the rules and laws of society were too strict. But today's young people seem to feel that laws are made to be broken. Parents complain that their children are impossible to control, that they do exactly as they please. Most teachers spend more time maintaining order than teaching. The police are busier with the antics of teen-agers than with adult criminality.

To members of the older generation who believe that to spare the rod is to spoil the child, the cause lies in the laxity of our child-training methods. This is too pat an explanation, although true in part. Corporal punishment is hardly the way to make a child into a law-abiding citizen, but sparing the child of any necessity for toeing the mark is a factor. Hence, the child believes he is a law unto himself; by adolescence he disregards the laws of the land as well as family rules and regulations. However, let us not forget that much of this disregard for laws is a reflection of the attitudes of our society. We cannot on one hand condone civil disobedience and the right to ignore so-called bad laws and expect youth to accept the limitations placed on him.

Adolescence is a time for dreaming, and today's adolescent is no exception. But he goes much further. He is convinced he will reach the pot of gold at the rainbow's end with a minimum of effort. If he fails, it will be someone else's fault. Today's adolescent feels anything is possible. It is very difficult to get young people to understand the despair of the Great Depression and a life without security.

Today's affluent adolescents may be a new species, but newness is not synonymous with superiority or contentment. Certainly they have more advantages, socially, culturally, and educationally, than in the past. It is true that the threat of atomic annihilation hovers over them, but every generation has had its tribulations. They have more knowledge and sophistication, but there is ample evidence that far too many whose hereditary endowments and cultural advantages would normally lead to high achievements are turning into second-rate students, workers, and citizens.

Many of today's adolescents are far from happy. They are bored, jaded, and disillusioned. Many turn to alcohol, drugs, and narcotics to relieve their anxieties and make them feel more adequate. There are far too many who suffer from feelings of inadequacy, question their own worth, wonder if life is worth living, and too often commit suicide as an escape from reality.

To be happy a person must not only have a feeling of confidence that he can achieve success within his capacities, but also he must retain a sense of individuality and identity. Too many of today's adolescents do not have this. They are slaves to the demands of their subculture and I fear are headed for a life where conformity to the herd will rule their every thought and act.

There is an increasing occurrence of vandalism, mugging, rape, burglaries, and crowd disturbances emanating from affluent youth. An apparent lack of logic characterizes most of the offenses. Often there is a kind of satisfying need of the moment, impulsiveness coupled with a complete disdain of authority. On apprehension, the typical reaction is defiance, unrepentance, and absence of anxiety.

Official statistics do not reflect the true incidence of delinquency among affluent youths because so much of it is never recorded. Most suburban teenagers never have any trouble with the police, but their lives seem to be affected by the same kind of random wandering and reaching out for thrills as motivates those who do get into trouble. "Where's the action?" is the motto. There is a ceaseless hunt for action. They cruise in their cars seeking parties to crash, pool-hopping in the summer, and racing on parkways.

Affluence brought the mobility of the car. As mentioned before, the family car has lost its prestige, and youth searches for a sports car, an aggressive car, stealing it for an evening's pleasure if necessary. The motorcycle has greater mobility and thrill. Wheels mean something to a boy in late adolescence, a self-concept he may not be able to achieve through more socially accepted channels.

Criminal behavior touches respectable parents to the quick. Some children often unconsciously select this kind of behavior to harass their parents. The youth who steals while he has money in his pockets is a headache to merchants in suburban communities. When caught they say, "Everyone's doing it, why pick on me?" Some observers blame TV shows for the disturbing patterns of violence in the first television-bred generation. But this is not limited to the affluent youth.

The pointlessness of most early teen-age vandalism without pilferage perplexes parents and police. When the vandals are asked what lies behind their actions, they say they "don't know." A common answer is, "For kicks," or "To get even." But they don't say with whom. Vandalism in schools has reached such proportions that wanton destruction must be provided for in the budgets. The telephone company is also victimized by culprits prying money out of coin boxes.

Riotous behavior of the affluent youth is an extension of rebellion. In itself rebellion may serve a constructive purpose, but it becomes destructive when it is expressed in ways that are permanently self-defeating to the individual, such as serious underachievement in school, antisocial behavior or sexual delinquency in girls, or when it results in property damage or physical injury to others.

Feelings of guilt or fear of eternal damnation simply do not have inhibiting and restricting effects on adolescents today. Of course there are still many young men and women for whom absolute morality has a meaning. There is a great deal of validity to the contention of many investigators that today's youth are more open, defiant, and daring in their sexual behavior. The prevailing college value is not chastity but fidelity.

Early child care attitudes and permissiveness, concern about frustration, and encouragement of immediate gratification of all desire in our affluent families have contributed to changing sexual mores. In addition, there is the significant female rebellion against traditional masculine sexual prerogatives, not to curb men but rather to release women. There are also the examples set by adults in our affluent society including wife swapping and rampant infidelity. The youth's affluence has contributed to the problem by creating opportunities for sexual involvement, making contraceptive pills available, the assurance that mother will pay for an abortion if necessary, and the basic feeling that money will take care of anything that may arise. The affluence of our society in turn has made the demand for babies for adoption so great that this solution for one's mistakes is always available to the white youth.

The large numbers of reported illegitimate births, the high percentage of women of all ages who are pregnant at the time they are married, the statistics on abortions, as well as the increase in venereal disease all indicate the depth of the problem.

The decline of the effectiveness of religious training seems to be a part of our affluent culture. Adolescents today, more than in earlier times, are demanding logical reasons for ethical standards. It is not enough to speak to them in terms of some kind of moral law or a feeling of what is right or wrong. Only those youths who realize that the consequences of their behavior are going to be harmful to their own welfare and the welfare of those they love are willing to restrain themselves and exert self-control.

As for the use of drugs by the young people today, there is evidence that the greater amount of cash in the hands of teen-agers has made this group attractive to pushers, although the spread is through social contagion, through "friends" rather that professional pushers. It is fallacious to try to contend with problems created by the use of marihuana, barbiturates, and amphetamines in the same way as LSD or heroin just because they are all illegal. The problems of psychological dependency must be differentiated from pharmacologic addiction. Much of the thrill attached to taking drugs is directly related to the satisfaction the participants gain from realizing how horrified their parents would be if they knew what was going on as well as creating a bond with their peers.

The social and moral implications involving the use of drugs are important. Apart from taking drugs to satisfy the rebellious impulses is the search for a change of mood to throw off the depression which is so often inherent in the low self-esteem in many young people. They have a need to be constantly happy: are searching for "instant happiness." Many adolescents are intrigued by death. In poetry and song they are often fascinated by tragedy and early death. This may be related to the pervasive feeling of alienation of many adolescents from affluent families. The availability of money, the boredom of leisure, the inability to find satisfactions and identity, and the permissiveness which invades our affluent society all add to the allure of drugs.

Comment

As a result of the philosophy of our socioeconomically affluent society which has incorporated the need to fulfill one's every desire immediately, the wish to avoid frustration at any cost, the urge to be constantly happy, and the peer acceptance of evasion as a way of life, many a youth has run away from the problems and frustrations of the realities of living. When the school grades do not live up to his expectations or what the youth considers the expectations of his parents, he sees himself as a failure and will drop out of school. When the academic failures become associated with social failures or failure of a love affair, he will run away from college. When the teen-ager's marriage does not allow for constantly being on the go and perpetual ecstasy he rushes to get a divorce. Too often, when the youth finds himself overwhelmed by life, he turns to drugs, alcohol, withdrawal, or suicide as escape.

When youth's rebellion takes the form of involvement and a sincere effort to effect reasonable changes in our society, then it can have meaning; but if it merely defies the patterns of our society as a way of attracting attention or escaping boredom, then it serves no social purpose. There can be little question that socioeconomic affluence is the cause of many problems of youth in one sector of our population, but so is our political affluence with its freedom of thinking, freedom of speech, and freedom of action. However, no one feels that the answer would be to relinquish any of these privileges. What we must do is to utilize our affluence and rights in a more constructive manner. Adult society must include youth in a meaningful way in various local committees and projects to help decide the many exciting and significant things that are going on in our communities. Young people should be accepted as individuals by adults to share their uncertainties, their troubles, and their triumphs. We must encourage a continued dialogue with adolescents and invite them to join us in finding solutions to their own crises and those of the society in which they live.

[43]   *Eli A. Rubinstein*   PARADOXES OF STUDENT PROTESTS

Early in the spring of 1968 when I was approached about making this presentation on student protests, I hesitated, primarily because my credentials in this field were neither very solid nor of any long duration. Had I anticipated the increased number and intensity of national and international incidents in this area the past year, I would have been even more reluctant to add still one more set of interpretations to the many statements which are now being published on student protests.

Since the recent turmoil at Columbia University and the riots in Paris, almost every periodical, professional as well as popular, which might have any relevance to the topic of student unrest, has published one or more articles on the subject. From the *American Scholar* to *Barrons Financial Weekly*, there have been specific descriptions and general interpretations of student protests. It is perhaps a measure of the complexity of this phenomenon that with everything that has been written subsequent to Berkeley in 1964, and the more recent incidents at Columbia and other universities here and abroad, we have only the most superficial and obvious understanding of the dynamics of the process of confrontation which is involved in these student protests.

Social influx is so intense these days that it reveals new depths of our ignorance of social systems more rapidly than we are able to add new knowledge. It reminds me of the classic *New Yorker* cartoon in which the gas station

FROM *American Psychologist*, 1969, 24, 133–141. COPYRIGHT 1969 BY THE AMERI-CAN PSYCHOLOGICAL ASSOCIATION, AND REPRODUCED BY PERMISSION OF THE AUTHOR AND THE PUBLISHER.

attendant, trying to fill the gas tank of an unbelievably high-powered and luxurious automobile, says to the driver, "Would you please turn off the motor, you're gaining on me."

As I read about the succession of incidents on campuses throughout the country, and think about the insights and understanding that we as behavioral scientists can offer to assist in solving the problems, I have the same uneasy feeling that they are gaining on us. It was partly because of that uneasiness and the belief that behavioral scientists can improve understanding of this phenomenon, that a group of scholars in July 1968 at the Center for Advanced Study in the Behavioral Sciences published a recommendation for a national study to examine the individual and group patterns of response to student protests (Abrams et al., 1968).

I would like to take just a moment to describe the background to that recommendation. In 1967, at the Center for Advanced Study in the Behavioral Sciences, a small group initiated a seminar which was entitled "The College Environment as a Place to Learn." Original discussions were devoted to various aspects of the relationship between the student and the institution which influence the learning experience. However, toward the end of the fall when student demonstrations began to occur on a number of college campuses around the country, we began to concentrate on that aspect of the college environment.

In keeping with the seminar format, and trying to take a somewhat different approach to an examination of student activism, we invited five college presidents—all from various California campuses—to come individually to meet with the seminar participants and give us their viewpoints on student activism. The five presidents included Robert Clark of San Jose State College, John Summerskill of San Francisco State College, Roger Heyns of the University of California at Berkeley, Dean McHenry of the University of California at Santa Cruz, and Louis Benezet of Claremont University Center. I will reveal my own biases when I characterize these five administrators as thoughtful, sensitive, and perceptive individuals who were aware of the stresses which now exist on the college campus and who were sincerely trying to respond to some of the demands being made by the student activists. It was the repercussions of those demands, incidentally, which forced John Summerskill to resign in the spring of 1968.

In preparation for meeting with these college presidents, a colleague and I visited six campuses around the country in February and March of 1968, on all of which some form of student demonstration had occurred. We interviewed representatives from the faculty, the administration, and the student body about student demonstrations on their respective campuses. At this point I must again mention the timing of my presentation here. My original intention in spring 1968 had been to use the meetings with the college presidents and my visits to the various campuses as a basis for commenting on some of the characteristics of student protests. Two things have happened since then which made me modify what I have to say. One, the events on campuses such as

Columbia and in Paris have changed and intensified the situation somewhat and, two, a number of recent articles have discussed some of the points I had intended to make.

I would like, therefore, to touch on some of the more recent interpretations of student unrest, relate these to some of the things I have been involved in this past year, and then try to raise some additional questions about this most intriguing development among the youth of today.

In July 1967 a series of papers on student activism in the *Journal of Social Issues* presented a perspective on some of the research done since the Berkeley days. It is interesting to note that in a summary article Sampson (1967) equivocates on the "future of student activism," but he suggests that activism will not be maintained. The year of 1968 at least suggests otherwise.

And it is within this past year that the statements and articles on student activism have become too numerous to follow. It would be an interesting statistic to know how many college—and high school—commencement addresses in June of 1968 were on student unrest or student power. My uninformed guess is that the vast majority were on some variant of that theme. And I would suspect that those addresses reflect an increasing degree of polarization on the subject. People are either for or against student protest per se. The issues on which the protests were initiated tend to be lost sight of in the intensity of the process of confrontation itself. It is not insignificant that the State Education Department in New York was recently reported as seeking an expert on college uprisings, who would be sent around to troubled campuses to interview persons involved in the riots.

The unanswered question in all this is what have been the factors which produced student protest? A number of themes run through much of the present literature. Sampson (1967), in the summary paper I mentioned earlier, discussed a number of "activism inducing contexts." It is obvious that the factors are multiple and interrelated: The affluent family, the unresponsive university environment, the political and social climate, the ever-present mass media, Vietnam and the draft, and the usual problems of adolescence are all invoked as the basis for protests.

More recently, Halleck (1968) has written a paper which summarizes the various hypotheses identified as the basis for, or influence on, student activism. Interestingly enough, Halleck's paper reflects the kind of polarization in attitude I just mentioned. He divided his hypotheses into groups, one of which he calls the "critical hypotheses." These are the hypotheses which find student activism a function of something which is wrong with the student protesters themselves; this would include permissive upbringing, too much affluence, or some family pathology. A second grouping of hypotheses is sympathetic to the student, finding him a victim of or a crusader against some external circumstance. This would include the war in Vietnam, the deterioration in the quality of life, and the problems of civil rights. And finally, Halleck has a group of neutral hypotheses, which include impersonal processes such as increased technology, mass media, and reliance on scientism. Halleck believes the neutral hypotheses are the most persuasive in understanding the student unrest.

Other recent writings have made an even more sweeping examination of the entire Zeitgeist and tried to describe youth in general from a broad over-view of our times. Rovit (1968) has written a very scholarly piece on "the contemporary apocalyptic image" in which he traces the history of the metaphor of the Apocalypse, and tries to relate it to the development of the newer revo-lutionary or radical thinking. He suggests, in language appropriately dramatic for the theme he is exploring, that

we may very well be on the brink of a brand new epistemology—a new technique and concept of rationality which may build on the advances of binary computation, field games theory, and include the irrationalities of extrasensory perception, mental telepathy, hallucinogenic drugs, and other open-ended nonteleological modes of understanding. This, of course, does not mean that man and his world have changed in any cardinal, unnatural way. Men will continue to be born, to suffer, and to die. The constants of human experience will remain inevitable and constant. But the dominant metaphor from which man draws his meanings and values may be in the throes of an explosive transformation [pp. 466–467].

Rovit retreats, however, from this apocalyptic metaphor, and ends by saying "the magic of man may after all lie in his capacity to enter into and exit from the metaphors that seek to capture him in rigid definitions. The ideal of poly-morphous perversity—an ideal of complete fluidity—can be as inflexible and inhuman as any other absolute [pp. 467–468]."

Keniston (1968), in a more direct effort to identify basic characteristics of today's young radicals, stresses the importance of *style*. He too sees fluidity and flux as a major attribute and believes that the way the younger generation approaches the world reveals more communality than their actual behavior. With the emphasis on change, it is difficult to find common or constant ide-ologies.

However, Keniston's central thesis—in its way as broad as Rovit's—is that the most important variable influencing the behavior of these young individ-uals is the threat of violence and their sensitivity to this issue. He believes "the issue of violence is to this generation what the issue of sex was to the Victorian world [p. 242]."

I would like to focus down from that level of broad generalization and touch on the dilemmas inherent in the process of protest itself. To this observer the student protesters reveal an unusual mixture of righteousness and wrongish-ness. This is exemplified in what I would call paradoxes of protest. I will cite just four. Many more could be found.

Perhaps the most central and prevalent paradox is that in the very effort to uphold their individual freedom the student activists forcibly abridge the freedom of others. It is on one or another variation of this point that university administrators have taken their stand. Almost uniformly, dissent has been permitted without punitive retaliation up to the point where college programs are disrupted or suspended, through acts of violence or coercion.

This point gets to the heart of the philosophy of the new left which is, interestingly enough, now being attacked by some of the social and political commentators whose earlier writings influenced the young activists. Thus, Paul Goodman (1968), the social critic, recently wrote on anarchism as a political framework for today's protesting students. At one point he does say, "The protesting students are anarchists because they are in an historical situation to which anarchism is their only possible response [p. 13]." However, he criticizes both the new left and the hippies because their philosophy ends up in the same kind of power struggle that they are presumably rebelling against.

I saw this dilemma regarding individual freedom acted out on a much smaller stage at one of the colleges I visited in the spring of 1968. Two of the students that I interviewed presented the opposing points of view very clearly. One student, who had sat in on a Dow demonstration, explained that for him it was a symbolic action that he had undergone because of his own personal conscience. He had made a moral judgment on genocide and felt that this was the only way he could express his point of view. All during the actual sit-in, which, incidentally, turned out to be less moral and less symbolic than he had anticipated, he was ambivalent about his action but did not leave for fear of disrupting the effect of the group behavior. The other student who had not sat in pointed out that he felt himself just as much involved in a moral judgment, but that it had been his position to consider the issue of freedom of choice more important than the issue of genocide. He did not want to do anything which would deny that freedom of moral judgment to others in pursuing their own moral conscience. Both students admitted the obvious conflict of moral issues and recognized that other students would decide in whichever direction they felt the moral value to be the greater.

The dilemma inherent in this situation was described in forceful language by Allen Wallis (1967), the president of the University of Rochester, at the time of their Dow demonstration:

To a community devoted to the life of the mind, carried on through reasoned discourse, persuasion and dialogue, nothing is more repugnant than coercion. Even the use of coercion to prevent coercion is abhorrent to us, not only in any specific instance, but because both reason and experience show the dangers of using coercion to protect freedom. We must recognize, however, that we may find ourselves face to face with the dilemma that through the ages has faced groups devoted to the free and peaceful life. The dilemma is that a small group which is determined to have its view prevail, even at the cost of obstruction and coercion, can guarantee that freedom and peace cannot both prevail. Such a willful group can certainly destroy one or the other temporarily.

Still another paradox is to be found in the intellectual antiintellectualism and the dogmatic antidogmatism. It is perfectly obvious that most of the student activists are, by definition as college students, considerably above average in intelligence. The leaders tend to be the brighter students in the better schools and if they are anything they are articulate.

One of the best examples of both the articulateness and the dogmatism can be found in reading a report of a conference held in August 1967 at the Center for the Study of Democratic Institutions at Santa Barbara. The conference, titled "Students and Society," was attended by 22 student leaders from universities around the country (Center for the Study of Democratic Institutions, 1968). At various points in the discussion, almost every American institution and ideology came under scathing criticism. One of the participants said, "I believe there is something fundamentally wrong with this country, and the wrong is caused by the institutions of this country. I sincerely believe that the institutions of this country must be destroyed [p. 26]." And a variation of this statement was repeated a number of times during the course of the three-day conference. One of the student participants himself best characterized the doctrinaire nature of this kind of extreme criticism:

Disruption of constructive dialogue results in intellectual dogmatism. Students, for example, who refuse to form a coalition, except on their own terms, who refuse to compromise at any level, frustrate the dialogue even while they labor under the illusion of communication. The refusal to listen, the intransigent style, the extremist position, the total conviction of one's own righteousness—all characterize the authoritarian personality and the lust for power. These are the very traits which the young find repugnant in adults [p. 41].

He goes on to point out that today's students will have to give way soon to a new generation of students whose ideas will again be different and that the only sensible way to continue a process is to establish a dialogue which permits communication with those who will follow.

A third paradox is that in the rebellion against what the activists see as an authoritarian and unresponsive politicized society they find themselves engaged in all kinds of complex political strategies and tactics. It is this aspect which troubles those student activists who are not part of the very extreme and very active core of the new left. While the Students for a Democratic Society (SDS) has successfully sponsored the major demonstrations of the past year, many of the idealist students with less extreme viewpoints are not in favor of the tactics of the demonstrations. Thus, a recent survey by Barton (1968) on the Columbia crisis shows that, while 51% of the faculty and 58% of the students were for the goals of the demonstration, only 10% of the faculty and 19% of the students supported the tactics.

The last dilemma I want to mention that relates to students is one that is difficult to label. It probably comes under the heading of "no matter what you do you can't win!" And this goes both for the students and the groups and institutions against which they are struggling. On the one hand, the students do want a confrontation. They want something definite and unyielding against which to resist. Today the so-called sincere liberal among the older population is probably, for the militant activist, the most scorned and the most detested of the adult types with whom they deal. As one activist student at a western state college said, "I know who my enemy is. He is the 'sincere liberal.' You talk to him and he agrees with everything you say and then he doesn't do a damn thing." At the same time, of course, if a college president, for example, takes a firm stand, such as Pusey at Harvard or Wallis at Rochester, the students view him as a perfect example of the entrenched establishment.

What happens when the institution provides the kind of environment that most, if not all, of the student body desires? The contrast between the situation at a prestigious eastern university and an equally prestigious eastern institute of technology gives some suggestion of an answer. The disenchantment of the students at the university is not duplicated in the environment of the institute of technology. As a matter of fact the faculty and administration in the institute of technology seem genuinely interested in encouraging the students to be more active and more involved in other than their strictly academic pursuits. At this institution there are no parietal regulations and the student body has a great deal of freedom. Furthermore, the institute, by virtue of its areas of specialization, provides for its students faculty models with whom the students can identify. In fact, the students identify so well with the role of a professional technician that both the faculty and the administration are working very hard to see that the students enlarge their view beyond that of just becoming a competent electrical engineer, biophysicist, or the like.

It is in this kind of climate that the following remarks were made in a final editorial of the outgoing editor of the student newspaper.

The administration is not guilty of denying students their rights, of suppressing them, or halting their actions. It is guilty of a system far more subtle and hence far less easy to detect or combat than any heavy-handed establishment. The administration has made a second-class partner of the student and especially of the so-called student leaders. But in forming the facade of partnership the students have not realized the consequences of their pact, nor have they been aware of the price they pay. The administration has crucified the students on a cross of responsibility. It has made incompetence (in the narrow, bureaucratic sense of the word) a cardinal sin.

He goes on to say that the newspaper itself has had excellent cooperation from the administration but then interprets this as follows:

The subtle favors granted—mailing rights through institute mail, briefings by the president from time to time; phone calls on important occasions—all work a subtle, unconscious allegiance to the administration's point of view. Such an allegiance is a more effective censor than any brute coercion.

In talking to the Dean of Students at the institute about the attitudes expressed in this editorial, I was told that he and other members of the administration were somewhat perplexed. His explanation was that the editor was expressing the frustration of the students at not having an issue on which to have a confrontation with the administration. I suspect the editor may have just finished reading Marcuse's (1965) now-famous article on "repressive tolerance."

These four paradoxes, which I have lightly touched on: one, the coercive efforts to uphold freedom; two, the highly intellectual form of the antiintellectualism; three, the political nature of the attack against today's politics; and four, the struggle to find a basis for confrontation, even in the most permissive of environments, are neither new nor of themselves the major variables in this phenomenon of student protest. I have not touched on any of the aspects of student activism which are not a function of the students themselves, but of the situation in which they find themselves and the people with whom they have to deal.

In this latter set of categories, a great deal more is now being written both as it relates to society at large, and to the state of the university in particular. The latter topic, for example, has been addressed in a recent issue of the *American Behavioral Scientist,* which is devoted to "The State of the University: Authority and Change" and includes a number of articles by a group of scholars using the history of the past four years at the University of California at Berkeley as their point of departure (Kruytbosch & Messinger, 1968).

In these articles, and in other recent examinations of the academic institutions, such as that of Jencks and Reisman (1967), the pressure for student participation in university governance is seen as a major force for change on campus. Jencks and Reisman point out that conflict on campus is not new. It was equally widespread at various times in the eighteenth and nineteenth centuries. What is a departure from the older confrontations, they believe, is the challenge to the legitimacy of adult authority. The distrust of the older generation has been the result of massing together, in colleges and high schools, very large numbers of young people whose common social background and generalized feelings of discontent have produced deep distrust of the adult generation.

The size of the student body is one aspect of the present state of the university which was mentioned in my visits around the country by almost everyone as a major source of the present tensions on campus. The growth of the college population in recent years has been phenomenal. By 1970, it will have doubled from the level it had reached in 1960! Another way of looking at it is to note the increasing proportion of 18- to 24-year-olds who are and will be going into our colleges and universities. In 1950, it was approximately 15%; in 1970 it is expected to be around 30%, and projections, tentative as they may be for 1985, indicate 40%. This rate of growth, in the face of an increasing population of 18- and 24-year-olds, makes for a staggering expectation. The effect of this one characteristic alone is extremely significant.

In the first chapter of his book entitled *The Revolt of the Masses,* the

Spanish philosopher, Ortego y Gasset (1932), talks about the fact of agglomeration and points out that towns are full of people, houses full of tenants, hotels full of guests, trains full of travelers, cafés full of customers, and so on. He says, "What previously was in general no problem, now begins to be an everyday one, namely to find room." After tracing the impact of that circumstance, Ortega y Gasset ends his book with the following statement:

The youth, as such, has always been considered exempt from doing or having done actions of importance. He has always lived on credit. It was a sort of false right, half ironic, half affectionate, which the no longer young conceded to their juniors. But the astounding thing at present is that these take it as an effective right, precisely in order to claim for themselves all those other rights which only belong to the man who has already done something. Though it may appear incredible, youth has become a *chantage*. We are, in truth, living in a time when this adopts two complementary attitudes—violence and caricature. One way or the other, the purpose is always the same, that the inferior—the man of the crowd—may feel himself exempt from all submission to superiors [p. 189].

It would be easy to dismiss this interpretation by pointing out that it was written some 35 years ago. In fact, immediately after the Berkeley Free Speech Movement (FSM) events in 1964, there was a sufficient positive reaction on that campus and others to the developments of that particular effort so that any misgivings about the extreme nature of the protest were lost in the sympathetic acceptance of the students' struggle against the inefficiencies and inequities in the university structure.

More and more, however, as additional incidents occur on other campuses and as individuals and groups who began in sympathy with the student protests find their own institutions threatened, there is an increasing reaction to the student protest movement. In January 1968, George Kennan (1968), the former ambassador to Russia, wrote a brief commentary in the *New York Times Magazine* called "Rebels Without a Program." It was published the day before I visited one of the eastern private universities and every faculty member and administrator on the campus with whom I spoke that Monday had read the article and was quoting from it. In it Kennan expressed his sympathy with the idealistic roles of the student activists, but he was sharply critical of the means they were using to achieve presumed goals.

The sequence of events in the past year accompanying some of the student protests has increased this kind of reaction. It is interesting to note the point at which each group of sympathetic faculty and older revolutionaries find their unwillingness to continue to support the more extreme student activities. A good example is a law professor, an active advisor to the local SDS chapter at a very liberal midwestern state university, who was appalled that the student activists made a mockery of a moot court trial of the student demonstrators involved in the protest at that university.

At this point, you may well ask what is the direct relevance of all this to clinical psychologists—especially when the author himself was trained as a clinical psychologist? I want to point out that I have deliberately omitted any suggestion that student protest is related to individual pathology, although some of the student activists are undoubtedly acting out certain personal problems. The spread and impact of student protests at the present time make them much more a sociological and a political phenomenon than a psychological one. And yet, one of the most powerful attributes that seems evident now is, in fact, psychological in nature. What seems to underline much of the force and vitality of these student protests is the sense of drama, the feeling of participation, and the excitement of being caught up in a group experience.

In a very vivid recent description of the FSM at Berkeley, Michael Rossman (1968), who played a prominent role in the 1964 events, described those days as having been "distinguished throughout by a fierce joy." There was a real sense of the theatre. More recently, one of my colleagues at the Center for Advanced Study in the Behavioral Sciences, who had been in Paris during the Paris student riots, emphasized how strongly the student participants felt that they were reenacting revolutionary days. There was a great deal of play acting, and overhanging all the events was the sense of history that this was where revolution had occurred in previous generations. The lecture halls in the Sorbonne were crowded all day and all night and it was a period of feverish and emotional general debate for all (Laslett, 1968). The activists themselves use such description at times. Rossman (1968), in the description of the FSM events mentioned a moment ago, talks about "a theatre of affirmation in joyful disruption; a theatre of social therapy."

Combine this social therapy with the violence of the confrontation and the implicit intent to shake up this society with the romantic expectation that the structure will somehow reorder itself into a more effective network of interrelationships and it would not be too far fetched to compare this with some kind of mass electroshock therapy. The convulsive nature of this kind of therapy is evident in the heat of the confrontation and the demonstration itself. What is not so clear, perhaps, is the subtle way in which this so-called therapeutic process is misinterpreted as being in itself an important and constructive way of life. There is a kind of reversal of figure and ground here. The confrontation itself is viewed as a most meaningful educational experience. The drama, the pseudo-event, all take on more significance than the day-by-day existence against which this is a reaction. Thus, the theatrical becomes reality and reality is dismissed as outmoded.

There is an interesting corollary to this reversal in the world of the theatre itself. Walter Kerr (1968), the well-known drama critic, who seems to be developing misgivings about today's advanced drama, wrote a recent commentary on the "delusion about illusion." He seems to be saying that the effort to make theatre as close to reality as possible and at the same time impress on the audience that everyone on the stage is really acting is a back and forth shuttling of identities which ignores the fact that the audience can never really be convinced of the reality of the play and does not need to be reminded of the reality of the players.

So, too, the student activists are deluding themselves if they believe confrontation is really living while at the same time taking refuge in their role as students. This kind of thinking was exemplified in a comment to me by one of the students at a midwestern university. At the end of a rather long and strong argument by the students in favor of student activism, he came up to say goodbye and said smilingly, "Don't take us too seriously, we're just students."

What all of this suggests is that with everything that is being written today, the major finding about student protests today is that we really have not been able to keep up with the fast-developing events in this process. I suspect that some of you have personal experiences with college students in your own family whose actions and views have left you at least a bit perplexed. In fact, it is just the children of parents in our category—professionals, well educated, liberal, and interested in society—who make up much of the student protest group. Lots of statements are being made about this phenomena, but careful studies of the process of confrontation itself are still very few in number.

In the recent paper in *Science* from the Behavioral Sciences Center, it was pointed out that there were a number of assertions being made about activism which had little or no nationwide data to support them (Abrams et al., 1968). These assertions relate to the numbers of students involved, the causes of the demonstrations, and the manner in which the demonstrations on campus actually proceed. It was suggested in the paper that

these assertions and many others that are now being made, need to be examined in broad perspective, and, in the light of recent events, the dynamics of protest itself need to be examined and understood. How does a handful of students enlist an increasing number of students and faculty in the sequence of events that occur during a student protest? Who stays and who leaves during the sequence of events in a campus crisis? In what way does the response by faculty, by administrators, and by the rest of the student body influence the process?

The entire matter of communication is a key variable. What is the nature of communication during the protest and after? What role do the communication media play in these demonstrations?

There are broad aspects of behavior and social process that need to be examined. If student unrest is a form of social movement, how are students recruited into it? What are some of the underlying value commitments? In what way does protest influence the future of those who participate? [p. 22]

While these and other questions are being addressed in some of the individual studies that have been done and are now being done, this entire phenomenon deserves a much more comprehensive examination, based on fact rather than opinion.

Is there any way of summarizing the present status of student protests? I think not. The situation continues to be extremely fluid. The forces that, on the one hand, are striving to contain student protests and those that are, on the other hand, stimulating new episodes are perhaps more polarized than they were a year ago. But for those university campuses that have not had a serious student protest it all remains somewhat academic until it actually occurs.

Not only are we in a period of rapid social change, but the effects of that change are amplified by the network of almost instantaneous communication that now surrounds the lives of all of us. Within hours after Martin Luther King is assassinated, the psychic shockwave is felt throughout the nation, leaving a frightening aftermath. Today's communication media by their visual and oral impact are undoubtedly influencing behavior. The full extent of that influence has not been evaluated. For example, what is the effect of the fact that among all the other kinds of worlds we live in, this is the world of instant replay. No sooner does something happen than it is predigested and regurgitated by the communication media as a new stimulus on top of the original real event. An example of this kind of instant regurgitation occurred on April 9, 1968, at 11:30 P.M., when the National Broadcasting Company (1968) had a special program entitled, "Ten Days in April." The program recapped the events beginning with President Johnson's announcement that he would not run, and included a review of the Martin Luther King assassination and the subsequent riots.

There is a paradox in that little incident which relates back to the paradoxes of student protest and which brings me to my final point. On the one hand, it is obviously grandiose and slightly premature to broadcast a program on April 9th, even at 11:30 P.M., which is entitled "Ten Days in April" and yet, at the same time, it was not only done but, within the constraints I have just indicated, it was done not too badly.

I would like to suggest that for many of the activist students there is the same grandiosity and impatience and yet within the constraints of what they are attempting they also manage to pull it off to some extent. The basic problem that we all face, however, is that there is a serious discontinuity between what the students believe they are trying to do and what actually seems to be happening.

In an earlier draft of this paper, I wanted to demonstrate another aspect of discontinuity by the very process of my presentation. I intended to give literally two talks simultaneously—a verbal presentation somewhat similar to the one I am giving now, and a visual presentation of a series of slides on a totally different topic, namely, mental health manpower. I was going to end my talk by trying to suggest in a kind of "the medium is the message" approach that this kind of disjunction is the way the student activists view the disparity between what they are told about their college education, and the way they actually see it. The two versions do not relate. It is for them truly a *double talk*.

That was one side of the message I wanted to give in that two-sided presentation. It was not too profound. I wanted to suggest something else, however, which I believe is somewhat less obvious.

In one of the many popularized accounts of the meaning of student activism, Irving Kristol (1965), who is himself a veteran of the old Left, sees these students as bored and totally unenthusiastic with the prospect of moving into a nice neat safe life in our present bureaucratic society. They have no difficulty in coping with the complexities of the organizational state. They are quite competent to deal with the IBM world they despise. They just do not see it as an exciting challenge. And I think here, with apologies to Marshall McLuhan, "the tedium is the message."

It is too easy either to be sympathetic and supportive of the somewhat romantic idealism of some of the student activists, or, on the other hand, to be sternly reproving of the methods that they are using in their efforts to be heard and responded to. Thus, they are called by one author a "prophetic minority," and, in contrast, "rebels without a program."

What is important in all of this is that these characterizations, positive and negative, result from the fact that student activists are doing more than just being students. And here everyone seems to agree that the current generation of college students is far and away the most competent, the best prepared, and the most dedicated. The student activists are often, although not always, from among the best students in their school. They can do more than they are being asked or allowed to do in their present status as college students.

They can look and listen to two distinct messages and get something out of both. In that sense the theoretical and the real can be mutually supportive rather than disjunctive.

If I may apply today's cliché term "rising expectations" to the student activists themselves, we should expect them to rise to the opportunity of helping us all find a way to be responsive to these seemingly disparate elements and, more importantly, to find some meaningful relationships among them. And this purpose requires a continuing reevaluation of what is said and what is seen, by them and by all the rest of us.

REFERENCES

Abrahams, M. H. ET AL., Student protest: A phenomenon for behavioral sciences research. *Science*, 1968, **161** (3836), 20–23.

Barton, A. H. *The Columbia crisis: Campus, veterans and the ghetto.* New York: Bureau of Applied Social Research, Columbia University, 1968.

Center for the Study of Democratic Institutions. Students and society, *Center Occasional Paper*, Vol. I, No. 1, Santa Barbara, California, 1968.

Goodman, P. The black flag of anarchism. *New York Times Magazine*, July 14, 1968, pp. 10–12.

Halleck, S. L. Hypotheses of student unrest. Address to American Association for Higher Education, March 4, 1968, Chicago, Illinois.

Jencks, C., & Reisman, D. The war between the generations. *The Record*, 1967, **69**(1), 1–21.

Keniston, K. Youth, change and violence. *The American Scholar*, 1968, **38**, 227–245.

Kennan, G. F. Rebels without a program. *New York Times Magazine,* January 21, 1968, pp. 1–4.

Kerr, W. The delusion about illusion. *New York Times,* July 21, 1968, pp. 1–3.

Kristol, I. What's bugging the students. In, *The troubled campus.* Boston: Atlantic, 1965.

Kruytbosch, C. E., & Messinger, S. L. (Eds.) The state of the university: Authority and change. *American Behavioral Scientist,* 1968, 11(5), 1–48.

Laslett, P. The Paris revolt. Informal address at Center for Advanced Study in the Behavioral Sciences, Stanford, California, July 1968.

Marcuse, H. Repressive tolerance. In R. Wolff (Ed.), *Critique of pure tolerance.* New York: Beacon, 1965.

National Broadcasting Company. Special news program, April 9, 1968.

Ortega Y Gassett, J. *The revolt of the masses.* New York: Norton, 1932.

Rossman, M. Breakthrough at Berkeley. *The Center Magazine,* 1968, 1(4), 40–49.

Rovit, E. On the contemporary apocalyptic imagination. *The American Scholar,* 1968, 453–468.

Sampson, E. E. Student activism and the decade of protest. In E. E. Sampson (Ed.), *Stirrings out of apathy. Journal of Social Issues,* 1967, 23(3), 1–33.

Wallis, W. A. Statement before College Cabinet, University of Rochester, November 6, 1967, Rochester, New York.

[44]   *Fred Davis & Laura Munoz*   HEADS AND FREAKS:

PATTERNS AND MEANINGS OF DRUG USE

AMONG HIPPIES

Regardless of whether the phenomenon is viewed in terms of a bohemian subculture, a social movement, a geographically based deviant community or some combination of these, there is substantial agreement among those who have studied hippies (Berger, 1967; Davis, 1967; Didion, 1967; Simon and Trout, 1967; von Hoffman, 1967) that drugs (or "dope," the term preferred by hippies)[1] play an important part in their lives. This generalization applies to nearly all segments of the hippie community for the reasons given below.

First, the patent empirical fact of widespread and frequent drug use *per se*[2] is easily ascertainable through even a brief stay in San Francisco's Haight-Ashbury, New York's East Village, Los Angeles' Fairfax, Vancouver's Fourth Avenue or wherever else hippie colonies have sprung up.[3] Second—and this importantly distinguishes hippie drug use from that of other drug-using sub-

FROM *Journal of Health and Social Behavior,* 1968, 9, 156–164. REPRINTED BY PERMISSION OF THE SENIOR AUTHOR AND THE AMERICAN SOCIOLOGICAL ASSOCIATION.

cultures—there are pronounced ideological overtones associated with it. Not only is it frequently asserted by many hippies that there is "nothing wrong" with certain of the drugs favored by them (chiefly marijuana and LSD, along with a number of other hallucinogens), or that their use is less harmful than alcohol or tobacco,[4] but that these drugs are positively beneficial, either as a pleasant relaxant, as with marijuana, or as a means for gaining insight with which to redirect the course of one's life along inwardly more satisfying and self-fulfilling lines (LSD). Among other manifestations, this spirit of ideological advocacy expresses itself in the conviction of some hippies that their ultimate social mission is to "turn the world on"—i.e., make everyone aware of the potential virtues of LSD for ushering in an era of universal peace, freedom, brotherhood and love. The last, and perhaps most crucial, circumstance for making drug use important in the lives of hippies is the simple and stark matter of the drugs' illegality. As contemporary deviance theory of the symbolic interactionist persuasion has shown in so many differing connections (Becker, 1963; Davis, 1961; Freidson, 1965; Goffman, 1963; Kitsuse, 1961; Lemert, 1962), the act by a community of successfully labeling a particular practice deviant and/or illegal almost invariably constrains the "deviant" to structure much of his identity and activity (Strauss, 1959) in terms of such imputations of deviance and law-breaking. Thus, the omnipresent threats of police harassment, of arrest and incarceration, as well as of a more diffuse social ostracism are "facts of life" which the hippie who uses drugs only occasionally must contend with fully as much as the regular user.

Beyond these rather global observations, all further generalizations concerning hippie drug use must be qualified carefully and treated as tentative. For not only are the actual patterns of drug use quite varied among individual hippies and different hippie sub-groups, but the patterns themselves are constantly undergoing change as the subculture evolves and gains greater experience with drugs (Becker, 1967). Further compounding the hazards of facile generalization are the following:

1. The apparent readiness of many hippies to experiment—if only once "to see what it's like"—with almost any drug or drug-like substance, be it Hawaiian wood rose seeds, opium or some esoteric, pharmacologically sophisticated psycho-active compound.

2. The periodic appearance on the hippie drug market of new drugs, usually of the hallucinogenic variety, which, like new fashions generally, excite a great flurry of initial interest and enthusiasm until they are either discredited, superseded or partially assimilated into a more "balanced" schedule of drug use. Thus, in the past year alone, for example, at least three new hallucinogenic type drugs have made much heralded, though short-lived, appearance in the Haight-Ashbury: STP (dimethoxymethyl-amphetamine), MDA (methylene-dioxy-amphetamine) and PCP, the "peace pill" (phencyclidine).

3. The vagaries, uncertainties, deceptions and misrepresentations of the illegal

drug market as such. Not only is it hard for a buyer to be sure that he is getting the drug he thinks he is getting—indeed, that he is getting any drug at all and not some placebo—but dosages, strengths and purity of compounding, even when not knowingly misrepresented by dealers, are likely to be unknown or poorly understood by dealer and buyer alike.[5] Thus, the ubiquitous possibility of an untoward reaction in which the user, or a whole aggregate of users, becomes violently ill or severely disoriented.

4. The fact, to be discussed later, that the very same drug (LSD, for example) can, depending on the intent of the user, his mood, the setting and the group context, be used to achieve very different drug experiences and subjective states. Though this "choice of drug experience" is never fully within the control of even the experienced user (see 3, above), it does exist, and thus facilitates differential use by different users as well as by the same user at different times.

Obliquely, these circumstances point to what is perhaps the chief obstacle to making firm generalizations concerning hippie drug use, namely, that the subculture is not (at least as yet) of a piece, that it includes many disparate social elements and ideational tendencies (Davis, 1967; Simon and Trout, 1967) and that, to the extent that drug use constitutes something of a core element in it, this must be seen in the context of these varying and constantly shifting socio-ideational subconfigurations. As has been characteristic of almost any expressive social movement in its formative stages (cf. Blumer, 1946), this diversity in the midst of a search for common definition is reflected in the frequent discussions among hippies on who is a "real" hippie, who a "plastic" hippie, and what "genuine" hipness consists of. Moral, behavioral and attitudinal boundaries of inclusion and exclusion are constantly being assessed and redrawn. But, in the absence of any recognized leadership group capable of issuing *ex cathedra* pronouncements on these matters, one man's, or one underground paper's, definition is as good as the next's. These ongoing discussions, debates and polemics extend, of course, to the place and use of drugs in the "new community," as hippie spokesmen like to refer to themselves. Some take a very permissive and inclusive stance, others a more restrictive one, and still others shift their ground from one encounter to the next. Inconclusive as this dialogue may be from an organizational standpoint, it nonetheless is important for the influences, albeit variable, it exerts on drug practices and attitudes within the subculture.

With these reservations in mind we wish to sketch here a rough sociological atlas, as it were, of patterns and meanings of drug use among San Francisco's Haight-Ashbury hippies, at least insofar as these manifested themselves through the summer and well into the fall of 1967. The data were gathered by the methods of ethnographic field work as part of a broader study of the interaction of Haight-Ashbury's hippie community with the larger San Francisco community. Although informed by a close-in familiarity with the hippie community, the data are, strictly speaking, impressionistic inasmuch as time, resources and certain situational peculiarities connected with doing research among hippies[6] militated against any exhaustive study of drug use *per se*.

LSD and methedrine

Since much of what follows deals with social psychological aspects of the use of the above two drugs, a few preliminary words are in order concerning the drugs themselves, their direct pharmacological effects, average dosages, modes of administration and frequency of use. No detailed description can be attempted here (see Blum, 1964; Kramer et al., 1967); rather, our aim is merely to touch on a few matters pertinent for the subsequent discussion of types of drug users. Inasmuch as we shall not be discussing marijuana, suffice it to say here that it is very widely used by all segments of the hippie community and constitutes the drug staple of the subculture. (Hashish, the purified and condensed forms of cannabis, though much preferred by those who have tried it, appears in the Haight-Ashbury only rarely and commands an exceedingly high price.)

The hallucinogenic LSD (lysergic acid diethylamide), one of a growing family of such drugs, is marketed in the Haight-Ashbury in tablet form. The shape, color and general appearance of tablets will vary considerably, from "well made" to "extremely crude," as new batches are produced by different illegal manufacturers. Taken orally, an average dose, usually one tablet, contains approximately 185 micrograms of LSD. Some users, though, are known to ingest considerably more than this amount, i.e., up to 1,000–1,250 micrograms, when they wish to "turn on." Street prices vary from about $2.50 per tablet in times of plentiful supply to $5.00 and $6.00 when supply is short. Typical users in the Haight-Ashbury "take a trip" once a week or thereabouts on the average; again, however, there is a considerable number who "drop acid" much more frequently, perhaps every three or four days, while still others resort to the drug only occasionally or episodically. The characteristic psychopharmacologic effects of the drug are described by Smith (1967:3) as follows:

When someone ingests an average dose of LSD, (150–250 micrograms) nothing happens for the first 30 or 45 minutes, and then after the sympathetic response the first thing the individual usually notices is a change in the way he perceives things. . . . Frequently . . . he notices that the walls and other objects become a bit wavy or seem to move. Then he might notice colors . . . about the room are looking much brighter or more intense than they usually do and, in fact, as times goes on these colors can seem exquisitely intense and more beautiful than any colors he has seen before. Also, it is common for individuals to see a halo effect around lights, also a rainbow effect. . . . There is another kind of rather remarkable perceptual change, referred to as a synesthesia. By this I mean the translation of one type of sensory experience into another, so that if one is listening to music, for example, one can sometimes feel the vibrations of the music in one's body, or one can sometimes see the actual notes moving, or the colors that he is seeing will beat in rhythm with the music.

More pronounced effects of an emotional, meditative or ratiocinative kind can, but need not, follow in the wake of these alterations in sense perception. In any case, the direct effects of the drug last on the average for an eight- to twelve-hour span.

Methedrine (generic name, methamphetamine) is a stimulant belonging to the sympathomimetic group of drugs. Its appearance is that of a fluffy white powder, referred to commonly as "crystals." In the Haight-Ashbury it is sold mainly in spoonful amounts (1–2 grams, approximately) and packaged in small transparent envelopes, prices ranging from $15.00 to $20.00 an envelope. Frequently, a user or small dealer in need of cash will repackage the powder and sell it in smaller amounts. Until a few years ago most users of Methedrine took it orally in capsule form. Among Haight-Ashbury hippies, however, the primary and preferred mode of administration is intravenous injection. Hence, the paraphernalia employed is almost identical to that of the heroin user: hypodermic needle, syringe, spoon for diluting the powder in tap water, and candle for heating the mixture. Because needles and associated equipment are often unsterilized or poorly sterilized, cases of serum hepatitis are quite common among Methedrine users. The physiological effects of the drug are elevated blood pressure, increased pulse rate, dilation of pupils and blurred vision— these accompanied by such behavioral states as euphoria, heightened spontaneous activity, wakefulness, loss of appetite and, following extended use, suspicion and acute apprehensiveness ("paranoia").

Although there is some disagreement among experts on whether regular use of Methedrine leads to addiction as, for example, in the case of heroin, it is well-established that a fair proportion of users become extremely dependent on the drug. Thus, whereas the episodic user will inject 25–50 milligrams for a "high," those who get badly "strung out" on a two to three week Methedrine binge will by the end be "shooting" as frequently as six times a day for a total daily intake of some 1,000 to 2,000 milligrams (1 to 2 grams). Needless to say, were it not for the steep increase in body tolerance levels built up through continuous use of the drug, such high daily dosages might well prove lethal.

Heads and freaks

A suitable starting point for our ethnographic sketch is those terms and references used by hippies themselves to distinguish certain types of drug users and patterns of drug use. Chief among these is the contrast drawn between "heads" and "freaks," sometimes explicitly, though more often implicitly with reference to a particular drug user or drug practice. While a whole penumbra of allusive imagery surrounds these terms, a "head" essentially is thought to be someone who uses drugs—and, here, it is mainly the hallucinogens that the speaker has in mind—for purposes of mind expansion, insight and the enhancement of personality attributes, i.e., he uses drugs to discover where "his head is at." For the "head," therefore, the drug experience is conceived of, much as during the first years of LSD experimentation by psychiatrists and psycho-pharmacologists (ca. 1956–1963), as a *means* for self-realization or self-fulfill-ment, and not as an end in itself. The term, "head," is, of course, not new with hippies. It has a long history among drug users generally, for whom it signified a regular, experienced user of any illegal drug—e.g., pot "head," meth "head," smack (heroin) "head." Although still sometimes used in this non-discriminat-ing way by hippies, what is novel about their usage of "head" is the extent to which it has become exclusively associated with certain of the more rarified facets of the LSD experience.

By contrast, the term "freak" refers usually to someone in search of drug kicks as such, especially if his craving carries him to the point of drug abuse where his health, sanity and relations with intimates are jeopardized. Though used primarily in the context of Methedrine abuse ("speed freak"), the refer-ence is frequently broadened to include all those whose use of any drug (be it Methedrine, LSD, marijuana or even alcohol) is so excessive and of such purely hedonistic bent as to cause them to "freak out," e.g., become ill or disoriented, behave violently or erratically, give evidence of a "paranoid" state of mind.

Whereas the primary connotative imagery of "head" and "freak" derives mainly from the subculture's experience with drugs, the terms themselves—given their evocative associations—have in a short course of time acquired great referential elasticity. Thus "head," for example, is extended to include any person (hip, "straight," or otherwise) who manifests great spontaneity, open-ness of manner, and a canny sensitivity to his own and other's moods and feel-ings. Indeed, hippies will claim that it is not strictly necessary to use hallu-cinogenic drugs—helpful though this is for many—to become a "head" and that, moreover, there are many persons in the straight world, in particular children, who are "really heads," but don't know it. Parenthetically, it might be noted that the concept of a *secret union* of attitude and sensibility, including even those ignorant of their inner grace, is a familiar attribute of expressive social movements of the deviant type; among other purposes, it helps to sub-jectively legitimate the proselytizing impulses of the movement. Homosexuals, too, are known to construct such quasi-conspiratorial versions of the world.

Similarly, the term "freak," while much less fertile in its connotative imagery than "head," is also extended to persons and situations outside the im-mediate context of drug use. Hence, anyone who is too aggressive or violent, who seems "hung up" on some idea, activity or interactional disposition, might be called a "freak." Accordingly, abnormal phases (e.g., high anxiety states, obsessiveness, intemperateness) in the life of one customarily thought a "head" will also be spoken of as "freaking" or "freaking out."

The two terms, therefore, have acquired a quality of ideal-typicality about them in the hippie subculture and have, at minimum, come to designate certain familiar social types (cf., Strong, 1946). At this level of indigenous typifica-tions, they can be seen to reflect certain ongoing value tensions in the sub-culture: a reflecting turning inward versus hedonism, Apollonian contentment versus Dionysian excess, a millenial vision of society versus an apocalyptic one. And that these generic extensions of the terms derive so intimately from drug experiences affords additional evidence of the symbolic centrality of drugs in the hippie subculture.[7]

Some social characteristics of heads and freaks

In the more restrictive, strict drug-using sense, who, then, are "heads" (LSD or "acid" users) and who "freaks" (Methedrine or "speed shooters")? Lacking accurate demographic data on the subject, our impression is that "heads" are found more often among older, more established and less transient segments of the Haight-Ashbury hippie community, i.e., persons of both sexes in their mid-to-late twenties who, while not exactly holding down full time jobs of the conventional sort, are more or less engaged in some regular line of vocational activity: artists, craftsmen, clerks in the hippie shops, some hippie merchants, writers with the underground press, graduate students, and sometimes mail carriers, to mention a few. It is mainly from this segment that such spokesmen and leaders as the "new community" has produced have come. By comparison, "freaks" are found more often among the more anomic and transient elements of the community, in particular those strata where "hipness" begins to shade off into such quasi-criminal and thrill-seeking conglomerates as the Hell's Angels and other motorcyclists (known locally as "bikeies"), many of whom now frequent the Haight-Ashbury and have taken up residence in and around the area. Some observers even attribute the growing use of Methedrine to the fact that it and closely related stimulants (e.g., Benzedrine, Dexedrine) were popular with West Coast motorcycle gangs well before the origins of the hippie community in the Haight-Ashbury. Unlike "acid," which is widely used by both males and females, "speed" appears to be predominantly a male drug.[8]

As these observations would suggest, it is our further impression that "heads" are by and large persons of middle and upper-middle class social origins whereas "freaks" are much more likely to be of working class background. Despite, therefore, the strong legal and moral proscriptions against both LSD and Methedrine, their differential use by hippies reflects, at one level at least, the basic contrast in expressive styles extant in the American class structure; put crudely, LSD equals self-exploration/self-improvement equals middle class, while Methedrine equals body stimulation/release of aggressive impulses equals working class.

These characterizations, however, afford but a gross approximation of drug use patterns in the Haight-Ashbury. The actual demography of use is complicated considerably by a variety of changing situational and attitudinal currents, some of which were alluded to earlier. Two additional matters especially deserve mention here. The first is the existence of a large, socially heterogeneous class of mixed drug users: persons who are neither "heads" nor "freaks" in any precise sense, but who regularly sample both LSD and Methedrine, as well as other drugs. Shifting intermittently or episodically from one to another, they may, save for continued smoking of marijuana, even undergo extended periods of drug abstinence. Of such users it can, perhaps, best be said that the very absence of any consistent pattern is the pattern. Secondly, it should be noted that this non-pattern pattern of drug use (this secondary anomie within a more inclusive deviant life scheme) has grown more pronounced in the Haight-Ashbury in recent months. Whereas prior to the summer of 1967 a newly arrived hippie would in all probability have been socialized into the LSD users' culture of "tripping," "mind-blowing" and meditation—"heads" then clearly constituted the socially, as well as numerically, dominant hippie group in the area—this kind of outcome became a good deal less certain following the publicity, confusion, congestion and increased social heterogeneity of recruits that attended the summer influx of youth from across the country (Davis, 1967). Not only did many of the settled hippies move away from the area in the wake of this massive intrusion, but new styles and tastes in drug use, notably "speed shooting," quickly established themselves. With the inundation and dispersal of the older "head" group, it became largely a matter of sheer for-tuitousness whether a novice hippie turned to "acid" or "speed," to some other drug or a combination of several. Whose "pad" he "crashed" on arrival or who befriended him the first time he set foot on Haight Street could have as much to do with his subsequent pattern of drug use as anything else. This was con-spicuously so in the instance of younger recruits, many of them runaways from home in the 14–17 age group, who, except perhaps for marijuana smoking, were completely naive to and inexperienced in drug use.

The prestige gradient of drug use

Nonetheless, to the extent that the hippie subculture has managed to con-serve elements of a core identity and to develop something of a common stance vis-à-vis "straight" society, it is still the "head" pattern of drug use that is idea-tionally, if not necessarily numerically, dominant within it. Thus, to be spoken of as a "head" is complimentary, whereas to be termed a "freak" or "speed freak" is, except in certain special contexts, derogating. Similarly, the under-ground press is forever extolling the virtues of "acid"; but, apart from an oc-casional piece of somewhat patronizing tone in which the author tries to "un-derstand" what "gives" with Methedrine users (Strauss, 1967), it almost invariably condemns "speed." Numerous posters on display in the Haight Street print and funny button shops announce in bold captions "SPEED KILLS."

The perceived dichotomy between mind-expansion and body-stimulation represented by the two drugs is sometimes reconceptualized to apply to LSD users alone so as to draw a distinction between those who use the drug mainly for purposes of "tripping" as against "true" or "real" "heads" who purport to use it for achieving insight and effecting personality changes within them-selves. While dosage levels of the drug seem to play some part in determining whether a "tripping" or "mind-expanding" experience will ensue—the larger the dose, the more likely the latter or, alternatively, a "bum trip," i.e., a panic reaction with severe disorientation—the intent and setting of the user also appear to have an important bearing on the outcome. Quiet surroundings, a contemplative mood and interesting objects upon which to focus (e.g., a mandala, a candle flame) are felt to be conducive to a mind-expanding experience; moving street scenes, an extroverted mood and the intense visual and auditory stimuli of the typical folk-rock dance and light show are thought conducive to "tripping." In any event, he who uses LSD only to "trip" (i.e., to intensify and refract his sensate experience of the environment) is regarded at best with a certain amused tolerance by "righteous acid heads." The latter, therefore, frequently counsel beginning users of LSD to move beyond mere "tripping" to where they can realize the higher meditative, revelatory and religious potentials of the drug. In this connection, a number of hippie groups, particularly those involved in the Eastern religions, advocate dispensing with LSD and other hallucinogens altogether following realization of these higher states; once the "doors of consciousness" have been opened, it is stated, it is no longer necessary to use drugs for recapturing the experience—newly discovered powers of meditation alone will suffice. Be that as it may, because the "head"—as both a certain kind of drug user and certain kind of human being—has emerged as the model citizen of the hippie movement, there are many who aspire to the status and aim to follow the true path that can lead them there.

Conclusion

In sum, drug use among Haight-Ashbury hippies reveals a number of contrary tendencies, the chief being the emergent social and symbolic contrast of the "head" and "freak" patterns—a contrast which, as we have seen, encompasses cultural elements well beyond the immediate realm of drug use *per se*. While the two patterns can, through several analytical levels removed, be traced back ultimately to certain historically persistent, subterranean expressive value strains in American society-at-large (see Matza, 1964), their surfacing and intimate co-existence within the hippie subculture serve to aggravate already difficult problems of member socialization, group integration and ideology that confront the community (Davis, 1967). Stated otherwise, the process of community formation is hindered, not wholly, or even primarily, by outside forces of repression—for, these will often solidify a social movement—but through the generation of anomie from within as well. If illegal and socially condemned drug use did not play so large a part in the subculture, these divisive tendencies could, perhaps, be better contained. As is, however, the pervasiveness of illegal drug use constantly opens up the subculture to a gamut of socially disparate, unassimilable elements and assorted predators, few of whom share the ethos of love, expressive freedom and disengagement from narrow materialistic pursuits that animated, and still animates, many within the movement. And, since it is highly unlikely that the drugs favored by hippies (again, possibly excepting marijuana) will soon be made legal, this situation is likely to get worse before it gets better.

As to the drug use patterns themselves, it can only be a matter of conjecture as to which—"head" or "freak"—if either, will come eventually to clearly prevail in the hippie community. Although the "head" pattern appears on the face of it to resonate more deeply with those broader philosophical and ideational themes that distinguish the movement,[9] it has, in the Haight-Ashbury at least, already lost much ground to the more exclusively hedonistic "freak" pattern. Should it continue to do so, what did have the earmarks of a culturally significant expressive social movement on the American scene could easily dissolve into little more than the sociologist's familiar "drug users' deviant subculture."

NOTES

1. As with earlier expressive social movements of a religious tendency, it is characteristic of hippies to employ, and thereby semantically reconstruct for initiates, a discredited term of pungent reference where, on purely denotative grounds, a more "acceptable" one would do as well or even better. The frequent public resort to sexual and scatological profanity by hippies (see Berger, 1967), most of whom were raised in homes where the use of such words would, to say the least, be frowned upon, is further evidence of this all but conscious tendency to linguistically celebrate the rejected and despised so as to cast them in a new moral light. Compare the remarks of Kenneth Burke (1954:125–147) on "organized bad taste."

2. This, of course, is not to say that drug use (and abuse) is not widespread among Americans generally. Rather, the obvious point is that the alcohol, tranquilizers, barbiturates, stimulants and common pain-relievers used in conventional society have not, despite the known injurious effects of some of them, been officially declared illegal or detrimental to health and morals as have the drugs favored by hippies. Hence, they are, except in extreme instances of abuse, treated as part of the everyday, taken-for-granted world of pharmaceutical products and household remedies to which little, if any, stigma is attached. Hippies, naturally, are forever pointing this out in their continuing campaign for drug law reform. "Why condemn us, when so many of you are constantly turning to drugs for almost every conceivable contingency of daily life? What makes your drug 'abuse' any better than ours?"

3. Exception must be made for a small number of hippie communes and settlements, most of them in rural areas, where, according to reports in the underground press, the use of all mind and mood-altering drugs is disapproved of.

4. As far as tobacco is concerned, the point is largely gratuitous. Our impression is that a great many hippies are heavy cigarette smokers.

5. A useful discussion of the hippie drug market—manufacture of drugs, distribution, pricing, types of drug dealers, relations with buyers, etc.—would require a lengthy paper in itself. Two points in particular, however, deserve mention

here for the special interest they hold for sociologists. 1) Much as in the legitimate drug trade, new drugs like STP and MDA are introduced selectively at first by manufacturers' and/or distributors' "detail men" making free samples available to the drug cognoscenti and opinion leaders in the hippie community (cf. Coleman et al., 1966). If favorably received in these élite circles, the drug is then put on the street market for "open" sale. 2) In line with the anti-hoarding sentiments of hippies, it is regarded as bad form not to share a "good thing," especially when one has a surplus on hand. It is not uncommon then, for hippie drug dealers, particularly non-commercial ones who only trade causally to earn a bit of extra cash, to give away gratis a fair portion of their stock to friends and favorities.

6. Above and beyond understandable sensitivities relating to illegal drug use, many hippies resent and deplore conventional modes of sociological inquiry—questionnaires schedules, formal interviews, etc.—directed at them. These, they state, reduce the respondent to a "thing," a mere statistical instance in an artificially constructed class of events, thereby denying him his individuality and possibilities for creative being. In line with certain prominent strains in the hippie ethos, the feeling is that it is never humane or just to relate to another in these terms. Tied in with these sentiments is the not wholly unfounded conviction of certain, more sophisticated hippies that social science investigators who do research among them are interested primarily in furthering their own careers; they "take" from the "new community" and return nothing to it by way of aid or comfort. Much as these attitudes make for difficulties in conducting research among hippies, they have the virtue of posing in a sharp and decidedly concrete manner a number of largely unexamined ethical, and epistemological, issues underlying social science research on human groups. (See Bruyn 1966; Seeley, 1967; Sjoberg, 1967).

7. Similarly, hippie art, poetry and folk-rock music are after appraised frequently in terms of their "druggy" qualities, i.e., how nearly they evoke the moods and sensations associated with drug experiences.

8. Some preliminary survey data gathered by Professor Frederick H. Meyers of the University of California Medical Center, San Francisco suggest, however, that the ratio of female Methedrine users (and abusers) among hippies is significantly higher than is commonly thought to be the case.

9. In this connection, a case could be made, and is by some hippies, that much which is distinctive about the hippie subculture (e.g., its music, aversion to physical violence, return to nature, communal sharing, etc.) are the product of the "acid" experience rather than psycho-cultural determinants of it. That is to say, the direct psycho-pharmacologic effects of LSD . . . are such as to lead people to selectively reconstitute their inner world of memory, feeling, percept, attitude, etc. in a new and *particularistic* way—in this instance a kind of Apollonian reconstruction of social reality. If true this opens up the interesting, and frightening, Huxleyan possibility of drugs not merely regulating culture but, in an important sense, generating it as well. Also, if true, this would call for certain qualifications in Becker's (1967) proposed thesis that it is the users' subculture, and not the direct effects of the drug *per se,* which largely determine the meaning and ideational content of the drug-induced experience.

REFERENCES

Becker, Howard S. 1963. Outsiders. New York: Free Press.

———. 1967. "History, culture and subjective experience: an exploration of the social bases of drug-induced experiences." Journal of Health and Social Behavior 8 (September):163–176.

Berger, Bennett M. 1967. "Hippie morality—more old than new." Trans-action 5 (December): 19–27.

Blum, Richard H. and Associates. 1964. Utopiates: The Use and Users of LSD-25. New York: Atherton.

Blumer, Herbert. 1946. "Collective behavior." Pp. 199–221 in Alfred McClung Lee (ed.) New Outline of the Principles of Sociology. New York: Barnes and Noble.

Burke, Kenneth. 1954. Permanence and Change. Los Altos, California: Hermes.

Bruyn, Severyn T. 1966. The Human Perspective in Sociology. Englewood Cliffs, New Jersey: Prentice-Hall.

Coleman, James S., Elihu Katz and Herbert Menzel. 1966. Medical Innovation, a Diffusion Study. Indianapolis: Bobbs-Merrill.

Davis, Fred. 1961. "Deviance disavowal." Social Problems 9 (Fall): 120–132.

———.1967. "Why all of us may be hippies someday." Trans-action 5 (December): 10–18.

Didion, Joan. 1967. "The hippie generation." Saturday Evening Post (September 23).

Freidson, Eliot. 1965. "Disability as social deviance." Pp. 71–99 in Marvin B. Sussman (ed.), Sociology and Rehabilitation. Washington: American Sociological Association.

Goffman, Erving. 1963. Stigma. Englewood Cliffs, New Jersey: Prentice-Hall.

Kitsuse, John I. 1962. "Societal reaction to deviant behavior." Social Problems 9 (Winter):247–256.

Kramer, John C., Vitezslav S. Fischman and Don C. Littlefield. 1967. "Amphetamine abuse." JAMA 201 (July 31):305–309.

Lemert, Edwin. 1962. "Paranoia and the dynamics of exclusion." Sociometry 25 (March):2–20.

Matza, David. 1964. "Position and behavior patterns of youth." In Robert E. L. Faris (ed.), Handbook of Modern Sociology. Chicago: Rand McNally.

Seeley, John 1967. The Americanization of the Unconscious. Philadelphia and New York: International Science Press.

Simon Geoffrey and Grafton Trout. 1967. "Hippies in college—from teeny-boppers to drug freaks." Trans-action 5 (December):27–32.

Sjoberg, Gideon (ed.). 1967. Ethics, Politics and Social Research. Cambridge, Massachusetts: Schenkman.

Smith, David E. 1967. "Lysergic acid diethyamide: an historical perspective." Journal of Psychedelic Drugs 1 (Summer):2–7.

Strauss, Anselm L. 1959. Mirrors and Masks. Glencoe, Illinois: The Free Press.

Strauss, Rick. 1967. "Confessions of a speedfreak." Los Angeles Oracle 1 (July).

Strong, Samuel M. 1946. "Negro-white relations as reflected in social types." American Journal of Sociology 52 (July):23–30.

van Hoffman, Nicholas. 1967. "Dope scene—big business in the Haight." San Francisco Chronicle (October 31).

INDEX

NAME INDEX

Abrahams, M. H., 499, 508, 510
Adams, E. B., 320, 325
Adams, J. F., 78, 81
Adelson, J., 150, 175–193
Adorno, T. W., 282, 290
Aldous, J., 320, 325
Allport, G. W., 253, 298–306, 320
Ames, L. B., 29, 31
Amthauer, R., 99, 100
Anastasi, A., 102–104, 116, 120
Anderson, L., 216, 234–242
Anderson, W. A., 455, 462
Angelino, H., 67, 81
Anthony, A., 425, 431, 433
Aquinas, St. T., 8
Aristotle, 3, 6–10, 16, 19, 20, 21
Arnhoff, F. N., 50, 82–87
Asch, S. E., 245, 249
Atkinson, J., 147, 375
Austin, G. A., 282, 290
Ausubel, D. P., 3, 22, 424, 432

Backman, G., 56, 62
Baker, F., 220, 224
Balinski, B., 103, 120
Bandura, A., vi, 1–2, 22–31, 364–365, 451
Barker, R. G., 8, 71, 82, 149, 151
Barton, A. H., 503, 510
Basedow, J. B., 16
Bass, B. M., 242, 249
Bayley, N., 70, 81, 151
Beach, F. A., 28, 31
Bealer, R. C., vi, 451, 454–463
Becker, H. S., 512, 521n, 522
Bellof, H., 83, 86, 87
Bellof, J., 83, 86, 87
Benedict R., 424–426, 428, 429, 432
Berenda, R. W., 243, 248, 249
Berg, I. A., 242, 249
Berger, B. M., 511, 520n, 522
Bergler, E., 345, 352

Bernstein, T. M., 477, 485
Berridge, W. L., 400, 417
Blaine, G. B., 302, 306, 417
Blatt, M., 209, 214
Block, J., 279, 290
Bloss, P., 43, 47
Blough, T. B., 460, 463
Blum, R. H., 514, 522
Blumer, H., 513, 522
Bonney, M. E., 237, 240, 242
Bowman, P. H., 455, 462
Boyd, W., 22
Boyne, A. W., 149, 151
Braaten, J., 400, 416
Brain, W. R., 83, 87
Brenman, M., 345, 348, 352
Brittain, C. V., 215, 224–234, 253, 420, 456, 463
Broderick, C. B., 59, 61–62, 309, 352–359
Broman, B., 52, 57, 62
Bronfenbrenner, U., 205, 214, 217, 218, 222, 223, 420, 433–441, 451
Bronson, G. W., 278, 279, 290
Brookover, W. B., 296, 298
Brown, D. G., 323, 325
Brown, J. K., 425, 426, 432
Bruner, J. S., 282, 290
Bruyn, H. B., 400, 402, 416
Bruyn, S. T., 521n, 522
Bryan, A. I., 102, 103, 120
Buck, R. C., 455, 456, 463
Buker, M. E., 150, 151, 175
Bullen, B. A., 77, 81
Burchinal, L., 217, 224
Burke, K., 520n, 522
Burt, C., 101–103, 119, 120
Burt, V., 78, 82
Burton, R. V., 218, 223

Calvin, J., 9, 10
Campbell, D. T., 243, 248
Campbell, E. Q., 481, 482, 485, 486

Canning, H., 78, 81
Carter, C. O., 54, 62
Cattell, R. B., 123, 143, 147
Chadderdon, H., 79, 81
Chaffey, J., 159, 170
Charlesworth, W. R., 40, 47
Christensen, H. T., 341, 351
Church, J., 254, 264
Clark, M. P., 102, 120
Clark, R., 147, 375
Cleveland, S. E., 83, 87
Cohen, A. K., 480, 485
Cohen, H., 81
Cohen, J., 103, 120
Cohen, Y. A., 327, 328, 339
Coleman, J. S., vi, 151, 224, 233, 420,
    451–452, 456, 463–475, 521n, 522
Comenius, J. A., 3, 11–12, 20, 22
Condillac, E. B., 13
Constanzo, P. R., 216, 242–249, 420
Cooley, W., 443, 445
Cowan, P. A., 40, 47
Criswell, J. H., 395, 397, 399
Cronbach, L. J., 102, 105, 120, 173, 175
Crutchfield, R. S., 244, 249

Dahlberg, G., 52, 57, 62
Damianopoulos, E. N., 50, 82–87
D'Andrade, R., 147
Darling, C., 400, 416
Darwin, C., 3, 7, 9, 18–19, 22
Datta, L. E., 133–134, 137–138
Dauw, D. C., 100, 133–138
Davis, A., 446, 450
Davis, F., vi, 453, 511–522
DeCharms, R., 282, 290
Deisher, R. W., 78, 79, 81
Descartes, R., 4
Despres, M. A., 22, 31
Deutsch, H., 310, 313, 317
Devereux, E. C., 433, 434, 441
De Vos, G., 415, 417
Dewey, J., 16, 193–194, 208, 211–212, 214
Dickinson, R. L., 328, 339
Dickson, L., 395, 399
Didion, J., 511, 522
Distler, L., 218, 224
Donohue, J. F., 477, 485
Donovan, B. T., 57, 62
Doppelt, J. E., 103, 120
Douvan, E., 307, 310–318, 362, 420
Drevdahl, J. E., 143, 147
Drews, E., 365, 375

Drought, N., 217, 224
Dublin, L. I., 401, 402, 404, 405, 417
Durkheim, E., 193, 212
Dwyer, J., 49, 50, 64–82
Dye, N. W., 99, 101–121

Easton, D., 176, 193
Edwards, A. M., 152, 153, 170
Ehrmann, W., 341, 351
Eisenberg, L., vi, 2, 31–39
Elkin, F., 25, 30, 224, 233
Elkind, D., 2, 39–48 49, 51
Emmerich, W., 217, 223
Engelman, W., 62, 63
Eppright, E. S., 79, 81
Erikson, E. H., vii, 2, 12, 29, 31, 35, 39,
    43, 46, 47, 149, 223, 251–264,
    265–277, 278, 280–281, 289–290,
    300, 306, 420, 433, 442, 446

Farberow, N. L., 415, 417
Faulkner, W., 423, 432
Federn, P., 83, 87
Feffer, M. H., 40, 48
Feldman, J. J., 76, 77, 81
Fenichel, O., 318
Fisher, R., 443, 446
Fisher, S., 83, 87
Fischman, V. S., 522
Flavell, J. H., 39
Foard, E. D., 80, 81
Ford, C. S., 28, 31
Fowler, S. E., 59, 62, 359
Frankel, E. A., 365, 375
Frazier, A., 50, 51, 88–98
Freedman, M. B., 341, 351
Freidson, E., 512, 522
French, J. W., 105, 120
Frenkel-Brunswik, E., 282, 290
Freud, A., 43, 47, 218, 223
Freud, S., 3, 4, 29, 31, 83, 87, 196, 212,
    255, 257, 305, 315, 318
Friedenberg, E., 8, 203, 361
Froebel, F., 3, 16, 18
Furfey, P. H., 170

Gagnon, J. H., 329, 333, 339
Galdston, I., 83, 87
Gallagher, J. R., 22, 31
Gardner, B., 217, 224
Garn, S. M., 60, 61, 63
Garrett, H. E., 101–104, 118, 120
Gesell, A., 3, 8, 20, 29, 31

Getzels, J. W., 100, 121–132, 143, 147, 362, 376–383
Gibbs, J. P., 405, 417
Gillespie, J. M., 304, 306
Goethe, J. W., 20, 45
Goffman, E., 512, 522
Goldblatt, I., 455, 462
Goodfield, B. A., 325
Goodman, P., 203, 361, 502, 510
Goodnow, I. J., 282, 290
Gordon, J. E., 243, 248, 249
Gottlieb, D., 362, 363, 384–399
Gourevitch, V., 40, 48
Gowan, J. C., 144, 147, 365, 375
Gray, S. W., 320, 325
Greenstein, F., 176, 193
Griffiths, K., 296, 298
Grim, P., 210, 214
Grinder, R. E., 215, 217–224, 341, 351, 432
Gronlund, N. E., 216, 234–242
Gruen, W., 278, 279, 290
Guilford, J. P., 99, 106, 116, 118–120, 123, 131–132, 142–143, 147

Haber, W. B., 83, 87
Haggard, E. A., 144, 147
Hall, G. S., 1–3, 8, 16, 18–22
Halleck, S. L., vi, 308–309, 339–352, 500, 510
Hampton, M. C., 81
Handltn, O., 476, 485
Hare, R. M., 207, 208, 214
Harman, H., 118, 120
Harms, E., 64, 81
Harris, D. B., 59, 63, 159, 164, 170, 455, 462
Harris, H. I., 22, 31
Harrower-Erikson, M. R., 379, 383
Hartley, R. E., 166, 170, 322, 325
Hartshorne, H., 194–196, 200–202, 208, 210, 212
Harvey, J., 243, 249
Hathaway, M. L., 80, 81
Havens, J., 303, 306
Havighurst, R. J., 12, 59, 63, 98, 100, 139–147, 149, 151, 196, 212, 446, 450, 455, 462
Hawkes, G., 217, 224
Head, H., 83, 87
Healy, S. L., 252, 253, 291–298
Heath, D. H., 62, 63
Heathers, G., 24, 31

Helvetius, C. A., 13
Herbart, J. F., 3
Hess, R. D., 176, 193, 217, 224, 455, 462
Hey, R. N., 477, 485
Hilgard, E. R., 325, 326
Hill, A. B., 402, 417
Himes, J. S., 452, 476–487
Hindsman, E., 365, 366, 374, 375
Hinton, M. A., 79, 81
Hobbes, T., 13, 22
Horrocks, J. E., 150–151, 173, 175
Houlihan, N. B., 59, 63
Huenenmann, R. L., 76, 81
Hulse, F. S., 58, 63
Humphreys, L., 60, 63
Hunt, J. M., 54, 63
Hunter, W. S., 60, 61, 63
Hurlock, E. B., 22, 31
Hyman, H. H., 176, 193, 461, 463

Ilg, F., 29, 31
Inhelder, B., 40, 42, 43, 47, 192, 193
Ipsen, J., 401, 417
Iscoe, J., 243 249, 250

Jackson, P. W., 100, 121–132, 143, 147, 362, 376–383
Jacob, P. E., 164, 170
James, W., 406
Jencks, C., 505, 510
Jennings, E., 365, 366, 374, 375
Jensen, A. R., 1, 2, 56–58, 63
Jensen, V. W., 400, 417
Jones, M. C., 59, 63, 70, 71, 81, 82, 149, 151, 152–170
Josselyn, I. M., 22, 31, 196, 212, 446, 449

Kagan, J., 217, 224
Kay, C. L., 175
Kaye, C., 311, 312, 317
Kell, L., 320, 325
Kelley, H., 244, 249
Keniston, K., 501, 510
Kennan, G. F., 506, 511
Kerlinger, F. N., 118, 120
Kerr, W., 507, 511
Kiell, N., 31
Kiil, V., 56, 58, 63
King, F. J., 365, 366, 374, 375
Kinsey, A. C., 341, 351, 459
Kitay, P. M., 323, 326
Kitsuse, J. L., 512, 522
Klaus, R., 320, 325

Kluckhohn, C., 456, 463
Kluckhohn, R., 425, 431, 433
Knott, V. B., 52, 60, 63
Kobrin, S., 420, 446–450, 452
Kohlberg, L., 41, 48, 150, 151, 193–214
Kohn, M., 203, 213
Kolb, L. C., 83, 87
Kramer, J. C., 514, 522
Krebs, R., 201, 203, 213
Kristol, I., 510, 511
Kroh, O., 7
Kruytbosch, C. E., 505, 511
Kubie, L. S., 60, 63
Kuhlen, R. G., 59, 63, 235, 237, 239, 242

Larson, W. R., 420, 442–446
Laslett, P., 507, 511
Latham, A. J., 68, 81
Laughlin, F., 235, 242
Lazowick, L. M., 319, 325
Lee, B. J., 235, 237, 239, 242
Lehman, H. C., 169n, 170
Leibnitz, G. W., 4
Lemert, E., 512, 522
Lenz, W., 56, 63
Lersch, P., 4
Lev, J., 156, 171
Levin, H., 218, 224
Levinson, D. J., 282, 290
Lewin, K., 8, 50, 252, 422, 432
Lewis, H. G., 477, 482, 485
Lichtenstein, A., 52, 57, 62
Lindzey, G., 83, 86, 87
Lippett, R., 206
Lipset, S. M., 454, 462
Lisonbee, L. K., 50, 51, 88–98
Littlefield, D. C., 522
Livson, N., 216, 217
Locke, J., 3, 4, 9, 13–14, 22
Loeb, M. B., 342, 351
Lohnes, P., 443, 445
Long, D., 45, 48
Lowell, E. L., 147, 375
Lundberg, G. A., 395, 399
Lynd, H. M., 44, 48, 442, 446
Lynd, R. S., 442, 446
Lynn, D. B., 308, 318–326

Maccoby, E. E., 218, 224
Mace, D., 327, 328
MacMahon, B., 401, 417
Maida, P. R., 451, 545–463
Maier, H. W., 296, 297
Makarenko, A. S., 434, 441

Mann, H., 16
Marcia, J. E., vii, 252, 253, 277–290
Marcuse, H., 505, 511
Marple, C. H., 243, 248, 249
Marshall, M., 169n, 170
Martin, W. T., 405, 417
Maslow, A., 342, 351
Matthews, G. B., 455, 462
Matza, D., 519, 522
May, M. A., 194–196, 200–202, 208, 210, 212
May, R., 346, 352
Mayer, J., 49, 50, 64–82
McArthur, C. C., 302, 306, 417
McClelland, D. C., 123, 125, 146–147, 365, 375
McCord, J., 223, 224
McCord, W., 223, 224
McDonald, F., 1, 2, 30, 31
McGuire, C., 365, 366, 374, 375
McKay, H. D., 480, 485
McKinney, J. P., 150, 171–175
McNemar, Q., 103, 120, 285, 290
Mead, M., 8, 28, 31, 419, 424–426, 428–432
Mech E. V., 67, 81
Meleny, H. E., 168, 169n, 170
Mendelson, M., 78, 82
Meredith, H. V., 52–55, 60, 63
Merton, R. K., 230, 234
Messinger, S. L., 505, 511
Miles, C. C., 171
Miller, W., 449, 450, 461, 463, 476, 485
Mills, C. A., 78, 79, 81
Mischel, W., 30
Mitchell, B. W., 81
Mohr, G. S., 22, 31
Monello, L. F., 77, 81
More, D. M., 72, 81
Morrow, W. R., 365, 375
Mosier, C. I., 220, 224
Mudd, E. H., 477, 485
Munoz, L., vi, 453, 511–522
Murray, H. A., 382, 383
Mussen, P. H., 70, 82, 218, 224, 339
Muuss, R. E., 1, 3–22, 49, 50, 51–64, 419, 421–433

Nicholson, M. C., 291, 297
Nixon, R. E., 12
Northway, M. L., 235, 238, 242

Oden, M., 143, 147

O'Neil, R., 150, 175–193
Ortega y Gassett, J., 505, 506, 511
Osgood, C. E., 443, 446
Ostlund, L. A., 452, 462
Otterstädt, H., 62, 63
Otto, H. A., 252, 253, 291–298

Parloff, M. B., 133, 134, 137, 138
Parrish, H. M., 400, 417
Parsons, T., 22, 31
Patel, A. A., 243, 248, 249
Paterson, A., 296, 298
Pearson, G. H. J., 22, 31
Peel, E. A., 42, 48
Perl, R., 102, 120
Pestalozzi, J. H., 3, 16
Piaget, J., 2, 11, 29, 31, 34, 39–43, 48,
    150, 151, 179, 191–193, 197, 203,
    213, 242, 249
Pierce, J. V., 455, 462
Plato, 3–7, 9–11, 13, 22
Pollitt, D. H., 483, 486
Power, S. H., 400, 417
Pressey, L. C., 163, 170
Pressey, S. L., 163, 169n, 170
Pugh, T. F., 401, 417
Putney, S., 455, 462

Radler, D. H., 164, 170, 454, 462
Ragsdale, R., 220, 224
Rank, O., 8
Raphael, T., 400, 417
Rasmussen, J. E., 218, 279, 290
Reichard, S., 102, 104, 120
Reik, T., 345, 352
Reisman, D., 505, 510
Reiss, I., 340, 351
Remmers, H. H., 164, 170, 454, 462
Remplein, H., 5, 7
Riddoch, G., 83, 87
Ringness, T. A., 361, 363–376
Robinson, L. H., 477, 479, 485
Rodgers, R. R., 433, 434, 441
Rose, A. M., 454, 462
Rosen, B. C., 146, 147
Rosenbaum, M. E., 282, 290
Rosenberg, B. G., 166, 170
Rosenthal, R., 280, 290
Rosenzweig, S., 383
Rossman, M., 507, 511
Rothacker, E., 4
Rotter, J. B., 289, 290
Rousseau, J. J., 3, 9, 10, 14–18, 20, 22

Rovit, E., 501, 511
Rubinstein, E. A., vi, 453, 498–511
Runner, K. R., 134–138

Salinger, J. D., 26, 31, 45
Sampson, E. E., 500, 511
Sanford, R. N., 164, 170, 282, 290
Sarason, I. G., 320, 325
Schilder, P., 83, 87
Schiller, B., 102, 103, 120
Schlosberg, H., 321, 325
Schmidt, S. S., 341, 351
Schneck, M. R., 102, 103, 120
Schonfeld, W. A., 452, 486–498
Schultz, H., 425, 427, 432
Searles, R., 482, 486
Sears, R. R., 218, 224
Seeley, J., 521n, 522
Seiden, R. H., vi, 363, 400–417
Seidmann, P., 62, 63
Seltzer, C. C., 76, 77, 81, 82
Seward, G. H., 420, 442–446
Shapping, L. R., 81
Shaw, C. R., 480, 485
Shaw, M. E., 216, 242–249
Sheldon, W., 84, 87
Shibutani, T., 224, 233
Shipman, G., 308, 326–339
Shneidman, E. S., 415, 417
Simon, G., 511, 513, 522
Simpson, R. L., 461, 463
Sjoberg, G., 521n, 522
Skorepa, C. A., 175
Smith, D. E., 514, 522
Smith, S., 323, 326
Smythies, J. R., 83, 87
Solomon, D., 456, 463
Souba, C. E., 291, 297
Spector, J. C., 215, 217–224
Spencer, H., 16
Spilka, B., 45, 48
Spillman, R. J., 383
Spinoza, B., 3
Stagner, R., 217, 224
Steiner, M. E., 379, 383
Stern, W., 99
Sternbach, R., 340, 341
Stolz, H. R., 66–68, 72–74, 82, 98, 159,
    170
Stolz, L. M., 66–68, 72–74, 82, 98
Stone, G. P., 71, 82, 149, 151
Stone, L. J., 254, 264
Strauss, A. L., 512, 518, 522

Strong, S. M., 516, 522
Stuart, H. C., 76, 82
Stunkard, A. J., 78, 82
Suci, G. J., 433, 434, 441
Suslow, S., 402, 417
Sutton-Smith, B., 166, 170
Symonds, P. S., 159, 169n, 170
Szasz, T. S., 83, 88

Taba, H., 196, 212
Tanner, J. M., 52, 54–58, 63, 168, 171
Taylor, R. G., 37, 365–366, 373–374, 376
Teahan, J., 365, 375
Temby, W. D., 400, 417
TenHouten, W. D., 362, 363, 384–399
Terman, L. M., 143, 147, 166, 171
Thomas, S., 296, 298
Thompson, G. G., 173, 175
Thorndike, E. L., 102, 121
Thorndike, R. L., 364, 376
Thrasher, F. M., 480, 485
Thurber, E., 223, 224
Thurstone, L. L., 102, 103, 121
Thurstone, T. G., 102, 103, 121
Torney, J. V., 217, 224
Torrance, E. P., 100, 133–138
Trout, G., 511, 513, 522
Tryon, C. M., 235, 239, 242
Tryon, R. C., 169n, 171
Tseng, S. C., 455, 462
Tuddenham, R. D., 60, 64, 244, 249
Tuma, E., 216, 217
Turiel, E., 208, 214
Tyler, L. E., 103, 121, 167, 171

Van Der Werff Ten Bosch, J. J., 62
Van Hoffman, N., 511, 522
Very, P. S., 99, 101–121
Volkart, E., 244, 249

Wakefield, D., 480, 485
Walker, H. M., 154, 171
Wallis, W. A., 502, 503, 511
Walters, R. H., 23, 30, 364, 365
Webster, H., 164, 171
Weick, K. E., 282, 290
Weir, M. W., 42, 48
Westley, W. A., 25, 30, 224, 233
White, S., 210, 214
Whiting, B. B., 328, 339
Whiting, J. W. M., 218, 223, 328, 339, 425, 431, 433
Whitney, A. P., 234, 242
Williams, J. A., Jr., 482, 486
Williams, M., 243, 249
Willits, F. K., 451, 454–463
Wilson, P. B., 455, 456, 463
Wilson, R. R., 365, 375
Withey, S. B., 311, 312, 318
Witty, P. A., 169n, 170
Wolff, W., 83, 86, 88
Wolins, L., 79, 81
Woodworth, R. S., 321, 325
Wylie, L., 431–433

Young, F. W., 425, 428, 433

Zeller, W., 7
Ziller, T., 18

SUBJECT INDEX

Achievement, 122–126, 142–146, 267, 311, 314, 361, 365, 370–380, 383, 421, 452, 465, 467, 468, 469, 470, 471, 477, 495
　academic, 122, 146, 361, 364, 365, 372–375, 406–409, 416, 463–475
　orientation, 100, 135–138
　school, 124–129, 144–146, 296, 362–376
Adolescence, the stormy decade, 22–31

Adolescent
　concepts of social sex roles, 442–446
　concern with physique, 88–98
　crises, 61–62, 253, 259, 452, 486, 487
　development in the middle and lower classes, 446–450
　dissatisfaction with school, 376–383
　egocentrism, 2, 39–49, 51
　growth, 32, 65–68, 75, 81
　　pattern, 64

spurt, 52, 54, 56
mental structure, 101–121
moral development, 150, 193–214, 315
perception of parental control, 217–224
self-perception, 253, 291–298
sense of community, 175–193
subculture, vi, 451–475, 487, 489–492
turmoil, 26, 35, 486–498
Affluence as a factor in adolescent development, 486–498
Age differentiation hypothesis, 101–104, 114, 117–119
Alienation, 343, 346, 396, 398, 489, 497
Athletics, 67–72, 126, 165–166, 302, 361, 362, 369–371, 389–392, 465, 471, 473–474, 481

Biological maturation, 33, 36
Body, build, 10, 71, 74, 76
changes, 50, 269, 424
image, 50, 78, 82–88, 492

Cognition, 40, 121, 203
Cognitive, abilities, 122, 191, 268
development, 2, 32, 99, 150, 203, 257, 361
functions, 124, 125, 131, 132
structure, 40, 47, 99, 151
Comenius' theory of development, 11–13
Concrete operations, 34, 41–43, 46, 192
Conformity, 2, 8, 22, 26, 64, 151, 197, 202, 206, 207, 210–212, 215–216, 222, 224, 260, 361, 371, 477, 490, 495
as a function of age level, 242–249
to parents, 226–227, 231–233
to peers, 226–227, 230–234, 490
Convergent thinking, 100, 131–132, 142
Courtship, 2, 34, 59, 61, 150, 326, 329, 337, 419
Creative adolescents, 100, 121–132, 133–138
Creativity, 34, 99–100, 121–128, 132–134, 142–143, 148, 258, 293–295
Crises in normal development, 253, 254, 260, 298–306, 487
Cross-cultural studies, 28, 200, 433–446
Cross-national differences, 442–446
Cultural conditioning, 28, 429, 447
Cultural factors, impact on adolescents, 446–450
Curriculum, vii, 11, 12, 16, 17, 59–61, 80, 97, 101, 203, 208, 211, 300, 326, 361, 375, 377, 378

Darwin's theory of evolution, 18–19
Dating, 2, 34, 52, 56, 59–61, 69, 238–240, 307, 353, 356, 361, 419, 455, 459, 464, 477, 488
Delinquency, 36, 45, 196, 252, 258, 260–262, 302, 457, 481, 486, 488, 495
origins of, 36–37
Delinquents, 26, 37, 146, 262, 270, 384, 391, 447
Dependence-independence conflict, 24–25
Developmental task, 32, 35, 149, 251, 257, 310
Disadvantaged, 36–38
Dissatisfaction with school, 376–383
Divergent thinking, 131–132, 142–143, 146
Dropouts, 302, 355, 370, 384, 455, 459–460
Drugs, 59–61, 424, 451–454, 495, 497, 501
barbiturates, 412, 497, 520n
freaks, 453, 454, 515–520
hallucinogens, 512, 514–516, 519
heads, 453, 515–520
heroin, 497, 515, 516
LSD, 453, 497, 512–519
marijuana, 344, 497, 512, 514, 516, 518
methedrine, 453, 514–518, 521n
use among hippies, 453, 511–521

Early and late maturation, 49, 50, 68–72
Early Greek concern with development, 4–9
Early maturation, 68–73, 165, 168
Ego, 83, 144, 202, 254, 263, 267, 289, 307, 310–316, 327–328
abilities, 195–196, 210
development, 312–313
identity, 251–252, 264–268, 277–290, 489
strength, 196, 262, 274, 279, 313
Egocentrism in adolescence, 2, 39–51, 259
Eight stages of man, 251, 256–257
Evolution, theory of, 7, 18, 19
Extracurricular activities, vii, 69, 361, 362, 387, 388, 455, 465

Fad behavior, 23–26, 44, 459
Family, structure, 37, 174, 217, 313, 327
matrifocal, 273, 309, 359, 452

Foreclosure, 251–252, 278–279, 281, 284–289
Formal operations, 42, 43, 46, 191, 192
Friendship, 6, 8, 21, 59, 69, 150, 215, 257, 313, 393, 395, 397, 456, 457
  stability in adolescents, 171–175

Generation gap, vi, 58, 420, 445, 489
Giftedness, 121, 122, 133
Growth, pattern, 51, 58, 59, 64, 73
  physical, 50, 52, 58, 59, 65
  spurt, 52, 54, 56

Hall's biogenetic psychology of adolescence, 19–22
Heterosexual, activity, 28–29, 52, 68, 309, 424
  behavior, 28–29
  interest, 59, 72, 149, 164, 169, 309, 359, 424
  orientation, 157, 159, 167, 309, 352, 356
Heterosexuality, 309, 352, 353, 355, 359
Hippies, 451, 453, 490, 502
  drug use, 511–522
Historical theories of adolescence, 3–22

Idealism, 2, 8, 20, 34, 489, 510
Identification patterns of boys, 363–376
Identity, 2, 4, 23, 36–37, 217, 223, 230, 251–252, 257–290, 296, 306, 317, 327, 328, 348, 420, 447, 452, 457, 489, 495
  achievement, 278, 279, 281, 284–289
  crisis, 252, 258–259, 261, 267, 278, 300, 442
  diffusion, 251–252, 257, 269, 277–279, 281, 284–289, 306, 343
  formation, vii, 149, 253, 262, 265, 268
  negative, 252, 261, 262, 270–272
Individual differences, 6, 10, 66, 233, 316n, 438, 439
Initiation ceremony, 28, 268, 421, 423–428
Intelligence, structure of, 99, 101–121
Intelligent adolescents, 100, 121–132, 139–147
Interpersonal relationships, 35, 308, 311, 414–416, 478
Intimacy, 46, 251, 257, 269, 316n, 319, 328, 340, 341, 344, 346, 350

Late maturation 68–72

Leadership, 36, 68–71, 144, 289, 361, 362, 379, 392–395, 444–445, 513
Lower class, 13, 54, 140, 178, 195, 203, 309, 343, 358, 359, 446–449, 460–462
  adolescent, 383, 421, 449, 452, 461
  parent, 146, 421, 449, 455

Marriage, 17, 33, 58, 61, 145, 301, 304, 326–329, 349, 414, 423, 426–430, 493
  attitude toward, 352, 355, 358, 359
  interest in, 59, 159
  roles, 477, 480
  sexual relationships before, 341–342, 346–347
  teen-age, 497
Mass media, 1, 26–28, 30, 60, 253, 347, 349, 476, 491, 501
  sensationalism, 26–27
Medieval Christian view of development, 9–11
Menarche, 33, 52, 54–56, 71, 327, 330–334, 419, 425–427
Mental, abilities, 10, 102, 139, 140, 146
  development, 32, 39, 40, 46, 47, 139
  structures, 39, 46, 47, 99, 101–121
Mentally superior children, 139–147
Middle class, 1, 13, 45, 57, 89, 139–141, 154, 178, 195, 203–307, 219, 343, 356, 393, 420, 446–449, 453, 460–462, 465, 476, 481, 492, 517
  adolescent, 421, 448, 449, 452
  parent, 420, 449
Minority groups, 33, 36, 77, 261, 303, 398
Moral, behavior, 150, 194, 200–204
  character, 7, 150–151, 194–204, 210, 212
  development, 150, 196, 199, 203–213, 315
  education, 150, 193–214
  judgment, 151, 195–214, 502
Morality, 122, 151, 196, 198, 207, 263, 273, 277, 340, 343, 348, 393, 431, 496
Moratorium, 251–252, 262, 269, 278, 281, 284–289
Motivation of high school boys, 363–376

Negro, and white, heterosexual development, 352–359
  adolescent, 252, 309, 383, 387, 452

minority, 388, 392, 395, 398, 452
student, 362–363, 386–390, 395–399,
    481
teen-age culture, 452, 476–487
youth, 52, 309, 384, 388, 390, 452
    and identity, 252, 265–277
Nonconformity, 25, 67, 248, 367, 372,
    490
Normality, 30, 50, 67, 79, 97, 349

Obesity and overweight, 74–77
Occupation, 131, 156, 169, 174, 280, 426
Occupational, adjustments, 447
    choices, 130, 278
    goals, 25
Over-achiever, 124, 125, 365, 366

Parent-child relationship, 27, 35, 218,
    305, 327, 365, 487
Parent-peer conflict, 25, 225, 231
Parent-peer cross-pressures, 224, 234, 420,
    433–441
Parental restrictiveness, 23–24
Peer group, 2, 35–37, 204–206, 224, 361–
    364, 371, 374, 420–421, 433, 440–
    441, 449, 451, 456, 491–492
    activities, 25, 159
    conformity, 22, 26, 64, 438
    dependency, 23, 366
    influence, 21, 36, 215
    popularity, 392–394
    pressures, 216, 361, 434
    racial composition of, 395–397
Peer pressures among Soviet and Amer-
    ican children, 433–441
Personal identity, 35–36, 251
Personalism, 179–181
Petting behavior, 335–336, 341, 349
Philosophical theories of adolescence, 3–
    22
Physical, appearance, 51, 64–82, 88–98
    change, 68, 88, 251, 424
    development, 37, 49–52, 58–61, 65, 69,
    150
    maturation, 32, 66, 70, 149, 361, 430,
    492
Political ideas in adolescence, 175–193
Popularity, 67, 69, 71, 144, 362, 371,
    374, 393, 489, 491
    criteria for, 392–394
Prejudice, 33, 77, 252, 323, 352, 452
Pressure from peers versus pressure from
    adults, 216, 433–441

Psychosexual development, 3, 262, 326–
    327
Puberty, 20, 29, 64–66, 73, 257, 315,
    326, 424–431
    as a new birth, 16
    beginning of, 7, 54
    crises, 330–334
    early, 80
    rites, 2, 33, 328, 419, 421–433
Pubescence, 10, 28–30, 49, 60, 216, 247,
    307, 359, 419, 424

Racial, composition of peer group, 395–
    397
    composition of school, 384–399
    integration, 386
    minority, 77, 252, 392, 398
    segregation, 388
Rebellion, 1, 22, 25, 27, 71, 215, 304,
    451, 454, 457, 459, 460, 496
Rebellious youth subculture, 454–463
Recapitulation theory, 3, 18–21, 310
Revolution, 20–21, 271, 506–507
    sexual, 308–309, 340, 342, 350, 351
Rites de passage, 332, 423, 425–429, 477

School, achievement in boys, 363–376
    dropouts, 355, 370, 455, 459–460
Secular trend in adolescent development,
    2, 51–64, 152–170
Self-body recognition, 82–88
Self-concept, 50, 90, 96, 251, 253, 279,
    297, 384, 409, 429, 445, 489, 495
Self-esteem, 17, 196, 252, 267, 268, 279,
    282, 287, 289, 346, 409, 487, 497
Self-fulfilling prophecy, 30
Self-image, 271, 296, 297, 303
Self-improvement, desire for, 88, 89, 92–
    94
Sex, and mental health, 339–352
    appropriateness of physique, 73–74
    conflicts, 304–305
    differences, 36, 78–80, 99–104, 107–
    110, 114–119, 156, 164–167, 175,
    177, 216, 222, 307–359, 382, 420,
    436, 488
    in youths character processes, 310–
    317
    in puberty rites, 425–427
    education, 60, 308, 326–339, 430–432
    role, 2, 35, 149, 157, 164–168, 307–
    359, 419, 420, 427, 428, 442
    behavior, 321–323

Sex, and mental health (*cont.*)
  differentiation, 217, 219
  identification, 223, 308, 318–326, 352
  identity, 36, 215, 223, 427
  preferences, 323, 324
Sexual, activity, 28, 29, 150, 307–309, 328, 341–342, 344, 347–348, 429–430
  behavior, 28–29, 35–36, 326–327, 340–343, 350–351, 451, 496
  development, 32–33, 35, 61, 67, 307–359
  identity, 35, 269, 332, 426, 428
  maturation, 32, 35, 49, 52, 54, 55, 149
  revolution, 308–309, 340, 342, 350–351
Sexuality, 8, 28, 36, 74, 275, 307, 308, 328–334, 337, 339–342, 346, 348–351
Sit-in protest, 483–484
Social, acceptability of junior high school pupils, 234–242
  class, 36, 57, 139–142, 152, 159, 195, 204, 384, 446, 460
  differences, 384, 393, 460–462
  development, 5, 19, 28, 30, 51, 61, 62, 69, 150, 164, 165, 193, 242, 359, 361
  heterosexual development, 352–359
  mobility, 14, 26, 67, 154, 361, 477, 481
  sex roles, 442–446
  systems of high schools, 384–399
Socialization, *vii*, 25, 28, 144, 163, 176, 222, 310, 332, 384, 399, 420, 421, 519

process, 216, 223, 247, 419, 433
Socio-economic, affluence, 486–498
  class, 54, 57, 367, 419, 452
  status, 52, 134, 140–142, 144, 154, 177, 354, 365, 367, 373, 422, 455, 460
Status-envy hypothesis, 215, 218–219, 223
Storm and stress, *vi*, 1, 20–23, 26–27
Student, activism, 451, 453, 499–505, 508–510
  protests, paradoxes of, 498–511
  suicide, 251, 344, 363, 400–417, 457, 495, 497

Tabula rasa, 3–4, 13–14
Theological view of development, 9–11
Tranquilizer, 412

Underachiever, 100, 143–145, 365–366, 496
Upper class, 57, 139, 140, 343, 460

Value system, 25, 149, 150, 252, 262, 340, 348, 364, 461, 469
Variations in physical appearance, 64–82
Vocational, achievement, 145, 490
  choices, 166, 167
  goals, 144, 451
  preparation, 362, 371, 372
  training, 37

Youth and the life cycle, 251, 253–264
Youth, culture, *vi*, 1, 490
  subculture, 384, 454–463